CAMBRIDGE GREEK AND

Silver bust of the Emperor Galba. Naples, Museo Archeologico Nazionale (inv. no. 110127). Reproduced by permission of the Soprintendenza per i Beni Archeologici delle province di Napoli e Caserta.

TACITUS

HISTORIES

BOOK I

EDITED BY

CYNTHIA DAMON

Associate Professor of Classics,
Amherst College

CAMBRIDGE UNIVERSITY PRESS
Cambridge, New York, Melbourne, Madrid, Cape Town, Singapore, São Paulo

Cambridge University Press
The Edinburgh Building, Cambridge CB2 2RU, UK

Published in the United States of America by Cambridge University Press, New York

www.cambridge.org
Information on this title: www.cambridge.org/9780521570725

First published 2003

A catalogue record for this publication is available from the British Library

Library of Congress Cataloguing in Publication data

Tacitus, Cornelius.
[Historiae. Liber 1]
Histories. Book I / Tacitus ; edited by Cynthia Damon.
p. cm. – (Cambridge Greek and Latin classics)
Text in Latin; commentary in English.
Includes bibliographical references (p.) and indexes.
ISBN 0 521 57072 7 – (hardback) ISBN 0 521 57822 1 (paperback)
1. Rome – History – Civil War, 68–69. 2. Galba, Servius Sulpicius, Emperor of Rome, 3 B.C.–A.D. 69 3. Vitellius, Aulus, Emperor of Rome, 15–69.
I. Damon, Cynthia, 1957– II. Title. III. Series.
PA6705.H6 B1 2003
937′.05 – dc21 2002073824

ISBN-13 978-0-521-57072-5 hardback
ISBN-10 0-521-57072-7 hardback

ISBN-13 978-0-521-57822-6 paperback
ISBN-10 0-521-57822-1 paperback

Transferred to digital printing 2005

CONTENTS

Preface *page* vii
List of abbreviations ix
Maps xi
1 Rome xi
2 The Roman forum xii
3 The Vitellian invasion xiii

Introduction 1
1 *The senator* 1
2 *The orator* 2
3 *The writer:* Agricola, Germania, Dialogus 2
4 *The historian* 4
5 Cura posteritatis 5
6 Ratio causaeque 6
7 Exempla 11
8 *Chronology* 11
9 Deinosis 12
10 *Elevation* 12
11 *Diction* 13
12 *Metaphor* 14
13 Sententiae 15
14 *Appendix sentences* 16
15 Variatio 19
16 Histories I 20
17 *The sources* 22
18 *The parallel tradition* 24
19 *The text* 30

CORNELI TACITI HISTORIARVM LIBER PRIMVS 33

Commentary 77
Appendices 291
1 *Parallel passages showing strong verbal similarities* 291
2 *Epigrams and* sententiae 302

3 *Notes pertaining to parallel incidents reported under two or more* principes 304

4 *Notes illustrating differences between* Histories I *and the parallel tradition* 305

Select bibliography 307

Indexes 319

1 *Latin words* 319

2 *General* 320

PREFACE

Simply put, the aim of the present commentary is to reintegrate *Histories* I into the corpus of teachable Latin texts. Tacitus is arguably the most powerful writer of Latin – to this day it requires great discipline to resist his interpretation of events – and the reader's best defence, and greatest pleasure, lie in an understanding of how his style works. This I try to supply. *Histories* I is particularly amenable to the attempt, owing to the chance survival of three parallel accounts (in Plutarch, Suetonius, and Dio), which render Tacitus' selection and stylization of material here capable of detailed analysis. The notes also introduce students to the historical and historiographical contexts in which *Histories* I was created; references are provided to more detailed discussions of both. Grammatical assistance is provided where necessary to elucidate Tacitus' sometimes difficult Latin.

Over the many years of this commentary's making I have been assisted and encouraged by friends, colleagues, and fellow Tacitus-enthusiasts; happily, in some cases all three labels apply. My gratitude for assistance for everything from interpretation of manuscript abbreviations to discussion of matters historiographical to advice on presentation and content goes to the following: John Bodel, Virginia Brown, Edward Courtney, Christopher Jones, Elizabeth Keitel, Christina Kraus, Leslie Murison, Francis Newton, Peter Pouncey, James Rives, Andreola Rossi, Richard Tarrant, and Richard Thomas. To my Amherst colleagues Elizabeth Keitel (at the University) and Alan Boegehold (at the College) go my thanks for giving the commentary a dry run at the draft stage. But my largest debt is to E. J. Kenney, who improved every page kindly, firmly, and with great good sense. I save for last the name of a colleague who did not live to see the completion of a work he had done much to aid: Peter Marshall.

My work has been generously supported by Amherst College, where over the past few (well, more than a few) years I have enjoyed a Miner D. Crary Summer Stipend and a Trustee Faculty Fellowship. Funding for student assistance – ably provided by Umit Dhuga, Amherst '01, and Seth Bernard and Jordan Holmes, both '03 – came from the Faculty Research Award Program.

This project was begun for the series under the encouragement of Pauline Hire at the Cambridge University Press; it appears thanks to the efforts and guidance of her successor Michael Sharp, and I am indebted to both of them. As I am to Stefano De Caro of the Soprintendenza Archeologica delle province di Napoli e Caserta, who kindly supplied a photograph of the Naples Museum's fine silver bust of Galba for the frontispiece.

ABBREVIATIONS

A&G	J. B. Greenough et al., edd. (1931). *Allen and Greenough's new Latin grammar.* Boston.
ALL	E. von Wölfflin, ed. (1884–1908). *Archiv fur lateinische Lexikographie und Grammatik mit Einschluss des alteren Mittellatein.* 15 vols. Leipzig.
ANRW	H. Temporini and W. Haase, edd. (1972–). *Aufstieg und Niedergang der römischen Welt.* Berlin.
app. crit.	*apparatus criticus*
CAH[2]	*Cambridge ancient history* (1970–). 2nd ed. Cambridge.
GG	A. Gerber and A. Greef, edd. (1887–90). *Lexicon Taciteum.* 2 vols. Leipzig.
HRR	H. Peter, ed. (1914). *Historicorum romanorum reliquiae.* 2 vols. 2nd ed. Leipzig.
K–H	R. Kühner and F. Holzweissig (1912). *Ausführliche Grammatik der lateinischen Sprache: erster Teil, Elementar-, Formen-, und Wortlehre.* 2nd ed. Hannover.
K–S	R. Kühner and C. Stegmann (1976). *Ausführliche Grammatik der lateinischen Sprache: zweiter Teil, Satzlehre.* 5th ed. by A. Thierfelder. 2 vols. Hannover.
lit.	literally
LSJ	H. G. Liddell, R. Scott, H. Stuart-Jones (1940). *A Greek–English lexicon.* 9th ed. Oxford.
M–W	R. H. Martin and A. J. Woodman (1989). *Tacitus, Annals book IV.* Cambridge Greek and Latin Classics. Cambridge.
McC–W	M. McCrum and A. G. Woodhead (1961). *Select documents of the principates of the Flavian emperors, including the year of revolution: A.D. 68–96.* Cambridge.
mod.	modern
NLS	E. C. Woodcock (1959). *A new Latin syntax.* London.
OLD	P. G. W. Glare, ed. (1982). *Oxford Latin dictionary.* Oxford.

ORF	H. Malcovati, ed. (1976). *Oratorum romanorum fragmenta liberae rei publicae*. 4th ed. Turin.
PIR	*Prosopographia imperii Romani saec. I, II, III*. (1897–8). 3 vols. Berlin.
PIR[2]	*Prosopographia imperii Romani saec. I, II, III*. (1933–). 2nd ed. Berlin.
RE	A. Pauly, G. Wissowa et al., edd. (1894–1979). *Paulys Real-Encyclopädie der classischen Altertumswissenschaft*. Stuttgart.
RG	Augustus, *Res gestae* (*Anc.* in the *OLD*, for *Monumentum Ancyranum*)
s.c.	*senatus consultum*
SCPP	*Senatus consultum de Cn. Pisone patre*. For text and discussion see W. Eck, A. Caballos, F. Fernández (1996). *Das senatus consultum de Cn. Pisone patre*. Vestigia 48. Munich.
TLL	*Thesaurus linguae latinae* (1900–). Munich.
W–M	A. J. Woodman and R. H. Martin (1996). *The Annals of Tacitus, book 3*. Cambridge.

The names and titles of classical authors and texts are abbreviated in accordance with *OLD* and LSJ, with the following (important) exceptions for Tacitus (T.) and his works: *Annals* (*A.*), *Agricola* (*Agr.*), *Dialogus* (*D.*), *Germania* (*G.*), *Histories* (*H.*). References to passages in Book 1 of the *Histories* use chapter and sentence number only. Journal titles are abbreviated in accordance with *L'année philologique*, slightly anglicized (e.g. *TAPA* for *TAPhA*).

MAPS

1 Rome (adapted from Marcel Le Glay, Jean-Louis Voisin and Yann Le Bohec, *A History of Rome* (English edition: Oxford, 1996), fig. 11.1, p. 332).

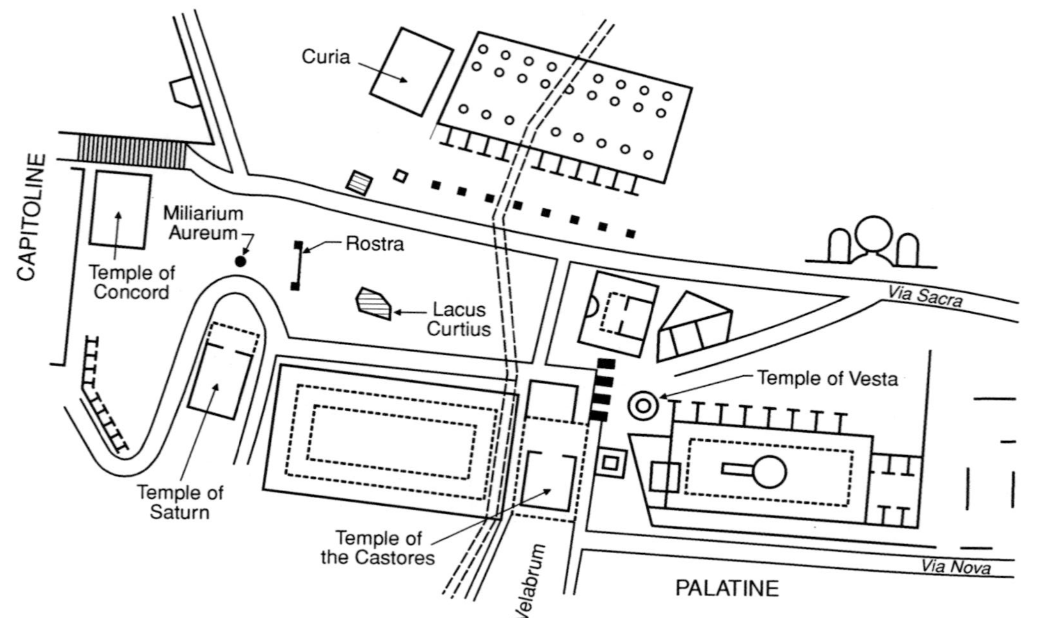

2 The Roman forum (adapted from Marcel Le Glay, Jean-Louis Voisin and Yann Le Bohec, *A History of Rome* (English edition: Oxford, 1996), fig. 13.1, p. 423).

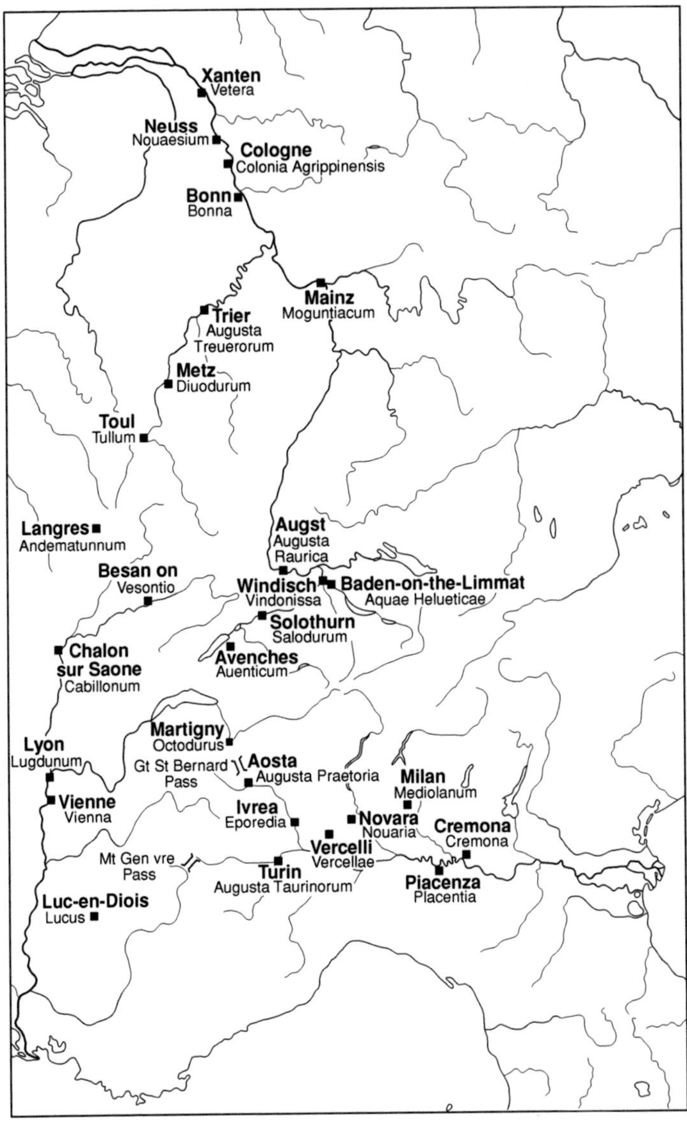

3 The Vitellian invasion (adapted from Charles L. Murison, *Galba, Otho and Vitellius* (Hildesheim, Zürich, New York, 1993), map 1).

INTRODUCTION

'Had forgetting been as much in our power as silence, we would have destroyed memory along with speech.' So writes T. of the dark days of Domitian's reign (A.D. 81–96; *Agr.* 2.3). But by 98 or so when he writes these words Domitian is dead and a new dynasty is in power. Silence (at least about the past) is no longer necessary nor is forgetting so much to be desired. T., now in middle age, nearly done with the senator's *cursus honorum*, devotes himself henceforth to *memoria*. There will even be pleasure, he predicts, in the story of the servitude that silenced senatorial speech, given the lively contrast between that past and a present of (he says) *princeps*-guaranteed *libertas* (*Agr.* 3.2). T. was well placed to write of both past and present.

1 THE SENATOR

'From Galba, Otho, and Vitellius I received neither benefit nor harm. That my career was initiated by Vespasian, advanced by Titus, and carried further by Domitian I do not deny' (*H.* 1.1.3). Birth in A.D. 56 or 57 is deduced from the dates of the political offices alluded to in the foregoing quotation (praetor in 88, suffect consul in 97, evidence that converges with a reference to himself as 'quite a young man' (*D.* 1.2 *iuuenis admodum*) at the dramatic date of the *Dialogus*, A.D. 74/5; see further Syme (1958) 59–74). T.'s father was perhaps the equestrian procurator of Gallia Belgica mentioned as a contemporary by Pliny the Elder (*Nat.* 7.76). His family's origin may lie in Transpadane Italy or, more probably, in Narbonese Gaul (Syme (1958) 618–24), but the earliest years of his life were passed in (for us) complete obscurity. Not even his praenomen is known with certainty: he may be a Gaius or a Publius. By 74/5 he was in Rome, training himself for a senatorial career by attending on the leading speakers of the day (*D.* 2.1). T. was granted the *latus clauus* (i.e. the right to wear a tunic with a broad purple stripe as a badge of prospective senatorial rank) by Vespasian (*H.* 1.1.3). The first (unattested) stages of his senatorial career must have been membership in the vigintivirate in Rome followed by military service as *tribunus laticlauius*. In 77 he married into the senatorial family of Cn. Julius Agricola (*Agr.* 9.6). T. is next attested in 88, when he was praetor and one of the *XV viri sacris faciundis* who, along with the emperor Domitian, organized the Secular Games in that year (*A.* 11.11.1). Abroad on public service when Agricola died on 23 August 93 (*Agr.* 45.5), T. returned to Rome after an absence of some three years to hold a suffect consulship in the second half of 97. An inscription in Asia Minor informs us that T. reached the summit of a senatorial career, the proconsulship of Asia, in 112/3 (*OGIS* 487, with Syme (1958) 664–5 for the date). He cannot have died before the extension of Roman dominion to the Red Sea, territory first conquered on Trajan's Parthian campaigns of 115/6, to which he refers at *A.* 2.61.2.[1]

2 THE ORATOR

By 98 T. had spent some two decades in service to the state. The Flavian peace had established itself, imperial power had passed from father to son and brother to brother. As one of the 'sad, submissive senators' of Domitian's reign he had had a share in the governance of the empire: in elections, legislation, trials, religious business, provincial affairs (Talbert (1984) 341–491; quotation from Syme (1958) 76). But for all this apparent activity these were years of intellectual and moral inertia according to T. (*Agr.* 3.1–2). After fifteen years of it Domitian's assassination gave the senate a greater charge: to choose a new *princeps*. And one year into Nerva's reign came T.'s suffect consulship (in September and October of 97, months that revealed the necessity of equipping Nerva with an heir quickly; see 15.1n. *in . . . fertur*). As consul T. also bade an official farewell to a survivor from the past, Verginius Rufus, an important, if enigmatic, figure in the civil war that brought the Flavian house to power (8.2n.). It was an honour befitting T.'s high reputation as an orator (Plin. *Ep.* 2.1.6 *laudator eloquentissimus*, cf. *Ep.* 1.20.24, 7.20.4, 9.23.2). In 100 he, with Pliny, successfully prosecuted an extortion case against a former governor of the province of Africa, Marius Priscus (Plin. *Ep.* 2.11).

3 THE WRITER: *AGRICOLA*, *GERMANIA*, *DIALOGUS*

With speaking came writing. In 98 he published the *Agricola*, a biography of his father-in-law, which tries to reclaim something from the moral wasteland

[1] A recent re-examination of a long-known inscription (*CIL* VI 1574) may have yielded further information on career and connections, but the identification of the stone's subject and our author is not firmly established. See Alföldy (1995).

of Domitian's principate (*Agr.* 42.4 *sciant...posse etiam sub malis principibus magnos uiros esse*). In close sequence, before or after, came the *Germania*, part ethnography of the Germani, Rome's most troublesome neighbours (*G.* 37.5 *triumphati magis quam uicti sunt*), part meditation on the ills besetting Rome. A third short work, the *Dialogue on Orators*, is variously dated (by conjecture) between 96 and 103.[2] Though its format distances the work from its author – it is ostensibly the report of a discussion heard by a young and silent T. – the *Dialogus* is in fact one of his most personal works and marks a crucial stage in his literary development.

T. announces the dialogue as a vehicle for explaining the decline of Roman oratory but begins it with a vignette advertising the effectiveness of poetry, specifically tragedy, as political commentary: the poet-provocateur Maternus hones his *Cato*, which had already offended many, and gives notice that his *Thyestes* will be stronger still (*D.* 3.2–3). But despite its striking picture of a contemporary poet, the defence of poetry as a genre in this work is curiously superficial. There is no reply, for example, to the charge that Maternus' tragedies cause offence without benefiting anyone, a charge that T. himself advances against other recalcitrants (*D.* 9.2, 9.4, 10.6, cf. *Agr.* 42.5 *in nullum rei publicae usum ambitiosa morte inclaruerunt*).[3] The decline of oratory receives more thorough scrutiny. Various causes are adduced; the final explanation is a political one: oratory flourishes in a state where decisions are collective because the orator's art enables him to sway assemblies, but it is empty in a state whose important decisions were made by a ruler who was *sapientissimus et unus* (*D.* 41.4).

The problem with oratory as a genre at the end of the first century A.D. was fundamentally a problem of audience. To whom could one speak? Or, more precisely, given the possible audiences, what was worth saying? The *plebs*, no longer called upon to decide anything, was better 'addressed' via *beneficia* (including 'bread and circuses': Juv. 10.78–81). The senate too often refused to decide matters that came before it. A *princeps* was swayed not by rhetorical skill but by associates – freedmen, family members, *delatores*, *socii laborum* – equipped with a keen sense of psychology. The courtroom (more

[2] For discussion and bibliography see C. O. Brink, 'Can the *Dialogus* be dated? Evidence and historical conclusions', *HSCP* 96 (1994) 251–80.

[3] The point of such sallies might be clearer if we knew what happened to Maternus between the dramatic date of the *Dialogus* (74/5) and its composition (*c.* 96–103), but we do not: see T. D. Barnes, 'The significance of Tacitus' *Dialogus de Oratoribus*', *HSCP* 90 (1986) 227–44.

specifically, the Centumviral court) remained a venue for speech-making, but if Pliny is an accurate guide it elicited a sadly diminished product. Practical barristers were eager to get their cases over with as quickly as possible (*Ep.* 6.2.5), ambitious ones hired claques to vaunt their praises (*Ep.* 2.14.4–11). One observer announced the death of oratory ('*centumuiri, hoc artificium periit*', *Ep.* 2.14.11), another brought Cato's famous definition of the orator (*uir bonus dicendi peritus*) up to date by saying '*orator est uir malus dicendi imperitus*' (*Ep.* 4.7.5). Epictetus describes contemporary senatorial utterance in terms that are perhaps appropriately bleak: 'a cold, miserable remnant suspended from idle argumentations by a hair' (*Diss.* 4.1.140). A popular signet ring emblem at this period was the figure of Harpocrates, who, according to Plutarch, 'keeps his finger on his lip in token of restrained speech or silence' (Plut. *Mor.* 378c; see Plin. *Nat.* 33.41 for the rings).

The subject of the *Dialogus* has been well described as 'the proper relationship between existing literary forms and public life in a depoliticized society' (Fantham (1996) 286). Rejecting poetry and oratory, two (but only two) of the 'existing literary forms', the *Dialogus* leaves the way open for a third genre, history.[4]

4 THE HISTORIAN

In the preface to *H.* T. maintains that the present is 'a happy age in which it is permitted to feel what you wish and say what you feel' (1.4). But he was not so rash as to test the limits of permissibility by writing about the present, a topic twice deferred (see n.). Instead, he offers a history of the period that coincided with his own youth and rising career, the brief reigns of Galba, Otho, and Vitellius, and the longer span of Flavian dominance, twenty-eight years all told (69–96), covered in some twelve or fourteen books.[5] We surmise from Pliny's letters on the A.D. 79 eruption of Vesuvius that T. was at work on *H.* in *c.* 106 (*Ep.* 6.16, 20). It is presumed that he completed *H.* before moving on to the *Annals*, a work that took him back to the Julio-Claudian period. But the extant books (1–4 and twenty-six

[4] The choice of literary form also exercised Pliny, who saw history as the genre most likely to yield its author lasting fame: *itaque diebus ac noctibus cogito, si 'qua me quoque possim tollere humo' . . . quod prope sola historia polliceri uidetur* (*Ep.* 5.8.3, cf. *Ep.* 9.27 on the *numen historiae*).

[5] For the historiographical tradition in which T. was writing see M–W 1–10. For discussion and bibliography on the number of books in the *Histories* see C. S. Kraus and A. J. Woodman (1997). *Latin Historians*. Oxford, 91–2.

chapters of Book 5) treat only the civil wars of 69 and the first few months of Vespasian's reign.

5 *CVRA POSTERITATIS*

Questions of aim and method appear with particular urgency at the outset of an author's work in a new genre. Some are answered by the programmatic preface to *H.*; for others elucidation comes from the narrative itself.

Book 1 begins on a sombre note. The histories of the period since the battle of Actium are a disappointing lot: the authors were small talents hampered by political ignorance and by the passions and pressures of life under a *princeps*. Truth suffered, and so did posterity, for subservience and hatred were selfish indulgences in an historian. There is a promise implicit in this brief paraphrase of 1.1–3 that T. will do better. He enunciates a general principle: integrity requires an historian to present the figures who appear in the narrative without favour or hatred (1.3 *incorruptam fidem professis neque amore quisquam et sine odio dicendus est*). The opening paragraph of his work thus presents history as a literary form with the potential to succeed where, according to the *Dialogus*, oratory and poetry fail: the truth can be told.

But the truth will benefit posterity only if it gets read, so the table of contents contained in the second and third paragraphs of the preface promises both exciting material (assassinations, civil war, natural disasters, human havoc) and broad coverage (in the empire, provinces from Britain to Parthia; in the natural world, land, sea, and sky; in society, ranks from noble to slave). The content of the projected work is closer to Thucydides' catalogue of suffering in the human and natural spheres (1.23) than to Herodotus' 'great and amazing deeds of both Greeks and barbarians' (1.1). But if T.'s chosen period is not happy, it is significant: even the adulteries are *magna adulteria* (2.2). There will be the occasional patch of something brighter (3.1 *bona exempla*), but as a whole the narrative will, he claims, illustrate an important fact, that 'it is not our peace that is of concern to the gods, but our punishment' (3.2 *non esse curae deis securitatem nostram, esse ultionem*).

Woodman argues that this table of contents advertises a disaster narrative with all the ingredients of 'pleasurable historiography' ((1988) 165–7). He makes the important point that T. is writing as a survivor in a state that survived all of the disasters he is about to relate, which means that the darkness of his chosen period is set off by the brighter frame of a glorious past and a happy present. But to say that 'his interest in the disasters centres primarily on their capacity to furnish gripping narrative material' (167) is to ignore the note of moral seriousness first sounded in *cura posteritatis* and heard on every page of T.'s historical work.

The inadequacy of the 'pleasure principle' for explaining T.'s achievement can be seen in one of the most gripping narratives in Book 1, the story of the collective mad-scene in chapters 80–5, where the praetorian rank-and-file runs amok and threatens, Ajax-like, to slaughter Otho's senatorial dinner guests. Disaster is in fact averted and the *status quo* is altered but little as a result of the uprising, yet T. gives the story full-dress treatment over more than five chapters, including a long speech, several fine epigrams, and memorable scenes such as that of senators and their wives creeping through the back streets of Rome in quest of anonymity, and a teary-eyed emperor standing on a dining couch to address frantic and blood-stained guardsmen. Here, if anywhere in Book 1, is an event told for its lively qualities. But it would be a mistake so to describe it. Although the year 69 gets more space than any other year covered by T. (three full books; A.D. 15 with forty-nine chapters in *Annals* 1 is the next fullest), T. has made a careful selection from the possible material (see below for omissions). The praetorian riot earned admission not only for its innate drama, but also for its connection to the single most prominent theme in the narrative of that 'long and single year', the collapse of military discipline. The uprising poses a challenge to the principle that Otho articulates at 83.3: *si, cur iubeantur, quaerere singulis liceat, pereunte obsequio etiam imperium intercidit.* By his own standards Otho's *auctoritas* will prove insufficient in Book 2, and understanding why he fails is essential preparation for understanding why Vespasian succeeds.

6 *RATIO CAVSAEQVE*

Besides telling the truth and offering an exciting story about a significant, if depressing, period, the historian aims to show cause and effect (4.1). To sample the quality of T.'s explanations we will look at one small and three large historical questions posed by the events narrated in Book 1.

The small question first: Why did the legions of Upper Germany despise their legate, Hordeonius Flaccus? To this question we have answers from both T. and Plutarch. According to T., old age, ill-health, and a weak character were Flaccus' undoing: 9.1 *Flaccum spernebat, senecta ac debilitate pedum inualidum, sine constantia, sine auctoritate.* In place of age and character Plutarch cites inexperience: *G.* 18.4 'Flaccus, physically incapacitated by acute gout and without practical experience, was a complete cipher to them.' These two sentences clearly reflect a single model and agree on the role of illness, but their content is not quite the same, indeed old age and inexperience might seem to be mutually exclusive (see further §§10, 18 below). The similarity of sentence structure suggests that the source both reported the soldiers' scorn and explained it. If T. reflects the source faithfully, then the source's explanation is fully borne out by Flaccus' behaviour in 69 and 70, which T. reports in great detail. On the other hand, if Plutarch's explanation, inexperience, is that of the source, then T. has discarded the source's implausible explanation – Flaccus commanded three legions in an important military zone – and added two new ones, one of which, old age, makes Flaccus resemble his principal, Galba, while the other, weak character, is justified by a damning train of events. (If neither author reflects the source all we can say is that T.'s story is internally consistent and well connected to the larger narrative.)

Character is also T.'s explanation for the first of the three larger questions we will consider, namely, why did Galba fall? In chh. 4–20 T. shows that Galba failed at the crucial task of building support for his rule: he did nothing to undo the alienation of the German legions arising from their conflict with his supporter Vindex (8.2), he threw away the nascent loyalty of the praetorians by refusing them a donative (18.3), he forfeited his title to moral leadership by allowing his associates free rein (6.1), and he chose a successor who brought him no new support (15.1 n. *in . . . fertur*). The essence of T.'s explanation appears in his famous epigram on Galba, 49.4 *consensu omnium capax imperii nisi imperasset* – he was not up to the job.

The second question is why Otho succeeded. To this T. gives a different sort of answer: it was not primarily character that brought Otho to the throne but external circumstances. Otho saw the discontent that Galba's inadequacy engendered and the breakdown of military discipline that civil discord allowed and capitalized on both problems, cultivating the goodwill of the praetorians and any other soldiers to whom he had access (chh. 23–4) and encouraging sedition (ch. 25). Not crippled by an out-of-date moral code, he suited his actions to the current situation and rose to the top on the strong shoulders of the praetorians. Intelligence had something to do with his success, and indeed his grasp of political realities allowed him to weather several crises once he was in power, but without the circumstances of discontent and indiscipline he would have achieved little.

A third question T.'s narrative prompts us to ask is why the German legions revolted. To this question, which was a crucial one given the military underpinnings of the *princeps*' power, T.'s answer is complex and rich in detail. The attitude of the legions is one factor: a recent easy victory had aroused their confidence and whetted their appetite for the rewards of victory (51.1). The difficulty of maintaining military discipline when loyalty was bought and sold and betrayal unpunished is another (51.2). Long-standing hostilities between Gallic tribes in the vicinity fed the legions' eagerness for a fight (51.4, 53.3), and the legions' insecurity about Galba's intentions for them kept the situation unsettled (51.5, 53.2). There was also the rivalry between the two armies of Germany (53.2), which was exacerbated by the selfish disloyalty of individual officers who had nothing to hope for in a stable state (52.3). Such men worked their will on the weak character of Vitellius (52.4), who had inherited a *dignitas* bigger than he could manage (9.1 n.). Then one has to consider human nature: T. cites the ease with which bad men come together for violent ends (54.3). And this is just the introduction to the narrative; further circumstantial factors are given as the story proceeds.

Comparison with Plutarch's explanation is again instructive. According to Plutarch, the German legions share the empire-wide disappointment over Galba's failure to pay a donative and are particularly offended by the fallout from Vindex' revolt (e.g. Galba's removal of Verginius Rufus from the German command and the rewards and honours that accrued to Vindex' memory and supporters, *G.* 22). Where the biographer mentions triggers specific to this occasion, the historian, while including specifics (and many more of them), looks beyond them to systemic conditions (civil war, inter-tribal and inter-army rivalries, personal ambition) that loosen the military discipline upon which the peace of the empire depends.

Causae for events of lesser moment in *Histories* 1 include human nature (12.2, 18.3, 32.1, 34.2, 38.3, 54.3, 55.1, 55.4, 56.2, 80.2, 87.2, 90.3) and, very occasionally, chance (*forte* at 7.1 and 31.1, *fortuitis ... causis* at 86.3). As a general explanation for the miseries of the Flavian period as a whole T. mentions divine punishment in the preface, but this theme is absent from the narrative so far as we have it. Fate is never cited except as a belief of historical figures (18.1 n. *fato manent*) or qualified by *uelut* (50.1, 71.2). There are also explanations that are strikingly modern in their attention to economic factors (46.2–4nn.) and natural causes (Tiber flood 86.2–3nn.). Some regrettable incidents are in the end inexplicable, particularly where human behaviour is involved, the behaviour of the Vitellian army commanded by Fabius Valens upon arrival in Divodurum, for example. Received amicably, they slaughter some four thousand Gauls and are with difficulty prevented from destroying the entire city. The monstrosity of their act defies rational explanation: 63.1 *non ob praedam aut spoliandi cupidine, sed furore et rabie et causis incertis*.

Apart from this last case, which has few parallels in *Histories* 1, the explanations that we have seen so far are by and large rational: evidence and explanation agree. Style, while it may enhance the impact of an explanation (as in the epigram on Galba), does not stand in for evidence. Some of T.'s other explanations, however, seem to demand assent rather than understanding. A single example will suffice here; the topic will be discussed more fully below. At 59.1 T. reports Vitellius' execution of four centurions. Nomen and cognomen are tolled for each. Then comes the explanation: they were 'condemned for the crime of loyalty' (*damnatos fidei crimine*). To the question, why were they killed? the neutral answer would have been 'because they were loyal to Galba', a fact that was documented at 56.1 *cum protegerent Galbae imagines*. In T.'s answer style – an oxymoron – weighs in to charge those responsible for the centurions' deaths with a perverse morality in which *fides* is a *crimen*. Here the explanation goes well beyond the evidence provided. Stylistic effects such as this are reserved for moments of special bitterness, where explanation is not enough.

At 2.101.1 T. himself points out an incident in the work of his predecessors where assertions pose as explanations. Apropos of the desertion of Vitellius for Vespasian by two key commanders, he says 'writers who composed histories of this war while the Flavian house was in power put this down as concern for peace and love of country, but these causes have been fabricated to please' (*corruptas in adulationem causas*). These *corruptae causae* involve the attribution of motive (*rei publicae cura, amor*) and are themselves explained as pursuit of favour in their authors. T.'s professions of impartiality – implicit here but explicit in his prologues – have provoked many readers (see Luce (1989)). Is he so naive as to believe that the causes of bias are limited to past or potential advantage or injury to the historian himself? And if he is not so naive, how, given the manifestly engagé character of his narrative, can we avoid charging him with hypocrisy? But in *Histories* 1, at least, T.'s explanations are for the most part qualitatively different from these *corruptae causae*. His passions come through rather in the colouring (see below). T.'s confidence in the historian's ability to explain is at a high-water mark here at the outset of the *Histories*; several passages in the *Annals* suggest a significant retreat (e.g. 3.18.4 *ludibria rerum mortalium*, 6.22.1 *mihi haec ac talia audienti in incerto iudicium est fatone res mortalium et necessitate immutabili an forte uoluantur*).

Some of T.'s explanations rely heavily on the reader. For example, the reader of *Histories* 1 needs to perceive the extent to which the description of the sedition given by Galba's advisors in sections 32–3 diverges from that given by T. himself in the preceding chapters in order to realize that T. means their advice to seem flawed. Readers of *H.* need to be particularly alert to repeated incidents, for Vespasian was preceded by three emperors who got as far as he did but failed to keep their footing there. In essence T. has to tell the stories of fall (Galba, Otho, Vitellius) and rise (Otho, Vitellius, Vespasian) three times each, and the mistakes of Vespasian's predecessors help explain Vespasian's success.

The events leading up to each emperor's proclamation, for example, reflect the claimants: Otho's is characterized by subterfuge and small numbers (chh. 24–7), Vitellius' by his passivity and the troops' disorder (55–57.1), Vespasian's by his own careful deliberations and the honest enthusiasm of his men (2.74–5, 2.79–80.1). Supporters can also be compared: Otho's are of low status (Maevius Pudens, Onomastus, and *duo manipulares*, 24–5), Vitellius' have rank but also crime and character flaws (Caecina Alienus, Fabius Valens), while Vespasian relies on Mucianus (whose record was mixed but in whom this enterprise brought out the best: 10.1 nn.) and his own son Titus. (Vespasian does end up with unsavoury supporters – Antonius Primus, for example (2.86.1 *legibus nocens*), and Cornelius Fuscus (he had a taste for *noua*, *ambigua*, and *ancipitia*: 2.86.3) – but these are opportunists who sign up once movement is under way, not the inner circle.) When they actually begin the business of governing, Otho and Vitellius are shown so subservient to their troops that they are unable to oppose the soldiers' (bloodthirsty) wishes except by guile (58.2n. *occidere . . . fallendo*); Vespasian's *initia* reveal an expert in the practical business of running a campaign: 2.82.1 conscription, recall of veterans, arrangements for weapons manufacture and coinage, 2.82.3 foreign borders secured, 2.84.1–2 revenue; in short, *ea cuncta per idoneos ministros suis quaeque locis festinabantur* (2.82.1). And finally there are mistakes that Vespasian does not make: absent from the account of Vespasian's start are the statue-smashing (41.1, 55.3; indeed

Antonius Primus has *imagines* of Galba re-erected at 3.7.2), the deaths of loyal centurions (43.1, 59.1), the paranoia (25.2, 51.5, 54.1), and the greed (24.1, 51.4; at 2.82.2 Vespasian's men get an appropriate donative but no inducement to hanker after more). Vespasian's party does not remain (and perhaps never was) a paragon, of course, but by T.'s account it begins well, and Book 1's account of the reigns that preceded his is crucial for showing how it did so. (Incidents that allow a comparison between two or more of the emperors of 69 are listed in App. 3.)

7 *EXEMPLA*

A fourth element of T.'s historiographical programme is moral evaluation. *Exempla* are promised in the preface to *H.*, and by the time T. was writing the *Annals* giving memory's due to virtues and making warnings of crimes had come to seem of primary importance (*A.* 3.65.1 *quod praecipuum munus annalium reor, ne uirtutes sileantur utque prauis dictis factisque ex posteritate et infamia metus sit*; see Luce (1991) and, for a different view, Woodman (1995)). In all of T.'s work *mala exempla* are more numerous than *bona*; this is particularly true of *Histories* 1. Of the virtuous acts listed in ch. 3 – mothers accompanying exiled children, wives accompanying exiled husbands, loyal assistance from friends, relatives, and even slaves, death bravely met – only the last figures in Book 1, and that only once. It gets suitable fanfare: 43.1 *insignem illa die uirum Sempronium Densum aetas nostra uidit. Mala exempla*, being so much more numerous, are woven into the narrative with greater subtlety (see below).

8 *CHRONOLOGY*

It remains to mention a matter that T. does not address explicitly in *H.* but that can be inferred from his practice. Chronological precision *per se* was clearly not a priority for T. Chronology matters in his account of Galba's decision to adopt Piso and in his version of the encounter of Julius Atticus and Galba, so he provides the necessary temporal indications (12.1n. *paucis . . . diebus*, 35.2n. *Iulius Atticus speculator*). But he leaves modern historians groping for the dates of the Vitellian crossings of the Alps (66.3n. *sic . . . peruentum*, 70.3n. *hibernis adhuc Alpibus*), the departure of Otho's naval expedition (87.1n. *Narbonensem . . . statuit*), the praetorian riot (80–5n.), and more. In the case of the last incident, which was discussed above, it is clear why: in T.'s view the story illustrates the consequences of the collapse of military discipline and for that purpose its date is irrelevant. Modern historians want to use the incident for other purposes (e.g. to fix the date of the departure of the navy for Narbonensis; see Chilver *ad loc.*) and are hindered by not knowing its date (see also 20.1 n. *proxima pecuniae cura*).

9 *DEINOSIS*

T.'s first major historical work is shaped both by the historiographical priorities just listed and by his attitude towards the world he has chosen to portray. Reason may tell him that the principate was a good or necessary system, but it does not console him for the system's effects. In the words of Eduard Norden, 'he glows with inner fervour' ((1909) 326). In those of Ronald Mellor (1993), 'The future is where historians exercise power, and T. revels in it' (2). As a result, *mala exempla* are not simply *mala*, but *pessima*. To convey his fervour and to exercise his power T. employs a style that eschews complacency. Diction is elevated to new levels of seriousness, syntax's boundaries are challenged, and the arrangement of words and clauses confounds expectations and becomes a major carrier of meaning. The effect of T.'s style is felt in every paragraph of his work and its elements are too various to be discussed in full here. An introductory example and a glance at some elements of style that are particularly effective in *Histories* 1 will suffice to prepare the reader for T.'s powerful prose.[6]

10 ELEVATION

Here again is the opening sentence of chapter 9 together with its parallel in Plutarch (discussed above):

> superior exercitus legatum Hordeonium Flaccum spernebat, senecta ac debilitate pedum inualidum, sine constantia, sine auctoritate.
>
> Flaccus, physically incapacitated by acute gout and without practical experience, was a complete cipher to them. (Plut. *G.* 18.4)

A small detail to begin with: where Plutarch specifies the disease's name, ποδάγρα, T. specifies its effect, *debilitate pedum*, making his expression both

[6] Word choice and arrangement will receive more attention here than syntax since T.'s syntax reflects the usage of his day as well as his own stylistic choices. For an overview of T.'s syntax see the introduction to Furneaux (1884–91), and Draeger (1882) *passim*.

more decorous and more relevant to his argument.[7] Other characteristically Tacitean touches are the compactness of the expression *superior exercitus* as a reference to the legions of Upper Germany, and the abstract nouns (*senecta, debilitate, constantia, auctoritate*). The concluding anaphora illustrates both T.'s deft hand with rhetorical special effects (Plutarch uses a somewhat muddy chiastic antithesis, literally 'incapacitated in body and of affairs inexperienced') and the liberties he takes with loosely attached ablative phrases. T.'s *inualidum* is more precise than Plutarch's ἀδύνατον (Flaccus was not incapacitated, since he did act); it is also a member of T.'s favourite class of adjectives, those compounded with privative *in-* (see below). And finally, the sentence structure consisting of a dense main clause followed by a longer and more elaborate appendix is distinctively Tacitean (Plutarch uses a regular verb-final period).

Put together, these elements yield a unique style that Pliny, speaking of T.'s oratorical style, labelled 'solemn' (*Ep.* 2.11.16 σεμνῶς). Its most important constituents – elevated diction and figured speech – are examined further below.

II DICTION

An elevated diction opens up to the reader the larger significance of the particulars at hand. Adjectives and nouns compounded by the privative prefix *in-*, for example, both describe something and point to a standard from which it deviates. They appear in great abundance in T.; there are more than sixty in Book I alone, ranging from the familiar *inops*, *inimicus*, and *infelix* to the more recherché *inexorabilis* and *infructuosus*.[8] The effect

7 The following analysis takes Plutarch's version not as a stand-in for the common source, from which T. can then be shown to have deviated, but as another way of developing the same information. If T. is in fact following the source verbatim here (which seems extremely improbable), then the verbal artistry we appreciate is not that of Cornelius Tacitus but of the source author.

8 Adjectives and adverbs: *ignarus, ignauus, ignorans, ignotus, illaesus, immemor, immensus, immoderatus, immodicus, immotus, impar, impatiens, impenetrabilis, imperitus, impiger, impius, improuidus, impudicus, impune, intempestus, inanimus, inauditus, incautus, incertus, incorruptus, incruentus, incuriosus, indecorus, indefensus, inermis, iners, inexorabilis, inexpertus, infamis, infaustus, infelix, infidus, infructuosus, ingratus, inhonestus, inimicus, innocens, inoffensus, inops, inquietus, insatiabilis, inscius, insolitus, intrepidus, intutus, inualidus* (3), *irritus*; nouns: *ignauia, ignorantia, impudentia, impunitas, incolumitas, inertia, infirmitas, iniuria, inopia, inscitia, intemperies*.

may be studied at 6.1 and 6.2, where T. uses *inualidus*, *ignauissumus*, *inauditus*, *indefensus*, *innocens*, *inermis*, *infaustus*, and *inertia*.

A larger category of words that insist on the general in the particular consists of abstract nouns. Especially characteristic is T.'s use of abstract nouns as subjects of active verbs, as at 80.2 *obsequia meliorum nox abstulerat*. Although the pluperfect *abstulerat* makes this explanation particular to the occasion (contrast the *sententiae* discussed below), *nox*, which encompasses notions ranging from darkness and confusion to danger and licence, gives it a certain amplitude. At 49.1 *Galbae corpus diu neglectum et licentia tenebrarum plurimis ludibriis uexatum* the ablative *licentia tenebrarum* expresses some (but only some) of what is implicit in *nox* at 80.2. (The tone of 80.2 is further elevated by the moral note provided by *obsequia* and *meliorum*.) Even in more common constructions such as *licentia tenebrarum*, abstract nouns, because of their frequency, realize the past as the interplay of large-scale forces. In the fairly typical ch. 12 T. uses *reuerentia*, *arbitrium*, *seditio*, *adoptio*, *sermo*, *licentia*, *libido*, *aetas*, *iudicium*, *amor*, *spes*, *odium*, *actus*, *fortuna*, *cupiditas*, *facilitas*, *metus*, and *praemium*.[9] Abstract nouns are more numerous in passages of analysis and characterization and less numerous in narrative proper – ch. 51, with thirty lines of analysis, has thirty-one abstract nouns, chh. 49–50.1, with thirty lines of character sketch, have thirty, ch. 79, with thirty lines of narrative, has eleven – but there is no paragraph in *Histories* 1 entirely without them. On rare occasions they provide more elevation than a situation calls for, as at 79.2 *lubrico itinerum adempta equorum pernicitate*, which describes an almost farcical scene of horses slipping on ice. A similar expansiveness of reference is provided by impersonal passives and substantive neuter adjectives.

12 METAPHOR

Metaphors, which imply an analogy, are another element of style that allows T. to expand the particular.[10] They are frequently found in combination with other elevation-producing expressions, as at 26.1 *infecit ea tabes legionum quoque et auxiliorum motas iam mentes, postquam uulgatum erat labare Germanici exercitus fidem*. Here T. uses two abstract nouns as subjects for active verbs (*tabes*, *fidem*), an impersonal passive (*uulgatum erat*), and three metaphorical verbs (*infecit*, *motas*, *labare*). Despite the accumulation, this is not a sentence

[9] See further Walker (1976) 116.

[10] For general lists of common Tacitean metaphors see Draeger (1882) §248 and Furneaux (1884–91) §66.

that draws attention to itself; rather, it is of a piece with the surrounding narrative. It is in fact the very ordinariness of metaphors in T. that is so distinctive: what in other prose authors would be ornaments introduced in suitable settings T. uses as basic building blocks. (Unusual metaphors are listed in the index s.v.)

13 *SENTENTIAE*

A more elaborate figure of speech that provides a generalizing and elevating effect is the *sententia*. T.'s contemporary Quintilian defines the *sententia* as a *uox uniuersalis* that is applicable and interesting beyond the particular context of an utterance (*Inst.* 8.5.3). A modern scholar, more concerned with tone than type, attributes to T.'s many *sententiae* the impression the historian gives of being 'master of all he surveys' (Sinclair (1995) 147). T. uses the *sententia* primarily to enunciate the principles governing the (bad) behaviour of groups and individuals. It is one component of what Mellor calls his 'rhetoric of exposure', his programme of revealing truths that had been hidden or simply lost sight of.[11] The groups in question are large (55.1 *insita mortalibus natura*), small (44.2 *tradito principibus more*), and in between (1.3 *incorruptam fidem professis*, 54.3 *faciliore inter malos consensu*, 90.3 *ut in familiis*). Quintilian's chapter on the *sententia* owes its length to the figure's popularity (8.5.1–35). He likens *sententiae* to eyes (*oculi eloquentiae*) even as he urges restraint in their use: 'I don't want eyes all over the body, nor do I want the other limbs to lose their function' (8.5.34). An historian has to exercise particular caution because the figure tends to bring the narrative to a full stop (8.5.27). T. is properly abstemious, and most of his *sententiae* punctuate as well as illuminate (see index s.v.).[12] But T.'s *sententiae* are not quite the sparkling brilliants that Quintilian seems to have in mind: what their light exposes is all too often a grim truth. Among T.'s themes are punishment (3.2, 41.2), crime (12.3, 39.2), misfortune (15.3), suspicion and hatred (21.1), danger (21.2, 56.3, 62.1), failure (39.1), violence (54.3), reluctance (55.1), and self-interest (15.4, 90.3). Master he may be, but his domain

[11] Mellor (1993) 126. Quintilian's favourite metaphor for the figure is that of light: *lumina . . . praecipueque in clausulis posita* (2, cf. 28, 34), *nitere* (19), *scintillae* (29), *oculos eloquentiae* (34), *clarescit* (19).

[12] For example, the sentences after the following *sententiae* are not connected to what precedes: 3.2 *non esse . . . ultionem*, 12.3 *apud infirmum . . . peccaretur*, 15.3 *secundae res . . . corrumpimur*, 39.1 *optima . . . effugerat*, 44.2 *tradito . . . ultionem*, 56.3 *minore discrimine . . . quaeri*, 62.1 *nihil in discordiis . . . esset*, 90.3 *priuata . . . decus publicum*.

appalls him. Some authors, including Quintilian himself in a later part of his chapter, treat epigrams (i.e. expressions of conspicuous verbal neatness, such as 25.1 *suscepere duo manipulares imperium populi Romani transferendum et transtulerunt*) as *sententiae*. Many epigrams, however, including this one, lack the elevating effect of *uoces uniuersales*. For a list of both types see App. 2.

As we have seen, the various elements of Tacitean elevation are generally used to emphasize the darker side of the Roman world in A.D. 69. Ancient rhetorical theory designates this procedure *deinosis*, or 'making terrible' (see Cousin (1951)). Quintilian defines it as 'style adding force to things that are undeserved, harsh, or hateful' (*Inst.* 6.2.24); its relevant emotions are anger, hatred, fear, jealousy, and grief (6.2.20). An orator uses it to involve a judge's passions, particularly in prooemia and epilogues (6.2.20). T. uses it throughout. It is obvious, perhaps too obvious, in a passage such as 40.2:

> igitur milites Romani, quasi Vologaesum aut Pacorum auito Arsacidarum solio depulsuri ac non imperatorem suum inermem et senem trucidare pergerent, disiecta plebe, proculcato senatu, truces armis, rapidi equis forum irrumpunt. nec illos Capitolii aspectus et imminentium templorum religio et priores et futuri principes terruere quo minus facerent scelus cuius ultor est quisquis successit.

The analogy between the Roman emperor and one of the interchangeable foreign dynasts, the venerability and vulnerability of the victim, the violent action (*disiecta, proculcato, irrumpunt*), the contempt for cultural touchstones (Capitol, temples, past and future *principes*), the moral labels (*scelus, ultor*), all of these elements plainly convey outrage. But the most effective medium for Tacitean *deinosis* is much more subtle.

14 APPENDIX SENTENCES

A sentence structure considered characteristic of T. consists of a pithy main clause complete in itself, followed by a subordinate appendix that overwhelms the main clause in length and complexity. There are some fifty-five such sentences in *Histories* 1, or about 13 per cent of its 432 sentences. A few examples will show how much such a structure can contribute to the impact of T.'s narrative. Consider this sentence, which follows the night-time expulsion of some civilians from a legionary camp (|| marks the end of the main clause):

> 54.2 inde atrox rumor, || affirmantibus plerisque interfectos, ac ni sibi ipsi consulerent, fore ut acerrimi militum et praesentia conquesti per tenebras et inscitiam ceterorum occiderentur.

The main clause, three short words, conveys the quality (*atrox* 'horrifying' 'alarming') of the soldiers' talk. What they actually said to one another is reported in the subordinate ablative absolute. *atrox* prepares the reader to interpret the inference the soldiers draw from the rumoured execution as evidence of the near-panic conditions of the camp.[13] A common variation on this structure reserves characterization for the appendix, as in the description of the Helvetii at 67.1:

> irritauerant turbidum ingenium Heluetii, || Gallica gens olim armis uirisque, mox memoria nominis clara, de caede Galbae ignari et Vitellii imperium abnuentes.[14]

In the examples just given the appendix supports the interpretation or attitude expressed in the main clause. Alarm, anger, ignorance, and obstruction all suit T.'s view of the period and this unsettling sentence structure combines with the other elements of style we have examined to give them due prominence. But at 55.1 he uses the same structure to undermine an apparent statement of facts:

> inferioris tamen Germaniae legiones sollemni kalendarum Ianuariarum sacramento pro Galbae adactae, || multa cunctatione et raris primorum ordinum uocibus, ceteri silentio proximi cuiusque audaciam exspectantes, insita mortalibus natura propere sequi quae piget inchoare.

That is, the legions of Lower Germany declared themselves loyal on 1 January, but the declaration meant little given its manner and cause (hesitation, expectant silence, nascent audacity, herd instinct).[15]

[13] In a similarly built sentence at 6.1 the appendix explains *tardum et cruentum*, likewise at 8.2 (*solliciti et irati*), 9.1 (*spernebat*), 13.4 (*spem . . . rapiebat*), 20.1 (*uix decuma portione*), 31.2 (*diffidebatur*).

[14] Cf. 18.1 *contemptorem . . . uitantur*, 26.2 *ignarus . . . peruicax*, 31.2 *infestae . . . Galba*, 45.2 *industriae . . . infensi*, 50.1 *ante . . . crederetur*, 51.4 *super . . . iactabant*, 66.2 *accensis . . . prodigus*, 71.3 *eandem . . . irascebantur*, 79.1 *ad . . . intenta*, 90.2 *crebro . . . sonans*. Still another variation is seen in sentences that seem to end, then offer a comment, either via a noun in apposition (44.2n. *munimentum . . . ultionem*) or a free-floating adverb (65.1n. *crebrius . . . ut*).

[15] Cf. 47.1n. *adnitentibus cunctis*.

The connection between sentence structure and tone is perhaps best illustrated by contrasting two sentences of similar content but different type. The weakening of military discipline is an important theme of the book and T. devotes a number of passages to analysing its causes in specific incidents. The first such occurs at 5.1:

> miles urbanus longo Caesarum sacramento imbutus et ad destituendum Neronem arte magis et impulsu quam suo ingenio traductus, postquam neque dari donatiuum sub nomine Galbae promissum neque magnis meritis ac praemiis eundem in pace quem in bello locum praeuentamque gratiam intellegit apud principem a legionibus factum, pronus ad nouas res scelere insuper Nymphidii Sabini praefecti imperium sibi molientis agitatur.

This is an ordinary historical period: it begins with its subject, ends with its verb, and packs a series of subordinate explanations between the two (*imbutus, traductus, postquam . . . intellegit, pronus*). The sentence is an efficient and fairly matter-of-fact statement of and explanation for the unsettled state of the praetorian guard. There are indeed some slight shadings of black (the selfishness of *praeuentam gratiam*, the moral label *scelere*, the ironic juxtaposition of *praefecti* and *imperium*), but there are also brighter tones (e.g. the antithesis *meritis~praemiis*, which reflects an accepted moral code, and the premise of real loyalty – *ingenio* – to the Julio-Claudian house). The assessment is balanced.

A more negative picture of unsettled loyalties occurs at 31.3:

> Germanica uexilla diu nutauere, || inualidis adhuc corporibus et placatis animis, quod eos a Nerone Alexandriam praemissos atque inde rursus longa nauigatione aegros impensiore cura Galba refouebat.

The main clause here characterizes the behaviour neutrally (see on *nutauere*), but the ablative absolute explains the soldiers' not very creditable reasons for not joining their confrères in abandoning Galba and the causal clause details the attentions they had received from Galba. Despite the element of balance inherent in *nutauere*, then, the appendix only explains why the troops favoured Galba; their inclination for revolt is taken for granted. It would have been possible to accommodate the contrast between *nutauere* and *refouebat* with a concessive clause ('although Galba was reviving the troops, their loyalty wavered'). T.'s sentence, disconcertingly, does not acknowledge that there is anything to explain away.

A majority of the appendix sentences give vivid expression to T.'s generally pessimistic view of the past. But like *sententiae*, these stylistically powerful structures can also provide punctuation, as at 47.2, which concludes the report of the first day of Otho's principate:

> Pisonem Verania uxor ac frater Scribonianus, Titum Vinium Crispina filia composuere, || quaesitis redemptisque capitibus, quae uenalia interfectores seruauerant.

The ablative absolute, chronologically anterior to the main clause, contains the more arresting material and more pungent expression (heads for sale, killers saving); in its posterior position it has a show-stopping effect.

Although appendix sentences are no more numerous than other types, their power is disproportionate. Two reasons may be suggested. First, the looseness of the syntactic connection between the main clause (which requires no supplement) and the appendix demands that the reader determine how the two are related in content: do they agree? conflict? contrast? Where Cicero would supply conjunctions and Caesar or Livy temporal indicators, T. leaves the reader to make sense of his juxtapositions. The reader who does so has been drawn into the text. Harder to analyse, but no less important, is the unsettling effect of having so often to qualify a main clause after the fact. However satisfying a main clause such as *irritauerant turbidum ingenium Heluetii* may seem in itself, it proves insufficient to the complexity that T. wants to convey, which contrasts glory past and future with a present of blind error (67.1, quoted above). These elements could have been presented in a regular period, neatly subordinated to the main event, *irritauerant*. As T. writes it, however, while the main event gets due prominence at the beginning of the sentence, blind error weighs just as heavily at the end and changes the significance of the main event substantially. As a rule in T., the more pithily expressed his main clause is, the more likely it is to be qualified before the sentence comes to an end; the style insists that first thoughts and initial appearances rarely suffice.

15 *VARIATIO*

Histories 1 is not a story of unrelieved gloom. *Bona exempla* are few, but rational analysis takes over at times (as at 5.1, quoted above). The four long speeches in Book 1 are also written in styles very different from that of the narrative (see their introductory notes). In fact, after elevation, variety is probably the most striking characteristic of T.'s style. As we have seen, even the most distinctive sentence type only accounts for some 13 per cent of his sentences.

The pursuit of variety is perceptible at every level of Tacitean composition from the smallest phrase – he uses both *ut mos est* and *ut moris est* (7.3n.), for example, and refers to the praetorian prefect with at least six different titles (46.1 n.) – to paragraphs-long type-scenes (4.2n. *finis Neronis*). *Variatio*'s most familiar manifestations occur where content and prior usage lead the reader to expect parallel phrases or clauses, as after *seu* (9.1 n.) or in adverbial expressions modifying a single verb. Plentiful examples of verbal inconcinnity can be found, neatly categorized, in Sörbom (1935) (for passages from Book 1 see index s.v. *uariatio*). Less numerous, but perhaps more significant for the tone of T.'s narrative, are expressions that display what might be called inconcinnity of thought, that is, expressions in which an innocuously parallel form contains two (or more) substantially different kinds of content. A simple (and frequent) type sets a concrete term in parallel with an abstraction, as in *plausus et immodica studia* (35.2) or *strepitus telorum et facies belli* (85.1). More subtle is a statement about the armies of Illyricum, *nec uitiis nec uiribus miscebantur* (9.3), where the alliteration reinforces the parallelism established by *nec* . . . *nec* but *uires*, when used of armies, denotes not (or not only) moral qualities (which would constitute a proper parallel to *uitia*), but strategic clout. More complex still is the description of Galba on 15 January: *inopia ueri et consensu errantium uictus*. Though *inopia* and *consensu* are parallel ablatives of cause explaining Galba's decision, Galba himself only experiences the *consensus errantium*; T. is the one who perceives *inopia ueri*. The effect of these non-parallel parallels is to roughen the surface of the narrative, to give the reader pause, to offer equivalencies that require thought. And that is really the essential point: T.'s style makes you think. He has been likened to both Cassandra (Mellor (1993) 112) and Oscar Wilde (Cousin (1951) 234), but neither comparison is perfect. T. is no divine mouthpiece, nor does he write to shock. This senator, who had witnessed the beginning of Rome's third dynasty and much else besides, wrote Latin with the depth and texture that were appropriate to the public act of writing history.

16 *HISTORIES* 1

With its story of the struggles of the short-lived emperors Galba, Otho, and Vitellius, and its hints about the off-stage Vespasian, *Histories* 1 is an exciting tale. Highlights are Galba's rationale for adopting a successor (chh. 15–16; this was the policy that replaced dynastic succession in the period when T. was writing), the ill-omened presentation of his heir to the troops (ch. 18), the growth of Otho's sedition (chh. 21–31), an advising scene replete with all the nastiness of court politics (chh. 32–3), the murder of Galba and his closest associates with the populace looking on as if it were a show (chh. 40–1), the distress of the senate in the face of rapid changes of rulers (chh. 45, 47), the first description of Vitellius, whose character plainly disgusted T. (ch. 62), and the unstoppable two-pronged crossing of the Vitellian armies into northern Italy (chh. 63–70). The book ends on a tense note, with Vitellius' forces north of the Po and Otho on his way to confront them.

The structure of *Histories* 1 is complex but always clear; it provides surprise and suspense, but also satisfactory endings. The book opens with a three-part preface: ch. 1 introduces the author, 2–4.1 the content, 4.2–11 the background to the narrative. The retrospective in chh. 4–11, which covers the period between Nero's suicide in June of 68 and 1 January 69, itself has two clearly articulated parts, the first intent on Rome (chh. 4–7), the second offering a broad sweep through the provinces of the empire (chh. 8–11). The concluding sentence is a miniature marvel: *hic fuit rerum Romanarum status cum Seruius Galba iterum Titus Vinius consules inchoauere annum sibi ultimum, rei publicae prope supremum.* This one sentence brings together what was diffused throughout the retrospective (*rerum Romanarum*), closes the introduction by returning it to its beginning (*Seruius Galba iterum Titus Vinius consules*, cf. 1.1), launches the narrative on 1 January, and alerts the reader as to what was at stake (*rei publicae prope supremum*).

The first large panel of the narrative (chh. 12–21) opens with a reminder of the unrest in Germany (12.1), but focuses on Rome and Galba. It is a story of failure, justifying T.'s negative assessment of Galba (49.4, quoted above). Galba's successor, Otho, makes a surprise appearance in ch. 13, which prepares the way for Otho's success story in chh. 21–6. The final clash between Galba and Otho, the work of a single day, yields a long and dramatic panel (chh. 27–47). Galba's story is brought to an end by obituaries, first his associates' (ch. 48), then, in more detail, his own (ch. 49). Ch. 50 reopens the German narrative from the perspective still of Rome (50.1 *trepidam urbem . . . nouus insuper de Vitellio nuntius exterruit*). It also reintroduces Vespasian, who will move into full view at the beginning of Book 2. But before Vespasian come Vitellius and the restless legions of Germany (chh. 51–70). This section begins with an analysis of causes and a muster of strength (chh. 51–4); it ends with the German armies moving inexorably towards Italy with Vitellius following ominously behind (61.2 *tota mole belli secuturus*). At ch. 71 we leave the Vitellians on the move and return to Rome and Otho's principate (chh. 71–90), a section that balances chh. 12–21 on Galba's *acta*: where Galba failed completely, Otho makes the best of a bad situation. The more positive tone here is set in relief by the storm approaching from the North. Though Otho himself remains in Rome until the end of this section, events bring many areas of the empire back into the narrative (in ch. 76 Illyricum, Spain, Gaul, Judaea, Syria, Egypt, Africa; in ch. 78 Spain, Cappadocia, Asia; in ch. 79 Moesia). The book ends with a concentration of focus: the date is 14 March 69 and Otho sets out for war (ch. 90).

17 THE SOURCES

The events of Book 1 took place when T. was about thirteen years old. When he came to write it *c.* A.D. 100 he was able to draw upon contemporary documents and some three decades' worth of retellings both oral and written.

The first category was probably the least important. Research in documentary archives is assumed of him for *H.* by Pliny, who had been consulted about an A.D. 93 trial in which he had played a prominent role (*Ep.* 7.33.3 *diligentiam tuam fugere non possit, cum sit in publicis actis*), but would have yielded little towards the narrative of Book 1. The items most likely to have come from official sources, especially senatorial archives, are the military *uacationes* (46.2n.), the senatorial embassies (19.2, 74.2), the restoration of senatorial rank to three men (77.3), the re-erection of Poppaea's statues *per senatus consultum* (78.2), the successful campaign against the Sarmatae (79.5n. *consularibus ornamentis donantur*), and the date of Otho's last acts in Rome (90.1n. *pridie Idus Martias commendata patribus res publica*), none of which appears in any other extant source. But the significant events of A.D. 69 did not occur at official meetings.

It is difficult to gauge the importance of oral report for this book. T. mentions eyewitness accounts for other books of *H.* (3.65.2, 4.81.3); at least some of these will have been oral only (90.2n. *erant qui . . . noscerent*). Suetonius, who wrote not long after T., has information from his father, who fought at Otho's defeat (Suet. *O.* 10.1). Plutarch, who probably wrote rather earlier, had spoken to an ex-consul who had tried to 'read' the battlefield shortly after that same battle (Plut. *O.* 14.1–2). Of people named in connection with the events of Book 1, some were active well into the 90s (Verginius Rufus 8.2n., Verania Gemina 47.2n.; possibly Pompeius Longinus 31.2n.) and at least one, Arrius Antoninus, seems to have survived into the period of the book's composition (77.2n.). But T. cites none of these nor any other oral source. It is possible, however, that he owes the story of Otho's naval expedition to Narbonensis (87.1–2nn.) to his father-in-law, Agricola, who lost his mother in that campaign and spent time in the area shortly after it (*Agr.* 7.1–2); the expedition is treated by no other source.[16]

As for written sources, Josephus, an older contemporary of T., tells us that the period from Nero's suicide to Vespasian's accession had been treated by many authors both Greek and Roman (*BJ* 4.492–6). But all indications in *Histories* 1 suggest that T. used a single written source as the basis of his narrative. He does have more information than the authors of the parallel tradition (discussed below), but his narrative of the events of 1 January–14 March is also the longest.[17] As we shall see, where the accounts overlap they are generally in agreement on events and they sometimes even share details of language; there are no significant differences in matters of fact. If T. did supplement the common source with documentary evidence or oral testimony or with material from another written source, his supplements bulk rather small.[18] The identity of the common source remains a matter of scholarly dispute and need not detain us here; T. considered none of his predecessors in the field satisfactory (1.1, cf. 2.101.1, quoted above).[19] It is more productive to examine the parallel tradition to learn how T. used this source.

[16] There is a bare mention in Dio (preserved at Zonaras 11.15: 'Otho sent a force by land and by sea').

[17] Chh. 12–90 have 44.5 large-format Teubner pages, Plutarch has 24 small-format Teubner pages (*G.* 16–29 and *O.* 1–5.2), Suetonius 8.5 small pages (*G.* 11.2–23, *O.* 4–8, *Vit.* 7.3–9), Dio 4 small pages (64.4–64.10.1).

[18] For items that may derive from a second written source see 6.1n. *Cornelius Laco*, 27.2n. *innixus liberto*, 31.1n. *insidiis et simulatione*, 41.2n. *uarie prodidere*, 43.1n. *insignem . . . uidit*, 73.1n. *Caluia Crispinilla*.

[19] Possible sources (and their principal supporters) are Cluvius Rufus (Mommsen (1870); see also Townend (1964)), Fabius Rusticus (Groag (1897)), and Pliny the Elder (Fabia (1893), Hardy (1890)). For discussion see Syme (1958) App. 29; he calls the source 'Ignotus'.

18 THE PARALLEL TRADITION

There are three parallel accounts of the events T. describes in Book 1: Plutarch's *Lives* of Galba and Otho, Suetonius' *Lives* of Galba, Otho, and Vitellius, and the excerpts and epitomes of Dio, Book 64. By careful comparison among the four one is able to see more clearly here than anywhere else in T.'s historical work the choices he makes in the selection, arrangement, and presentation of his material.[20] (The most significant parallel passages are printed in Appendix 1 and will be referred to by T.'s chapter and sentence number here.)

Where the separate accounts show parallels of language and even sentence structure it is clear that each author has followed the common source closely.[21] Some such passages plainly involve must-have anecdotes and *bons mots*: Galba's famous phrases (5.2, 35.2, 41.2), Claudius' clever revenge on the despicable Vinius (48.3), Otho's tears (82.1). For some of these items two or more accounts are essentially the same (22.1b, 24.1, 24.2, 25.1, 25.1b, 27.1–2, 27.2, 41.2, 41.2b, 44.2, 49.1, 57.1 (T. and Plutarch, but not Suetonius), 72.1, 74.1, 77.2). For example, all four authors know about the elaborate plan that Otho and his associates concocted to extract him from the palace on the morning of the coup and three of them report it step-by-step, even though none of the steps was particularly important to the outcome (see on ch. 27 in App. 1). T., Plutarch, and Suetonius each begin with Galba sacrificing and the seer's warning, each brings out the irony of Otho's presence and explains the property-inspection ruse. They even trace the route by which Otho made his way out of the palace, and describe his destination in nearly identical terms: *in Velabrum, inde ad miliarium aureum sub aedem Saturni pergit* (27.2), 'He came to the forum, where stands the gilded column at which all the roads that cut across Italy terminate' (Plut. *G.* 24.2), *in foro sub aede Saturni ad miliarium aureum* (Suet. *O.* 6.2).

Close attention to the source is also apparent on a smaller scale. At 57.1, for example, T. and Plutarch report the same sequence of ideas:

> superior exercitus speciosis senatus populique Romani nominibus relictis tertium nonas Ianuarias Vitellio accessit.

[20] The discussion in Martin (1981) 189–96 is judicious but draws primarily on material from Book 2.

[21] It is unlikely that T. used Plutarch as a principal source or that Plutarch used T. or that Suetonius so used either. Dio's sources are more difficult to ascertain. See Hardy (1890) xxiv–xxxv, lvi–lx.

> And straight away Flaccus' force cast aside their fine and democratic oaths of allegiance to the senate and swore to Vitellius that they would do what he commanded. (Plut. *G.* 22.8)

The two versions share the identification of the military forces, the specious oaths, the declaration for Vitellius, the scornful tone. There are differences of detail – T.'s date is more precise than 'straight away' and *accessit* is more compact than 'swore to do what he commanded' – but there has been no major rethinking in either. Suetonius omits the scorn.

Another category of close parallels shows shared ornaments of style: antithesis (22.1, 88.1), metaphor and simile (12.1, 13.3, 32.1, 37.5, 40.1), epigram (19.1, 45.1, 49.2, 72.1 b, 74.1, 81.1). The epigram at 81.1, *cum timeret Otho timebatur*, for example, adds no essential information to the story of the praetorian riot, but its felicity won it acceptance from Plutarch as well as T.: *O.* 3.5 'Fearing for these men he himself was fearful to them.'

Other parallel narratives have been adapted to their context in either content (5.2, 13.4, 28, 35.2, 41.3, 43.1, 89.3) or phrasing (48.3, 71.2, 77.3, 82.1). Thus T.'s version of a disreputable anecdote about Vinius, although it contains the same basic elements as Plutarch's, is noticeably neater in expression:

> seruili deinceps probro respersus est, tamquam scyphum aureum in conuiuio Claudio furatus, et Claudius postera die soli omnium Vinio fictilibus ministrari iussit. (48.3)
>
> Dining with Claudius Caesar he carried off a silver cup. When Claudius heard, he invited him back to dinner the next day, and when Vinius came he ordered the servants to bring out and set before him nothing silver but only earthenware. (Plut. *G.* 12.2)

soli omnium Vinio is more pointed than 'when Vinius came', and the impersonal passive *ministrari* allows T. to leave out the superfluous servants.[22] T. also makes the diagnostic value of the anecdote clear at the outset: *seruili probro respersus est.* Occasionally T., Plutarch, and Suetonius will use a successful expression differently: with general and specific applications, for example (7.3n. *tamquam . . . festinantes*), or in connection with different events (8.1 n. *tamquam . . . multitudine*, 19.1 n. *quadriduo*, 45.1 n. *aliud . . . populum*, 47.2n. *cruento . . . iacentium*, etc. For further examples see App. 1).

[22] The material of the stolen cup differs in the two accounts. Suetonius, in a different context, tells the story with a gold cup (*Cl.* 32), which suggests that Plutarch normalized the cup's material.

An adaptation of content can be seen in the reports about the prodigies heralding Otho's loss of control:

> in uestibulo Capitolii omissas habenas bigae cui Victoria institerat. (86.1)
>
> Everyone saw that in the Capitolium the reins of the Nike standing on a chariot had been loosed from her hands as if she was no longer able to control it. (Plut. *O.* 4.4)
>
> statuam Diui Iuli in insula Tiberini amnis sereno et immoto die ab occidente in orientem conuersam. (86.1 b)
>
> The statue of Gaius Caesar on the island in the river Tiber, without the occurrence of either seismic movement or wind, turned from west to east. (Plut. *O.* 4.4)
>
> statuam Diui Iuli ad orientem sponte conuersam. (Suet. *Ves.* 5.7)

These and other prodigies are reported by T. with annalistic fullness (86n.), but Plutarch selects and analyses ('Everyone saw . . . '). T. and Suetonius give different dates for the statue prodigy (see n.). But the language used to report the signs remains very close: *omissas habenas* ≈ τὰς ἡνίας . . . ἀφειμένας, *statuam Diui Iuli . . . conuersam* ≈ *statuam Diui Iuli . . . conuersam.*[23] Similarly, the language with which T. and Plutarch herald Sempronius Densus' heroics (*insignem illa die uirum Sempronium Densum aetas nostra uidit*; Plut. *G.* 26.4–5 'No one kept them off or supported him except one man, the only one among the thousands seen by the sun who was worthy of the Roman empire. He was Sempronius Densus, a centurion') is closely related even though the content differs: in Plutarch he dies defending Galba, while T. has him defending Piso (43.1).

The parallels examined so far give the impression that T. weighed each sentence in the source and either adopted its essence (for points that didn't merit his special handling), or took it as it was (for signal stylistic successes), or recast or reset it, depending on whether form or context or both needed redoing. The most striking example of retained language and content is perhaps that at 41.3:

> de percussore non satis constat: quidam Terentium euocatum, alii Laecanium, crebrior fama tradidit Camurium quintae decimae legionis militem.

[23] For a more extensive passage in which T. uses a more lively rhetoric than Plutarch does for the same material see 45.2nn. *Marium . . . subtraxit.*

> The man who killed him, according to most writers, was a certain Camurius from Legio xv. Some report that it was Terentius, others Lecaenius, still others Fabius Fabullus, who they also say cut off Galba's head and carried it wrapped in a cloak, since its baldness made it difficult to hold. (Plut. *G.* 27.2)

Included in the shared material here is what looks like a claim by both T. and Plutarch to have checked numerous sources, but that job must in fact have been done (or fabricated) at an earlier stage of the tradition.[24] The content of the statement – that Galba's assassin was variously identified – may well be true, but there is nothing to suggest that either T. or Plutarch verified it for himself. Which is not to say that the passage was adopted without thought. In fact, P. has dropped the military rank of one of the possible assassins (*euocatum*), and T. has omitted one of the four names and the rather gruesome story that went with it (49.1 n. *plurimis* . . . *uexatum*). But source criticism, even the rudimentary sort that T. applies immediately above (41.2 *ut cuique odium aut admiratio fuit, uarie prodidere*), would have been counterproductive here, for the assassination is chilling precisely because almost any Roman soldier could have done it and done it quite casually. Indeed fully 120 people claimed rewards from Otho for services rendered in connection with the assassination of his predecessor (44.2). Loyalty such as that shown by Sempronius Densus, not betrayal, was the surprising thing on 15 January in 69.[25]

Differences on plain matters of fact do occur, but the information is generally of small importance (see App. 4). In some cases – that concerning the number of members on Galba's property reclamation board, for example, where Suetonius says fifty, T. thirty (21.1 n.) – we lack independent evidence for deciding which is correct. For others we have reason to believe that T. gives the correct version.

A more significant sort of difference may be illustrated by the abortive plan to proclaim Otho before 15 January. Both T. and Suetonius report such a plan, but the details are rather different (26.1, Suet. *O.* 6.1). Suetonius dates it to immediately following (*statim*) Piso's adoption (which took place on the 10th) and says that it was called off as a courtesy to the praetorian

24 At 41.2 he shares a similar claim with Suetonius: *plures prodidere* (see n.).

25 Suetonius' expectations were more sanguine: *G.* 20.1 *illud mirum admodum fuerit, neque praesentium quemquam opem imperatori ferre conatum et omnes qui arcesserentur spreuisse nuntium excepta Germanicianorum uexillatione.*

cohort on guard duty that day and further delayed on the advice of a seer. In T. the proclamation was set for the evening of the 14th but postponed until the following morning because of the potential for confusion in the darkness when the troops were drunk and dispersed in their separate camps. The significant difference between the two accounts is not so much the date – Suetonius' *statim* is too vague to be taken as a reference to the day of Piso's adoption, as some have done (see Murison (1991 b) *ad loc.*) – but rather the explanation for the plan's cancellation, the *causa*: Suetonius' Otho defers to (presumed) praetorian sensibility, while T. cites more practical considerations.[26]

An historian who goes looking for explanations will not always find sufficient ones. Another measure of T.'s quality as an historian (and another source of differences between T. and the parallel tradition), is that unresolvable dubieties are declared as such. The principal vehicles are alternative questions and disquieting rumours (App. 4). The different sources' treatment of Fonteius Capito, for example, is instructive. Capito, commander of the legions of Lower Germany, was executed in 68, ostensibly in Galba's interest if not at his behest (7.1). All of the sources tell a simple story, according to which Capito was a rebel and was executed by a loyal Galba supporter, Fabius Valens. But T. is suspicious: he knows that Valens has backed and then betrayed other coup attempts, and that the winners of conflicts get to write the records, so he mentions another version of what happened, introducing it with the words *fuere qui crederent* (7.2). Besides preserving a second explanation of Capito's death, this sentence contributes to the theme of the disinformation that circulated during a period of civil war. Much has been written deprecating T.'s use of loaded alternatives and rumour-based innuendo in the *Annals*, but here at least, because the reasoning behind the alternative is so clear, there is little to criticize.

Still other differences between T.'s account and the rest of the tradition arise from his omissions. The most significant omissions stem from his choice of starting date (App. 4), but some occur during his chosen period as well. Many are plainly due to his sense of generic decorum: the biographers report things beneath history's notice, such as the name of the condition from which Hordeonius Flaccus suffered (gout: 9.1 n. *debilitate pedum*), the amount of Otho's debt (200 million sesterces: Plut. *G.* 21.1), the sum Vinius' daughter paid for her father's head (47.2n.), Tigellinus shaving (Plut. *O.* 2.3), and the sensational details of the abuse of Galba's head (49.1 n. *plurimis ludibriis uexatum*). Suetonius, whose focus is more strictly biographical than

[26] See further 39.2n. *agitasse ... dicitur*, 55.4n. *non ... locutus*.

Plutarch's (cf. Plut. *G.* 2.3), also provides information about Galba's eating habits (Suet. *G.* 22.1), omens of his fall (Suet. *G.* 18.3, 19.1), dreams (Suet. *G.* 18.2, *O.* 7.2), and more sums of money (Suet. *O.* 5.2, 7.1). Much of this we are glad to learn, but we do not learn it from T.

Finally, some differences are due to T.'s inclusion (or creation) of material absent from the other sources. There are several categories. The material possibly owed to senatorial archives or to oral report has already been mentioned. Another important category is names of individuals. In chh. 29–31, for example, T. describes the measures taken in response to the first news of Otho's proclamation: supporters were sent to secure the allegiance of troops dispersed throughout the city. Plutarch has the same incident in *G.* 25.4. Where Plutarch gives two names (Piso and Marius Celsus), T. gives seven with details to match (including a speech by Piso and reports about the missions of the rest). At 7.1 and 43.2 T. has two names to Plutarch's one (*G.* 15.2 and 27.4). Other names are omitted by all sources but T.: Otho's praetorian prefects (46.1) and speech writer (90.2), Calvia Crispinilla (73.1), three men restored to the senate (77.3), four tribunes discharged from the urban troops (20.1), and a scout aided by Otho (24.1). Many others occur in connection with provincial affairs (see below). T. is also more generous in describing the emotional state of the city of Rome (e.g. 32.1, 35.1, 36.1–2, 40.1, 45.1, 50, 85.1–3, 88.2–89.2, 90.2–3), descriptions that have no parallels in Plutarch or Suetonius.

The two most significant categories of material absent from the parallel tradition are speeches and provincial activity. Plutarch does have one short speech (*G.* 22.4–5; 55.4n. *non... locutus*), but nothing equivalent to the speeches in *Histories* 1. Plutarch mentions both Piso's address to the *speculatores* (*G.* 26.4) and Otho's post-riot speech (*O.* 3.8), but T. makes the men speak for nearly two chapters each (29.2–30, 83.2–84). Suetonius gives the gist of Otho's first address in the praetorian camp in a few short words (*O.* 6.3 *nihil magis pro contione testatus est, quam id demum se habiturum, quod sibi illi reliquissent*); T. again devotes two chapters (37–38.2). Galba's adoption speech (15–16) is not even mentioned elsewhere. These are all free compositions that contribute to the historian's analysis and delineation of character (see introductory notes).[27]

The parallel sources show a minimal interest in events occurring in or policies pertaining to Rome's provinces. T. establishes the theme with the

[27] T. passes up at least one occasion for a speech in the senate: Suet. *O.* 7.1 *ingressus senatum positaque breui oratione quasi raptus de publico et suscipere imperium ui coactus gesturusque communi omnium arbitrio.*

geographical survey in chh. 8–11 (see introductory note for its uniqueness). The provinces are surveyed again, more briefly, in ch. 76, and 78.1 is devoted to measures affecting the provinces. Ch. 79, a long chapter, covers a foreign attack on Moesia and the province's successful defence. Bulking still larger is the Vitellian panel (especially chh. 56–70), which has, as we have seen, an inadequate counterpart in Plutarch's *G.* 22 (among other things, Plutarch omits four names: 56.1 n. *quattuor centuriones*). There is nothing equivalent in Suetonius and only a tantalizing hint in Dio (a single mention of Fabius Valens at 64.10).

Ronald Martin's excellent chapter on T.'s use of his sources in *H.* was mentioned at the beginning of this section; his concluding words ((1981) 198) may be given now:

> Whatever the source or sources from which he has gathered his material, Tacitus has imposed on it his own over-view of the events, their causes, and their interrelationship. Moreover, the treatment of the whole section bears his own unmistakable imprint, in which moral judgment and dramatic impact unite to give a peculiarly Tacitean emphasis and profile to the narrative.

19 THE TEXT

The fundamental source for our text of *H.* is a single eleventh-century manuscript, Laurentianus 68.2.[28] This manuscript, referred to by the siglum **M**, is now preserved in the Biblioteca Mediceo-Laurentiana in Florence. It was written in Beneventan script at Montecassino and contains, besides *H.*, Books 11–16 of the *Annals* and the major works of Apuleius; *Histories* 1–5, in fact, is presented as Books 17–21 of the *Annals*, following the chronology of the subject matter rather than that of composition. Some 900 years had passed since T.'s writing; in that period his text was copied into different scripts with different degrees of diligence. At each stage errors entered. Two stages of the transmission prior to **M** can be identified from errors found in **M**: there was once a copy in minuscules, before that one in rustic capitals. The latter was a copy made in late antiquity; closer to T.'s own text we cannot get.

M was itself copied. From its copies and their descendants (the '*recentiores*') one can fill in the gaps that arose in **M** owing to physical damage

[28] The following is largely derived from the account of Tarrant (1983) 407–9.

subsequent to the copying (e.g. 1.69–75.2, 1.86.2–2.2.2). Establishing the text of **M** was the first stage of producing our modern text. Some of the errors that centuries of copyists generated in **M** have been emended by further centuries of readers and scholars.

The text printed here adopts the paragraph and sentence numeration of the Teubner text of H. Heubner (Stuttgart, 1978), but differs from both that edition and the *OCT* of C. D. Fisher (Oxford, 1911) in spelling, punctuation, and occasionally paragraphing. Where the text is substantively different from that in these standard editions the notes explain (15.4 *et iam*, 18.1 *dirumpendis*, 30.3 *perinde*, 31.1 *apud signa*, 33.2 *proinde*, 46.4 *ex fisco suo*, 49.1 *e prioribus*, 52.2 *auiditate imperandi*, 53.1 *cito*, 55.4 [*in modum contionis aut*], 58.2 *satiatis*, 58.2 *sanguine se*, 70.1 *exciti*, 74.1 *quietis locum*, 77.3 †*Saeuino Promquo*†, 87.2 †*immutatus*†, 88.3 *ac*). Spelling has been regularized according to the *OLD* (e.g. prepositional prefixes are assimilated to initial consonants) and minuscule 'v' has been replaced by consonantal 'u'. The principles of punctuation are as follows. Semicolons separate syntactically complete antitheses. Colons precede indirect statement and text that refers explicitly back to what precedes the colon. Commas set off appositions and ablative absolute phrases, especially at the end or in mid-sentence. They also set off phrases that are T.'s comments on the text. They are omitted when particles or other structures (e.g. relative clauses, purpose clauses, anaphora, etc.) punctuate sufficiently.

CORNELI TACITI HISTORIARVM
LIBER PRIMVS

CORNELI TACITI HISTORIARVM
LIBER PRIMVS

Initium mihi operis Seruius Galba iterum Titus Vinius consules **1**
erunt. nam post conditam urbem octingentos et uiginti prioris
aeui annos multi auctores rettulerunt, dum res populi Romani me-
morabantur, pari eloquentia ac libertate; postquam bellatum apud
Actium atque omnem potentiam ad unum conferri pacis interfuit,
magna illa ingenia cessere. simul ueritas pluribus modis infracta,
primum inscitia rei publicae ut alienae, mox libidine assentandi
aut rursus odio aduersus dominantes. ita neutris cura posteritatis
inter infensos uel obnoxios. sed ambitionem scriptoris facile 2
auerseris, obtrectatio et liuor pronis auribus accipiuntur. quippe
adulationi foedum crimen seruitutis, malignitati falsa species libertatis inest. mihi Galba Otho Vitellius nec beneficio nec iniuria cog- 3
niti. dignitatem nostram a Vespasiano inchoatam, a Tito auctam, a
Domitiano longius prouectam non abnuerim, sed incorruptam fidem professis neque amore quisquam et sine odio dicendus est.
quod si uita suppeditet, principatum diui Neruae et imperium 4
Traiani, uberiorem securioremque materiam, senectuti seposui,
rara temporum felicitate ubi sentire quae uelis et quae sentias
dicere licet.

Opus aggredior opimum casibus, atrox proeliis, discors sedi- **2**
tionibus, ipsa etiam pace saeuum. quattuor principes ferro
interempti. trina bella ciuilia, plura externa ac plerumque permixta. prosperae in Oriente, aduersae in Occidente res: turbatum Illyricum, Galliae nutantes, perdomita Britannia et statim
missa. coortae in nos Sarmatarum ac Sueborum gentes, nobilitatus cladibus mutuis Dacus, mota prope etiam Parthorum arma
falsi Neronis ludibrio. iam uero Italia nouis cladibus uel post lon 2
gam saeculorum seriem repetitis afflicta. haustae aut obrutae urbes
fecundissima Campaniae ora. et urbs incendiis uastata, consumptis
antiquissimis delubris, ipso Capitolio ciuium manibus incenso. pollutae caerimoniae, magna adulteria. plenum exiliis mare, infecti

3 caedibus scopuli. atrocius in urbe saeuitum: nobilitas, opes, omissi
gestique honores pro crimine, et ob uirtutes certissimum exitium.
nec minus praemia delatorum inuisa quam scelera, cum alii sacer-
dotia et consulatus ut spolia adepti, procurationes alii et interiorem
potentiam, agerent uerterent cuncta odio et terrore. corrupti in
dominos serui, in patronos liberti. et quibus deerat inimicus per
amicos oppressi.

3 Non tamen adeo uirtutum sterile saeculum ut non et bona
exempla prodiderit. comitatae profugos liberos matres, secutae
maritos in exilia coniuges. propinqui audentes, constantes generi,
contumax etiam aduersus tormenta seruorum fides. supremae
clarorum uirorum necessitates, ipsa necessitas fortiter tolerata et
2 laudatis antiquorum mortibus pares exitus. praeter multiplices
rerum humanarum casus caelo terraque prodigia et fulminum
monitus et futurorum praesagia, laeta tristia, ambigua manifesta.
nec enim umquam atrocioribus populi Romani cladibus magis-
ue iustis indiciis approbatum est non esse curae deis securitatem
nostram, esse ultionem.

4 Ceterum antequam destinata componam, repetendum uidetur
qualis status urbis, quae mens exercituum, quis habitus prouinciarum, quid in toto terrarum orbe ualidum, quid aegrum fuerit,
ut non modo casus euentusque rerum, qui plerumque fortuiti sunt,
sed ratio etiam causaeque noscantur.

2 Finis Neronis ut laetus primo gaudentium impetu fuerat ita
uarios motus animorum non modo in urbe apud patres aut populum aut urbanum militem sed omnes legiones ducesque conciuerat, euulgato imperii arcano posse principem alibi quam Romae
3 fieri. sed patres laeti, usurpata statim libertate licentius ut erga
principem nouum et absentem; primores equitum proximi gaudio
patrum; pars populi integra et magnis domibus adnexa, clientes
libertique damnatorum et exulum in spem erecti; plebs sordida et
circo ac theatris sueta, simul deterrimi seruorum, aut qui adesis
bonis per dedecus Neronis alebantur, maesti et rumorum auidi.

5 Miles urbanus longo Caesarum sacramento imbutus et ad
destituendum Neronem arte magis et impulsu quam suo ingenio

traductus, postquam neque dari donatiuum sub nomine Galbae
promissum neque magnis meritis ac praemiis eundem in pace
quem in bello locum praeuentamque gratiam intellegit apud
principem a legionibus factum, pronus ad nouas res scelere insuper Nymphidii Sabini praefecti imperium sibi molientis agitatur.
et Nymphidius quidem in ipso conatu oppressus, sed quamuis 2
capite defectionis ablato manebat plerisque militum conscientia,
nec deerant sermones senium atque auaritiam Galbae increpantium. laudata olim et militari fama celebrata seueritas eius angebat
aspernantes ueterem disciplinam atque ita quattuordecim annis a
Nerone assuefactos ut haud minus uitia principum amarent quam
olim uirtutes uerebantur. accessit Galbae uox pro re publica honesta, ipsi anceps, legi a se militem, non emi. nec enim ad hanc formam cetera erant:inualidum senem Titus Vinius et Cornelius 6
Laco, alter deterrimus mortalium alter ignauissimus, odio flagitiorum oneratum contemptu inertiae destruebant.

Tardum Galbae iter et cruentum, interfectis Cingonio Varrone
consule designato et Petronio Turpiliano consulari. ille ut
Nymphidii socius hic ut dux Neronis inauditi atque indefensi
tamquam innocentes perierant. introitus in urbem trucidatis 2
tot milibus inermium militum infaustus omine atque ipsis etiam qui
occiderant formidolosus.

Inducta legione Hispana, remanente ea quam e classe Nero conscripserat, plena urbs exercitu insolito. multi ad hoc numeri e Germania ac Britannia et Illyrico, quos idem Nero electos praemissosque ad claustra Caspiarum et bellum quod in Albanos parabat opprimendis Vindicis coeptis reuocauerat. ingens nouis rebus materia, ut non in unum aliquem prono fauore ita audenti parata.

Forte congruerat ut Clodii Macri et Fontei Capitonis caedes 7
nuntiarentur. Macrum in Africa haud dubie turbantem Trebonius
Garutianus procurator iussu Galbae, Capitonem in Germania, cum
similia coeptaret, Cornelius Aquinus et Fabius Valens legati
legionum interfecerant antequam iuberentur. fuere qui crederent 2
Capitonem ut auaritia et libidine foedum ac maculosum ita cogitatione rerum nouarum abstinuisse, sed a legatis bellum suadentibus,

postquam impellere nequiuerint, crimen ac dolum ultro compositum, et Galbam mobilitate ingenii, an ne altius scrutaretur, quoquo modo acta, quia mutari non poterant, comprobasse. ceterum
utraque caedes sinistre accepta, et inuiso semel principi seu bene
seu male facta parem inuidiam afferebant.

3 Venalia cuncta, praepotentes liberti, seruorum manus subitis
auidae et tamquam apud senem festinantes, eademque nouae aulae
mala, aeque grauia, non aeque excusata. ipsa aetas Galbae irrisui
ac fastidio erat assuetis iuuentae Neronis et imperatores forma ac
decore corporis, ut est mos uulgi, comparantibus.

8 Et hic quidem Romae, tamquam in tanta multitudine, habitus animorum fuit. e prouinciis Hispaniae praeerat Cluuius Rufus,
uir facundus et pacis artibus, bellis inexpertus. Galliae super
memoriam Vindicis obligatae recenti dono Romanae ciuitatis et
in posterum tributi leuamento. proximae tamen Germanicis exercitibus Galliarum ciuitates non eodem honore habitae, quaedam
etiam finibus ademptis, pari dolore commoda aliena ac suas in-
2 iurias metiebantur. Germanici exercitus, quod periculosissi-
mum in tantis uiribus, solliciti et irati, superbia recentis uictoriae
et metu tamquam alias partes fouissent. tarde a Nerone desciuerant, nec statim pro Galba Verginius. an imperare noluisset dubium;
delatum ei a milite imperium conueniebat. Fonteium Capitonem
occisum etiam qui queri non poterant tamen indignabantur. dux
deerat, abducto Verginio per simulationem amicitiae. quem non
remitti atque etiam reum esse tamquam suum crimen accipiebant.

9 Superior exercitus legatum Hordeonium Flaccum spernebat, senecta ac debilitate pedum inualidum, sine constantia, sine
auctoritate. ne quieto quidem milite regimen; adeo furentes infir-
mitate retinentis ultro accendebantur. inferioris Germaniae legiones
diutius sine consulari fuere, donec missu Galbae A. Vitellius aderat,
censoris Vitellii ac ter consulis filius. id satis uidebatur.

2 In Britannico exercitu nihil irarum. non sane aliae legiones per omnes ciuilium bellorum motus innocentius egerunt, seu
quia procul et Oceano diuisae, seu crebris expeditionibus doc-
3 tae hostem potius odisse. quies et Illyrico, quamquam excitae a

Nerone legiones, dum in Italia cunctantur, Verginium legationibus adissent. sed longis spatiis discreti exercitus, quod saluberrimum est ad continendam militarem fidem, nec uitiis nec uiribus miscebantur.

Oriens adhuc immotus.Syriam et quattuor legiones obti- **10**
nebat Licinius Mucianus, uir secundis aduersisque iuxta famosus.
insignes amicitias iuuenis ambitiose coluerat. mox attritis opibus,
lubrico statu, suspecta etiam Claudii iracundia, in secretum Asiae
sepositus tam prope ab exule fuit quam postea a principe. lux- 2
uria industria, comitate arrogantia, malis bonisque artibus mixtus.
nimiae uoluptates, cum uacaret; quotiens expedierat, magnae uirtutes. palam laudares, secreta male audiebant. sed apud subiectos
apud proximos apud collegas uariis illecebris potens, et cui expeditius fuerit tradere imperium quam obtinere. bellum Iudaicum 3
Flauius Vespasianus (ducem eum Nero delegerat) tribus legionibus administrabat. nec Vespasiano aduersus Galbam uotum aut
animus. quippe Titum filium ad uenerationem cultumque eius miserat, ut suo loco memorabimus. occulta fati et ostentis ac responsis destinatum Vespasiano liberisque eius imperium post fortunam
credidimus.

Aegyptum copiasque quibus coerceretur iam inde a diuo **11**
Augusto equites Romani obtinent loco regum. ita uisum expedire,
prouinciam aditu difficilem, annonae fecundam, superstitione ac
lasciuia discordem et mobilem, insciam legum, ignaram magistratuum, domui retinere. regebat tum Tiberius Alexander, eiusdem
nationis. Africa ac legiones in ea interfecto Clodio Macro contenta 2
qualicumque principe post experimentum domini minoris. duae
Mauretaniae Raetia Noricum Thracia et quae aliae procuratoribus
cohibentur ut cuique exercitui uicinae ita in fauorem aut odium
contactu ualentiorum agebantur. inermes prouinciae atque ipsa in 3
primis Italia, cuicumque seruitio exposita, in pretium belli cessurae
erant.

Hic fuit rerum Romanarum status cum Seruius Galba iterum Titus Vinius consules inchoauere annum sibi ultimum, rei publicae prope supremum.

12 Paucis post kalendas Ianuarias diebus Pompei Propinqui
procuratoris e Belgica litterae afferuntur: superioris Germaniae
legiones rupta sacramenti reuerentia imperatorem alium flagitare
et senatui ac populo Romano arbitrium eligendi permittere quo
seditio mollius acciperetur.
2 Maturauit ea res consilium Galbae iam pridem de adoptione
secum et cum proximis agitantis. non sane crebrior tota ciuitate
sermo per illos menses fuerat, primum licentia ac libidine talia
3 loquendi, dein fessa iam aetate Galbae. paucis iudicium aut rei
publicae amor; multi stulta spe, prout quis amicus uel cliens, hunc
uel illum ambitiosis rumoribus destinabant, etiam in Titi Vinii
odium, qui in dies quanto potentior eodem actu inuisior erat. quippe
hiantes in magna fortuna amicorum cupiditates ipsa Galbae facilitas intendebat, cum apud infirmum et credulum minore metu et
maiore praemio peccaretur.
13 Potentia principatus diuisa in Titum Vinium consulem
Cornelium Laconem praetorii praefectum; nec minor gratia Icelo
Galbae liberto, quem anulis donatum equestri nomine Marcianum
uocitabant. hi discordes et rebus minoribus sibi quisque tendentes,
circa consilium eligendi successoris in duas factiones scindeban-
2 tur: Vinius pro M. Othone, Laco atque Icelus consensu non
tam unum aliquem fouebant quam alium. neque erat Galbae ignota Othonis ac Titi Vinii amicitia; et rumoribus nihil silentio
transmittentium, quia Vinio uidua filia, caelebs Otho, gener ac
socer destinabantur. credo et rei publicae curam subisse, frustra
3 a Nerone translatae si apud Othonem relinqueretur. namque
Otho pueritiam incuriose adulescentiam petulanter egerat, gratus
Neroni aemulatione luxus. eoque Poppaeam Sabinam, principale
scortum, ut apud conscium libidinum deposuerat donec Octauiam
uxorem amoliretur. mox suspectum in eadem Poppaea in
4 prouinciam Lusitaniam specie legationis seposuit. Otho comiter
administrata prouincia primus in partes transgressus nec segnis et,
donec bellum fuit, inter praesentes splendidissimus, spem adoptionis statim conceptam acrius in dies rapiebat, fauentibus plerisque
militum, prona in eum aula Neronis ut similem.

Sed Galba post nuntios Germanicae seditionis, quamquam **14**
nihil adhuc de Vitellio certum, anxius quonam exercituum uis
erumperet, ne urbano quidem militi confisus, quod remedium
unicum rebatur, comitia imperii transigit, adhibitoque super
Vinium ac Laconem Mario Celso consule designato ac Ducenio
Gemino praefecto urbis, pauca praefatus de sua senectute, Pisonem
Licinianum arcessiri iubet, seu propria electione siue, ut quidam
crediderunt, Lacone instante, cui apud Rubellium Plautum exercita cum Pisone amicitia. sed callide ut ignotum fouebat, et prospera de Pisone fama consilio eius fidem addiderat. Piso M. Crasso 2
et Scribonia genitus, nobilis utrimque, uultu habituque moris antiqui et aestimatione recta seuerus, deterius interpretantibus tristior
habebatur. ea pars morum eius quo suspectior sollicitis adoptanti
placebat.

Igitur Galba apprehensa Pisonis manu in hunc modum **15**
locutus fertur: 'si te priuatus lege curiata apud pontifices, ut moris
est, adoptarem, et mihi egregium erat Cn. Pompei et M. Crassi subolem in penates meos asciscere, et tibi insigne Sulpiciae ac Lutatiae
decora nobilitati tuae adiecisse. nunc me deorum hominumque
consensu ad imperium uocatum praeclara indoles tua et amor patriae impulit ut principatum, de quo maiores nostri armis certabant, bello adeptus quiescenti offeram, exemplo diui Augusti qui
sororis filium Marcellum dein generum Agrippam mox nepotes suos
postremo Tiberium Neronem priuignum in proximo sibi fastigio
collocauit.

'Sed Augustus in domo successorem quaesiuit, ego in re publica, 2
non quia propinquos aut socios belli non habeam, sed neque ipse
imperium ambitione accepi, et iudicii mei documentum sit non
meae tantum necessitudines, quas tibi postposui, sed et tuae. est tibi
frater pari nobilitate, natu maior, dignus hac fortuna nisi tu potior
esses. ea aetas tua quae cupiditates adulescentiae iam effugerit, ea 3
uita in qua nihil praeteritum excusandum habeas.

'Fortunam adhuc tantum aduersam tulisti; secundae res acrio-
ribus stimulis animos explorant, quia miseriae tolerantur, felicitate
corrumpimur. fidem libertatem amicitiam, praecipua humani 4

animi bona, tu quidem eadem constantia retinebis, sed alii per obsequium imminuent. irrumpet adulatio blanditiae et pessimum ueri affectus uenenum, sua cuique utilitas. et iam ego ac tu simplicissime inter nos hodie loquimur; ceteri libentius cum fortuna nostra quam nobiscum. nam suadere principi quod oporteat multi laboris, assentatio erga quemcumque principem sine affectu peragitur.

16 'Si immensum imperii corpus stare ac librari sine rectore posset, dignus eram a quo res publica inciperet. nunc eo necessitatis iam pridem uentum est ut nec mea senectus conferre plus populo Romano possit quam bonum successorem nec tua plus iuuenta quam bonum principem. sub Tiberio et Gaio et Claudio unius familiae quasi hereditas fuimus; loco libertatis erit quod eligi coepimus. et finita Iuliorum Claudiorumque domo optimum
2 quemque adoptio inueniet. nam generari et nasci a principibus fortuitum, nec ultra aestimatur; adoptandi iudicium integrum et, si uelis eligere, consensu monstratur.

'Sit ante oculos Nero, quem longa Caesarum serie tumentem non Vindex cum inermi prouincia aut ego cum una legione sed sua immanitas sua luxuria ceruicibus publicis depulerunt. neque erat
3 adhuc damnati principis exemplum. nos bello et ab aestimantibus asciti cum inuidia quamuis egregii erimus.

'Ne tamen territus fueris si duae legiones in hoc concussi orbis motu nondum quiescunt. ne ipse quidem ad securas res accessi, et audita adoptione desinam uideri senex, quod nunc mihi unum obicitur. Nero a pessimo quoque semper desiderabitur; mihi ac tibi prouidendum est ne etiam a bonis desideretur.

4 'Monere diutius neque temporis huius, et impletum est omne consilium si te bene elegi. utilissimus idem ac breuissimus bonarum malarumque rerum dilectus est cogitare quid aut uolueris sub alio principe aut nolueris. neque enim hic, ut gentibus quae regnantur, certa dominorum domus et ceteri serui, sed imperaturus es hominibus qui nec totam seruitutem pati possunt nec totam libertatem.' et Galba quidem haec ac talia, tamquam principem faceret, ceteri tamquam cum facto loquebantur.

17 Pisonem ferunt statim intuentibus et mox coniectis in eum omnium oculis nullum turbati aut exsultantis animi motum

prodidisse. sermo erga patrem imperatoremque reuerens, de se
moderatus; nihil in uultu habituque mutatum, quasi imperare
posset magis quam uellet. consultatum inde, pro rostris an in 2
senatu an in castris adoptio nuncuparetur. iri in castra placuit: honorificum id militibus fore, quorum fauorem ut largitione et ambitu
male acquiri ita per bonas artes haud spernendum. circumsteterat
interim Palatium publica exspectatio, magni secreti impatiens. et
male coercitam famam supprimentes augebant.

Quartum idus Ianuarias, foedum imbribus diem, tonitrua et **18**
fulgura et caelestes minae ultra solitum turbauerant. obseruatum
id antiquitus comitiis dirumpendis non terruit Galbam quo minus
in castra pergeret, contemptorem talium ut fortuitorum, seu quae
fato manent, quamuis significata non uitantur. apud frequentem 2
militum contionem imperatoria breuitate adoptari a se Pisonem
exemplo diui Augusti et more militari quo uir uirum legeret pro-
nuntiat. ac ne dissimulata seditio in maius crederetur ultro asseuerat
quartam et duoetuicensimam legiones, paucis seditionis auctoribus,
non ultra uerba ac uoces errasse et breui in officio fore. nec ullum
orationi aut lenocinium addit aut pretium. tribuni tamen cen- 3
turionesque et proximi militum grata auditu respondent; per ceteros
maestitia ac silentium, tamquam usurpatam etiam in pace donatiui
necessitatem bello perdidissent. constat potuisse conciliari animos
quantulacumque parci senis liberalitate; nocuit antiquus rigor et
nimia seueritas, cui iam pares non sumus.

Inde apud senatum non comptior Galbae non longior quam **19**
apud militem sermo; Pisonis comis oratio. et patrum fauor aderat:
multi uoluntate, effusius qui noluerant, medii ac plurimi obuio obsequio, priuatas spes agitantes sine publica cura. nec aliud sequenti
quadriduo, quod medium inter adoptionem et caedem fuit, dictum
a Pisone in publico factumue.

Crebrioribus in dies Germanicae defectionis nuntiis et facili 2
ciuitate ad accipienda credendaque omnia noua cum tristia sunt,
censuerant patres mittendos ad Germanicum exercitum legatos;
agitatum secreto num et Piso proficisceretur, maiore praetextu, illi
auctoritatem senatus hic dignationem Caesaris laturus. placebat et
Laconem praetorii praefectum simul mitti. is consilio intercessit.

legati quoque (nam senatus electionem Galbae permiserat) foeda inconstantia nominati excusati substituti, ambitu remanendi aut eundi, ut quemque metus uel spes impulerat.

20 Proxima pecuniae cura. et cuncta scrutantibus iustissimum
uisum est inde repeti ubi inopiae causa erat. bis et uiciens miliens
sestertium donationibus Nero effuderat; appellari singulos iussit,
decima parte liberalitatis apud quemque eorum relicta. at illis uix
decimae super portiones erant, isdem erga aliena sumptibus quibus
sua prodegerant, cum rapacissimo cuique ac perditissimo non
2 agri aut faenus sed sola instrumenta uitiorum manerent. exactioni
triginta equites Romani praepositi, nouum officii genus et ambitu
ac numero onerosum. ubique hasta et sector, et inquieta urbs actio-
nibus. ac tamen grande gaudium quod tam pauperes forent quibus
donasset Nero quam quibus abstulisset.

3 Exauctorati per eos dies tribuni: e praetorio Antonius Taurus et Antonius Naso, ex urbanis cohortibus Aemilius Pacensis, e uigilibus Iulius Fronto. nec remedium in ceteros fuit sed metus initium, tamquam per artem et formidine singuli pellerentur, omnibus suspectis.

21 Interea Othonem, cui compositis rebus nulla spes, omne
in turbido consilium, multa simul exstimulabant: luxuria etiam
principi onerosa, inopia uix priuato toleranda, in Galbam ira,
in Pisonem inuidia. fingebat et metum quo magis concupisceret:
praegrauem se Neroni fuisse, nec Lusitaniam rursus et alterius
exilii honorem exspectandum. suspectum semper inuisumque do-
minantibus qui proximus destinaretur. nocuisse id sibi apud senem
principem, magis nociturum apud iuuenem ingenio trucem et
2 longo exilio efferatum; occidi Othonem posse. proinde agen-
dum audendumque dum Galbae auctoritas fluxa, Pisonis nondum
coaluisset. opportunos magnis conatibus transitus rerum, nec cunctatione opus ubi perniciosior sit quies quam temeritas. mortem
omnibus ex natura aequalem obliuione apud posteros uel gloria
distingui; ac si nocentem innocentemque idem exitus maneat,
acrioris uiri esse merito perire.

22 Non erat Othonis mollis et corpori similis animus. et intimi libertorum seruorumque, corruptius quam in priuata domo habiti,

aulam Neronis et luxus adulteria matrimonia ceterasque regno-
rum libidines auido talium, si auderet, ut sua ostentantes, quiescenti ut aliena exprobrabant, urgentibus etiam mathematicis, dum
nouos motus et clarum Othoni annum obseruatione siderum affir-
mant, genus hominum potentibus infidum sperantibus fallax,
quod in ciuitate nostra et uetabitur semper et retinebitur. multos 2
secreta Poppaeae mathematicos, pessimum principalis matrimonii
instrumentum, habuerant. e quibus Ptolemaeus Othoni in Hispania
comes, cum superfuturum eum Neroni promisisset, postquam ex
euentu fides, coniectura iam et rumore senium Galbae et iuuentam
Othonis computantium persuaserat fore ut in imperium ascisceretur. sed Otho tamquam peritia et monitu fatorum praedicta 3
accipiebat, cupidine ingenii humani libentius obscura credendi. nec
deerat Ptolemaeus, iam et sceleris instinctor, ad quod facillime ab
eius modi uoto transitur.

Sed sceleris cogitatio incertum an repens. studia militum iam **23**
pridem spe successionis aut paratu facinoris affectauerat, in
itinere in agmine in stationibus uetustissimum quemque militum
nomine uocans ac memoria Neroniani comitatus contubernales
appellando; alios agnoscere, quosdam requirere et pecunia
aut gratia iuuare, inserendo saepius querelas et ambiguos de
Galba sermones quaeque alia turbamenta uulgi.labores itinerum, 2
inopia commeatuum, duritia imperii atrocius accipiebantur, cum
Campaniae lacus et Achaiae urbes classibus adire soliti Pyrenaeum
et Alpes et immensa uiarum spatia aegre sub armis eniterentur.

Flagrantibus iam militum animis uelut faces addiderat Maeuius **24**
Pudens, e proximis Tigellini. is mobilissimum quemque ingenio
aut pecuniae indigum et in nouas cupiditates praecipitem alliciendo
eo paulatim progressus est ut per speciem conuiuii, quotiens Galba
apud Othonem epularetur, cohorti excubias agenti uiritim centenos nummos diuideret. quam uelut publicam largitionem Otho 2
secretioribus apud singulos praemiis intendebat, adeo animosus
corruptor ut Cocceio Proculo speculatori de parte finium cum
uicino ambigenti uniuersum uicini agrum sua pecunia emptum
dono dederit, per socordiam praefecti, quem nota pariter et occulta
fallebant.

25 Sed tum e libertis Onomastum futuro sceleri praefecit. a
quo Barbium Proculum tesserarium speculatorum et Veturium
optionem eorundem perductos, postquam uario sermone calli-
dos audacesque cognouit, pretio et promissis onerat, data pecunia
ad pertemptandos plurium animos. suscepere duo manipu-
2 lares imperium populi Romani transferendum et transtulerunt.
in conscientiam facinoris pauci asciti. suspensos ceterorum animos diuersis artibus stimulant: primores militum per beneficia
Nymphidii ut suspectos, uulgus et ceteros ira et desperatione dilati
totiens donatiui. erant quos memoria Neronis ac desiderium prioris
licentiae accenderet. in commune omnes metu mutandae militiae
terrebantur.

26 Infecit ea tabes legionum quoque et auxiliorum motas iam mentes postquam uulgatum erat labare Germanici exercitus fidem. adeoque parata apud malos seditio, etiam apud integros dissimulatio fuit, ut postero iduum die redeuntem a cena Othonem rapturi fuerint, ni incerta noctis et tota urbe sparsa militum castra nec facilem inter temulentos consensum timuissent, non rei publicae cura, quam foedare principis sui sanguine sobrii parabant, sed ne per tenebras, ut quisque Pannonici uel Germanici exercitus militibus oblatus esset, ignorantibus plerisque, pro Othone destinaretur.

2 Multa erumpentis seditionis indicia per conscios oppressa; quaedam apud Galbae aures praefectus Laco elusit, ignarus militarium animorum consiliique quamuis egregii, quod non ipse afferret, inimicus et aduersus peritos peruicax.

27 Octauo decimo kalendas Februarias sacrificanti pro aede
Apollinis Galbae haruspex Vmbricius tristia exta et instantes insidias ac domesticum hostem praedicit, audiente Othone (nam
proximus astiterat) idque ut laetum e contrario et suis cogitationi-
bus prosperum interpretante. nec multo post libertus Onomastus
nuntiat exspectari eum ab architecto et redemptoribus, quae
significatio coeuntium iam militum et paratae coniurationis con-
2 uenerat. Otho, causam digressus requirentibus, cum emi sibi
praedia uetustate suspecta eoque prius exploranda finxisset, innixus

liberto per Tiberianam domum in Velabrum, inde ad miliarium aureum sub aedem Saturni pergit. ibi tres et uiginti speculatores consalutatum imperatorem ac paucitate salutantium trepidum et sellae festinanter impositum strictis mucronibus rapiunt. totidem ferme milites in itinere aggregantur: alii conscientia plerique miraculo, pars clamore et gladiis pars silentio, animum ex euentu sumpturi.

Stationem in castris agebat Iulius Martialis tribunus. is magnitu- **28**
dine subiti sceleris, an corrupta latius castra et, si contra tenderet, exitium metuens, praebuit plerisque suspicionem conscientiae. anteposuere ceteri quoque tribuni centurionesque praesentia dubiis et honestis, isque habitus animorum fuit ut pessimum facinus auderent pauci, plures uellent, omnes paterentur.

Ignarus interim Galba et sacris intentus fatigabat alieni iam **29**
imperii deos, cum affertur rumor rapi in castra incertum quem senatorem, mox Othonem esse qui raperetur, simul ex tota urbe, ut quisque obuius fuerat, alii formidine augentes, quidam minora uero, ne tum quidem obliti adulationis. igitur consultantibus placuit pertemptari animum cohortis quae in Palatio stationem agebat, nec per ipsum Galbam, cuius integra auctoritas maioribus remediis seruabatur.

Piso pro gradibus domus uocatos in hunc modum allocutus 2
est: 'sextus dies agitur, commilitones, ex quo ignarus futuri, et siue optandum hoc nomen siue timendum erat, Caesar ascitus sum. quo domus nostrae aut rei publicae fato, in uestra manu positum est, non quia meo nomine tristiorem casum paueam, ut qui aduersas res expertus cum maxime discam ne secundas quidem minus discriminis habere; patris et senatus et ipsius imperii uicem doleo si nobis aut perire hodie necesse est aut, quod aeque apud bonos miserum est, occidere. solacium proximi motus habebamus incruentam urbem et res sine discordia translatas; prouisum adoptione uidebatur ut ne post Galbam quidem bello locus esset.

'Nihil arrogabo mihi nobilitatis aut modestiae; neque enim **30**
relatu uirtutum in comparatione Othonis opus est. uitia, quibus solis gloriatur, euertere imperium, etiam cum amicum imperatoris

ageret. habitune et incessu an illo muliebri ornatu mereretur imperium? falluntur quibus luxuria specie liberalitatis imponit: perdere iste sciet, donare nesciet. stupra nunc et comissationes et feminarum coetus uoluit animo: haec principatus praemia putat, quorum libido ac uoluptas penes ipsum sit, rubor ac dedecus penes omnes. nemo enim umquam imperium flagitio quaesitum bonis artibus exercuit.

2 'Galbam consensus generis humani, me Galba consentientibus uobis Caesarem dixit. si res publica et senatus et populus uacua nomina sunt, uestra, commilitones, interest ne imperatorem pessimi faciant. legionum seditio aduersus duces suos audita est aliquando; uestra fides famaque illaesa ad hunc diem mansit. et Nero
3 quoque uos destituit, non uos Neronem. minus triginta transfugae et desertores, quos centurionem aut tribunum sibi eligentes nemo ferret, imperium assignabunt? admittitis exemplum et quiescendo commune crimen facitis? transcendet haec licentia in prouincias, et ad nos scelerum exitus, bellorum ad uos pertinebunt. nec est plus quod pro caede principis quam quod innocentibus datur, sed perinde a nobis donatiuum ob fidem quam ab aliis pro facinore
31 accipietis.' dilapsis speculatoribus cetera cohors non aspernata contionantem, ut turbidis rebus euenit, timore magis et nullo adhuc consilio apud signa quam, quod postea creditum est, insidiis et simulatione.

2 Missus et Celsus Marius ad electos Illyrici exercitus Vipsania in porticu tendentes; praeceptum Amullio Sereno et Domitio Sabino primipilaribus ut Germanicos milites e Libertatis atrio arcesserent. legioni classicae diffidebatur, infestae ob caedem commilitonum, quos primo statim introitu trucidauerat Galba. pergunt etiam in castra praetorianorum tribuni Cetrius Seuerus, Subrius Dexter, Pompeius Longinus, si incipiens adhuc necdum
3 adulta seditio melioribus consiliis flecteretur. tribunorum Subrium et Cetrium adorti milites minis, Longinum manibus coercent exarmantque quia non ordine militiae sed e Galbae amicis fidus principi suo et desciscentibus suspectior erat. legio classica

nihil cunctata praetorianis adiungitur. Illyrici exercitus electi
Celsum infestis pilis proturbant. Germanica uexilla diu nutauere,
inualidis adhuc corporibus et placatis animis, quod eos a Nerone
Alexandriam praemissos atque inde rursus longa nauigatione
aegros impensiore cura Galba refouebat.

Vniuersa iam plebs Palatium implebat, mixtis seruitiis et dissono **32**
clamore caedem Othonis et coniuratorum exitium poscentium,
ut si in circo aut theatro ludicrum aliquod postularent. neque illis iudicium aut ueritas, quippe eodem die diuersa pari certamine
postulaturis, sed tradito more quemcumque principem adulandi
licentia acclamationum et studiis inanibus.

Interim Galbam duae sententiae distinebant. Titus Vinius 2
manendum intra domum, opponenda seruitia, firmandos aditus,
non eundum ad iratos censebat. daret malorum paenitentiae, daret
bonorum consensui spatium: scelera impetu, bona consilia mora
ualescere. denique eundi ultro, si ratio sit, eandem mox facultatem,
regressus, si paeniteat, in aliena potestate.

Festinandum ceteris uidebatur, antequam cresceret inualida **33**
adhuc coniuratio paucorum: trepidaturum etiam Othonem, qui
furtim digressus, ad ignaros illatus, cunctatione nunc et segnitia
terentium tempus imitari principem discat. non exspectandum ut
compositis castris forum inuadat et prospectante Galba Capitolium
adeat, dum egregius imperator cum fortibus amicis ianua ac limine tenus domum cludit, obsidionem nimirum toleraturus. et 2
praeclarum in seruis auxilium, si consensus tantae multitudinis et,
quae plurimum ualet, prima indignatio languescat. proinde intuta
quae indecora; uel si cadere necesse sit, occurrendum discrimini.
id Othoni inuidiosius et ipsis honestum. repugnantem huic sententiae Vinium Laco minaciter inuasit, stimulante Icelo priuati odii
pertinacia in publicum exitium.

Nec diutius Galba cunctatus speciosiora suadentibus accessit. **34**
praemissus tamen in castra Piso, ut iuuenis magno nomine, recenti
fauore et infensus Tito Vinio, seu quia erat seu quia irati ita uole-
bant. et facilius de odio creditur.

2 Vixdum egresso Pisone occisum in castris Othonem uagus primum et incertus rumor. mox, ut in magnis mendaciis, interfuisse se quidam et uidisse affirmabant, credula fama inter gaudentes et incuriosos. multi arbitrabantur compositum auctumque rumorem mixtis iam Othonianis, qui ad euocandum Galbam laeta falso uulgauerint.

35 Tum uero non populus tantum et imperita plebs in plausus et immodica studia, sed equitum plerique ac senatorum, posito metu incauti, refractis Palatii foribus ruere intus ac se Galbae ostentare, praereptam sibi ultionem querentes, ignauissimus quisque et, ut res docuit, in periculo non ausurus, nimii uerbis, linguae feroces. nemo scire et omnes affirmare, donec inopia ueri et consensu errantium uictus sumpto thorace Galba irruenti turbae neque aetate neque corpore resistens sella leuaretur.

2 Obuius in Palatio Iulius Atticus speculator cruentum gladium ostentans occisum a se Othonem exclamauit. et Galba 'commilito,' inquit 'quis iussit?' insigni animo ad coercendam militarem licentiam, minantibus intrepidus, aduersus blandientes incorruptus.

36 Haud dubiae iam in castris omnium mentes tantusque ardor
ut non contenti agmine et corporibus in suggestu, in quo
paulo ante aurea Galbae statua fuerat, medium inter signa
Othonem uexillis circumdarent. nec tribunis aut centurionibus
2 adeundi locus; gregarius miles caueri insuper praepositos iubebat.
strepere cuncta clamoribus et tumultu et exhortatione mutua, non
tamquam in populo ac plebe uariis segni adulatione uocibus, sed
ut quemque affluentium militum aspexerant, prensare manibus,
complectiarmis, collocare iuxta, praeire sacramentum, modo
imperatorem militibus, modo milites imperatori commendare.

3 Nec deerat Otho protendens manus adorare uulgum iacere
oscula et omnia seruiliter pro dominatione. postquam uniuersa classicorum legio sacramentum eius accepit, fidens uiribus, et quos
adhuc singulos exstimulauerat accendendos in commune ratus,
37 pro uallo castrorum ita coepit: 'quis ad uos processerim, commilitones, dicere non possum, quia nec priuatum me uocare sustineo

princeps a uobis nominatus, nec principem alio imperante. uestrum
quoque nomen in incerto erit donec dubitabitur imperatorem
populi Romani in castris an hostem habeatis.

'Auditisne ut poena mea et supplicium uestrum simul pos- 2
tulentur? adeo manifestum est neque perire nos neque saluos
esse nisi una posse. et, cuius lenitatis est Galba, iam fortasse
promisit, ut qui nullo exposcente tot milia innocentissimorum militum trucidauerit. horror animum subit quotiens recordor feralem 3
introitum et hanc solam Galbae uictoriam, cum in oculis urbis
decimari deditos iuberet, quos deprecantes in fidem acceperat. his
auspiciis urbem ingressus, quam gloriam ad principatum attulit
nisi occisi Obultronii Sabini et Cornelii Marcelli in Hispania,
Betui Cilonis in Gallia, Fontei Capitonis in Germania, Clodii
Macri in Africa, Cingonii in uia, Turpiliani in urbe, Nymphidii in
castris? quae usquam prouincia, quae castra sunt nisi cruenta et ma- 4
culata aut, ut ipse praedicat, emendata et correcta? nam quae alii
scelera, hic remedia uocat, dum falsis nominibus seueritatem pro
saeuitia, parsimoniam pro auaritia, supplicia et contumelias uestras
disciplinam appellat.

'Septem a Neronis fine menses sunt, et iam plus rapuit Icelus 5
quam quod Polycliti et Vatinii et Aegiali petierunt. minore auaritia ac licentia grassatus esset T. Vinius si ipse imperasset: nunc et
subiectos nos habuit tamquam suos et uiles ut alienos. una illa
domus sufficit donatiuo quod uobis numquam datur et cotidie
exprobratur.

'Ac ne qua saltem in successore Galbae spes esset arcessit ab **38**
exilio quem tristitia et auaritia sui simillimum iudicabat. uidis-
tis, commilitones, notabili tempestate etiam deos infaustam adoptionem auersantes. idem senatus idem populi Romani animus est.
uestra uirtus exspectatur, apud quos omne honestis consiliis robur
et sine quibus quamuis egregia inualida sunt.

'Non ad bellum uos nec ad periculum uoco; omnium mili- 2
tum arma nobiscum sunt. nec una cohors togata defendit nunc
Galbam sed detinet. cum uos aspexerit, cum signum meum accepe-
rit, hoc solum erit certamen, quis mihi plurimum imputet. nullus

cunctationis locus est in eo consilio quod non potest laudari nisi peractum.'

3 Aperire deinde armamentarium iussit. rapta statim arma sine more et ordine militiae, ut praetorianus aut legionarius insignibus suis distingueretur; miscentur auxiliaribus galeis scutisque, nullo tribunorum centurionumue adhortante, sibi quisque dux et instigator. et praecipuum pessimorum incitamentum quod boni maerebant.

39 Iam exterritus Piso fremitu crebrescentis seditionis et uocibus in urbem usque resonantibus, egressum interim Galbam et foro appropinquantem assecutus erat. iam Marius Celsus haud laeta rettulerat, cum alii in Palatium redire alii Capitolium petere plerique rostra occupanda censerent, plures tantum sententiis aliorum contra dicerent, utque euenit in consiliis infelicibus, optima
2 uiderentur quorum tempus effugerat. agitasse Laco ignaro Galba de occidendo Tito Vinio dicitur, siue ut poena eius animos militum mulceret, seu conscium Othonis credebat, ad postremum uel odio. haesitationem attulit tempus ac locus, quia initio caedis orto difficilis modus. et turbauere consilium trepidi nuntii ac proximorum diffugia, languentibus omnium studiis qui primo alacres fidem atque animum ostentauerant.

40 Agebatur huc illuc Galba uario turbae fluctuantis impulsu, completis undique basilicis ac templis, lugubri prospectu. neque populi aut plebis ulla uox, sed attoniti uultus et conuersae ad omnia aures; non tumultus, non quies, quale magni metus et magnae irae silentium est. Othoni tamen armari plebem nuntiabatur; ire praecipites et occupare pericula iubet.

2 Igitur milites Romani, quasi Vologaesum aut Pacorum auito Arsacidarum solio depulsuri ac non imperatorem suum inermem et senem trucidare pergerent, disiecta plebe, proculcato senatu, truces armis, rapidi equis forum irrumpunt. nec illos Capitolii aspectus et imminentium templorum religio et priores et futuri principes terruere quo minus facerent scelus cuius ultor est quisquis successit.

41 Viso comminus armatorum agmine uexillarius comitatae Galbam cohortis (Atilium Vercilionem fuisse tradunt) dereptam

Galbae imaginem solo afflixit. eo signo manifesta in Othonem
omnium militum studia, desertum fuga populi forum, destricta
aduersus dubitantes tela. iuxta Curtii lacum trepidatione ferentium 2
Galba proiectus e sella ac prouolutus est. extremam eius uocem,
ut cuique odium aut admiratio fuit, uarie prodidere. alii suppliciter
interrogasse quid mali meruisset, paucos dies exsoluendo donatiuo
deprecatum. plures obtulisse ultro percussoribus iugulum: agerent ac ferirent, si ita e re publica uideretur. non interfuit occidentium quid diceret. de percussore non satis constat: quidam 3
Terentium euocatum, alii Laecanium, crebrior fama tradidit
Camurium quintae decimae legionis militem impresso gladio iugulum eius hausisse. ceteri crura bracchiaque (nam pectus tegebatur)
foede laniauere; pleraque uulnera feritate et saeuitia trunco iam
corpori adiecta.

Titum inde Vinium inuasere, de quo et ipso ambigitur con- **42**
sumpseritne uocem eius instans metus an proclamauerit non esse
ab Othone mandatum ut occideretur. quod seu finxit formidine
seu conscientiam coniurationis confessus est, huc potius eius uita
famaque inclinat, ut conscius sceleris fuerit cuius causa erat. ante
aedem diui Iulii iacuit primo ictu in poplitem mox ab Iulio Caro
legionario milite in utrumque latus transuerberatus.

Insignem illa die uirum Sempronium Densum aetas nostra **43**
uidit. centurio is praetoriae cohortis a Galba custodiae Pisonis
additus stricto pugione occurrens armatis et scelus exprobrans ac
modo manu modo uoce uertendo in se percussores quamquam
uulnerato Pisoni effugium dedit. Piso in aedem Vestae peruasit, 2
exceptusque misericordia publici serui et contubernio eius abditus non religione nec caerimoniis sed latebra imminens exitium
differebat, cum aduenere missu Othonis nominatim in caedem
eius ardentis Sulpicius Florus e Britannicis cohortibus, nuper a
Galba ciuitate donatus, et Staius Murcus speculator, a quibus pro-
tractus Piso in foribus templi trucidatus. nullam caedem Otho **44**
maiore laetitia excepisse nullum caput tam insatiabilibus oculis
perlustrasse dicitur, seu tum primum leuata omni sollicitudine
mens uacare gaudio coeperat, seu recordatio maiestatis in Galba
amicitiae in Tito Vinio quamuis immitem animum imagine tristi

confuderat, Pisonis ut inimici et aemuli caede laetari ius fasque
credebat.
2 Praefixa contis capita gestabantur inter signa cohortium iuxta
aquilam legionis, certatim ostentantibus cruentas manus qui occiderant, qui interfuerant, qui uere qui falso ut pulchrum et memorabile facinus iactabant. plures quam centum uiginti libellos
praemium exposcentium ob aliquam notabilem illa die operam
Vitellius postea inuenit, omnesque conquiri et interfici iussit, non
honore Galbae sed tradito principibus more munimentum ad praesens, in posterum ultionem.
45 Alium crederes senatum, alium populum: ruere cuncti in castra,
anteire proximos, certare cum praecurrentibus, increpare Galbam,
laudare militum iudicium, exosculari Othonis manum, quantoque
magis falsa erant quae fiebant tanto plura facere. nec aspern-
abatur singulos Otho, auidum et minacem militum animum uoce
2 uultuque temperans. Marium Celsum, consulem designatum et
Galbae usque in extremas res amicum fidumque, ad supplicium
expostulabant, industriae eius innocentiaeque quasi malis artibus
infensi. caedis et praedarum initium et optimo cuique perniciem
quaeri apparebat, sed Othoni nondum auctoritas inerat ad prohibendum scelus; iubere iam poterat. ita simulatione irae uinciri iussum et maiores poenas daturum affirmans praesenti exitio
subtraxit.
46 Omnia deinde arbitrio militum acta. praetorii praefectos sibi
ipsi legere: Plotium Firmum e manipularibus quondam, tum uigilibus praepositum et incolumi adhuc Galba partes Othonis se-
cutum; adiungitur Licinius Proculus, intima familiaritate Othonis
suspectus consilia eius fouisse. urbi Flauium Sabinum praefecere, iudicium Neronis secuti, sub quo eandem curam obtinuerat,
2 plerisque Vespasianum fratrem in eo respicientibus. flagitatum ut
uacationes praestari centurionibus solitae remitterentur. namque
gregarius miles ut tributum annuum pendebat. quarta pars manipuli sparsa per commeatus aut in ipsis castris uaga dum mercedem centurioni exsolueret, neque modum oneris quisquam neque
genus quaestus pensi habebat: per latrocinia et raptus aut seruilibus
3 ministeriis militare otium redimebant. tum locupletissimus quisque

miles labore ac saeuitia fatigari donec uacationem emeret. ubi
sumptibus exhaustus socordia insuper elanguerat, inops pro locu-
plete et iners pro strenuo in manipulum redibat, ac rursus alius
atque alius, eadem egestate ac licentia corrupti, ad seditiones et discordias et ad extremum bella ciuilia ruebant. sed Otho, ne uulgi 4
largitione centurionum animos auerteret, ex fisco suo uacationes annuas exsoluturum promisit, rem haud dubie utilem et a
bonis postea principibus perpetuitate disciplinae firmatam. Laco 5
praefectus, tamquam in insulam seponeretur, ab euocato quem ad
caedem eius Otho praemiserat confossus; in Marcianum Icelum ut
in libertum palam animaduersum.

Exacto per scelera die nouissimum malorum fuit laetitia. uocat **47**
senatum praetor urbanus, certant adulationibus ceteri magistratus,
accurrunt patres. decernitur Othoni tribunicia potestas et nomen
Augusti et omnes principum honores, adnitentibus cunctis abolere
conuicia ac probra, quae promisce iacta haesisse animo eius nemo
sensit: omisisset offensas an distulisset, breuitate imperii in incerto
fuit.

Otho cruento adhuc foro per stragem iacentium in Capitolium 2
atque inde in Palatium uectus concedi corpora sepulturae cre-
marique permisit. Pisonem Verania uxor ac frater Scribonianus,
Titum Vinium Crispina filia composuere, quaesitis redemptisque
capitibus, quae uenalia interfectores seruauerant.

Piso unum et tricensimum aetatis annum explebat, fama me- **48**
liore quam fortuna. fratres eius Magnum Claudius, Crassum
Nero interfecerant. ipse diu exul, quadriduo Caesar, properata
adoptione ad hoc tantum maiori fratri praelatus est ut prior
occideretur.

Titus Vinius quinquaginta septem annos uariis moribus egit. 2
pater illi praetoria familia, maternus auus e proscriptis. prima militia infamis. legatum Caluisium Sabinum habuerat, cuius uxor mala
cupidine uisendi situm castrorum per noctem militari habitu ingressa, cum uigilias et cetera militiae munia eadem lasciuia temptasset, in ipsis principiis stuprum ausa. et criminis huius reus
Titus Vinius arguebatur. igitur iussu C. Caesaris oneratus cate- 3
nis, mox mutatione temporum dimissus, cursu honorum inoffenso

legioni post praeturam praepositus probatusque seruili deinceps
probro respersus est, tamquam scyphum aureum in conuiuio
Claudii furatus. et Claudius postera die soli omnium Vinio fictilibus
4 ministrari iussit. sed Vinius proconsulatu Galliam Narbonensem
seuere integreque rexit; mox Galbae amicitia in abruptum tractus. audax callidus promptus et, prout animum intendisset,
prauus aut industrius eadem ui. testamentum Titi Vinii magnitudine opum irritum, Pisonis supremam uoluntatem paupertas
firmauit.

49 Galbae corpus diu neglectum et licentia tenebrarum plurimis
ludibriis uexatum dispensator Argius e prioribus seruis humili
sepultura in priuatis eius hortis contexit. caput per lixas calonesque
suffixum laceratumque ante Patrobii tumulum (libertus is Neronis
punitus a Galba fuerat) postera demum die repertum et cremato
iam corpori admixtum est.

2 Hunc exitum habuit Seruius Galba, tribus et septuaginta annis quinque principes prospera fortuna emensus et alieno imperio felicior quam suo. uetus in familia nobilitas, magnae opes. ipsi
3 medium ingenium, magis extra uitia quam cum uirtutibus. famae
nec incuriosus nec uenditator; pecuniae alienae non appetens, suae
parcus, publicae auarus; amicorum libertorumque, ubi in bonos
incidisset, sine reprehensione patiens, si mali forent, usque ad culpam ignarus. sed claritas natalium et metus temporum obtentui, ut,
4 quod segnitia erat, sapientia uocaretur. dum uigebat aetas militari
laude apud Germanias floruit. pro consule Africam moderate, iam
senior citeriorem Hispaniam pari iustitia continuit, maior priuato
uisus dum priuatus fuit, et omnium consensu capax imperii, nisi
imperasset.

50 Trepidam urbem ac simul atrocitatem recentis sceleris simul
ueteres Othonis mores pauentem nouus insuper de Vitellio nuntius
exterruit, ante caedem Galbae suppressus ut tantum superioris
Germaniae exercitum desciuisse crederetur. tum duos omnium
mortalium impudicitia ignauia luxuria deterrimos uelut ad perden-
dum imperium fataliter electos non senatus modo et eques, quis
aliqua pars et cura rei publicae, sed uulgus quoque palam maerere.

nec iam recentia saeuae pacis exempla sed repetita bellorum ciuil- 2
ium memoria captam totiens suis exercitibus urbem, uastitatem
Italiae, direptiones prouinciarum, Pharsaliam Philippos et Perusiam
ac Mutinam, nota publicarum cladium nomina, loquebantur. 3
prope euersum orbem etiam cum de principatu inter bonos certare-
tur, sed mansisse C. Iulio, mansisse Caesare Augusto uictore imperium; mansuram fuisse sub Pompeio Brutoque rem publicam.
nunc pro Othone an pro Vitellio in templa ituros: utrasque impias
preces, utraque detestanda uota inter duos quorum bello solum
id scires, deteriorem fore qui uicisset. erant qui Vespasianum et 4
arma Orientis augurarentur, et ut potior utroque Vespasianus, ita
bellum aliud atque alias clades horrebant. et ambigua de Vespasiano
fama, solusque omnium ante se principum in melius mutatus est.

Nunc initia causasque motus Vitelliani expediam. caeso cum **51**
omnibus copiis Iulio Vindice ferox praeda gloriaque exercitus,
ut cui sine labore ac periculo ditissimi belli uictoria euenisset,
expeditionem et aciem, praemia quam stipendia malebat. diu 2
infructuosam et asperam militiam tolerauerant ingenio loci caelique
et seueritate disciplinae, quam in pace inexorabilem discordiae
ciuium resoluunt, paratis utrimque corruptoribus et perfidia impunita. uiri arma equi ad usum et ad decus supererant. sed 3
ante bellum centurias tantum suas turmasque nouerant; exercitus
finibus prouinciarum discernebantur. tum aduersus Vindicem contractae legiones, seque et Gallias expertae, quaerere rursus arma
nouasque discordias; nec socios, ut olim, sed hostes et uictos uocabant. nec deerat pars Galliarum quae Rhenum accolit, easdem
partes secuta ac tum acerrima instigatrix aduersum Galbianos
(hoc enim nomen fastidito Vindice indiderant). igitur Sequanis 4
Aeduisque ac deinde prout opulentia ciuitatibus erat infensi, expugnationes urbium populationes agrorum raptus penatium hauserunt
animo, super auaritiam et arrogantiam, praecipua ualidiorum
uitia, contumacia Gallorum irritati, qui remissam sibi a Galba
quartam tributorum partem et publice donatos in ignominiam
exercitus iactabant. accessit callide uulgatum, temere creditum, de- 5
cimari legiones et promptissimum quemque centurionum dimitti.

undique atroces nuntii, sinistra ex urbe fama; infensa Lugdunensis colonia et pertinaci pro Nerone fide fecunda rumoribus. sed plurima ad fingendum credendumque materies in ipsis castris, odio metu et, ubi uires suas respexerant, securitate.

52 Sub ipsas superioris anni kalendas Decembres Aulus Vitellius inferiorem Germaniam ingressus hiberna legionum cum cura adierat: redditi plerisque ordines, remissa ignominia, alleuatae notae; plura ambitione, quaedam iudicio, in quibus sordes et auaritiam Fontei Capitonis adimendis assignandisue militiae ordinibus
2 integre mutauerat. nec consularis legati mensura sed in maius omnia accipiebantur. et ut Vitellius apud seueros humilis, ita comitatem bonitatemque fauentes uocabant quod sine modo sine iudicio donaret sua largiretur aliena; simul auiditate imperandi ipsa uitia pro uirtutibus interpretabantur.

3 Multi in utroque exercitu sicut modesti quietique ita mali et strenui. sed profusa cupidine et insigni temeritate legati legionum Alienus Caecina et Fabius Valens. e quibus Valens infensus Galbae, tamquam detectam a se Verginii cunctationem, oppressa Capitonis consilia ingrate tulisset, instigare Vitellium, ardorem militum ostentans: ipsum celebri ubique fama, nullam in Flacco Hordeonio moram; adfore Britanniam, secutura Germanorum auxilia; male fidas prouincias, precarium seni imperium et breui transiturum.
4 panderet modo sinum et uenienti Fortunae occurreret. merito dubitasse Verginium equestri familia, ignoto patre, imparem si recepisset imperium, tutum si recusasset; Vitellio tres patris consulatus, censuram, collegium Caesaris et imponere iam pridem imperatoris dignationem et auferre priuati securitatem. quatiebatur his
53 segne ingenium, ut concupisceret magis quam ut speraret. at in superiore Germania Caecina, decorus iuuenta, corpore ingens, animi immodicus, cito sermone, erecto incessu, studia militum illexerat. hunc iuuenem Galba, quaestorem in Baetica impigre in partes suas transgressum, legioni praeposuit. mox compertum publicam
2 pecuniam auertisse ut peculatorem flagitari iussit. Caecina aegre passus miscere cuncta et priuata uulnera rei publicae malis operire statuit.

Nec deerant in exercitu semina discordiae, quod et bello aduersus Vindicem uniuersus adfuerat, nec nisi occiso Nerone translatus
in Galbam atque in eo ipso sacramento uexillis inferioris Germaniae
praeuentus erat. et Treueri ac Lingones quasque alias ciuitates atro- 3
cibus edictis aut damno finium Galba perculerat hibernis legionum
propius miscentur; unde seditiosa colloquia et inter paganos cor-
ruptior miles et in Verginium fauor cuicumque alii profuturus.

Miserat ciuitas Lingonum uetere instituto dona legionibus dex- **54**
tras, hospitii insigne. legati eorum in squalorem maestitiamque
compositi per principia per contubernia modo suas iniurias modo
uicinarum ciuitatium praemia et, ubi pronis militum auribus
accipiebantur, ipsius exercitus pericula et contumelias conquerentes accendebant animos. nec procul seditione aberant, cum 2
Hordeonius Flaccus abire legatos, utque occultior digressus esset, nocte castris excedere iubet. inde atrox rumor, affirmantibus
plerisque interfectos, ac ni sibi ipsi consulerent, fore ut acerrimi militum et praesentia conquesti per tenebras et inscitiam ceterorum
occiderentur. obstringuntur inter se tacito foedere legiones, ascisc- 3
itur auxiliorum miles, primo suspectus tamquam circumdatis cohortibus alisque impetus in legiones pararetur, mox eadem acrius
uoluens, faciliore inter malos consensu ad bellum quam in pace ad
concordiam.

Inferioris tamen Germaniae legiones sollemni kalendarum **55**
Ianuariarum sacramento pro Galba adactae, multa cunctatione et
raris primorum ordinum uocibus, ceteri silentio proximi cuiusque
audaciam exspectantes, insita mortalibus natura propere sequi quae
piget inchoare. sed ipsis legionibus inerat diuersitas animorum: 2
primani quintanique turbidi adeo ut quidam saxa in Galbae imagines iecerint; quinta decima ac sexta decima legiones nihil ultra
fremitum et minas ausae initium erumpendi circumspectabant.

At in superiore exercitu quarta ac duoetuicensima legiones, 3
isdem hibernis tendentes, ipso kalendarum Ianuariarum die
dirumpunt imagines Galbae, quarta legio promptius, duoetuicensima cunctanter, mox consensu. ac ne reuerentiam imperii 4
exuere uiderentur, senatus populique Romani oblitterata iam

nomina sacramento aduocabant, nullo legatorum tribunorumue pro Galba nitente, quibusdam, ut in tumultu, notabilius turbantibus. (non tamen quisquam [in modum contionis aut] suggestu
56 locutus; neque enim erat adhuc cui imputaretur.) spectator flagitii Hordeonius Flaccus consularis legatus aderat, non compescere ruentes, non retinere dubios, non cohortari bonos ausus, sed segnis pauidus et socordia innocens. quattuor centuriones duoetuicensimae legionis, Nonius Receptus, Donatius Valens, Romilius Marcellus, Calpurnius Repentinus, cum protegerent Galbae imagines, impetu militum abrepti uinctique. nec cuiquam ultra fides aut memoria prioris sacramenti sed, quod in seditionibus accidit, unde plures erant omnes fuere.

2 Nocte quae kalendas Ianuarias secuta est in coloniam Agrippinensem aquilifer quartae legionis epulanti Vitellio nuntiat quartam et duoetuicensimam legiones proiectis Galbae imaginibus in senatus ac populi Romani uerba iurasse. id sacramentum inane uisum; occupari nutantem fortunam et offerri principem placuit.
3 missi a Vitellio ad legiones legatosque qui desciuisse a Galba superiorem exercitum nuntiarent: proinde aut bellandum aduersus desciscentes aut, si concordia et pax placeat, faciendum imperatorem. et minore discrimine sumi principem quam quaeri.

57 Proxima legionis primae hiberna erant et promptissimus e legatis Fabius Valens. is die postero coloniam Agrippinensem cum equitibus legionis auxiliariorumque ingressus imperatorem Vitellium consalutauit. secutae ingenti certamine eiusdem prouinciae legiones. et superior exercitus, speciosis senatus populique Romani nominibus relictis, tertium nonas Ianuarias Vitellio accessit; scires illum priore biduo non penes rem publicam fuisse.

2 Ardorem exercituum Agrippinenses Treueri Lingones aequabant, auxilia equos arma pecuniam offerentes ut quisque corpore opibus ingenio ualidus. nec principes modo coloniarum aut castrorum, quibus praesentia ex affluenti et parta uictoria magnae spes, sed manipuli quoque et gregarius miles uiatica sua et balteos phalerasque, insignia armorum argento decora, loco pecuniae tradebant, instinctu et impetu et auaritia.

Igitur laudata militum alacritate Vitellius ministeria principa- 58
tus per libertos agi solita in equites Romanos disponit, uacationes
centurionibus ex fisco numerat, saeuitiam militum plerosque ad
poenam exposcentium saepius approbat, raro simulatione uinculorum frustratur. Pompeius Propinquus procurator Belgicae statim interfectus; Iulium Burdonem Germanicae classis praefectum
astu subtraxit. exarserat in eum iracundia exercitus tamquam 2
crimen ac mox insidias Fonteio Capitoni struxisset. grata erat
memoria Capitonis, et apud saeuientes occidere palam, ignoscere
non nisi fallendo licebat. ita in custodia habitus et post uictoriam
demum, satiatis iam militum odiis, dimissus est. interim ut piaculum obicitur centurio Crispinus; sanguine se Capitonis cruentauerat eoque et postulantibus manifestior et punienti uilior fuit.
Iulius deinde Ciuilis periculo exemptus, praepotens inter Batauos, 59
ne supplicio eius ferox gens alienaretur. (et erant in ciuitate
Lingonum octo Batauorum cohortes, quartae decimae legionis
auxilia, tum discordia temporum a legione digressae, prout inclinassent, grande momentum sociae aut aduersae.) Nonium,
Donatium, Romilium, Calpurnium centuriones, de quibus supra
rettulimus, occidi iussit, damnatos fidei crimine, grauissimo inter
desciscentes.

Accessere partibus Valerius Asiaticus, Belgicae prouinciae 2
legatus, quem mox Vitellius generum asciuit, et Iunius Blaesus,
Lugdunensis Galliae rector, cum Italica legione e ala Tauriana
Lugduni tendentibus. nec in Raeticis copiis mora quo minus statim adiungerentur. ne in Britannia quidem dubitatum. praeerat 60
Trebellius Maximus, per auaritiam ac sordes contemptus exercitui inuisusque. accendebat odium eius Roscius Coelius legatus
uicensimae legionis, olim discors, sed occasione ciuilium armorum
atrocius proruperant. Trebellius seditionem et confusum ordinem
disciplinae Coelio, spoliatas et inopes legiones Coelius Trebellio
obiectabat, cum interim foedis legatorum certaminibus modestia
exercitus corrupta eoque discordiae uentum ut auxiliarium quoque
militum conuiciis proturbatus et aggregantibus se Coelio cohortibus
alisque desertus Trebellius ad Vitellium perfugerit. quies prouinciae

quamquam remoto consulari mansit; rexere legati legionum, pares iure, Coelius audendo potentior.

61 Adiuncto Britannico exercitu ingens uiribus opibusque Vitellius duos duces duo itinera bello destinauit. Fabius Valens allicere uel, si abnuerent, uastare Gallias et Cottianis Alpibus Italiam irrumpere, Caecina propiore transitu Poeninis iugis degredi iussus.
2 Valenti inferioris exercitus electi cum aquila quintae legionis et cohortibus alisque, ad quadraginta milia armatorum data; triginta milia Caecina e superiore Germania ducebat, quorum robur legio unaetuicensima fuit. addita utrique Germanorum auxilia, e quibus Vitellius suas quoque copias suppleuit, tota mole belli secuturus.

62 Mira inter exercitum imperatoremque diuersitas. instare miles, arma poscere, dum Galliae trepident, dum Hispaniae cunctentur: non obstare hiemem neque ignauae pacis moras; inuadendam Italiam, occupandam urbem; nihil in discordiis ciuilibus festina-
2 tione tutius, ubi facto magis quam consulto opus esset. torpebat Vitellius et fortunam principatus inerti luxu ac prodigis epulis praesumebat, medio diei temulentus et sagina grauis, cum tamen ardor et uis militum ultro ducis munia implebat, ut si adesset imperator et strenuis uel ignauis spem metumue adderet. instructi intentique signum profectionis exposcunt. nomen Germanici Vitellio statim additum; Caesarem se appellari etiam uictor prohibuit.

3 Laetum augurium Fabio Valenti exercituique quem in bellum agebat, ipso profectionis die aquila leni meatu prout agmen incederet uelut dux uiae praeuolauit, longumque per spatium is gaudentium militum clamor, ea quies interritae alitis fuit ut haud dubium magnae et prosperae rei omen acciperetur.

63 Et Treueros quidem ut socios securi adiere. Diuoduri (Mediomatricorum id oppidum est) quamquam omni comitate exceptos subitus pauor terruit, raptis repente armis ad caedem innoxiae ciuitatis, non ob praedam aut spoliandi cupidine sed furore et rabie et causis incertis eoque difficilioribus remediis, donec precibus ducis mitigati ab excidio ciuitatis temperauere. caesa
2 tamen ad quattuor milia hominum. isque terror Gallias inuasit

ut uenienti mox agmini uniuersae ciuitates cum magistratibus et precibus occurrerent, stratis per uias feminis puerisque quaeque alia placamenta hostilis irae non quidem in bello sed pro pace tendebantur.

Nuntium de caede Galbae et imperio Othonis Fabius Valens **64**
in ciuitate Leucorum accepit. nec militum animus in gaudium aut formidine permotus; bellum uoluebat. Gallis cunctatio exempta est; in Othonem ac Vitellium odium par, ex Vitellio et metus.

Proxima Lingonum ciuitas erat, fida partibus. benigne excepti 2
modestia certauere, sed breuis laetitia fuit cohortium intemperie quas a legione quarta decima, ut supra memorauimus, digressas exercitui suo Fabius Valens adiunxerat. iurgia primum, mox rixa inter Batauos et legionarios, dum his aut illis studia militum aggregantur, prope in proelium exarsere, ni Valens animaduersione paucorum oblitos iam Batauos imperii admonuisset.

Frustra aduersus Aeduos quaesita belli causa; iussi pecuniam 3
atque arma deferre gratuitos insuper commeatus praebuere. quod Aedui formidine Lugdunenses gaudio fecere. sed legio Italica et ala Tauriana abductae; cohortem duodeuicensimam Lugduni, solitis sibi hibernis, relinqui placuit. Manlius Valens 4
legatus Italicae legionis, quamquam bene de partibus meritus, nullo apud Vitellium honore fuit; secretis eum criminationibus infamauerat Fabius ignarum et, quo incautior deciperetur, palam laudatum.

Veterem inter Lugdunenses et Viennenses discordiam pro- **65**
ximum bellum accenderat. multae in uicem clades, crebrius infestiusque quam ut tantum propter Neronem Galbamque pugnaretur. et Galba reditus Lugdunensium occasione irae in fiscum uerterat; multus contra in Viennenses honor. unde aemulatio et inuidia et uno amne discretis conexum odium.

Igitur Lugdunenses exstimulare singulos militum et in 2
euersionem Viennensium impellere, obsessam ab illis coloniam suam, adiutos Vindicis conatus, conscriptas nuper legiones in praesidium Galbae referendo. et ubi causas odiorum praetenderant, magnitudinem praedae ostendebant, nec iam secreta exhortatio sed

publicae preces: irent ultores, exscinderent sedem Gallici belli.
cuncta illic externa et hostilia; se, coloniam Romanam et partem
exercitus et prosperarum aduersarumque rerum socios, si fortuna
66 contra daret, iratis ne relinquerent. his et pluribus in eundem
modum perpulerant ut ne legati quidem ac duces partium restingui
posse iracundiam exercitus arbitrarentur, cum haud ignari discriminis sui Viennenses, uelamenta et infulas praeferentes, ubi agmen
incesserat, arma genua uestigia prensando flexere militum animos.
addidit Valens trecenos singulis militibus sestertios. tum uetustas
dignitasque coloniae ualuit et uerba Fabi salutem incolumitatemque
Viennensium commendantis aequis auribus accepta. publice tamen
2 armis multati priuatis et promiscuis copiis iuuere militem. sed fama
constans fuit ipsum Valentem magna pecunia emptum. is diu sor-
didus repente diues mutationem fortunae male tegebat, accensis
egestate longa cupidinibus immoderatus et inopi iuuenta senex
prodigus.

3 Lento deinde agmine per fines Allobrogum ac Vocontiorum
ductus exercitus, ipsa itinerum spatia et statiuorum mutationes
uenditante duce foedis pactionibus aduersus possessores agrorum
et magistratus ciuitatum, adeo minaciter ut Luco (municipium id
Vocontiorum est) faces admouerit donec pecunia mitigaretur. quotiens pecuniae materia deesset, stupris et adulteriis exorabatur. sic
ad Alpes peruentum.

67 Plus praedae ac sanguinis Caecina hausit. irritauerant turbidum ingenium Heluetii, Gallica gens olim armis uirisque mox
memoria nominis clara, de caede Galbae ignari et Vitellii imperium
abnuentes. initium bello fuit auaritia ac festinatio unaetuicensimae
legionis: rapuerant pecuniam missam in stipendium castelli quod
2 olim Heluetii suis militibus ac stipendiis tuebantur. aegre id passi
Heluetii, interceptis epistulis quae nomine Germanici exercitus ad
Pannonicas legiones ferebantur, centurionem et quosdam militum
in custodia retinebant.

Caecina belli auidus proximam quamque culpam, antequam
paeniteret, ultum ibat. mota propere castra; uastati agri; direptus longa pace in modum municipii exstructus locus, amoeno

salubrium aquarum usu frequens; missi ad Raetica auxilia nuntii ut uersos in legionem Heluetios a tergo aggrederentur.

Illi ante discrimen feroces, in periculo pauidi. quamquam **68**
primo tumultu Claudium Seuerum ducem legerant, non arma noscere, non ordines sequi, non in unum consulere. exitiosum aduersus ueteranos proelium, intuta obsidio dilapsis uetustate moenibus; hinc Caecina cum ualido exercitu, inde Raeticae alae cohortesque et ipsorum Raetorum iuuentus, sueta armis et more militiae exercita.

Undique populatio et caedes. ipsi medio uagi, abiectis armis, magna pars saucii aut palantes, in montem Vocetium perfugere.
ac statim immissa cohorte Thracum depulsi et consectantibus 2
Germanis Raetisque per siluas atque in ipsis latebris trucidati. multa hominum milia caesa, multa sub corona uenundata. cumque dirutis omnibus Auenticum gentis caput infesto agmine peteretur, missi qui dederent ciuitatem, et deditio accepta. in Iulium Alpinum e principibus ut concitorem belli Caecina animaduertit; ceteros ueniae uel saeuitiae Vitellii reliquit.

Haud facile dictu est, legati Heluetiorum minus placabilem **69**
imperatorem an militem inuenerint. ciuitatis excidium poscunt, tela ac manus in ora legatorum intentant. ne Vitellius quidem uerbis et minis temperabat, cum Claudius Cossus, unus e legatis, notae facundiae sed dicendi artem apta trepidatione occultans atque eo ualidior, militis animum mitigauit. ut est mos, uulgus mutabile subitis et tam pronum in misericordiam quam immodicum saeuitia fuerat; effusis lacrimis et meliora constantius postulando impunitatem salutemque ciuitati impetrauere.

Caecina paucos in Heluetiis moratus dies dum sententiae **70**
Vitellii certior fieret, simul transitum Alpium parans, laetum ex Italia nuntium accipit alam Silianam circa Padum agentem sacramento Vitellii accessisse. pro consule Vitellium Siliani in Africa habuerant; mox a Nerone, ut in Aegyptum praemitterentur, exciti et ob bellum Vindicis reuocati ac tum in Italia manentes, instinctu decurionum, qui Othonis ignari Vitellio obstricti robur aduentantium legionum et famam Germanici exercitus attollebant, transiere in

partes et ut donum aliquod nouo principi firmissima Transpadanae
regionis municipia, Mediolanum ac Nouariam et Eporediam et
2 Vercellas, adiunxere. id Caecinae per ipsos compertum. et (quia
praesidio alae unius latissima Italiae pars defendi nequibat) praemissis Gallorum Lusitanorumque et Britannorum cohortibus et
Germanorum uexillis cum ala Petriana, ipse paulum cunctatus
est num Raeticis iugis in Noricum flecteret aduersus Petronium
Vrbicum procuratorem, qui concitis auxiliis et interruptis fluminum
3 pontibus fidus Othoni putabatur. sed metu ne amitteret prae-
missas iam cohortes alasque, simul reputans plus gloriae retenta
Italia et, ubicumque certatum foret, Noricos in certa uictoriae
praemia cessuros, Poenino itinere subsignanum militem et graue
legionum agmen hibernis adhuc Alpibus transduxit.

71 Otho interim contra spem omnium non deliciis neque desidia
torpescere. dilatae uoluptates, dissimulata luxuria et cuncta ad
decorem imperii composita, eoque plus formidinis afferebant falsae
uirtutes et uitia reditura.

Marium Celsum consulem designatum, per speciem uinculorum
saeuitiae militum subtractum, acciri in Capitolium iubet; clemen-
2 tiae titulus e uiro claro et partibus inuiso petebatur. Celsus constanter seruatae erga Galbam fidei crimen confessus, exemplum ultro
imputauit. nec Otho quasi ignosceret sed ne hostem metueret conciliationes adhibens statim inter intimos amicos habuit et mox
bello inter duces delegit, mansitque Celso uelut fataliter etiam pro
3 Othone fides integra et infelix. laeta primoribus ciuitatis, celebrata
in uulgus Celsi salus ne militibus quidem ingrata fuit, eandem
uirtutem admirantibus cui irascebantur.

72 Par inde exsultatio disparibus causis consecuta impetrato
Tigellini exitio. Ofonius Tigellinus obscuris parentibus, foeda pueritia, impudica senecta, praefecturam uigilum et praetorii et alia
praemia uirtutum, quia uelocius erat, uitiis adeptus, crudelitatem
mox, deinde auaritiam, uirilia scelera, exercuit, corrupto ad omne
facinus Nerone, quaedam ignaro ausus, ac postremo eiusdem desertor ac proditor. unde non alium pertinacius ad poenam flagitauere,
diuerso affectu, quibus odium Neronis inerat et quibus desiderium.

apud Galbam Titi Vini potentia defensus, praetexentis ser- 2
uatam ab eo filiam. (haud dubie seruauerat, non clementia, quippe
tot interfectis, sed effugium in futurum, quia pessimus quisque diffi-
dentia praesentium mutationem pauens aduersus publicum odium
priuatam gratiam praeparat. unde nulla innocentiae cura sed uices
impunitatis.) eo infensior populus, addita ad uetus Tigellini odium 3
recenti Titi Vini inuidia, concurrere ex tota urbe in Palatium ac
fora et, ubi plurima uulgi licentia, in circum ac theatra effusi seditiosis uocibus strepere, donec Tigellinus, accepto apud Sinuessanas
aquas supremae necessitatis nuntio, inter stupra concubinarum et
oscula et deformes moras sectis nouacula faucibus infamem uitam
foedauit etiam exitu sero et inhonesto.

Per idem tempus expostulata ad supplicium Caluia Crispinilla **73**
uariis frustrationibus et aduersa dissimulantis principis fama periculo exempta est. magistra libidinum Neronis, transgressa in
Africam ad instigandum in arma Clodium Macrum, famem populo Romano haud obscure molita, totius postea ciuitatis gratiam
obtinuit, consulari matrimonio subnixa et apud Galbam Othonem
Vitellium illaesa, mox potens pecunia et orbitate, quae bonis ma-
lisque temporibus iuxta ualent.

Crebrae interim et muliebribus blandimentis infectae ab Othone **74**
ad Vitellium epistulae offerebant pecuniam et gratiam et quemcumque quietis locum prodigae uitae legisset. paria Vitellius
ostentabat, primo mollius, stulta utrimque et indecora simulatione; mox quasi rixantes stupra ac flagitia inuicem obiectauere,
neuter falso. Otho, reuocatis quos Galba miserat legatis, rursus 2
ad utrumque Germanicum exercitum et ad legionem Italicam
easque quae Lugduni agebant copias specie senatus misit. legati
apud Vitellium remansere, promptius quam ut retenti uiderentur;
praetoriani, quos per simulationem officii legatis Otho adiunxerat, remissi antequam legionibus miscerentur. addidit epis- 3
tulas Fabius Valens nomine Germanici exercitus ad praetorias
et urbanas cohortes de uiribus partium magnificas et concordiam offerentes. increpabat ultro quod tanto ante traditum
Vitellio imperium ad Othonem uertissent. ita promissis simul ac **75**

minis temptabantur, ut bello impares, in pace nihil amissuri; neque ideo praetorianorum fides mutata. sed insidiatores ab Othone in Germaniam, a Vitellio in urbem missi. utrisque frustra fuit, Vitellianis impune, per tantam hominum multitudinem mutua ignorantia fallentibus; Othoniani nouitate uultus, omnibus inuicem
2 gnaris, prodebantur. Vitellius litteras ad Titianum fratrem Othonis composuit, exitium ipsi filioque eius minitans ni incolumes sibi mater ac liberi seruarentur. et stetit domus utraque, sub Othone incertum an metu; Vitellius uictor clementiae gloriam tulit.

76 Primus Othoni fiduciam addidit ex Illyrico nuntius iurasse in eum Dalmatiae ac Pannoniae et Moesiae legiones. idem ex Hispania allatum laudatusque per edictum Cluuius Rufus; et statim cognitum est conuersam ad Vitellium Hispaniam. ne Aquitania quidem, quamquam ab Iulio Cordo in uerba Othonis obstricta, diu mansit. nusquam fides aut amor; metu ac necessitate huc illuc mutabantur. eadem formido prouinciam Narbonensem ad
2 Vitellium uertit, facili transitu ad proximos et ualidiores. longinquae prouinciae et quicquid armorum mari dirimitur penes Othonem manebat, non partium studio, sed erat grande momentum in nomine urbis ac praetexto senatus, et occupauerat animos prior auditus. Iudaicum exercitum Vespasianus, Syriae legiones Mucianus sacramento Othonis adegere. simul Aegyptus omnesque
3 uersae in Orientem prouinciae nomine eius tenebantur. idem Africae obsequium, initio Carthagine orto neque exspectata Vipstani Aproniani proconsulis auctoritate. Crescens Neronis libertus (nam et hi malis temporibus partem se rei publicae faciunt) epulum plebi ob laetitiam recentis imperii obtulerat, et populus pleraque sine modo festinauit. Carthaginem ceterae ciuitates secutae.

77 Sic distractis exercitibus ac prouinciis Vitellio quidem ad capessendam principatus fortunam bello opus erat, Otho ut in multa pace munia imperii obibat, quaedam ex dignitate rei
2 publicae, pleraque contra decus ex praesenti usu properando. consul cum Titiano fratre in kalendas Martias ipse, proximos menses Verginio destinat ut aliquod exercitui Germanico delenimentum. iungitur Verginio Pompeius Vopiscus praetexto ueteris

amicitiae; plerique Viennensium honori datum interpretabantur.
ceteri consulatus ex destinatione Neronis aut Galbae mansere,
Caelio ac Flauio Sabinis in Iulias, Arrio Antonino et Mario Celso in
Septembres, quorum honoribus ne Vitellius quidem uictor intercessit. sed Otho pontificatus auguratusque honoratis iam senibus 3
cumulum dignitatis addidit, aut recens ab exilio reuersos nobiles
adulescentulos auitis ac paternis sacerdotiis in solacium recoluit.
redditus Cadio Rufo, Pedio Blaeso, †Saeuino Promquo† senatorius
locus. repetundarum criminibus sub Claudio ac Nerone ceciderant.
placuit ignoscentibus uerso nomine, quod auaritia fuerat, uideri
maiestatem, cuius tum odio etiam bonae leges peribant.

Eadem largitione ciuitatum quoque ac prouinciarum animos **78**
aggressus Hispalensibus et Emeritensibus familiarum adiectiones,
Lingonibus uniuersis ciuitatem Romanam, prouinciae Baeticae
Maurorum ciuitates dono dedit; noua iura Cappadociae, noua
Africae, ostentata magis quam mansura. inter quae necessitate 2
praesentium rerum et instantibus curis excusata ne tum quidem
immemor amorum statuas Poppaeae per senatus consultum repo-
suit. creditus est etiam de celebranda Neronis memoria agitauisse
spe uulgum alliciendi. et fuere qui imagines Neronis proponerent.
atque etiam Othoni quibusdam diebus populus et miles, tamquam
nobilitatem ac decus astruerent, Neroni Othoni acclamauit. ipse in
suspenso tenuit, uetandi metu uel agnoscendi pudore.

Conuersis ad ciuile bellum animis externa sine cura habe- **79**
tbantur. eo audentius Rhoxolani, Sarmatica gens, priore hieme
caesis duabus cohortibus, magna spe Moesiam irruperant, ad
nouem milia equitum, ex ferocia et successu praedae magis quam
pugnae intenta. igitur uagos et incuriosos tertia legio adiunctis auxiliis repente inuasit. apud Romanos omnia proelio apta; Sarmatae 2
dispersi cupidine praedae aut graues onere sarcinarum et lubrico
itinerum adempta equorum pernicitate uelut uincti caedebantur.
namque mirum dictu ut sit omnis Sarmatarum uirtus uelut extra
ipsos. nihil ad pedestrem pugnam tam ignauum; ubi per turmas
aduenere uix ulla acies obstiterit. sed tum umido die et soluto 3
gelu neque conti neque gladii, quos praelongos utraque manu

regunt, usui, lapsantibus equis et catafractarum pondere. (id principibus et nobilissimo cuique tegimen, ferreis lamminis aut prae-
duro corio consertum, ut aduersus ictus impenetrabile ita impetu
hostium prouolutis inhabile ad resurgendum.) simul altitudine et
4 mollitia niuis hauriebantur. Romanus miles facilis lorica et mis-
sili pilo aut lanceis assultans, ubi res posceret leui gladio inermem
Sarmatam (neque enim scuto defendi mos est) comminus fodiebat,
donec pauci qui proelio superfuerant paludibus abderentur.
5 ibi saeuitia hiemis aut uulnerum absumpti. postquam id Romae
compertum, M. Aponius Moesiam obtinens triumphali statua,
Fuluus Aurelius et Iulianus Tettius ac Numisius Lupus, legati legionum, consularibus ornamentis donantur, laeto Othone et gloriam in se trahente tamquam et ipse felix bello et suis ducibus suisque
exercitibus rem publicam auxisset.

80 Paruo interim initio, unde nihil timebatur orta seditio prope
urbi excidio fuit. septimam decimam cohortem e colonia Ostiensi
in urbem acciri Otho iusserat. armandae eius cura Vario Crispino
tribuno e praetorianis data. is quo magis uacuus quietis castris
iussa exsequeretur, uehicula cohortis incipiente nocte onerari aperto
armamentario iubet. tempus in suspicionem, causa in crimen,
affectatio quietis in tumultum eualuit, et uisa inter temulentos
2 arma cupidinem sui mouere. fremit miles et tribunos centurionesque proditionis arguit, tamquam familiae senatorum ad perniciem Othonis armarentur, pars ignari et uino graues, pessimus
quisque in occasionem praedarum, uulgus, ut mos est, cuiuscumque
motus noui cupidum; et obsequia meliorum nox abstulerat. re-
sistentem seditioni tribunum et seuerissimos centurionum obtrun-
cant. rapta arma, nudati gladii. insidentes equis urbem ac Palatium
petunt.

81 Erat Othoni celebre conuiuium primoribus feminis uirisque,
qui trepidi fortuitusne militum furor an dolus imperatoris, manere
ac deprehendi an fugere et dispergi periculosius foret, modo constantiam simulare modo formidine detegi, simul Othonis uultum intueri. utque euenit inclinatis ad suspicionem mentibus,
2 cum timeret Otho, timebatur. sed haud secus discrimine senatus

quam suo territus et praefectos praetorii ad mitigandas militum iras
statim miserat et abire propere omnes e conuiuio iussit. tum uero
passim magistratus proiectis insignibus, uitata comitum et seruorum
frequentia, senes feminaeque per tenebras diuersa urbis itinera, rari
domos, plurimi amicorum tecta et, ut cuique humillimus cliens, incertas latebras petiuere.

Militum impetus ne foribus quidem Palatii coercitus quo **82**
minus conuiuium irrumperent, ostendi sibi Othonem expostu-
lantes, uulnerato Iulio Martiale tribuno et Vitellio Saturnino
praefecto legionis dum ruentibus obsistunt. undique arma et minae, modo in centuriones tribunosque modo in senatum uniuersum,
lymphatis caeco pauore animis et, quia neminem unum destinare
irae poterant, licentiam in omnes poscentibus, donec Otho contra decus imperii toro insistens precibus et lacrimis aegre cohibuit,
redieruntque in castra inuiti neque innocentes.

Postera die uelut capta urbe clausae domus, rarus per uias 2
populus, maesta plebs; deiecti in terram militum uultus ac plus tristitiae quam paenitentiae. manipulatim allocuti sunt Licinius Proculus
et Plotius Firmus praefecti, ex suo quisque ingenio mitius aut
horridius. finis sermonis in eo ut quina milia nummum singulis 3
militibus numerarentur. tum Otho ingredi castra ausus. atque illum
tribuni centurionesque circumsistunt, abiectis militiae insignibus
otium et salutem flagitantes. sensit inuidiam miles et compositus in
obsequium auctores seditionis ad supplicium ultro postulabat.

Otho, quamquam turbidis rebus et diuersis militum animis, **83**
cum optimus quisque remedium praesentis licentiae posceret, uulgus et plures seditionibus et ambitioso imperio laeti per turbas
et raptus facilius ad ciuile bellum impellerentur, simul reputans
non posse principatum scelere quaesitum subita modestia et prisca
grauitate retineri, sed discrimine urbis et periculo senatus anxius, postremo ita disseruit: ‘neque ut affectus uestros in amorem 2
mei accenderem, commilitones, neque ut animum ad uirtutem co-
hortarer (utraque enim egregie supersunt) sed ueni postulaturus
a uobis temperamentum uestrae fortitudinis et erga me modum
caritatis. tumultus proximi initium non cupiditate uel odio, quae

multos exercitus in discordiam egere, ac ne detrectatione quidem
aut formidine periculorum: nimia pietas uestra acrius quam considerate excitauit. nam saepe honestas rerum causas, ni iudicium
adhibeas, perniciosi exitus consequuntur.
3 'Imus ad bellum. num omnes nuntios palam audiri, omnia
consilia cunctis praesentibus tractari ratio rerum aut occasionum
uelocitas patitur? tam nescire quaedam milites quam scire oportet.
ita se ducum auctoritas, sic rigor disciplinae habet, ut multa etiam
centuriones tribunosque tantum iuberi expediat. si cur iubeantur
quaerere singulis liceat, pereunte obsequio etiam imperium inter-
4 cidit. an et illic nocte intempesta rapientur arma? unus alterue
perditus ac temulentus (neque enim plures consternatione proxima
insanisse crediderim) centurionis ac tribuni sanguine manus imbuet,
imperatoris sui tentorium irrumpet?
84 'Vos quidem istud pro me; sed in discursu ac tenebris et rerum
omnium confusione patefieri occasio etiam aduersus me potest.
si Vitellio et satellitibus eius eligendi facultas detur, quem nobis
animum, quas mentes imprecentur? quid aliud quam seditionem et
discordiam optabunt, ne miles centurioni, ne centurio tribuno ob-
2 sequatur, ut confusi pedites equitesque in exitium ruamus? parendo
potius, commilitones, quam imperia ducum sciscitando res militares continentur, et fortissimus in ipso discrimine exercitus est qui
ante discrimen quietissimus. uobis arma et animus sit; mihi consilium et uirtutis uestrae regimen relinquite. paucorum culpa fuit,
duorum poena erit; ceteri abolete memoriam foedissimae noctis.
3 'Nec illas aduersus senatum uoces ullus usquam exercitus au-
diat. caput imperii et decora omnium prouinciarum ad poenam
uocare non hercule illi, quos cum maxime Vitellius in nos ciet,
Germani audeant. ulline Italiae alumni et Romana uere iuuentus ad
sanguinem et caedem depoposcerit ordinem cuius splendore et gloria sordes et obscuritatem Vitellianarum partium praestringimus?
nationes aliquas occupauit Vitellius, imaginem quandam exercitus habet; senatus nobiscum est. sic fit ut hinc res publica, inde
4 hostes rei publicae constiterint. quid? uos pulcherrimam hanc
urbem domibus et tectis et congestu lapidum stare creditis? muta

ista et inanima intercidere ac reparari promisca sunt; aeternitas rerum et pax gentium et mea cum uestra salus incolumitate senatus firmatur. hunc auspicato a parente et conditore urbis nostrae institutum et a regibus usque ad principes continuum et immortalem, sicut a maioribus accepimus, sic posteris tradamus. nam ut ex uobis senatores, ita ex senatoribus principes nascuntur.'

Et oratio ad perstringendos mulcendosque militum animos 85
et seueritatis modus (neque enim in plures quam in duos animaduerti iusserat) grate accepta compositique ad praesens qui
coerceri non poterant. non tamen quies urbi redierat: strepitus
telorum et facies belli, militibus ut nihil in commune turbantibus,
ita sparsis per domos occulto habitu et maligna cura in omnes
quos nobilitas aut opes aut aliqua insignis claritudo rumoribus
obiecerat. Vitellianos quoque milites uenisse in urbem ad studia par- 2
tium noscenda plerique credebant. unde plena omnia suspicionum
et uix secreta domuum sine formidine. sed plurimum trepidationis in publico, ut quemque nuntium fama attulisset animum uul-
tumque conuersis, ne diffidere dubiis ac parum gaudere prosperis
uiderentur. coacto uero in curiam senatu arduus rerum omnium 3
modus, ne contumax silentium, ne suspecta libertas; et priuato
Othoni nuper atque eadem dicenti nota adulatio. igitur uersare sen-
tentias et huc atque illuc torquere, hostem et parricidam Vitellium
uocantes, prouidentissimus quisque uulgaribus conuiciis, quidam
uera probra iacere, in clamore tamen et ubi plurimae uoces, aut
tumultu uerborum sibi ipsi obstrepentes.

Prodigia insuper terrebant diuersis auctoribus uulgata: in 86
uestibulo Capitolii omissas habenas bigae cui Victoria institerat,
erupisse cella Iunonis maiorem humana speciem, statuam diui Iulii
in insula Tiberini amnis sereno et immoto die ab occidente in orientem conuersam, prolocutum in Etruria bouem, insolitos animalium
partus et plura alia rudibus saeculis etiam in pace obseruata, quae
nunc tantum in metu audiuntur. sed praecipuus et cum praesenti 2
exitio etiam futuri pauor subita inundatione Tiberis, qui immenso
auctu proruto ponte sublicio ac strage obstantis molis refusus non
modo iacentia et plana urbis loca sed secura eius modi casuum

impleuit. rapti e publico plerique, plures in tabernis et cubilibus intercepti. fames in uulgus inopia quaestus et penuria alimentorum. corrupta stagnantibus aquis insularum fundamenta, dein remeante
3 flumine dilapsa. utque primum uacuus a periculo animus fuit, id ipsum quod paranti expeditionem Othoni campus Martius et uia Flaminia iter belli esset obstructum, a fortuitis uel naturalibus causis in prodigium et omen imminentium cladium uertebatur.

87 Otho lustrata urbe et expensis bello consiliis, quando Poeninae Cottiaeque Alpes et ceteri Galliarum aditus Vitellianis exercitibus claudebantur, Narbonensem Galliam aggredi statuit classe ualida et partibus fida quod reliquos caesorum ad pontem Muluium et saeuitia Galbae in custodia habitos in numeros legionis composuerat, facta et ceteris spe honoratae in posterum militiae. addidit classi urbanas cohortes et plerosque e praetorianis, uires et robur exercitus atque ipsis ducibus consilium et custodes.
2 summa expeditionis Antonio Nouello, Suedio Clementi primipilaribus, Aemilio Pacensi, cui ademptum a Galba tribunatum reddiderat, permissa. curam nauium Moschus libertus retinebat ad obseruandam honestiorum fidem †immutatus†. peditum equitumque copiis Suetonius Paulinus, Marius Celsus, Annius Gallus rectores destinati, sed plurima fides Licinio Proculo praetorii praefecto. is urbanae militiae impiger, bellorum insolens, auctoritatem Paulini, uigorem Celsi, maturitatem Galli, ut cuique erat, criminando, quod facillimum factu est, prauus et callidus bonos et modestos anteibat.

88 Sepositus per eos dies Cornelius Dolabella in coloniam Aquinatem, neque arta custodia neque obscura, nullum ob crimen, sed uetusto nomine et propinquitate Galbae monstratus.

Multos e magistratibus, magnam consularium partem Otho non participes aut ministros bello sed comitum specie secum expedire iubet, in quis et Lucium Vitellium, eodem quo ceteros cultu, nec ut
2 imperatoris fratrem nec ut hostis. igitur motae urbis curae, nullus ordo metu aut periculo uacuus. primores senatus aetate inualidi et longa pace desides, segnis et oblita bellorum nobilitas, ignarus militiae eques, quanto magis occultare et abdere pauorem nitebantur,

manifestius pauidi. nec deerant e contrario qui ambitione sto- 3
lida conspicua arma, insignes equos, quidam luxuriosos apparatus conuiuiorum et irritamenta libidinum ut instrumentum belli mercarentur. sapientibus quietis et rei publicae cura, leuissimus quisque et futuri improuidus spe uana tumens, multi afflicta fide in pace ac turbatis rebus alacres, et per incerta tutissimi.

Sed uulgus et magnitudine nimia communium curarum ex- **89**
pers populus sentire paulatim belli mala, conuersa in militum usum omni pecunia, intentis alimentorum pretiis, quae motu Vindicis haud perinde plebem attriuerant, secura tum urbe et prouinciali
bello, quod inter legiones Galliasque uelut externum fuit. nam 2
ex quo diuus Augustus res Caesarum composuit, procul et in unius sollicitudinem aut decus populus Romanus bellauerat. sub Tiberio et Gaio tantum pacis aduersa ad rem publicam pertinuere. Scriboniani contra Claudium incepta simul audita et coercita. Nero nuntiis magis et rumoribus quam armis depulsus. tum legiones classesque et, quod raro alias, praetorianus urbanusque miles in aciem deducti, Oriens Occidensque et quicquid utrimque uirium est a
tergo. si ducibus aliis bellatum foret, longo bello materia. fuere 3
qui proficiscenti Othoni moras religionemque nondum conditorum ancilium afferrent; aspernatus est omnem cunctationem ut Neroni quoque exitiosam. et Caecina iam Alpes transgressus exstimulabat.

Pridie idus Martias commendata patribus re publica reliquias **90**
Neronianarum sectionum nondum in fiscum conuersas reuocatis ab exilio concessit, iustissimum donum et in speciem magnificum,
sed festinata iam pridem exactione usu sterile. mox uocata con- 2
tione maiestatem urbis et consensum populi ac senatus pro se attollens, aduersum Vitellianas partes modeste disseruit, inscitiam potius legionum quam audaciam increpans, nulla Vitellii mentione, siue ipsius ea moderatio, seu scriptor orationis sibi metuens contumeliis in Vitellium abstinuit, quando, ut in consiliis militiae Suetonio Paulino et Mario Celso, ita in rebus urbanis Galeri Trachali ingenio Othonem uti credebatur. et erant qui genus ipsum orandi noscerent, crebro fori usu celebre et ad implendas
populi aures latum et sonans. clamor uocesque uulgi ex more 3

adulandi nimiae et falsae. quasi dictatorem Caesarem aut imperatorem Augustum prosequerentur, ita studiis uotisque certabant, nec metu aut amore, sed ex libidine seruitii, ut in familiis, priuata cuique stimulatio, et uile iam decus publicum. profectus Otho quietem urbis curasque imperii Saluio Titiano fratri permisit.

COMMENTARY

1 *Initium mihi operis*

The first chapter of the *Histories* is a masterpiece of indirection. It communicates the work's topic (Rome under the principate) and chronological scope (Galba to Domitian), the author's credentials and aspirations, and his promises of concern for posterity and fidelity to truth, but his points will be apparent only to readers who infer them from what T. says about other authors, on other subjects, and in generalizations (see nn.). His affiliation to the annalistic tradition is directly declared (1.1 n. *consules*), but even here the message is oblique: the annalistic framework, with its presumption of the significance of the republican yearly cycle, is in constant tension with the imperial and dynastic realities of the period. From the outset, then, it is clear that T.'s aim is not to illuminate (contrast Sal. *Jug.* 5.3 *quo ad cognoscendum omnia illustria magis ... sint*, Liv. *praef.* 10 *documenta in illustri posita monumento*) but rather to uncover.

Missing from this chapter are several of the standard prefatory topoi: the magnitude of the task (e.g. Liv. *praef.* 4 *res ... immensi operis*), the historian's desire for personal glory (e.g. Sal. *Cat.* 1.3 *memoria nostri*, 3.5 *honoris cupido*, Liv. *praef.* 3 *mea fama*, Plin. *Ep.* 5.8.1 *aliorum ... famam cum sua extendere*), and his fears about the work's reception (e.g. Liv. *praef.* 4 *legentium plerisque ... minus praebitura uoluptatis sint*, Jos. *BJ* 1.12 'a critic too severe for pity', T. *Agr.* 1.4 *narraturo mihi ... uenia opus fuit*, etc.); reticence is a mark of T.'s historiographical style.

As is brevity of his Latin style. In this first chapter we get a glimpse of its power, its potential for breadth of implication (see 1.1 nn. *magna ... cessere*, *ut alienae*). In a felicitous phrase originally applied to Virgil but equally true of our author, T. achieves a 'style precisely attuning syntactic ambiguity and semantic richness' (Glenn Most, in Spence (2001) 189).

Recent discussions include Leeman (1973), Woodman (1988), Christes (1995), Marincola (1999); for prefatory topoi see Herkommer (1968).

1.1 Seruius Galba iterum: his first consulship was in 33 under Tiberius (*A.* 6.15.1; sources at *PIR* s 723). For his background, career, and character see the obituary at 49.2–4. In 69 Galba was seventy-three (5.2n. *senium atque auaritiam*). **T. Vinius,** an undistinguished senator and commander of the single legion in Tarraconensis, was catapulted into power in 68 when the province's governor, Galba, was proclaimed emperor. For his *cursus* see Sumner (1976) and 6.1n., for his obituary 48.2–4. **consules:** cf. Sal. *Hist.* fr. 1.1 *res populi Romani M. Lepido Q. Catulo consulibus ac deinde... composui.* Like Sallust T. begins his *Histories* with a consular date, and like Livy he marks the beginning of each year with the consuls' names (42 of T.'s year-beginnings are extant; 31 have an abl. abs. formula (e.g. *A.* 6.15.1 *Ser. Galba L. Sulla consulibus*), the rest variations; see W–M *ad A.* 3.2.3. The only other year-beginning in *H.* is 4.38.1 *interea Vespasianus iterum ac Titus consulatum absentes inierunt* (A.D. 70). On the year 69 cf. also *D.* 17.3 *illum Galbae et Othonis et Vitellii longum et unum annum.* On 1 January as a starting date (in preference to Nero's suicide or the beginning of Galba's principate) see Syme (1958) 145 ('vital and inevitable') and, for criticisms, Chilver *ad loc.* **erunt** agrees with the predicate nouns (*A&G* §316b). **nam... inest:** the sequence of thought has caused difficulty. It begins simply enough: T. starts his history with the year 69, for (*nam*) many have told the story of Rome's previous 820 years (roughly 753 B.C.–A.D. 69). What follows is essentially parenthetic (*dum... inest*): a discussion of the work, both good and bad, of the historians of the earlier period (*dum... obnoxios*) and advice on how a reader can compensate for their various failings (*sed... inest*). At 1.3 T. returns to his own work, reviewing possible sources of one failing, bias, and declaring his intention of avoiding it (*mihi... dicendus est*). The logic of the sentence has seemed to some to require a starting date of 31 B.C. (when historical talent dried up) rather than A.D. 69; for full discussion and bibliography see Chilver, Hellegouarc'h, and Marincola (1999). Although T. does not mention the fact here, his chosen period already had its historians (2.101.1). **post conditam urbem** depends on *annos*; cf. 11.2n. *Africa... contenta.* **octingentos et uiginti... annos:** 821 years separate Rome's foundation (on Varro's date, 753 B.C.) and A.D. 69. T. uses the same round figure for the period of Rome's existence at 4.58.6. For another cf. 4.74.3 *octingentorum annorum fortuna*, as well as *D.* 17.3 *centum et uiginti* (for 117). **rettulerunt** 'related' *OLD* 18. **res populi Romani** 'the history of the Republic' (Chilver), so defined by the antithesis with post-Actium history. For the gen. cf. *Tiberii Gaique et Claudii ac Neronis res* (*A.* 1.1.2), the subject of the *Annals*. On histories of the Republic see also *A.* 1.1.2 *ueteris populi Romani prospera uel aduersa claris scriptoribus memorata sunt.* Both Sallust (fr. 1.1, quoted above) and Livy (*praef.* 1 *si a primordio urbis res populi Romani perscripserim*) define their subjects with this phrase. **pari eloquentia ac libertate:** for the association of eloquence and Republican *libertas* see Maternus' speech at *D.* 36–8, which ends with this assessment of the principate: *eloquentiam... depacauerat.* **postquam bellatum:** sc. *est*, impersonal pass. (2.3n. *saeuitum*). The battle of Actium was fought on 2 September 31 B.C. **ad unum:** on the *princeps*' unique responsibility cf. 89.2 *in unius sollicitudinem*, *D.* 36.2 *moderatore uno*, 41.4 *sapientissimus et unus*, *A.* 1.9.4 *non aliud discordantis patriae remedium fuisse quam ut ab uno regeretur.* **potentiam... conferri pacis interfuit:** *interfuit* 'it was expedient' (*OLD* 9b) is a non-committal author's minimum of praise. For the abstract noun with *interest* cf. Plin. *Nat.* 9.56 *aiunt et si teratur gurges, interesse capturae* (sc. *piscium*), Plin. *Ep.* 9.13.25 *interest... exempli, ut uera uiderentur.* For the acc. + inf. subject cf. 3.86.2 *rei publicae... intererat Vitellium uinci.* **magna illa ingenia cessere:** 'These *magna ingenia* are... not named, but they hardly needed to be; they were the great historians of the Republican era, beginning with Cato, and going through to Sallust and Livy' (Marincola (1999) 402). When writing the *Annals* T. found the historiographical landscape of the Augustan period less bleak: *A.* 1.1.2 *temporibusque Augusti dicendis non defuere decora ingenia, donec gliscente adulatione deterrerentur* (cf. on Livy *A.* 4.34.2 *eloquentiae ac fidei praeclarus in primis*). And he is not uncomplimentary about individual historians writing under the Julio-Claudians: on Cluvius Rufus see 8.1 nn., on Fabius Rusticus (and Livy) *Agr.* 10.3 *eloquentissimi*, on Servilius Nonianus *A.* 14.19 *tradendis rebus Romanis celebris.* However, 'his concern is not with these immediate predecessors at all' (Marincola (1999) 401), rather, like that of Sallust (who uses *magna ingenia* of the giants of Greek historiography at *Cat.* 8.3), with the best ones, as the echoes of their work throughout this preface show. **cessere** = *cesserunt.* T. follows Sallust (following Cato) in using both *-erunt* and *-ere* in prose. Cicero, Caesar, Nepos, and Quintilian, *inter alios*, avoided *-ere* (K–H §163.2). The absolute use of *cedere* is poetic; here both 'withdraw' (*OLD* 3) and 'recede' (*OLD* 4) are possible translations. **ueritas... infracta:** sc. *est*; cf. Seneca describing the starting point of his father's history, *HRR* 2.98 *unde primum ueritas retro abiit*, and Dio 53.19 on the unreliability of information available to historians of the empire. On *infringo* cf. Don. *ad* Ter. *Eun.* 336 *'infractos'... ualde fractos significat*; T. uses it again with abstract nouns at 2.99.2 *uirtus*, 3.42.2 *fides*, *A.* 4.19.2 *ius*, 15.21.4 *auaritia.* **pluribus** = *compluribus* 'several', introducing *primum... mox.* **ut alienae:** either *quia aliena erat* or *ut si aliena esset*; the brevity allows both. The former, which implies that the *res publica* was now the *res priuata* (or *propria*) of the *princeps* (cf. 29.1 *alieni . . . imperii*, 89.2 *res Caesarum*, *A.* 1.1.2 *cuncta* (sc. *Augustus*) . . . *sub imperium accepit*; *A.* 1.1.2 (quoted on *res populi Romani* above); Plin. *Pan.* 66.4 *ubi erat autem omnino res publica?*), leaves little hope for historiography; the latter suggests that a properly informed historian, i.e. one who has had a public career, can deliver *ueritas*, within limits (see e.g. 7.2n. *fuere . . . abstinuisse*). Over time T. became increasingly aware of the limits: *A.* 3.19.2 *adeo maxima quaeque ambigua sunt* with W–M *ad loc.* **libidine assentandi:** crowd behaviour (12.2 *libidine talia loquendi*, 4.49.3 *indiligentia ueri et adulandi libidine*). **odio aduersus dominantes:** on the delayed expression of hatred for emperors cf. *A.* 1.1.2 *res . . . postquam occiderant recentibus odiis compositae sunt.* **neutris:** sc. *erat*, looking forward to the *infensi* and *obnoxii*. **cura posteritatis:** claimed, implicitly, for T. himself; cf. *A.* 4.11.3 for *cura nostra* of the *Annals*. **inter infensos uel obnoxios** 'among the hostile and the subservient', the former motivated by *odium*, the latter by *libido assentandi*. For *inter* cf. 34.2 *inter gaudentes et incuriosos*, *Agr.* 32.3 *inter male parentes et iniuste imperantes*.

1.2 ambitionem . . . obtrectatio et liuor: this pair supplements *libidine assentandi . . . odio* – love of flattery yields profit, hatred 'envious disparagement' (Alford) – and is further developed in the next sentence with *seruitus* added to the first, *species libertatis* to the second. **auerseris . . . accipiuntur:** for the *uariatio* see Sörbom (1935) 108–10. **auerseris:** for the address to the reader see 10.2n. *palam . . . audiebant.* The potential subj. refers to possible future encounters with a flattering narrative (*A&G* §446). **pronis auribus:** cf. Stat. *Silu.* 5.2.58–9 *bibe talia pronis | auribus*; more vivid than the common *aequis auribus* (66.1) and its equivalents *promptis auribus*, *propitiis auribus*, *secundis auribus*, etc. (*TLL* s.v. 1509.2–1510.5). **quippe** typically introduces an explanatory clause or sentence (here: why we reject laudatory histories and welcome hostile ones; cf. 12.3 *quippe . . . intendebat*) but with *falsa* T. incorporates a further point: we welcome hostile histories because we think they show *libertas*, *but we are wrong* (they are just the product of human *malignitas*). The formal parallelism is belied by the variation in content. On *malignitas* as an explanation for historical bias see Luce (1989) 24–5.

1.3 nec beneficio nec iniuria cogniti: authorial bias was generally credited to material causes of the kind T. mentions here (cf. Sen. *Apoc.* 1.1 *nihil nec offensae nec gratiae dabitur*) rather than to abstract ones (e.g. differences of outlook on philosophical, political, or moral grounds, or emotions resulting from personal experience); see Luce (1989). **dignitatem**

nostram 'my career'. Membership in the governing elite – for T.'s *cursus* see below – is a traditional prerequisite for writing history at Rome, with Livy the principal exception. T.'s work will not suffer from *inscitia rei publicae*, at least insofar as knowledge is available outside the imperial inner circle (1.1 n. *ut alienae*). **inchoatam . . . auctam . . . prouectam:** sc. *esse*. The passives emphasize T.'s receipt (rather than pursuit) of benefits from the Flavians. Dates for the various steps in T.'s career, particularly the early ones (*latus clauus*, military tribunate, vigintivirate, quaestorship, tribunate or aedileship) are uncertain. His praetorship belongs to Domitian's reign, A.D. 88, by which date he also held a priesthood in the *XVviri* (*A.* 11.11.1). For discussion see Chilver *ad loc.* and Syme (1958) 59–74. **non abnuerim:** a more modest assertion (*A&G* §447.1) than Sallust's declarations in *Cat.* (4.2 *mihi a spe metu partibus rei publicae animus liber erat*) and *Hist.* (fr. 1.6 *neque me diuorsa pars in ciuilibus armis mouit a uero*). **fidem professis . . . dicendus est:** *professis* (= *eis qui profitentur*) is a compact dat. of agent. Implicit in this generalization is the historian's own promise (*OLD* s.v. *profiteor* 3) of fidelity to the truth. His comment about Livy's *fides* is quoted above (1.1 n. *magna . . . cessere*); cf. also Josephus' more explicit 'having set truth as my target' (*AJ* 20.157 σκοπὸν προθέμενοι τὴν ἀλήθειαν). T.'s phrase is imitated by Ammianus, who claims an *opus ueritatem professum* (27.4.2 and again at 31.16.9 in his final sentence). **neque amore quisquam et sine odio dicendus est:** T. abruptly abandons the rhetorical polish (parallel structures, tricolon crescendo) of the preceding sentences; here the *amor*~*odium* antithesis is complicated by *uariatio* in the negative (*neque . . . quisquam*~*et sine*) and abl. expressions (*amore . . . sine odio*). *A.* 1.1.3 *sine ira et studio* is more simply expressed.

1.4 principatum diui Neruae et imperium Traiani: *imperium* here may reflect Trajan's military accomplishments (Irvine *ad loc.*) but it is paired with *principatus* rather casually at 56.3; see Chilver *ad loc.* for possible contemporary resonances. **uberiorem:** 2.1 n. *opimum casibus.* **securiorem . . . materiam:** flattering to a *ciuilis princeps*, no doubt, but, as T. would show in his account of the trial of Cremutius Cordus, who wrote on the civil wars and principate of Augustus under Tiberius, the risk to the historian came from the period in which he was writing, not from his subject matter (*A.* 4.34–5). **seposui:** for T.'s other announcements of future topics see *Agr.* 3.3 (presumably Domitian to Trajan) and *A.* 3.24.3 (Augustus' principate); none came to fruition. **rara temporum felicitate:** similarly of the post-Domitian years at *Agr.* 3.1 *felicitatem* *temporum*. Nerva himself mentions *felicitas temporum* in an edict quoted by Pliny (*Ep.* 10.58.7). On the effect here cf. Woodman (1988) 167 'the mere fact of referring to the happy present means that T. denies in advance that any permanent damage was done to the Roman constitution by the disasters which he is about to catalogue'. On the abl. abs. see Intro. §14. **ubi...licet:** for the flattering sentiment cf. Plin. *Pan.* 66.4 *iubes, quae sentimus, promere in medium: proferemus.* For chiasmus in a terminal sentence see, in App. 2, 2.3, 45.2, 77.3; also 28 *auderent pauci, plures uellent.*

2–3 *Opus aggredior*

After the general introduction of ch. 1, chh. 2–3 introduce the work's particular themes: wars (internal, external, *permixta*), natural disasters, the disintegration of the social fabric, human character (base and admirable), and divine retribution. The thematic focus of this 'table of contents' distinguishes it from other ancient content lists, which usually mirror the organization of the books they introduce. The list in the *Bellum Judaicum* of Josephus, for example, offers a précis of the narrative, mentioning events in the order in which they occur in the work's seven books (*BJ* 1.19–29), and Pliny's *Natural History* has a long table of contents indicating *quid singulis contineretur libris* (*praef.* 33). Similar to these, but less detailed, is the announcement of topics for the seventeen books of Appian's *Roman History* (*praef.* 14–15). T.'s thematic list is less informative but more colourful than such lists and, as Woodman suggests, entices the reader ((1988) 167 'indeed the whole of the second section of T.'s preface... heralds a "disaster narrative" of the most vivid and dramatic type'; Intro. §5). As befits a table of contents, the syntax is simple. Only in the last sentence does T. return to a fuller style.

The prevailing colours are dark. The tone set by the opening sentence (*atrox... discors... saeuum*) is maintained by references to violence (*interempti, perdomita, afflicta, saeuitum, spolia, oppressi, tormenta*), disorder and disease (*turbatum, nutantes, pollutae, infecti, scelera, agerent uerterent, corrupti, casus*), and destruction (*cladibus* (3x), *haustae, obrutae, uastata, consumptis, exitium, exitus*), and fittingly capped by the final word, *ultionem*. To convey the disastrousness of the period T. exaggerates negative and omits positive features reported in other sources. The exaggerated negatives are mentioned in the notes, the omissions, briefly, here.

Chief among the omitted positives is stability. With T.'s characterization of the period as *opimum casibus* contrast Suet. *Ves.* 1.1 *incertum diu et quasi uagum imperium suscepit firmauitque tandem gens Flauia*, 8.1 *per totum imperii tempus nihil habuit antiquius quam prope afflictam nutantemque rem p. stabilire primo, deinde et ornare.* (Suetonius' *ornare* is also omitted by T.: there is nothing here on the Flavian building programme, for which see *CAH*[2] XI 967–71.) Stability was secured, at least in part, by financial and administrative reforms (*Ves.* 8.4, 9.2, 10.1, 16.3, *Dom.* 8), by military discipline and an increase in military pay (*Ves.* 8.3, *Dom.* 7.3, Dio 67.3.5), and by the proper functioning of the judicial system (e.g. Plin. *Ep.* 7.33, cf. also Suet. *Dom.* 8.1). Flavian generosity to the populace in the form of games was also a factor (Suet. *Ves.* 19.1, *Tit.* 7.3–8.2, *Dom.* 4, Dio 66.15.2, 66.25, 67.8.1–9.6, cf. also *Ves.* 17), and was celebrated by contemporary poets (e.g. Martial's *Liber spectaculorum* on the opening of the Colosseum); for Augustus' precedent see *RG* 22–3. Moral leadership, something T. himself credits Vespasian with at *A.* 3.55.4, is also absent from the positives here. For other omissions see 2.1 n. *aduersae in Occidente*, 3.2n. *prodigia . . . praesagia.*

T.'s overview of the period here is as dark as that given by Pliny in the *Panegyricus* (see nn. and Bruère), but in Pliny Flavian gloom serves as foil to the bright new day of Trajan's reign. The themes announced here continue to engage T.'s attention in the *Annals*, which he characterizes as a narrative of *saeua iussa, continuas accusationes, fallaces amicitias, perniciem innocentium* (*A.* 4.33.3).

2.1 opus . . . opimum . . . atrox . . . discors . . . saeuum: the adjectives increasingly suit the period better than they do *opus*. **opimum casibus:** *opimum* is an emendation for M's *opibus* (itself corrected to *plenum* by a later hand) found already in M's descendants (see Wellesley's app. crit.). Though much beleaguered (Wellesley lists eleven challengers, Chilver obelizes, Syme (1987) 111 pronounces it 'alien to the usage of Tacitus and incongruous if yoked to *casibus*'), it is right; so Baldwin (1981) and Hellegouarc'h *ad loc.* *opimus* ('abounding in' 'abundant' *OLD* 6) is commonly applied to fields and their produce (*TLL* s.v. 710.27–52). The metaphor here is recalled at 3.1 *sterile saeculum*, which opens the second panel of the table of contents; for a similar combination of metaphor and antithesis cf. Cic. *Att.* 2.7.3 *illa opima* (sc. *legatio*) . . . *epuloni Vatinio reseruatur, haec ieiuna . . . datur ei cuius*, etc.). T. does not use *opimus* elsewhere, but cf. 1.4 *uberiorem . . . materiam.* For *opus* with a similar adjective (indeed with one of the challengers to *opimum*) cf. Hor. *Carm.* 2.1.6 *periculosae plenum opus aleae*, and for a similarly introductory phrase cf. Luc. 1.68 *immensum ... aperitur opus.* **casibus** 'occurrences'; cf. 4.1 *casus euentusque*, 29.2 *tristiorem casum. casus* often acquires a more precise meaning from its context: 'disasters' at 86.2 *eius modi casuum* (it is used of other natural disasters at *A.* 2.47.1 earthquake, 4.63.1 amphitheatre collapse, 16.13.3 fire), 'chance event' at *A.* 1.70.3 *nihil ... consilia a casu differre*, 'experiences' at *Agr.* 25.1 *sua quisque facta, suos casus*, 'opportunity' at *A.* 1.13.2 *Arruntium ... si casus daretur, ausurum.* Relevant to its meaning here is its recurrence at the end of the table of contents (3.2 *praeter multiplices rerum humanarum casus*), where *casus* sums up everything in chh. 2–3, *res* both *prosperae* and *aduersae.* 'Disasters' might better suit the darkness of the list that follows here (*atrox ... discors ... saeuum*) and make a nice paradox with *opimum* (contrast e.g. Lucr. 1.728 *insula rebus opima bonis* and Liv. 3.7.3 *agrum opimum copiis*), but it seems a shame to anticipate the concluding paradox *pace saeuum.* **pace saeuum:** 50.2n. *saeuae pacis.* **quattuor principes ferro interempti:** sc. *sunt.* Three *principes* were killed in 69 (Galba on 15 January, Otho on 16 April, Vitellius on 20 December), one in 96 (Domitian on 18 September). **trina bella ciuilia:** sc. *erant*; two in 69 (Otho versus Vitellius, Vitellius versus Vespasian), a third under Domitian, who faced a (modest) challenge in 89 from the governor of Upper Germany, L. Antonius Saturninus (Suet. *Dom.* 6.2 *bellum ciuile motum a L. Antonio*; 10.5 *ciuilis belli*); according to B. W. Jones (1992) 144–9 'the insurrection was brief and miscarried'. Forms of *trini, -ae, -a*, used here for *tria* to avoid parallelism with *quattuor*, originally modified plurals such as *annales, ludi, catenae, litterae, castra*, and *comitia* (*A&G* §137b, K–S §121.5). Its usage expanded to other contexts (both cardinal, as here, and distributive, as at 3.82.2 *trinis ... praesidiis*) largely owing to the experiments of poets. **plura externa:** under the Flavians, war (coupled with diplomacy and followed by consolidation) extended the empire on many fronts, the principal being N. Africa, Britain, the Rhine, the Danube, and the border with Parthia. For Vespasian's wars see Levick (1999) 156–69, for Domitian's see B. W. Jones (1992) 126–59. **plerumque permixta:** notably the Batavian uprising, to which T. devotes a substantial narrative in Books 4 and 5 (cf. 2.69.1 *interno simul externoque bello*). The *bellum ciuile* of Saturninus (see above on *trina ... ciuilia*) was also labelled *Germanicum* (*ILS* 1006, 2127, 2710), i.e. foreign. See also 79.1n. *ciuile bellum ... externa.* **prosperae in Oriente:** foremost the Flavian success in Judaea, to the crowning achievement of which, the capture of Jerusalem, T. must have devoted a large part of Book 5: 5.2.1 *famosae urbis supremum diem tradituri sumus.* For other Flavian activity in the East see Levick (1999) 163–9, B. W. Jones (1992) 155–9. **aduersae in Occidente res:** sc. *erant.* The reverses (*turbatum Illyricum*, etc.) are listed in roughly chronological order. T. omits both the concomitant successes (see nn. below) and the areas that remained calm and prospered (e.g. Spain and Africa, and the Rhine region after the military zone was reorganized into regular provinces; see *CAH*² XI 444–61, 514–46, 495–513 respectively). **turbatum Illyricum:** Illyricum denotes (roughly) the Danubian provinces Dalmatia, Pannonia, and Moesia, an area that under the Flavians superseded Germany as a focus for military activity (*CAH*² XI 577–85). Already in 68 it was garrisoned by seven legions (9.2n. *excitae ... legiones*). The reference here may be to the Danubian legions' declaration for Vespasian in the spring of 69 (2.85–6, ending *momento ... temporis flagrabat ingens bellum, Illyricis exercitibus palam desciscentibus*; contrast 9.3 *quies et Illyrico*, describing the local situation in January 69) and the disturbances consequent upon it (3.46.1, an incursion from Dacia). Subsequent disturbances seem to be covered by *coortae in nos Sarmatarum ac Sueborum gentes* below. **Galliae nutantes,** here and at 4.49.1, refers to the precarious situation in Gaul just before important tribes abandoned Rome for Civilis and proclaimed an *imperium Galliarum* complete with a Gallic Caesar (4.67.1; see further 8.1 n. *proximae ... ciuitates*, 53.3n. *Treueri ac Lingones*). On *nutantes* see 31.3n. T.'s choice of focus is instructive: what mattered was not that a Batavian rebelled (cf. 5.25.1 *quotam partem generis humani Batauos esse?*) but that the rich and generally reliable provinces of Gaul joined him. Gallic tribes are first solicited by Civilis at 4.28.1; the balance begins to tip in his favour with the news of the burning of the Capitol (4.54). His defeat, an operation requiring eight legions, was an early Flavian success; T.'s narrative occupies thirty-nine chapters (4.55–79, 85–6, 5.14–26) and is not quite complete when our text gives out; for discussion see Levick (1999) 107–19. **perdomita Britannia et statim missa:** T. uses *perdomo* again at *Agr.* 10.1 *tum primum perdomita est*, but the conquest of Britain was never completed. *statim missa* 'immediately abandoned' (*OLD* 4) also overstates the speed and extent of the Roman pull-back that followed rapid expansion under Agricola. What was abandoned was the goal of complete subjugation of the island (cf. e.g. *Agr.* 27.1 *penetrandam Caledoniam inueniendumque tandem Britanniae terminum*): the island's garrison was reduced and a fortress in the far north, Inchtuthil, demolished within two or three years of Agricola's departure (*statim*); the process continued throughout T.'s lifetime and after. The initial phase of withdrawal T. ascribed to Domitian's jealousy and paranoia (*Agr.* 39, 41). See further Chilver *ad loc.*, B. W. Jones (1992) 131–5, *CAH*² xi 559–66. **coortae . . . Sarmatarum ac Sueborum gentes:** sc. *sunt*. Early in 69 a Sarmatian tribe, the Iazyges, made a plundering raid into Moesia but was repelled (79.1–5). Later that year Flavian leaders took precautions against incursions by the Sarmatae and the Suebi (3.5.1), but 70 saw trouble both rumoured (4.54.1) and real (Jos. *BJ* 7.89–96 on a raid resulting in the death of the governor of Moesia and prompting permanent reinforcement of the provincial garrison; Levick (1999) 114–15). Trouble materialized again under Domitian, who fought a campaign labelled *Suebicum et Sarmaticum* (*CIL* iii suppl. 1 6818 = *ILS* 1017; *CIL* x 135 = *ILS* 2719; Suet. *Dom.* 6.1; cf. Dio 67.5.2) and other less well-attested campaigns in this area (cf. *Agr.* 41.2 *tot exercitibus in Moesia Daciaque et Germania et Pannonia . . . amissi* with Ogilvie and Richmond (1967) *ad loc.* and B. W. Jones (1992) 150–5). A victory was marked in 93 by the dedication of a laurel wreath in the Capitoline temple (Suet. *Dom.* 6.1) and pronounced 'worthy of a triumph' by both Statius (*Silu.* 3.3.170–1) and Martial (8.15.5–6), but the area was still the focus of military activity into the reigns of Nerva and Trajan (*CAH*² xi 577–85). **Sarmatarum:** at *G.* 1.1 the territory of the Sarmatae is distinguished from that of the Germani, at 46.1–2 their culture is contrasted (unfavourably) with that of the Germani: they live *in plaustro equoque*, are filthy, and have inert leaders (see Rives (1999) 101 for the territory, 322–4 on the textually difficult 46.1). Statius, too, refers to their nomadic life (3.3.170–1 *uagos Sauromatas*), and Josephus calls them Scythians (*BJ* 7.89). **Sueborum:** in T.'s account at *G.* 38.1 the Suebi are 'a supra-tribal grouping' comprising 'all the tribes whom the Romans regarded as living beyond the Danube, rather than beyond the Rhine' (Rives (1999) *ad loc.*). **nobilitatus cladibus mutuis Dacus:** in the extant books the advantage is decidedly with the Romans (e.g. 3.46.3 *adfuit, ut saepe alias, fortuna populi Romani*, on Mucianus' defeat of a Dacian invasion), but Suet. *Dom.* 6.1 records two expeditions *in Dacos* resulting in Roman losses (cf. also *Agr.* 41.2 quoted above). Victories leading to some seven imperatorial salutations, two triumphs (86, 89) and an *ecus maximus* in the Forum (Stat. *Silu.* 1.1) redressed the balance (B. W. Jones (1992) 138–9, 141–3; Murison (1999) on Dio 67.6–10). Dacian campaigns are closely connected with those against the Suebi and Sarmatae, the western neighbours of Dacia (roughly modern Romania): 'preparations for war against the first two inevitably involved defensive measures against the third' (B. W. Jones (1992) 135). **nobilitatus:** cf. Liv. 22.43.9 *ad nobilitandas clade Romana Cannas*, 42.49.7 *Romano . . . nobilitatus bello* (sc. *Philippo*), Vell. 2.8.3 *Cimbri et Teutoni . . . multis mox nostris suisque cladibus nobiles*, 2.105.1 *gentes utinam minus mox nostra clade nobiles*, Tac. *D.* 37.8 *nobilitata discriminibus* (sc. *eloquentia*). Paradox seems to adhere to *nobilito* (cf. Ter. *Eun.* 1021 *qui stultum adulescentulum nobilitas flagitiis*); here it describes an enemy with whom Rome was engaged as T. was writing (Trajan conducted numerous campaigns in Dacia between 100 and the capture of its capital in 106: Dio 68.6–14). **falsi Neronis ludibrio:** both Dio (66.19.3b on an imposture in Titus' reign; see Murison (1999) *ad loc.*) and Suetonius (*Ner.* 57.2 on one in 88; see Bradley (1978b) *ad loc.*) mention false Neros with Parthian support; at 2.8–9 T. mentions one who appeared in 69 (without Parthians) and gives a forward reference to other discussions, presumably his narratives of those that appeared under Titus and Domitian. See Tuplin (1989). For *ludibrium* 'imposture' (*OLD* 4) cf. the metaphorical extensions of the term at 4.15.2 *Gaianarum expeditionum ludibrium*, also *per ludibrium* at *A.* 1.10.5 *consulti per ludibrium pontifices* (on Octavian's marriage to a pregnant Livia). T. takes the impact of the first imposter, at least, as a sign of the times: 2.8.2 *multi ad celebritatem nominis erecti rerum nouarum cupidine et odio praesentium.*

2.2 iam uero connects and emphasizes the second (or later) item in a list (*OLD* 8a); it is frequent in Cicero (see *TLL* s.v. *iam* 123.6–49) and appears 5 times in *D.*, twice in *Agr.*, once in *G.*, only here in *H.*, never in the *Annals.* **nouis cladibus:** exemplified by the eruption of Vesuvius in 79. Pliny's famous letters (6.16, 6.20) on the eruption were solicited by T. as raw material for *H.* The surviving books include no other natural disasters, but the *Annals* have many: earthquakes (2.47.1, 15.22.2), storms (2.23–4, esp. 24.1 *illa clades nouitate et magnitudine excessit*, 15.46.2, 16.13.1), plague (16.13.1), fires (4.64, 13.57.3, 15.38–45, 16.13.3), cf. also the *malum improuisum*, an amphitheatre collapse, at *A.* 4.62–3. On novelty as a historiographical topos see Woodman (1988) 191 n. 17. **repetitis:** exemplified by the burning of the Capitoline temple (see below). **afflicta:** sc. *est.* **haustae aut obrutae**: sc. *sunt*, 'were swallowed up or buried' *OLD* 7b and 3 respectively; cf. Sen. *Nat.* 6.1.7 (of an earthquake) *gentes totas regionesque . . . modo ruinis operit, modo in altam uoraginem condit.* **urbes:** the destruction of human life and habitat in this eruption was much commented upon: e.g. Stat. *Silu.* 4.4.81–3 *credetne uirum uentura propago, | cum segetes iterum, cum iam haec deserta uirebunt, | infra urbes populosque premi?* Plin. *Ep.* 6.16.2 *ut populi ut urbes memorabile casu*, Dio 66.23.3 'it buried two entire cities, Herculaneum and Pompeii'. Therefore the inclination of some editors to delete *urbes* and take *hausta aut obruta* (thus emended) with *ora* (see Heraeus' and Wellesley's app. crit.) is misguided. **fecundissima . . . ora:** nom. or abl.? A local abl. is more accurate historically: Pompeii and Herculaneum suffered the permanent destruction implied in *haustae aut obrutae*, but the Campanian shore as a whole, both its other cities (Misenum, Naples, Puteoli, even Stabiae (cf. Stat. *Silu.* 3.5.104 *Stabias . . . renatas*) and its countryside, recovered: Stat. *Silu.* 3.5.74 *stant populisque uigent.* Some editors put a comma after *urbes*, making *ora* nominative and gaining emotional impact from the asyndeton (see Alford). For the phrase cf. 3.60.2 *pulcherrimam Campaniae oram.* **urbs incendiis uastata:** sc. *est.* Fire destroyed the Capitoline temple in 69 (see below), and in 80 a fire that burned *per triduum totidemque noctes* (Suet. *Tit.* 8.3) swept through 'a wedge-shaped area extending in a generally North-West direction from the Capitol' destroying, among other buildings, the temple of Isis and Serapis, the Saepta, the temple of Neptune, Agrippa's baths and Pantheon, the Diribitorium, the theatre of Balbus, the stage building of Pompey's theatre, the *porticus Octaviae* together with their books, and the Capitoline temple (again); the principal source is Dio 66.24.1–3, on which see Murison (1999), from whom the quotation is taken. **Capitolio ciuium manibus incenso:** described at 3.71 and lamented at 3.72: *id facinus post conditam urbem luctuosissimum foedissimum rei publicae populi Romani accidit*, etc. Fire destroyed an earlier Capitoline temple in 83 B.C. (3.72.1). **pollutae caerimoniae:** sc. *sunt*, most notably by sexual activity among the Vestal Virgins, four of whom were executed as *incestae* under Domitian (Suet. *Dom.* 8.4, Plin. *Ep.* 4.11.6–9, Dio 67.3.3, cf. Stat. *Silu.* 1.1.32–6, Philostr. *VA* 7.6; see B. W. Jones (1992) 101–2). There were two trials. At the first, in 83, three of the six priestesses were condemned; a fourth, acquitted on that occasion, was condemned and executed *more ueteri* (by burial alive: Plut. *Num.* 10.4–7, D.H. 2.67.3–4, 9.40.3) in 89 or 90 (for the dates see Sherwin-White (1966) *ad loc.*). In Suetonius the executions come in a section of praise (*Dom.* 8.3 *suscepta correctione morum . . .*) and are followed (8.5) by reference to an action undertaken *ne qua religio deum impune contaminaretur*; in Dio they illustrate Domitian's cruelty ('he did not spare even the Vestal Virgins . . . '). T. focuses on the religious observances, not the *princeps*. *caerimoniae*, though few in the surviving portions of *H.* (4.53 on the restoration of the Capitoline temple is the longest notice), are a regular topic in the *Annals*: 3.58 on the *flamen Dialis*, 3.60–3 on asylum, 4.16 on the *flamen Dialis* again, 4.55–6 on imperial cult, 11.11 on *ludi saeculares* (where T. says that he gave a more detailed account in the Domitianic books of *H.*), 12.23–4 on the *pomerium*, etc. *pollutae caerimoniae* (for the expression cf. *A.* 14.22.4 on Nero bathing in the aqua Marcia *uidebatur ... potus sacros et caerimoniam loci corpore loto polluisse*, and Cic. *S. Rosc.* 113 *qui ... perfidia legationis ipsius caerimoniam polluerit*) were also a theme for declamations (e.g. Sen. *Contr.* 1.2 and 1.4; see Woodman (1988) 166–7). **magna adulteria:** sc. *erant*, including Domitian's with his niece Julia (Plin. *Ep.* 4.11.6 *ipse fratris filiam incesto ... polluisset*; cf. *Pan.* 52.3, Suet. *Dom.* 22). Dio, too, generalizes: 67.12.1 'Many persons of wealth, both men and women, were punished for adultery.' Politically significant adultery is a subject in the *Annals* (e.g. Julia~Sempronius Gracchus, Sejanus~Livilla, Messalina). For *magnus* indicating the involvement of eminent folk cf. 2.53.1 *magnis inimicitiis*. **plenum exiliis mare:** Helvidius Priscus (Suet. *Ves.* 15) was exiled under Vespasian; known exiles from Domitian's principate are Acilius Glabrio (Suet. *Dom.* 10.2, cf. Dio. 67.14.3), Mettius Pompusianus (to Corsica, Dio 67.12.2–3, cf. Suet. *Dom.* 10.3), Epaphroditus (Nero's killer, 67.14.4), Salvidienus Orfitus and Apollonius of Tyana (to unspecified islands: Philostr. *VA* 7.8, cf. Suet. *Dom.* 10.2), Mettius Modestus (Plin. *Ep.* 1.5.5), Julius Bassus (Plin. *Ep.* 4.9.1), Baebius Massa (Plin. *Ep.* 7.33.4), the father of Claudius Etruscus and his superior (the one to Campania, the other *horrida supra aequora ... procul Itala rura*, Stat. *Silu.* 3.3.160–4), Flavia Domitilla and others accused of 'atheism' (Domitilla to Pandateria, Dio 67.14.2), the sexual partners of the Vestal Virgins tried in 83 (see above and Plin. *Ep.* 4.11.1 on one sent to Sicily), philosophers (Suet. *Dom.* 10.3 *philosophos omnes urbe Italiaque summouit*, cf. Plin. *Ep.* 3.11.2; Epictetus was one: Arr. *Epict.* 1.2.19–24), members of the 'philosophic' opposition (Dio 67.13.3 with Murison (1999) *ad loc.* for names), and 'many noble women' (*Agr.* 45.1 *tot nobilissimarum feminarum exilia et fugas*, with Ogilvie and Richmond (1967) *ad loc.* for names); others can be surmised (see B. W. Jones (1992) 188–91, who concludes, citing Dio 68.1.2, 'ultimately, many of those exiled were recalled by Nerva'; see below for the rest). The sentences of exile reported in the surviving portion of *H.* (Octavius Sagitta and Antistius Sosianus at 4.44.2–3, Antonius Flamma at 4.45.2) are deemed just by T., but also indicative of the Flavian failure to rein in the really dangerous citizens, the *delatores* (4.45.3). In the *Annals* the long catalogue of exiles (see Walker (1968) appendix II for the Tiberian books) is a by-product of T.'s attention to relations between *princeps* and the senatorial *ordo*. For *exiliis* ≈ *exulibus* cf. Luc. 5.784–5 *notescent litora clari nominis exilio*; for other abstract nouns similarly used cf. 17.2 *publica exspectatio*, 64.2 *studia militum*. **infecti caedibus scopuli:** cf. 3.70.2

stratam innocentium caedibus celeberrimam urbis partem, 2.55.1 *quem locum Galba moriens sanguine infecerat*. The language has a strongly poetical tinge: cf. Ov. *Met.* 3.143 *mons erat infectus uariarum caede ferarum*, Stat. *Theb.* 5.353 *infectos caedibus enses* and *TLL* s.v. *inficio* 1412.30–50. Of the exiles listed above the first five, at least, were eventually executed; similarly Cornelius Laco in 69 (46.5). Plin. *Pan.* 34.5 uses similar language to speak (gleefully) of *delatores* suffering under Trajan the punishments, cliffs included, suffered by their victims under Domitian: *si quem* (sc. *delatorem*) *fluctus ac procellae scopulis reseruassent, hic nuda saxa et inhospitale litus incoleret* (he uses *scopulos* again at 35.1, and cf. 35.2 *quantum diuersitas temporum posset tum maxime cognitum est cum isdem quibus antea cautibus innocentissimus quisque, tunc nocentissimus affigeretur, cumque insulas omnes, quas modo senatorum, iam delatorum turba compleret*). Cf. also Juv. 13.246–7 *maris Aegaei rupem scopulosque frequentes | exulibus magnis*.

2.3 saeuitum: sc. *est*; cf. *A.* 4.20.1 *saeuitum ... in bona*. Impersonal passives are useful for rapid sketches (cf. 1.1 *bellatum apud Actium*, 31.2 *praeceptum* and *diffidebatur*, 40.1 *nuntiabatur*, 59.2 *dubitatum*) and summaries, particularly dark ones (cf. 12.3 *peccaretur*, 22.3 *transitur*, 46.2 *flagitatum*, 51.5 *callide uulgatum, temere creditum*). See also 1.2n. *potentiam ... interfuit*, 85.1n. *animaduerti*. **nobilitas, opes, omissi gestique honores pro crimine:** cf. 85.1 for the dangers of distinction under Otho; for Nero's reign see Dio 62.26.1 'Thrasea and Soranus, at the pinnacle of birth and wealth and every virtue ... perished because they were such.' For the security of poverty see 4.42.3 *te securum reliquerat exul pater et diuisa inter creditores bona, nondum honorum capax aetas*. **nobilitas:** in the Flavian period it was not so much *nobilitas* (14.2n. *nobilis utrimque*) as imperial connections that were dangerous. Connection by birth to the imperial house marked out two men eventually executed by Domitian (sons of his cousin Flavius Sabinus: 77.2n.), connection by marriage another (L. Aelius Lamia (*PIR*[2] A 205); cf. Juv. 4.152 on Domitian: *Lamiarum caede madenti*). Connection with Galba endangers Cornelius Dolabella (88.1n.) and Otho warns his nephew Salvius Cocceianus of the danger their connection will pose to him (2.48.2; for the nephew's execution see below on *ob uirtutes certissimum exitium*). T. points out the new attitude at *A.* 13.1.1 (on M. Junius Silanus) *insontem, nobilem et, quod tunc spectaretur, e Caesarum posteris* (cf. 15.35.1 *Torquatus Silanus mori adigitur, quia super Iuniae familiae claritudinem diuum Augustum abauum ferebat*). *Nobiles* of long standing were in fact few in number by this period (Hopkins (1983), esp. 171–6), though some survived (and were deemed threatening) through the Julio-Claudian period (Galba was one: 49.2n.; see also

14.1 nn. *Pisonem Licinianum* and *Rubellium Plautum*). At [Sen.] *Oct.* 495–8 the character Nero gives voice to the problem: *seruare ciues principi et patriae graues, | claro tumentes genere quae dementia est, | cum liceat una uoce suspectos sibi | mori iubere?* The clash between emperor and elite, however defined, is a theme in both of T.'s historical works. **opes:** for the civil war period cf. 4.1.2 *nec deerat egentissimus quisque ... prodere ultro dites dominos.* Less violent but equally deadly were the fiscally motivated convictions alleged against both Vespasian (Suet. *Ves.* 16.2) and Domitian (Suet. *Dom.* 12.1 with 12.2 on delation for failure to make payments to the *fiscus Iudaicus*; cf. Plin. *Pan.* 34.2, 35.3, 42.1, 50.5, Dio 67.4.5, and D. Chry. *Or.* 46.8). Particulars are rare (see Suet. *Dom.* 12.2 for one), indeed Suetonius credits Vespasian with indifference to at least one defendant's wealth (*Ves.* 13), Titus with respect for property (*Tit.* 7.3), and Domitian with restraining such cases early on (*Dom.* 9.3 *fiscales calumnias ... repressit*). But Nerva takes credit for reform in coins of 96 with the legend *fisci Iudaici calumnia sublata* (see *CAH*[2] XI 74), as does Trajan in a rescript (*Dig.* 48.22.1 (Pomponius)). For this theme in the *Annals* cf. 4.20.1 *saeuitum ... in bona,* 11.1.1 and 12.59.1 (both on *horti* as partial motivation for prosecutions), 12.22.2 *materiam sceleri detrahendam,* etc. **omissi gestique:** for *-que* 'or' see *OLD* 7. In the first category Pliny places Helvidius Priscus' son (*Ep.* 9.13.3 *metu temporum nomen ingens paresque uirtutes secessu tegebat*), and Dio 67.13.2 Herennius Senecio, who stopped his *cursus* at the quaestorship though he was active in senatorial trials under Domitian. T. himself reports that Agricola, after his command in Britain, refused the proconsulship of Asia (*Agr.* 42.1–2). Political withdrawal may also underlie the *inertia* alleged of Domitian's victims Flavius Clemens (Suet. *Dom.* 15.1) and Salvidienus Orfitus (Philostr. *VA* 7.33, 8.7). Quint. *Inst.* 11.1.35 has a scathing aside on the withdrawal of the self-styled 'philosophers' from public service, Pliny a comment on the risks they ran even so: *Pan.* 45.2 *bonos autem otio aut situ abstrusos et quasi sepultos non nisi delationibus et periculis in lucem et diem proferebant.* In the *Annals* T. notes the existence of disengagement at the end of the reigns of Tiberius (6.27.3) and Nero (16.27.2; cf. also 15.45.3 where Seneca's request for *secessus* is denied, 16.22.1–2 on Thrasea Paetus, who absented himself from public ceremonies and senate meetings, and *H.* 2.86.3 *Cornelius Fuscus ... quietis cupidine senatorium ordinem exuerat*). For the second category Suetonius gives a list of *complures senatores, in iis aliquot consulares,* who were executed, including one *in ipso Asiae proconsulatu* (*Dom.* 10.2) and another while legate of Britain (*Dom.* 10.3). According to Dio 67.14.4 Domitian also indicted standing praetorian prefects. **pro crimine:**

sc. *erant.* **ob uirtutes certissimum exitium:** the climax of the indictment, emphasized by paradox (virtue causing death) and the clash of abstract and concrete. For the charge cf. *Agr.* 1.4 *saeua et infesta uirtutibus tempora*, 41.1 *causa periculi... infensus uirtutibus princeps*, Plin. *Pan.* 45.1 *et priores quidem principes... uitiis potius ciuium quam uirtutibus laetabantur*, 90.5 *ille optimi cuiusque spoliator et carnifex*; cf. also 4.50.2 on the *delator* Baebius Massa, *optimo cuique exitiosus.* Examples: *fides* characterizes Junius Blaesus, whose *famosa mors* T. relates at length (3.38–9), and kills outright the four centurions whose names T. preserves for posterity (56.1 n. *quattuor... Repentinus*) as well as Sempronius Densus (43.1 n. *insignem... uidit*); the same virtue proves nearly fatal for Marius Celsus (14.1 n., cf. also 59.1 n. *fidei crimine*). *pietas* gets Salvius Cocceianus killed (Suet. *Dom.* 10.3 *quod Othonis imperatoris patrui sui diem natalem celebrauerat*). According to the *Panegyricus*, Trajan, unlike Domitian, provided incentives to virtue: 46.8 *boni prouehuntur*, cf. *Pan.* 44.6–8. **praemia delatorum inuisa:** sc. *erant.* In the *Annals*, which have more on this theme than does the extant portion of *H.*, T. regularly reports the rewards of successful prosecutors (e.g. after the trial of Cn. Piso, *A.* 3.19.1); see further below on *alii... adepti.* He introduces the theme in that work at *A.* 1.74.1–2, a passage that echoes many features mentioned here. **scelera:** *delatores* were responsible for exiles and executions in both the Flavian and Julio-Claudian periods; Rutledge (2001) gives a good overview of the individuals and activities involved. Revenge against them was contemplated at the beginning of Galba's reign (4.6.2), pursued at the beginning of Vespasian's (4.42–4), and achieved, in small measure, under Titus (Suet. *Tit.* 8.5), early Domitian (Suet. *Dom.* 9.3 quoting Domitian's *mot* '*princeps qui delatores non castigat, irritat*'), Nerva (Plin. *Ep.* 9.13, etc.), and Trajan (Plin. *Pan.* 34–5). T. was not impressed: *A.* 4.30.3 *delatores, genus hominum publico exitio repertum et ne poenis quidem umquam satis coercitum per praemia eliciebantur.* He also extends blame for their *scelera* to the senatorial court in which the cases were tried: *Agr.* 45.1 *nostrae duxere Heluidium in carcerem manus, nos Maurici Rusticique uisus, nos innocenti sanguine Senecio perfudit.* **alii sacerdotia et consulatus... adepti:** the statutory award for successful prosecutors in *maiestas* cases was a quarter of the condemned man's property (*A.* 4.20.2; see Rutledge (2001) 35–7), but political advancement (*consulatus, procurationes*; cf. *A.* 2.32.1 *praeturae extra ordinem*, *A.* 3.19.1 *suffragium ad honores*, 11.4.3 *insignia praeturae*, 16.33.2 *quaestoria insignia*) and priestly office (*sacerdotia*; cf. 4.42.4 *sacerdotio fulgens*) are also known (Rutledge (2001) 20–53). In the *Dialogus* the worldly success of the *delatores* Eprius Marcellus and Vibius Crispus 'proves' the worth of rhetorical pursuits (8.3). For *praemia* as a motive for delation cf. *H.* 4.42.4 *libidine sanguinis et hiatu praemiorum*, *A.* 4.30.3 *delatores . . . per praemia eliciebantur*, Plin. *Ep.* 9.13.23 *reddat praemium sub optimo principe quod a pessimo accepit.* **ut spolia:** for the equation of political success and *spolia* cf. Sal. *Jug.* 84.1 *sese consulatum ex uictis illis spolia cepisse*; for the (bitter) analogy between delation and military success cf. *Agr.* 45.1 *una adhuc uictoria Carus Mettius* (a Domitianic *delator*) *censebatur*, and Cic. *S. Rosc.* 89–90, where he refers to delation under Sulla as a second *pugna Cannensis*. Traditional *spolia* were displayed in the vestibules of victorious generals (e.g. Liv. 38.43.11 *spolia . . . fixurus in postibus suis*); the ostentation implicit in the simile stands in antithesis with *interiorem potentiam* below. **procurationes:** for a *delator* of equestrian rank who might have aspired to one of these equestrian posts see 2.10.1 on Annius Faustus (with Rutledge (2001) 189–90). Accusers of less than senatorial rank are also implied in Juvenal's (exaggerated) picture of *delatores* lining the shores of the Adriatic (*Sat.* 4.47–52 with Courtney (1980) *ad loc.*); an infamous example from the Neronian period is the philosopher P. Egnatius Celer, whose betrayal of his patron and friend Barea Soranus was rewarded with 'money and honours' (Dio 62.26.2; *A.* 16.32.2–3). Of similarly modest rank were the men, including his son's tutor, who accused Josephus (without avail) to Vespasian, Titus, and Domitian (*Vita* 424, 428–9). **interiorem potentiam** 'power behind the scenes' (Chilver); for the position cf. *A.* 3.30.2 (on Sallustius Crispus) *praecipuus cui secreta imperatorum inniterentur*. The expression here has no exact parallel, but cf. Suet. *Cal.* 19.3 *interioribus aulicis* (of courtiers with an inside story), Nep. *Hann.* 2.2 *interioribus consiliis* and Liv. 42.17.4 *amicitiae interioris* (of intimacy with kings), and, for Domitian's court, the last line of the surviving fragment of Statius' epic on Domitian's wars, *Caesareae confinis Acilius aulae*. For the deadly use of *interior potentia* cf. Juvenal's description of an otherwise unknown courtier Pompeius: *saeuior illo | Pompeius tenui iugulos aperire susurro* (4.109–10) and Plin. *Pan.* 62.9 *clandestinas existimationes . . . insidiantes susurros*. For Flavian *amici* see Crook (1955) 48–52; on the role and constitution of the inner circle more generally see *CAH*[2] XI 195–213. **agerent uerterent cuncta:** 'the phrase is . . . made forcible by simplicity and vagueness' (Alford); like Virgil's *uertere . . . cuncta* (*Aen.* 2.652–3) and T.'s own *agunt feruntque cuncta* (*D.* 8.3, also of *delatores*) and *miscere cuncta* (53.2n.), it expresses general upheaval rather than particular actions. For the asyndetic pair expressing mob activity cf. 2.70.3 *intueri mirari*, 3.83.3 *exsultabant fruebantur*, 4.11.1 *ambiri coli*, *A.* 1.41.3 *orant obsistunt rediret maneret* (with Goodyear's comment 'T. is again attempting to present the soldiers' tumultuous excitement'), *A.* 2.19.1 *incursant turbant*; similarly Sal. *Cat.* 20.12 *pecuniam trahunt uexant.* **cuncta:** on the formal and artificial tone of this synonym for *omnia* see Adams (1973) 129–31. **odio et terrore:** abl. of manner, but of the victims of delation rather than the *delatores* themselves; for adverbial ablatives external to the subject see 12.2n. *licentia ... Galbae.* **corrupti:** cf. 85.2 *uix secreta domuum sine formidine.* On the *accusator domesticus* under Domitian see Plin. *Pan.* 42 (e.g. 42.4 on Domitian as *principem illum in capita dominorum seruos subornantem*) and (by implication) Dio 68.1.2 'Nerva put to death all the slaves and freedmen who had conspired against their masters and allowed such persons to lodge no other sort of complaint against their masters.' The formal parallel between *corrupti* and *oppressi*, though the former refers to agents of destruction, the latter to victims, suggests what Pliny states (above, *principem ... subornantem*) and Dio implies ('conspired'), namely, that the *princeps* or those acting on his behalf actively encouraged domestic betrayal. **quibus deerat inimicus, per amicos oppressi:** a *sententia* employing antithesis (cf. Cic. *Ver.* 4.31 *per amicum aliud aliud per inimicum inueniebant*) and paradox (*per amicos oppressi*); cf. 4.1.2 *alii ab amicis monstrabantur.* Exemplified in the betrayal of Dolabella (88.1 n.) by Plancius Varus (2.63.1 *ex intimis Dolabellae amicis*), and in charges laid against P. Egnatius Celer in 70 for the betrayal, under Nero, of Barea Soranus (4.10.1 *proditor corruptorque amicitiae*; cf. *A.* 16.32.2 *cliens ... ad opprimendum amicum emptus*, and 16.32.3 *amicitiae fallaces*); cf. *A.* 2.27–32 on the entrapment of Libo. Among Pliny's praises for Trajan is *reddita ... amicis fides* (*Pan.* 42.2).

3.1 uirtutum sterile saeculum: sc. *fuit.* The metaphor stands in antithesis to *opimum casibus* at 2.1 (see n., and cf. 90.1 *usu sterile*); cf. Plin. *Pan.* 56.2 (on Trajan's reign) *quod momentum, quod immo temporis punctum, aut beneficio sterile, aut uacuum laude?* and *Ep.* 5.17.6 *faueo enim saeculo, ne sit sterile et effetum.* For the gen. cf. Vell. 1.18.3 *quae urbes ... studiorum fuere steriles* and *OLD* 2d. **bona exempla:** Pliny offers to T. one of his own actions from this period as an *exemplum simile antiquis* (*Ep.* 7.33.9), but even Pliny concedes that *bona* are rarer than *mala*: *Ep.* 5.8.13 *plura culpanda sunt quam laudanda.* For T. on the didactic function of *exempla* see *A.* 4.33.2 *pauci prudentia honesta ab deterioribus, utilia ab noxiis discernunt, plures aliorum euentis docentur* with M–W *ad loc.* **comitatae ... secutae:** cf. *Agr.* 45.1 *non uidit Agricola ... tot nobilissimarum feminarum exilia et fugas.* Agricola died 23 August 93. **comitatae profugos liberos:** no examples are known from this period, but cf. Sen. *Dial.* 12.16.7 on the mother of a man exiled in 91 B.C., an *exemplum* that he cites in writing to his own mother in the first years of Claudius' principate: *Rutilia Cottam filium secuta est in exilium et usque eo fuit indulgentia constricta ut mallet exilium pati quam desiderium.* **secutae maritos:** best known is Fannia, wife of Helvidius Priscus (Plin. *Ep.* 7.19.4 *bis maritum secuta in exsilium est, tertio ipsa propter maritum relegata* with Sherwin-White (1966) *ad loc.* for the dates; cf. *Ep.* 7.19.7 for Fannia as an *exemplum* for posterity both female and male; sources in *PIR*² F 118). *secutae* seems to refer both to wives who voluntarily accompanied exiled husbands and to wives who were themselves exiled. Of the latter Pliny mentions two relegated in 93 (*Ep.* 3.11.6, 9.13.5): Arria (wife of Thrasea Paetus and credited by T. with the desire to follow her husband even into the grave at *A.* 16.34.2; see further *PIR*² A 1114) and Verulana Gratilla (wife, it is presumed, of Arulenus Rusticus; sources, including *H.* 3.69.3, in Raepsaet-Charlier (1987) 790). Accompanying an exiled husband merits mention in the *Annals*, too: *A.* 15.71.3 *Priscum Artoria Flaccilla coniunx comitata est, Gallum Egnatia Maximilla.* **exilia** 'various places of exile'; cf. Virg. *Aen.* 2.780 *longa* . . . *exilia*, 3.4 *diuersa exilia* (both of Aeneas' wanderings). **propinqui audentes:** Fannia is exemplary here, too: she commissioned a biography of her executed husband based on his *commentarii* and was relegated in consequence (Plin. *Ep.* 7.19.5: her boldness emerges clearly from the trial scene Pliny describes there). For the links of blood and marriage among members of the 'philosophic opposition', whose boldness probably underlies this generalization (e.g. 4.5.2 on Helvidius Priscus: *recti peruicax, constans aduersus metus*), see Sherwin-White (1966) *ad* Plin. *Ep.* 3.11.3. **constantes generi:** the particularity of *generi* is odd – why not sons or brothers? – and suggests that this rubric, like others in the table of contents (e.g. *nutantes Galliae, nouis cladibus, cladibus* . . . *repetitis, pollutae caerimoniae, magna adulteria, contumax* . . . *fides*), is not a generalization about the period but rather an oblique reference to a precise incident. The obvious referent here is Helvidius Priscus, son-in-law of Thrasea Paetus, relegated at the time of Paetus' condemnation under Nero (4.6.1 *ruina soceri in exilium pulsus*; cf. *A.* 16.35.1), and faithful under the Flavians to Paetus' political programme (4.5.2 *e moribus soceri nihil aeque ac libertatem hausit*). **contumax . . . seruorum fides:** exemplified (note *egregio*) at 4.50.2: *seruus egregio mendacio se Pisonem esse respondit ac statim obtruncatur.* Cf. Sen. *Dial.* 3.35.1 *si tacuit* (sc. *seruus*) *interrogatus, contumaciam uocas.* Here *contumacia* 'defiance' seems admirable and at 85.3 (where frightened senators speak lest their silence be adjudged *contumax*) lack of it contemptible, but elsewhere in T. it is closer to pointless and often harmful provocation

(51.4n.). **supremae ... necessitates** 'final straits'; first found at Sal. *Hist.* fr. 1.55.15 *neque quisquam extremam necessitatem nihil ausus ... exspectat.* In T. both singular and plural forms occur and suicide usually follows: 72.3 (on Tigellinus) *accepto ... supremae necessitatis nuntio, A.* 11.37.3 (on Messalina, who in the event (11.38.1) lacks the fortitude for suicide) *supremis eius necessitatibus, A.* 15.61.4 (on Seneca) *necessitatem ultimam denuntiaret*; cf. Sen. *Ep.* 17.9 *si necessitates ultimae inciderint, iamdudum exibit e uita et molestus sibi esse desinet.* This expression is less ironic than *mortis arbitrium*, a synonymous expression also used by T. and others (see below on *laudatis ... exitus*). **ipsa necessitas ... exitus:** a restatement of the two components of 'compulsory death'. Some editors delete *ipsa necessitas* and print *toleratae*; see Alford's and Wellesley's app. crit. **laudatis antiquorum mortibus pares exitus:** the only *mors laudata* in the extant books of *H.* is Otho's (2.49; for the praise see 2.31.1 *egregiam ... famam*), and that was not compulsory. For the rich theme of enforced suicide in the *Annals* see e.g. *A.* 11.3.1 (on Valerius Asiaticus) *liberum mortis arbitrium ei permisit*, 15.60.1 (on Plautius Lateranus) *non illud breue mortis arbitrium permitteret*, 16.33.2 *Thraseae Soranoque et Seruiliae datur mortis arbitrium*; on praiseworthy death more generally, *A.* 4.33.3 *clari ducum exitus retinent ac redintegrant legentium animum* and Pomeroy (1991) 192–225. A contemporary, Titinius Capito, wrote a work consisting entirely, it seems, of *exitus illustrium uirorum* (Plin. *Ep.* 8.12.5; cf. 5.5.3 on C. Fannius, who *scribebat ... exitus occisorum aut relegatorum a Nerone*).

3.2 caelo terraque: cf. *A.* 6.37.2 *quae terra caeloue portenderentur* and, on the tone of this prepositionless local abl., Cic. *Fin.* 5.9.2 *caelo mari terra, ut poetice loquar.* Among the portents of Vitellius' end were a comet (cf. *A.* 14.22.1 *sidus cometes effulsit, de quo uulgi opinio est tamquam mutationem regis portendat*), two lunar eclipses, and a double sun (Dio 65.8.1; see Murison (1999) *ad loc.* for parallels). **prodigia ... monitus ... praesagia:** for the largest collection in *H.* see 86.1–3 (with introductory note, which lists the relevant *Annals* passages); see also 10.3n. *ostentis ac responsis*, 18.1n. *tonitrua et fulgura et caelestes minae*, 22.2nn., 62.3n. *laetum augurium ... acciperetur*, 2.1.2 *praesaga responsa*, 4.26.2 *prodigii loco*, 5.13.1 *euenerant prodigia.* Other sources on this period have a wealth of material (particularly in connection with the ends and beginnings of reigns), some of which we can see T. to have omitted: e.g. Suet. *G.* 18.3 (not in T.), *O.* 7.2 (not in T.), *Vit.* 9 (not in T.), *Ves.* 5.2–7, *Tit.* 10.1, *Dom.* 15.2–3, 23.2; Plut. *O.* 4.4 (see 86.1 nn. *bigae* and *ab occidente*); Dio 64.7.1–2 (on the end of Otho, not in T.), 65.8.1 and 65.16.1 (on the end of Vitellius' reign, not in T.), 66.1.1–4 (on Vespasian's advent), 66.17.2

(on Vespasian's death), 67.12.1, 67.16.1–2, and 67.18.1 (all on Domitian's death). **fulminum monitus:** cf. 18.1 *tonitrua et fulgura et caelestes minae* (with n.). Lightning omens are also attested during Domitian's reign (Suet. *Dom.* 15.2). In the *Annals* T. reports lightning prodigies in connection with Agrippina's death (14.12.2, with the authorial comment *quae adeo sine cura deum eueniebant ut multos postea annos Nero imperium et scelera continuauerit*; on T.'s view of the attitude of the gods see below on *non . . . ultionem*). **laeta tristia, ambigua manifesta:** cf. 10.2 *luxuria industria, comitate arrogantia.* **laeta:** cf. 62.3 *laetum augurium*, and Suet. *Dom.* 6.2 (on the defeat of Antonius Saturninus in 89) *aquila . . . clangores laetissimos edidit.* T.'s emphasis, however, is on the *tristia* (cf. *cladibus* and *ultionem* in the following sentence, which purports (*enim*) to explain this one). **cladibus . . . indiciis approbatum est:** *cladibus* sums up (with a negative colour) the events listed in the table of contents, *indiciis* the reference to divine portents that concludes it. **magisue iustis indiciis** 'or with fuller portents'; for other passages in T. where the standard of *iustus* is something other than *iustitia* (*OLD* 6–9, *TLL* 720.33–722.54) cf. 4.21.1 *iusti iam exercitus ductor*, 4.46.4 *quibus aetas et iusta stipendia*, *A.* 14.32.2 *sine iustis armis*; cf. Liv. 40.6.6 *iustam belli speciem*; in both Velleius (2.89.1 etc.) and Pliny (*Nat. praef.* 19) *iustum opus* refers to a 'full-scale' history. *magisue iustis* is Rhenanus' emendation for the MS reading *magis uetustis*; other emendations for this phrase and for *indiciis* have been suggested, none as successful (see Wellesley's app. crit.). For *indicia* as 'portents' (*OLD* 3b) cf. Vell. 2.57.1 *plurima ei praesagia atque indicia di immortales futuri obtulissent periculi.* **non esse curae deis securitatem nostram, esse ultionem** 'that heaven cares not for our peace, only for our punishment' (Irvine); similar in expression but in content more explicitly political is Luc. 4.807–9 *felix Roma quidem ciuesque habitura beatos, | si libertatis superis tam cura placeret | quam uindicta placet.* Pliny uses the same antithesis to express a completely different world view: *Pan.* 35.4 *diuus Titus securitati nostrae ultionique prospexerat ideoque numinibus aequatus est. nostram* is active with *securitatem*, passive with *ultionem*. With antithesis, nimble syntax, and surprise (*esse ultionem* caps an apparently complete *sententia*) T. makes an epigram. On the attitude of the gods towards Rome T. is inconsistent: he shows them vengeful (2.38.2 *eadem illos deum ira, eadem hominum rabies, eaedem scelerum in discordiam egere*, *A.* 4.1.2 *deum ira in rem Romanam* with M–W *ad loc.* for further references), benificent (or potentially so: 3.72.1 *propitiis si per mores nostros liceret deis*, 4.78.2 *ope diuina*), and indifferent (*A.* 14.12.1 *quae* (sc. *prodigia*) . . . *sine cura deum eueniebant*, 16.33.1 *aequitate deum erga bona* *malaque documenta*). Perhaps most helpful is 4.26.2 *quod in pace fors seu natura, tunc fatum et ira dei uocabatur* (on contemporary interpretations of a drought in Germany; cf. *A.* 13.17.1 on a storm: *uulgus iram deum portendi crediderit*), which suggests that the *ira* explanation, at least, says more about the despair of those who advance it (including the author) than about the nature of the world. Cf. Goodyear (1972) on expressions such as *deum ira* (*ad A.* 1.39.6): 'devices of style, calculated to enhance his presentation of particular scenes and serving as convenient ways of expressing pathos and indignation'. For an extended discussion of the relevant passages in *H.* see Scott (1968) 45–106.

4–11 Chronological retrospective and geographical survey

In chh. 4–11 T. provides an overview of the state of the empire at Galba's accession, chh. 4–7 treating Rome, chh. 8–11 the armed provinces. The end of the section is signalled by an echo of the opening words of the work. Content, structure, and style make these chapters a masterly piece of historical writing.

The section introduces itself as a retrospective (4.1 *repetendum uidetur*). Ch. 4 duly looks back to Nero's suicide on 9 June 68. The ensuing months are represented by Rome's increasing familiarity with Galba: in ch. 5 he is known only by reputation, ch. 6 contains his march to Rome, in ch. 7 his aging physique is a source of ridicule to those who see him. No event is dated, and even relative chronology is fuzzy (7.1 n. *forte congruerat*). As defined by chh. 4–7 the significant elements in the *status urbis* were the attitudes towards Galba in the various groups surveyed and the general instability of a city crowded with the disaffected and the armed.

These two themes also dominate chh. 8–11. Galba is mentioned only twice (8.2, 10.3) but the potential for turbulence is measured province by province, moving roughly clockwise around the Mediterranean: Spain is rated low, Gaul rather higher, the German military zone higher still. By contrast, calm reigns in Britain, Illyricum, and, at least for the moment, the East (chh. 8–10). Egypt, as always, is a special case (11.1). Africa's potential for turbulence has already been expended (11.2 *Africa . . . contenta*). All of these provinces are garrisoned by legions. Next come the lesser provinces, with Mauretania as the hinge. Due west of Africa, it heads the list of provinces administered by imperial procurators, none of which poses any independent threat to the *status quo* (11.2). Bringing up the rear are the unarmed provinces, none even mentioned by name, and Italy, not a province at all but like the unarmed provinces in its defencelessness before the legions.

With this reference to Italy T. completes the geographical circuit; with the following reference to the new consulships of Galba and Vinius he completes his chronological coverage and poises the narrative on 1 January 69.

Comparison with the parallel sources (here, chiefly Plutarch's *Galba*) sheds light on T.'s selection and presentation. Simple omission is one feature of T.'s account; more significant is its concentration on details essential to his chosen themes (both procedures are noted below).

T. and Plutarch part company after ch. 8: the biographer of Galba and Otho did not need to look beyond Germany. In fact, Plutarch treats the report of trouble in East and South as an alarmist fiction (*G.* 13.3). But internal evidence reveals further details of T.'s compositional policy. The geographical survey, so simple in outline, is rich in purposeful variations that introduce themes prominent in Books 1–3: the independence of the soldiers and the superiority of Vespasian to all previous contenders. Otho, by contrast, a historical actor who unexpectedly capitalized on the potential for turbulence in Rome, is reserved for a surprise appearance in ch. 13; literary art and historical analysis converge in his omission from the retrospective.

Roman literary art generally involves the application of creative innovation to sound tradition. A number of verbal and structural allusions declare T.'s debt to Sallust in chh. 4–11. *repetundum*, for instance, which introduces the chronological retrospective, alludes to programmatic statements at the beginning of both of Sallust's monographs and to what can be discerned of his practice in the *Histories* (*Cat.* 5.9 *supra repetere, Jug.* 5.3 *supra repetam*; *Hist.* frr. 1.11–51). But T.'s retrospective is very different from those of his 'model'. Where in the *Bellum Catilinae* Sallust sweeps grandly from the regal period to the first century B.C. reviewing Rome's moral and political health, T. looks back a few short months and focuses on power and unrest. The geographical survey, on the other hand, which Syme declared to 'lack precedent or parallel in ancient historiography' ((1958) 146), may owe something to a document drafted by Augustus and described by Suetonius as 'an overview of the whole empire', the first half of which treated the strength and disposition of the military forces (*Aug.* 101.4 *breuiarium totius imperii, quantum militum sub signis ubique esset*). But as we have seen, T.'s survey provides far more than numbers and places.

Another element of Sallust's programme for retrospectives, namely brevity (*Cat.* 5.9 *paucis*, *Jug.* 5.3 *pauca*), shows up in T.'s practice unannounced. Sallust's retrospectives are not in fact markedly more concise than his narratives but in chh. 4–11 we find, in addition to T.'s ordinary brevities, expressions showing remarkable compression (noted below). In both style and content, then, T. produces a more challenging text than Sallust. If the table of contents advertises the attractions of the coming narrative, the retrospective reveals something of what will be required of the reader: an eagerness for understanding historical processes and an appreciation for a style of unparalleled density.

T. also opens the *Annals* with a retrospective, but a much simpler one (*A.* 1.2–3). The state of the Roman world is summarized there in two short sentences (3.6–7): military activity was almost nil (a single war) and on the domestic front all was tranquil. The early books of the *Annals* chronicle the gradual development of the imperial system and its attendant evils; in *H.* 1–3, by contrast, T. offers action, a series of events unrolling without pause through three full books of narrative with a geographic span matching that of the empire itself. (The main events of Books 4 and 5, the revolt of Civilis and the siege of Jerusalem, are not introduced by the retrospective.) The necessary background for all of it is given in chh. 4–11, a piece of writing that shows T. already a master of his craft.

4.1 ceterum . . . noscantur: a leisurely period providing bland relief from the dazzling lists of the table of contents and the memorable epigram that closed it. The indirect questions are parallel in form and increasing in length (6 syllables, then 7, 9, and 17), obeying classical, not Tacitean, norms. *status*, *mens*, and *habitus* are properties of the human body, and prepare for the 'health of the body politic' metaphor that becomes explicit in *ualidum* and *aegrum*. For *status urbis* cf. *Agr.* 7.2 *statum urbis Mucianus regebat* and the fuller expression at *A.* 1.16.1 *hic rerum urbanarum status erat*. *mens* 'attitude' (*OLD* 8) refers to the different attitudes of the various armies described in chh. 8–11 (cf. *A.* 2.36.3 *unde prospici posse quae cuique . . . mens*). On *habitus* see 8.1 n. **quid aegrum:** cf. 2.86.4 *quidquid usquam aegrum foret aggrediuntur*. Disease in the body politic (cf. 16.1 *immensum imperii corpus*) is a recurrent metaphor in *H.* 1–3; in Book 1 it appears at 11.2 *contactu*, 26.1 *tabes*, and in the remedies mentioned at 9.3, 14.1, 20.3, 29.1, 37.4, 63.1, 74.1, 83.1. **non modo casus euentusque rerum, qui plerumque fortuiti sunt, sed ratio etiam causaeque:** the pair *casus euentusque* 'occurrences and outcomes' is used again at 5.10.2 and *A.* 2.26.2, shorter formulas at 51.1 *initia causasque motus Vitelliani expediam* and 3.46.1 *id bellum cum causis et euentibus . . . mox memorabimus*. The emphasis on explanation (*ratio causaeque*) links *H.* to a tradition of ancient historiography indebted to Polybius, which defined itself in the Roman world by opposition to the first generation of 'annalistic' histories that simply recorded each year's events.

4.2 finis Neronis: *finis* indicates an emphasis on the effects of Nero's death; its cause and manner T. had declared insignificant by beginning *H.* on 1 January 69 (1.1 n. *consules*). In Rome the end of Nero (9 June 68) was not the beginning of Galba, who was still *en route* from Spain. Comparable situations arose at the deaths of Otho and Vitellius, whose successors began to rule when still far from Rome (Vitellius in Germany, Vespasian in Egypt). T. lends a different emphasis to each scene: here variety is the theme, at Otho's death the senseless joy in Rome is contrasted with the devastation of Italy (2.54–5), at Vitellius' death Rome herself experiences devastation (4.1.1–3). **ut . . . ita:** 'though . . . yet'; the antithesis between the universal joy of *laetus* and the fragmented *motus animorum* turns a comparative into a concessive expression (*NLS* §253iiia, *OLD ut* 5b). So also at 7.2, 17.2, 50.4, 52.2, 79.3, 85.1; cf. 6.2n. *ut non . . . ita*. **primo gaudentium impetu** 'in the initial surge of (people) rejoicing'; cf. 2.23.3 *uincentium impetu*, *A.* 11.37.4 *impetu uenientium*, *A.* 3.74.4 *gaudio et impetu uictoris exercitus*. The substantive participle is a compact equivalent for a clause (e.g. *eorum qui gaudebant*) and a concrete alternative to an abstraction (Cic. *Lael.* 63 *impetum beneuolentiae*, V. Max. 5.9.1 *impetu irae*). T. gives us emotional people rather than emotion *per se*. The construction, prominent in Livy beginning with *praef.* 4 *et legentium plerisque* 'and for most readers', is particularly suited to representing public opinion: 5.2 *increpantium*, 7.3 *comparantibus*, 13.2 *transmittentium*, 14.2 *interpretantibus*, 22.2 *computantium*, 27.2 *requirentibus*, 32.1 *poscentium*, 41.2 *ferentium*. **uarios motus animorum . . . conciuerat:** *concieo* 'arouse' (*OLD* 2b) is commonly used of summoning troops (70.2 *concitis auxiliis*), but here, as at *A.* 1.23.1, 14.17.2, 16.32.2, its object is abstract (*pace OLD* 3). **apud** governs the accs. from *patres* to *duces*; cf. 46.3 *ad seditiones et discordias et . . . bella ciuilia* and *A.* 2.68.1 *effugere ad Armenios, inde Albanos Heniochosque.* **urbanum militem:** the praetorian guard was the most powerful element of the forces in Rome (see ch. 5): T. credits them with *iudicium* (45.1) and *arbitrium* (46.1). The other regular city forces were the urban cohorts; in extraordinary circumstances the *uigiles* also counted (46.1 n. *Plotium Firmum*; cf. 3.64.1 with 46.1 n. *Flauium Sabinum*). In *H.* T. uses *miles urbanus* of praetorian and urban cohorts together (5.1, 14.1, 2.19.1, 2.94.1), of the urban cohorts alone (89.2, 3.69.1), and in contexts where the praetorians alone seem relevant (2.19.1); he differentiates the urbans from the praetorians at 20.3, 74.3, 87.1, 89.2, 2.21.4, 2.93.2. The undifferentiated reference, besides being brief, reflects reality, since the two corps, though under the command of praetorian and urban prefects respectively, lived together in the *castra praetoria* in Rome, appeared together in lists of veterans, and shared their numeration (cohorts I–IX being praetorian, X and above urban in the Augustan organization); see O. Robinson (1992) 181–8, Freis (1967) 36–46. **euulgato imperii arcano:** T. was alert to incidents that exposed the unstated conditions of the emperor's power. Other *arcana*: the principle that the emperor should not render account for his acts (*A.* 1.6.3 *arcana domus*), the emperor's practice of designating future magistrates (*A.* 2.36.1 *arcana imperii*), the exclusion of high-ranking Romans from Egypt (*A.* 2.59.3 *dominationis arcana*). **posse principem alibi quam Romae fieri:** 'elsewhere than in Rome' implies 'by the legions' (5.1 *principem a legionibus factum*, cf. 2.76.4 *posse ab exercitu principem fieri* (of Vitellius), and 5.16.3 *principem Galbam sextae legionis auctoritate factum*). Hitherto only the praetorian guard had chosen or approved a *princeps*.

4.3 patres . . . deterrimi seruorum: attitudes in Rome are again surveyed from top to bottom at 88.2–3. **patres laeti:** sc. *erant.* **usurpata statim libertate:** primarily in trials of Neronian agents: 4.42.6 *senatus . . . occiso Nerone delatores et ministros more maiorum puniendos flagitabat*; cf. 2.10.1–2, 4.6.1–2. Implicit in *statim* is a temporal antithesis, but T. leaves for later the senate's subsequent showing as obsequious, self-serving, and craven (19.1–3, 35.1) and omits altogether their subservience to Nymphidius Sabinius (Plut. *G.* 8.3–4). Senatorial experimentation with *libertas* is more fully documented at the outset of Vespasian's reign (4.6.3–4.10) but that phase, too, came quickly to an end. **ut** 'inasmuch as' *OLD* 21a. **erga principem nouum et absentem** 'towards a new and distant ruler', cf. 4.49.1 *alienato erga Vespasianum animo.* **primores equitum:** cf. 25.2 *primores militum.* In the imperial period *equites* were increasingly involved in government (50.1 *cura rei publicae*, 58.1 *ministeria*, 5.9.3 *prouincia*, *A.* 16.27.2 *munia publica*) and were therefore exposed to the dangers of eminence under a despot. During Nero's reign the suffering of *equites* frequently mirrored that of senators (*A.* 14.14.4, 15.57.2, 16.13.2, 16.17.1, 16.27.2). Vespasian restocked both orders (Suet. *Ves.* 9.2; cf. Dio 59.9.5). For the equestrian elite cf. *A.* 2.59.3 *senatoribus aut equitibus Romanis illustribus* and see Brunt (1983) 62. **pars populi integra et magnis domibus adnexa:** contrasted with the *plebs sordida*, whose desires (*panem et circenses*, Juv. 10.81) obliged them directly to the emperor (see below); in Suetonius the rejoicing *plebs* is undifferentiated (*Ner.* 57.1). At 12.3 adoption by Galba for their patron appears as one object of client hopes. On several occasions in 69 dependants were called upon to hide their patrons (81.2n. *incertas latebras*). For *integer* cf. 4.64.3 *sincerus et integer et seruitutis oblitus populus* (of Germans), also Vell. 2.3.2 *intacta perniciosis consiliis plebs*; for the contrast cf. Liv. 9.46.13 *in duas partes discessit ciuitas: aliud integer populus, fautor et cultor bonorum, aliud forensis factio, tenebat.* **clientes libertique damnatorum et exulum in spem erecti:** among the props at Galba's proclamation were *imagines* of Nero's victims and an exiled *puer nobilis* (Suet. *G.* 10.1, cf. Plut. *G.* 5.2). Nero's exiles, including Galba's eventual heir Piso Licinianus (48.1), Vespasian's gadfly Helvidius Priscus (4.6.1), and one Cassius Asclepiodotus (possibly an ancestor of the historian Dio: cf. his 62.26.2 and *A.* 16.33.1) returned under Galba, but most encountered difficulties in recovering confiscated property (90.1n. *reuocatis ab exilio*). **plebs sordida et circo ac theatris sueta:** cf. 3.74.2 *sordida pars plebis*, and contrast *A.* 11.7.3 *plebem, quae toga enitesceret*; for the pairing with slaves cf. 4.1.2 *egentissimus quisque e plebe et pessimi seruitiorum*. Public entertainment was financed primarily by the *princeps* (Millar (1977) 368–75). **deterrimi seruorum:** the construction emphasizes quality (*deterrimi*) over rank (*serui*); cf. 22.1 *intimi libertorum* and, more generally, 10.1 *secretum Asiae*, 25.1 *incerta noctis*, 79.2 *lubrico itinerum*, 85.2 *secreta domuum*. **qui adesis bonis per dedecus Neronis alebantur:** also reported, again without names, at *A.* 14.14.3. The consumption metaphor in *adesis bonis* (cf. *A.* 13.21.2 *adesis omnibus fortunis*) and *alebantur* suggests that these *ingenui* have been debased by their own actions to the status of parasites: cf. Hor. *Ep.* 1.15.26–7 *rebus maternis atque paternis | fortiter absumptis urbanus coepit haberi.*

5.1 miles urbanus: 4.2n. Only praetorians are mentioned in connection with Sabinus' coup attempt, but it took place in the camp shared by praetorian and urban cohorts, so both corps may be meant here. **longo Caesarum sacramento imbutus** 'steeped in their long-standing oath to the emperors', substituting fact (long service to the Caesars) for concept (loyalty *uel sim.*). For praetorian loyalty cf. 30.2 *uestra fides . . . illaesa ad hunc diem mansit*, *A.* 14.7.4 *praetorianos toti Caesarum domui obstrictos*. For the metaphor cf. 2.85.1 *imbutae fauore Othonis* (sc. *legiones*) and 3.15.2 *ut . . . ciuili praeda miles imbueretur.* **ad destituendum Neronem . . . traductus:**

details in Plutarch and Suetonius: the praetorians aligned themselves with Galba only after their prefect Nymphidius Sabinus (see below) led them to believe, wrongly, that Nero had abandoned Rome for Egypt, and promised them a donative in Galba's name (Plut. *G.* 2.2, Suet. *G.* 16.1). The phrase *arte et impulsu* reflects T.'s focus on the emotional after-effects of Nymphidius' failed coup; the man himself he allows little significance. **neque dari donatiuum:** the donative promised, 30,000 HS to each praetorian and 5,000 for legionaries, was double the highest known precedent, higher, perhaps, than could be paid (Plut. *G.* 2.2). Galba refused to pay it, or indeed anything at all, for which decision T. faults him at 18.3. Vespasian paid, but modestly (2.82.2). The annual salary for a praetorian soldier at this period was 3,000 HS, for a legionary 900 (Alston (1994)). For other bribes see 24.1–2, 25.1, 66.1, 82.3. **eundem:** sc. *esse.* **eundem in pace quem in bello locum:** *quem* functions as a connective (= *atque*) rather than as a true relative here and is therefore attracted into the case of its antecedent (cf. *Agr.* 32.1 *eandem Romanis in bello uirtutem quam in pace lasciuiam adesse creditis? A.* 6.7.1 *placitum eandem poenam irrogari quam in Aruseium*; *NLS* §289). **praeuentamque gratiam:** sc. *esse.* Illustrated for individuals by the installation of Galba's staff member Cornelius Laco as sole praetorian prefect, a post one of the existing prefects had wanted for himself (see below). But nothing indicates that Galba showed favour to his original legion (VI *Victrix*), which remained in Spain, or to his newly conscripted legion (VII *Galbiana*), which was dispatched to Pannonia. T. in fact exaggerates praetorian disaffection; in Plutarch they establish a claim on Galba's gratitude by suppressing a coup attempt (Plut. *G.* 14.3 'let us show ourselves Galba's true and faithful Guard'). The competition for temporal priority in winning the emperor's favour operates between both individuals (45.1 *anteire proximos*) and armies (53.2 *praeuentus erat*, 57.1 *ingenti certamine*). **Nymphidii Sabini praefecti:** a freedwoman's son, C. Nymphidius Sabinus was the colleague of Tigellinus (72.1 n.) as praetorian prefect from 65 (*PIR*^{2} N 250). In that year he also received *consularia ornamenta*, probably for services in suppressing the Pisonian conspiracy. From August 66 to March 68 he appears to have been in sole command of the praetorians in Rome, as Tigellinus was with Nero in Greece; after Nero's death he forced Tigellinus from office (Plut. *G.* 8.3). His lacunose biography at *A.* 15.72.2 owes its composition to the fact that *et ipse pars Romanarum cladium erit*, but here T. reduces his story to a minimum: he sought supreme power and failed. Plutarch, by contrast, allots four substantial chapters (*G.* 8–9, 13–4). In 68 Nymphidius was instrumental in securing ratification in Rome for Galba's proclamation as emperor (Plut. *G.* 2.1) and sent Galba Neronian paraphernalia to use *en route* (Plut. *G.* 11.1). He turned against Galba when passed over in the distribution of posts (Plut. *G.* 8.2, 9.8–9, Suet. *G.* 11.1) but when he urged the praetorians to make him emperor they killed him instead (Plut. *G.* 14.1, cf. 37.3).

5.2 et Nymphidius quidem: '*quidem* emphasizes one statement... while directing our attention to another which contrasts with the first' (Solodow (1978) 13), similarly at 8.1 *et hic quidem Romae*, 16.4 *et Galba quidem*, 63.1 *et quidem Treueros*. **oppressus:** sc. *est.* **quamuis capite... ablato:** *quamuis*, which qualifies the abl. abs., reinforces the concessive relation indicated by the antithesis *ablato*~*manebat*; cf. 32.1n. *quippe... postulaturis*, 60 *quamquam remoto consulari*, 83.1 *quamquam turbidis rebus et diuersis militum animis.* **manebat... nec deerant:** the subjects of the two verbs joined by *nec* are very different entities (*conscientia, sermones*). Chilver says it is 'almost certainly wrong' not to infer a break between the two parts of the sentence, but the sentence's form does its best to bridge the break in content, creating a continuous accumulation of disaffection. **manebat... conscientia:** with concomitant fear of punishment (20.3n. *exauctorati*). **senium atque auaritiam:** T. distils these two general criticisms from the specific irritants mentioned in the following sentences: *senium* from Galba's *uetus disciplina*, *auaritia* from his refusal to buy the loyalty of his troops. Sources disagree on the year of Galba's birth, but T. and Plutarch believed him 73 at his death (49.2, Plut. *G.* 8.1 (born 6 B.C.); cf. Suet. *G.* 23, Dio 64.6.5 (5 B.C.), Suet. *G.* 4.1 (3 B.C.); see further 6.1n. *inualidum senem*). T. himself agrees with the charge of *auaritia*, within limits (49.3 *pecuniae alienae non appetens, suae parcus, publicae auarus*; see below on *legi a se militem, non emi*). Plutarch (*G.* 13.4) develops the critique of *senium* very differently, quoting the ridicule of Galba's aged physique voiced not by a crowd (*increpantium*) but by a single individual, Mithridates of Pontus, to whom T. denies a place in history. **increpantium:** 4.2n. *primo gaudentium impetu.* **laudata olim... seueritas:** cf. 49.4 *militari laude*; illustrated in Suetonius by Galba's imposition of hard physical labour (*G.* 6.3) and strict discipline (6.3, 7.2) on his troops during his governorships of Upper Germany (A.D. 40) and Africa (A.D. 45–6). Official praise included triumphal regalia and three priesthoods, plus esteem from two emperors (Suet. *G.* 8.1; 6.3 (Gaius), 7.1 (Claudius)). His *seueritas*, though relaxed under Nero (*olim*, cf. Suet. *G.* 9.1 *in desidiam segnitiamque conuersus est*), was fatal to his principate: 18.3 *nocuit antiquus rigor et nimia seueritas*. Otho (36.3) and Vitellius (62.2) occupy the opposite extreme; on Flavian moderation in disciplinary matters see 2.76.4, 2.77.3, 2.82.1. **militari fama celebrata** 'much talked about among the soldiers'; *fama* is abl. of means, as in Liv. 33.44.8 *fama celebratos tyrannos* and *Agr.* 39.1 *uictoriam . . . ingenti fama celebrari*. Its modifier indicates the source of the talk (cf. [Q. Cicero] *Comm. pet.* 17 *forensem famam* and the common expression *popularis fama* 'public opinion') and is equivalent to the subjective gen. in expressions such as Cic. *Phil.* 9.10 *omnium mortalium fama* and Cic. *Div.* 1.88 *fama Graeciae*. **legi a se militem, non emi:** also recorded at Plut. *G.* 18.2 ('an utterance befitting a great commander'), Suet. *G.* 16.1, and Dio 64.3.3 (see App. 1). **nec enim . . . ad hanc formam cetera:** T. charges Galba with failing to maintain a standard he himself had set, Plutarch with acting contrary to his promises (*G.* 15.1); specifics appear in 6–7. For *ad formam* 'in accordance with a standard' cf. Vell. 2.109.1 *ad Romanae disciplinae formam*, Varro *L* 8.32 *lectos* (beds) . . . *ad unam formam*, etc.; 9.37 *formam, ad quam . . . accomodari debeant uerba*; Lucr. 2.379 *facta . . . ad certam formam primordia*.

6.1 inualidum senem: while Galba's combination of age and physical weakness is mentioned by both Plutarch (*G.* 15.4 'weak and elderly in appearance') and Dio (64.3.4 'old and weak in the sinews'; cf. 64.3.2) and his age and subjection to Vinius and Laco occur side by side in the revolutionary rhetoric of Plutarch's Nymphidius Sabinus (*G.* 13.2 'Galba himself was a reasonable and moderate old man but did not follow his own counsels in the least and was badly directed by Vinius and Laco'), only T. connects Galba's physical state and his choice of associates in explaining his growing unpopularity. With *inualidus* T. may allude to the old men of Latinus' doomed city: Virg. *Aen.* 12.132 *inualidique senes* (Miller (1987b) 92–3). **Titus Vinius:** see 1.1 n., 42n. *conscius sceleris*, and the obituary at 48.2–4, where T. gives a more balanced assessment. *deterrimus mortalium* distils Vinius' conduct under Galba: he was greedy (12.3n. *hiantes . . . cupiditates*, 37.5 *auaritia ac licentia*) and compromised by association with the hated Tigellinus (72.2n.); for Vinius as a liability to Galba's party see further 8.1 n. *recenti dono Romanae ciuitatis*, 12.3, 34.1, 37.5, 39.2, 42; Plut. *G.* 11.2, 12.1–2, 17.1–5, 18.1; Suet. *G.* 14.2. **Cornelius Laco**, an equestrian member of Galba's staff in Spain (Suet. *G.* 14.2 *assessor* 'aide'; *PIR*² C 1374). Earlier he had been a familiar of Rubellius Plautus, who was executed at Tigellinus' urging in 62 (14.1 n.). Galba raised Laco to near the top of the equestrian *cursus* in making him praetorian prefect (Suet. *G.* 14.2); at that time only the prefect of Egypt ranked higher (Turner (1954) 63–4). T. depicts him as deceitful (14.1, 39.2), incompetent

(24.2n. *per socordiam praefecti*, 26.2n. *consilii ... inimicus*), and combative (33.2, cf. Suet. *G.* 14.2 *arrogantia socordiaque intolerabilis*); he is killed without much ado at 46.5. In T.'s references to Laco style often adds sting to an already damning content. T. shares with the parallel sources the notices about Laco's influence with Galba (13.1 *potentia principatus*) and his successful support for the plan of leaving the Palace for the Forum (33.2), but he reports much more: Laco's (also successful) support for Piso (14.1), his appointment to and withdrawal from the embassy to the German legions (19.2), his culpable ignorance of the troops he commanded (24.2, 26.2), the abortive plan to sacrifice Vinius (39.2), and the sentence of exile that was superseded by his assassination (46.5). T. insists that the commander of the praetorians, who transferred their loyalty to Otho, share the blame for Galba's failure with them. Criticisms such as 24.2 *quem nota pariter et occulta fallebant* and 26.2 *consilii quamuis egregii, quod non ipse afferret, inimicus et aduersus peritos peruicax* may be the product of Tacitean inference, but the rest of the material seems to be drawn from a different source or sources (the official material (19.2, 46.5) may come from senatorial archives (see Intro. §18); Townend (1964) 354 credits Cluvius Rufus with both these data and the information at 14.1 and 39.3). The two details in Suetonius and Plutarch that T. omits (Laco's lowly status in Spain and his loyal defence of Galba in the Palace: 35.1n. *ruere*) conflict with T.'s picture of Laco as both significant and pernicious. **alter deterrimus mortalium alter ignauissimus, odio flagitiorum oneratum contemptu inertiae destruebant:** in each of the two antithetical pairs (*deterrimus~ignauissimus, odio ~contemptu*) the first member refers to Vinius, the second to Laco. This elaborate structure is further complicated by the temporal sequence of the verbs, which convey the background (*odio ... oneratum*) and the proximate cause (*contemptu ... destruebant*) of Galba's collapse, creating a miniature narrative that will be developed in chh. 12–46 with evidence of the widespread hatred for Vinius and praetorian contempt for Laco. (Valmaggi 147 excised *oneratum* in order to remove the latter complication.) For this distribution of paired terms some fifteen parallels in T. and Augustan poetry are cited by Brink (1944), including two in Book 1 (62.2 *strenuis uel ignauis spem metumue adderet*, 79.3 *neque conti neque gladii ... usui, lapsantibus equis et catafractarum pondere*, to which add 60 *per auaritiam ac sordes contemptus ... inuisusque*; see also 82.2n. *allocuti ... horridius*). Only in our passage (a summary) does asyndeton maximize *breuitas*. Vespasian's suite, unlike Galba's, provides support: 2.76.1 *et alii legati amicique firmabant et Mucianus.* **tardum Galbae iter:** sc. *erat.* Setting out from Spain in mid-July, Galba crossed the Pyrenees (23.2), met the senate's delegation at Narbo Martius (Plut. *G.* 11.1), went inland at least as far as Vienne, across the Cottian Alps (23.2), and so down to Rome, a journey of about 1,700 km (Murison (1993) 27–30). At marching speed (*c.* 22 km/day) this would require at least seventy-eight days, putting his arrival in early October at the earliest. It was probably during this journey that he distributed rewards and punishments to communities of Spain and Gaul that aided or resisted him (Suet. *G.* 12.1); Lyon, which opposed Vindex and contained an important mint, will have required particular attention (51.5n.). **cruentum:** in Suetonius' version Galba is an active aggressor complete with military dress and a dagger within easy reach (*G.* 11.1 *paludatus ac dependente a ceruicibus pugione*; cf. 2.89.1 on Vitellius approaching Rome *paludatus accinctusque*). In T.'s version the killings are curiously impersonal. With the disfavour generated by these killings contrast the popular affection for Vespasian's generals Antonius Primus and Arrius Varus, *quia in nemimen ultra aciem saeuierant* (4.39.3). *cruentus* is an affective word emphasizing the painful, ugly side of fighting; Caesar does not use it, but Sallust (four times), Livy (twenty-one times), and T. (sixteen times) do. Cicero has it sixteen times in speeches, only once in the letters. It is most at home in epic, where the tone is right and the clausula welcome (Virg. *Aen.* twenty-three times, Stat. *Theb.* fifty-four times). **Cingonio Varrone consule designato:** designated by Nero for a suffect consulship in 68 (Townend (1962) 117) notwithstanding an earlier conflict (*A.* 14.45.2), Varro wrote a speech for Nymphidius Sabinus' projected acclamation (Plut. *G.* 14.4). His execution took place *in uia* (37.3); he may have approached Galba for a pardon (cf. the Othonian generals with Vitellius, 2.60.1–2). Plutarch pairs Varro's execution not with Turpilianus' (see below) but with that of another of Nymphidius' supporters, Mithridates of Pontus (Plut. *G.* 15.1). **Petronio Turpiliano consulari:** he led the larger part of the forces that Nero mustered in response to the defections of Galba and Verginius (Dio 63.27.1[a]; *PIR*[2] P 315). His troops went over to Galba even before Nero's death (Murison (1993) 24); Turpilianus himself returned to Rome where, despite his powerlessness, he was ordered to die (37.3 *Turpiliani in urbe*, Plut. *G.* 15.2, with 17.3 implying that Vinius was responsible). **inauditi atque indefensi:** the same alliterative pair at *D.* 16.4, 2.10.2, *A.* 2.77.2; later simple *inauditus* suffices (*A.* 4.11.1, 12.22.2). On the adjectives see Intro. §11. **tamquam innocentes** adds a wry twist to the outrage-inducing report of summary executions: cf. Pliny on one of Domitian's victims: *Ep.* 4.11.8 *nescio an innocens, certe tamquam innocens.* Plutarch's 'albeit justly' (*G.* 15.1 εἰ καὶ δικαίως).

6.2 introitus . . . infaustus omine: sc. *erat* 'his entry was inauspicious'; cf. Plut. *G.* 15.4 'entering the city through so much slaughter, so many corpses, was not a good or auspicious omen for Galba' (οὐ χρηστὸν οὐδὲ αἴσιον . . . τῶι Γάλβαι τὸν οἰωνόν). T. does not limit the omen to Galba but adapts a more general expression first found in Virgil: *Aen.* 11.589 *tristis* (sc. *Diana*) *ubi infausto committitur omine pugna* (Miller (1987b) 93–4). *omine*, abl. of respect (*NLS* §55), projects the bad luck of *infaustus* (cf. 38.1 *infaustam adoptionem* 'unlucky adoption') into the future. For other omens and the crowd reactions they provoke see, in Book 1, 62.3 and 86.3. **trucidatis tot milibus inermium militum:** the killing took place at the Mulvian Bridge (87.1, cf. 37.3 *in oculis urbis*); the victims were marines, soldiers attached to the Roman fleet (Plut. *G.* 15.4, Suet. *G.* 12.2), who were demanding either confirmation or amelioration of their status. Dio gives the improbably high number of 7,000 (64.3.2; he also identifies the victims as praetorians); according to Plutarch they were armed at least with swords. For the survivors see 87.1 *in custodia habitos*. The historical record on marines in 68–9 is confused (see Chilver). Vitellius' troops commit a similar atrocity upon arrival at the seventh milestone (2.88.1–2), but Mucianus succeeds in saying no to ex-praetorians clamouring for restoration to their posts by spending money and proceeding gradually (4.46). **ipsis etiam qui occiderant formidolosus:** T. alone describes the reaction of Galba's soldiers (a legion newly recruited in Spain, VII *Galbiana*, and possibly some detachments of praetorians; 23.1n. *studia . . . affectauerat*), a detail consistent with his emphasis on military opinion in this survey. **legione Hispana:** VII *Galbiana* played no part in the disturbances of 15 January; it was probably already on the Danube, from which it marched against Vitellius for Otho in March 69 (2.11.1). Here T. implies that its presence contributed to the rebellion-potential in Rome on 1 January, an error perhaps to be ascribed to the primarily topical rather than chronological organization of this survey. **ea, quam e classe Nero conscripserat:** similarly Vitellius at 3.55.1 *e classicis legio*. Galba confirmed the unit's new status on 22 December 68 (Dio 55.24.1, supported by discharge diplomas of that date *CIL* III 2.847, 848, III suppl. 3.1958 (= XVI 7–9); Ritterling (1924) 1381–3). They join Otho at 36.3. **plena:** sc. *erat*. **numeri** 'detachments' from legions and auxiliary units stationed in Germany, Britain, and Illyricum; see further 38.3n. *miscentur*. **claustra Caspiarum:** both here and at *A.* 6.33.4 (*Caspia uia*) T. is referring to the pass through which runs the modern road between Tbilisi and Vladikavkas (= Dariel pass); cf. Luc. 8.222–3 *si uos, o Parthi, peterem cum Caspia claustra | et sequerer duros* *aeterni Martis Alanos.* **in Albanos:** Pliny sites the Albani on the west coast of the Caspian Sea, just north of the Kur river (*Nat.* 6.29, 6.39). See Chilver for the problems arising from T.'s assertion. **opprimendis Vindicis coeptis:** dat. gerundive expressing purpose, cf. 18.1 *comitiis dirimendis*, 41.2 *exsoluendo donatiuo*: Draeger (1882) §206 'There are three occurrences of this construction in T.'s minor works and thirteen in the *Histories* but the *Annals* are full of it.' C. Julius Vindex, a senator's son and praetorian governor in 68 of the lightly garrisoned province of Gallia Lugdunensis (*PIR*[2] I 628), declared against Nero in early March (see Brunt (1959) and Murison (1993) 1–3). He sought military backing from fellow governors, some of whom reported him to Nero (Galba refrained: Plut. *G.* 4.2), and from Gallic leaders (Jos. *BJ* 4.440). His force eventually numbered more than 20,000 (Plut. *G.* 6.3). Verginius Rufus, the governor of the nearest armed province (Upper Germany), leading units from both Germanies, overwhelmed Vindex at Vesontio (mod. Besançon) in mid-May (Murison (1993) 26). **ut non ... ita** 'though not ... yet'. The prominent negative turns a comparative into a concessive expression; cf. 85.1 *militibus ut nihil in commune turbantibus, ita sparsis per domos* and 4.2n. *ut ... ita.* **prono fauore ... parata:** the *uariatio* abl. of respect ~ adjective is common; cf. 8.1 *facundus et pacis artibus*, 53.1 on Caecina, 88.2 *aetate inualida et ... desides*, and Sörbom (1935) 90. **audenti** describes Otho (for his boldness see 21.1, 22.1, 38.2) but does not identify him; soldiers, not leaders, were the decisive factor.

7.1 forte congruerat: either with Galba's arrival or simply with one another; T. depicts an accumulation of dissatisfaction instead of giving a precise chronology. **Clodii Macri:** L. Clodius Macer (*PIR*[2] C 1170) was Nero's legate commanding the legion stationed in the province of Africa (for the unusual power structure there and the ambition it encouraged in legates see 4.48.1–2). When Galba's proclamation in Spain offered Romans a respectable alternative to Nero, most governors and legates (including, probably, the governor of Africa) aligned themselves with him; Macer, however, imitated him. He too had one legion (III *Augusta*), conscripted another (2.97.2), and minted '*libertas*' coins acknowledging the authority of the Senate (cf. McC–W 24 '*s(enatus) c(onsulto)*'). His strategic position in one of Rome's 'breadbasket' provinces was superior, but he lacked Galba's experience and prestige (his earlier career has left no record) and his ally in Nero's court, Calvia Crispinilla (73n.), did not match the clout of Nymphidius Sabinus, who supported Galba (5.1n.). According to Plutarch, Macer's rebellion was an attempt to avoid punishment for his crimes (*G.* 6.2, a stock explanation, cf. 53.1 on Caecina); T. labels him a petty tyrant (11.2n. *domini minoris*). See further Murison (1993) 48. Vitellius, too, had an upstart in Africa killed (2.58.2). **Fontei Capitonis:** an obscure (to us) consular (cos. 67; *PIR*² F 467–8). Governor of Lower Germany from mid-67 to 68, he removed potential leaders of a rumoured Batavian revolt (4.13.1; see 59.1n. *Iulius... exemptus*), won the support of his army (58.2n. *grata... memoria*), and was plotted against by his subordinates (see below, 58.1, and 7.2n. *fuere... abstinuisse*). **haud dubie**, syntactically superfluous, signals the historian's judgment (cf. 46.6 *rem haud dubie utilem*, *A.* 2.88.2 *liberator haud dubie Germaniae*), which distinguishes the clear case of Macer's rebellion from the murky and inconsistent reports about Capito's actions. **turbantem:** one word, used absolutely, suffices for Macer's dead-end rebellion; by 1 January his murder was the significant fact. For the *uariatio* participle~temporal clause see Sörbom (1935) 117. **Trebonius Garutianus procurator:** only here and in Plutarch (*G.* 15.2 Τρεβωνιανός). *procuratores* were administrators charged by the emperor with a wide range of tasks, from managing the emperor's private estates to governing small provinces. For executions carried out by other *procuratores* see Chilver *ad loc.* **Cornelius Aquinus:** only here; possibly legate of the legion at Novaesium (mod. Neuss; Syme (1982b) 468). **Fabius Valens:** a major figure in *H.* 1–3, though barely noticed in the parallel tradition (cf. 6.1n. *Cornelius Laco*), he flourished both under Nero and in 68–9 (*PIR*² F 68) and was accorded by T. a devastating obituary: 3.62.2 *natus erat Valens Anagniae equestri familia. procax moribus neque absurdus ingenio famam urbanitatis per lasciuiam petere. ludicro Iuuenalium sub Nerone uelut ex necessitate, mox sponte mimos actitauit, scite magis quam probe. legatus legionis et fouit Verginium et infamauit; Fonteium Capitonem corruptum, seu quia corrumpere nequiuerat, interfecit, Galbae proditor, Vitellio fidus et aliorum perfidia illustratus.* In 68 he and his legion joined Galba's party (Plut. *G.* 10.3) but he later urged Verginius (unsuccessfully) and Vitellius (successfully, 57.1n.) to depose him. His march to Italy occupies chh. 62–6 of Book 1, his role in the defeat of Otho 2.27–45, his period of supremacy 2.51–3.40. He was suffect consul in the fall of 69 and dead by November or December (3.62.1). **antequam iuberentur:** for Galba's reaction to a similar anticipation cf. 35.2 *'commilito', inquit, 'quis iussit?'*; see 52.3 for his coolness to Valens. For *antequam* + subj. in a purely temporal clause (i.e. not indicating purpose) see *NLS* §228b.

7.2 fuere qui crederent Capitonem... abstinuisse: Plutarch (*G.* 15.2) and Suetonius (*G.* 11) consider both Capito and Macer rebels; a rather obscure notice in Dio shows Capito arrogating the title 'Caesar' (64.2.3). In the preceding sentence and at 52.3 T. follows this common version, but suspicion about Valens' motives in arranging for Capito's death appears here and in the obituary for Valens (quoted above), supplemented there by the evidence of Valens' career of treachery: he supported Galba's coup only to abandon him for Vitellius, and urged Verginius to claim supreme power then gave evidence against him; Capito would be a third victim. A parallel to Valens' alleged failure with Capito is narrated in unwonted detail at 4.49–50.3 (still another more briefly at 4.27.2), where T. remarks on the difficulty of ascertaining the truth in such events (4.49.1). Plutarch and Dio are content to assign ultimate responsibility for Capito's death to Galba; Suetonius does not raise the question. **ut...ita:** concessive (4.2n.); greed and loose morals were regularly ascribed to revolutionaries in Rome (e.g. Sal. *Cat.* 5.7 on Catiline and 14.2–3, 23.1–3 on his associates); for Capito cf. 52.1 *sordes et auaritiam Fontei Capitonis.* **postquam... nequiuerint:** primary sequence shifts the point of view to that of the *legati* as they came to terms with Capito's refusal, a rhetorical device – *repraesentatio* 'making present (to the mind)' (*NLS* §284) – favoured by T. In Book 1: 21.2 *sit*, 32.2 *sit*, 33.1 *discat*, 34.2 *uulgauerint*, 79.2 *obstiterit*; for a comparable situation cf. 2.41.1. For the abrupt derivation of the subject from a preceding agent (*legatis*) cf. 15.3n. *felicitate corrumpimur* and Sörbom (1935) 138. **compositum:** sc. *esse.* **mobilitate ingenii:** twice used of Vitellius apropos of specific changes of mind (2.57.2, 3.84.4), but not echoed in any other description of Galba's character; here it may indicate that Galba's initial approval of Capito and ratification of his command were effectively reversed by acquiescence in his murder. For the *uariatio* causal abl. ~ purpose clause cf. 26.1 *non... cura... sed ne... destinaretur*, 39.2 *siue ut... mulceret,... uel odio* and Sörbom (1935) 114. **an ne... scrutaretur:** *scrutari* 'investigate' *OLD* 2. *an* adds an alternative explanation, as at 28 *magnitudine subiti sceleris, an... metuens.* For the explanatory purpose clause cf. *A.* 3.3.1 *inferius maiestate sua rati... an ne... falsi intellegerentur*, 4.8.2 *nullo metu an ut firmitudinem animi ostentaret*, 13.9.1. This construction – 'T. is most conspicuous in its use', Goodyear (1972) *ad A.* 1.13.6 – is an abbreviated alternative indirect question: 'it is uncertain whether from... or...'. At 49.3 *usque ad culpam ignarus* T. himself charges Galba with failure to investigate and curtail the crimes of his associates. Vitellius had the same weakness (2.59.1). On behalf of the absent Vespasian, however, Mucianus kept a vigilant eye on important Flavian supporters and made many prudent adjustments to the constellation of powers, moving the praetorian prefect to *cura annonae* (4.68.2), stripping a general of his legion but rewarding his friends (Antonius Primus, 4.39.4, cf. 4.80.1–2 for Vespasian's cooperation), reining in young Domitian (4.51.2, 4.68.3, 4.85.2), etc. **quoquo modo acta** 'the deeds, however done', obj. of *comprobasse* 'sanction' *OLD* 4b. **seu bene seu mala facta:** in Plutarch a comparable consequence (18.1 'even Galba's moderate measures were criticized' καὶ τὰ μετρίως πραττόμενα διαβολὴν εἶχεν) follows instead upon Vinius' association with Tigellinus, which T. reserves for later (72.2). For other displacements of source material see App. 4. **parem inuidiam:** Bezzenberger's satisfying emendation for M's *premi-nuit iam* (see Wellesley's app.crit.).

7.3 uenalia cuncta: sc. *erant*; details in Plutarch and Suetonius: protection for Tigellinus and Turpilianus' death (Plut. *G.* 17.2–3, cf. Suet. *G.* 15.2 *impunitates noxiorum, poenas innocentium*), remission of tribute and grants of citizenship in Gaul (Plut. *G.* 18.1, cf. Suet. *G.* 15.2 *uectigalia, immunitates*), backing for Otho (Plut. *G.* 20.3, 21.1). **praepotentes liberti:** only Icelus is named in the sources (13.1 n.; Plutarch mistakenly mentions Vitellius' freedman Asiaticus, *G.* 20.4, cf. Suet. *Vit.* 12). For the expression cf. 3.47.1 *Anicetus Polemonis libertus, praepotens olim.* **subitis** 'in unforeseen circumstances'; the concision of this substantival adj. made it useful to T.: 69 *uulgus mutabile subitis, A.* 15.59.2 *subitis terreri, A.* 14.55.1 *subita expedire.* **tamquam apud senem festinantes:** for causal *tamquam* without a finite verb ('on the ground of being' *OLD* 7b) cf. 48.3 *tamquam . . . furatus. apud* 'in dealing with' *OLD* 15. In Plutarch it is Vinius who exhibited haste (*G.* 16.4 'Seeing that Galba was old and weak, Vinius took his fill of good luck on the ground that its beginning practically coincided with its ending'); for the same motive, differently phrased, cf. 3.41.1 *ruentis fortunae nouissima libido* and the *sententia* at 2.47.1 *difficilius est temperare felicitati, qua te non putes diu usurum.* **eademque nouae aulae mala** 'the evils of the new court were the same' (sc. as those of the old). *aula* 'court' is shorthand for 'the emperor's household and closest associates'. Used elsewhere of the courts of mythological kings and eastern dynasts, in T. (who is the first to use *aula* of a Roman ruler) particularly of Nero (13.4, 22.1, 2.7.1., *A.* 15.34.2, cf. 2.95.2 (Vitellius), *A.* 1.7.5 and *A.* 2.43.5 (Tiberius), *A.* 6.43.1 (Tiridates)). The reference to Nero's court signals the end of the compositional unit begun with *finis Neronis.* **imperatores forma ac decore corporis . . . comparantibus:** Plutarch specifies baldness and wrinkles (*G.* 13.4), Suetonius adds a hooked nose, severe deformity of the joints, and a pendulous hernia (*G.* 21). Age and appearance are also factors in the soldiers' comparison of the Vitellian commanders Fabius Valens and Caecina Alienus (52.3n., cf. 53.1 *decorus iuuenta*, 66.2 *senex prodigus*). Age compounded by infirmity hobbles Hordeonius Flaccus in the estimation of his troops (9.1n.). **ut est mos:** in Book 1 at 69, 79.4, 80.2; T. also uses *ut moris est* (15.1), simple *ut in* (55.4), and a variety of abl. expressions (90.3 *ex more*, 18.2 *more militari*, 32.1 and 44.2 *tradito more*, 55.1 *insita mortalibus natura*); cf. also 56.1 *quod . . . accidit.*

8.1 et hic quidem Romae: 5.2n. **hic . . . habitus animorum fuit** 'this was the array of opinions'; cf. 28 *isque habitus animorum fuit ut pessimum facinus auderent pauci, plures uellent, omnes paterentur.* **tamquam in tanta multitudine** 'as is (sc. normal) in such a large population'; Plutarch uses a similar expression in an actual crowd scene at *G.* 26.3 'as was (sc. normal) in so great a crowd' οἷα δὲ ἐν πλήθει τοσούτωι. The use of *tamquam* to compare entities that are nearly identical (here *Roma* and *multitudo*, cf. 33.2 and 75.1 for *tanta multitudo* of Rome's population) is peculiar: no parallels are listed at *OLD* 1c, and the ostensible parallel in GG (36.2 *tamquam in populo ac plebe*) compares the populace with soldiers. **Hispaniae praeerat Cluuius Rufus:** in 68 the governors of the three provinces of Roman Spain (Tarraconensis, Lusitania, Baetica) were Galba, Otho, and an unknown (perhaps one of Galba's two victims in Spain (37.3n. *occisi . . . in Hispania*). The singular of *Hispania* suggests that when Galba and Otho left for Rome Cluvius Rufus (on whom see below) assumed the command of all three provinces, as does a later allegation that the style of the edicts he signed as governor betrayed a claim to 'control of the provinces of Spain' (2.65.1 *possessio Hispaniarum*). Spain remained under his authority through the reign of Vitellius (76.1, 4.39.4, 2.97.1). T. does not mention the forces at the governor's disposal (Galba's *legio* VI and eventually X *Gemina*; Syme (1982b) 469); Cluvius did not use them (2.58.2–59.1). No new threat to imperial stability would arise in Spain; later Vitellius affirmed Rufus' position *nulla formidine* (2.65.2). **Cluuius Rufus:** a former consul, he served as herald for Nero's singing tours in Italy and Greece (Suet. *Ner.* 21.2, Dio 63.14.3; *PIR*^{2} C 1206). The date of his consulship is not known (but see Syme (1958) 293–4 and Townend (1961) 234–5). Subsequently he received a command from Galba, praise from both Otho (76.1) and Helvidius Priscus (4.43.1), vindication from Vitellius (2.65.2), and, apparently, a secure retirement from Vespasian (Plin. *Ep.* 9.19.5 records an anecdote from the Flavian period). Obsequiousness (2.65.1) and avoiding offence (4.43.1) seem to have been his hallmarks. For his *History*, possibly among T.'s sources, see Intro. §17. **uir facundus et pacis artibus, bellis inexpertus** 'a man of eloquence and civility but untried in war'. For Rufus' speaking ability cf. 4.43.1 *eloquentia clarus*, for his avoidance of military activity in this period see 2.58.2–59.1. The description rests on a civilian~military antithesis (cf. *A.* 13.2.1 *diuersa arte ex aequo pollebant, Burrus militaribus curis et seueritate morum, Seneca praeceptis eloquentiae et comitate honesta*), which suggests that *facundus* and *pacis artibus*, which are linked by *et*, are contrasted as a unit with *bellis inexpertus*, which stands in asyndeton with the pair. For the combination of eloquence with other *artes*, particularly the ability to please, cf. the description of Seneca quoted above, 2.5.1 *aptior sermone, dispositu prouisuque rerum ciuilium peritus*, and 3.10.3 *et facundia aderat mulcendique uulgum artes et auctoritas*; for Rufus' ability to please see 2.65.1. For *artibus* cf. *A.* 1.13.1 *diuitem promptum, artibus egregiis*. For the picture here (minus the eloquence) cf. *Agr.* 16.3 *Trebellius segnior et nullis castrorum experimentis, comitate quadam curandi prouinciam tenuit*. If one supplies, as Chilver, Heubner, and others do, a notional *expertus* from *inexpertus* ('eloquent and experienced in the arts of peace, untried in war'), or, as Wellesley does, an actual <*aptus*>, *facundus* is left dangling. **proximae tamen Germanicis exercitibus Galliarum ciuitates:** cf. 11.2 *ut cuique exercitui uicinae* (sc. *prouinciae*). **super memoriam Vindicis:** Galba's contribution to Vindex' cause was limited (6.2n. *opprimendis . . . coeptis*), but as emperor Galba publicly honoured Vindex' memory (Plut. *G.* 22.2), rewarded his partisans, and punished his opponents (see below). *super* 'over and above' (*OLD* 7) also at 14.1 and 51.4. **obligatae:** sc. *sunt*. **recenti dono Romanae ciuitatis:** the recipients are not known; it was certainly not all of Gaul, as tribute was still being paid, albeit at a reduced rate (see below), and the Lingones received citizenship from Otho after Galba's death (78.1n.). Pliny records only a grant of Latin status to two Alpine tribes (*Nat.* 3.37). Plutarch lists the concession of citizenship among the 'moderate acts' of Galba (*G.* 18.1) but it was at odds with normal Roman policy in Tres Galliae, where only the citizens of Lugdunum (mod. Lyon) had full Roman citizenship. The grants of both Galba and Otho were instances of a more general pattern of extraordinary favours designed to attract the support of various provincial groups. In addition to the substantial benefactions listed here, Galba cancelled the trade tariffs for Gaul (see below) and gave a consulship to a man from Vienne (65.1n. *et Viennenses*). Vitellius married his daughter to a prominent senator from Vienne, Valerius Asiaticus (59.2n.). Otho was even more generous with what T. calls his *largitio* (78.1n.). Vespasian granted colonial status to the *ciuitas*-capital of the Helvetii (68.2). **in posterum tributi leuamento**: tribute, paid by all Gallic tribes since the reign of Tiberius, was reduced by a quarter (51.4; cf. 4.57.2 *infracta tributa*). Galba also cancelled border tolls (Suet. *Ves.* 16.1 *omissa sub Galba uectigalia*; de Laet (1949) 170–3). Tribute, a monetary symbol of subjugation, was still a grievance under Vespasian (4.17.4, 4.26.1, 4.32.2, 4.64.1, 4.65.3), but rather than sacrifice income from this source Vespasian relieved the Gauls of conscription: 4.71.2 *recepta iuuentute facilius tributa tolerauere*. T. puts a defence of *tributum* in the mouth of Vespasian's general Cerialis at 4.74.1–2. **proximae tamen Germanicis exercitibus Galliarum ciuitates:** the Treveri (of Trier, equidistant from the legionary bases at Moguntiacum and Bonna) and the Lingones (of Andemantunnum, mod. Langres, not adjacent to any base but evidently in contact with the legions: 54.1n.) incite the Vitellians at 53.3; to these are linked the Ubii of Cologne (Vitellius' base, 57.2). The Mediomatrici of Metz (63.1) and the Leuci of Toul (64.1) also supported the forces gathering against Galba. **quaedam etiam finibus ademptis:** cf. 53.3 *damno finium*. Suetonius (*G.* 12.1) also reports increased tribute, dismantled fortifications, and executions. **pari dolore commoda aliena ac suas iniurias metiebantur:** rephrased at 54.1 *modo suas iniurias modo uicinarum ciuitatium praemia ... conquerentes. dolore* names the scale on which the measure is taken, cf. Cic. *Fin.* 5.93 *isti ipsi* (sc. *Epicurei*) *qui uoluptate et dolore omnia metiuntur.*

8.2 quod 'a circumstance that'; the antecedent is the main clause (*NLS* §230.6); cf. 14.1 *quod remedium unicum rebatur*, 56.1 *quod in seditionibus accidit.* **tantis uiribus:** seven legions were quartered along the Rhine at this date, three in Upper Germany (one at Vindonissa, two at Moguntiacum), four in Lower Germany (one each at Bonna and Novaesium, two at Vetera). **solliciti et irati:** sc. *erant. solliciti* 'anxious' is explained chiastically by *metu*, *irati* by *superbia*. The state of mind is more fully described in 51.1–5. **superbia recentis uictoriae:** cf. *A.* 14.38.3 *superbia uictoris*; here the gen. does duty for a causal clause, producing *uariatio* in the modifiers of the parallel abl. *superbia* and *metu*. T. is briefer and more abstract than Plutarch: *G.* 18.3 'thinking themselves deserving of great rewards on account of the battle they had fought against Vindex'. For their resentment of *contumeliae* see 54.1. **metu tamquam alias partes fouissent:** for particulars see 51.5. For *tamquam* ('on the grounds that' *OLD* 7b) after *metus*, expressing past or present causes of fear – a construction unique to T. – cf. 20.3 *metus initium, tamquam ... singuli pellerentur*, 4.46.3 *metus per omnes et praecipua Germanici militis formido tamquam ... ad caedem destinaretur.* **tarde a Nerone desciuerant:** the vagueness of *tarde* obstructs attempts to fix the chronology of the second quarter of 68 (Murison (1993) 17–26) but should not obscure the content of *desciuerant*: the German armies abandoned Nero while he was still alive. (The point is reinforced by *partes fouissent* in the preceding sentence – this cannot refer to support for Nero, their legitimate ruler.) Verginius Rufus, the commander of the army of Upper Germany, was their initial candidate for replacing Nero. *desciuerant* reflects their rudderless predicament after Verginius referred the choice of *princeps* to the Senate: they were detached from Nero but lacked direction. Both here and at Plut. *G.* 6.3–4 the soldiers' choice is separated from that of their commander(s). **nec statim pro Galba Verginius:** cf. 52.3 *Verginii cunctationem*. L. Verginius Rufus was one of the many talented Italians who prospered in imperial service. Born into an equestrian family from Transpadane Italy in Augustus' last year (A.D. 13/4), he reached the consulship under Nero at the relatively late age of forty-nine or fifty (cos. 63, *A.* 15.23.1; *PIR* v 284). In 68 he was in command of the three-legion army of Upper Germany and, against Vindex, also of units from the Lower army and Gallic auxiliaries (51.3, 53.2, 4.17.3; Murison (1993) 9 n. 25). Victorious, they offered to make their commander emperor. The sources agree in placing the acclamation of Verginius before Nero's death (Dio 63.25.1, Plut. *G.* 6.1, cf. Suet. *Ner.* 47.1, with Murison (1993) 16–20). Verginius refused, and eventually accepted Galba, the senate's choice, as his emperor. T. gave the eulogy at Verginius' public funeral as consul in 97, but from the *Histories*' fragmented account of him in 68/9 no laudable picture emerges. See further Shotter (1967). **an imperare noluisset dubium:** sc. *erat. dubium* challenges the report of Pliny, Verginius' ward and protégé (*Ep.* 2.1.2 *noluisset*). Only one of the alternative questions implied here is expressed. In such constructions the content of the other is usually obvious either from the context (cf. e.g. *A.* 15.64.1 *incertum an ignarae* (sc. *an gnarae*), *A.* 5.1.2 *incertum an inuitam* (sc. *an uolentem*)). Here supply *uoluisse*. Dio 63.25.3 is much fuller: 'whether because he did not think it right that soldiers should confer imperial power (for he said that this was the business of the senate and people) or because he was entirely high-minded and had no need of the autocratic power that other men did their all for'. **delatum ei a milite imperium:** sc. *esse*. The first of at least two such abortive acclamations. T. reports another after Otho's defeat at Bedriacum (2.51, cf. πολλάκις 'often' at Plut. *G.* 6.1, Dio 63.25.1. See further Levick (1985) 334–5). **conueniebat** 'it was agreed' *OLD* 7. **Fonteium Capitonem occisum:** sc. *esse*. 7.1–2nn. **dux deerat:** cf. 53.3 *in Verginium fauor cuicumque alii profuturus*. The situation in Rome was comparable: 6.2 *ut non in unum aliquem prono fauore*. **abducto Verginio per simulationem amicitiae:** Verginius, replaced by Hordeonius Flaccus in Upper Germany, travelled to Rome in Galba's entourage. No further military commands are attested for him. T.'s expression, darker than Plutarch's (*G.* 10.3 'turned back in Galba's company without receiving any indication of anger or esteem'), reflects the mood of the soldiers (cf. *indignabantur*, and *in suum crimen accipiebant*). **quem:** connecting relative (= *et eum*), a construction of which T. makes sparing use in Book 1: 22.2 *e quibus*, 24.2 *quam*, 25.1 *a quo*, 37.2 *cuius*, 52.3 *e quibus*, 65.1 *unde*. **reum esse:** an exaggerated reference to hostile reports made by Fabius Valens (3.62.2 *Verginium . . . infamauit*).

9.1 legatum Hordeonium Flaccum: Galba's replacement for Verginius Rufus; *PIR*[2] H 202. He retained his command under Vitellius (2.57.1) and Vespasian (4.31.1). The failings listed here are amply documented in the narrative, where Flaccus is unable to impose his will on his troops (54.2, 56.1, 4.19.2). He was, in T.'s repeatedly expressed opinion, compliant to a fault (4.19.2, 4.24.3, 4.25.1, 4.36.2). His change of mind at 4.19.2 was disastrous to Roman resistance to Civilis and his poor health encouraged him to delegate important commands to subordinates, whose leadership and courage contrasted with his own *segnitia* and *ignauia* (56.1, 4.19.2, cf. 4.18.1, 4.24.1, 4.25.4, 4.27.2). On top of all this, he was a traitor to the emperor chosen by his own troops, encouraging Civilis' defection and thus aiding Vespasian (4.24.2, cf. 2.97.1, 4.13.3, 4.27.3, 5.26.3). His troops followed his lead in taking the oath to Vespasian with obvious reluctance, and the donative he paid in Vespasian's name (but with Vitellius' money) financed a night of celebration in which Flaccus was dragged from his quarters and killed by his own men (4.31.2, 4.36.1–2). The present passage suggests that the explanation for the whole shocking story of Flaccus' behaviour in 69–70 lies in his character, *sine constantia, sine auctoritate*. In Plutarch's account (*G.* 18.4) gout and inexperience explain the legions' scorn for their commander, but T. would have known that a governor of Germany was unlikely to have lacked experience of command.

On a possible background for Flaccus see D'Arms (1998). For a similarly incompetent governor see 79.5 *M. Aponius.* **debilitate pedum:** presumably T. felt 'gout' (*podagra*, cf. Plut. *G.* 18.3) unsuited to the dignity of history. **ne quieto quidem milite regimen:** sc. *ei erat.* **adeo furentes . . . accendebantur:** *adeo* 'all the more' (*OLD* 7) after a negative (*ne . . . quidem*) is a form of antithesis favoured only by T. and the elder Pliny (*TLL* s.v. 607.45–67). The inconcinnity of the phrases forming the antithesis here (*quieto milite~furentes*) makes this the most difficult example in T. **inferioris Germaniae legiones:** 55.2nn. **A. Vitellius:** born in either A.D. 12 (3.86.1, Suet. *Vit.* 18) or 15 (Suet. *Vit.* 3, Dio 65.22), as a youth one of Tiberius' ill-famed companions on Capri (Suet. *Vit.* 3.2; cf. Dio 64.4.2); he later made himself agreeable to Caligula (via chariot-driving), Claudius (via gambling), and Nero (in connection with his singing, all in Suet. *Vit.* 4), and to Galba's associate T. Vinius (as a fan of the same racing team, Suet. *Vit.* 7.1; *PIR* V 499). His first consulship came early (cos. 48), in the year following his father's third. He later filled his deceased father's spot as one of the Arval Brethren. His success was variously ascribed to his father's influence (3.86.1) or to sexual favours (Suet. *Vit.* 3.2). Before being chosen by Galba for Lower Germany he spent two years in Africa, one as governor, one as legate during his brother's governorship, and held the office of *curator operum publicorum* (Suet. *Vit.* 5; for his brother see 88.1 n.). Suetonius reports that his appointment to Germany was a surprise, and was motivated by Galba's belief that a man who spent all his time thinking about eating would pose no threat to his own position (*Vit.* 7.1). T., whose portrait of Vitellius is equally, but differently, negative, credits him with the virtues of *simplicitas* and *liberalitas* (3.86.1–2). See further 52.4n. *segne ingenium* and Engel. **censoris Vitellii ac ter consulis:** Vitellius' father had an exceptional *cursus*: cos. 34, cos. iterum 43, cos. III 47, censor 47–8; *PIR* V 500; see also App. 1.

9.2 in Britannico exercitu nihil irarum: Britain itself saw no action in the civil war (60nn.) but its legions – II *Augusta*, IX *Hispana*, XX *Valeria* (3.22.2) – sent detachments to Nero (6.2) and Vitellius (2.57.2, 2.100.1, cf. 4.46.2). **seu quia procul et Oceano diuisae, seu crebris expeditionibus doctae hostem potius odisse:** cf. 2.32.1 *Britannicum militem hoste et mari distineri*, 3.2.2 *Britanniam freto dirimi*, *Agr.* 16.3 *assuetus expeditionibus miles* (sc. *Britannicus*). With *procul* read *erant. Oceano* is abl. of means; cf. *A.* 2.43.1 *prouinciae quae mari diuiderentur.* For the *uariatio* of causal clause ~ predicate adj. see Sörbom (1935) 115.

9.3 quies et Illyrico: sc. *erat. Illyrico* is dat.; cf. 60 *quies prouinciae . . . mansit.* **quamquam . . . adissent:** in Book 1 T. uses *quamquam* once with the indicative (this was the construction used by authors before Livy), once with the subj. (the construction common, though not exclusive, in Livy and T.), and often with the verb in ellipsis (14.1, 43.1n.). **excitae a Nerone legiones:** the provinces of the area called Illyricum were garrisoned as follows: Pannonia with VII *Galbiana*, XIII *Gemina*, XIV *Gemina Martia Victrix*, Dalmatia with XI *Claudia*, Moesia with III *Gallica*, VII *Claudia*, VIII *Augusta*. Vexillations dispatched from Illyricum for Nero's Caspian war had been recalled to face Vindex and were apparently in Rome in early January (6.2, 31.3). **quod:** 8.2n. **nec uitiis nec uiribus miscebantur** 'they shared with one another neither their weaknesses nor their strength', implicitly contrasting these legions with those of Germany, where both Vetera and Moguntiacum housed two legions. For a similar syllepsis cf. *Agr.* 25.1 *mixti copiis et laetitia.* The alliterative pair *uitiis~uiribus* (abl. of respect) is a variation on the more common antithesis *uitia ac uirtutes* (5.2, 30.1, 49.2, 52.2, 71.1, etc.).

10.1 Oriens adhuc immotus: sc. *erat.* The lightly garrisoned provinces of the area are not mentioned in the survey: Galatia, Cappadocia, perhaps Lycia-Pamphylia; these lay on or near Mucianus' route to Italy (Jos. *BJ* 4.632). See also 11.3n. *inermes prouinciae.* **Syriam et quattuor legiones:** on 1 January there were in fact only three legions in Syria (IV *Scythica*, VI *Ferrata*, XII *Fulminata*). The fourth, III *Gallica*, had been transferred to Moesia, but Mucianus reckoned on its continued loyalty (2.74.1 *suam numerabat*), correctly (2.85.1); its legate was unchanged (79.5n. *Fuluus Aurelius*). **Licinius Mucianus:** despite Mucianus' notoriety, little is known about his family and early career: *PIR*[2] L 216. He governed the province of Lycia under Nero (Plin. *Nat.* 12.10, 13.88) and held a suffect consulship some time before his appointment in 68 to the heavily garrisoned province of Syria. Under Vespasian he served two further suffect consulships in 70 and 72. His death seems to fall between 75 (the dramatic date of *D.*, in which he is alive: 37.2) and 77 or 78, when Pliny was writing Book 32 of *Nat.* (32.62). In the extant books of *H.* he is an effective administrator and regent (3.66.3 *specimen partium Mucianus*, cf. 2.76–7, 2.83.1, 4.46.2–4, Dio 66.2). His tactics, however, are frighteningly unscrupulous: confiscations (2.84.1), secret letters (3.52.2–3, 4.80.2, cf. 3.53.3), murders (4.11.2, 4.49.2–4, 4.80.1). Such actions contributed to his reputation for arrogance (2.5.1 *cuncta priuatum modum supergressa*, 4.4.1, 4.80.1). T. does not allude to the charge of effeminate sexuality (Suet. *Ves.* 13 *impudicitia*; see below on *nimiae uoluptates*) or to the most famous of Mucianus' writings, the collection of *mirabilia* mined by Pliny for *Nat.* (e.g. 12.10, 13.88). He does, however, mention Mucianus' collection of the *Acta* (eleven books) and *Epistulae* (three books) of prominent figures from the Republic (*D.* 37.2). See further 76.2. For Mucianus' origin see Syme (1958) App. 85. **secundis aduersisque iuxta famosus** 'equally notorious in success and failure' (Martin (1981) 217); cf. Plin. *Ep.* 4.9.1 *aduersis suis clarus.* The abls. indicate that *famosus* is used *in malam partem*; cf. *A.* 3.7.2 *famosam ueneficiis Martinam*, and *A.* 6.30.1 *Seruilius Corneliusque perdito Scauro famosi.* **attritis opibus:** for the metaphor cf. Sal. *Jug.* 5.4 *Hannibal... Italiae opes maxume attriuerat* and 89.2 *plebem... attriuerat.* **in secretum Asiae sepositus:** for *sepono* of informal exile cf. 13.3 *seposuit* and *A.* 4.44.3 *hunc... seposuit Augustus in ciuitatem Massiliensem, ubi specie studiorum nomen exilii tegeretur.* **prope ab** 'near' *OLD* 1b; for Mucianus' later position cf. 2.83.1 *socium magis imperii quam ministrum agens.*

10.2 luxuria industria, comitate arrogantia, malis bonisque artibus mixtus: sc. *est.* For the contrasts cf. *A.* 4.1.3 *illi... iuxta adulatio et superbia... modo largitio et luxus, saepius industria ac uigilantia*; like this description of Sejanus, that of Mucianus harks back to Sallust's characterization of Catiline (see M–W on *A.* 4.1.3, and on *uariis illecebris potens* below). For the source abl. with *misceo* ('produce by mixing' *OLD* 2) cf. *Agr.* 4.2 *locum Graeca comitate et prouinciali parsimonia mixtum.* The balance between energy and laxity that characterizes Mucianus contrasts with the (excessive) vigour of Galba's associate, T. Vinius, in whom virtues and vices were likewise mixed (48.4). **nimiae uoluptates:** sc. *ei erant.* None is mentioned in the extant books, which cover the period of Mucianus' greatest activity. Suetonius reports his reputation for *impudicitia*; a quip attributed to Vespasian ('*ego tamen uir sum*') suggests that effeminacy is meant (Suet. *Ves.* 13). The asymmetry of the adj. in the antithesis (*nimiae~magnae*) reflects the Roman attitude towards pleasure: *uoluptas* was inherently excessive. **cum uacaret; quotiens expedierat:** for the *uariatio* of conjunction and mood cf. *A.* 1.44.5 *si... approbauerant... ubi... obiectauissent.* From the antithesis Chilver infers that *expedierat* does not have its ordinary impersonal construction ('it was advantageous') but means rather 'was on campaign' (as at 88.1 *expedire*), but in antithesis *uacare* is usually paired with a general, not a specific, term for activity (e.g. Sen. *Dial.* 4.13.2 *uacat pudicitia, libido occupatissima est*, Sen. *Ep.* 49.9 *non uaco ad istas ineptias; ingens negotium in manibus est,* etc.) and Mucianus' *uirtutes* were not in fact limited to the military sphere. To the familiar contrast between inactivity and activity T. has added the idea of activity's potential for profit. His antithesis elides the middle term (activity). **palam laudares, secreta male audiebant** 'in public you would praise him but his private life was criticized'; similar in expression to 64.4 *secretis eum criminationibus infamauerat Fabius ignarum, et . . . palam laudatum*, but here with the double antithesis complicated by the change of mood and subject and the variation *palam~secreta*. The potential subj. of *laudares* stimulates (and directs) the reader's moral judgment (cf. 45.1 *alium crederes senatum, alium populum*, 57.1 *scires illum . . . non penes rem publicam fuisse*; for further examples and discussion see Gilmartin (1975) and Kenney (1990) *ad* Apul. *Met.* 5.1.3). The non-personal subject of *male audiebant* is unusual but not unprecedented (cf. Ov. *Tr.* 5.11.3 *mea . . . fortuna male audit*). Past editors have argued for a precise antithesis between *palam* and *secreta* by assuming that *palam* = *palam facta* (thus Valmaggi, Heubner, Alford, Chilver, the last with reservations), but for this assumption no parallel has been found in T., bold as he is with this adverb (Goodyear (1972) on *A.* 1.3.3), or elsewhere. Emendation has not been attempted since the antitheses protect the text; it seems better to assume that in this condensation of material T. has allowed himself to merge the concepts of public deeds and public praise. That is, one need not assume that *palam* = *palam facta* but should rather infer from *palam laudares* that the object of public praise is Mucianus' public record. For his *secreta* see above on *nimiae uoluptates.* **uariis illecebris potens, et cui expeditius fuerit tradere imperium quam obtinere:** with *potens* read *erat.* The primary sequence of *fuerit* reflects the author's overall judgment of a character: *A.* 2.88.2 *liberator haud dubie Germaniae et qui non primordia populi Romani . . . sed florentissimum imperium lacessierit*, an obituary. Power gained via *illecebrae* is a feature of Catiline's characterization in both Cicero (*Cat.* 2.8) and Sallust (*Cat.* 14.4, 16.1, with details at 14.6: to some associates he provided women, for others he bought dogs and horses, etc.) but elsewhere it is attributed principally to women (Caecil. 234–6 Ribbeck^3 *istam in uicinitatem te meretriciam cur contulisti? cur illecebris cognitis non . . . refugisti?*, Virg. *G.* 3.217 *dulcibus . . . illecebris iuuencae*, Tac. *A.* 14.2.1 *muliebres illecebras*, *A.* 12.3.1 *Agrippinae illecebris*). Mucianus' technique is not illustrated in the extant books.

10.3 bellum Iudaicum: Josephus places the outbreak of this war for independence in May 66 (*BJ* 2.284, cf. Suet. *Ves.* 4.5). By 69 the principal task remaining was the capture of Jerusalem (2.4.3). **Flauius**

Vespasianus: the future Imperator Caesar Vespasianus Augustus, born T. Flavius Vespasianus (*PIR*[2] F 398). For his background and early career see Suet. *Ves.* 1–4.4. His virtues, according to T., were those of the typical *uir militaris*, his principal fault *auaritia* (2.5.1; 50.4n. *ambigua* . . . *fama*). This first mention of the man who will be the focus of ten years of the *Histories*' narrative is very brief; his partner, Mucianus, receives more attention in the extant books (Syme (1958) 195). **nec . . . aduersus Galbam uotum aut animus:** sc. *erat* 'toward Galba neither his wish nor his attitude was hostile'. **suo loco:** *H.* 2.1–3. **occulta fati . . . destinatum . . . imperium:** with *destinatum* read *esse*. For the *uariatio* substantive ~ acc. + inf. in the objects of *credidimus* see Sörbom (1935) 111. **ostentis ac responsis:** *ostenta* are signs, *responsa* oracular responses; cf. *Agr.* 13.5 *monstratus fatis Vespasianus*. Flavian propaganda was effective in getting both into the historical record: 2.4.2, 2.78.2–4, 4.81–2, 5.13.1, Suet. *Ves.* 5.2–7, 7.1–3. **post fortunam:** *fortuna* is a brief and abstract reference to the possession of imperial power, eliding the complicated and messy business whereby it was acquired (for Vitellius see 62.2 and 77.1). For *post* cf. Sal. *Jug.* 5.4 *post magnitudinem nominis Romani*. **credidimus**: for the 'associative we' marking collective connivance in the evils of the imperial system cf. *Agr.* 2.3, 45.1 and see Sinclair (1995) 53–62.

11.1 copiasque quibus coerceretur: two legions, III *Cyrenaica* and XXII *Deiotariana*, and auxiliary units, amounting to some 17,000–18,000 men (*CAH*[2] X 687, Lewis (1983) 19–20). *coercere* is used frequently for a government's control of its citizens' excesses (e.g. 35.2, 89.2) but rarely of the control of territory (*A.* 4.5.2 *cetera Africae per duas legiones parique numero Aegyptus . . . coercita*, elsewhere only at Ov. *Pont.* 3.3.61 *sic regat imperium terrasque coerceat omnes*). **loco regum** 'in place of the pharaohs' *OLD* 20 s.v. *locus*; cf. Strabo 17.797 'the prefect has the position of the pharaoh'. **uisum:** sc. *est*. **aditu difficilem:** cf. *B. Alex.* 26.2 *tota Aegyptus maritimo accessu Pharo, pedestri Pelusio, uelut claustris munita existimatur.* **superstitione ac lasciuia discordem et mobilem:** Egyptian *superstitio* and an instance of the resulting social discord form the subject of Juvenal *Sat.* 15; see Courtney (1980) *ad* 15.2–12 for the poem's historicity. **insciam legum, ignarum magistratuum:** magistrates and laws defined a free state for the Romans; T. may be elaborating on Polybius' first-hand assessment of the native population as 'quick to anger and apolitical' (ὀξὺ καὶ ἀπολιτικόν, quoted by Strabo 17.797). Egypt was never free on the Roman definition but it was not without laws and an elaborate administrative structure (Lewis (1983) 156–95, CAH^2 x 684–6). **domui** 'under the control of the imperial house' (Ricklefs, Halm: *domi* MSS); possession indicated by the loc. *domi* is concrete (e.g. *domi habuisti pecuniam*) not metaphorical (*TLL* s.v. 1956.71–1957.4). **regebat tum Tiberius Alexander, eiusdem nationis:** Tiberius Julius Alexander (PIR^2 I 139) was born in Alexandria but with the label 'Egyptian' (*eiusdem nationis*) T. short-changes him. He was a member of a prominent Jewish family of Alexandria; for T.'s hostility to his Jewish material see Syme (1958) 467–9, 530; *contra*, Feldman. He pursued an equestrian career, necessarily abandoning Jewish observances to do so (Jos. *AJ* 20.100). Offices are attested for him under Claudius, Nero, Galba, and Vespasian. As prefect of Egypt in 68–9 he was naturally sought as a supporter by the imperial contenders. His choices were prudent: after Nero's suicide he issued an edict proclaiming Galba 'benefactor of all races of humankind' (6 July 68; *OGI* 669, lines 7 and 66; for text see Evelyn White and Oliver (1938) 23–44, for discussion Chalon (1964) 43–52, 78–88), in the struggle between Vitellius and Vespasian he backed East against West. He gave Vespasian his first public show of support by administering to the troops of Alexandria an oath of loyalty to Vespasian on 1 July 69, a date that became the official beginning of the Flavian era. In January of 69 he was still loyal to Galba (*P. Oxy.* 899, line 28). For his early discussions with Vespasian see 2.74.1, Jos. *BJ* 4.616–19.

11.2 Africa ac legiones in ea . . . contenta: sc. *erat.* On 1 January Africa had one official legion, III *Augusta*, and one legion in limbo, I *Macriana* (raised by Clodius Macer, disbanded by Galba, soon to be reconstituted by Vitellius (2.97.2); 7.1n. *Clodi Macri*). The compound subject shows the same juxtaposition as the items immediately preceding it in T.'s list: *Syriam et quattuor legiones* (10.1), *bellum Iudaicum . . . tribus legionibus* (10.3), and *Aegyptum copiasque* (11.1), all of which emphasize the political clout of the military in 68–9. Here a prepositional phrase is dependent directly on the noun, a construction that serves the twin goals of *uariatio* and brevity. *contenta* agrees with the more general member of the compound subject rather than the nearer one (K–S §15e). See Chilver for objections to the Latinity. **interfecto Clodio Macro:** 7.1n. **duae Mauretaniae:** Tingitana and Caesariensis, garrisoned by nineteen cohorts and five *alae* (2.58.1); for subsequent disturbances see 2.58–9. **Raetia, Noricum, Thracia:** Raetia bordered the Rhine military zone and supported Vitellius (59.2n. *Raeticis copiis*); its neighbour across the river Inn, Noricum, aligned itself with the legions of Illyricum in support of first Otho then Vespasian (70.2n. *Noricum*). Thrace, lying to the east of Illyricum, is not mentioned in the narrative but will have had its course decided late in 69, when Mucianus marched his forces through *en route* from Syria to Italy (Wellesley (1972) 211–15). **quae aliae procuratoribus cohibentur:** procuratorial provinces appearing in the narrative are Corsica, where loyalty was determined by the proximity of Otho's fleet (2.16.1–3; when the procurator Decumius Picarius flouted provincial opinion and based policy on his antipathy to Otho he paid with his life), and Alpes Maritimae, where the procurator, Marius Maturus, was steadfastly loyal to Vitellius (3.42.1). The remaining two, the other Alpine provinces, lay on or close to Valens' path to Italy and Valens made a point of demonstrating the penalty for non-compliance (61.1, 63.1). *cohibere* is not elsewhere used of civil government. **ut cuique exercitui uicinae:** sc. *erant*; for the persuasiveness of proximity cf. 64.1, 76.1.

11.3 inermes prouinciae: T. has mentioned the principal provinces ruled by imperial legates and procurators and the special cases of Judaea, Egypt, and Africa; remaining are the legionless provinces: Sicily, Sardinia, Narbonensis, Macedonia, Achaea, Asia, Bithynia/Pontus, Cyprus, Crete/Cyrene (4.45.2). They are explicitly dismissed at 2.81.2. **cuicumque seruitio exposita** 'available for the service of each and every (master)'. For subjection to an emperor not of one's choosing as *seruitium* cf. 2.6.2 *ne penes ceteros imperii praemia, penes ipsos tantum seruitii necessitas esset, fremere miles*, 4.2.2 *ciuitas pauida et seruitio parata*. The modifier here indicates the master, as at 4.54.1 *Vitellianae legiones uel externum seruitium quam imperatorem Vespasianum malle.* **in pretium belli cessurae erant** 'would become a prize of the war'; *cedere* 'turn into' *OLD* 17. For the idea cf. 70.3 *Noricos in certa uictoriae praemia cessuros*, 3.64.1 *omnia prona uictoribus*, 4.76.1 *Gallos quid aliud quam praedam uictoribus?* and *A.* 15.45.1 *inque eam praedam etiam di cessere, spoliatis in urbe templis.* **Seruius Galba iterum Titus Vinius consules:** cf. 1.1 *initium mihi operis Seruius Galba iterum Titus Vinius consules erunt.* The repetition signals the end of the preliminaries. For the structural device cf. the repetition Sallust uses to end the first digression in the *Bellum Catilinae*: 14.1 *in tanta tamque corrupta ciuitate Catilina* ~ 5.8 *incitabant praeterea corrupti ciuitatis mores.*

12–20 Galba's *acta*

After reviewing Galba's gradual loss of favour in Rome and the potential for turbulence in the provinces, T. allots chh. 12–20 to Galba's efforts to shore up his position. Principal among these was the adoption of a son to succeed him (chh. 12–19), but financial and disciplinary measures also appear (ch. 20). Throughout this section T.'s material is fuller, more accurate, and more richly elaborated than that in the parallel sources, with the exception of details dear to biographers. The disciplinary measure with which T. concludes, involving the praetorians, provides an easy transition to the following section on the origins of Otho's praetorian-backed coup (chh. 21–6). For the narrative proper, which begins here, T. uses a style much less abrupt than that of the summary. The composition of this section is discussed in Morgan (1993d).

12.1 paucis post kalendas Ianuarias diebus: nine events are dated precisely in Book 1, more than in any other of T.'s books. All but the last (90.1, 14 March) occur during the period 1–15 January, which is covered by simultaneous narratives, one set in Rome (12–47), the other on the Rhine (51–63). **Pompei Propinqui procuratoris:** only here. Loyal to Galba, he was murdered by Vitellians (58.1), whom the governor of his province supported (59.2n. *Valerius Asiaticus*). For the responsibilities of his post, which T.'s father might have held earlier (Plin. *Nat.* 7.76), see Drinkwater (1983) 98–102. **litterae afferuntur:** later in the year a Vitellian governor writes to Vitellius about the defection of a legion to Vespasian, and saves his skin by joining them (2.96.1; see 79.5n. *M. Aponius*). **rupta sacramenti reuerentia:** *reuerentia* functions as a kind of ethical brake, blocking actions that an individual or group is otherwise eager for: *reuerentia matris* keeps Nero from indulging passions (*A.* 14.13.2), *reuerentia ducis* keeps Vitellians from changing sides (*H.* 3.41.2), *reuerentia foederis* keeps the Parthian king Vologaeses from avenging a Roman insult (*A.* 15.1.1). In adapting the common phrase *rumpere foedus* (*TLL* s.v. *foedus* 1007.32–9) by applying *rupta* instead to the abstract noun *reuerentia* T. refers the particular act of breaking an oath to a more general ethical collapse (55.4n. *reuerentiam imperii exuere*). Suetonius uses a similar expression of this same event: *G.* 16.2 *obsequium rumpere*. Plutarch uses the idea in a speech (*G.* 22.4): 'It is as though we were averse, not to Galba, but to all rule and obedience'; for displacements of source material see App. 4. **arbitrium eligendi** 'the decision of the choice'. For the idea cf. Liv. 43.15.5 *praetores consulis in eligendo arbitrium fecerunt*, where the praetors allow a consul to decide the choice of legions for his command. For the objective gen. cf. Liv. 4.7.6 *arbitrium ... senatui leuandae iniuriae permittant.* In contrast to the parallel tradition, T. has the legions of Upper Germany echo the 'constitutionalist' line of their former commander, Verginius Rufus (Plut. *G.* 6.2 'Verginius ... declared that he would neither assume the imperial power himself nor allow it to be given to anyone else whom the senate did not elect'; 8.2n. *an ... dubium*).

12.2 maturauit 'brought to fruition' *OLD* 1c; for the metaphor cf. *D.* 3.3 *maturare libri huius editionem festino.* **iam pridem ... agitantis** 'deliberating for some time' *OLD* 18c. **tota ciuitate:** locative abl. (*NLS* §51 iii). **sermo:** e.g. the rumours about the adoption of Titus reported at 2.1.1. **licentia ac libidine ... dein fessa iam aetate Galbae:** causal abl., *licentia* and *libidine* being internal to the notional subject, the populace, *aetate* external. Setting the two types in parallel makes the explanation compact (cf. the much longer description of Augustus' decline and the hopes it raised at *A.* 1.4.2). T. follows poetic usage in applying *fessus* to abstractions (*aetas* 3.67.1, *A.* 1.46.3, 3.59.4, 14.33.1, 15.38.4; *res A.* 15.50.1; *imperium A.* 11.24.3; cf. Virg. *Aen.* 2.596 *fessum aetate parentem*, Sen. *H.F.* 1250 and *Ph.* 267 *anni fessi*, Luc. 2.128 *fessa senectus*). When used with nouns meaning 'age', a Virgilian innovation, *fessus* 'has a strong emotive force, with overtones of compassion for the helplessness of age' (Miller (1987b) 94).

12.3 paucis: sc. *erat.* **stulta** implies misguided expectations: 74.1 *stulta ... simulatione*, 3.54.1 *stulta dissimulatione*, *A.* 4.52.2 *sola exitii causa sit, quod Agrippinam stulte ... ad cultum delegerit.* **prout quis amicus uel cliens**: sc. *erat* 'according as he was anyone's friend or dependant'. *quis* = *quibus*, plural in preparation for *hunc uel illum.* Exemplified in the astrologer Ptolemaeus at 22.2. **ambitiosis** 'self-serving' (*OLD* 2) stands in antithesis to both *rei publicae amor* and *in T. Vini odium*; for the former cf. 19.1 *multi ... priuatas spes agitantes sine publica cura.* Sörbom (1935) cites no parallels for the *uariatio* adj. ~ *in* + acc. of purpose. **destinabant** 'marked out' *OLD* 7. **odium:** for the *uariatio* with the causal abl. (*spe*) cf. 72.2 *clementia ... effugium*, 76.1 *fides ... necessitate*, 76.2 *studio ... momentum.* **eodem actu** 'with the same force', the most innovative of T.'s several variations in the correlative pair *quanto ... tanto* (cf. 88.2n. *quanto*), is not found elsewhere. **hiantes ... cupiditates:** cf. Sen. *Ben.* 7.26.3 *aspice quemadmodum ... hominum cupiditates hient.* The verb *hiare*, apt for satire (Hor. *Sat.* 1.2.88 *emptorem ... hiantem*, 2.5.56 *coruum* (i.e. *captatorem*) ... *hiantem*, Pers. 5.176 *ducit hiantem cretata ambitio*), appears in a similar context of imperial profit-sharing at 3.55.2 *uulgus ad magnitudinem beneficiorum hiabat.* **ipsa Galbae facilitas:** 49.3n. *amicorum ... ignarus.*

13.1 potentia principatus: 'the real power of the throne' (Fyfe); cf. Plut. *G.* 20.4 'for these were the most powerful (ἐν δυνάμει μάλιστα) of those at court'. Another parallel text, Suet. *G.* 14 *regebatur trium arbitrio*, suggests 'over the *princeps*' as the meaning of the gen., but the reference to the offices held by Vinius and Laco and the parallel situations reported for Otho (e.g. 2.39.1 *honor imperii penes Titianum fratrem, uis ac potestas penes Proculum praefectum*) and Vitellius (13.2n. *discordes*) makes 'of the regime' or even 'in the government' more likely. Plutarch has a similar charge in his Nymphidius Sabinus narrative (*G.* 13.2) and again in his obituary for Galba (*G.* 29.4). **diuisa:** sc. *est.* **nec minor gratia:** sc. *erat.* **Icelo Galbae liberto:** imprisoned by Nero at the outbreak of Vindex' rebellion, in June of 68 Icelus was viewed as the new emperor's man-on-the-spot for instructions about the disposal of Nero's corpse (Suet. *Ner.* 49.4; *PIR*[2] I 16). He made the Rome to Clunia journey to inform Galba of Nero's suicide in a remarkable seven days (Plut. *G.* 7, Suet. *G.* 22; Murison (1993) 27). Galba's favour (to which Suetonius ascribes a sexual origin: *G.* 22) won Icelus equestrian rank (see below). For T. there was an inverse relation between the influence of freedmen and the *libertas* of the traditional ruling classes (76.3n. *nam . . . faciunt*). **anulis donatum:** the (right to wear gold) rings marks membership in the *ordo equester* (for the plural *anuli* see Nutting (1928)). Since equestrian status required free birth going back two generations, this privilege effectively erased Icelus' servile past. T. refuses to endorse the erasure: when the fiction of free birth by imperial fiat has lost its effectiveness with Galba's death and Icelus is executed *ut libertus*, T. gives the man his servile name along with his 'equestrian' cognomen (46.5 *Marcianus Icelus*). T. registers inflation in this particular form of flattery with two parallel episodes. At 2.57.3 Vitellius' soldiers themselves urge Vitellius to make a freedman a Roman knight and at 4.39.1 the senate bestows equestrian rank unasked on Vespasian's freedman Hormus. **equestri nomine:** 'Marcianus', a name proclaiming affiliation with the gens Marcia, did not of itself indicate equestrian status; rather, when substituted for 'Icelus' (Plut. *G.* 7.3) it removed the allusion to a servile or non-citizen past that could be read into a foreign cognomen. Parallels cited by Kajanto (1965) 34–5 and Weaver (1972) 90–2 suggest that 'Marcianus', if it was not simply an arbitrary choice, was derived from a previous owner's name. **uocitabant:** unspecified 'they' as subject of verb of naming is a common usage (e.g. *Agr.* 10.4 *insulas quas Orcadas uocant*; *A.* 3.43.2 *cruppellarios uocant*; K–S §3c). In its other two occurrences in T. *uocitare* also has a sarcastic edge:

D. 17.6 (on improper labelling) *antiquos ac ueteres uocitetis oratores* and *H.* 5.2.1 (on an unconvincing etymology) *accolas Idaeos aucto in barbarum cognomento Iudaeos uocitari.* **hi** indicates change of subject from 'they' (indefinite) to 'Vinius, Laco, and Icelus'. **discordes:** cf. 2.92.1 *inter discordes Vitellio nihil auctoritatis.* **sibi quisque** 'each one for himself'. For the singular distributive pronoun with a plural antecedent (*A&G* §317e) cf. 82.2*allocuti sunt... praefecti ex suo quisque ingenio mitius aut horridius.* **circa** 'in connection with' *OLD* 9; the meaning is first common in the elder Pliny (*TLL* s.v. 1093.69–1095.31). **scindebantur** 'were split' *OLD* 6; the metaphor is first found at Virg. *Aen.* 2.39 *scinditur incertum studia in contraria uulgus.*

13.2 Vinius pro M. Othone sc. *erat,* cf. 2.86.4 *utraque legio pro Othone... fuerat.* The *praenomen* marks this as the first reference to Otho, who was omitted from the retrospective, and is even here subordinated to Vinius. **M. Othone:** M. Salvius Otho, the short-lived emperor, was born in 32 into a family whose fortunes had risen rapidly under the principate: his great-grandfather was an *eques* in Etruria, his grandfather a praetorian senator under the patronage of Livia, his father a suffect consul loved by Tiberius, maintained by Gaius, and given patrician status by Claudius (2.50.1, Suet. *O.* 1.1–3; *PIR* s 109). Once Otho made Nero's acquaintance (which, according to Suetonius, he managed by means of an affair with an unattractive imperial freedwoman: *O.* 2.2), he was well suited by age and character to keep company with the heir apparent (b. 37; see 13.3nn. *petulanter* and *aemulatione luxus* and 22.1n. *mollis*). Familiarity was established by 55 (*A.* 13.12.1). By 57 Otho had followed his father and elder brother (on whom see 75.2n.) into the college of Arval Brethren (*CIL* VI 2039 = Smallwood (1967) 19). The date of his quaestorship is not known (he would have been twenty-five in 57; see Murison (1991 b) 97–8). After his marriage with Poppaea Sabina (13.3n.) he spent ten years as Nero's legate in Lusitania (59–68; 13.3n. *seposuit*), which he governed in such a way as to yield no unfavourable report (13.4). Lusitania provided a convenient springboard for joining Galba (13.4n. *primus... transgressus*). **non tam unum aliquem** conveys the in-fighting among Galba's courtiers better than a named alternative would have done. For the expression cf. 6.2 *non in unum aliquem prono fauore,* 82.1 *neminem unum destinare irae poterant.* The only known adoption candidate other than Otho and Galba's eventual choice Piso Licinianus (who may have had Laco's support: 14.1n. *siue... Lacone instante*) is Cornelius Dolabella (88.1n.). **neque erat Galbae ignota... amicitia:** both had connections with Tigellinus (72.2n.; see also 24.1n. *Maeuius Pudens*). T. uses the internal deliberations of Galba (here and with *curam subisse*) as a hook on which to hang information necessary to the narrative (the *amicitia* and material introduced by *namque* below), creating a tight narrative flow. The same procedure is used in 13.4, where Otho's growing expectations (*spem ... rapiebat*) give occasion for mentioning his supporters (*fauentibus plerisque militum, prona ... aula*). **rumoribus ... transmittentium:** cf. 22.2 *rumore ... computantium* and 4.2n. *primo gaudentium impetu.* **quia Vinio:** sc. *erat.* **uidua filia:** Vinia Crispina, whose filial piety is recorded at 47.2. In the days of his power Tigellinus had saved her from Nero (72.2n.). *uidua* may mean either 'lacking a husband' or 'widowed' *OLD* 1–2; no husband is on record (Raepsaet-Charlier (1987) #807). **gener ac socer:** a famous combination since Catul. 29.24 *socer generque perdidistis omnia*, where it neatly captures the tension between personal alliance and political strife that enmeshed Pompey and Caesar in the 50s B.C. (for parallels see *TLL* s.v. *gener* 1770.47–68). **destinabantur:** 12.3n. For the predicate nom. cf. 21.1 *qui proximus destinaretur*, for the abl. cf. 12.3 *hunc uel illum ambitiosis rumoribus destinabant.* Where T. has rumours, Plutarch has assertion: *G.* 21.1 'It had been agreed that Otho should marry her when he had been adopted by Galba and declared his successor.' For the role of rumour see recently Gibson ((1998) with bibliography). **rei publicae curam subisse:** sc. *Galbam*; cf. 2.70.3 *erant quos uaria sors rerum lacrimaeque et misericordia subiret* and *A.* 11.28.2 *subibat ... metus reputantes hebetem* (sc. *esse*) *Claudium*; for the omitted object cf. *Agr.* 3.1 *subit* (sc. *nos*) ... *ipsius inertiae dulcedo*, *A.* 2.2.2 *mox subiit pudor* (sc. *barbaros*), and *A.* 3.31.3 *subit recordatio* (sc. *uictores*). See also 37.3n. *horror animum subit.* T.'s version is shorter and more abstract than Plut. *G.* 21.1 'putting the common good above his own' πρὸ τοῦ ἰδίου τὸ κοινὸν τιθέμενος. **translatae:** an explanatory participle ('since ...') added when the syntax of its substantive, *rei publicae*, was already complete, it acquires a conditional nuance ('would have been transferred') from the following *si.*

13.3 incuriose 'heedlessly'; in T. (for whom *incuriose* and *incuriosus* replace the classical pair *neglegenter* and *neglegens*: the former eighteen times in T., never in Cic., the latter twice in T., thirty-three times in Cic.; cf. Liv. 27.8.5 *adulescentiam neglegentem luxuriosamque*) often of soldiers who have abandoned routine: 79.1, 2.88.2, 3.6.3, 5.22.1, *A.* 4.45.1. It is first found in Sallust (*Hist.* fr. 2.42 *Octauius languide et incuriose fuit*, 4.36 *infrequentem stationem nostram incuriosamque tum ab armis*), but its frequency in Gellius (thirteen times) suggests a Catonian original. Certainly a censorious tone is appropriate here and elsewhere in T. (in Book 1, 34.2, 49.3, 79.1, cf. *Agr.* 1.1 *incuriosa suorum aetas*). **petulanter** 'wildly'. In T. *petulantia* signifies aggression that falls short of dangerous: 2.27.2, 3.11.3, 3.32.2, 4.1.3, *Agr.* 16.4. A detail from Suetonius (*O.* 2.1): prowling through the streets of Rome by night Otho (and presumably a band of other *petulanter agentes*) would humiliate weak souls and lonely inebriates by tossing them in a cloak. **aemulatione luxus:** T.'s severely abstract expression eschews the sillinesses reported by Pliny (*Nat.* 13.22 Nero learned to perfume the soles of his feet from Otho) and Plutarch (*G.*19.3 Otho dispensed perfume from gold and silver pipes, Nero merely sprinked it). Even in Otho's obituary T. gives no details (2.50.1). *luxuria* is one of the two causes for Nero's downfall identified in Galba's speech (16.2); at 21.1 Otho's *luxuria* is characterized as *etiam principi onerosa*. **eoque . . . seposuit:** the story of the Otho-Poppaea-Nero triangle survives in five accounts, none of which agrees in all details with any other (*A.* 13.45–6, Plut. *G.* 19.2–20.2, Suet. *O.* 3, Dio 61.11.2–4; for discrepancies and sources see Townend (1961) 242–8, Murison (1993) 75–80, Morgan (1993d) 567–70). The *Annals* account has more (prejudicial) detail of characterization and event than the present one and a different narrative purpose; for it T. seems to have adapted a different source. Closest to the present version is Plutarch's, by comparison with which T. has abbreviated drastically (four lines versus twenty) and with strict attention to the needs of his narrative: his version heightens the likeness between Otho and Nero (which made him an unsuitable candidate for adoption) and explains how Otho found himself in Spain (whence he could join Galba early). For the biographers the story explains why a wanton Otho betrayed Nero for the reputedly straight-laced Galba (Plut. *G.* 20.2, Suet. *O.* 4.1 *occasio ultionis*). **eoque** 'and for that reason' *OLD* 1; lit. 'and by that (fact)', the antecedent of *eo* being the preceding statement. **Poppaeam Sabinam:** the most successful scion of a courtier family of varied fortune (*PIR*[2] P 850), she was both attractive and ambitious (13.45.1–4; cf. 16.7.1 *impudicitia* and *saeuitia*). Otho was her second husband, Nero her third. She bore the latter a short-lived daughter in 63 (*A.* 15.23.1) and died pregnant in 65, allegedly as a result of her husband's kick (*A.* 16.6.1, Suet. *Ner.* 35.3, Dio 63.28.1). As empress and Augusta she figured in statues (78.2; *A.* 14.61.1), coins, and Pompeian graffiti; after her death her image was reproduced on theatrical masks (Dio 63.9.5). Nero had her deified (Dio 63.26.3, cf. *A.* 16.21.2). **principale scortum:** a piquant combination of elevated and base. In

T. the adj. is applied (scornfully) to entities whose importance is unduly inflated by a connection with the *princeps*: 22.2 *matrimonium*, 2.59.2 *paratus*, 2.59.3 and 2.81.3 *fortuna*, 4.40.3 *commentarii*. *scortum*, foreign to T.'s elevated diction, is used for its shock value in juxtapositions (3.83.2 *cruor et strues corporum, iuxta scorta et scortis similes*; cf. *A.* 15.37.3, 15.72.2). Livy (twice) and Valerius Maximus (4.3.ext.3) use the phrase *nobile scortum* of a well-born and well-behaved sexual dependant; Cicero's *scortum populare* (*Dom.* 49, of Clodius) is closer in spirit to T.'s phrase. **conscium libidinum:** Otho had filled a similar role as early as 55 (*A.* 13.12.1 *conscientiam*). T. omits all reference to the tradition of Otho's sexual relationship with Nero (Suet. *O.* 2.2 *consuetudine mutui stupri*), but for an imputation of effeminacy see 30.1 n. *illo muliebri ornatu*. **deposuerat:** sc. *Nero*. The metaphor, also present in Suetonius (*O.* 3.1 *abductam marito demandatamque* (sc. *Othoni*), 3.2 *depositum*) and, less clearly, Dio (61.11.2 'he gave' ἔδωκε), implies a marriage between Otho and Poppaea, and their marriage is mentioned explicitly by Plutarch (*G.* 19.2), Suetonius (*O.* 3.2), and Tacitus (*A.* 13.45.4). Chilver's misgivings about its occurrence, based on the phrase *nuptiarum specie* at Suet. *O.* 3.1 and Suetonius' failure to mention Otho as Poppaea's husband at *Ner.* 35.2, are unwarranted: the former suggests that the marriage was for Nero's convenience but does not deny its occurrence, for the latter see Bradley (1978b) *ad loc.* **Octauiam uxorem amoliretur:** daughter of Claudius and Messalina, she was married young to the heir-apparent in 53. They had no children. *amoliretur* 'rid himself of' is a restrained but not inaccurate summary of Nero's actions as T. describes them in the *Annals* (14.59–64, esp. *A.* 14.59.3 *parat Octauiam . . . coniugem amoliri*). The subjunctive with *donec* 'marks the limit which it is the aim of the subject . . . to reach' (*NLS* §224). **suspectum:** in the biographers Otho falls prey to Poppaea's attractions and begrudges Nero access (Plut. *G.* 19.4, Suet. *O.* 3.2). T. alludes to this story at 78.2 when he describes Otho, who had by then resurrected Poppaea's statues, as *ne tum quidem immemor amorum*. But here Otho's sentiments are irrelevant. **in prouinciam Lusitaniam:** the south-west corner of the Iberian peninsula, facing the Atlantic, at that period the most insignificant of the imperial provinces in the West (Alföldy (1969) 218–29; Edmonson (1990)). It had no legionary garrison and its governors for the most part enjoyed only modest success in their later careers. T. has no other occasion to mention it. **specie legationis:** *specie* 'pretext' stresses the discrepancy between Otho's appointment (*legatus Augusti pro praetore*) and Nero's motive in appointing him (see below and cf. *A.* 2.5.1 *ea specie* on Germanicus' mission in the East and *A.* 12.41.2 *per speciem honoris*). **seposuit:** as at 10.1, of a *de facto* exile. Suetonius uses the same verb: *O.* 3.2 *sepositus est per causam legationis.* Plutarch speaks of exile proper (*G.* 20.1 φυγῆς).

13.4 comiter 'amiably', a style of governance recommended by Cicero to his brother (*Qfr.* 1.1.22 *quam iucunda ... praetoris comitas in Asia potest esse*). *comitas* was the opposite quality to Galba's *seueritas* (5.2n., with Cic. *Orat.* 34; Morgan (1993d) 570–4). Though welcome, it was also suspect, particularly in a figure of authority; too much of it aroused contempt (Quint. *Inst.* 10.2.25), hence the qualifiers in T.'s praise of Seneca (*A.* 13.2.1 *comitate honesta*) and Titus (*H.* 5.1.1 *comitate ... incorrupto ducis honore*); 52.2n. Plutarch records the same general idea (*G.* 20.1 'not unpleasant or hateful to his subjects' οὐκ ἄχαριν οὐδὲ ἐπαχθῆ τοῖς ὑπηκόοις); elsewhere Otho's governorship is characterized by different virtues: *A.* 13.46.3 *integre sancteque*, Suet. *O.* 3.2 *moderatione atque abstinentia singulari.* No details are given anywhere. **primus in partes transgressus nec segnis et ... splendidissimus:** details in Plut. *G.* 20.2–3: Otho (who had no troops but had been Galba's provincial neighbour for some eight or nine years) provided Galba with precious metals for coinage and with waiters fit to serve an emperor (cf. 22.1 on Otho's household: *corruptius quam in priuata domo habiti*). His prominence in Galba's entourage on the march to Rome and assiduity in services to potential friends (23.1–2nn.) later redounded to his own advantage. **bellum** refers to Galba's revolt; cf. 15.1 *principatum ... bello adeptus*, 15.2 *socios belli*, 16.3 *nos bello ... asciti*, 18.3 *bello perdidissent* and *A.* 3.55.1 *ea arma quis Seruius Galba rerum adeptus est*; also *CIL* VIII 13 (cf. p. 979) = *ILS* 1014 *bello quod imp(erator) Galba pro re p(ublica) gessit* with Alföldy (1969) 71–5. **spem adoptionis statim conceptam ... rapiebat:** *rapiebat* 'clutched, grasped', is more violent than Suet. *O.* 4.1 *eodem ... momento et ipse spem imperii cepit magnam.* See also 13.2n. *neque ... amicitia.* **ut similem** is the sting in the tail of an otherwise not unflattering description, justifying Galba's *cura. congruentia morum* is adduced by Suetonius and Dio to explain Otho's high place in Nero's favour (*O.* 2.2; 61.11.2); on support accruing to Otho from their connection see also 78.2n. *creditus ... agitauisse.*

14.1 sed ... transigit: a perfectly periodic sentence: subject, subordinate clauses, verb. **nihil adhuc de Vitellio certum:** sc. *erat.* The legions of Upper Germany refused to swear allegiance to Galba on 1 January (55.3), Vitellius received his first acclamation on 2 January (57.1) and was joined by the Upper Germany legions on the 3rd (57.2). Here T. specifies the time precisely (and differently from Plut. *G.* 23.1–2: 'Thus was

Vitellius proclaimed emperor in Germany. Hearing of the revolution there Galba postponed adoption no longer') in order to keep Vitellius out of the narrative during the Galba/Otho conflict (Fuhrmann 263–5). There are references to the German sedition in 12–49 (16.3, 18.2, 19.2) but none to Vitellius himself (44.2 is a digression about future events). **anxius quonam exercituum uis erumperet:** *anxius* governs an indirect question only in T. (*A.* 11.25.3, 14.13.1) and his imitator Ammianus (21.7.1, 31.4.13); cf. 81.1 *trepidi fortuitusne...foret.* **ne urbano quidem militi confisus:** rightly so, as the sequel proved: 25.2, 36–38, 40.2, cf. 5.1. **quod...rebatur:** 8.2n. **remedium:** 4.1n. *quid...ualidum, quid aegrum*; cf. Plin. *Pan.* 8.3 (on the adoption of Trajan) *unicum auxilium fessis rebus.* **comitia imperii transigit** 'he brought about a meeting to decide on a ruler', a distortion of the constitutional language of the Republic: *comitia,* properly of an assembly of the *populus Romanus*, here refers to a gathering of five high-ranking officials. In place of the precise genitives used elsewhere with *comitia* to indicate the election or law or trial to be decided (e.g. *creandi consulis, ferendae legis, perduellionis*; *TLL* s.v. *comitium* 1806.31–1807.6) T. uses the abstract *imperii*; no comparably bold expression appears until the fifth century (*comitia purpurae*, Symm. *Or.* 3.3). The verb, too, is unparalleled (*TLL* s.v. *comitium* 1808.61–1809.4). Real *comitia* were crucial institutions of popular sovereignty during the Republic but in the principate (as T. describes it) the term rings hollow: *A.* 1.81.4 (about rules governing consular elections) *speciosa uerbis, re inania aut subdola*; cf. 2.91.2, 3.55.2, *A.* 1.15.1, 14.28.1. See further 16.1 n. *optimum...inueniet.* **Mario Celso consule designato:** his background is uncertain (*PIR*² M 296), his career primarily military: *legatus legionis* in Pannonia and Syria in 63 (*A.* 15.25.3), *dux* against Vitellius in 69 (71.2), *legatus Augusti* in Lower Germany in 72 (see Rüger (1979)). He is last attested as governor of Syria in 73 (*ILS* 8903). Celsus may be the author quoted on how to fight the Parthians at Lyd. *Mag.* 3.33.4 ('Celsus the Roman tactician'). Active service to five successive emperors was counted a virtue in him (for his *fides* see 45.2, 71.2–3; cf. 31.2–3, 39.1, 87.2, etc. with Shotter (1978)). For his leadership of Othonian forces see, in Book 2, 23–5, 33, 39–40, 44, with 25.1 and 39.1 for his *prudentia.* From the consulship held under Vitellius (2.60.2; during July and August according to Townend (1962) 118–19) no record remains. But Vespasian appointed him to Lower Germany after the defeat of the Batavian rebel Civilis and later to Syria, both important military provinces (Eck (1982) 287–91). **Ducenio Gemino praefecto urbis:** like Celsus, apparently from a family with no long history of service in the government (*PIR*² D 201); the distinctive *nomen* is associated with Padua (Syme (1982b) 479). As Galba's *praefectus urbis* he replaced Vespasian's brother, Flavius Sabinus, who had been in office since 61 (46.1 n.). No trace of activity hereafter unless he is correctly credited with the governorship of Asia in 73/4 (Syme (1982b) 479). If so, his success under Vespasian is a further parallel with Marius Celsus. **Pisonem Licinianum:** by his full name, L. Calpurnius Piso Frugi Licinianus (*PIR*² C 300). He was born in 38, the fourth of four sons. His family had as long and varied a record of public service as Galba's own (see below on *nobilis utrimque*). His father (M. Licinius Crassus Frugi, cos. 27), mother (Scribonia), and eldest brother (Cn. Pompeius Magnus, named, as were all the brothers, 'in ostentation of pedigree', Syme (1986) 277) fell victim to Messalina (48.1 n.). A second brother, M. Licinius Crassus Frugi (cos. 64), fell to the *delator* M. Aquillius Regulus in the last years of Nero's reign (48.1 n.). For the third brother see 15.2n. Despite his ancestry Piso Licinianus had not embarked on the *cursus honorum* by the time of his adoption at age thirty; the *titulus* to his tomb records only membership in the *XVviri* (*ILS* 240 = McC–W 76 = *CIL* VI 31723). For his 'long exile' (21.1 *longo exilio*, 48.1 *diu exul*; cf. 38.1 *accersit ab exilio*) neither dates nor cause is known. A wife, Verania Gemina, is on record (47.2n.), but no children. **seu propria electione:** according to Suetonius, Piso was Galba's heir long before 10 January 69 (*G.* 17; see Murison (1993) 62–74). Galba had lost wife and sons some thirty years earlier (Suet. *G.* 5.1); as a Roman proud of his family tradition it would be surprising if he had not chosen an heir to the name. Piso's ill-fated father and eldest brother had, like Galba, accompanied Claudius to Britain (Suet. *Cl.* 17.3, *G.* 7.1; Dio 60.21.5). **siue . . . Lacone instante:** T. does not decide between the alternatives; the second, which is unknown to the parallel tradition, is given in more detail but its significance is undercut by 13.2 *Laco atque Icelus . . . non tam unum aliquem fouebant quam alium.* In both versions Galba bears the ultimate responsibility for this disastrous choice (*adoptanti placebat*; for Piso's inadequacy see 29.2–30n.). On the *uariatio* abl. ~ abl. abs. cf. 44.2 *non honore . . . sed tradito principibus more* with Martin (1953) 92, 79.3 *lapsantibus equis et . . . pondere*, 86.2 *proruto ponte sublicio . . . strage*, and Sörbom (1935) 79. **Rubellium Plautum:** possession of Claudian ancestry (see below and 16.2n. *longa . . . tumentem*; *PIR* R 85) got him killed in 62 (*A.* 14.57–9). Friendship with Rubellius Plautus had lasting consequences: in 66 it was one of the formal charges against Barea Soranus (*A.* 16.23.1, 30.1), while for Plutarch Nero's persecution of Plautus' friends was a familiar *exemplum*, comparable to Alexander's treatment of the friends and relatives of Philotas and Parmenio (*Mor.* 96c).

14.2 nobilis utrimque: *nobilis* indicated descent by birth or adoption from consuls elected by the people, i.e. those who held office before 15 (Syme (1986) 51–3; *pace* Chilver *ad* 1.30.1). Transmission of the claims of birth was now possible via the maternal line (*A.* 14.22.1). Among the consular forebears in the line of Piso's mother was Cn. Pompeius Magnus (see stemma XIV in Syme (1986); for his consul father's consular ancestors see stemma XVII). **moris antiqui . . . seuerus:** in this 'correct assessment' Piso resembles Galba (18.3 *antiquus rigor et nimia seueritas*, with 5.2n.) more closely than he does in Plutarch's version: *G.* 23.2 'predisposed to every virtue, but showing most conspicuously orderliness (τὸ κόσμιον) and austerity (αὐστηρόν)'. *antiqui moris* also describes Vitellius' mother, who viewed her son's elevation with misgivings (2.64.2). For the common *uariatio* gen. of characteristic ~ adj. see Sörbom (1935) 88–9. **aestimatione recta . . . deterius interpretantibus:** *recta* (with *aestimatio* only in T.) has a stronger moral cast than *uera* (Liv. 28.16.10, 38.51.14, V. Max. 6.8.6, Sen. *Ep.* 90.34). Grammarians distinguish between *deterius* 'less well' and *peius* 'worse': *peius* is for comparison with *malum*, *deterius* with *bonum* (Non. p. 432M, Serv. *ad G.* 4.89, Claud. Don. *ad Aen.* 8.326). Here the 'good' is given in *recta*. For the *uariatio* noun ~ participle see, in general, Sörbom (1935) 89–91; the particular pattern here, an abstract noun parallel to a substantive participle, has no precise equivalent, but 15.4 *suadere . . . assentatio*, with an infinitive in place of the participle, is close. **quo** 'insofar as'; its correlative *eo* is omitted (Draeger (1882) §181). **suspectior:** sc. *erat.*

15.1 in hunc modum locutus fertur: in this, the first of four speeches in *oratio recta* in Book 1, Galba grooms Piso for the succession. The focus on the pair is reinforced by a gesture (15.1 *apprehensa Pisonis manu*). The book's other speeches are addressed to the praetorians (Piso at 29.2–30, Otho at 37–38.2 and 83.2–84). Galba's narrative space is curtailed by the starting date of *H.*, so this speech, which only T. reports, contributes essential background.

Galba claims knowledge of the behaviour of a ruler's inner circle, but the narrative shows him incapable of capitalizing on it (7.2, 32.2–33; see further Keitel (1991) 2774–5). Comparison of speech and narrative also reveals his blindness to larger issues of governance such as the qualities desirable in a successor and the nature of the opposition. A still larger question broached here, namely, how the succession should be decided, is reexamined in later books (and indeed throughout the *Annals*). Galba makes a case for adoption, but not a very good case. *Libertas*, *aestimatio*, and *consensus* (16.1–2) are all conspicuously absent or hollow in his own choice; conversely, *inuidia* is a ludicrous understatement of the problems facing him (16.3). Pliny's *Panegyricus*, after the much more successful adoption of Trajan, makes a better case, emphasizing stability, for example, over *uirtus* (8.4–6; on the relationship with *Pan.* see Sage (1990) 861–2). The succession question does not arise in T.'s account of Otho's reign (though Otho's brother looms large: 75.2n.) but the claims of dynasty are revived under Vitellius, who vaunted a young son (75.2n. *mater ac liberi*). They are pressed on Vespasian with more justification at 2.77.1 *tuae domui... duo iuuenes, capax iam imperii alter et... apud Germanicos quoque exercitus clarus*. But not even this can be the last word, as Mucianus' argument here is based only on circumstantial factors (Titus' age and training), while the experience of Domitian's principate will have reinforced the lessons learned under Nero. Galba's speech is the first phase of a major political debate. Its hortatory purpose generates language that elevates the positive and understates the negative. For this un-Tacitean point of view T. creates a suitably distinct style characterized by predictability, concinnity, and amplitude. **si... offeram:** neatly periodic. **si... adoptarem:** the contrafactual expression frustrates inquiry into the procedure employed for this adoption (Murison (1993) 69–74). T. and the parallel sources focus instead on its announcement: Plut. *G.* 23.3 'he went down to the camp to present (ἀποδείξων) him as Caesar and successor', Suet. *G.* 17.1 *perduxit in castra ac pro contione adoptauit.* **lege curiata apud pontifices:** because adoption of a person *sui iuris* abolished his line, normal procedure required the sanction of the *populus Romanus* via the curiate assembly: *leges curiatae* were enacted for the adoptions of Octavian (App. *BC* 3.94), Agrippa Postumus and Tiberius (Suet. *Aug.* 65.1), and Nero (*A.* 12.26.1). For the presence of *pontifices* see Gel. 5.19.5 *comitia arbitris pontificibus praebentur.* **ut moris est:** 7.2n. **egregium erat:** for the mood see *NLS* §200i. **Cn. Pompei et M. Crassi:** 14.1n. *Pisonem Licinianum.* **Sulpiciae ac Lutatiae:** sc. *gentis*; 49.2n. *uetus... nobilitas.* **deorum hominumque consensu** rings hollow after the survey of growing dissent in chh. 4–11. *deorum*, the regular form at this date but less common in T. than *deum* (in the proportion 9:32; see Adams (1973) 129), is an instance of the normalized vocabulary of T.'s speeches. *consensus*, a political slogan of the period, appears unusually often in Book 1 (twelve occurrences, against eight in Books 2–5 and fourteen total in the *Annals*). It is attested on coins, but on Vitellius' coins (e.g. *consensus exercituum BMC* #81–5, 99–102, 110–12) not Galba's; Galba favoured *concordia* (*BMC* #1–2, 55–61). T. later points to the superficiality of two such slogans (2.20.2 *postquam pax et concordia speciosis et irritis nominibus iactata sunt*). **in proximo sibi fastigio collocauit:** via adoption only for the grandsons and Tiberius; Marcellus and Agrippa received tribunician power. *fastigium* 'degree of eminence, rank' (*OLD* 7) can serve for both groups.

15.2 non quia ... non habeam sed ... accepi: for the change of mood cf. 29.2 *non quia ... non paueam ... doleo*, 2.17.1 *nec quia ... mallent, sed longa pax ... fregerat*; a variation on the (Ciceronian) norm *non quia* + subj., *sed quod* + ind. **propinquos:** only (so far as is known) Cornelius Dolabella (88.1 n.). **documentum sit:** the potential subj. expresses Galba's expectation for the future (*NLS* §118) by contrast with the ind. *accepi* of the *fait accompli*; cf. 84.3 *audeant*. *sit* is singular by attraction to the predicate nom. *documentum* (K–S §12.8). **est tibi frater:** an older brother, now known only by his *cognomina*, Crassus Scribonianus; *PIR*[2] L 192. As for Piso, so for Scribonianus no offices are known. He joined Verania Gemina in burying his brother after 15 January (47.2). In 70 a disgruntled Flavian general urged him unsuccessfully to make a bid for the purple (4.39.3); an earlier connection with Vespasian for both Scribonianus and Licinianus is implied by *CIL* VI 1268). His death (of unknown date) is alluded to at 48.1. **nisi tu potior esses:** for *potior* 'preferable' (*OLD* 5) cf. 50.4 *potior utroque Vespasianus*. According to Galba the qualities that would make Piso a *bonus princeps* (16.1) are character, patriotism, maturity, and a clean record (15.1, 3). T.'s Otho points out Piso's resemblance to Galba: 38.1 *sui simillimum*; see also 14.2n. *moris antiqui ... seuerus*.

15.3 ea: sc. *est*. **quae ... effugerit ... in qua ... habeas:** consecutive relative clauses ('such that ...'; *NLS* §156, 158). **nihil ... excusandum habeas:** for *habere* + gerundive see *NLS* §207.3, Draeger (1882) §27e. **explorant** 'test' *OLD* 3. The paradox (echoed in Piso's speech to the praetorians, 29.2) goes back at least as far as Cato's speech for the Rhodians: *secundae res laetitia transuorsum trudere solent a recte consulendo atque intellegendo* (fr. 163.8–9 Malcovati); cf. the more banal thought (but similar language) of Sil. *Pun.* 6.403 *explorant aduersa uiros*. The commonplace (Otto s.v. *uirtus* (4)) also appears with similar wording at Plin. *Pan.* 31.1 *cum secunda felices aduersa magnos probent*. **miseriae tolerantur, felicitate corrumpimur:** an epigrammatic restatement of the foregoing. The (effective) change of person is unparalleled.

15.4 alii . . . utilitas: borne out for Galba himself (32.2–33n.) and for the two subsequent *principes*: Otho's advisors give him bad advice before the final engagement (2.33.1), while the rivalry among Vitellius' legates (2.30.2) leads to his eventual betrayal by Caecina (2.99.2). By contrast Vespasian, the *princeps* who survives, has a single advisor (Mucianus, 2.76–7) and the ability to think for himself (2.74–5). **irrumpet adulatio:** word order reflects the violence of the metaphor; for effective use of word order see also 47.1n. *laetitia*. **et iam:** a slight correction of M's *etiam*, already in Puteolanus' 1476 edition; see Wellesley's app. crit. **simplicissime** 'very frankly' *OLD* 4. T. rarely cites frankness as a virtue in emperors (3.86.2 on Vitellius: *inerat . . . simplicitas ac liberalitas, quae, ni adsit modus, in exitium uertuntur*; cf. Plin. *Pan.* 4.6, 54.5, 84.1 *illa tua simplicitas, tua ueritas, tuus candor*) though its absence is often decried. **ceteri libentius cum fortuna nostra quam nobiscum:** sc. *loquuntur*. The antithesis between rank and individual is a commonplace in discussions of courtly interactions: cf. *A.* 2.71.3 *si me potius quam fortunam meam fouebatis*, Plin. *Pan.* 2.8 *agnoscit enim sentitque sibi non principi dici*, 83.6 *non potentiam tuam sed ipsum te reueretur*. **suadere . . . multi laboris:** sc. *est*; cf. 16.4 *monere . . . neque temporis huius* (sc. *est*). Parallel in function to *assentatio . . . sine affectu peragitur*; for the formal *uariatio* see Sörbom (1935) 110. **assentatio . . . peragitur:** a purposeful periphrasis for *assentari*: with its prefix indicating successful completion *peragitur* 'is accomplished' strengthens the contrast between the continuous effort required in giving good advice and the ease of simply saying yes. For its use in other periphrases see *TLL* s.v. 1177.54–65.

16.1 immensum imperii corpus: cf. the equally fulsome language (also from a speech) at *A.* 1.12.3 *unum esse rei publicae corpus atque unius animo regendum*. **stare ac librari sine rectore:** *librari* 'keep one's balance' (*OLD* 2b), commonly applied to the physical world (e.g. Ov. *Met.* 1.13 *pendebat in aere tellus ponderibus librata suis*; see *TLL* s.v. 1351.24–52), suits the description of the political world as an *immensum corpus*. For the pair *stare~librari* cf. Plin. *Nat.* 2.11 (a description of the universe) *terram . . . stare pendentem librantemque per quae pendeat*. *rector* is an elevated label for persons in authority (twenty-two times in T.). T. sometimes uses it in place of a technical title (e.g. 59.2 *Blaesus, Lugdunensis Galliae rector*, for *legatus Augusti pro praetore*; cf. 87.2n.), but more often, as here, to highlight the gap between the utility and good intentions implicit in the metaphor ('helmsman' *OLD* 1) and the reality of the authority so labelled. Thus in a sarcastic comment about Drusus at *A.* 3.59.3 *sic imbui rectorem generis humani*, and in the bland (but perhaps not very helpful) advice offered by Claudius to a newly made Parthian king at 12.11.2 *ut non dominationem et seruos, sed rectorem et ciues cogitaret.* The euphemism is used, without T.'s sardonic edge, of a divinity by Cicero (*N.D.* 2.90 *rectorem et moderatorem*), of Augustus by Ovid (*Met.* 15.860 *patriae rector*, cf. *Tr.* 2.39) and *CIL* XII 4333 (*orbi terrarum rector*), and of Vespasian by the elder Pliny (*Nat.* 2.18 *maximus omnis aeui rector*). **dignus eram:** 15.1 n. *egregium erat.* **res publica:** used specifically with reference to the Republican period also at 50.3 *mansuram fuisse sub Pompeio Brutoque rem publicam* and *A.* 1.3.7 *quotus quisque reliquus, qui rem publicam uidisset?* See also 1.1 n. *res populi Romani.* **eo necessitatis:** 1.1 n. *potentiam ... interfuit.* **bonum successorem:** applied to Trajan in Pliny's more fulsome rhetoric: *Pan.* 11.3 *in principe ... certissima diuinitatis fides est bonus successor.* **quasi hereditas fuimus:** *quasi*, which in Cicero excuses a non-technical use of a technical term (e.g. *Prov.* 15 *constabat Graecum hominem ac leuem ... quasi triumphasse*) but is not so used elsewhere in T., contributes to the rhetorical flavour of the passage; contrast 13.3 *deposuerat*, a technical term used without apology in narrative. **loco libertatis** 'a substitute for freedom' *OLD* 20; cf. 57.2 *insignia armorum argento decora, loco pecuniae tradebant.* **eligi coepimus:** T. regularly uses active *coepi* with passive infinitives (Draeger (1882) §26b; classical usage required *coeptus sum*). **optimum quemque adoptio inueniet:** *optimus* indicates a moral scale (on which Piso easily surpassed Otho and Vitellius: 50.1 *duos omnium mortalium impudicitia ignauia luxuria deterrimos*), but cf. Syme (1958) x: 'In that selection Sulpicius Galba looked to ancestry and the negative virtues, advertising thereby his own incompetence.' A choice based on *uirtus* harks back to Livy's fairy tales about the succession of Rome's kings, in which there were *comitia rege creando* (14.1 n. *comitia imperii transegit*) and the *consensus* deciding the election was based on the candidate's moral worth: thus at the accession of Numa Pompilius (1.18.5) and the elections of Tullus Hostilius (1.22.1) and Ancus Marcius (1.32.1). In these stories hereditary succession never determined the choice and was not even an issue until the death of the fourth king, Ancus Marcius (1.40.2, 1.48.2).

16.2 fortuitum: sc. *est.* **integrum:** sc. *est.* **consensu monstratur:** the subject, 'a desirable adoption candidate' *uel sim.*, must be inferred from the context (*si uelis eligere*). Galba's assertion is neither true in Piso's case nor likely in any other; in 12.2–3 T. sketched the 'the miraculous temptation for plot and intrigue' at play in an impending adoption (Syme (1958) 2). **sit ... depulerunt:** cartoonlike in its exaggerated language and physical imagery. **longa Caesarum serie tumentem:** *tumens* 'puffed up' (*OLD* 4) refers to expectations disproportionate to their basis; cf. 88.3 *leuissimus quisque... spe uana tumens. intumescere* is used similarly at 4.19.1 *intumuere statim* (sc. *cohortes*) *superbia ferociaque.* The connection with dynastic pride is more at home in epic: Stat. *Theb.* 4.121 *genero tumuit Ioue*; 8.429 *proauoque tumebat Achille*, Sil. 10.176 *antiquo tumentem nomine.* Such bombast is parodied at Juv. 8.40–1 *tumes alto Drusorum stemmate, tamquam | feceris ipse aliquid propter quid nobilis esses.* For *series* cf. Sen. *Ep.* 76.12 *auorum proauorumque serie* and especially Luc. 4.823–4 *Caesareaeque domus series, cui tanta potestas | concessa est.* **immanitas** designates behaviour of which a human being ought to be incapable; it is used of Nero again at *A.* 14.11.3 *immanitas omnium questus anteibat*, of his mother at 14.2.2, and of his agents at 16.26.2. **ceruicibus publicis depulerunt:** the public 'neck' and its vulnerability are commonplaces of ancient political language (e.g. Liv. 4.12.6 *regno... in ceruicibus accepto*, Suet. *Cal.* 30.2 *utinam populus Romanus unam ceruicem haberet!*). For the personal subject favoured in this phrase by e.g. Cicero (*Cat.* 3.17 *hanc tantam molem mali a ceruicibus uestris depulissem*, *Dom.* 63 *hanc ego uim... ab omnium bonorum ceruicibus depuli*; cf. *Sulla* 28, *Mil.* 77, *Phil.* 3.8) T. substitutes abstract nouns. **damnati principis:** Nero was declared a *hostis* by the senate on 8 June (Suet. *Ner.* 49.2); Caligula's *acta* were annulled and his coins melted down but he was not condemned.

16.3 nos bello et ab aestimantibus asciti: more nuanced than the claim Dio attributes to Galba: 64.2.1 'he considered that he had not seized power but had had it given to him (this was his constant refrain)'; cf. Plut. *G.* 29.2 'summoned to be ruler' κληθεὶς... αὐτοκράτωρ. **inuidia** is inadequate to describe contemporary discontent with Galba's rule, as is *quod nunc mihi unum obicitur.* For T.'s own description see chh. 4–11 *passim*, with further details in 21 and 25.2.

16.4 temporis huius: sc. *est.* **utilissimus... nolueris:** a rather inadequate 'golden rule' for running the empire; young Nero's comprehensive and practical *forma futuri principatus* at *A.* 13.4.2 specifies refraining from judicial abuses, preventing corruption in his household, maintaining a distinction between *domus Augusti* and *res publica*, supporting the senate and consuls in their traditional roles, and looking after the army. **neque enim hic:** sc. *est.* **et Galba quidem:** 5.2n.

17.1 statim... oculis: the *statim~mox* antithesis is complicated by the *uariatio* between the substantive participle *intuentibus* (dat.) and the abl. abs. *coniectis... oculis*, an abrupt change from the glib regularity of Galba's speech. *omnium* seems odd with only five others present, so T. may be alluding to Piso's subsequent appearances before the praetorians (18.2) and the senate (19.1–2). Plutarch, who does not mention a preliminary *consilium*, places the visual evaluation of Piso in the praetorian camp (*G.* 23.3). **reuerens:** sc. *erat.* **se:** reflects the notional subject, Piso, not the grammatical subject, *sermo.* **mutatum:** sc. *est* (or *esse*, dependent on *ferunt*).

17.2 consultatum . . . augebant: a showpiece of compression, with omissions (*utrum*, forms of *esse*), impersonal verbs (*consultatum, iri*), an abstract noun (*exspectatio*), a connecting relative pronoun (*quorum*), and a substantive participle (*supprimentes*). **consultatum:** sc. *est.* **pro rostris an in senatu:** T. regularly omits *utrum* in disjunctive indirect questions. In Book 1: 7.2n. *an . . . scrutaretur*, 37.1, 47.1, 69.1. **honorificum . . . fore:** indirect statement depending on the notion of thinking in *placuit.* **quorum fauorem . . . haud spernendum:** sc. *esse. quorum*, though formally a relative pronoun, functions as a connective + demonstrative (*et eorum*), introducing a second acc. + inf. (*fauorem . . . haud spernendum*); *NLS* §289. *fauorem* is also the subject of *acquiri*, which is aligned with *spernendum* by the particles *ut . . . ita* ('although . . . yet' 4.2n.). **ambitu** denotes solicitation: the emperor is a petitioner to his own troops (see also 83.1 n. *ambitioso imperio*); cf. the senators' petitions to Galba at 19.2 *ambitu remanendi aut eundi.* **circumsteterat . . . publica exspectatio:** only Cicero is similarly bold with this personification: *Clu.* 63 *uocat me . . . tacita uestra exspectatio.* Here there is an effective overlap between the figure of speech (comparable to e.g. Virg. *Aen.* 2.559 *circumstetit horror*) and reality (crowds were in fact 'standing around'; cf. 32.1 *uniuersa iam plebs Palatium implebat*).

18.1 quartum idus Ianuarias 'the fourth [day] before the Ides of January'; the Ides being the 13th, the fourth day previous, counting inclusively, is 10 January. *ante diem* is often omitted from the dating formula (as at *CIL* VI 2051.25 referring to this date: *IIII idus Ian(uarias) adoptio facta*; cf. *TLL* s.v. *Idus* 242.67–243.7), but T. tightens further by making the date the direct object. **foedum imbribus diem:** 'more likely to come from Virgil than from any of the other sources', Miller (1987b) 91, with reference to *G.* 1.323–4 *foedam glomerant tempestatem imbribus atris | collectae ex alto nubes.* **tonitrua et fulgura et caelestes minae:** unusually full for T. but still tauter than Plutarch *G.* 23.1 'as soon as Galba set out, great signs from heaven (διοσημίαι) accompanied him . . . There was so much thunder and lightning, and so much rain and darkness poured down on camp and city that it was plain that the heavenly powers did not sanction or approve this inauspicious adoption.' *caelestes minae*, which recalls 3.2 with its *fulminum monitus* and the reference to the gods, has no exact parallel in T.; parallels are found in the poets generally and at Sen. *Nat.* 2.59.11, 6 praef. 6 *tonitrua et minas caeli*; see *TLL* s.v. 993.49–63. **turbauerant:** the tense retrojects the description back over chh. 15–17, the events of which all took place on the 10th. **obseruatum id antiquitus comitiis dirumpendis** 'observation of this (i.e. the celestial disturbance) traditionally causing assemblies to be broken up'. *obseruatum id* is the subject of *terruit*, an instance of the so-called '*ab urbe condita*' construction (*NLS* §95; cf. 89.3 *Caecina ... transgressus exstimulabat*); an equivalent abstract noun is also used by T.: 22.1 *obseruatione siderum*, *G.* 10.3 *obseruatio auspiciorum*, *A.* 15.55.2 *dierum obseruatione*. For the dat. of purpose with gerundives (~ 'causing') see 6.2n. *opprimendis Vindicis coeptis*. The statement simplifies and idealizes Republican (~ *antiquitus*) response to divine signs, which was 'consciously contrived and politically motivated' (Gruen (1974) 256). *dirumpendis* is the reading of M; most editors follow its descendants in correcting to *dirimendis* '... to be dispersed', which is the *uox propria* for the dissolution of public assemblies for religious reasons (*TLL* s.v. 1260.26–55). **non terruit Galbam quo minus ... pergeret:** *quo minus* indicates that the force of *terruit* here is preventive 'deterred' (cf. 40.2 and *NLS* §184). **ut** 'inasmuch as' *OLD* 21a. **seu quae fato manent ... non uitantur:** *seu* sets this sentence in parallel with what precedes (the explanatory apposition *contemptorem*) as an alternative explanation for Galba's persistence. As often in T., the second explanation is less flattering than the first. For T.'s frequent omission of *siue* / *seu* with the first of alternative explanations see GG s.v. *siue* I(B) with Sörbom (1935) 125. **fato manent** 'are fated'; *manere* 'be in store' *OLD* 4. For *fato* cf. *A.* 6.22.1 *mihi haec ac talia audienti in incerto iudicium est, fatone res mortalium et necessitate immutabili an forte uoluantur*, T.'s comment on an incident that led Tiberius to believe that a seer was *praescius periculorum*.

18.2 imperatoria breuitate: for the ideal of the rhetoric-free Roman general, a commonplace (as in Marius' boast at Sal. *Jug.* 85.31 *non sunt composita uerba mea; parui id facio. ipsa se uirtus satis ostendit*, etc.), cf. the opening words of a speech by the most successful military figure of *H.*, Petillius Cerialis: 4.73.1 *neque ego umquam facundiam exercui.* **more militari, quo uir uirum legeret:** referring to the *lex sacrata* (cf. Liv. 9.39.5 *lege sacrata coacto exercitu, cum uir uirum legisset*), which was 'manifestly an Italic practice whereby all able men who failed to report for military service were declared *sacer*' (Ogilvie (1965) *ad* 4.26.3). No writer uses the phrase for contemporary military recruitment; Galba is again appealing to the 'good old days', as

Augustus did in recruiting a new senate in 18 B.C. (Suet. *Aug.* 35.1 *quo uir uirum legit*, cf. *Aug.* 54, with Dio 54.13–14. for the date and details). **ne dissimulata seditio in maius crederetur** 'so that a concealed rebellion would not be believed to be on a larger scale'. **quartam . . . fore:** Galba downplays the disaffection in addressing his soldiers, but Vitellius, upon receipt of similar news, is himself the addressee of such talk (2.96.1). **quartam et duoetuicensimam legiones:** 55.3nn.

18.3 maestitia ac silentium: sc. *est.* **tamquam** 'on the grounds that' *OLD* 7b. **donatiui necessitatem:** donatives were offered even on hereditary successions such as that of Nero (*A.* 12.69.2). See further 5.1n. and Millar (1977) 195–6. **quantulacumque . . . liberalitate** 'with a very little generosity'. **antiquus rigor:** cf. Plut. *G.* 29.3–4 'an old-fashioned ruler' (ἀρχαῖος αὐτοκράτωρ), who 'determined to rule men petted by Tigellinus and Nymphidius as Scipio and Fabricius and Camillus ruled the Romans of their day'. **seueritas:** 5.2n. *legi . . . emi*, 49.2n. *magis . . . uirtutibus.* **sumus:** 10.3n. *credidimus.*

19.1 non comptior: sc. *erat.* Neither this speech nor that of Piso nor the senatorial deputation of 19.2 is mentioned in any other source. In 19–20, chapters with a marked brevity of style, T. concentrates material given either earlier by Plutarch and Suetonius or not at all. **comis oratio:** 13.4n. *comiter.* **multi . . . cura:** for the (unflattering) list cf. 80.2 *pars . . . pessimus quisque . . . uulgus.* **multi:** sc. *fauebant.* **priuatas spes agitantes sine publica cura:** the senators' attitude is comparable to that of the *uulgus* under Otho: 90.3 *priuata cuique stimulatio et uile iam decus publicum.* **quadriduo:** Plutarch's reference to the four-day interval between adoption and assassination (24.1 'it was not the work of four days to change the allegiance of a healthy army, and only so many days intervened . . .') accompanies material T. places in ch. 25. **dictum:** sc. *est.*

19.2 facili ciuitate ad accipienda credendaque omnia noua cum tristia sunt: cf. 34.2 *credula fama inter gaudentes et incuriosos.* **mittendos:** sc. *esse.* **legatos:** the embassy set out but cannot have reached Germany before Galba's death; Otho sent a new commission (74.2n. *rursus . . . misit*). An earlier senatorial deputation had gone to meet Galba *en route* to Rome (Plut. *G.* 9.1); later ones go to the legions (3.80.1) and to Vespasian (4.6–8, where the selection process is described in great detail). **agitatum:** sc. *est.* **maiore praetextu, illi auctoritatem senatus hic dignationem Caesaris laturus** 'the trappings (of authority) being more impressive with the senators bearing the prestige of the senate, he the rank of Caesar'. T. uses both *praetextus* and *praetextum*; for the meaning here cf. 76.2 *erat grande momentum in nomine urbis ac praetexto senatus* and 3.80.1 *praetexto rei publicae*; cf. also 3.4.2 *ut consulare nomen ... partibus honesta specie praetenderetur*. *dignatio* characterizes another senatorial emissary at 3.80.2. **ambitu remanendi aut eundi, ut quemque metus uel spes impulerat** 'people sought to stay or go, each according as fear or hope moved him'; 6.1 n. *alter ... destruebant*.

20.1 proxima pecuniae cura: sc. *erat*. The reclamation of money comes 'next' after the adoption and the embassy only in T.; it must actually have begun earlier to have progressed to the numerous trials T. describes (Intro. §8; cf. Plut. *G*. 16.2, Suet. *G*. 15.1, Dio 63.14; for a possible reclamation effort mentioned only by T. see *Agr*. 6.5). Placed here it adds substance to his account of Galba's principate. **scrutantibus:** Plutarch specifies the involvement of Vinius (*G*. 16.3–4). **repeti:** its subject, *pecuniam*, is supplied from the preceding sentence. For a similar measure under Claudius cf. Dio 60.17.2 'what had been given away by Gaius without justice or reason he demanded back from the recipients'. Plutarch and Suetonius add the important detail that Galba's commission also sought to recover property from those who had received it from Nero's beneficiaries (Plut. *G*. 16.2, Suet. *G*. 15.1), a procedure perhaps modelled on extortion law, which allowed recovery from such parties. Pliny and Tacitus were involved in a number of important extortion cases in the early years of Trajan's reign, including one in which this procedure was followed (*Ep*. 3.9.17). **bis et uiciens miliens sestertium:** 2,200,000,000 HS (22 × 1,000 × *centena milia*). Large sums of money were reckoned in units of 100,000 HS. Only T. gives an amount. **appellari singulos iussit:** sc. *Galba*. *appello* 'summon to pay' *OLD* 5. By omitting the amount at stake and by describing the targets as 'denizens of stage and gym' (Plut. *G*. 16.2, cf. Suet. *G*. 15.1 *scaenici ac xystici*), the parallel sources make the reclamation project seem petty. But from Dio we learn that among those assessed were the Hellanodikai, to whom Nero had given 1,000,000 HS for a generous first prize in an Olympic event, and the Pythia at Delphi, who had received 400,000 for some gratifying oracles (63.14.1–2). For other substantial Neronian gifts see Suet. *Ner*. 30.2 with Bradley (1978b) *ad loc*. **decima parte ... relicta:** both here and in the following sentence with *isdem ... sumptibus* the abl. abs. appendix surpasses the main clause in both length and complexity (Intro. §14). **super ... erant:** the only instance of tmesis in T. **isdem erga aliena**

sumptibus quibus sua prodegerant, cum . . . non agri aut faenus sed sola instrumenta uitiorum manerent: Plut. *G.* 16.2 'most of the recipients, living satyr-like in the present (ἐφήμεροι καὶ σατυρικοί), had squandered their largess' lacks T.'s antitheses. **faenus** 'capital' *OLD* 2. **instrumenta uitiorum:** a periphrasis (comparable to *A.* 1.65.7 *per quae egeritur humus* for shovel or spade) but with ethical colouring added; cf. 4.3 *deterrimi seruorum* and 88.3 *irritamenta libidinum.*

20.2 triginta equites . . . praepositi: sc. *sunt.* Suetonius says there were fifty members (*G.* 15.1), but even thirty was a large number for a Roman commission. **nouum officii genus:** in T.'s day the centumviral court dealt with property cases. Nothing is known about the procedure in Claudius' reclamation action (see above). **et ambitu ac numero onerosum** 'burdensome (to its members) because of the scope and number (of cases)'; admirably brief, but capable of various interpretations depending on how one fills in the blanks occasioned by the general terms *ambitus* and *numerus.* The parallel passage in Plutarch (16.2 'a boundless task (πράγματος ὅρον οὐκ ἔχοντος) which ranged far and touched many') prompts the translation suggested above. *onerosum* is referred to the commissioners because of the antithesis with *gaudium* (i.e. the commission was hard work for its members but a source of satisfaction to the public at large). So taken, this notice agrees with the positive cast of 19–20. Against it is the boldness of *ambitus* 'scope' as applied to *officium,* since elsewhere it has physical or temporal referents (*TLL* s.v. 1859.10–1860.20). For other views see Alford, Chilver, and Valmaggi. **hasta et sector:** sc. *erat.* The spear signified an auction in progress; the *sector* was the profiteer who bought up auctioned goods (90.1 n. *reliquias . . . conuersas*). **gaudium:** sc. *erat.* The epigram, the content of which is absent from the parallel sources, rounds off the section; cf. 82.1 n. *inuiti neque innocentes.* For terminal epigrams cf., in App. 2, 1.4, 3.2, 6.1, 11.3, 24.2, 38.3, 39.1, 48.1, 48.4, 49.4, 50.3, 52.4, 54.3, 56.1, 63.2, 71.2, 87.2.

20.3 exauctorati: sc. *sunt,* a technical expression for military discharge (*TLL* s.v. 1188.55–1189.10). No grounds are given here but the parallel tradition suggests that these officers were discharged for involvement with Nymphidius Sabinus. If so, this incident, too, is postponed, since Galba is unlikely to have left suspect commanders in their posts for months after the failed coup. (The postponement may in fact be the reason behind T.'s omission of the Nymphidius Sabinus connection.) Both Plutarch (*G.* 23.4

'a large number of adherents of Tigellinus and Nymphidius Sabinus, men who had been in high positions but were now cast aside and humbled, were lured onto Otho's side') and Suetonius (*G.* 16.1 *praetorianos etiam metu et indignitate commouit* (sc. *Galba*), *remouens subinde plerosque ut suspectos et Nymphidi socios*) imply that large numbers were involved and treat the event as yet another of Galba's errors. Plutarch adds the detail, supported by T.'s own narrative (see below on Aemilius Pacensis and Julius Fronto), that those discharged joined Otho (similarly the praetorians cashiered, *en masse*, by Vitellius, take up the Flavian cause (3.43.1); for their identity see Wellesley's note *ad loc.*). T. presents the measure in a less negative light by naming the punishment (contrast 'cast aside and humbled'), by naming names (only four), and by specifying Galba's intention (*remedium*). Vespasian behaves similarly (4.46.4). Discharges from the legions, too, are perhaps to be inferred from 37.4 *castra . . . emendata et correcta* but no details are known. For an unintended consequence of this disciplinary measure see 51.5n. *decimari . . . dimitti.* **tribuni** commanded cohorts of the city's garrison, which in early 69 included twelve praetorian cohorts, four urban, and seven of the watch. Of the four men mentioned here two reappear in the narrative. **Antonius Naso:** a praetorian tribune not mentioned again by T. but known to have been a career soldier from inscriptions and coins (*PIR*[2] A 854); he survived this blow to serve again. **Aemilius Pacensis,** having regained his post under Otho (87.2), was put in charge of the urban cohorts in the attack on Narbonensis, but was unable to control them (2.12.1). For his death see 3.73.2. **e uigilibus Iulius Fronto:** Fronto was restored to office by Otho but treated with suspicion because his brother served on the Vitellian side (2.26.1); on the *uigiles* see 46.1 n. **per artem et formidine:** for the *uariatio* cf. *A.* 1.11.4 *incertum metu an per inuidiam* and Sörbom (1935) 84.

21–26 Otho's conspiracy

After Galba's *acta* T. gives us the seeds of Otho's defection, beginning with Otho's personal motivations and the close associates who fostered huge hopes in him (chh. 21–2), but also encompassing praetorian attitudes (chh. 23–5). The situation is brought to a head by news of sedition in Germany (ch. 26). The panel moves from the immediate aftermath of the adoption (ch. 21) back to Otho's stay in Lusitania (22.2) then gradually forward through the march to Rome (chh. 23–4) and back to the post-adoption present (25.1 *sed tum*); verb tenses neatly articulate the various phases. The few available facts about the conspiracy are similarly reported in Plutarch and Suetonius, but T. alone has the internal deliberations with which Otho goads himself to his *flagitiosissimum facinus* (ch. 21; cf. 2.50.1) and the moral censure for Otho's associates (ch. 22).

21.1 nulla spes: sc. *erat*. **in turbido:** *res turbidae* generally involve political turmoil: 31.1, 55.2, 83.1. For the substantive adj. cf. Liv. 3.40.10 *nisi quid in turbido minus perspicuum fore putent quid agatur* (also of political turmoil). **inopia . . . uix toleranda:** the pairing *luxuria~inopia* is Sallustian (e.g. *Cat.* 25.4 *luxuria atque inopia praeceps abierat*) and like Sallust T. uses *inopia* of debt (e.g. *Jug.* 41.7 *populus militia atque inopia urgebatur*; *TLL* s.v. 1744.62–4). For Otho's debt see Suet. *O.* 5.1–2 *instigante . . . magnitudine aeris alieni*, and Plut. *G.* 21.1, where Otho's 200,000,000 HS debt is given as a reason for Galba's disinclination to adopt him. For *tolerare* 'support (financially)' see *OLD* 2b. **fingebat et metum** 'he also contemplated what he feared'; cf. 2.74.2 (on Vespasian) *aliquando aduersa reputabat*. For *fingere* of the visualization or mental review of fears (*OLD* 8; in T. at 4.54.1, *A.* 5.10.2) cf. Cic. *Tusc.* 1.36 *ignoratio finxit inferos easque formidines*, Tib. 2.6.51–2 *tunc mens mihi perdita fingit, quis . . . meam teneret*, Ov. *Her.* 2.21–2 *fidus amor quidquid properantibus obstat | finxit*. **praegrauem . . . perire:** indirect statement dependent on *metum*. Infinitives of *esse* are omitted throughout. **praegrauem:** cf. *A.* 14.3.1 *praegrauem ratus* (sc. *matrem*), *interficere constituit*. Six of the fifteen metaphorical uses of this adj. occur in T., three in Pliny the Elder. **alterius exilii honorem:** oxymoron; 13.3n. *seposuit*. **proximus destinaretur** 'was marked out as next in succession'. Plutarch reports this as fact, not Othonian revery: *G.* 23.3 he was 'the first thought worthy' (πρῶτος ἀξιωθείς; i.e. of being chosen successor). For Otho's popularity see Suet. *O.* 4.2 *iam uix ullus esset qui non et sentiret et praedicaret solum* (sc. *Othonem*) *successione imperii dignum* and Plut. *G.* 23.1 'some of his supporters backed Dolabella, most of them Otho'. **apud senem** 'with an elderly *princeps*'; for *apud* 'in the estimation of' or 'with' see *OLD* 12. **efferatum:** commonly (and apparently first) applied to humans by Livy, both of persons rendered generally sub-human by their circumstances and with specific reference to the aggrieved person's potential for cruelty (e.g. 2.29.9 *Ap. Claudius et natura immitis et efferatus*). The latter sense is particularly relevant to Otho's fears. But neither sense fits T.'s picture of Piso: 14.2 *moris antiqui*, *seuerus*, 17.1

sermo ... *reuerens* ... *moderatus*, 19.1 *comis oratio*; cf. his non-violence at 29.2. **occidi Othonem posse:** for the third-person reference by Otho to himself cf. 2.47.2 and 2.48.2.

21.2 proinde 'accordingly' effects the transition from analysis to exhortation (cf. 33.2, 56.3). Such particles contribute to a rhetorical tone even in indirect speech (Adams (1973) 131–3); T. uses *proinde* thus seventeen times in speeches or indirect speech, only five times in narrative, though narrative occupies much more space in the historical works than speech. **fluxa:** sc. *esset*; *fluxa* 'tottering' is so defined by the antithesis with *coalescere* 'become established'; cf. *A.* 13.19.1 *nihil* ... *tam instabile ac fluxum est quam fama.* **nec cunctatione opus:** sc. *esse* 'delay was not called for', lit. 'there was no need for delay' (*OLD* s.v. *opus* 12); for Otho's haste cf. 38.2 *nullus cunctationis locus est*, and the command *ire praecipites et occupare pericula* at 40.1. **sit ... maneat:** *repraesentatio* (7.2n. *postquam* ... *nequiuerint*). **merito perire** 'to deserve to perish' (lit. 'to perish deservedly'), subject of *esse*, with *acrioris uiri* as the predicate. At 33.2 similar words, there labelled *speciosiora*, persuade Galba.

22.1 non erat Othonis mollis ... animus: cf. 71.1 and 2.11.3 (of his march to the front) *nec illi segne aut corruptum luxu iter, sed lorica ferrea usus est et ante signa pedes ire, horridus, incomptus famaeque dissimilis*. Otho's reputation for softness (cf. Martial 6.32.2 *mollis Otho*) stems from matters of dress (30.1 n. *illo muliebri ornatu*), grooming (Suet. *O.* 12.1 reports a facial treatment used *ne barbatus umquam esset*), and, perhaps, sexuality (Suet. *O.* 2.2 with Murison (1991b) *ad loc.*; Juv. 2.99 *pathici* ... *Othonis*). **corruptius quam in priuata domo habiti:** cf. Juv. 4.66 *priuatis maiora focis*; both passages show a wry appreciation of the fact that the slaves of the most powerful man were the least restrained; see also 13.4 *primus* ... *spendidissimus* and, for the analogy, 90.3 *ut in familiis*. *quam* 'than (was suitable)' *OLD* 8. **si auderet, ut sua ostentantes, quiescenti ut aliena exprobrabant:** the ironic note of moral censure in *exprobrabant* (they 'reproached' him with passing up what it was virtuous to reject) evokes a topsy-turvy household. *ut sua* depends on *si auderet* ('his, if he dared') as *ut aliena* on *quiescenti*. For the *uariatio* of conditional clause and dat. see Sörbom (1935) 118. Piso gives a more specific list of Othonian *libidines*: 30.1 *stupra, comissationes, feminarum coetus.* But Otho surprised everyone (71.1). **urgentibus ... retinebitur:** a twenty-nine-word two-part appendix (Intro. §14). **urgentibus etiam mathematicis:** for other astrologers involved in treasonable activities see e.g. *A.* 2.27 (A.D. 16), 3.22 (A.D. 20), 12.52.1 (A.D. 52), 16.14–15 (A.D. 66), with Cramer (1964) and Potter (1994) 171–82. Individual punishment, as in the case of the astrologers associated with Libo (*A.* 2.32.3), was reinforced by collective banishment (see below on *uetabitur*), but the exiles only gained authority thereby: Juv. 6.557 *praecipuus tamen est horum, qui saepius exul*, cf. *A.* 16.14.1 *Pammenem ... exulem et Chaldaeorum arte famosum eoque multorum amicitiis innexum.* **nouos motus** ≈ *nouas res* 'change of government'; cf. 80.2. Astrology concerned itself with the horoscopes of nations as well as individuals (Ptol. *Tetr.* 2.1, Firmicus Maternus 2.30.4; Barton (1994) 180). **clarum ... annum:** uniquely Tacitean, despite the frequency with which years are summarily characterized, esp. in annals-based histories (e.g. *A.* 4.64.1 *feralem ... annum*; see *TLL* s.v. *annus* 118.13–50). *clarus* 'illustrious' (*OLD* 8) has a prophecy's characteristic flexibility of meaning. The parallel sources predict Otho's rule (see App. 1). **genus hominum potentibus infidum, sperantibus fallax, quod in ciuitate nostra et uetabitur semper et retinebitur:** a neat, if somewhat overstated, *sententia*. Prohibition was not blanket: in 33 B.C. astrologers were expelled from Rome itself but not forbidden to practice (Dio 49.43.4), in A.D. 11 Augustus restricted the conditions and subjects of consultation but did not make consultation illegal *per se* (Dio 56.25.5). Tighter control was essayed in 17 with citizen-astrologers expelled from Italy with loss of property; foreigners were executed (*A.* 2.32.3 with Goodyear (1981) *ad loc.*). A similar measure, *atrox et irrita*, was enacted in 52 (*A.* 12.52.3, Dio. 60.33.3). Between 68 and the end of the Flavian period several other expulsions from Rome and Italy are attested but dating them is more difficult (Cramer (1964) 241–6). On still later attempts at controlling astrology and the related prognostical arts see Potter (1994) 176–82. Elsewhere, too, T. criticizes the use of astrologers as advisors (cf. 2.78.1 (on Vespasian) and *A.* 2.27.2). But alongside his scorn for astrological advice T. reports the occasional accuracy of their predictions: *A.* 6.20.2 gives Tiberius' correct *praesagium* about Galba's brief principate, at 6.22.4 we find a correct prediction of Nero's principate. At 6.22.3 T. even maintains that both past and present offer *clara documenta* of the reliability of the astrological art, *fidem artis* (cf. *A.* 4.20.3 for the possibility that only some aspects of fate are determined by the *sors nascendi*). The difficulty lay in interpretation. When *periti caelestium* foretold in 26 that Tiberius would not return to Rome (*A.* 4.58.2–3), they were technically correct, but failed to add the important fact that he would live on outside of Rome for a further eleven years.

22.2 secreta Poppaeae . . . habuerant: *secreta* has been taken as Poppaea's rooms (Heubner, Spooner, Valmaggi) or her private deliberations (Alford, Church and Brodribb); 85.2 *secreta domuum* is formally similar but *secreta* is more precisely delimited by the gen. Other advisers without portfolio are described in similar terms: Sallustius Crispus was *praecipuus cui secreta imperatorum inniterentur* (*A.* 3.30.3, cf. 1.6.3 *particeps secretorum*), Livilla's doctor was *frequens secretis* (*A.* 4.3.4), Piso's friend Antonius Natalis was *particeps ad omni secretum Pisoni* (*A.* 15.50.2). **pessimum principalis matrimonii instrumentum** 'the worst possible tool for an imperial spouse'; 13.3n. *principale scortum.* For *instrumentum* of those who do imperial dirty work cf. *A.* 12.66.2 *diu inter instrumenta regni habita.* We know nothing about Poppaea's astrologers. Of the other imperial wives only Agrippina is connected with astrologers (*A.* 6.22.4, 12.68.3, 14.9.3, Suet. *Ner.* 6). Non-imperial wives making objectionable use of astrologers were satirized by Juvenal: 6.565 *consulit . . . de te Tanaquil tua.* **principalis matrimonii:** T. uses abstract *matrimonium* for concrete *uxor* at 73 *consulari matrimonio subnixa* and *A.* 2.13.3 *matrimonia ac pecunias hostium praedae destinare*; cf. *TLL* s.v. 480.45–481.9. **e quibus:** connecting relative (= *et ex eis*); cf. 52.1n. *in quibus.* It is odd that one of Poppaea's associates accompanied Otho in his quasi-exile. Suetonius accounts for the astrologer's presence in Spain differently: *O.* 4.1 *ultro inopinatus aduenerat* (Suetonius also differs from both Plutarch and T. in naming the astrologer Seleucus, perhaps confusing him with Vespasian's astrologer of that name: *H.* 2.78.1). **Othoni . . . comes:** for the dative dependent directly on a noun (adnominal dat., a construction 'used by no one more frequently than by T.' (Draeger (1882) §53); see also *NLS* §67, K–S II §77.4 n. 5) cf. 38.1 *honestis consiliis robur*, 61.1 *itinera bello*, 67.1 *initium bello*, 77.2 *exercitui delenimentum*, 87.1 *bello consiliis*, 88.1 *ministros bello.* **superfuturum:** sc. *esse.* **postquam . . . fides:** sc. *erat.* **coniectura iam et rumore:** instrumental abl. *coniectura* 'interpretation (of dreams, etc.)' (*OLD* 3), which presumably refers to Ptolemaeus, is a surprising partner for *rumore*, the talk of the town (*computantium*); cf. 12.2n. *licentia . . . Galbae.* **fore ut in imperium adsisceretur:** i.e. by adoption; cf. 15.1 *subolem in penates meos asciscere*, 29.2 *Caesar ascitus sum.*

22.3 credendi: the MSS read *credi*; emendation corrects the sense. *cupido* with the gerund is common: in Book 1, 48.2 *cupidine uisendi*, 63.1 *spoliandi cupidine.* For the whole phrase cf. Sal. *Hist.* fr. 1.103 *more humanae* *cupidinis ignara uisendi* and *Jug.* 93.3 *more ingeni humani cupido difficilia faciundi.* **instinctor:** the earliest occurrence of this verbal derivative. T. uses it again at 4.68.5 *acerrimo instinctore belli*, a passage twice echoed by Ammianus (21.12.20, 30.1.2). Personal agency is unusual for *instinguere* and its derivatives: passion or experience usually provides the spur (70.1n. *instinctu decurionum*). In Book 1 T. also initiates *instigator* (38.3) and *instigatrix* (51.3) and uses *instinctus* (57.2, 70.1).

23.1 incertum: sc. *est.* **an repens:** sc. *fuerit.* The unexpressed alternative appears in the next sentence, *iam pridem*; cf. 8.2n. *an... dubium*, 75.2n. *repens*, in antithesis with *iam pridem*, means 'recent' *OLD* 2. **studia militum... affectauerat:** the question is, which soldiers? Throughout chh. 23–5 Otho seems to be dealing with praetorians (see below on *uetustissimum quemque* and *Campaniae lacus et Achaiae urbes* and note the contrast at 26.1 *legionum quoque et auxiliorum*), but no source includes praetorians on Galba's march to Rome. Either T. has mistaken the troops whose support Otho courted *en route* (so Chilver (1957) 33) or the historical tradition is lacunose (so Heubner *ad loc.*; Murison (1993) 29–30) and T. has simply focused Otho's rhetoric on the troops who made a difference in January 69. In either case, the arguments that Otho uses here, unlike the monetary transactions in ch. 24 (which are also known to Plutarch and Suetonius), are supplied by T. **in itinere in agmine:** the doublet appears at Cic. *Att.* 6.4.3 *haec festinans scripsi in itinere atque agmine* and, in circumstances like those of the present passage, at *A.* 3.9.1 *in agmine atque itinere crebro se militibus ostentauisset.* **uetustissimum quemque militum nomine uocans:** a carefully chosen detail: a decade of service in Lusitania separated Otho from his last contact with the Rome-based praetorians (37.1n. *commilitones*); since praetorian service lasted sixteen years, he would only know the old-timers. **uocans... appellando:** for the *uariatio* thus far cf. 43.1 *occurrens... exprobrans... uertendo* and Sörbom (1935) 91. But the list of Otho's tactics continues with three historic infinitives (*agnoscere, requirere, iuuare*) and a second gerund (*inserendo*), a form of *uariatio* used by T. only here. **quaeque alia turbamenta** = *et ea alia quae turbamenta* (sc. *erant*); for the form see 63.2n. *turbamenta* is a rare word with a Sallustian past (*Hist.* fr. 1.55.25 *maxuma turbamenta rei publicae*) and a future in Ammianus (25.7.12, 26.7.8). **uulgi:** 25.2n.

23.2 Campaniae lacus et Achaiae urbes classibus adire soliti: frequent trips to Campania are on record for Nero and therefore for the praetorian detachments who guarded him (A.D. 59, *A.* 14.4–13;

A.D. 64, *A.* 15.33, Suet. *Ner.* 20; A.D. 65, *A.* 16.10; A.D. 66 *A.* 16.19.1; see Millar (1977) 61–6 for the role of the praetorians). The lakes in question were the lagoon of Baiae (*lacus Baianus*) and lake Avernus. Nero was in Greece from August of 66 through November of 67 (Bradley (1978a)). One of the praetorian prefects, Tigellinus, accompanied him (72.1 n); the troops themselves participated in an abortive canal project at the Isthmus (Suet. *Ner.* 19.2, Dio 63.10.1–3). **eniterentur** 'struggled over' *OLD* 1 b; cf. *A.* 2.20.1 *aggerem eniteretur.*

24.1 Maeuius Pudens: named only by T., though the bribe is recorded by both Plutarch and Suetonius (see below). **per speciem conuiuii** 'on a pretext of (giving them) dinner'. Prior attempts to bribe praetorians are rare indeed: apart from the donative offered by Nymphidius Sabinus (5.1 n.), the machinations of Nero's mother are the best attested (*A.* 13.18.2, 13.21.4). **centenos nummos:** Plutarch and Suetonius report an equivalent bribe of 1 (denarius) aureus = 25 silver denarii = 100 HS. This sum represents about 3 per cent of the regular praetorian's 750 denarius annual salary at this period, or eleven days' wages. For other bribes see 5.1 n. *neque dari donatiuum*, 66.1 n. *addidit . . . sestertios.*

24.2 quam: connecting relative (= *et eam*). **uelut publicam largitionem . . . intendebat:** the object of *intendebat* 'intensified' (*OLD* 5) is *largitionem* 'bribery'; *uelut publicam* is a predicate modifier ('which was so to speak wholesale'); cf. *A.* 3.12.3 *an falsa haec in maius uulgauerint accusatores*, where *falsa* ('which were false') is a predicate. **animosus** 'energetic' *OLD* 3; cf. Plin. *Nat.* 10.83 *animosa contentio* (of birds vying in singing). **Cocceio Proculo speculatori:** for the role of the *speculatores* in Otho's coup see further 25.1, 27.2, 31.1, 35.2. *speculatores* worked with the praetorian cohorts, particularly as imperial bodyguards (2.11.3 *ipsum Othonem comitabantur speculatorum lecta corpora*; Suet. *Cl.* 35.1, *G.* 18.1; cf. *Cal.* 44.2), but were not of them (see McC–W 400). Their different loyalties are illustrated in ch. 31 ff., where the *speculatores* desert, while the praetorian cohort on guard duty remains at its post. **per socordiam praefecti:** as the second appendix in this sentence and following on the neatly terminated result clause *ut . . . dederit* this characterization of Laco comes as a (damning) surprise. T. joins Suetonius (*G.* 14.2) in applying to him a Sallustian term of opprobrium (*socors* and *socordia* occur nineteen times in Sallust); 6.1 n. *Cornelius Laco.*

25.1 sed tum brings the narrative back to the post-adoption present. **Onomastum:** he reappears at 27.1. **sceleri . . . praefecit:** with the formal term *praefecit* 'put in charge of' *sceleri* is unexpected; for the effect cf. Plaut. *St.* 683 *cado te praeficio, Stiche*, and Cic. *Red. Sen.* 15 *quasi praefectis libidinum.* **a quo:** connecting relative (= *et ab eo*). **Barbium Proculum tesserarium et Veturium optionem eorundem:** Plutarch says that they were among the now-suspect adherents of Tigellinus and Nymphidius Sabinus (*G.* 24.1; 25.2n. *primores . . . suspectos*). T. emphasizes instead their subordinate rank; cf. below *manipulares.* The duties of a *tesserarius* involved the daily watchword (Veget. 2.7); the *optio* was a kind of ADC: Festus 184 M *optio in re militari appellatus is quem decurio aut centurio sibi rerum priuatarum administrum, quo facilius obeat publica officia.* Suetonius reports the source of Otho's funds (a kickback of a million HS from a slave whom Otho had arranged a lucrative post) and the careful planning of the solicitation (*O.* 5.2). Omitting the former and much of the latter T. emphasizes the small numbers involved (*duo*). **perductos** 'won over' *OLD* 3. **pretio et promissis:** T.'s alliterative phrase is more compact than Plut. *G.* 24.1 'some with money, others with hopes' and less detailed than Suet. *O.* 5.2 *omnibus dena sestertia repraesentata et quinquagena promissa.* **pertemptandos:** cf. 29.2 *pertemptari*; T. uses *temptari* with the same meaning (75.1). **transferendum et transtulerunt:** for paronomasiac epigrams in Book 1 see (in App. 2). 6.1, 16.4, 45.1, 48.1, 49.4, 81.1.

25.2 asciti: sc. *sunt.* **suspensos . . . animos:** cf. 2.4 *suspensis prouinciarum et exercituum mentibus.* **primores militum:** T. uses *primores* as both substantive (4.3 *primores equitum*, 71.2 *primoribus ciuitatis*, 88.2 *primores senatus*) and adj. 81.1 *primoribus feminis uirisque*). **uulgus** is an insulting label for soldiers, rare elsewhere, but not in T. (GG IA(b); 'two-fifths of the occurrences of *uulgus* in the *Histories* refer to soldiers' Newbold (1976) 85). In Book 1: 23.1, 46.4, 69, 80.2, 83.1. **mutandae militiae:** compared with legionary soldiers, praetorians had an easier job (*A.* 1.17.6 *urbanas excubias*), higher pay (750 denarii per annum versus 375), a shorter term of service (sixteen years versus twenty), and more influence, so any change would be a loss. A worse change than transfer to the legions (which seems to be envisaged here) awaited them under Vitellius, who discharged them (2.67.1). They were easily won over by Vespasian (2.82.3; cf. 2.96.2, 3.43.1).

26.1 infecit: with the infecting agent as the subject this is bolder than 3.11.1 *legiones uelut tabe infectae* and closer to Sal. *Cat.* 36.5 *tanta uis morbi ac ueluti tabes plerosque ciuium animos inuaserat* (cf. *Jug.* 32.4 *ueluti tabes inuaserat, Hist.* fr. 4.46 *qui quidem mos ut tabes in urbem conuectus*). For other medical metaphors in Book I see 4.1n. *quid... aegrum.* **legionum quoque et auxiliorum:** those in Rome in January of 69 (6.2nn.); see also 54.3n. *asciscitur auxiliorum miles.* **labare... fidem:** a Livian metaphor (22.61.10, 27.1.5, 32.30.9). **postero iduum die:** sc. *Ianuarium*; the day after the Ides is 14 January. *postridie eius die* is found occasionally (*TLL* s.v. *postridie* 254.69–74), but for forward reckoning from a named day only Cic. *Sull.* 52 *posterum diem nonarum* is cited as a parallel. Pliny's *pridie posteroue pleniluni die* (*Nat.* 7.38) is, however, similar, and such expressions are an easy extension of usages such as Cic. *Fam.* 3.8.10 *nonis Octobribus... profecti sumus; haec scripsi postridie eius die*, *Fam.* 16.20 *aut nonis aut postridie*, *Att.* 12.5.4 *Tiro idibus reuertetur, te exspectabo postridie*, and Colum. 11.2.84 *kalendis Nouembribus et postridie*. The transmitted text has, however, been doubted on chronological grounds and variously emended. Mommsen (1866) argued (and many agree) that *postquam uulgatum erat* is a reference to Galba's announcement of the German sedition in his speech to the praetorians (18.2) and that the abortive proclamation took place *postridie*, i.e. on 11 January (for support for *postridie* and other emendations see Wellesley's Appendix Critica). But news about the German sedition kept arriving after the 10th (19.2 *crebrioribus in dies Germanicae defectionis nuntiis*) and *postquam uulgatum erat* is not precise enough to make *postridie* alone a reference to 11 January. **rapturi fuerint** serves both as the verb of a secondary sequence result clause and as the apodosis of a past contrary-to-fact condition. The tension between the perf. subj., denoting an actual result (3.1n. *prodiderit*), and the fut. participle, denoting a potential occurrence, makes this periphrastic form suitable for 'near-miss' conditionals here and at Liv. 26.10.7 *ea res tantum tumultum ac fugum praebuit, ut, nisi castra Punica extra urbem fuissent, effusura se omnis pauida multitudo fuerit.* For further examples see K–S II §215.6a. **incerta... castra... consensum:** the objects of *timuissent* appear parallel but imply different structures: *incerta* is a direct object, *sparsa... castra* an '*ab urbe condita*' expression (18.1n. *obseruatum... dirumpendis*), *nec facilem... consensum* abbreviates a fearing clause (e.g. *ut consensus facilis fieret*). **incerta noctis:** 4.3n. *deterrimi seruorum.* For substantive *incerta* cf. 2.77.2 (*proeliorum*), *A.* 3.54.4 (*maris et tempestatium*), 4.23.2 *belli*; cf. Sal. *Hist.* fr. 1.24 *per... incerta humani generis*, fr. 2.87 *ceteris fuga tuta fuit incerto noctis et metu insidiarum.* With *noctis* T. also uses *obscurum* (2.14.3). **temulentos:** praetorian drunkenness and disorder will figure prominently in chh. 80–5. **sed ne per tenebras... destinaretur** 'but lest in the darkness somebody else, whoever might be presented to the troops from Pannonia or Germany (most of whom did not know Otho), be proclaimed in Otho's stead'; for the addition of a object clause to a verb already supplied with a direct object cf. 84.1 n. *ne . . . ne . . . ut.*

26.2 oppressa: sc. *sunt.* **elusit** 'made light of'; cf. 29.1 *quidam minora uero, ne tum quidem obliti adulationis.* In connecting *eludere* with the elderly Galba T. evokes a typical plot element of Roman comedy, the gulling of the *senex* (e.g. Ter. *Ph.* 885 *summa eludendi occasiost mihi nunc senes*; cf. Hor. *S.* 1.10.40–1 *Dauoque Chremeta | eludente senem*, Manil. 5.473 *elusos senes*). Similar forces were at work in Vitellius' court: 2.96.1 *amici adulantes mollius interpretabantur.* **consilii quamuis egregii . . . inimicus:** if this is not simply a general critique, it is perhaps a reference to Laco's (otherwise unattested) opposition to the only plan T. recommends vis-à-vis the praetorians, namely, the payment of a donative, however small (18.3). For the silence of all but T. on much pertaining to Laco see 6.1 n.

27–35 The beginning of Galba's end

The narrative of January 69 moves forward again in ch. 27. At the outset Galba and Otho are juxtaposed, with Galba dignified but unrealistic and ineffective, Otho hiding tumultuous emotion. The prosecution of Otho's plans and his proclamation as emperor are noted briefly but develop no momentum as yet (27.2–28). At ch. 29 the focus returns to Galba and the successful adoption candidate, Piso, who makes his cameo appearance in speech (29.2–30). The remainder of the panel is devoted to Galba's response to Otho's challenge (31.1–2, 32.2–33) and to the mood in Rome, both military (31.3) and civilian (32.1, 34–5). As T.'s material gets more exciting forward progress slows: chh. 27–47 report the events of a single day, 15 January 69. T. develops the details available to him by drawing on other memorable stories (29.1 n. *fatigabat*) and story patterns (27.1 n. *audiente . . . interpretante*), by writing a speech for Piso (29.2–30) and a debate for Galba's court (32.2–33), and by describing the behaviour of various segments of the Roman populace. For the parallel tradition see App. 1.

27.1 octauo decimo kalendas Februarias: between *decimo* and *kalendas* understand *die ante*: 15 January. **haruspex Vmbricius:** perhaps Umbricius Melior – *haruspicum in nostro aeuo peritissimus* (Plin. *Nat.* 10.19) – who was one of Pliny's authorities for Books 10 (birds) and 11 (insects), in the latter as author of a treatise *de Etrusca disciplina.* **instantes insidias ac**

domesticum hostem: for Umbricius' rather melodramatic utterance T. personifies *insidiae* and uses an oxymoron that Cicero applied to Catilinarian conspirators (*Cat.* 3.14, 22, 28; cf. *Flac.* 95). T.'s *domesticus hostis* points more directly to Otho than does Plutarch's 'danger of treachery' (*G.* 24.2 δόλου κίνδυνον). For the connection between *exta* and domestic disaster cf. Liv. 8.9.1 *Decio caput iocineris a familiari parte caesum haruspex dicitur ostendisse.* On the liver see Meer (1987) with the review by Linderski (1995) 595–9. **praedicit** 'announces' (*OLD* 2), a technical term for prophecy. **audiente . . . interpretante:** this appendix recounts Otho's opportunistic reinterpretation of the omens. In contrast to Galba, Otho is a believer in omens (22.2 *persuaserat*, cf. 18.1 *contemptorem talium*). In Plutarch's version his belief brings on panic, not confidence (*G.* 24.3). Structurally the scene resembles *peripeteia*-producing messenger speeches such as that at Soph. *OT* 1008ff., where Jocasta hears news of which only she understands the significance then rushes off to take drastic action. **architecto et redemptoribus** 'architect and agents'; *redemptor* is a technical term for the purchaser of a public contract (Fest. 270M) but T. uses it here as an agent noun for *redimere*, whose semantic range includes private transactions. Plutarch has 'builders and sellers' (*G.* 24.4). Hellegouarc'h suggests that T.'s words double as a reference to the 'mastermind and agents' of the plot. **conuenerat** 'had been agreed upon' *OLD* 7; cf. Suet. *O.* 6.2 *quod signum conuenerat.*

27.2 eoque: 13.3n. **innixus liberto:** a peculiar detail, which has been taken variously as further characterization of Otho as either *mollis* (Alford) or casual (Heubner) and as an unassimilated remnant of a variant story recorded in Suetonius, that Otho excused his departure with a sudden attack of illness (*O.* 6.3; Townend (1964) 357). For the retention of details that conflict with T.'s narrative see also 31.1n. *insidiis et simulatione*, 62.2n. *nomine . . . prohibuit.* **Tiberianam domum:** an imperial residence initiated by Tiberius on the north-facing slope of the Palatine, overlooking the Forum (Richardson (1992) 136–7). The palace adjoined the Velabrum at its north-west corner (see map 2). **Velabrum:** a vaguely defined area south of the Forum and west of the Palatine, the site of a busy market (see map 2 and Richardson (1992) 406–7). In T.'s version Otho skirts the Forum, which will shortly see Galba's assassination (41.2); Plutarch sends him right into it (*G.* 24.4 εἰς ἀγοράν). **miliarium aureum:** it stood *in capite Romani fori* (Plin. *Nat.* 3.66–7); for Pliny it was a logical point from which to measure the lengths of roads leading from the centre of Rome to its various gates.

It might have been chosen as a rallying point for its symbolic value as the centre of Rome's arterial network (though that symbolism is not explicitly attested anywhere); it lay a considerable distance from the *castra praetoria*, to which Otho was eventually carried (see map 1). **tres et uiginti:** a small number as measured against the hundreds in the cohort on guard at the Palatine, but perhaps the full complement of its *speculatores* (apart from the opportunistic Julius Atticus; 35.2n.). For the numbers see Chilver *ad loc.* **sellae:** Suetonius (*O.* 6.3) has a *sella muliebris* and other colourful details not used by T.: when the bearers grew tired Otho continued on foot until a sandal came loose, whereupon he was carried to the barracks on the shoulders of his supporters. **mucronibus:** T. uses both *mucro* and *gladius* of the praetorian weapon (cf. 80.2 *rapta arma, nudati gladii*). **rapiunt:** sc. *in castra praetoria*; cf. Suet. *O.* 7.1 *quasi raptus de publico.* **miraculo** 'amazement' *OLD* 4. Like T., Suetonius is hard put to explain the eager adherence of non-conspirators to Otho's cause: *O.* 6.3 *obuio quoque non aliter ac si conscius et particeps foret adhaerente.* The same combination of planning and surprise characterizes Caecina's defection from Vitellius: 3.13.1 *incipientibus qui conscii aderant ceteros re noua attonitos in uerba Vespasiani adigit.* **clamore et gladiis:** the same double reference to swords appears at Plut. *G.* 25.2. **sumpturi:** agrees with plural sense of *pars.*

28 Iulius Martialis tribunus: only here and at 82.1. **magnitudine subiti sceleris:** causal abl. with *praebuit*, referring to the scale of Otho's uprising as it developed over the course of the day (by leaps and bounds), not just to its state upon arrival at the *castra praetoria* (which, on T.'s reckoning, was still small: the initial twenty-three soldiers plus *totidem*, 27.2). In focusing on *why* Martialis acted as he did T. omits *what* he did, namely, admit Otho and his train into the praetorian camp: cf. Plut. *G.* 25.3 'Of tribunes the one on guard at the camp, Martialis ... allowed them to enter.' **an ... metuens:** an alternative explanation for Martialis' action. For the structure cf. *A.* 15.56.3 (on a conspirator naming names) *Scaeuinus ... imbecillitate, an cuncta iam patefacta credens ... edidit ceteros.* **contra tenderet** 'exerted himself against; resisted' *OLD* 12. **suspicionem conscientiae:** where T. explains how suspicions might have arisen (cf. 3.10.2 *nimius pauor conscientiam argueret*), Plutarch reports consensus on Martialis' innocence: *G.* 25.3 'not himself a conspirator, so they say, but confounded by the unexpected event and afraid'. For more after-the-fact speculation about loyalties see 31.1 *quod postea creditum est, insidiis et simulatione*, and ch. 42 on T. Vinius.

29.1 ignarus: *nescius* is used with like irony at 2.57.1 *Vitellius uictoriae suae nescius*. *ignarus* is applied to Galba again at 39.2 and 49.3. **fatigabat** 'importuned' (*OLD* 3b) conveys the futility of Galba's persistence in what was a standard response to unfavourable omens, i.e. repeating the sacrifice until a sign of divine favour – a *litatio* – was obtained (Gel. 4.6.6, Cic. *Div.* 2.36). The scene may be modelled on literary treatments of the prelude to Caesar's assassination, e.g. Suet. *Jul.* 81.4 *pluribus hostiis caesis, cum litare non posset, introiit curiam spreta religione Spurinnamque* (sc. *haruspicem*) *irridens*. If so, it will be the first in a series of analogies to memorable Republican deaths: Otho's suicide, paradoxically enough, wins accolades approaching those of Cato (cf. Martial 6.32), and the *deformitas* of Vitellius' end matches that of Pompey's (3.84.5). **rumor rapi . . . senatorem, . . . Othonem esse:** for acc. + inf. supplying the content of *rumor* cf. 34.2 *occisum* (sc. *esse*) *in castris Othonem uagus . . . rumor*. **incertum quem senatorem** 'some unidentified senator' (Irvine), a compressed expression for *senatorem quendam, quis senator incertum est* (cf. Virg. *Aen.* 8.352 *collem, quis deus incertum est, habitat deus*); *quem* has been attracted into the case of its antecedent. **ex tota urbe** reflects the course of Otho's progress from the head of the Forum to the *castra praetoria* on the north-east outskirts of the city (see map 1). **obuius:** sc. *Othoni*. **alii . . . quidam:** T. regularly varies the pronouns used with *alii*: in Book 1, 27.2 *alii . . . plerique*, 39.1 *alii . . . alii . . . plerique . . . plures*, 41.2 *alii . . . plures*, 41.3 *quidam . . . alii . . . crebrior fama*. The construction here is further complicated by the different omissions in the parallel participial phrases: the object (e.g. *uisa*, cf. *A.* 12.40.1 *illo augente audita*) is missing in the first, the participle itself (e.g. *referentes*) in the second. **integra auctoritas maioribus remediis seruabatur:** *integra* is a predicate adj. 'preserved *intact*'. Otho receives similar advice at 2.33.2. For the medical metaphor see 4.1 n. *quid . . . aegrum*.

29.2 Piso . . . in hunc modum allocutus est: as he had done for Galba, so for Piso T. deepens his characterization by means of a speech. Like that earlier speech, this one lacks an equivalent in the parallel tradition. But whereas the earlier speech depended for its effect on its 'dissonance with the surrounding narrative' (Keitel (1991) 2775), this one must be read in conjunction with the speeches that bracket it, both of which include descriptions of Piso (15.2–3, 38.1; see also 21.1 n. *efferatum*). Piso's purpose in this speech is to secure the loyalty of the on-duty cohort. In short order he claims a link between himself and his audience (*sextus . . . esset*), attacks his rival (*nihil . . . exercuit*), and explains what is in his audience's best interests

(*Galba . . . accipietis*), a structure mirrored in Otho's first speech (37–8; Fabia (1893) 285, Keitel (1991) 2778). The first section contains some remarkably false notes (see nn. on *commilitones, incruentam*) and the invective verges on the hysterical (*euertere imperium, transfugae ac desertores*) and even misfires (cf. 71.1 *Otho . . . non deliciis neque desidia torpescere*). The third section has to its credit predictions that are borne out by subsequent events (*uacua nomina; transcendet haec licentia in prouincias*), but begins with another false claim (see n. on *consensus generis humani*) and ends with a misstep (see n. on *donatiuum*). This does not add up to an impressive performance. Of the four qualities in Piso that Galba cites in explaining his selection, the first and fourth – *praeclara indoles tua* and *ea uita in qua nihil praeteritum excusandum habeas* – appear to have been irrelevant (15.2–3, cf. 30.1 *nihil arrogabo . . . nobilitatis aut modestiae*). The second, *amor patriae*, is echoed but not confirmed in *senatus et ipsius imperii uicem doleo* (29.2), while the third, *aetas tua quae cupiditates adulescentiae iam effugerit*, undermines Piso's prediction of *libidines* in Otho, six years his elder (30.1). More to the point is Otho's observation that Galba selected a son *sui simillimus* (38.1). In the course of this speech it becomes apparent that Piso resembles Galba not so much in *disciplina* and *parsimonia* as in his refusal to acknowledge a reality that falls short of ideal. He emulates Galba in glossing over unpalatable situations with appealing words (29.2 *solacium*, 30.2 *consensus*) and, more significantly, he fails to see that his epigram *nemo . . . umquam imperium flagitio quaesitum bonis artibus exercuit* (30.1) is as applicable to the facts of Galba's principate as to Otho's. In style the speech distinguishes itself from the surrounding narrative by its bland antitheses and parallel structures, the simplicity of the *uariatio*, the rhetorical ornaments, and the pleonasms. For further discussion and bibliography see Keitel (1991) 2776–9. **commilitones:** a form of address not justified by Piso's career (14.1 n.); Otho uses it with (slightly) more justification at 37.1 (see n.) and 83.2, Galba with full entitlement at 35.2. In the first three passages it introduces a request and therefore promises a future in which the speaker will be under obligation to the *milites* rather than, as in the last case, reflecting shared experience. **siue optandum . . . siue timendum erat:** a parenthetical comment on his adoption; for the verbs cf. Sen. *Dial.* 10.7.9 *at ille . . . nec optat crastinum nec timet.* **quo . . . fato:** sc. *ascitus sim*; indirect question, subject of *positum est.* **non quia** 'not that' (*OLD* 3b) + subj. rebuts a listener's inference about the speaker's reason for the preceding statement; here it denies a selfish motivation for the question *quo . . . fato.* **cum maxime** 'at this very moment' *OLD* 6b.

uicem 'on (someone's) account' + gen. *OLD* 8. **incruentam urbem et res sine discordia translatas:** belied by the retrospective, esp. 6.2 *introitus* (sc. *Galbae*) *in urbem trucidatis tot milibus inermium militum infaustus* and 8–9.1. Otho, in his response, supplies more evidence of bloodshed (37.2–4).

30.1 uitia . . . euertere imperium: echoing Galba (on Nero): 16.2 *sua immanitas, sua luxuria ceruicibus publicis depulerunt*; cf. the author himself at 89.2 *Nero nuntiis magis et rumoribus quam armis depulsus.* **habitune et incessu:** 22.1 n. *mollis.* **illo muliebri ornatu:** cf. Suet. *O.* 12.1 *munditiarum uere paene muliebrium.* Feminine attire is not ascribed to Otho elsewhere (Suet. *O.* 12.1 has him wearing linen in public for Isiac rites) but rather to Nero (Suet. *Ner.* 51, cf. Dio 63.13.3 'he used to welcome senators wearing a short flowered tunic and a muslin drape around his neck'). The topic of men in women's dress (i.e. in silk or transparent fabric) was addressed by sumptuary legislation and debate under Tiberius (*A.* 2.33.1, 3.53.4) and lived on as a topos for moralists (e.g. Sen. *Ep.* 122.7, Plin. *Nat.* 11.8, Juv. 2.65–78; for further references see Courtney (1980) *ad loc.* and W–M *ad A.* 3.53.4). **mereretur** 'could he have earned?' For the impf. potential subj. referring to 'what could have or might have happened' see *NLS* §121. For the oxymoron cf. 2.10.3 *Faustus . . . pessimis moribus meruerat* and 4.34.1 *dux uterque pari culpa meritus.* **imponit** 'deceive' *OLD* 16.

30.2 consensus generis humani: another false claim (15.1 n. *deorum hominumque consensu*). **uacua nomina:** cf. 55.4 *oblitterata iam nomina.* **Nero . . . uos destituit, non uos Neronem:** the desertion in question, Nero's move to Alexandria (Plut. *G.* 2.1, Suet. *Ner.* 47.2, Dio 63.27.2), was never carried out (5.1 n. *ad destituendum Neronem . . . traductus*). Plutarch puts a similar charge in the mouth of the tribune Antonius Honoratus, who persuaded the praetorians to show their loyalty to Galba by killing Nymphidius Sabinus: *G.* 14.2 'Not even on account of these things (i.e. Nero's criminal and shameful deeds) did we tolerate deserting him, but only when we believed Nymphidius' story that he deserted us first and fled to Egypt.' T.'s neat turn of phrase echoes words written by Caesar about Nero's great-great-grandfather, L. Domitius Ahenobarbus: *Ciu.* 2.32.8 *uosne uero L. Domitium an uos Domitius deseruit?*

30.3 minus triginta: presumably a reference to the twenty-four absent *speculatores.* After *minus* (and *plus*) *quam* is frequently omitted (*A&G* §407c). **centurionem aut tribunum sibi eligentes:** as they do at 46.1. **exitus** 'consequences, results' *OLD* 5; used by Otho at 21.2

si nocentem innocentemque idem exitus maneat, and again at 83.2 *perniciosi exitus consequuntur*. **perinde** indicates an equivalence between the two potential donatives (*OLD* 3). It is the reading of a single MS (Harleianus 2764), where the rest (and Heubner) read *proinde*. For confusion between the two words cf. 33.2n. **donatiuum:** mentioned at long last, but in terms too vague to be effective for long. Otho takes up the topic at 37.5. **ob fidem . . . pro facinore:** for the antithesis between different routes to gratitude cf. Thuc. 3.58.1 'earn an honourable gratitude rather than a shameful one'.

31.1 aspernata: sc. *est*. **ut . . . euenit, timore magis et nullo adhuc consilio apud signa quam, quod postea creditum est, insidiis et simulatione:** badly garbled in transmission. M reads *ut . . . euentior te magis et nonnullo adhuc consilio par signas quod postea creditum est insidiis et simulatione. ut . . . euenit timore* is the reading of one branch of M's descendants (see Wellesley's app. crit.). A correction found in another branch of the tradition (*nullo* for *nonnullo*) yields an acceptable (if not inevitable) antithesis between *timore magis et nullo adhuc consilio* and *insidiis et simulatione*. One must then supply *quam* before *quod* to go with *magis* (52.2n. *ut Vitellius*). *apud signa* (for M's *par signas*) is an attributive prepositional phrase modifying *cohors*; cf. 3.35.1 *sua quemque apud signa*, 4.35.2 = 4.77.2 *rarum apud signa militem*. It is clear from 41.1 and 43.1 that at least two of the praetorians, Atilius Vercilio and Sempronius Densus, stayed on duty; probably the majority did (cf. 38.2 (quoted below), 41.1 *comitatae Galbam cohortis*, 43.1 *custodiae Pisonis*). Thus reconstructed the sentence denies these praetorians any credit for remaining on duty. For the historian's difficulty in discerning motives during these tumultuous hours cf. 28n. *suspicionem conscientiae*. For other textual remedies see Wellesley's Appendix Critica and Morgan (1992) 56 n. 5. **insidiis et simulatione:** despite T.'s denial here of complicity on the part of this cohort, there are traces of that version of the story elsewhere in his text, as at 38.2 *nec una cohors togata defendit iam Galbam, sed detinet* (which may of course be a bluff), and 41.1 *eo signo* (see n.).

31.2 Celsus Marius: 14.1 n.; his career included a legionary command in an Illyrian province (Pannonia, A.D. 63). His mission was unsuccessful (39.1 *Marius Celsus haud laeta rettulerit*). **Vipsania in porticu:** no remains of this building are known, but its approximate location on the south-east side of the Campus Agrippae just outside the Servian wall at the base of the Quirinal can be determined from literary references

(Richardson (1992) 319–20). On the troop dispositions and their significance for T.'s narrative see Morgan (1992), esp. 57–8 'an arc running from north-west to north to north-east of the Palace'. **tendentes** 'encamped' *OLD* 3. **praeceptum:** sc. *est.* **Amullio Sereno et Domitio Sabino primipilaribus:** only here. *primipilares* were former chief centurions. That office was normally held for a year at a time but might be iterated in different legions (Webster (1998) 114). It is presumably men waiting for such renewals who are occasionally found carrying out special military assignments such as this one and Otho's naval expedition (87.2; cf. 3.70.1, *A.* 4.72.1). **Libertatis atrio:** the German vexillations were billeted in a lavishly decorated public library that was situated just outside the *porta Fontinalis* (Richardson (1992) 41). They were therefore much closer to the Palatine and the Forum than either the Illyrian troops or the praetorians (see map 1). **caedem commilitonum:** 6.2n. *trucidatis . . . militum.* **pergunt . . . in castra praetorianorum tribuni:** the current prefect, Laco, was presumably too unpopular (6.1 n.); cf. 81.2 *praefectos praetorii ad mitigandas militum iras statim miserat.* **Cetrius Seuerus . . . Subrius Dexter:** both are attested epigraphically (*PIR*[2] C 703, *PIR* S 683); the latter was promoted to the equestrian bureaucracy under the Flavians. **Pompeius Longinus:** see below and *PIR*[2] P 622. **si** 'to see if' *OLD* 11. **incipiens adhuc necdum adulta:** for the deletion of M's *et* before *necdum* see Nipperdey (1877) 199 and Fletcher (1971) 384.

31.3 quia non ordine militiae sed e Galbae amicis fidus principi suo et desciscentibus suspectior erat: *ordine militiae* 'with military status' (a typically bold abl. of description; Draeger (1882) §61) and the parallel attributive prepositional phrase *e Galbae amicis* (cf. 24.1 *e proximis Tigellini*, 25.1 *e libertis*) describe Longinus ('being . . . '); cf. *A.* 4.66.2 *quia claris maioribus et Varo conexus.* For *ordo militiae* as 'military status' cf. *Cod. Theod.* 8.1.11 *sumere cingulum et militiae ordinem tenere numerarios iubemus*; it is not strictly true of Longinus, a praetorian tribune, for the time of the narrative, but refers rather to his background ('not a military man'), an unusual one. Praetorian tribunes were typically career soldiers (20.3nn.; cf. also the label *uir militaris* that T. applies to other praetorian tribunes: 3.73.2, *A.* 4.42.2, 15.67.3). For other explanations of the syntax see Chilver. **nutauere** 'remained undecided' (*OLD* 6) is a bald rendering of the metaphor here, which evokes an object, usually a heavy one, moving in response to opposing forces but still centred on a balance point (e.g. Juvenal's picture of great tree trunks swaying through the streets of Rome on carts, 3.256 *nutant alte populoque minantur*). *nuto* appears in an explicit statement of the competing alternatives of loyalty and rebellion at 2.98.1 *nutabat, palam... Vitellium, occultis nuntiis Vespasianum fouens* and again at 2.1 *Galliae nutantes*, 56.2 *nutantem fortunam*, 2.9.2 *trierarchi... nutantes*, 2.76.1 *nutantem* (sc. *Vespasianum*), 3.40.1 *nutantem Caecinam*, etc. Suetonius' story (*G.* 20.1) that these troops tried to join Galba but lost their (short) way does not square with T.'s story of *primipilares* sent to fetch them (Fabia (1912) 95). At least one member of the group made it to the Forum in time to incur suspicion of being Galba's assassin (41.3). **inde rursus** 'from there back again'. **longa nauigatione:** the west–east leg could be accomplished in as little as nine days but the return journey might take as many as seventy owing to the etesian winds (see 2.98.2 and Rickman (1980) 128–9). On the chronology of the vexillations' travels see Morgan (1992) 58–60, with his conclusion 'On January 15 the German troops must have been back in Rome for a minimum of four months.' Whatever the precise nature of their malaise (about which T. is vague), the important point was that Galba did not have the loyalty even of the few troops he had coddled (Morgan (1992) 62).

32.1 Palatium: the Palatine hill, not the palace; cf. *A.* 14.61.1 (of a Roman crowd rejoicing) *et Palatium multitudine et clamoribus complebant.* **mixtis... postularent:** the five-word main clause is dwarfed by the twenty-word appendix (abl. abs., participial phrase, comparative clause), emphasizing the negative characterization of the crowd over the fact of their gathering on the Palatine. **mixtis** 'mixed' (sc. with the *plebs*); for brevity's sake *mixtis* appears without either the dat. complement or the prefix that usually completes the sense (cf. 34.2 *mixtis iam Othonianis*, contrast 2.1 *permixta*, 38.3 *miscentur auxiliaribus galeis scutisque*, 53.3, 74.2). *miscere* (eighty-three times in T.) evokes disorder, contributing to the dark atmosphere that T. favours: in Book 1, 9.3, 10.2, 34.2, 38.3, 53.2, 53.3, 74.2. Caesar, by contrast, never uses *miscere*, and uses compounds only six times. **seruitiis:** more elevated than *seruis*. **dissono clamore** is formally parallel to *mixtis seruitiis*, but different in content, since *seruitiis* describes a portion of the crowd, *clamore* the commotion of the whole gathering. *dissono* is distributive, i.e. some were calling for *caedes Othonis*, others for *exitium coniuratorum* (cf. *A.* 1.34.2, 14.45.1 *ita dissonae uoces respondebant numerum aut aetatem aut sexum ac plurimorum indubiam innocentiam miserantium*). The abstract and therefore more elevated *clamor* ('din', forty-seven times) is commoner in T. than *clamores* ('shouts', nine times); here it is used even in a situation involving distinct shouts. **exitium** (Acidalius) is preferable to the MS reading *exilium*, which credits the crowd with a capacity for drawing nice distinctions (death for the rival, exile for his supporters) that is wholly foreign to T's picture; cf. Otho's reprise at 37.1 *auditisne ut poena mea et supplicium uestrum simul postulentur?* **poscentium** 'of people calling for'; 4.2n. *primo gaudentium impetu.* **in circo aut theatro:** cf. 4.3 *plebs sordida et circo ac theatris sueta.* In the circus there were chariot racing and gladiatorial games (2.94.3), in the theatre, dramatic performances. For unruly behaviour cf. 72.3, where a theatre crowd calls for a political execution. For rivalry between elements of theatre crowds see *A.* 1.77.1–4 and 11.11.2; according to 13.25.4 Nero encouraged it. The image of the populace as mere spectators of political upheaval recurs at 40.1, where the crowd finally gets a bloody show; *eodem die* here links the two 'shows'; for another see 3.83 (with Shumate (1997)), and cf. Luc. 3.128–9 *turba . . . | spectatrix scelerum.* **postularent:** Seneca mentions a gladiatorial event called the *par postulaticium* that seems to have involved crowd requests (*Ep.* 7, cf. Suet. *Cal.* 30.3 *cumque Tetrinius Latro postularetur*, where the context is again gladiatorial). **neque illis iudicium aut ueritas** 'in them was no judgment or sincerity' (for *ueritas* see *OLD* 7); the negative creates a gap between the possible (*iudicium* and *ueritas*) and the real (*neque illis*) that expresses T.'s scorn for the crowd's behaviour. With the crowd's mindless enthusiasm (cf. 90.3 *studiis uotisque certabant, nec metu aut amore, sed ex libidine seruitii*) one may contrast the senate's equally unappealing but more prudent dissimulation (45.1 n. *alium . . . populum*); cf. also 90.3 *clamor uocesque ex more adulandi nimiae et falsae.* **quippe . . . postulaturis** 'in that they were going to demand'. *quippe* here simply reinforces the explanatory participle (cf. 72.2 *quippe tot interfectis*). See also 5.2n. *quamuis . . . ablato* and 7.3n. *tamquam . . . festinantes.* **diuersa** 'different things', among them the death of Marius Celsus (45.2). The generalization is darker than precise information would be (Walker (1968) 51–2). Fickleness (*diuersa*) is a regular attribute of Tacitean crowds (cf. 45.1 *alium crederes senatum, alium populum*; 69 *uulgus mutabile*, 3.85 (quoted below), 5.8.3 *mobilitate uulgi expulsi* (sc. *reges*), etc.). **pari certamine** 'with equal enthusiasm', cf. 57.1 *secutae ingenti certamine eiusdem prouinciae legiones.* For this paradoxical critique of the fickle crowd's unchanging behaviour cf. 3.85 *uulgus eadem prauitate insectabatur interfectum qua fouerat uiuentem.* **sed tradito more quemcumque principem adulandi** 'adulation of any *princeps* whomsoever having become customary'. *sed* is prepared for by *neque*, but instead of introducing a phrase parallel to *iudicium aut ueritas* it is followed by an abl. abs. *adulandi* is a defining gen. dependent on *more* (cf. 90.3 *ex more adulandi*); the phrase implies that adulation has become part of the *mos maiorum*, comparable to the traditional procedures for e.g. choosing the *flamen Dialis* (*A.* 4.16.2 *uetusto more*) or extending the pomerium (12.23.2 *more prisco*). See also 44.2n. *tradito... more.* **licentia acclamationum** 'unruly shouts of approval' (lit. 'with the lack of restraint characteristic of acclamations'; cf. 49.1 *licentia tenebrarum*). *licentia* is an instrumental abl. parallel with *studiis*; the one noun is modified by a gen., the other by an adj.

32.2 duae sententiae: the scene now shifts from outside the palace to inside, the council of war. The debate or *agon* features in most genres of Greek literature; in historiography from the time of Herodotus it is used as a framework for the rhetorical presentation of arguments for and against a particular course of action. The form provides analysis rather than narrative (most obviously, perhaps, in the constitutional debates in Herodotus (3.80–3) and Dio (52.1–40)). The particular type found here – an *in camera* discussion among a leader's councillors – derives plausibility in histories of Rome from the Roman institution of the *consilium*, the group of family members, friends, and subordinates that a Roman would consult with before making important decisions, and is widespread in them. Caesar has some notable examples (e.g. *Gal.* 5.28.2–31.4, *Ciu.* 1.67, 2.30), and Livy, too, liked the form, even reading it into non-Roman discussions such as Antiochus' council of war (35.17–19). For other debates in T. see 2.32–3, 3.1–2, 4.76, *A.* 2.76–78.1, 16.25–6. Here the two *sententiae* are distinct in tone. Vinius offers a bland rhetoric of unrealistic plans, inaccurate assessments, facile moral labels, and unlikely projections, all couched in un-Tacitean parallel clauses. Given Otho's haste, delay was an unpromising alternative. In this whole disingenuous speech, in fact, T. is laying the foundation for his claim that Vinius was already working for Otho (42n. *conscius sceleris*). The opposing argument, *occurrendum discrimini*, receives a much more lively presentation: the language is forceful and the sarcasm palpable. The scorn with which *ceteri* counter Vinius' points is striking – little heat is generated in most *agones* – and conveys the hostility among Galba's advisors. The debate thus contributes to a leitmotiv of *H.*, the exposure of *principes* to self-interested and competitive advisors (15.4n. *alii... utilitas*). For discussion and bibliography see Keitel (1991) 2790–4. **Titus Vinius:** 1.1n., 6.1n. **opponenda seruitia:** *opponere* 'deploy' *OLD* 3. A few months later Vitellius' desperate attempt to hide himself in the Palace failed when his slaves fled (3.84.4). **firmandos aditus:** cf. Virg. *Aen.* 11.466 *pars aditus urbis firmet* with Miller (1987b). T. has a similar expression at 3.76.2 *intuta moenium firmare*. For the impracticality of the plan, see 33.1 n. *dum ... cludit.* **non eundum:** by listing the rejected action last Tacitus keeps his sentence structure from being predictable (i.e. periodic). **iratos** seriously underestimates the soldiers' mood. At 24.1 their *animi* are *flagrantes* and about to be inflamed further, at 25.2 they feel *ira* and *desperatio* and are terrified at the prospect of a transfer, at 26.1 their minds are crazed and infected by a *tabes.* **daret ... potestate:** this excerpt of reported speech with the anaphora of *daret*, the parallel structure of three successive pairs of clauses (*daret ... spatium*; *scelera ... ualescere*; *si ratio sit ... si paeniteat*), and the use of the place-marker *denique* is highly rhetorical (Adams (1973) 132). **daret:** jussive subj. in indirect statement (*NLS* §109 and 266.3). **malorum paenitentiae ... spatium** 'room (i.e. time) for the wrongdoers to repent'. **bonorum consensui:** the events of 15 January showed that the support of the *boni* on whom Galba relied (16.3) was no use to him: they did nothing (26.1, 28.1) and his association with them only spurred on the sedition (38.3 *praecipuum pessimorum incitamentum quod boni maerebant*). For *consensus* see 15.1 n. *deorum hominumque consensu.* **scelera impetu, bona consilia mora ualescere:** indirect statement of a neatly expressed but badly reasoned *sententia*; prompt response was called for (21.2n. *nec cunctatione opus*). **ualescere:** this inchoative verb (eight times in T., more than in all other authors combined; *conualescere* is preferred elsewhere) is responded to by its opposite, *languescere*, in the speech of Vinius' opponents (33.2) and by a word of kindred meaning applied by the narrator to the sedition as it developed (39.1 *crebrescentis*). For other striking inchoative verbs in Book 1 see 21.1 *concupisceret*, 71.1 *torpescere*, 80.1 *eualuit.* **ultro** 'at will' (Wellesley; *OLD* 5), is balanced by *in aliena potestate*. For the alternation adverb ~ prep. phrase cf. 89.2 and see Sörbom (1935) 95. **sit:** the immediacy and urgency of the rhetoric is enhanced by the *repraesentatio* (7.2n. *postquam ... nequiuerint*). **eandem facultatem:** sc. *fore.* **regressus** is best taken as a gen. parallel to *eundi* and dependent on *facultatem*, despite the slight redundancy of *facultas regressus* 'opportunity for retreat' where *regressus* alone would suffice (cf. *A.* 4.11.1 *nullo ad paenitendum regressu* and 12.10.2 *ut ... sit regressus ad principem patresque*). For the thought cf. 3.66.1 *fidem in libidine uictoris. regressus* has also been taken as an acc. pl. (parallel to *facultatem*), and emended to *regressum*; see Chilver.

33.1 festinandum: cf. 62.1 *nihil in discordiis ciuilibus festinatione tutius.* **ceteris:** two names are given at 33.2: Laco (the commander of the praetorian guard) and Icelus (a powerful freedman). Here the vague but inclusive *ceteris* makes Vinius, who is named, look isolated. **inualida adhuc coniuratio paucorum:** these advisors, too, underestimate the strength of the movement, perhaps deliberately (26.2n. *elusit*). T. himself has described Otho's conspiracy as small (25.2 *pauci*, 27.2 *tres et uiginti*), but the praetorians were only waiting for a leader (6.2n. *audenti parata*). The miscalculation (or misinformation) proved fatal to both Galba and his advisors. **trepidaturum etiam Othonem:** sc. *esse*, 'Otho would even be frightened'; infinitives of *esse* are omitted in the indirect statement, which continues through 33.2 *honestum. trepidaturum* is the apodosis of a condition whose protasis is implicit: *si festinatum fuerit.* For *etiam* see *OLD* 4. **qui** introduces a causal relative clause that explains why Otho would be frightened by a prompt resistance (*NLS* §157b). **ignaros** is active in sense ('men who didn't know him') and at present untrue (chh. 23–5, but cf. 70.1 *Othonis ignari* (sc. *decuriones*). **cunctatione nunc et segnitia:** circumstantial abl. *segnitia* denotes a failure of leadership (e.g. 49.3, 52.4, 56.1, 2.40, 3.3, *A.* 1.58.2, etc.) and rephrases *cunctatione*: to hesitate is to fail your side (5.2n. *laudata ... celebrata*). **terentium tempus** 'of those wasting time'; i.e. Vinius. **imitari principem:** a partisan expression; one who imitates an emperor cannot yet be an emperor. The first proclamation of Otho as *princeps* has already taken place in Tacitus' account (27.2). **discat:** 7.2n. *postquam ... nequiuerint.* The process of learning to be *princeps* is described in minute (and discreditable) detail for Vitellius at 2.60–4, cf. 2.63.1 *dominationis magistris.* **compositis castris:** this had already happened: 36.1 *haud dubiae iam in castris omnium mentes.* **prospectante Galba:** they paint a humiliating picture of Galba looking on while Otho takes possession of the symbolic 'keys' of Rome, the Forum and the Capitol, the places that Galba will want to seize when his situation becomes more precarious (39.1), and the ones that Otho will in fact take: 40.2 *forum irrumpunt*, 47.2 *Otho ... in Capitolium ... uectus.* **dum ... ianua ac limine tenus domum cludit** 'while he (sc. Galba) shut off the house, to the extent of a door and doorframe'; highly sarcastic. The Palace doors could not even be held against well-wishers: 35.1 *refractis Palatii foribus*, cf. 82.1. For *claudo* 'make inaccessible' see *OLD* 3b; for *tenus* 'to the extent of' *OLD* 3. For the purely temporal *dum* + ind. in indirect statement see *NLS* §221 iv. **obsidionem nimirum toleraturus:** more sarcasm; on *obsidio* see 68.1n.

33.2 praeclarum in seruis auxilium responds (with scorn) to Vinius' *opponenda seruitia* (q.v.). **si consensus tantae multitudinis et . . . indignatio languescat:** *consensus* refers to support for Galba (32.2n. *bonorum consensui*), *indignatio* to resentment of anyone who tried to take the highest place for himself; both sentiments contributed to the preservation of the *status quo*. What is described here will shortly come to pass: 39.1 *languentibus omnium studiis*. On *languescat* see 32.2n. *ualescere*. Some editors emend to *elanguescat*, which T. uses at 46.3 and 4.42.6, but the uncompounded form (which he uses eight times) responds precisely to *ualescere*. **consensus tantae multitudinis** responds (with sarcasm) to Vinius' *bonorum consensui*. In the view of these advisors, the *boni* are neither many nor reliable. **proinde** 'accordingly' introduces a summary of the argument thus far as preparation for the exhortation to come (21.2n.). Heubner prints the variant *perinde*. **intuta quae indecora** 'the shameful course was not (even) safe'; cf. 68.1 *intuta obsidio*, again in a context of decision-making. T. follows Sallust and Livy in his predilection for *intutus* ('unsure' *OLD* 2), which is rare outside the historians: T. nine times, Sal. once, Liv. twice, Amm. six times. **id Othoni inuidiosius:** cf. 4.1.3 *Othoniani Vitellianique militis inuidiosa antea petulantia*. **ipsis honestum:** T. will later say that Galba and Piso perished by an honourable death, *tamquam in acie* (3.68.1; cf. 2.44.2 *honestius in acie perituros*). With the plural *ipsis* the advisors profess willingness to die with Galba. In fact they survive him, but are later executed by Otho's partisans (46.5). **repugnantem** 'fighting back', a strong word, followed by the even more virulent *minaciter inuasit* and reinforced by *stimulante* ('egging on'); the debate becomes (metaphorically) a brawl. Galba, T. suggests, was moved not by reasoned argument, but by the force of personalities and by in-fighting among his supporters. The battle lines were drawn within Galba's party over the question of Galba's heir (13.1 *in duas factiones scindebantur*). Vinius (who urged Galba to adopt Otho) also lost the earlier fight. **Laco:** 6.1n. **Icelo:** 13.1n. **in publicum exitium:** an ominous sounding phrase in a neat antithesis, but only vaguely relevant to the situation. Icelus might have disregarded public welfare in pursuing his private feud with Vinius, but it is hard to see how he damaged the state. T. cannot suggest that Galba should have followed Vinius' advice, since Galba's cause was a lost one (29.1 *alieni iam imperii*).

34.1 nec: with *cunctatus*, not *accessit*; cf. 71.2 *nec Otho quasi ignosceret*. **speciosiora:** internal acc. (*NLS* §1.iv) with *suadentibus* (cf. Liv. 22.3.8 *omnibus in consilio salutaria magis quam speciosa suadentibus*, from a similar context). See further 49.3n. *famae ... nec uenditator.* **accessit** 'went along with' + dat., *OLD* 8. **praemissus:** sc. *est*; the prefix implies that Galba meant subsequently to go himself, a plan short-circuited by the rumours of Otho's death (see below). From Piso's mission (which no other source reports; Townend (1964) 357) to the deaths of Galba and Piso, T.'s account diverges considerably from the other sources, particularly Plutarch, who is elsewhere close to T. **tamen** points out the oddity of Piso going instead of Galba. At 29.1 Galba was being kept in reserve for a crisis, but that crisis is at hand. **in castra:** sc. *praetorianorum*. Piso turned back before he got there (39.1). **ut** 'in accordance with the fact that'. **iuuenis:** sc. *erat.* **magno nomine:** 14.1n. *Pisonem Licinianum.* **recenti fauore:** when Piso was presented to the troops their *fauor* was lukewarm at best (18.1–2); the cohort on the Palatine was no more enthusiastic (31.1). **infensus** 'hostile to' *OLD* 2. Vinius' misdeeds had helped make Galba unpopular (6.1n.), and Galba was unwilling to recognize the man's faults (49.3), so Laco and Icelus may have thought that Piso's hostility to Vinius would produce two desirable results, both the satisfaction of some of the conspirators' grievances and the removal of their own rival (cf. 39.2 *agitasse Laco ignaro Galba de occidendo Tito Vinio dicitur*). **et facilius de odio creditur:** cf. 2.60.1 *et Vitellius credidit de perfidia.* In *creditur* it is unclear whose beliefs are meant. Is it a statement about what T. believes? Or is it a generalization ('people very easily believe in enmity between others')? T. normally uses *credo* to express his own views (e.g. 13.2 *credo*) or *crediderim* if he is rebutting someone else's view (e.g. *Agr.* 12.6 *ego facilius crediderim*). But he later uses a similarly vague expression (42.1 *huc potius eius uita famaque inclinat*) for his own judgment between alternatives, and T. would have found it easy to believe that the upright Piso hated Vinius, *deterrimus mortalium.*

34.2 The scene shifts back to the crowd outside the Palace. **uixdum:** this adverb and the absence of connectives convey the speed with which events were unrolling. **occisum:** sc. *esse*, indirect statement dependent on *rumor.* Another faked report of a death (Vespasian's) is devised by Civilis and Classicus to persuade Cerealis to head the Gallic revolt at 4.75.1. **rumor:** sc. *erat.* With *rumor* postponed to the end of the clause the reader gets the news of Otho's death before the source is discredited, an effect that evokes the uncertainties of the time, the difficulty of getting reliable information (cf. 35.2 *inopia ueri*). **ut in magnis mendaciis** 'as so often in tall tales', cf. Sen. *Ben.* 7.30.2 *nec quisquam fingere contentus est leuia, cum magnitudine mendacii fidem quaereat.* The alliteration gives this cynical aside a colloquial tone comparable to that in Plaut. *Rud.* 515 *dum tuis ausculto magnidicis mendaciis* (cf. *Capt.* 671 *falsidicis fallaciis*) and *Ps.* 943 *mera mendacia iam fundes.* For the self-perpetuation of lies cf. 4.50.1 *ueraque et falsa more famae in maius innotuere.* For *magnis* cf. *A.* 15.36.4 *quae natura magnis timoribus, deterius credebant quod euenerat.* **interfuisse . . . et uidisse:** an almost tautological doublet emphasizing the insistence with which these liars pressed their fabrications on the credulous. **credula fama inter gaudentes et incuriosos** 'among people who rejoice without thinking rumour finds credence'; cf. *A.* 14.4.1 *facili feminarum credulitate ad gaudia.* Bad news, too, found ready belief (19.2). For the irresponsibility cf. 2.90.2 *uulgus . . . uacuum curis et sine falsi uerique discrimine. . . . clamore et uocibus astrepebat* and 4.49.3 *gaudio clamoribusque cuncta miscebant indiligentia ueri et adulandi libidine. fama* is personified and characterized as gullible; she hears news and, believing it, spreads it; cf. 2.78.4 *has ambages et statim exceperat fama et tunc aperiebat.* **multi arbitrabantur:** Suetonius asserts on his own authority what T. says people were thinking at the time: *G.* 19.2 *sed extractus* (sc. *Galba*) *rumoribus falsis, quos conspirati, ut eum in publicum elicerent, de industria dissiparant.* T., like Suetonius, will have found the notion that the rumour was part of Otho's plan in his sources, but it does not fit with T.'s assertion that Vinius was one of Otho's conspirators (42n. *conscius sceleris*) since the conspirators' plan cannot have involved both luring Galba out with the rumour and keeping him in through pressure from Vinius. Authorial support is therefore withheld from the claim that the rumour was deliberately spread. (Neither Plutarch nor Dio mentions a plan for luring Galba out.) For authorial distancing cf. also 7.2 *fuere qui crederent* and 85.2 *plerique credebant.* **compositum auctumque:** sc. *esse.* **mixtis iam Othonianis:** dat. of agent (used more than thirty times by T.; *A&G* §375, Draeger (1882) §51). **uulgauerint:** *repraesentatio* (7.2n. *postquam . . . nequiuerint*). For rumour as an instrument of policy cf. 51.5 *callide uulgatum.*

35.1 tum uero introduces similarly shocking scenes at 81.2, 4.29.2 *tum uero strepitus dissoni* etc., *Agr.* 37.2 *tum uero . . . grande et atrox spectaculum,* and *A.* 1.35.4 *tum uero, quasi scelere contaminaretur*; it often begins sentence, line, and revelation in Virgil (e.g. *Ecl.* 6.27 *tum uero . . . uideres, Aen.* 2.105 *tum uero ardemus,* 2.228 *tum uero . . . pauor,* 2.309 *tum uero manifesta,* 2.624 *tum uero . . . uisum,* etc.); cf. Sal. *Cat.* 61.1 *tum uero cerneres,* Liv. 28.20.6 *tum uero apparuit,* and see further Chausserie-Laprée 520–31. **non populus tantum** 'not only the populace'. **populus . . . plebs:** again at 36.2, 40.1, 82.1, etc. With these subjects *ruere* (modified by *in plausus et studia*) is used metaphorically, while with *plerique* it is literal (modified by *intus*). For the syllepsis cf. 9.2 *nec uitiis nec uiribus miscebantur* and 67.1 *plus praedae ac sanguinis Caecina hausit.* **imperita plebs:** cf. 89.1 *uulgus et . . . communium curarum expers populus* and 50.1 n. *non senatus . . . uulgus*. Under the imperial constitution the *plebs*, being deprived of the decision-making responsibilities it had enjoyed during the Republic, was necessarily inexperienced. T. does not have the same regret for its reduced role in the state (cf. *A.* 1.15.1 *neque populus ademptum ius questus est, nisi inani rumore*) that he has for the likewise diminished senate (45.2n. *alium . . . populum*, 85.3n. *uersare . . . torquere*). **in plausus et immodica studia:** *plausus* is the concrete form of the abstract (and therefore more elevated) *immodica studia* 'lavish enthusiasm'; 5.2n. *laudata . . . celebrata*. **ruere** is the first of a series of historic infinitives (*ostentare, scire, affirmare*) that convey the urgency of the moment (an effect enhanced by the frequentative *ostentare*): everyone was in a hurry to have his presence registered to prove that he had not been among the *Othoniani*. At 45.1 a similar scene, again with a series of historic infinitives, shows the transfer of loyalty to Otho (see n.). Plutarch (*G.* 25.4) has the crowd arrive while Galba is still sacrificing (cf. 29.1 *affertur rumor*) and adds the detail that Vinius, Laco, and some freedmen drew swords to protect Galba (6.1 n. Laco). **praereptam sibi ultionem querentes:** sc. *esse*. **ignauissimus quisque:** subject of *querentes*, modified by *nimii*; its form is singular but its meaning plural ('all the cowards'). Modifiers take their form accordingly (*A&G* §317e); cf. 2.44.1, 2.66.3, 2.84.2, 4.62.1 *ignauissimus quisque . . . pauentes.* **nimii** is an adj. with more feel ('excessive') than content; *uerbis* indicates its sphere of applicability: cf. 3.75.1 *sermonis nimius* and 4.23.3 *praeferoces initio et rebus secundis nimii.* **linguae feroces** 'fierce in tongue', a bold and typically Tacitean gen. of reference (*NLS* §73.6); cf. *A.* 1.32.2 *animi ferox*, 4.7 *occultus odii*, 12.22.1 *atrox odii*, with Harrison (1994). **donec . . . leuaretur:** T. regularly uses the subj. after *donec*, even when, as here, there is no sense of purpose involved (*NLS* §224iii). **inopia ueri . . . consensu errantium:** Galba's decision is based solely on *consensus errantium*; T. is the one who perceives *inopia ueri.* **thorace:** only here in T. Suetonius says Galba's corselet was made of cloth (*G.* 19.1 *lorica lintea*), but T. credits the garment with protecting Galba's chest from wounds (41.3). **neque aetate neque corpore:** Galba is deficient in both energy and strength (cf. 12.2 *fessa iam aetate Galbae*, 12.3 *apud infirmum*). Otho, by contrast, reacts with vigour to an even more dangerous irruption when a band of misguided soldiers break into the Palace looking for their *princeps* (82.1), and even the middle-aged Vitellius can handle unruly soldiers who rush in upon him while he is at a party (2.68.4). **resistens** is an emendation for M's *sistens*, with which *aetate* and *corpore* are hard to understand, since ablatives with *sisto* in the active voice elsewhere in T. are locative. It is not Galba's ability to stand that is important here, but his ability to withstand the pressures, both physical and psychological, that surround him. *neque . . . resistens* marks his incapacity for the former, *uictus* (in the preceding sentence) for the latter. The initial syllable will have been lost after *corpore*. For a defence of *sistens* see Morgan (1993b) 374.

35.2 obuius: the absence of any connective (asyndeton) contributes to the rapidity of the narrative. **Iulius Atticus speculator:** only here. For *speculatores* see 24.2n. Atticus, the boldest of the rumour-mongers, does not succeed, since Galba snubs him. The effect is reinforced by the distribution of T.'s narrative: in Plutarch Galba's departure follows immediately on Atticus' revelation (*G.* 26.2), but in T. Galba is already on his way out when Atticus arrives, and his departure is not mentioned again until 39.1. **cruentum . . . exclamauit:** cf. Sal. *Jug.* 101.6, where a Numidian claims to have killed the Roman general Marius. That passage, too, has a bloody sword: *simul gladium sanguine oblitum ostentans . . . quem in pugna . . . cruentauerat.* On *cruentus* see 6.1n. **occisum:** sc. *esse.* **'commilito,' inquit 'quis iussit?':** Galba's *bon mot* is reported, to various ends, in all surviving accounts of his reign (Plut. *G.* 26.2, Suet. *G.* 19.2, Dio 64.6.2; see App. 1). In T. it illustrates Galba's ostentatious imperviousness to the more obvious manifestations of adulation. **insigni . . . incorruptus:** this description, which gives a foretaste of the full obituary (49.2–4), generalizes from the events just narrated: Galba intends to resist the seditious soldiers who have put Otho at their head (*minantibus intrepidus*) and refuses to be flattered by the opportunistic Julius Atticus (*aduersus blandientes incorruptus*).

36–43 The *coup d'état*

The scene now returns to the praetorian barracks, where the coup is gathering momentum. After a paragraph illustrating the breakdown of traditional military discipline, which ends with Otho playing the slave to his own troops (36.3 *omnia seruiliter pro dominatione*), comes a speech in which Otho is held up to Piso's measure (chh. 37–8). With ch. 39 the focus shifts back to Galba's party; their final frantic discussions end with the arrival of news about Otho. A brief glance back at the barracks shows Otho dispatching the troops (40.1); after a rhetorical flourish to fill time (40.2) the soldiers arrive in the Forum to murder first Galba (ch. 41), then Vinius (ch. 42) and Piso (ch. 43).

36.1 haud dubiae iam: sc. *erant*. **non contenti agmine et corporibus . . . Othonem uexillis circumdarent:** the sense of *non contenti* is completed by an implicit inf. (*circumdare*) modified by *agmine et corporibus* 'with a throng of bodies' (hendiadys); for the scene thus summarized see 27.2 and cf. 2.29.3 *laudantes gratantesque circumdatum* (sc. *Valentem*) *aquilis signisque in tribunal ferunt*. T. makes Otho look like a puppet, Plutarch has Otho hang back at the last moment (*G*. 25.1–2), while Suetonius' Otho is more decisive (*O*. 6.3 *in castra contendit . . . ad principia deuenit*). **suggestu:** the raised platform from which a commander addressed his troops in camp (cf. 55.4) and on which symbols of power were displayed (cf. *A*. 16.29.2). T. uses both *suggestus* and *tribunal* to designate the structure, as does Caesar. **signa . . . uexillis:** praetorian *signa* were ornamental pikes bearing symbols (fashioned in silver: Plin. *Nat*. 33.58) of a unit's identity and history (founder, decorations, commemorative insignia) and *imagines* of emperors (Durry (1938) 198–206). The *uexillum* was a pennant associated with the praetorian cavalry units (Durry (1938) 203 'qui dit uexillum dit cavalerie'; cf. 2.11.2 *quinque praetoriae cohortes et equitum uexilla*). Both recur in the story of Otho's coup (41.1n. *uexillarius*, 44.2 *inter signa cohortium*). **tribunis aut centurionibus:** praetorian officers (a tribune and six centurions for each of the twelve cohorts) would have been placed or confirmed in their ranks by Galba after Nero's death; for specific purges and appointments see 20.3 and compare the purge of Othonian centurions after Vitellius' victory at 2.60.1. Earlier these officers had made pro-Galba noises (18.3), so when the sedition developed momentum and many of them, including the tribune on duty, Julius Martialis, went along with it they were not trusted (28.1). The tribunes sent from the Palace to the praetorian camp to reclaim the troops' loyalty for Galba met with a hostile reception (31.3). Conflict between men and officers also dominates the story of the praetorian riot in chh. 80–5. **gregarius miles . . . iubebat:** soldiers were now acting the commander's part; cf. 36.2n. *exhortatione mutua*, 46.1 *omnia deinde arbitrio militum acta*. **caueri . . . praepositos** 'that precautions be taken against the officers'; lit. 'that the officers be guarded against', a passive inversion of expressions such as *A*. 11.1.1 *moneret Claudium cauere uim atque opes* *principibus infensas* and 13.13.3 *amici orabant* (sc. *Neronem*) *cauere insidias mulieris.* For the warning cf. Plut. *O.* 3.2, where the praetorians urge Otho not to trust leading men (τοὺς ἀξιολόγους). Such suspicions contribute later to the riot: cf. 80.2 *fremit miles et tribunos centurionesque proditionis arguit*, 82.1 *undique arma et minae, modo in centuriones tribunosque.* Discord between ranks is a constant theme in T.'s account of the civil wars, leading, in Book 1, to the deaths of at least eight officers (59.1 four centurions, 58.2 one centurion, 80.2 a tribune and two centurions); at 82.3 praetorian officers demand discharge, so impossible has their position become. In A.D. 70 a conciliatory officer trying to signal the end of civil war ascribes such discord to fate: 4.72.3 *fato acta dictitans quae militum ducumque discordia... euenissent.* **insuper:** with *iubebat.* T. uses this adverb some thirty-one times (Cicero never, Sallust once, Caesar four times); like Livy, who uses it forty-eight times, he found it useful for conveying exasperation, indignation, and outrage (e.g. 46.3, 50.1, 64.3, 86.1).

36.2 strepere is the first of a long string of historic infinitives that extend the description begun with *iubebat.* **exhortatione mutua:** these soldiers, instead of being exhorted by their leader, are exhorting one another, another indication that they have taken command of the situation; contrast 3.27.3, 5.16.2 *exhortatio ducum*, *A.* 14.36.1 *Suetonius... exhortationes et preces miscebat.* **uariis segni adulatione uocibus** 'the changeable cries of aimless adulation'. *segni adulatione* explains *uariis.* The construction is hard to parallel (Virg. *Aen.* 4.701, 5.89 *uarios aduerso sole colores*, is close), but for the meaning cf. 4.6.2 *uariis, ut sunt hominum ingenia, sermonibus.* **ut... aspexerant** 'whenever they saw' *NLS* §217.2c. **prensare** is an emendation; M has *pressare.* Comparable scenes elsewhere in T. involve embracing, not just touching: 66.1 *arma genua uestigia prensando*, 2.46.2 *proximi prensare genua*, 4.46.3 *prensare commanipularium pectora*, *A.* 14.10.2 *centurionum tribunorumque... prensantium manum gratantiumque.* The term, like *complecti armis* below, may be borrowed from Virgil (*Aen.* 6.360 *prensantem... uncis manibus capita aspera montis*) though the context differs from Virgil's (Miller (1987b) 95–6). **complecti armis:** modelled on Virg. *Aen.* 12.433 *Ascanius fusis circum complectitur armis*, where with *armis* (from *armus*, *-i* 'upper arm' as well as *arma*) Virgil 'has furnished a notable ambiguity' (Pease on *Aen.* 4.11). Virgil's line concludes an arming scene and is followed by Aeneas kissing his son *per galeam* (12.434), so *arma* is perhaps predominant; in T., after *manibus*, *armis* is most easily taken as a body part, but Virgil's *arma* adds the point that Otho's original supporters, the on-duty *speculatores*, were armed, while those who joined in camp were not (until 38.1). **iuxta:** adverbial. **praeire sacramentum** 'dictated the oath', combining two technical expressions. *praeire* is used for the dictation of a formula by a priest (e.g. Liv. 42.28.9 *praeeunte uerba . . . pontifice maximo id uotum susceptum est*; Varro *L* 6.45 *augur consuli . . . praeit, quid eum dicere oporteat*) or other magistrate (V. Max. 4.1.10 *scriba . . . sollemne ei censori precationis carmen praeiret*). It is not elsewhere used of a soldier's oath of obedience to his commander; for this the regular expression is *sacramento* (or *sacramentum*) *dicere* or *rogare*: Caes. *Ciu.* 1.23.5 *milites Domitianos sacramentum apud se dicere iubet*; *Gal.* 6.1.2 *sacramento rogauissent*; Tac. *A.* 1.28.3 *Percennio et Vibuleno sacramentum dicturi sumus?* Both here and at 2.74.1 T. adds the religious solemnity of *praeire* to the taking of the soldier's oath.

36.3 nec deerat Otho . . . adorare 'nor did Otho fail to salute'. *desum* + inf., a construction that T. also uses at 3.58.3, 4.1.2, 4.11.1, and 4.80.3, is more common in poetry than in prose. **uulgum:** 25.2n. **omnia seruiliter pro dominatione:** sc. *facere*; cf. 84.1n. *pro me*. For the antithesis cf. Sal. *Hist.* fr. 1.55.2 *dominationis in uos seruitium suum mercedem dant.* **uniuersa classicorum legio:** 6.2n. *trucidatis . . . militum.* **ita coepit:** Suetonius reports the content of Otho's speech in a single sentence: *O.* 6.3 *ad conciliandos pollicitationibus militum animos nihil magis pro contione testatus est quam id demum se habiturum quod sibi illi reliquissent.* This accords reasonably well with T.'s *omnia seruiliter pro dominatione* (36.3), but does not match the range of material in the speech T. gives Otho. According to T., Otho's ostensible purpose was to rouse further his already eager supporters (36.3 *accendendos . . . ratus*). To do so he employs many of the topoi of battle exhortations which, when used to incite Roman soldiers to overthrow a Roman ruler, generate for the reader both a general irony and a specific reminiscence of Sallust's Catiline (Keitel (1987)). But the speech also derives effect from comparison with the speech of Otho's rival, Piso, and with T.'s own retrospective of events (chh. 4–11), which covers some of the same ground. The speech draws on the hostile tradition about Galba that Plutarch and Suetonius transmit via anecdotes and moral labels (see nn. on ch. 49.2–4). In criticizing Galba T.'s Otho uses stronger language than T. allowed himself and cites more names in the long list of *occisi* (37.3), but his criticisms hit the mark much better than Piso's did (29.2n. *Piso . . . allocutus est*). Only occasionally does his rhetoric go beyond what the narrative warrants. But ignorance and exaggeration mar his description of the contemporary situation and his view of the future is short-sighted in the extreme (perhaps deliberately so), contrasting unfavourably with Piso's accuracy. Perhaps inevitably Otho shares his opponents' recourse to *falsa nomina*, yet he ends well, discarding moral claims and offering a pragmatic epigram. Stylistically the speech has more in common with the two preceding speeches than with the narrative, containing a wealth of parallels and antitheses, several instances of anaphora and pleonasm, and two neat epigrams.

37.1 quis ad uos processerim: names and labels represent stability; that they fail in revolutionary times, a topos since Thucydides at least (3.82–3), is a theme of the narrative of 15 January: 29.2 *Caesar ascitus sum*, 29.2 *solacium*, 31.1 *consensus*, 37.4–5, 40.2 *pulchrum et memorabile facinus*, 42n. *Sulpicius Florus . . . ciuitate donatus.* The present passage may allude more specifically (and utterly ironically) to Scipio's speech recalling mutinous soldiers to traditional discipline (Liv. 28.27.3–4; see Keitel (1987) 74). **commilitones:** before his quaestorship (see 13.1 n.) Otho presumably did the years of military service that customarily preceded a senatorial career, which gives some slight justification for his use of the term. But see 29.2n. **imperatorem . . . an hostem:** 17.2n. *pro . . . senatu.*

37.2 poena mea et supplicium uestrum: cf. 32.1 *caedem Othonis et coniuratorum exitium.* **poena . . . postulentur:** in Book I T. pairs *poena* with four different verbs: cf. 58.1 *ad poenam exposcentium*, 72.1 *ad poenam flagitauerunt*, 84.3 *ad poenam uocare.* **et . . . promisit:** the obj., *poenam et supplicium*, can be supplied from the context, but Galba did not in fact promise punishment (see 35.2). **cuius lenitatis est Galba** 'for such is Galba's clemency'; lit. 'for he is of this clemency'; the rel. pronoun introduces a parenthetic comment (*OLD* 12b, K–S II §195.5). T. uses gen. where abl. is standard. **nullo exposcente** forms a neat antithesis with *postulentur* but is irrelevant to the scene referred to (6.2n. *trucidatis . . . militum*). **tot milia innocentissimorum militum trucidauerit:** at 6.2 they are simply *inermes.*

37.3 horror animum subit: *horror* occurs only here in T. The best parallels are poetic: V. Fl. 8.67 *ille silet, tantus subiit* (sc. *Iasonem*) *tum uirginis horror*, Stat. *Theb.* 10.160–1 *ecce repens . . . horror | Theiodamanta subit*, 9.861–2 *sic iuuenem saeui conspecta mole Dryantis | iam non ira subit, sed leti nuntius horror*. For *subire* see 13.2n. *rei . . . subisse.* **feralem**, which describes things associated with death or the underworld, occurs eight times in T.; before T. (but not after) the word is more common in poetry than in prose, though it is found in a declamation (Sen. *Contr.* 9.2.2) and in Pliny the Elder (three times). In the retrospective T. characterized the *introitus* as *infaustus* and *formidolosus* (6.2). **Galbae:** sc. *esse.* **decimari deditos iuberet, quos deprecantes**

in fidem acceperat: in the retrospective T. reported none of these damning details; Suet. *G.* 12.2 also mentions decimation. For the procedure see Polybius 6.38. See also 51.5n. *decimari legiones.* **his auspiciis:** for the metaphor cf. *A.* 15.74.2, where a dedication to Jupiter Vindex is interpreted after the fact as an *auspicium et praesagium* of the revolt of Julius Vindex. **occisi . . . castris:** like T.'s retrospective, this list surveys the empire then focuses on Rome. Here again Otho gives details – the first three deaths on his list – omitted in the retrospective. **occisi Obultronii Sabini et Cornelii Marcelli in Hispania:** both men were senators, both get brief mentions in the *Annals* (13.28.3, 16.8.3). Various posts have been conjectured for them in Spain, including governor and legate of Baetica (see *PIR*² O 4 and Chilver *ad loc.* for discussion and bibliography; on Marcellus see also *PIR*² C 1403). By analogy the third name, Betuus Cilo, is assigned to the governor of Aquitania; the man is otherwise unknown (*PIR*² B 124). **Fontei Capitonis:** 7.1–2nn. **Clodii Macri:** 7.1n. **Cingonii:** 6.1n. **Turpiliani:** 6.1n. **Nymphidii:** 5.1n.

37.4 quae usquam prouincia . . . correcta: considerably exaggerated, judging by T.'s provincial overview in chh. 8–11. **emendata et correcta:** contrast T.'s assessment at 20.3 *nec remedium in ceteros fuit.* **supplicia et contumelias uestras:** Galba discharged some praetorian officers (20.2) and forbore to bribe or flatter the guard (5.2; 18.2 *nec ullum orationi aut lenocinium addit aut pretium*).

37.5 Polycliti . . . Vatinii . . . Aegiali: in the sing., Neronian agents (*A.* 14.39.1–2, *A.* 15.34.2; cf. *PIR*² P 561, *PIR* V 208; Aegialius only here). T. uses pl. proper names with the same tone of outrage at 2.95.2 *Polyclitos* and *A.* 12.60.4 *Matios posthac et Vedios* (cf. also *A.* 15.14.2). **petierunt**, an emendation for M's *perierunt*, is accepted by Goelzer (cf. *petiuerunt*, Ritter (1836), citing *A.* 15.25.2 *qui peterent quod eripuerant*). Syntax requires a transitive verb and sense a verb that suits the antithesis with *rapuit.* One family of descendants has *parauerunt*, but that is both inherently vague and feeble as a contrast for 'grabbed'. For a long list of other conjectures see Wellesley's app. crit.; Heubner prints *perdiderunt*, which ruins Otho's rhetoric: Nero's henchmen undoubtedly grabbed more than they wasted, too, so there is little point in saying that Icelus did. **grassatus esset** 'would have proceeded' *OLD* 3; the word is also associated with predatory violence (*OLD* 2). In T. it is paired with instrumental abl. such as *ueneno* (3.39.1), *dolo* (4.16.1), *dissimulatione* (4.56.2), and *ferro* (*A.* 15.60.2) and is used both of Nero prowling the back streets of Rome and assaulting passers-by (*A.* 13.25.2) and of the great fire (*A.* 15.40.1). The agent noun *grassator* is attested in Cato (cited at Gel. 11.2.5); Cicero and Caesar ignore the word-group almost entirely, while Sallust uses it three times (cf. esp. *Jug.* 64.5 *cupidine atque ira ... grassari*). It abounds in imperial prose. Suetonius, who uses *grassari* and related words eleven times, applies it to Galba's henchmen (Vinius among them) at *G.* 14.2 *his diuerso uitiorum genere grassantibus*, which may indicate that T. transferred the term from its context in the source to his independent creation, Otho's speech. **uiles** 'of little account' *OLD* 4. **una illa domus:** for *domus* 'property, wealth' (not in *OLD*) cf. *A.* 2.33.2 *angustas ciuium domos* with its context and Juv. 3.10 *sed dum tota domus raeda componitur una* and especially 14.259 *incrementa domus* (with Courtney (1980) *ad loc.*). **quod uobis numquam datur et cotidie exprobratur:** a neatly balanced homoioteleuton to conclude the rehearsal of the present regime's crimes. *cotidie exprobratur* 'is a daily source of reproaches' refers, presumably, to quips like Galba's '*legi a se militem, non emi*' (5.2).

38.1 tristitia: 14.2n. *moris antiqui ... seuerus.* **notabili tempestate ... auersantes:** see 18.1. **infaustam:** 6.2n. *introitus ... infaustus omine.* **auersantes** 'expressing aversion to'; cf. *A.* 1.28.2 (soldiers interpreting a lunar eclipse) *auersari deos lamentantur.* **idem ... animus:** sc. *ac uester*. For their actual state of mind see 35.1. **apud quos:** sc. *est*; the antecedent *uos* is derived from *uestra.* **honestis consiliis robur:** 22.2n. *Othoni ... comes.*

38.2 non ad bellum ... uoco: contrast Piso at 30.3 *transcendet haec licentia in prouincias, et ad nos scelerum exitus, bellorum ad uos pertinebunt.* **omnium militum arma nobiscum sunt** reveals either surprising ignorance about the situation in Germany or extreme duplicity. See 50.1n. *nouus ... nuntius.* **una cohors ... detinet**, together with *signum meum* below, conflicts with 31.1 *nullo adhuc consilio.* They may be imperfectly assimilated bits of a different version of the story, or Othonian bluff. A second reference to the *signum* at 41.1 *eo signo manifesta ... studia* makes the former the more likely. **cohors togata:** Durry ((1938) 207) infers from this passage that on the praetorians guarding the Palace formal civilian dress (i.e. a toga) normally concealed a sword; he contrasts *A.* 16.27.1 (on the trial of Thrasea Paetus) *aditum senatus globus togatorum obsederat non occultis gladiis.* **imputet** 'claim credit for' + acc. of the favour, dat. of the beneficiary; cf. *G.* 21.4 *gaudent muneribus, sed nec data imputant nec acceptis obligantur*, 55.4 *cui imputaretur*, 71.2 *exemplum ... imputauit.* On competition for a new emperor's favour see also 5.1n. *praeuentamque gratiam.* **non potest laudari nisi**

peractum: the epigram offers a 'dual focus' (Plass (1988) 29) – an absolute moral category (that which is praiseworthy) clashes with a contingent pragmatic category (success or no success) – and neatly completes the speech with the word 'complete'. Aristotle recommends this type of antithesis (*Rhet.* 1399a30–4); T. uses it again at 45.2 *Othoni nondum auctoritas inerat ad prohibendum scelus; iubere iam poterat.* For the thought cf. *A.* 12.67.2 *haud ignarus summa scelera incipi cum periculo, peragi cum praemio.*

38.3 aperire . . . iussit: for the omission of the subject of the inf. after *iubere* see *OLD* 1 a. **armamentarium:** presumably an arsenal, but little is known about such buildings (see Bishop and Coulston (1993) 199–201). An attempt to remove weapons from this one for a routine troop transfer initiates the praetorian riot of chh. 80–5. **rapta:** sc. *sunt.* **sine more et ordine militiae** 'without [regard for] military custom and hierarchy'. **ut praetorianus aut legionarius insignibus suis distingueretur** explains *more et ordine*: cf. *Agr.* 14.1 *uetere . . . populi Romani consuetudine, ut haberet instrumenta seruitutis et reges.* Military custom prescribed a visual (and hierarchical) distinction between praetorian and legionary based not on their equipment, which was very similar, but on ornamental devices (*insignia*), which had to be affixed to battle kit (cf. Caes. *Gal.* 2.21.5 *temporis tanta fuit exiguitas . . . ut non modo ad insignia accomodanda sed etiam ad galeas induendas scutisque tegimenta detrahenda tempus defuerit*; Bishop and Coulston (1993) 61 suggest helmet crests, in particular); see also 57.2 *insignia armorum argento decora.* **miscentur auxiliaribus galeis scutisque:** praetorian and legionary soldiers 'were mixed in with auxiliary helmets and shields' (presumably on auxiliary soldiers; on their distinctive gear see Bishop and Coulston (1993) 206–9). Individuals from legionary and auxiliary units play important roles in the praetorian proclamation of Otho (e.g. 41.3 *Camurium quintae decimae legionis militem*, 42 *Iulio Caro legionario milite*, 43.1 *Sulpicius Florus e Britannicis cohortibus*) and the mixing of troops is, in T.'s view, a symptom of civil war (54.3n. *asciscitur auxiliorum miles*; also 32.1n. *mixtis*). Others (Alford, Irvine, Heubner, Fyfe, etc.) suggest that praetorians and legionaries equipped *themselves* with auxiliary gear. **instigator:** this is its earliest known occurrence; cf. 22.3n. *instinctor.* **incitamentum:** sc. *erat.* An *incitamentum* is usually a spur to virtuous action (e.g. *G.* 7.2 *fortitudinis incitamentum*; Cic. *Arch.* 23 *hoc* (sc. *gloria*) *maximum et periculorum incitamentum et laborum*; Sen. *Ep.* 64.9 *quidni ego magnorum uirorum . . . imagines habeam incitamenta animi*; Curt. 4.14.1 *ingentia spei gloriaeque incitamenta*) but T. likes to reverse its valence, often as part of an epigram, as here and at *A.* 1.55.3 *quae . . . apud* *concordes uincula caritatis incitamenta irarum apud infensos erant*, 3.10.2, *A.* 2.38.1, 6.1.2, 14.14.3. **quod boni maerebant:** a Ciceronian *querela* (*Pis.* 26 *maerebant boni*; *Dom* 26. *maerentibus bonis omnibus*; *Dom.* 129 *lugerent semper boni*), but in a military context.

39.1 iam exterritus Piso: the scene moves outside of the camp, which Piso is approaching from the Palatine. T. does not make explicit the consequence of what Piso hears, which is that he abandons the idea of approaching the praetorians and returns (a long way) to the Forum, but relies on the deterrent effect implicit in *exterrere* (e.g. *A.* 1.42.3 *uultu et aspectu Actiacas legiones exterruit*; *A.* 1.56.5 *exterruit Caecina ... ferens arma*). **rostra occupanda:** sc. *esse.* Another symbolic rallying point (27.2n. *miliarium aureum*). The same plan is recommended to another conspirator at *A.* 15.59.1. **utque ... effugerat:** this *sententia* shares elements with others at 3.84.4 *quae natura pauoris est, cum omnia metuenti praesentia maxime displicerent* and *A.* 15.36.4 *quae natura magnis timoribus, deterius crederent quae euenerat.*

39.2 ignaro Galba: 29.1n. **siue ut ... mulceret, seu ... credebat ... uel odio:** 7.2n. *mobilitate ingenii.* **mulceret:** *mulcere* is used by T. four times in this context: 85.1, 3.10.3 *facundia aderat mulcendique uulgum artes*, 4.72.3 *donec Cerealis mulceret animos.* Always more common in poetry, it is used by a variety of imperial prose authors (Livy, Velleius, Seneca, Pliny the Elder, Quintilian, Apuleius) and was memorably applied to a political context at Virg. *Aen.* 1.153 *regit dictis animos et pectora mulcet* (cf. 1.197, 5.464). As in the Virgilian passages, the soothing is often accomplished by words (e.g. Vell. 2.85.4 *Caesar quos ferro poterat interimere uerbis mulcere cupiens*; see *TLL* s.v. 1562.63–81); only T. suggests murder as a solace. **seu conscium Othonis credebat:** 42n. *huc ... fuerit.* **haesitationem attulit:** *haesitatio* also appears at 2.45.2 *ea res haesitationem attulit* and *A.* 1.80.3. It is Ciceronian (*Fam.* 3.12.2). T. generally prefers *cunctatio* (thirty times; also Ciceronian) and *mora* (passim; cf. 89.3 *moras afferrent*). **difficilis:** sc. *est* (or *esset*, if the causal clause is Vinius' reasoning: *NLS* §285); cf. 85.3 *arduus ... modus.* **trepidi nuntii** 'frightening news' *OLD* 3a; cf. 51.5 *atroces nuntii. nuntii* and *diffugia* are syntactically parallel but actually sequential – the former presumably precipitate the latter (cf. *Agr.* 34.3 *nouissimae res et extremo metu torpor*). **diffugia:** *diffugere* is common but the noun occurs only here; for the scene cf. 3.84.4 *dilapsis etiam infimis seruitiorum.* **languentibus ... ostentauerant:** *studiis* and *ostentauerant* link this abl. appendix with the scene at 35.1 (*studia, ostentare*).

40.1 fluctuantis: only here in T., though common in both prose and poetry (see *TLL* s.v.). The wave analogy is also used by Plutarch, though less boldly: *G.* 26.3 'His litter was swept hither and thither (δεῦρο κἀκεῖ) as if in a swell and often threatened to capsize.' **completis undique basilicis ac templis, lugubri prospectu:** T. uses a similar pair of abl. appendixes at *A.* 3.7.1 *erectis omnium animis petendae e Pisone ultione et crebro questu.* **lugubri prospectu** 'the view being a dismal one' (Alford); for *prospectus* as 'that which is seen from a vantage point' (*OLD* 2) cf. Cic. *Luc.* 80 *o praeclarum prospectum: Puteolos uidemus*, *Att.* 12.9.1 *prospectu maris.* Only Statius uses it with a similarly dark modifier: *Theb.* 6.205 *prospectu... nefasto.* More commonly the view is pleasant: Plin. *Ep.* 5.6.30 *iucundum prospectum*, Vitr. 1.2.6 *prospectus... elegantes*, Apul. *Met.* 10.29 *prospectu gratissimo.* A different analysis of *lugubri prospectu*, argued most thoroughly by Morgan (1994b), makes the phrase an editorializing apposition: 'The expectancy of the crowd... struck him – and was meant to strike the reader – as a lugubrious prospect' (241). *prospectus* is, on this view, a metaphor for the author's perspective on his material. **neque... ulla uox:** sc. *erat.* **populi aut plebis:** 35.1 n. **non tumultus:** sc. *erat.* **quale magni metus et magnae irae silentium est** clarifies the paradox of *non tumultus, non quies.* The *sententia* is modelled on a battle scene in Xenophon's *Agesilaus*: 2.12 'There was no battle cry there, nor again silence, but the sound was such as (φωνὴ δέ τις ἦν τοιαύτη οἵαν...) anger and battle supply'; Xenophon's fuller syntax is simpler and devoid of paradox. Some make the phrase dependent on *quies* alone (Chilver, Husband (1915), citing a parallel at Liv. 1.29.2). As such, it describes an indifferent crowd, one not moved by fear or anger. See further Morgan (1994b) 238–9. **tamen** marks the inaccuracy of the report. **occupare pericula** boldly combines two distinct senses of *occupare.* 'Seize' (*OLD* 2) is used elsewhere with intangible objects (e.g. 56.2 *fortunam*) including *pericula*: Sen. *Ep.* 24.5 (on Mucius Scaevola holding his hand in the flames) *acrior... ad occupanda pericula uirtus.* But 'get ahead of' or 'forestall' (*OLD* 11 c) is suggested by the preceding *praecipites ire* and is proverbial: Otto s.v. *principium* (1). The closest parallel is Stat. *Theb.* 10.671 *i, precor, accelera, ne proximus occupet Haemon* (sc. *fatum*). With *pericula* as object it is hard to see this as a metaphorical chariot race (*pace* Morgan (1994b) 240).

40.2 Vologaesum aut Pacorum auito Arsacidarum solio: Vologaeses (or -us) was a contemporary of Nero mentioned in *Annals* 12–15, esp. 15.2 and 15.11–17; Pacorus was his brother (*A.* 15.2, 14, 31).

solium Arsacidarum is used again at *A.* 2.2.2. **inermem et senem:** cf. Plut. *G.* 15.2 (on Petronius Turpilianus) 'an old man alone and unarmed' (γέροντα γυμνὸν καὶ ἄνοπλον). **disiecta plebe:** cf. Suet. *G.* 19.2 *dimota paganorum turba*, Plut. *G.* 26.4 'the soldiers ordered all private citizens out of their way'. **proculcato senatu:** Virgil uses *proculcare* for the heedless trampling of a master by his slave (*Aen.* 12.532–4). Morgan (1994b) 244 observes that 'the collective *senatu* (rather than *senatoribus*) is meant to balance *plebe*'. **rapidi equis:** each praetorian cohort had ninety mounted soldiers, the *equites praetoriani* (Durry (1938) 99). Suetonius agrees with T. in mentioning only mounted soldiers here (*G.* 19.2 *equites*); Plutarch and Dio also mention soldiers on foot (*G.* 26.3; 64.6.3). **nec illos . . . religio:** contrast Liv. 7.6.3–4 *tum M. Curtium . . . templa deorum immortalium, qua foro imminent, Capitoliumque intuentem . . . se deuouisse.* **terruere quo minus facerent scelus:** 18.1 n. **scelus cuius ultor est quisquis successit:** Vitellius did in fact execute anyone who claimed credit for the crime (44.2). The victory of Vitellius was treated (however implausibly) as a kind of vindication of Galba (2.55.1), but the Flavians, too, made a show of vindicating him (3.7.2, 4.40.1). Nobody avenged Otho. Of other emperors, Gaius was avenged by Claudius (Jos. *AJ* 19.265), Nero by Domitian (Suet. *Dom.* 14.4), and Domitian himself by Nerva, albeit reluctantly (Suet. *Dom.* 23.1; Dio 68.3.3).

41.1 comminus 'close at hand' (*OLD* 2) is a usage developed first in poetry (e.g. Lucr. 4.406–7 *supra sol montis esse uidetur | comminus*; Ov. *Pont.* 1.5.74 *aspicit hirsutos comminus Vrsa Getas*, Luc. 1.206 *uiso leo comminus hoste*; cf. Stat. *Silu.* 3.5.38 *Lethaeos audirem comminus amnes*); its original meaning was military 'hand to hand'. **uexillarius . . . dereptam Galbae imaginem:** *imagines* of emperors were fastened to praetorian standards amidst the unit's insignia and to *uexilla* below the pennant; an *imago* is visible beneath the *uexillum* in scenes 32 and 103 of Trajan's column (see Reinach (1909–12) I: 342, 366; also p. 244). The same symbolic act marks Caecina's defection from Vitellius (3.13.1 *simul Vitellii imagines dereptae*); the defection of the sixteenth legion from Rome itself was even more thorough: 4.62.2 *reuulsae imperatorum imagines.* **Atilium Vercilionem:** only here and at Plut. *G.* 26.4. The spelling of his cognomen is not certain (*PIR*² A 1310). **eo signo:** 31.1 n. *insidiis et simulatione.* Plutarch does not have this detail. **manifesta:** sc. *erant.*

41.2 iuxta Curtii lacum: the combination of event and location has a symbolic power that T. exploits again at 2.55.1, 2.88.3, and 3.85.1. Three aetiological accounts of the place name survive (see Richardson (1992)); the basin was long since dry. The most well-known story concerns the *deuotio* of M. Curtius (e.g. Liv. 7.6.1–6): 'The self-immolation of Curtius closed the chasm that threatened the destruction of Rome, but the murder of Galba can only symbolize its reopening' (Scott (1968) 57–62; quotation from p. 58). The murder of an emperor on that spot had a particular irony since people marked the fulfilment of annual vows for an emperor's safety there (Suet. *Aug.* 57.1). **trepidatione ferentium:** Plut. *G.* 27.1 'the litter having been upset' lacks this detail, which contributes to the picture of Galba's abandonment by all close to him. **uarie prodidere:** in chh. 41–6 the principal figures of Galba's reign are killed: Galba at 41.3, T. Vinius in 42, Piso at 43.2, Laco and Icelus at 46.5. Galba's murder is also reported by Plutarch, Suetonius, and Dio (*G.* 27.1–2; *G.* 19.2–2.1; 64.6.3), those of Piso, Vinius, and Laco by Plutarch alone and only briefly (*G.* 27.4); the fate of Icelus is not noted by any other source. Accounts of these deaths, particularly that of Galba, apparently existed in some numbers and with details that were not always compatible. The source used by both T. and Plutarch for Galba's death already knew three different names for the assassin, and there are different versions of both Galba's last words (here) and Vinius' (42). The most striking discrepancy in surviving accounts concerns a praetorian centurion, Sempronius Densus, whose glorious death is a prelude to Galba's death in Plutarch and Dio, and to Piso's in T. (43.1). Inferences about the sources underlying the accounts of these deaths (see 43.1 n. *insignem . . . uidit*) are of limited value for the book as a whole, since such stories might well have survived independently of the larger historical narrative of the year 69; *exitus*-scenes were a popular literary form in the period (Pomeroy (1991)). **alii suppliciter interrogasse:** sc. *prodiderunt eum.* **quid mali meruisset** 'what harm did he deserve?' (*OLD* s.v. *mereo* 4b); cf. Dio 64.6.4 'but what evil have I done?' (καὶ τί κακὸν ἐποίησα). **plures obtulisse ultro percussoribus iugulum:** thus at Plut. *G.* 27.1. Suetonius reports that this was the more common of the two versions in nearly identical words (see App. 1). **agerent ac ferirent:** indirect statement of '*agite, ferite*'. **si ita e re publica uideretur:** cf. Plut. *G.* 27.1 'Strike, if this is better for the Roman people.' Scott ((1968) 57) detects an allusion here to the patriotic *deuotio* of M. Curtius (see above). **non interfuit occidentium quid diceret:** a moment of supreme Tacitean cynicism.

41.3 de percussore non satis constat: at 2.23.5 T. assigns a kind of collective guilt to all involved by referring to a disruptive element of the

Othonian army as the '*interfectores Galbae*'. **Terentium euocatum:** ordinarily *euocatus* would designate a veteran of the praetorian or urban cohorts (*OLD*), but Galba had revived an older use of the term ('soldier selected by a commander') for his elite bodyguard: Suet. *G.* 10.3 *delegit et equestris ordinis iuuenes qui ... euocati appellarentur excubiasque circa cubiculum suum uice militum agerent.* It would suit T.'s theme of betrayal if a member of Galba's select bodyguard turned on him (cf. 31.3n. *longa nauigatione*, 43.2n. *Sulpicius Florus ... donatus*), but T. does not provide enough information to show which meaning is active here and Plutarch omits the label altogether. **quintae decimae legionis:** stationed at Vetera: 9.1 n. *inferioris Germaniae legiones.* **impresso gladio iugulum eius hausisse**: told in slow motion by comparison with Suet. *G.* 20.2 *iugulatus est ad lacum Curtii* and Plut. *G.* 27.2 'slit his throat' ἀπέσφαξε δὲ αὐτόν. *impresso gladio* is a detail appropriate to deaths of high drama in poetry (e.g. Sen. *Oed.* 1036–7 *utrumne pectori infigam meo* | *telum an patenti conditum iugulo imprimam?* cf. *Herc.* 1312, *Thy.* 1057) and prose (Petr. 80.4 *nudo ecce iugulum; conuertite huc manus, imprimite mucrones. ego mori debeo qui amicitiae sacramentum deleui*; cf. Sen. *Contr.* 1.7.4, V. Max. 5.4. ext. 6). *haurire* 'to gouge' (*OLD* 3) belongs to the same tonal register (*TLL* s.v. 2573.70–83). T. uses neither elsewhere. **adiecta:** sc. *sunt.*

42 de quo et ipso ambigitur: *et* connects the uncertainties about Galba's assassination with the uncertainty about Vinius' last words. For the detailed development of one of two alternatives – in this case speechlessness and speech – between which T. professes himself unable to decide cf. 14.1 n. *siue ... Lacone instante* and also 3.71.4 *hic ambigitur ... depulerint.* Plutarch again accepts the second version without demur: *G.* 27.4 'he cried out that his death was contrary to Otho's intention'; cf. 41.2n. *plures ... iugulum*, and see 43.1 n. *insignem ... uidit.* **consumpseritne ... metus:** a bold and original expression for fear-induced speechlessness, indebted to but utterly different from Virgil's famous lines at *Aen.* 4.279–80 *at uero Aeneas aspectu obmutuit amens* | *arrectaeque horrore coma et uox faucibus haesit.* There are parallels for fear as the subject of *consumere* (e.g. Stat. *Theb.* 10.563 *consumpsit uentura timor*) and sound as its object (e.g. Plin. *Ep.* 2.17.22 *omnem sonum media inanitate consumit*), but there is nothing equivalent to T.'s fear-swallowed words. **proclamauerit:** sc. *Vinius.* **finxit formidine:** for this alternative there is a closely comparable passage later. Where Vinius failed in his bid to claim allegiance with the victor, two Othonian generals succeed, defending themselves to Vitellius by saying (falsely) that they had gone over to him even before the final battle (2.60.1). **huc potius eius uita famaque inclinat, ut . . . fuerit:** T. uses *inclinare* 'to favour belief' (cf. *OLD* 9d) in deciding between alternatives again at *A.* 14.2.2 *eadem ceteri quoque auctores prodidere, et fama huc inclinat* (cf. Liv. 29.33.10 *haec animum inclinat ut . . . credam.* For Vinius' disreputable past see 48.2–3. **conscius sceleris:** this verdict underlies details of the preceding narrative, including Vinius' disingenuous advice to Galba during the debate and Otho's easy betrayal of him (37.5n.; see also 34.2n. *multi arbitrabantur*). Vinius cast his lot in with Otho's before the adoption (13.2) and could expect nothing from Piso (34.1n. *infensus*). Plutarch's verdict is more elaborate but less clear: *G.* 12.3 'of tragic events and great disasters he provided for some a cause (τοῖς μὲν αἰτίαν), for others a pretext (τοῖς δὲ πρόφασιν)'. **causa:** *a* cause (cf. αἰτίαν above), but not *the* cause. For Vinius as a liability to Galba see 6.1n. **ante aedem diui Iulii iacuit:** a temple dedicated in 29 B.C. on the site of Caesar's cremation at the hands of the populace (Aug. *RG* 19.1; Dio 51.22.2); it lay near the *lacus Curtii* (see map) and offered asylum (Dio 47.19.2; see Richardson (1992) 213–14). **Iulio Caro legionario milite:** only here. **in utrumque latus** 'from one side to the other'; cf. Virg. *Aen.* 12.508 *transadigit costas et crates pectoris ensem.* **transuerberatus:** sc. *est*; again at 3.17.1 *uexillarium fugientem hasta transuerberaret.*

43.1 insignem . . . uidit: an abrupt transition from the possibly craven and certainly criminal Vinius to the shining virtue of a Roman centurion. A later laudatory chapter begins with a similar sentence 4.42.1 *magnam eo die pietatis eloquentiaeque famam Vipstanus Messalla adeptus est.* In Book 1 only Galba merits the adj. *insignis* (35.2), but see also *A.* 2.17.4 (quoted in n. on *modo manu* below). Densus' heroics are reported with a similar rhetorical enhancement in Plutarch and Dio (see App. 1), but in both authors he was defending Galba, not Piso. Apropos of Galba's death T. is closer to Suetonius, who maintains that no one even tried to assist the emperor (*G.* 20.1, cf. *G.* 19.1 *desertum a suis*). Suetonius does not mention Piso's death or Densus, but it has reasonably been inferred that in describing Galba's solitary death he and T. were following a source not used by Plutarch or Dio (see also 41.2n. *plures . . . iugulum* and 42n. *de quo . . . ambigitur*). As to whether that second source paired Densus' resistance with Piso's death or whether the pairing is T.'s, it is impossible to say. At some point the version in Plutarch (*G.* 27.5, with Piso wounded, fleeing, and killed by a certain Murcus at the temple of Vesta) was melded with the Densus story to produce the causally coherent sequence we see in T. **aetas nostra**

uidit: Plutarch uses a different personification: *G.* 26.4–5 'the only one among the thousands seen by the sun who was worthy of the Roman empire'. For T.'s phrase cf. *Agr.* 2.3 *sicut uetus aetas uidit quid ultimum in libertate esset, ita nos quid in seruitute* and *A.* 4.3.1 *quem uidit sequens aetas praepotentem* and, for the pride in positive evidence about the present, *A.* 3.55.5 *nostra quoque aetas multa . . . imitanda posteris tulit.* **modo manu modo uoce:** for the scene cf. *A.* 2.17.4 *Arminius manu uoce uulnere sustentabat pugnam.* The pair *manus~uox* is common (*TLL* s.v. *manus* 358.56–69). **quamquam:** with *uulnerato* (*OLD* 4); cf. 63.1 *quamquam . . . exceptos*, 64.4 *quamquam bene de parte meritus*, 76.1 *quamquam . . . obstricta.* **effugium dedit:** cf. *A.* 2.17.5 *uirtus seu fraus . . . Inguiomero effugium dedit* (a passage that follows shortly after the description of Arminius quoted above). On T.'s self-imitation see Woodman (1988) 176–9. T. uses *effugium* again at 72.2 and altogether sixteen times, more than twice as often as any other author.

43.2 aedem Vestae: further from the centre of the Forum than the spots where Galba and Vinius were killed (see map). **contubernio . . . abditus:** cf. 3.74.1 *Domitianus . . . apud aedituum occultans* and *contubernio* later in that passage. **nominatim:** cf. Suet. *O.* 6.3 *missis qui Galbam et Pisonem trucidarent.* Plutarch specifies Piso's name via a vignette: *G.* 27.3 'They say that Otho, when the head (sc. of Galba) was brought to him, cried out, "This is nothing, comrades. Show me the head of Piso!"' **in caedem eius ardentis:** imitated at Amm. 22.3.11 *in Siluani necem . . . arsisse.* T. uses *ardescere* similarly at *A.* 11.25.5 *ardesceret in nuptias incestas* (sc. *Claudius*). *ardentis*, an emendation for *ardentes*, brings the passage into line with the parallel tradition (see n. above) and with T.'s usage (for which cf., in Book 1, 5.1 *Nymphidii Sabini . . . molientis*, 12.2 *Galbae . . . agitantis*, 66.1 *Fabi . . . commendantis*, 72.2 *Vini . . . praetexantis*). **Sulpicius Florus e Britannicis cohortibus, nuper a Galba ciuitate donatus:** an auxiliary soldier (32.1n. *mixtis*). Only T. reports his name (Sulpicius from Sulpicius Galba) and citizenship grant, which are further evidence of Galba's failure to hold even those he had benefited (31.3n. *longa nauigatione*, 43.1n. *Terentium euocatum*). **Statius Murcus speculator:** Plutarch gives this story only briefly: *G.* 27.4 'he was pursued and slain by a certain Murcus at the temple of Vesta' (43.1n. *insignem . . . uidit*). The *nomen* is sometimes emended to Staius to align this name with one attested a century earlier (see *MMR* v. 3, p. 200; the earlier Staius' *nomen*, attested on stone, is frequently corrupted to Statius in the MSS). **trucidatus:** sc. *est.*

44–50 Setting the stage for Otho's reign

Galba's reign ends in ch. 43. Otho's begins, effectively, in ch. 71. The intervening chapters set the stage (darkly) for Otho's reign (chh. 44–50) and describe Vitellius' gathering force (chh. 51–70). In content and pace these two panels are very different: the first stands still in time (15 January) and place (Rome), the second moves steadily forward from the death of Vindex in the late spring of 68 to the early spring of 69 and carries Vitellius' legions from their bases along the Rhine to the brink of and then over the Alps. The present chapters thus form an interlude between two sections of great activity, a pause for burying the dead (46.5, 47.2–49), sampling emotions (joy 44.1, 47.1; fear 50.1, 50.4; sorrow 50.1), and watching Rome's various groups reorient themselves around the new *princeps* (45–6, 50).

Scanty in events, these chapters are lavish in style. Epigrams abound (twelve in seven chapters; see App. 2). There is a profusion of asyndeton and alliteration, and much repetition. Both Sallust and Virgil contribute their own unhappy tints to T.'s scene. Judging by chh. 44–50, the outlook for Otho's principate is gloomy indeed; the good news does not begin to register until ch. 71. In these highly stylized chapters T. is relatively distant from the parallel tradition.

44.1 nullam caedem Otho maiore laetitia excepisse . . . dicitur: cf. 3.75.2 *caedem eius laetam fuisse Muciano accepimus.* **insatiabilibus:** elsewhere in T. only *A.* 4.38.4 *insatiabiliter.* **perlustrasse** 'to have scrutinized' *OLD* 2b. **confuderat** 'had troubled' (*OLD* 10) is also paired with *imagine* at Virg. *Aen.* 12.665 *obstipuit uaria confusus imagine rerum* (cf. *TLL* s.v. 262.45–8). For the situation cf. *A.* 15.36.2 *seu facinorum recordatione numquam timore uacuus* (sc. *Nero*). Suetonius conveys Otho's state of mind with less psychological analysis but still memorable effect via a dream in which he is driven from the throne by Galba's ghost (*O.* 7.2; cf. Dio 64.7.2). **Pisonis . . . credebat:** after the neat parallel structures of the beginning (*nullam . . . nullum, seu . . . seu, maiestatis in Galba . . . amicitiae in Tito Vinio*) the asyndeton and shift of construction (*Pisonis* in place of the abl., indirect statement in place of direct) are abrupt.

44.2 praefixa contis capita: cf. Virg. *Aen.* 9.465–7 *ipsa arrectis (uisu miserabile) in hastis | praefigunt capita . . . | Euryali et Nisi*; Miller (1987b) 96. Virgil's tableau, however, concludes a tale, sad but glorious, of courage and devotion, very different from the present scene of three solitary deaths variously sullied. **gestabantur inter signa:** cf. 36.1 *medium inter signa Othonem.* **aquilam legionis:** sc. *classicorum* (36.3). **certatim ... ultionem:** to the facts shared with Plutarch and Suetonius (bloody display, 120 affidavits demanding rewards, executions; see App. 1) T. adds the four-fold anaphora of *qui*, the hollow claim of virtue (*ut pulchrum ... facinus*), and the elaborate appendix (*non ... ultionem*). For the claimants' behaviour cf. 3.69.3 (on having been in the besieged Capitol) *uictore Vespasiano multi id meritum erga partes simulauere.* **tradito ... more,** both here and at 32.1, suggests that the *mos maiorum* was yielding to a new imperial *mos* less estimable than the old. For the *uariatio* see 14.1n. *siue ... instante.* **munimentum ... ultionem:** stands in apposition to and comments on the principal action of the sentence (the ordering of executions for all who claimed part in Galba's assassination); cf. 46.4 *rem ... utilem*, 59.1 *grande momentum*, 62.3 *laetum augurium* (with n.), 90.1 *iustissimum donum*, 3.31.2 *extremum malorum*, *A.*1.49.3 *piaculum furoris* and see Draeger (1882) §77 and Goodyear (1972) *ad A.* 1.27.1. Here the abstract nouns lend only specious elevation since Vitellius neither protected himself nor was avenged but was rather forced to contemplate Galba's death at his own cruel end (3.85.1). Vespasian constituted himself Galba's true successor (40.2n. *scelus ... successit*).

45.1 alium crederes senatum, alium populum: cf. 2.90.1 *tamquam apud alterius ciuitatis senatum populumque* and see also 32.1n. *pari certamine* and 90.3n. *priuata cuique.* T.'s interest in the social chaos of the period (see below on *ruere cuncti*) is not shared by Plutarch, who uses the same anaphora with reference to the senate and gods: *G.* 28.1 'As if they were now other men or the gods were other gods, the senate met and swore loyalty to Otho.' For *crederes* see 10.2n. *palam laudares.* **ruere ... anteire ... certare ... increpare ... laudare ... exosculari ... facere:** the long string of historic infinitives in asyndeton is a stylistic reference to Sallust (e.g. *Cat.* 6.5, 12.2, *Jug.* 6.1, 23.1, 38.5, 94.3–6). See also 35.1n. *ruere.* **cuncti:** the collapse of hierarchies both social (see also 32.1 *mixtis seruitiis*) and military (46.1n. *arbitrio militum*, 84.1 *confusi pedites equitesque*) was a side-effect of the political crisis, but as Otho secures his power the traditional order begins to re-emerge: 71.2 *primoribus ciuitatis ... in uulgus ... militibus*, 83.1 *optimus quisque ... uulgus et plures.* The full panoply of distinctions does not appear until the restoration of the Capitolium: 4.53.3 *magistratus et sacerdotes et senatus et eques et magna pars populi.* **militum iudicium:** ironic, in view of the motivations and methods T. attributes to Otho and his supporters (see chh. 23–5); T.'s own word is *arbitrium* (46.1). **exosculari** recalls Otho's kisses for the crowd (36.3) and, more poignantly, is recalled by the praetorians' kisses for Otho's corpse: 2.49.3 *uulnus manusque eius exosculantes.* **quantoque magis falsa erant quae fiebant tanto plura facere:** for the form of the epigram cf. *A.* 1.7.1 *quanto quis illustrio tanto magis falsi ac festinantes.* For the notion of hiding oneself behind an illusion, a tactic adopted by both ruled and ruler (cf. *A.* 1.11.2 *ut sensus suos penitus abderet* (sc. *Tiberius*), with Goodyear (1972) *ad loc.*), T. has a wide variety of expressions. In Book 1 see also 19.1 *effusius qui noluerant,* 69 *dicendi artem apta trepidatione occultans,* 81.1 *modo constantiam simulare.* Sincerity, as in the soldiers' affection for Otho (2.46.1 *neque erat adulatio*) or in the mourning for Germanicus (*A.* 3.2.3 *aberat quippe adulatio*) was the surprising thing. See also 32.1n. *neque... ueritas.* **nec... temperans:** an effective picture of Otho as the sole defence for civilians (who have been reduced to atom-like singularity – *singulos*) against the collective *animus militum,* a role he plays again at the end of his life (2.49.1). Contrast the Flavian leaders, *temperandae uictoriae impares* (4.1.3). **uoce uultuque:** again at 3.58.3, *A.* 3.67.3, 15.55.4, 16.29.1.

45.2 Marium Celsum: 14.1n. **expostulabant:** the subject, *milites,* is understood from *auidum et minacem militum animum.* **industriae... innocentiaeque... infensi:** reversed at 71.3 *eandem uirtutem admirantibus cui irascebantur.* Here alliteration helps convey moral outrage, but the abstract nouns, which lack precise referents in the narrative, are somewhat weak. For other epigrams based on inverted standards see (in App. 2) 2.3, 38.3, 49.3, 50.3, 52.2, 59.1, 71.2, 77.3, 88.2. **caedis et praedarum initium:** similar phrasing at 39.2 *initio caedis orto difficilis modus* and 2.52.1 *causam et initium caedis quaerebant,* cf. also 64.3 *quaesita belli causa.* For slaughter of civilians later in the year see 4.1.1–3, where cruelty and greed are again twin motivators: *quae saeuitia sanguine explebatur, dein uerterat in auaritiam.* **apparebat:** presumably to Otho. **Othoni nondum auctoritas inerat ad prohibendum scelus; iubere iam poterat:** Otho's most recent orders had opened the arsenal (38.3) and killed Piso (43.2). As is common in epigrams, the second member is more laconic: here *poterat* replaces *auctoritas inerat* and the obj. is omitted (cf. in App. 2: 5.2, 10.2, 13.2, 25.1, 38.2, 49.4; see further Plass (1988) 31). Similar constraints are shown for Vitellius (58.2) and predicted for the Flavians (3.66.3). In the parallel to the present passage Plutarch simply notes that Otho was afraid to oppose his soldiers (*G.* 27.6). T.'s *nondum* contrasts with Piso's absolute *nemo umquam* (30.1). The story of Otho's principate does show a gradual reaffirmation of the social hierarchy (45.1 n. *ruere cuncti*), but the praetorian outbreak of chh. 80–5 shows how fragile it was. At 83.1 *reputans non posse principatum scelere quaesitum subita modestia et prisca grauitate retineri* Otho is no better off than he is here; *subita* points again to the future but the notion is less plausible the second time round. **ita . . . subtraxit:** *iussum* (sc. *Celsum*) is the obj. of *subtraxit*, *daturum* goes with *affirmans*, which is a parenthetic supplement to *simulatione irae*, so *et* is 'indeed' or 'in fact' *OLD* 2b. For other views see Alford, Heubner. **simulatione irae uinciri iussum:** rephrased at 71.1 *per speciem uinculorum saeuitiae militum subtractum* (sc. *Celsum*). Vitellius uses a similar tactic: 58.1 *simulatione uinculorum*. The ruse fails for Antonius Primus (3.10.3). Plutarch's Otho (*G.* 27.6) gives the soldiers a rational argument for delaying Celsus' execution – he had questions to ask him, he said. T.'s scene, by contrast, pits one concealed motive against another: Otho's strategic simulation is matched by the calculations of the soldiers, whose demand for Celsus' punishment actually aimed at a more general (and more profitable) slaughter (*caedis et praedarum initium . . . quaeri apparebat*). **daturum:** sc. *esse*.

46.1 arbitrio militum: *arbitrium* was properly an attribute of the senate (4.9.1, *A.* 1.26.1, 13.5.1, 14.28.1) and the *princeps* (*A.* 1.15.1, 1.26.1). **acta:** sc. *sunt*. **Plotium Firmum:** also in Plutarch (by emendation; *PIR*[2] P 503). His promotion from *praefectus uigilum* to *praefectus praetorio* mirrors that of Tigellinus before him (72.1 n.) and others after, but his rise from the ranks (of the praetorians, it is usually assumed, to explain their favour for him here) to an equestrian post is unusual for this period (Baillie Reynolds (1926) 33, 122–7). For his character see 82.2n. *allocuti . . . horridius*. **adiungitur:** even in reporting the selection of two prefects of equal rank T. varies the construction; cf. 48.3 below on the wills of Piso and Vinius. **Licinius Proculus:** known from T., Plutarch, and Dio, none of whom says anything about his prior career (*PIR*[2] L 233). T. gives the impression that friendship with Otho was his only recommendation for the job. His subsequent power was great (87.2 *plurima fides Licinio Proculo*; 2.39.1 *uis ac potestas pene Proculum praefectum*; cf. Plut. *O.* 7.4) but ill-placed. Later scenes reveal lack of experience (87.2 *bellorum insolens*; 2.33.1 *imperitia*) and of moral compass (2.60.1 *necessariis magis defensionibus quam honestis*; cf. 2.44.1). Plutarch adds the charge of cowardice (*O.* 13.1). Proculus survived Otho but presumably lost his post when Vitellius discharged the praetorians (2.67.1). For his character see further

82.2n. *allocuti . . . horridius.* **suspectus . . . fouisse:** cf. 4.34.4 *suspectus bellum malle.* **Flauium Sabinum:** elder brother of Vespasian, prominent in the events of 69 (*PIR*[2] F 352 and 356). The thirty-five years' service to the state mentioned in his obituary at 3.75 included a command during Claudius' expedition to Britain in 43, seven years as imperial legate in Moesia (perhaps A.D. 49–56), involvement with the census in Gaul, and twelve years as urban prefect (perhaps 57–60, 62–8, 69). His praetorship and suffect consulship presumably fall some time before those of Vespasian (A.D. 39 and 51 respectively). Despite T.'s eulogy *domi militiaeque clarus* Sabinus has no known military successes. His long tenure as urban prefect never earns T.'s notice in the *Annals* (he apparently had no role in the suppression of the Pisonian conspiracy, for example). Galba replaced Sabinus with Ducenius Geminus in 68 (14.1n.). Sabinus' return to office is dated by its collocation here to 15 January; Plutarch, giving it a different context, seems to put it as late as March (*O.* 5.2), which is unlikely. As the year proceeds Sabinus' official post and his connection with Vespasian push him further into prominence: after Otho's death he administers to troops in Rome the oath of loyalty to Vitellius (2.55.1) and facilitates the execution of Cornelius Dolabella, a man spared by both Galba and Otho (2.63.1–2; on Dolabella see 88.1n.). The latter action T. portrays as a failure of nerve: 2.63.2 *Sabinus . . . facilis mutatu et in alieno discrimine sibi pauens.* For the mid-year consulship of Sabinus' homonymous son see 77.2n. *Caelio ac Flauio Sabinis* and, on both men, Townend (1961). After the Flavian victory at Cremona in October Sabinus began discussions with Vitellius about a negotiated peace (3.65.2), but the plan was foiled by a riot that resulted, eventually, in the burning of the Capitol (3.69–71) and in Sabinus' lynching (3.74.2). His handling of the situation was sharply criticized (3.78.2), unjustly so, according to T.: *haud facile quis uni assignauerit culpam quae omnium fuit.* His death made a peaceful transfer of power more difficult (3.81.2). After his brother's accession he was honoured with a state funeral (4.47). As Vespasian's brother, Sabinus had been urged to claim a share of influence (3.64–5); his lack of enthusiasm was viewed by some as fraternal jealousy (3.65.1), but again T. offers a more favourable interpretation. Two, in fact: frailty (3.65.1 *inualidus senecta*, cf. 3.59.2) and character (3.65.2 *mitem uirum*; cf. 2.63.2 *Sabinus suopte ingenio mitis*). Further rumours arose from the prospect of conflict with Mucianus (3.75.2). T.'s *laudatio* is curiously lukewarm: 3.75.1 *uiri haud sane spernendi*; *innocentiam iustitiamque eius non argueres.* Public opinion may have preferred Sabinus to Vespasian (*quod inter* *omnes constiterit, ante principatum Vespasiani decus domus penes Sabinum erat*; see also Suet. *Ves.* 2.2), but in T.'s eyes he did not quite measure up (see further Gilmartin Wallace (1987)). **praefecere:** presumably the urban cohorts, who were under the command of the *praefectus urbis*, a consular with more status than the (equestrian) praetorian prefects, but much less power (O. F. Robinson (1992) 183–4). Plutarch, by contrast, says that Sabinus was Otho's choice (*O.* 5.2). T.'s topic here – *arbitrium militum* – and the moralizing fervour it engenders in his prose leads him away from the parallel tradition. **iudicium Neronis secuti:** the same motive is ascribed by Plutarch to Otho (see App. 1). **plerisque . . . respicientibus:** *respicere* 'take account of' *OLD* 7; in Plutarch this is Otho's precaution (App. 1).

46.2 flagitatum: sc. *est.* **uacationes** 'exemptions from fatigues' *OLD* 1, rephrased less technically below as *militare otium*. After Otho's concessions to the city troops comes a subsidy of particular interest to the legions. Vitellius, at the head of the German legions, adopts the same policy (58.1; Otho may in fact be matching rather than anticipating Vitellius). T.'s account, the source of which is unknown, has more details than the narrative requires – indeed no other author mentions the measure. The situation is nevertheless not wholly clear. Webster (1998) 118 and Chilver *ad loc.* speak of bribes for relief from unpleasant work, but what T. describes is an annual exaction (*tributum annuum*; *uacationes annuas*), and it is hard to see how Otho's subsidy would have rendered bribes obsolete. Credit for a permanent solution seems in fact due to Hadrian, who designated a category of soldiers, the *immunes*, permanently exempt from fatigues (Webster (1998) 118–20). Abuses in the allocation of exemptions were among the grievances expressed by mutinous legions in A.D. 14 (*A.* 1.35.1, 1.17.4). Both the historical analysis and the language of this passage share much with Sallust's rhetoric of moral decline (see nn.). **sparsa:** sc. *erat.* **neque . . . quisquam . . . pensi habebat** 'nor did anyone have any scruples about' (*OLD* s.v. *pendo* 7), a Sallustian expression (*Cat.* 5.6, 12.2, 23.2, 52.34, *Jug.* 41.9) used to characterize moral lapses by both Livy (e.g. 26.15.4, 43.7.11) and T. (*D.* 27.1, *A.* 13.15.3). The negative *neque . . . quisquam* intensifies the tone of outrage. **per latrocinia et raptus . . . redimebant:** the subject, *gregarii milites*, is understood from the context. The epigram, built around twin antitheses (thief/slave ~ soldier, activity ~ leisure) caps the expression of outrage. The end of the epigram juxtaposes clashing concepts, first *militare* and *otium*, words nowhere else united, then *otium* and *redimebant*, which are from equally disparate semantic spheres; for the first compare Vell. 2.78.2 *ne res disciplinae inimicissima, otium, corrumperet militem* and 87.2n. *urbanae militiae.* T. pairs *raptus* and *latrocinia* again at 35.2 and 2.58.1. Conditions appear to have worsened since Augustus' principate, when the *uacatio* fee was deducted from the regular stipendium (*A.* 1.17.4). For the *uariatio* prep. phrase ~ abl. see Sörbom (1935) 84–5.

46.3 fatigari: historic infinitives are also used singly at 50.1 *maerere*, 51.3 *quaerere*, 52.3 *instigare*, 71.1 *torpescere*, 89.1 *sentire.* **socordia:** cf. Sal. *Jug.* 2.4 *ingenium ... incultu atque socordia torpescere sinunt*, with 24.2n. *per socordiam praefecti*, and 2.73, 2.98.2, etc. **insuper:** 36.1n. **alius atque alius:** only here in T. (cf. *Rhet. Her.* 4.54, 4.63). **corrupti** agrees with the plural notion of *alius atque alius* (cf. 27.2 *sumpturi*, 35.1 *nimii*). **ad seditiones ... discordias ... bella ciuilia:** for the progression cf. Sal. *Hist.* fr. 1.12 *plurumae turbae, seditiones et ad postremum bella ciuilia orta sunt.*

46.4 uulgi largitione: the objective gen. is based on a dat. 'object'; cf. *A.* 15.48.3 *uoluptatum parsimonia* (≈ *uoluptati parcere*), *H.* 2.59.1 *in appulsu litoris* (≈ *litori appellens*). **ex fisco suo**, the reading of one branch of MSS (see Wellesley's app. crit. and cf. 58.1 *uacationes centurionibus ex fisco numerat*), is preferred over M's *et fiscum suum*, in which *et* has no function. **exsoluturum:** sc. *se esse.* **rem haud dubie utilem:** on *haud dubie* see 7.1n. For the acc. see 44.2n. *munimentum.* **bonis postea principibus:** for adverbs – particularly those of time and place – used attributively, a usage in which T. follows Livy's lead and that, like the attributive use of prepositional phrases (e.g. 50.4 *omnium ante se principum*), aids brevity, see K–S II§59.2 and cf. 65.1n. *multae inuicem clades.* **perpetuitate disciplinae** 'as a permanent rule of the service' (Church and Brodribb). For *disciplina* 'military regulations' see *TLL* s.v. 1324.73–1325.74. T. uses *fas disciplinae* to allude to the totality of the military code at *A.* 1.19.3; cf. *H.* 2.68.1 *apud Vitellium omnia indisposita temulenta, peruigiliis ac bacchanalibus quam disciplinae et castris propiora.*

46.5 Laco praefectus ... confossus: sc. *est.* On Laco see 6.1n. This sentence is either elliptical even by Tacitean standards or corrupt. The difficulty lies in making a connection between *tamquam ... seponeretur* and *confossus. A.* 16.9.1 *Silanus tamquam Naxum deueheretur Ostiam amotus, post municipio Apuliae ... clauditur* has spurred emendations here, of which the simplest is replacing *praefectus* with *profectus*, which then governs *tamquam* (for this and other repairs see Wellesley's app. crit.). But Laco's title is balanced by the reference to Icelus' status, *ut libertum*, in the following sentence, and *profectus* gives Laco surprising freedom of movement amidst the bloodbath of 15 January. A better repair inserts *amotus* before *ab euocato*, but the loss of the word is hard to explain and, once in, seems cloyingly regular. Better to explain the connection as lying in Otho: Otho created the pretence of exile for Laco while preparing his execution (this view is implicit in Alford's 'while professedly being removed to an island'). The connection is elided when T. makes Laco the subject and the verbs passive. **tamquam** 'as if' revives the theme of duplicity: as with the rescue of Marius Celsus, Otho effects something he gives no indication of intending. **Marcianum Icelum:** 13.1 n. **ut in libertum palam animaduersum:** sc. *est*; cf. 68.2 *in Iulium Alpinum*... *Caecina animaduertit.* For executions of other freedmen see 4.11.3 *seruili supplicio* and 4.3.2 *patibulo affixus.*

47.1 exacto per scelera die nouissimum malorum fuit laetitia: cf. *A.* 4.50.1 *rebus turbatis malum extremum discordia accessit.* T.'s *laetitia* is more pungent than Dio's 'pretence of gladness' (64.6.5a). **praetor urbanus:** with both consuls dead, the praetor was the senior magistrate with the power to convene the senate; for other such occasions see Talbert (1984) 185–6. **omnes principum honores:** of the remaining *honores* – the term covers titles, offices and powers, and prerogatives – the principal were *imperium*, the right to convene the senate, the office of *pontifex maximus*, and the name Imperator (Brunt (1977) 95–107). The formal transfer of imperial power was effected by one or more senatorial decrees that were ratified by a series of *leges* passed between January and March in *comitia* (Brunt (1977) 98–101). Here and for the accessions of Vitellius (2.55.2 *in senatu cuncta longis aliorum principatibus composita statim decernuntur*; cf. 2.90.2) and Vespasian (4.3.3 *at Romae senatus cuncta principibus solita Vespasiano decernit*), varying the expression each time, T. omits the legislative phase (so too Plut. *G.* 28.1 and Suet. *O.* 7.1), over-emphasizing, perhaps, the senate's role (and its servility). T.'s phrasing also stresses the similarity of the three senatorial decrees, obscuring somewhat the fact that Otho, unlike Vitellius or Vespasian, was present at the meeting. Indeed he spoke, according to Suet. *O.* 7.1; see also Dio 64.8.1. **adnitentibus cunctis:** T.'s evocation of senatorial aims and anxieties in this appended abl. abs. is not paralleled – apart from Dio's 'pretence of gladness' (see on *laetitia* above) – in the other sources, which focus instead on Otho's self-justifying speech (Suet. *O.* 7.1) or the irony of his accepting declarations of a loyalty he had not shown to Galba (Plut. *G.* 28.1). T. shows a similarly ingratiating senate welcoming the Flavians (4.4.3). **abolere** 'efface the memory of' *OLD* 3; first attested in Virgil (four times), it proved useful during the imperial period (Liv. eleven times, Sen. eight, Plin. *Nat.* ten, Suet. twenty-two times), particularly to T. (twenty-six times, plus twice of *abolitio*). See Wölfflin (1888) 118–19. **conuicia ac probra:** another near doublet (cf. *raptus et latrocinia*), used again at 2.52.1 and 3.10.3. On long-remembered insults see also *A.* 5.2.2 *quarum* (sc. *facetiarum*) *apud praepotentes in longum memoria est.* **promisce** is used differently at each of its three appearances in Book 1; for 'from many sources' (here) cf. *A.* 4.37.3 *promiscis adulationibus.* Some of the criticisms of Otho probably occurred at 35.1 *posito metu incauti . . . nimii uerbis, linguae feroces,* a scene of similar social chaos. See also 66.1n. and 84.4n. **nemo sensit:** since Otho was not present to hear the insults (see above) his (eventual) knowledge of them came from later reports. *nemo sensit* refers then to perceptions not on 15 January, but in the balance of Otho's reign, as is made clear in the final words of the sentence. That is, he caused no one to feel that the insults were fixed in his memory. Emendation (see Wellesley's app. crit.) is not needed. Plutarch's version is simpler and more complimentary: *O.* 3.1 'he did not remember personal grievances against anyone at all'. **omisisset:** for the omission of *utrum* see 17.2n. *pro . . . senatu.*

47.2 cruento adhuc foro per stragem iacentium: Plutarch (*G.* 28.1) exploits the detail differently, synchronizing it with the senate meeting and singling out 'headless bodies in consular robes' (i.e. Galba and Vinius). The death toll is unknown. **in Capitolium . . . uectus:** for a sacrifice. Both Plutarch (*O.* 1.1) and Suetonius (*O.* 7.1) place Otho's sacrifice on the next morning, the latter connecting it with an ominous dream from the night of the 15th. Dio reverses the order of sacrifice and dream (64.7.1; cf. 64.7.2 'after this'). T. does not mention the sacrifice specifically, nor does he report Otho's dream or his regret for the position he found himself in (expressed by a Greek proverb quoted by both Suetonius and Dio *ad. locc.*). For Vitellius' ascent to the Capitolium see 2.89.2; the temple burned before Vespasian's arrival in Rome. **concedi corpora sepulturae:** an unusual expression modelled on the last words of Mezentius: Virg. *Aen.* 10.906 '*me consortem nati concede sepulcro*'; Miller (1987b) 96. **Verania uxor** survived Piso by many years. Pliny's gossip of *c.* A.D. 104 includes a story about how she was inveigled into giving a legacy to a man accused in the Senate of having gnawed her husband's head (*Ep.* 2.20.1–5; cf. *H.* 4.42.2). **frater Scribonianus:** 15.2n. *est tibi* *frater.* **Crispina filia:** 13.2n. *uidua filia.* **composuere** 'buried' *OLD* 4c. **quaesitis redemptisque capitibus:** according to Plutarch, Verania got Piso's head for the asking, but Crispina had to pay 10,000 HS for Vinius' (*G.* 28.2). Plutarch also mentions Laco's head and specifies that they were all delivered to Otho (*G.* 27.5), but on Laco's death see 46.5n.

48.1 Magnum Claudius, Crassum Nero interfecerant: famous Republican names (14.1 n. *Pisonem Licinianum*) neatly interleaved with those of emperors. For the death of Magnus see Suet. *Cl.* 29.1–2, for that of Crassus see Plin. *Ep.* 1.5.3, Tac. *H.* 4.42.1. **ad hoc tantum... praelatus est ut prior occideretur:** the equation of preferment (*praelatus*) and death generates a wry tone; for the paronomasia (*prae- ... prior*) see 25.1 n. *transferendum ... transtulerunt.*

48.2 Titus Vinius: 1.1 n. The style of this obituary is blander than that of Piso's: much information is packaged in periods (*legatum ... ausa, igitur ... furatus*). Its content matches Plut. *G.* 12.1–2 closely, but Plutarch uses the material instead to introduce Vinius; for some stylistic differences see Intro. §18. **quinquaginta septem:** this number implies that Vinius was a very old twenty-six or twenty-seven at the time of his first military service (*c.* A.D. 39 under Calvisius Sabinus; see below) and should perhaps be emended to forty-seven (Sumner (1976) 431–2). **pater illi:** sc. *erat.* Forms of *esse* are frequently omitted in these obituaries. **maternus auus e proscriptis:** another suspect datum (Chilver *ad loc.*). **Caluisium Sabinum:** legate of Pannonia under Gaius (*c.* 39; Thomasson (1984) I: 100 and *PIR*[2] C 354). His wife's name was Cornelia. **uxor ... ingressa ... temptasset ... ausa:** Plutarch makes Vinius the subject (see App. 1). **mala cupidine uisendi:** female involvement in military affairs earns T.'s disapprobation at e.g. *A.* 1.69.2 and 2.55.6. At *A.* 3.33–4 he recounts a senatorial debate on the subject. **uigilias et cetera militiae munia ... temptasset:** cf. Dio 58.18.4 'she was charged with making the rounds of the sentries and viewing the soldiers' exercises'; Plut. omits this detail. *temptasset,* an emendation for M's nonsensical *temperasset,* suits T.'s picture of a woman taking the initiative (cf. *A.* 1.69.4 *nihil relictum imperatoribus, ubi femina manipulos interuisat, signa adeat, largitionem temptet*). Another possible emendation is *temerasset*: cf. 58.6 *castra incorrupta et intemerata, A.* 1.30.3 *castra infausta temerataque*; see Wellesley's app. crit. **principiis** 'headquarters building' *OLD* 10. **ausa:** sc. *est.*

48.3 mutatione temporum: i.e. by the assassination of Gaius in 41. **cursu honorum inoffenso:** *inoffensus* commonly characterizes a path or motion (*A.* 1.56.2 *siccitate et amnibus modicis inoffensum iter properauerat*; *TLL* 1735.10–44) but T.'s application of it to a metaphorical *cursus* is not found again until much later (*TLL* 1736.36–50). **tamquam** 'on the grounds that' 7.3n. **furatus:** sc. *est.* The story also appears (without Vinius' name) at Suet. *Cl.* 32. **fictilibus:** modest dinnerware (Juv. 3.161, 10.25).

48.4 proconsulatu: abl. of time when. **in abruptum tractus:** a metaphorical adaptation of Virgilian physical hazards: *Aen.* 3.422 *sorbet in abruptum fluctus* (sc. *Charybdis*), 12.687 *fertur in abruptum magno mons improbus actu*; the Virgilian images suggest a downward plunge. Cf. also *Agr.* 42.4 *plerique per abrupta . . . ambitiosa morte inclaruerunt* and *A.* 2.55.4 *orta tempestas raperet* (sc. *Pisonem*) *in abrupta.* For a similar metaphor cf. 78.2 *in suspenso.* **prout . . . intendisset:** *prout* 'according as' *OLD* 1; cf. 59.1 *prout inclinassent.* For *intendere* 'direct' see *OLD* 9. **prauus aut industrius eadem ui:** an abrupt and epigrammatic conclusion to the obituary, juxtaposing opposites (depravity ~ industry) and asserting a connection between them (*eadem*); cf. *A.* 2.2.4 *perinde odium prauis et honestis* (also a concluding epigram) and 11.33 *ad honesta seu praua iuxta leui* (sc. *praefecto*).

49.1 corpus diu neglectum et licentia tenebrarum plurimis ludibriis uexatum: *diu* 'for a long time' is odd, given that burial was on the 16th (see below), so some take *diu* as 'by day' and the antithesis *diu . . . licentia tenebrarum* as a variant of the common doublet *diu noctuque* (2.5.1, *A.* 15.12.4, *H.* 3.76.2 *noctu dieque*; *TLL* s.v. 1557.18–44). Others alter the word order (see Wellesley's app. crit.). For *licentia tenebrarum* cf. 32.1 *licentia acclamationum* – here too the basic meaning lies in the gen. ('in the darkness'), while *licentia* characterizes. **plurimis ludibriis uexatum:** see 41.3. Plutarch identifies the offenders as slaves of Patrobius (see below): *G.* 28.3 'after mutilating and insulting it in every way they cast it where those condemned by emperors die'. **dispensator Argius . . . contexit:** Plutarch reports that Helvidius Priscus, to whom T. gives a full introduction at 4.5–6, was an intermediary (see App. 1). Suetonius identifies the place of Galba's tomb (*Aurelia uia*) rather than its character (*humili*). **e prioribus seruis:** longwinded for *libertus*, if that is indeed what it means (cf. Plut. *G.* 28.3 ἀπελεύθερος) and odd if it denotes rather a slave owned before Galba's accession (so Hellegouarc'h). *primoribus* has been suggested as a repair (see Wellesley's app. crit.), but *dispensator* 'steward' has already explained, more precisely than 'high-ranking' would, Argius' position. **caput . . . ante Patrobii tumulum . . . repertum:** the other sources ascribe the mutilation of Galba's head to the slaves (Plut. *G.* 28.2–3) or a freedman (Suet. *G.* 20.2) of Patrobius and, stressing retribution, make the place of its disposal the place where Patrobius died. T.'s *postera demum die repertum*, by contrast, emphasizes the head's abandonment. **punitus a Galba:** presumably in 68 (Dio 64.3.4); for Galba's victims see Murison (1993) 56 n. 32.

49.2 hunc exitum habuit Seruius Galba: Galba, who died first, is remembered last. Plutarch's obituary begins similarly 'such was what happened to Galba' (*G.* 29.1) but, apart from a few shared details of language, is very different, T.'s being a character sketch and career outline, Plutarch's a review of Galba's place in history. Despite its shorter compass (109 words vs 156) T.'s obituary both incorporates material that Plutarch placed at the beginning of his *Life* and draws together threads spun in his own narrative. Almost nothing is not illustrated earlier. **quinque principes . . . emensus** 'having traversed [the times of] five emperors' (Alford) is more compact and conveys the extent of time better than Plut. *G.* 29.2 'having lived during five emperors' reigns'. For the participle cf. V. Max. 8.13. ext.1 *Masinissa . . . excessit, regni spatium LX annis emensus.* **uetus in familia nobilitas:** alluded to by Galba himself at 15.1 *Sulpiciae et Lutatiae decora* and by Mucianus at 2.76.2 *Galbae imagines*. In introducing their *Lives* both Plutarch (*G.* 3.1) and Suetonius (*G.* 2.3) discuss some of the Sulpicii and trace Galba's connections with Q. Lutatius Catulus (cos. 78 B.C.) and Livia. Like Suetonius, Silius credits Galba with a genealogy stretching back to Minos and Pasiphae (8.468–70). In Juvenal's satire on nobility Galba represents ancient nobility of birth (8.5). **magnae opes:** briefer than Plut. *G.* 3.1 'agreed to have been the wealthiest private individual to attain the house of the Caesars'. **medium ingenium:** cf. Liv. 1.32.4 *medium erat in Anco ingenium, et Romuli et Numae memor.* Plutarch (*G.* 3.2) limits the sphere of Galba's 'avoidance of extremes' (ἀπέριττον) to expenditures (see below on 49.3 *pecunia . . . parcus*). **magis extra uitia quam cum uirtutibus:** *saeuitia* and *auaritia* are charges advanced by Otho (37.4, cf. Suet. *G.* 12.1 *de eo fama saeuitiae simul atque auaritiae*), but as he had done in the narrative, so here T. denies (or moderates) them: 5.2n. *senium atque auaritiam*, 6.1 n. *et . . . trucidatis*, 37.2n. *cuius . . . Galba*; see also 5.2n. *legi . . . emi* and 87.1 n. *saeuitia Galbae*. The virtues credited to Galba in the narrative – 18.3

antiquus rigor and *nimia seueritas* – are annulled by their inappropriateness to conditions (*antiquus*, *nimia*).

49.3 famae nec incuriosus nec uenditator: more pungent than Plut. *G.* 11.1 'a large-minded man, apparently above vulgarity'. Plutarch illustrates this phrase with Galba's refusal to use Nero's trappings *en route* to Rome in 68. In T. the first quality can be seen at 34.1 *speciosiora suadentibus accessit*, the second at 16.3 *cum inuidia quamis egregii erimus*, 18.2 *nec ullum orationi... lenocinium addit*, 19.1 *apud senatum non comptior... sermo* (and for a like trait in Piso see 30.1 *nihil arrogabo mihi nobilitatis aut modestiae*). For *uenditator* 'touter' cf. Gel. 18.4.1–2, which describes a *iactator* and *uenditator Sallustianae lectionis*, and 5.14.3 (describing another boastful scholarly type) *in praedicandis doctrinis sui uenditator.* **pecuniae alienae non appetens, suae parcus:** modelled on but opposite to Sal. *Cat.* 5.4 *alieni appetens, sui profusus*, briefer than Plut. *G.* 3.2 'the restraint of his manner of life and his thrift in expenditures gave him the reputation of parsimony once he became emperor'. The second trait is illustrated by anecdotes in Plutarch (*G.* 16.1) and Suetonius (*G.* 12.3, 13); in T. it is a criticism expressed by Otho at 37.4 *parsimoniam pro auaritia.* **publicae auarus:** illustrated in ch. 20; see also *O.* 12.1. For a critique of the text see Wellesley (1967) 211–15. **amicorum... ignarus:** cf. 12.3 *ipsa Galbae facilitas*, there in connection with the peculation of *mali*, and 7.2 *Galbam... comprobasse*, apropos of their crimes. Plutarch (*G.* 29.4) and Suetonius (*G.* 14.2) make similar charges with specific reference to Galba's handling of Vinius, Laco, and Icelus. The only friends in the narrative who could be considered *boni* are Piso and Marius Celsus. **obtentui:** sc. *erat*, used without the metaphor at 2.14.3 *obscurum noctis, obtentui fugientibus.* **segnitia:** according to Suet. *G.* 9.2 (on Galba as governor of Spain) showing *segnitia* was a form of self-defence, *quod nemo rationem otii sui reddere cogeretur.* For the antithesis cf. *Agr.* 6.3 *gnarus sub Nerone temporum, quibus inertia pro sapientia fuit.*

49.4 militari laude: 5.2n. *laudata... seueritas.* **apud Germanias... Africam... Hispaniam:** Plutarch (*G.* 3.2–3) and Suetonius (*G.* 6–8) give more details about Galba's provincial commands. **omnium consensu capax imperii, nisi imperasset:** lists of *capaces imperii* generated by Augustus (*A.* 1.13.2) and Trajan (Dio 69.17.3) are on record; according to T., Tiberius predicted that Galba would be emperor, but not that he was *capax* (*A.* 6.20.3 '*degustabis imperium*'; cf. Suet. *G.* 4.1 with Murison (1991 b) *ad loc.*). The famous epigram on Galba employs a 'slightly off-center logic' (Plass (1988) 95): by omitting the main clause of the contrary-to-fact condition ('he would have retained his reputation' *uel sim.*) T. juxtaposes a widely held belief about Galba's potential (*omnium consensu capax imperii*) with the circumstances that proved it utterly wrong (*imperasset*). The abruptness and completeness of the reversal makes T.'s epigram more forceful than Suetonius' antithesis: *G.* 14.1 *maiore adeo et fauore et auctoritate adeptus est quam gessit imperium*, which admits of degrees (*maiore*). Plutarch expresses a similar point still more diffusely: Galba had leadership qualities (*G.* 29.2 ἀνδρὸς ἡγεμονικοῦ) but left behind none still eager for his rule (29.4). Epigram form is used for similar reversals at 10.3, 38.2, and 39.1 (see App. 2).

50.1 nouus insuper de Vitellio nuntius: it is news to the reader, too (14.1 n. *nihil ... certum*); the details come in chh. 55–7. **uelut ... fataliter electos:** similarly 71.2 *uelut fataliter.* **uulgus quoque:** for the *uulgus*' exclusion from governance cf. 35.1 *imperita plebs*, 89.1 *communium curarum expers populus*, and 4.38.3 *uulgus ... cui una ex re publica annonae cura*, with Newbold (1976). **maerere:** 46.3n. *fatigari.*

50.2 saeuae pacis: at 2.1 of the Flavian period (*ipsa etiam pace saeuum*), here, presumably, of the Julio-Claudian past; cf. 89.2 *sub Tiberio et Gaio ... pacis aduersa*, *A.* 1.10.4 *pacem ... cruentam.* **repetita ... memoria:** for the abl. abs. cf. Liv. 8.18.12 *memoria ex annalibus repetita.* **captam totiens suis exercitibus urbem:** the known dates (all B.C.) are 88 (Sulla), 87 (Cinna and Marius), 82 (Sulla), 49 (Caesar), 43 (Octavian), 41 (L. Antonius); the first three occasions were particularly bloody. **uastitatem Italiae:** a much used phrase, most memorably by Livy for Hannibal's dream of the fate of Italy (21.22.9), but also in connection with civil war (Cic. *Sest.* 12, Sal. *Jug.* 5.2). **Pharsaliam Philippos et Perusiam ac Mutinam:** the dates (all B.C.) are 48, 42, 40, 43. For the connectives cf. *A.* 1.1.2 *Tiberii Gaique et Claudii ac Neronis*, 12.64.1 *quaestore aedili tribuno ac praetore et consule ... defunctis.*

50.3 euersum: sc. *esse.* **ituros:** sc. *se esse.* In indirect statement T. often omits subject *se*: here with *ituros*, at 51.4 with *donatos*; see Adams (1972) 370–1 'The omission ... is common in historians other than Velleius. The ellipse is usually an easy one. T.'s liking for the usage increases: in the minor works he rarely allows it, but in the *Annals* in particular it becomes very frequent.' *ituros* is often treated as a rhetorical question, but in the absence of an interrogative particle (contrast 2.75.1 *quid enim profuturas* (sc. *esse*) *cohortes alasque?* and *A.* 2.2.2 *ubi illam gloriam* (sc. *esse*)*?*) it is preferable to take it as a grimly sardonic statement. For the syntax and tone cf. *A.* 1.26.3 *eundum ergo senatum consulendum* (sc. *esse*) *quotiens supplicia aut proelia indicantur.* *an* 'or perhaps' introduces a second possibility (*OLD* 9; cf. 3.25.1 *uagus inde an consilio ducis subditus rumor*), not a disjunctive question (17.2n. *pro … senatu*). **deteriorem fore qui uicisset:** cf. Sen. *Ep.* 14.13 apropos of the struggle between Pompey and Caesar: *potest melior uincere, non potest non peior esse qui uicerit.*

50.4 augurarentur: elsewhere in T. only at *G.* 3.1 *futurae … pugnae fortunam ipso cantu augurantur.* **ambigua de Vespasiano fama:** sc. *erat.* Criticisms collected by Suetonius include lack of ambition (*Ves.* 2.2), difficulty in attaining the aedileship (2.3), servility towards Gaius (2.3), unpopularity as governor of Africa (4.3; he was pelted with turnips), going to excessive lengths to get money (4.3–4), obscure family (4.5). T. focuses on Vespasian's *auaritia*: 2.5.1 *si auaritia abesset, antiquis ducibus par.* **solus omnium ante se principum:** the logical flaw (Vespasian wasn't one of his own predecessors) is like that at Thuc. 1.1.1 on a war 'most noteworthy of those that preceded' (ἀξιολογώτατον τῶν προγεγενημένων); the expression is compressed but perfectly intelligible. See also 46.4n. *bonis postea principibus.*

51–54 Disaffection in Germany and Gaul: *causae*

T. turns away from the foreboding of ch. 50 to provide background for the *motus Vitellianus.* In addition to answering the questions why here? and why now? this section characterizes the forces from which Vitellius drew his armies and the men who led them.

Ch. 51 is devoted to the currents of emotion in the German armies in the aftermath of their easy victory over Vindex: a sense of power and greed for the profits of power clashed with a consciousness of having backed a loser in Nero. The resulting discontent was fanned by the Gauls. Lax discipline facilitated the growth of sedition, ominous rumours added urgency. Chh. 52–53.2 introduce Vitellius, newly arrived in the area, and his principal legates, Fabius Valens and Caecina Alienus. In ch. 54 a small incident illustrates the tinderbox atmosphere of the two-legion camp at Moguntiacum.

51.1 initia causasque: 4.1n. *non … causaeque.* **expediam**, introducing background material (cf. 4.12.1, 4.48.1, *G.* 27.2, *A.* 4.1.1), varies Sal. *Jug.* 5.3 *prius quam huiusce modi rei initium expedio, pauca supra repetam.*

The formula is Virgilian: Miller (1987b) 97. **caeso cum omnibus copiis Iulio Vindice:** 6.2n. *opprimendis Vindicis coeptis*, 8.1n. *super memoriam Vindicis*. Vindex took his own life, so T.'s expression is more brief than precise. **ferox praeda gloriaque exercitus:** cf. 8.2. For *ferocia* of eagerness, often ill-advised, for battle and its rewards cf. 79.1 *ex ferocia et successu praedae magis quam pugnae intenta*, 2.43.1 *ferox et noui decoris auida*, 5.11.2 *poscebant ... pericula, pars uirtute, multi ferocia et cupidine praemiorum*. The adj. is so used by Sallust (*Jug.* 94.4 *Numidae ... secundis rebus feroces*) and Livy (e.g. 1.25.11 *geminata uictoria ferocem*, 3.61.13 *feroces ab re ... bene gesta*, 25.39.9 *feroces ... uictoria proelium ineunt*) but not Caesar. **expeditionem et aciem, praemia quam stipendia malebat** 'preferred campaign and battle – the rewards (sc. of war) – over regular pay'. *praemia* shows an abrupt pragmatism (war = rewards) echoed in *stipendia*, which parallels the (elided) antithesis to war, *pax*. The sentence as a whole emulates the antithesis and the inconcinnity, if not the precise form, of Sal. *Cat.* 17.6 *incerta pro certis, bellum quam pacem malebant*. For the military doublet cf. *Agr.* 33.2 *tot expeditionibus, tot proeliis*, Liv. 3.12.5. *nunc in expeditionibus, nunc in acie*, 37.53.18 *nulla expeditio, nullum equestre proelium*, Suet. *Dom.* 19 *in expeditione et agmine*, 4.58.1 *proelium et acies*, 4.50.4 *per arma atque acies*. For the abrupt change in terminology cf. 5.2n. *laudata ... seueritas* and 33.1n. *cunctatione ... segnitia*.

51.2 infructuosam 'unprofitable'(*OLD* 2) voices the seditious soldier's view of military service; cf. *A.* 1.17.4 *militiam ipsam grauem, infructuosam* (and *sterilem pacem* later in this seditious speech). At *D.* 9.1 *laudem inanem et infructuosam* the adj. again contributes to a negative characterization of its speaker, Aper. **ingenio ... seueritate:** causal abl. with *infructuosam* and *asperam*, appended to an already complete main clause. Further unannounced clauses follow. **ingenio loci** occurs first in Sallust (*Hist.* fr. 3.28 *pugna ... ingenio loci prohibebatur*, cf. fr. 1.100 *quas duas insulas ... constabat suopte ingenio alimenta mortalibus gignere*). Cicero uses *natura*: *Ver.* 5.26 *hic situs atque haec natura esse loci caelique dicitur*. For similar expressions in T. cf. 2.4.3 *arduo opere ob ingenium montis*, 5.14.2 *camporum suo ingenio umentium*, *A.* 6.41.1 *locorum ... ingenio sese ... tutabatur*. **caeli** 'climate' (*OLD* 7) is used again in Mucianus' description of the rigours of a posting to Germany: 2.80.3 *Germanica hiberna caelo ac laboribus dura*. **inexorabilem:** in Livy, too, of a fundamental Roman institution viewed through seditious eyes (those of Tarquinius' *sodales*): 2.3.4 *leges rem surdam, rem inexorabilem esse*. **paratis utrimque corruptoribus et perfidia impunita:** stated more strongly later: 3.61.3 *nec ulla . . . flagitii poena, et praemiis defectorum uersa fides ac reliquum perfidiae certamen.* **uiri arma equi:** formulaic: *A.* 12.37.2 *habui equos uiros, arma opes,* Liv. 23.24.9 *arma uiros equos obruerunt,* etc. See Heubner (1963). **ad usum et ad decus supererant** 'more than sufficed for use and show'. *decus,* an emendation for M's nonsensical *dedecus,* often has a utilitarian partner, as at [Sal.] *ad Caes.* 1.7.3 *usum atque decus* and Vegetius 4.31 *decore et utilitate*; cf. also *Agr.* 6.1 *decus ac robur,* 33.6 *incolumitas ac decus, G.* 13.3 *in pace decus in bello praesidium.*

51.3 aduersus Vindicem contractae legiones: the three legions of Upper Germany (IV and XXII from Moguntiacum, mod. Mainz, XXI from Vindonissa, mod. Windisch; cf. 53.2 *bello aduersus Vindicem uniuersus adfuerat*) and at least one legion in strength from Lower Germany (probably I from Bonna; see further 53.2n. *praeuentus erat*). These troops were probably together for at least three months (assuming a joint march to Vesontio beginning in late March and the force's continued existence until after news of Nero's suicide arrived in mid-June; see Murison (1993) 7–11. **quaerere**: 46.3n. *fatigari.* **instigatrix**: 22.3n. *instinctor,* and cf. *A.* 3.40.1 *exstimulator acerrimus.* **Galbianos**: cf. *legio Galbiana* (2.86.1, 3.7.1, 3.10.1). Partisan groups were frequently named from their leader's nomen or cognomen, both by opponents (e.g. *Pompeiani* in Caesar's *Ciu. passim*) and by themselves: *SCPP* 55–6 *milites alios Pisonianos, alios Caesarianos dici laetatus sit* (sc. *Piso*); see further Wölfflin (1898). **hoc enim nomen fastidito Vindice indiderant:** the omission of subject (*Galli, milites,* former *Vindiciani*?) and dat. complement (*iis* or *sibi*?) obscures the meaning. Retaining *Galli* (i.e. Gauls who had opposed Vindex) as subject is the simplest solution. Heubner (and Wölfflin (1898)) take the Rhine legions as the subject, but T. presented the legions' view of their opponents in 51.3. *indere* is used by T. of self-naming (2.61.4 *iamque assertor Galliarum et deus* (*nam id sibi indiderat*), *A.* 14.61.2 *plebis sibi nomen indiderint,* etc.) as well as name-calling (*A* 1.23.3 *cui . . . uocabulum 'Cedo alteram' indiderant,* 2.56.3 *illi* (sc. *Artaxiae*) *uocabulum indiderant ex nomine urbis,* etc.), so former *Vindiciani* are another possible subject, though the omission of *sibi* is difficult.

51.4 Sequanis Aeduisque: the Sequani are not mentioned again; for the Aedui see 64.3n. **ac deinde . . . infensi:** i.e. *ac deinde ciuitatibus prout opulentia cuique erat infensi.* **prout opulentia . . . infensi:** for Vitellian exactions from Vienna, the capital of the Allobroges, and Lucus, the capital of the Vocontii, see 65.2–66. *En route* to Italy Vitellius' armies would have passed through still other tribal centres and cities (see Murison (1993) 86–91). For the wealth of the area generally see Suet. *Ner.* 40.4 *opulentissima prouincia*, and Duncan-Jones (1981). **expugnationes . . . hauserunt animo:** only *animo* reveals that the damage is intended, not actual; cf. Virg. *Aen.* 10.648 *animo spem turbidus hausit inanem*, 12.26 *hoc animo hauri*; contrast 3.84.1 *quidquid tot proeliis laboris ac periculi hausissent.* Stylistic elevation (tricolon, metaphor, abstraction) conveys the *arrogantia* (see below) of the Vitellians; for tone and image cf. Cic. *Phil.* 11.10 *quid eum non sorbere animo, quid non haurire cogitatione, cuius sanguinem non bibere censetis?* **raptus penatium,** even if *penates* are unlikely in Gallic households, suggests a lack of moral scruple (cf. *auaritia* below) fully evidenced in the subsequent narrative. **super:** 8.1 n. *super memoriam Vindicis.* **contumacia** 'provocation', usually pointless and sometimes harmful: thus in the elder Agrippina (*A.* 5.3.2 *arrogantiam oris et contumacem animum*), her son Nero (*A.* 4.60.1 *uoces . . . contumaces et inconsultae*), Cn. Calpurnius Piso (*A.* 3.12.1 *contumacia et certaminibus asperasset iuuenem*; cf. *A.* 2.57.3 *precibus contumacibus*), and Thrasea Paetus (*A.* 16.22.2 *contumaciam sententiarum*). T.'s warmest praises go to those who show how to avoid it: Agricola (*Agr.* 42.3 *non contumacia neque inani iactatione libertatis famam fatumque prouocabat*) and M. Lepidus (*A.* 4.20.3 *liceat . . . inter abruptam contumaciam et deforme obsequium pergere iter ambitione ac periculis uacuum*). See also 3.1 n. *contumax . . . seruorum fides.* **remissam . . . donatos:** sc. *esse*; with *donatos* supply also *se* (50.3n. *ituros*). For some details see 8.1 nn. *recenti dono Romanae ciuitatis* and *in posterum tributi leuamento.*

51.5 accessit . . . dimitti: for the structure cf. 5.2 *accessit . . . emi.* **decimari legiones et promptissimum quemque . . . dimitti:** both rumours were extrapolated from Galba's actual disciplinary measures: 37.3n. *decimari . . . acceperat*, 20.3n. *exauctorati.* T.'s language implies a common cause between soldiers and centurions that is both at odds with the course of earlier seditions (e.g. *A.* 1.20.1 *centuriones . . . insectantur*, *A.* 1.32.1 *in centuriones inuadunt*) and belied by the present one (see 56.1). **atroces nuntii, sinistra . . . fama:** 5.2–7.3. **infensa:** sc. *Galbae erat.* **Lugdunensis colonia:** mod. Lyon. Officially established at the confluence of the Rhone and the Saône in 43 B.C. on a site earlier settled by colonists who had been driven out of Vienna (Dio 46.50.4; 65.1 n. *et Viennenses*), Lugdunum received significant investments of capital both practical (walls, forum, theatre, quays, dikes, roads, aqueduct, etc.) and symbolic (imperial mint, altar and *sacerdos* of Rome and Augustus, federal sanctuary of the Gauls) under the Julio-Claudians, emerging as 'the virtual capital of the Three Gauls under the High Empire' (Drinkwater (1983) 21). Based there were the governor of Lugdunensis, the procurators of Lugdunensis and Aquitania, and, unusually, an urban cohort (64.3n.; for the enlarged garrison in 69 see 59.2nn. *Italica legione* and *ala Tauriana*). After a devastating fire in 65 the city received compensation from Nero (*A.* 16.13.3). It remained loyal to him during the revolt of Vindex – probably the governor of Lugdunensis at the time – and was punished by Galba (65.1n. *reditus Lugdunensium*). In January of 69 Lugdunum followed its then governor, Junius Blaesus, in joining the Vitellian cause (59.2 for Blaesus, 64.3 for Lugdunum); the city contributed *materiel* to Valens (64.3, note *gaudio*) and served as a temporary capital for Vitellius (2.59.3; similarly in 70 for young Domitian (4.85.2)). See further Drinkwater (1975), Chevallier (1975) 912–39, Fishwick (1987) 97–137, *CAH*² XI 493–500. **plurima ad fingendum credendumque materies:** sc. *erat*; cf. 89.2 *longo bello materia.* T. uses both *materia* (twenty-two times before and three times in the *Annals*) and *materies* (here and nine times in the *Annals*); as with the omission of *se* above, so here his practice anticipates that of the *Annals.* **odio metu et, ubi uires suas respexerant, securitate:** the reference to *uires* (cf. 8.2 *in tantis uiribus*), highlighted by the list's inconcinnity, ends the paragraph on an ominous note. For similar abl. lists see 57.2n. *instinctu et impetu et auaritia.* For *et* see, in Book 1, 56.1 *segnis pauidus et socordia innocens* and 71.1 *dilatae uoluptates dissimulata luxuria et cuncta ad decorem imperii composita* and GG s.v. *et* 390–1.

52.1 hiberna legionum: Bonna (Bonn), Novaesium (Neuss), and Vetera (Xanten). His administrative base was *colonia Agrippinensis* (Cologne: 56.2n.). **cum cura adierat:** cf. *A.* 11.18.2 *Corbulo prouinciam ingressus magna cum cura et mox gloria.* Both *cum cura,* which expresses general approbation (unusual in T.), and some of the details that follow present Vitellius more favourably than does Suetonius (e.g. *Vit.* 8.1: *castra uero ingressus nihil cuique poscenti negauit*). **redditi . . . ordines:** sc. *erant. ordo* means 'military rank' (*OLD* 3b), especially that of centurion (*TLL* 964.1–21, 33–45). A possible beneficiary is Claudius Faventinus, *centurio per ignominiam a Galba dimissus* (3.57.1). For the focus on centurions cf. *A.* 1.44.5. **remissa ignominia, alleuatae notae:** the distinction between *ignominia* and *notae*, if there is one, is collapsed in Suetonius' version: *Vit.* 8.1 *ignominiosis notas . . . dempsit.* Military punishments included both permanent measures (demotion, dismissal) and temporary ones, including barley rations (Liv. 27.13.9, Suet. *Aug.* 24), quarters outside camp (Liv. 10.4.4, *A.* 13.36.5), harder service (Liv. 23.25.8), and stoppage of pay (Festus 69M); cf. the list at *Dig.* 49.16.3.1 (Modestinus) *poenae militum huiuscemodi sunt: castigatio, pecuniaria multa, munerum indictio, militiae mutatio, gradus deiectio, ignominiosa missio.* **plura ... quaedam:** objects of *mutauerat.* **in quibus** 'among them', connecting relative (cf. 22.2 *e quibus*) introducing a parenthetical example of Vitellius' judicious measures. **sordes et auaritiam** 'sordid greed' (hendiadys; cf. 60 *per auaritiam ac sordes*), with *mutauerat,* which serves in both main clause (*plura ... mutauerat*) and parenthesis (*sordes ... mutauerat*). A rhetorically elaborate and morally emphatic reference to extortion in the distribution of military posts, which, though technically the responsibility of the emperor, was in practice carried out by the commanding officer (see e.g. *A.* 2.55.5, 3.49.2). T. uses the technical term for extortion only in connection with actual charges (e.g. 77.3 *repetundarum criminibus ... ceciderant*). **adimendis assignandisque ... ordinibus:** for the abl. gerundive phrase with *sordes et auaritiam* cf. *A.* 3.19.2 *finis ... ulciscenda Germanici morte* (another difficult passage) and see *NLS* §207.4d. **integre:** of provincial administration at 48.4 *Vinius proconsulatu Galliam Narbonensem seuere integreque rexit, A.* 13.46.3 (of Otho in Lusitania) *integre sancteque egit,* Suet. *Ves.* 4.3 *sortitus Africam integerrime ... administrauit,* Quint. *Inst.* 12.1.16 *integerrime prouincia administrata,* Plin. *Ep.* 7.25.2 *procuratione ... prouinciae integerrime functus.*

52.2 consularis legati mensura: cf. Quint. *Inst.* 2.3.7 *praeceptorem ... summittentem se ad mensuram discentis.* **ut ... humilis:** sc. *erat.* **ut Vitellius:** *ut* is added to emend the text. For the loss of VT before VIT cf. the loss of *quam* before *quod* at 31.1, *se* after *sanguine* at 58.2, *-ta* after *ostenta* at 78.1, and *-que* before *quos* at 5.1.2. For *ut ... ita* see 4.2n. **apud** 'in the estimation of' *OLD* 12. **apud seueros ... fauentes:** for the variety of views cf. Plut. *G.* 22.4–5 'In the poverty for which he is reproached by some, Vitellius offers clear proof of his probity and magnanimity.' **comitatem bonitatemque:** the doublet, unique in T. though he uses *comitas* eighteen times, voices gushing approval. Suetonius reports a more sober estimate (*Vit.* 7.3 *facili ac prodigo animo*) and his details illustrate camaraderie rather than generosity: greeting soldiers with a kiss, inquiring whether they had had breakfast, and showing with a belch that he had done so. **donaret sua largiretur aliena:** the words of the *fauentes,* as the subjunctives show. *sine modo* and *sine iudicio* are T.'s additions (Heubner *ad loc.* 'two separate utterances are layered together'), perhaps replacing a more favourable adverb ('unstintingly' *uel sim.*). Generosity is one of the qualities mentioned by Sallust's Cato apropos of the changed meanings of words: *Cat.* 52.11 *bona aliena largiri liberalitas . . . uocatur*; both passages look back to Thucydides (37.1 n. *quis ad uos processerim*). **auiditate imperandi** 'in their greed for control'; for selfish motives in a would-be emperor's entourage cf. 7.3 (Galba), 24.1 (Otho), 2.99.2 (Vespasian). Heubner deletes *auiditate imperandi* as a gloss, and the phrase, even when not deleted, is often emended (see Wellesley's app. crit.; of the emendations the best is Nipperdey's (1877) *imperi dandi*, based on *A.* 12.64.3 *Agrippina, quae filio dare imperium, tolerare imperitantem nequibat*; see also Wellesley (1967) 215–17). But *imperare* is apt: it represents the control consequent on winning a war at e.g. Cic. *Phil.* 8.12 *maiores . . . ut imperent arma capiebant*, *Off.* 1.38 *cum Cimbris bellum . . . gerebat uter esset, non uter imperet*, *Rep.* 5.1 *fuse lateque imperantem rem publicam*, Sal. *Jug.* 18.12 *uicti omnes in gentem nomenque imperantium concessere.* **ipsa uitia pro uirtutibus interpretabantur:** sc. *fauentes*; cf. 5.2 *haud minus uitia principum amarent quem olim uirtutes uerebantur* and, for the expression, Sal. *Jug.* 92.2 (of Marius' failings) *omnia non bene consulta in uirtutem trahebantur.* Dio, likewise connecting *uitia* and support for Vitellius, specifies: 64.4.2 'That he had been a sex object for Tiberius and continued to live in accordance with that licentiousness concerned them not at all, or rather, they deemed that he suited them for precisely this reason.'

52.3 modesti quietique: sc. *erant.* These qualities surface later: 2.20.1 *modesto agmine per Italiam incessit*, 2.19.1 *totis castris modesti sermones.* For *modestia* and *quies* as military virtues cf. 84.2 *fortissimus in ipso discrimine exercitus est qui ante discrimen quietissimus* and see 60n. **strenui:** paired with a negative adj. only here; *strenuus et fortis*, by contrast, is formulaic (e.g. Cato *Hist.* fr. 83 *operam rei publicae fortem atque strenuam perhibuit*, twice in Sallust, fifteen times in Livy, four times in Seneca; cf. also Sal. *Jug.* 67.3 *iuxta boni malique strenui et imbelles inulti obtruncari*). **profusa cupidine et insigni temeritate:** sc. *erant.* **Alienus Caecina:** the more attractive and energetic of Vitellius' two *legati* (cf. 2.30.2 *studia . . . militum in Caecinam inclinabant*, 2.56.2 *minus auaritiae in Caecina, plus ambitionis*; *PIR*² C 99). Formally named here at his introduction into the text, he is elsewhere simply Caecina (eighty-five times). For his character and prior career see 53.1–2, for his progress to the Alps chh. 67–70. His legion was probably IV *Macedonica* (55.3n.) based at Moguntiacum. Though successful against Otho's forces and rewarded by Vitellius with both power (2.92.1; including a suffect consulship: 2.71.2) and possessions (3.13.3 *domos hortos opes*), he declared for Vespasian before the second battle of Bedriacum (3.13.1). This timely betrayal prolonged his life (though perhaps not his career: no further offices or honours are attested, despite Jos. *BJ* 4.644 'honours beyond expectation'), but he was killed at Titus' behest before the end of Vespasian's reign on suspicions of further treachery (Suet. *Tit.* 6.2, Dio 66.16.3 with Murison (1999) *ad loc*). **Valens:** 7.1n. **detectam . . . cunctationem:** 8.2n. *nec statim pro Galba Verginius.* **oppressa . . . consilia:** 7.1n. *Fontei Capitonis.* **instigare:** 46.3n. *fatigari.* **ipsum:** sc. *esse* (forms of *esse* are omitted in the indirect statement, which continues through *securitatem*). This 'seducer's rhetoric' (Irvine 133) is functionally equivalent to but formally distinct from Otho's silent soliloquy (21.1–2), Galba's *consilium* (32.2–33), and the musings of Vespasian's supporters (2.6.1–2). A closer formal parallel is Mucianus' speech to Vespasian (2.76–7), but its context is different (2.76.1 *coram ita locutus*). See further 15.4n. *alii . . . utilitas* and 32.2n. *duae sententiae.* The style here is hard-hitting at first: three asyndetic, exaggerated (*ubique*, *nullam*), paired phrases in which each second member is longer than its first build to the exhortation *panderet modo sinum.* This exhilarating picture is reinforced by the seemingly flattering comparison of Vitellius and Verginius Rufus, which modulates smoothly into a warning about the dangers of such pre-eminence. The effect? *quatiebatur his . . . segne ingenium* (51.4). The exhortation is absent from the parallel tradition, but see 55.4n. *non . . . locutus.* **nullam in Flacco Hordeonio moram:** 9.1n.; cf. Plut. *G.* 22.5 'Flaccus Hordeonius . . . should be ignored.' **adfore Britanniam:** a true prediction: 59.2 *ne in Britannia quidem dubitatum.* **secutura Germanorum auxilia:** also true: 61.2n. **precarium seni imperium:** for the adj. 'on sufferance' (*OLD* 1) cf. Sen. *Thy.* 215 *precario regnatur.* **panderet modo sinum:** for image and exhortation cf. Sen. *Thy.* 430 *cur bonis tantis sinum subducis? Ep.* 119.1 *sinum laxa, merum lucrum est*; cf. also 3.69.1 *tamquam omnis res publica in Vespasianum sinum cessisset*, Sen. *Ep.* 74.6 *ad haec quae a Fortuna sparguntur sinum expandit*, Juv. 1.88 *quando maior auaritiae pandit sinus?*, 14.327–9 *si nondum impleui gremium, si panditur ultra, | nec Croesi fortuna umquam nec Persica regna | sufficient animo.* **uenienti Fortunae occurreret:** for *fortuna* cf. 56.2 *occupari nutantem fortunam . . . placuit*, 77.1 *Vitellio . . . ad capessendam principatus fortunam bello opus erat*; for *occurrere* cf. 33.2 *occurrendum discrimini* and *A.* 15.5.2 *uenienti matri occurrere* (of Nero intercepting Agrippina), parallels that, with Pers. 3.64 *uenienti occurrite morbo*, bode ill for Vitellius' encounter with *fortuna.*

52.4 dubitasse Verginium: 8.2n. *nec statim pro Galba Verginius.* **tres patris consulatus, censuram, collegium Caesaris:** 9.1n., and cf. the similar list given by an unnamed speaker at Plut. *G.* 22.5

'his father [having been] censor, three times consul, and colleague, in a manner of speaking, of Claudius Caesar'; see further 55.4n. *non... locutus.* **quatiebatur** 'roused' *OLD* 5b; cf. 2.86.4 *igitur mouere et quatere quidquid usquam aegrum foret* (where *aegrum* means 'liable to abandon Vitellius') and 4.28.1 *aliam manum Mosam amnem transire iubet* (sc. *Ciuilis*), *ut Menapios et Morinos et extra Galliarum quateret.* **segne ingenium:** Vitellius' *segnitia*, in abeyance during the exciting days of early January, returns at 62.2 *torpebat Vitellius*; cf. 2.59.1 *nihil... Vitellio conquirenti*, 2.73 *socordiae... Vitellio adoleuerit*, 2.90.1 *somno et luxu pudendus*, 2.94.2 *insitam animo ignauiam*, 2.97.1 *auxilia... exciuit, segniter et necessitatem dissimulans*, 3.55.1 *Vitellius ut et somno excitus*, 3.36.2 *praeterita instantia futura pari obliuione dimiserat*, 3.56.2 *summi discriminis incuriosus*, and finally 3.86.1 *nomen locumque inter primores nulla sua industria, sed cuncta patris claritudine adeptus.* On *segnitia* itself see 33.1 n. *cunctatione nunc et segnitia.*

53.1 decorus... incessu: Plutarch's description of Caecina (*O.* 6.3) mentions his size and manner of speaking, but not his youth, spirit, or stride. T., emphasizing youthful energy (and excess) here, reserves other traits for 2.20.1. **decorus iuuenta:** *decorus* is an emendation for M's *decori*; cf. 57.2 *insignia... argento decora*, 2.80.2 *decorus etiam... facundia*, 4.40.1 *decorus habitu*, *A.* 11.16.1 *ipse forma decorus.* A case can also be made for *decora*, a correction found already in M's descendants: *A.* 12.44.3 *Radamistus, decora proceritate, ui corporis insignis*, *A.* 2.73.2 *utrumque corpore decoro, genere insigni*, *A.* 11.36.3 *is modesta iuuenta sed corpore insigni*, cf. 4.11.2 *nomen insigne et decora ipsius iuuenta... celebrabantur.* **cito sermone** 'with a rapid manner of speaking' *OLD* s.v. *sermo* 6; cf. Cic. *de Orat.* 3.216 *uox cita tarda*, Jer. *Ep.* 33.6 *cito sed non cauto sermone*, 43.2 *uelocior pes, citus sermo, auris attentior*, [Acro] on Hor. *Carm.* 4.3.5 *Pindarum... in dicendo citum.* Sallust uses *citus* of Catiline's hectic demeanour: *Cat.* 15.5 *citus modo modo tardus incessus.* Tacitus uses it eleven times, more than any other prose author (seven times in Ammianus); the adjective is favoured by poets, the adverb more generally popular. Haste was characteristic of Caecina: 67.1 *turbidum ingenium*, 67.2 *belli auidus*, 67.2 *propere*, 68.2 *statim*, 70.2 *agmen hibernis adhuc Alpibus transduxit*, cf. 2.99.2 *Caecinae ambitio uetus, torpor recens. cito* has, however, been suspected: how does rapidity of speech attract *studia militum? scito*, Lipsius' widely accepted emendation, describes a more obviously attractive quality (cf. Cic. *N.D.* 1.93 *scito illo sermone et Attico*). According to Plutarch, Caecina's speech, like his style of dress, was 'uncommon' (*O.* 6.3 οὐ... δημοτικός), but the example he provides is confused (see Hardy (1890) *ad loc.*) and sheds no light on the modifier here. **iuuenem** 'as a young man'; legionary legates were ordinarily praetorian in rank and age ('at least in their thirties, though Agricola was only twenty-eight', Webster (1998) 112). **impigre:** frequent and favourable in Livy (forty-eight times, paired with e.g. *oboedienter, fideliter*), generally of attention to duty: 3.27.5 *impigre . . . omnes . . . praesto fuere*, 21.12.1 *Maharbale . . . impigre rem agente*; cf. *Agr.* 13.1 *Britanni dilectum ac tributa et iniuncta imperii munia impigre obeunt* and Sal. *Jug.* 88.2 *Marius impigre prudenterque suorum et hostium res pariter attendere*. Used here, wryly, of treachery (compare 52.3 *mali et strenui*, 87.2n. *urbanae militiae impiger*). No details are known, but see 37.3n. *occisi . . . in Hispania* for the fate of Caecina's immediate superiors in Baetica. **compertum** 'having been found (to have committed an offence)' *OLD* 3. **flagitari:** *flagito* 'summon to stand trial' (*OLD* 1b; cf. 4.42.6 *delatores . . . puniendos flagitabat*), like *arcesso* (cf. *A.* 2.50.1 *Varillam . . . delator arcessebat*), is briefer, livelier, and less technical than expressions with *uoco* (e.g. 2.10.1 *Vibius Crispus . . . Annium Faustum . . . ad cognitionem senatus uocabat*, 4.45.2 *uocati qui arguebantur*, *A.* 2.34.2 *uocata in ius Vrgulania*) and *cito* (which T. avoids). Galba's procedure compares favourably with Vitellius': 2.64.1 *uocatum* (sc. *Dolabellam*) *per epistulas . . . interfici iussit.*

53.2 miscere cuncta: adapted from Sallust (*Cat.* 10.1 *saeuire fortuna ac miscere omnia coepit*) and much used: 3.73.2 *cuncta miscent*, 4.29.2 *misceri cuncta*, 4.49.3 *cuncta miscebant*, etc.; see also 32.1n. *mixtis*, 2.3n. *agerent uerterent cuncta.* **priuata uulnera rei publicae malis operire statuit:** similarly Catiline (Sal. *Cat.* 31.9 '*incendium meum ruina restinguam*') and Civilis (5.25.3 *illum domesticis malis excidium gentis opposuisse*); for the commonplace see Woodman (1983) *ad* Vell. 2.91.3–4. **operire:** cf. Cato fr. 59 (*ORF*³) *tuum nefarium facinus peiore facinore operire postulas.* **translatus:** 8.2n. *tarde . . . desciuerant.* **praeuentus erat:** T., focusing on the army's psychology, omits a detail: it was Fabius Valens, commander of a legion (and presumably the *uexilla*) from Lower Germany, who first took the oath of allegiance to Galba (Plut. *G.* 10.3). For the competition for temporal priority in winning the emperor's favour see 5.1n. *praeuentamque gratiam.*

53.3 Treueri ac Lingones: 8.1n. *proximae . . . ciuitates.* Treveran support for Vitellius is mentioned at 57.2, 63.1, 2.14.1–3 (where an *ala Treuerorum* resists the Othonian expedition into Narbonensis), 3.35.2 (a Treveran officer), that of the Lingones at 57.2, 64.2. Otho apparently tried to win over the latter with citizenship (78.1n.). Both groups became prominent in Civilis' rebellion (see Heubner's *Index historicus*). When the Lingones eventually capitulated they numbered 70,000 (Front. *Strat.* 4.3.14), but T. is dismissive: 4.67.1 *fortuna melioribus affuit: fusi Lingones.* **atrocibus edictis aut damno finium:** 8.1 n. *non . . . ademptis.* **propius** 'more intimately' *OLD* 3a. **seditiosa colloquia:** illustrated at 54.1. **paganos** 'civilians' *OLD* 2; cf. 3.24.3 (addressed to the praetorians) '*nisi uincitis, pagani*'. One sign of the confusion of civil war is their presence in battle: 2.14.2, 2.14.3, 2.88.1, 3.77.2, 4.20.2. T. does not use *paganus* outside *H.*; cf. *A.* 3.46.1 *oppidani.* **in Verginium fauor:** 8.2n. *nec . . . Verginius.*

54.1 miserat ciuitas Lingonum . . . dona legionibus: the legions seem to be those at Flaccus' base, Moguntiacum, but for traders from the Lingones at Vetera see *CAH*[2] x 529 with note 29. At 59.1 T. reports that the Batavian cohorts (see n.) were *in ciuitate Lingonum*; he does not connect their presence with the Lingones' initiative here. **dextras** 'metal models of a hand or clasped hands' *OLD* 1c; cf. 2.8.2 *dextras, concordiae insignia.* **ipsius exercitus pericula et contumelias:** the former only rumoured (51.5), the latter quite real (e.g. 51.4 *in ignominiam exercitus iactabant*).

54.2 nec procul seditione aberant: cf. 26.1 *adeo parata apud malos seditio*, introducing an incident that, like this one, reveals the temper of the troops. Otho's supporters show more control. **Hordeonius Flaccus:** 9.1 n. **nocte . . . excedere iubet:** for a similar tactical error see 80.1. **atrox:** sc. *erat.* **interfectos:** sc. *eos esse.* **per tenebras et inscitiam ceterorum** 'under cover of darkness and their comrades' ignorance' (Godley); cf. 3.22.2 *agminis disiecti per iram ac tenebras.*

54.3 obstringuntur . . . legiones: cf. 4.76.3 *legiones foederibus Galliarum obstrictas.* Presumably the soldiers bound themselves to resist the rumoured *pericula* (51.5, 54.2), but T. conveys the conspiracy's surreptitious (*tacito*) and brooding (*suspectus, uoluens*) atmosphere rather than its aims. **tacito foedere:** for *tacitus* 'secret' see *OLD* 8, but that translation enfeebles T.'s oxymoron, which exploits the tension between the utterance necessary for an agreement and the silence necessary for conspiracy; cf. Prop. 4.7.21–2 *foederis heu taciti, cuius fallacia uerba | non audituri diripuere noti.* **asciscitur auxiliorum miles:** for auxiliary involvement in legionary sedition see also 26.1, 38.3, 60. **circumdatis cohortibus alisque:** to have aroused suspicion *circumdatis* must indicate an unusual position. That separate legionary and auxiliary *castra* was standard for the permanent Rhine camps is implied at 4.61.3 (cf. 3.46.2), but the fortification by auxiliaries of a marching camp separate from that of the legions is prelude to treachery at 4.57.1: *tumque primum discreti a legionibus proprio uallo castra sua circumdant.* The setting here is Moguntiacum, where the *alae* and *cohortes* ought to be outside the legionary *castra*, but how *circumdatis* differs from that arrangement is not clear. **faciliore . . . concordiam:** 20.2n. *gaudium.*

55–62 Vitellius' preparations: *initia*

In ch. 55 discontent develops into open revolt. Drawn up to renew the *sacramentum* on the first day of the year, the four legions of Lower Germany in their three separate camps are reluctant and restive: *initium erumpendi circumspectabant.* An *initium* comes from Upper Germany (55.3), but the absence there of a suitable leader brings a temporary halt to rebellion and a clearly specious oath of loyalty to the SPQR (55.4). Back in Lower Germany Vitellius' willingness to lead sets things moving again (56.2) and momentum then gathers quickly: support accrues first from one, then the other legions of Lower Germany, then from the legions of Upper Germany, and finally from Gallic peoples (57.1–2). The pacing of the narrative is masterful and Tacitus' own: no other source begins the narrative of 1 January in Lower Germany (see, e.g., 55.1 n. *adactae*) or conveys the snowballing at the end. How accurately T. reflects the actual events is another question (Murison (1979)).

In chh. 58–9 Vitellius begins to rule. Deference to the demands of his soldiers is apparent at every turn, and support begins to arrive from more distant parts: Belgica, Lugdunum, Raetia, Britannia.

In ch. 60, on Britain, the narrative again pauses. The province was a standing interest of T.'s, generously chronicled in the *Annals* as well as the *Agricola.* The episode described here illustrates the collapse of *disciplina* in Rome's armies. The chapter ends with a tag generalizable to the civil war as a whole: *audendo potentior.*

By ch. 61 Vitellius has developed a plan of attack: *duo duces, duo itinera bello,* a plan that gives shape to the subsequent narrative, where chh. 62.3–66 cover Valens' *iter,* 67–70 Caecina's. Ch. 62, which sketches the *mira diuersitas* between Vitellius (*torpebat Vitellius*) and his men (*instructi intentique*), provides an ominous backdrop to the invasion. The invasion itself begins in a falsely bright light (62.3 *laetum augurium*).

The start of the Vitellian movement should be read in conjunction with Otho's beginning (chh. 23–47) and especially with Vespasian's (2.74–86).

Numerous parallels of theme and language, and also some striking differences, are mentioned in the notes.

55.1 adactae: sc. *sunt.* For *adigo* 'cause (a person) to take (an oath)' *OLD* 9a, cf. Suet. *G.* 16.2 on the legions of *Upper* Germany on 1 January: *adigi sacramento nisi in nomen senatus recusarunt.* **raris primorum ordinum uocibus, ceteri . . . exspectantes:** for the *uariatio* abl. abs. ~ adj. cf. 79.2 *Sarmatae . . . graues . . . adempta equorum pernicitate* and see Sörbom (1935) 91. **primorum ordinum** may indicate 'front ranks' (*OLD* 2, cf. Caes. *Gal.* 7.62.4 *cum primi ordines hostium . . . occidissent*), 'centurions of the first cohort' (*OLD* 3b, 52.1 n.), or 'centuries of the first cohort' (*OLD* 3c, cf. 3.22.4). The first fits T.'s impressionistic scene best. **silentio:** pregnant silence also characterizes the scene where Vespasian leads his men in an oath of loyalty to Vitellius (2.74.1). **insita mortalibus natura . . . sequi:** causal abl. abs. 'it being human nature to follow' (lit. 'the nature fixed in mortals being to follow'); for the inf. (*A&G* §452) cf. 2.20.1 *insita mortalibus natura . . . introspicere* and 2.38.1 *uetus ac iam pridem insita mortalibus potentiae cupido*; see further 7.3n. *ut est mos.*

55.2 legionibus inerat diuersitas animorum: cf. 62.1 *mira inter exercitum imperatoremque diuersitas*, 4.27.3 *tanta illi exercitui diuersitas inerat licentiae patientiaeque*, and Sen. *Suas.* 2.15 *in quibus quanta fuerit animorum diuersitas*, the earliest attestation of the abstract noun. **primani quintanique:** based in Bonna (mod. Bonn) and Vetera (mod. Xanten) respectively. *Legio* I, together with its commander, Fabius Valens (7.1 n.), probably served under Verginius Rufus at Vesontio (51.3n. *tum . . . legiones*). A vexillation went with Valens into Italy (2.100.1) but the eagle remained in Bonna (4.19–20), where the legion became embroiled in the Batavian uprising, eventually swearing fealty to the *imperium Galliarum* (4.59.2), seeing its legate killed (4.70.5), and returning to the Roman side (4.70.5). It failed to redeem itself in battle (4.77.3; cf. 61.2n. *legio unaetuicensima*) and was one of the four legions dissolved by Vespasian in the sequel. V *Alaudae* was the senior of the two legions based at Vetera (see below on *quinta decima*). Six decades earlier the *quintani* had led the disturbances on the Rhine (A.D. 14: *A.* 1.31.3). The eagle accompanied Valens to Italy (2.43.2, 68.2, 100.1), where the legion was tenaciously loyal to Vitellius (3.14). Some of the legion's troops remained at Vetera to be besieged, defeated, and betrayed by Civilis (4.18.1, 35.3, 60.2). The legion was later deployed on the Danube. See further Ritterling (1924) 1376–80 on *legio* I, 1564–71 on V *Alaudae.* **Galbae imagines:**

41.1n. *uexillarius . . . imaginem.* **quinta decima ac sexta decima legiones . . . circumspectabant:** based in Vetera and Novaesium (mod. Neuss) respectively. XV *Primigenia* was more cautious than its senior partner at Vetera (see above). It had never seen much real action. A vexillation accompanied Valens to Italy (2.100.1, 3.22–3) but the bulk of the unit remained at Vetera, where they shared the fate of the soldiers from V *Alaudae* (see above). The legion was dissolved by Vespasian. One of the alleged killers of Galba, Camurius, might have been a member of this legion (41.3n.). *Legio* XVI, like XV, sent a vexillation to Italy with Valens (2.100.1, 3.22). The fate of those who remained on the Rhine matched that of the *primani* (see above). The legion was dissolved by Vespasian. See further Ritterling (1924) 1758–60 on XV, 1761–5 on XVI. **circumspectabant** 'sought' *OLD* 3; for the scene cf. 2.29.2 *torpere cuncti, circumspectare inter se attoniti et id ipsum, quod nemo regeret, pauentes.*

55.3 quarta ac duoetuicensima legiones, isdem hibernis tendentes: as at Vetera, so at Moguntiacum, mod. Mainz, a long-established unit (IV *Macedonica,* created by Julius Caesar) was quartered with a newer one (XXII *Primigenia,* created by Caligula), and here too the senior unit took the lead. Double camps were later banned (Suet. *Dom.* 7.3). IV *Macedonica* sent a vexillation to Italy with Caecina (2.100.1). The remainder shared the unhappy fate of the first and sixteenth legions (see above); the unit was dissolved by Vespasian. The history of XXII *Primigenia* probably included first-hand experience of Galba's *seueritas* during his period as governor in A.D. 40 (5.2n. *laudata . . . seueritas*). The legion's initial hesitancy was soon overcome: the four centurions who were imprisoned and eventually killed for loyalty to Galba came from XXII (56.1, 59.1). A vexillation set out for Italy with Caecina (2.100.1); the eagle followed with Vitellius (2.89.1 with Chilver's note *ad loc.*). Though some soldiers remained in Germany (4.37.2), the majority escaped the shameful developments on the Rhine and the legion was redeployed rather than dissolved. See further Ritterling (1924) 1549–56 on IV, 1797–1820 on XXII. For the MS variations *duoetuicensima~duodeuicensima* see Wellesley's Appendix Critica; the identity of the unit is not in doubt. **dirumpunt . . . turbantibus:** Plutarch is much briefer: *G.* 22.3 'Going up to the statues of Galba they overturned them and dragged them down. After swearing allegiance to the senate and the Roman people they dispersed.' While similar in information, T.'s version incorporates themes important in the *Histories* – the infectious spread of sedition (*ut in tumultu*), political posturing (*ne . . . uiderentur*), the collapse of the military leadership (*nullo legatorum tribunorumue pro Galba nitente*) – and a sharp note of regret (*oblitterata iam nomina*). Suetonius' version differs in both content and expression: *G.* 16.2 *obsequium rumpere ausi Kal. Ian. adigi sacramento nisi in nomen senatus recusarunt. statimque legationem ad praetorianos cum mandatis destinauerunt: . . . eligant ipsi* (sc. *praetoriani*) *quem cuncti exercitus comprobarent.* The content can be reconciled if here (and at 12.3 *senatui ac populo Romano arbitrium eligendi*) T. means that the choice of the senate and people would ratify that of the praetorians, as happened in A.D. 41 and 54 (see Murison (1991b) on Suet. *G.* 16.2). T. will then have omitted the embassy because in his narrative the praetorians have already declared for Otho (36.1–2). *dirumpunt* 'break apart' (*OLD*; cf. Sen. *NQ* 6.30.4 *aes unius statuae . . . diruptum est*) specifies more destruction than do Plutarch's verbs and links the scene both with 12.1 *rupta sacramenti reuerentia* and with Otho's proclamation (41.1 *dereptam Galbae imaginem solo afflixit*). Vitellius' *imagines* are smashed when the fleet at Ravenna goes over to Vespasian (3.12.1–3) and again when that sedition begins to spread to the legions (3.13.1), but T. does not mention any comparable episode in connection with Vespasian's initial proclamation in the East; instead, the series ends with Vitellius watching the destruction of his own statues in Rome: 3.85.1 *coactum . . . cadentes statuas suas . . . intueri.*

55.4 ne reuerentiam imperii exuere uiderentur: reported in more detail at 12.1. This public relations effort was short-lived: 57.1 *speciosis senatus populique Romani nominibus relictis.* As the rebellion winds down *reuerentia* regains persuasive force, at least for provincials (see 4.69.1); for *reuerentia imperii* cf. *G.* 29.2. **oblitterata** 'fallen into disuse'; cf. *D.* 8.1 *libentius . . . nouis et recentibus quam remotis et oblitteratis exemplis utor*, 22.5 *oblitterata et olentia*, *A.* 2.83.4 (on the honours for Germanicus) *quaedam . . . uetustas oblitterauit*; with constitutional entities Gaius 1.111 *ius . . . ipsa desuetudine oblitteratum est*, 8.2.2 *iudicium . . . oblitteratum silentio.* See also 30.2 *uacua nomina.* **aduocabant** 'invoked' *OLD* 5b. **nullo legatorum tribunorumue pro Galba nitente:** four centurions, by contrast, were loyal (see 56.1). **ut in tumultu:** 7.3n. *ut est mos.* For the contagion of sedition see 26.1n. *infecit.* **non tamen quisquam . . . locutus:** Plutarch places a speech here (*G.* 22.4–5); Jones (1971) 78 suggests that T. corrects Plutarch and supplies his reasoning in the following clause: *neque enim erat adhuc cui imputaretur.* The correction may be rather to the common source; see further Intro. §18. Some of the content of Plutarch's speech is used by T. in the reasoning of those with closer ties to Vitellius: 52.2n. *apud seueros . . . fauentes*, 52.3n. *nullam . . . moram*, 52.4n. *tres . . .*

Caesaris. **[in modum contionis aut] suggestu:** for *suggestus* see 36.1 n. Since *contio* is the proper word for an assembly of soldiers (*OLD* 1 b, cf. 2.82.2 *donatiuum militi . . . Mucianus prima contione . . . ostenderat*), *in modum contionis* is otiose; it may have entered the text as a gloss for *suggestu*. Editors generally replace *aut* with a preposition or add one (see Wellesley's app. crit.), but Draeger (1882) §57 gives parallels for the loc. abl. without preposition in T. See also 57.2n. *manipuli* and 61.2n. *unaetuicensima.* **locutus:** sc. *est.* **cui imputaretur** 'from whom credit might be claimed' (38.2n., 71.2n.); cf. 2.85.1 *posse imputari Vespasiano quae apud Vitellio excusanda erant.*

56.1 spectator . . . innocens: faced with sedition, Flaccus did nothing. Style conveys T.'s contempt (cf. 6.1 n. *Cornelius Laco*). *spectator flagitii* aligns the consular commander of three legions with the *uulgus* in Rome (32.1 n. *in circo aut theatro*). Flaccus' rank (and the responsibilities implicit therein) replaces the adj. found in similar expressions: Cic. *Off.* 2.26 *spectatores se otiosos praebuerunt Leuctricae calamitatis*, Plin. *Ep.* 10.33.2 *otiosos et immobiles tanti mali spectatores*, Luc. 2.207–8 *sedit securus . . . spectator sceleris*). Flaccus' failure to act is restated with anaphora (*non . . . non . . . non . . .*) and again with a paradox, *socordia innocens.* For the combination of passivity and innocence cf. *A.* 14.51.2 on the *segnis innocentia* of Faenius Rufus, whose 'innocence' consisted in refraining from peculation, and *Agr.* 16.5 on that of Vettius Bolanus: *innocens Bolanus et nullis delictis inuisus.* Flaccus' conduct was culpably irresponsible, but he refrained, if only through *socordia*, from sedition. **compescere ruentes:** cf. *A.* 1.42.3 *diuus Iulius seditionem exercitus uno uerbo compescuit.* **quattuor . . . Repentinus:** their execution is noted at 59.1, again with a tolling of names. None is attested elsewhere. **abrepti uinctique:** sc. *sunt.* **nec cuiquam ultra:** sc. *erat.* **quod in seditionibus accidit:** 7.3n. *ut est mos.* **unde plures erant omnes fuere:** for the characterization of sedition cf. 28 *pessimum facinus auderent pauci, plures uellent, omnes paterentur*, 55.1 *insita mortalibus natura propere sequi quae piget inchoare.* **unde** 'on the side (sc. in a dispute) where' *OLD* 6g.

56.2 nocte . . . epulanti Vitellio nuntiat: the date is 1 January. For the scene cf. Plut. *G.* 22.6 'He announced it to Vitellius in the evening, while many were feasting with him.' Suet. *Vit.* 8.1, though different in detail, also includes a hint of dining: *uespere, subito a militibus e cubiculo raptus, ita ut erat in ueste domestica, imperator est consalutatus circumlatusque per celeberrimos uicos, strictum Diui Iuli gladium tenens . . . . nec ante in praetorium rediit quam flagrante triclinio ex conceptu camini.* On Vitellius' gluttony see 62.2n. *inerti . . . epulis.* For Suetonius' divergences see Murison (1991 b) *ad loc.* **coloniam Agrippinensem:**

site of the headquarters of the provincial governor, but Vitellius had no significant forces there. The city backed Vitellius warmly (57.1 *ardorem exercituum Agrippinenses . . . aequabant*) but its mixed population of Germans and Romans (4.28.1, 4.65.2) made for difficulties during the Batavian revolt. T. devotes three dramatic chapters to a representative episode: at the height of Civilis' success his army threatened to sack Cologne (4.63), then invited it to prove its Germanness by razing its walls and killing Roman residents (4.64), whereupon Cologne temporized, limiting its concessions to economic ones (4.65). Later the city reasserted its Roman loyalty by entrapping and killing some of Civilis' best troops (4.79.2). On the city's history and Roman amenities see Doppelfeld (1975). **uisum:** sc. *esse* or *est*? With this ambiguity, with the omission of a dative for *placuit*, and with the passive infinitives T. reduces to nil Vitellius' part in the decision to challenge Galba. For T.'s historical acumen in this see Murison (1979) 188–94.

56.3 missi: sc. *sunt.* **proinde:** 21.2n. **bellandum:** sc. *esse*; for the ultimatum cf. 2.85.1. **concordia et pax:** 15.1n. *deorum hominumque consensu.* 'The irony shows to perfection T.'s understanding of revolutionary slogans' (Chilver *ad loc.*). **minore discrimine sumi principem quam quaeri:** for Vespasian the alternatives are more sharply differentiated and the choice belongs to the leader, not the troops: 2.74.2 *imperium cupientibus nihil medium inter summa et praecipitia.* For the construction cf. Sal. *Jug.* 54.5 *minore detrimento illos uinci quam suos uincere*, *A.* 1.18.3 *leuiore flagitio legatum interficietis quam ab imperatore desciscitis* with Goodyear (1972) *ad loc.* 'a condensed form of expression, in which the modal abl. is equivalent to a predicate'; i.e. *minore discrimine* = '(is) less dangerous'.

57.1 legionis primae: 55.2n. Bonna was some 30 km distant, more than a day's march for foot soldiers. **die postero:** 2 January. **secutae:** sc. *sunt.* **certamine:** 5.1n. *praeuentam gratiam.* **speciosis . . . relictis:** see Intro. §18. **tertium nonas Ianuarias:** 3 January. **scires:** 10.2n. *palam . . . audiebant.* **penes rem publicam:** for *penes* 'within the power of' (*OLD* 2) with *rem publicam* (which rephrases *senatus populusque Romanus* of 55.4 and 56.2) cf. Cic. *apud* Asc. *Scaur.* 21.15 (Clark) *iudicia penes equestrem ordinem*, Ampel. 50.2 *penes senatum consilii publici summa est*, Liv. 6.41.5 *penes quos igitur sunt auspicia . . . ? nempe penes patres.*

57.2 auxilia: these native levies (68.1n. *Raeticae . . . iuuentus*) were dismissed at the first opportunity (2.69.1). The Flavian party turned down a similar offer at 3.5.1 and, given the sequel in Gaul – an *imperium*

Galliarum (4.58.1, 4.59.2, etc.) – its restraint looks prescient. **ualidus:** sc. *erat.* **ex affluenti:** sc. *erant*; the adj. with *ex* indicates the state of affairs (*OLD* 8 s.v. *ex*); for the expression as predicate cf. 3.49.1 *ratus ... cetera ex facili* (sc. *esse*). **manipuli** 'common soldiers' *OLD* 3b; cf. 25.1 *manipulares. gregarius miles*, a more straightforward expression, may be a gloss; cf. 55.4n. *in modum ... suggestu.* **uiatica:** properly of funds for travel (e.g. for a new recruit to join his unit), but often of soldiers' funds more generally (*OLD* 1b). **insignia armorum argento decora:** 38.3n. *sine ... distingueretur.* **loco pecuniae:** 16.1n. *loco libertatis.* **instinctu et impetu et auaritia:** the vagueness of *instinctu* and *impetu*, which convey passionate enthusiasm (cf. Plin. *Ep.* 1.22.10 *impetu quodam et instinctu procurrere ad mortem*, Tac. *H.* 2.46.1 *furore quodam et instinctu flagrabant*) but, lacking modifiers (cf. 4.2 *primo gaudentium impetu*, 70.1 *instinctu decurionum*), not much more, sets *auaritia*, which is both precise and cynical, into relief. For other lists of causal abl. cf. 12.2 *licentia et libidine ... dein fessa iam aetate Galbae*, 51.1 *odio metu et ... securitate*, 63.1 *furore et rabie et causis incertis*, 67.1 *olim armis uirisque mox memoria nominis clara.* For other lists that conclude on a pragmatic note see 46.1n. *plerisque ... respicientibus*, 66.1n. *addidit ... sestertios.*

58.1 ministeria principatus ... in equites Romanos disponit: *ministeria* are 'functions' (*OLD* 2) related to e.g. correspondence (*ab epistulis*), petitions (*a libellis*), and rhetoric (*a studiis*). An epigraphically attested Vitellian functionary is Sex. Caesius Propertianus, who rose from the equestrian office of tribune of IV *Macedonica* to be procurator of Vitellius' private fortune (*a patrimonio*), his inheritances (*ab hereditatibus*), and petitions (*a libellis*): *ILS* 1447 = McC–W 338. Chilver suggests *ad loc.* that such appointments made a virtue of necessity, Vitellius not having a suitable corps of *liberti* at his disposal in January of 69 (2.59.2). Perhaps so, but in T.'s view keeping freedmen out of public service is a commendable policy here, at *Agr.* 19.2 *nihil per libertos seruosque publicae rei* (sc. *agit Agricola*), and at *A.* 13.4.2 *discretam domum et rem publicam*; for his resentment of freedmen civil servants see 76.3 *nam et hi* (sc. *libertini*) *malis temporibus partem se rei publicae faciunt* with note. His attitude matches that of Trajan (Plin. *Pan.* 88.1–2 with its conclusion *scis enim praecipuum indicem non magni principis magnos libertos*, and cf. *Ep.* 6.31.9). See further Millar (1977) 69–83 on imperial freedmen, 83–100 on equestrian functionaries. **uacationes:** 46.2n. **saeuitiam ... approbat:** the antithesis with *frustratur* makes *approbat* denote passive assent rather than active endorsement, but with *saeuitiam* even assent is disturbing. **simulatione uinculorum:** 45.2n. *simulatione irae uinciri iussum*. For Julius Burdo, at least (see below), the shackles were quite real; what was simulated was the intent to punish. **Pompeius Propinquus:** 12.1n. **interfectus:** sc. *est*. **Iulium Burdonem Germanicae classis praefectum:** the fleet's base, like Vitellius', was Cologne (more precisely, Alteburg, 3 km south); proximity may explain the presence of its commander in a plot against Vitellius' predecessor (for the plot's other leaders see 7.1; for its confused record see 7.2n. *fuere... abstinuisse*). After dismissal (see 58.2) Burdo might have ended up a municipal magistrate in Narbonensis (*CIL* XII 1050; see *PIR*[2] I 214). A twenty-four-ship detachment of the fleet with Batavians among the rowers provided an early victory for Civilis' Batavian uprising (4.16.3). **astu subtraxit:** in describing a similar rescue in the Flavian army T. omits the invidious word *astu* (3.7.1).

58.2 exarserat in eum iracundia exercitus: i.e. against Burdo, though his superior officers were responsible (7.1). **crimen ac mox insidias:** cf. 7.2 *crimen ac dolum*; the charge was rebellion against Galba. No details besides the involvement of the centurion Crispinus (see below) are known. **grata... memoria:** the source of Capito's popularity is not known; possibly it was his willingness, contrary to the reluctance of Verginius Rufus in Upper Germany, to head a challenge to Galba (7.1n. *Fontei Capitonis*). **occidere palam, ignoscere non nisi fallendo:** Vitellius behaves as did Otho (45.2). Where Otho's reign sees a gradual increase in control, however (see n.), Vitellius' sees a decline: 3.70.4 *ipse neque iubendi neque uetandi potens non iam imperator sed tantum belli causa erat* (sc. *Vitellius*). By 3.74.2 Vitellius is unable to save Flavius Sabinus from lynching (46.1n.). **satiatis... odiis:** *satiatis* is an emendation (Freinsheim's) for M's *statis*; for the phrase cf. Cic. *Flac.* 95 *sanguine... odium satiaueritis*, *Part.* 96 *ad odium satiandum*, Sen. *Ben.* 5.16.1 *uetera et ingenita odia satiauerit*; for the image cf. *A.* 15.52.3 *Nero uetus aduersum insontem odium expleuerit*, *H.* 4.1.1 *saeuitia recentibus odiis sanguine explebatur*. For discussion of *satiatis* and other emendations see Morgan (1993b), who defends *statis*. **ut piaculum obicitur centurio Crispinus:** there is a sharp change of tone between *piaculum* ('expiatory offering') and *obicitur* ('is tossed') and the metaphor of the latter evokes a punishment inappropriate to a Roman centurion (cf. 2.61 *Mariccus quidam... feris obiectus*, and, for the tone, Cic. *Fam.* 10.32.3 *bestiis... ciues Romanos... obiecit Balbus*; see *OLD* 1b); both effects convey T.'s indignation, as does *punienti uilior*. See also 63.2n. *placamenta*. **sanguine se**

Capitonis: 52.2n. *ut Vitellius.* **cruentauerat:** for the event cf. 2.85.1, from Vitellius' principate, where, in order to settle a private quarrel, the governor of Moesia sends a centurion to kill one of his legionary legates. **eoque:** 13.3n. **uilior:** 37.5n.

59.1 Iulius deinde Ciuilis periculo exemptus: sc. *est.* T. gives the background at 4.13.1: before Nero's death Civilis, a Batavian prince with Roman citizenship and command of an auxiliary cohort of his tribesmen, was arrested, perhaps on grounds of support for Vindex, by Fonteius Capito (see Chilver and Townend (1985) *ad loc.*). Although Galba had pardoned him the Rhine army demanded his punishment from Vitellius (his brother, similarly charged, had been executed: 4.13.1, 4.32.2). In releasing him Vitellius does not in fact reconcile the Batavians to Roman rule or even to effective cooperation with the invasion (see below). **ferox gens:** T. gives background information on this tribe at the opening of his account of the Batavian revolt (4.12.2–3); see Chilver and Townend (1985) *ad loc.* and Hassall (1970). **et** 'and in fact', introducing a parenthesis, *OLD* 2b. **in ciuitate Lingonum:** Andemantunnum, mod. Langres, an important junction of the roads connecting Italy and Narbonensis with Britain and the Rhine area. Valens passes through at 64.1. **octo Batauorum cohortes:** *en route* back to Britain, whence Nero had summoned them for his Eastern campaign, they stopped to join Valens (2.27.2). Batavian units had contributed to Rome's fighting force since Germanicus' German campaigns (*A.* 2.11.1, cf. 2.8.3), perhaps since those of Drusus (Saddington (1975) 191); for their military prowess cf. *G.* 29.1 *uirtute praecipue Bataui* (with Rives (1999) *ad loc.*). The cohorts mentioned here include mounted soldiers (4.19.1) and are probably quingenary in size. Though their service record was distinguished (2.28.2 *ueteres illos et tot bellorum uictores*, 4.12.3 *aucta per Britanniam gloria*), their behaviour was disruptive (64.2n. *intemperie*). Having contributed to a Vitellian victory in N. Italy (2.43.1) they were given the job of escorting the *legio* XIV to Britain (2.66.1), a plan that backfired badly (2.66.2). They were then sent to Moguntiacum. Their accession thence to Civilis' revolt (4.19.2) made him *iusti iam exercitus ductor* (4.21.1). For their motives see Brunt (1960) 501–2. These cohorts were probably disbanded by Vespasian but Batavian units remained in use (Cichorius (1900) s.v. *cohors* 249–53). **grande momentum sociae aut aduersae** 'significant in the scales, for or against'; cf. 76.2 *grande momentum in nomine urbis ac praetexto senatu*, 2.86.2 *labantibus Vitellii rebus Vespasianum secutus grande momentum addidit* (sc. *Antonius Primus*), 3.8.1 *magni momenti locum obtinuit.* The diction is traditional (cf. Liv. 3.12.6 *iuuenem ... maximum momentum rerum eius ciuitatis in quamcumque uenisset*, Justin 17.2.11 *Pyrrhus ingens momentum futurus utri parti socius accessisset*, Luc. 4.819 *momentumque fuit mutatus Curio rerum*, and *TLL* s.v. 1393.45–50), the phrasing, an appositional comment, unusually terse (44.2n. *munimentum ... ultionem*). The effect of these cohorts is significant at 2.43.1, more so at 4.21.1 (see note above, cf. also 2.69.1 where their dispatch to Germany is labelled *principium interno simul externoque bello*). When Valens detached them from his invasion column to (*a*) counter the Othonian offensive in Narbonensis and (*b*) rid his army of an unruly group, his soldiers not only complained that the army was losing valuable forces (2.28.1) but also began to riot (2.29). The power of these eight cohorts is vividly illustrated at 4.19–20 where, caught between two (admittedly weakened) Roman legions, they frighten one into inaction and defeat the other. **supra rettulimus:** at 56.1. **fidei crimine:** under Otho *fides* leads to suspicion (31.3 *fidus principi suo et eo desciscentibus suspectior*) and threats (45.2 *Galbae ... fidum ... ad supplicium expostulabant*, 71.2 *fidei crimen confessus*), under Vitellius to death (here and at 3.39.2, but cf. 2.60.1 *fidem absoluit*), under the Flavians to effective but bloodless precautionary measures (see 3.5.2 on *Porcius Septiminus, incorruptae erga Vitellium fidei*).

59.2 accessere 'joined' *OLD* 7b; cf. 2.58.1 *accessisse partibus*, 2.86.1 *tertia decima legio ac septima Galbiana ... haud cunctanter Vespasiano accessere* and see 70.1n. **generum asciuit:** cf. *A.* 5.6.2 *collegam* (sc. *Seianum*) *et generum asciuerat*, Virg. *Aen.* 11.472 *generumque asciuerit urbi*, Liv. 21.2.4 *Hasdrubal gener ... ascitus.* **Valerius Asiaticus, Belgicae prouinciae legatus:** a surprising Vitellian, given the responsibility of Vitellius' father for the death of Asiaticus' father (*A.* 11.1–3). Vitellius' choice of Asiaticus as son-in-law may have been a sop to Vienne, his city of origin (so also, perhaps, the consulship of 70, for which Galba had designated him; see Townend (1962) 127 with n. 23, and cf. 77.2 on the consulship of Pompeius Vopiscus), but he despaired of protecting the city from an enraged Vitellian army (65–6, esp. 66.1 *ne legati quidem ac duces partium restingui posse iracundiam exercitus arbitrabantur*). He might have abandoned Vitellius even before the Flavian victory, since Vitellius' daughter is offered to another potential partisan at 3.78.1. After Vitellius' death Asiaticus, now senior consul designate, proposed honours for the Flavian victors and restrained the Senate in their interest (4.4.3, cf. also 4.6.3, 4.8.1, 4.9.1 with Townend (1962) 125–9). See further Wiedemann (1999). **Iunius Blaesus, Lugdunensis Galliae rector:** *rector* is used of provincial governors only under the empire

(*OLD* 4a). This post was praetorian. T. describes Blaesus more fully at 2.59.2 *genere illustri, largus animo et par opibus* and gives his ancestry at 3.38.3 *Iunios Antoniosque auos; stirpe imperatoria*; for the Antonian connection see Syme (1982b) 466. Descent from a dynast and deep pockets worried Vitellius even in a supporter (3.38.4 *aemulum principis*, cf. 2.59.2 *eo ipso* (sc. *Vitellio*) *ingratus*), so Blaesus was poisoned (3.39.1). T. sends him out with praise: 3.39.2 *Blaeso super claritatem natalium et elegantiam morum fidei obstinatio fuit. integris quoque rebus a Caecina et primoribus partium iam Vitellium aspernantibus ambitus abnuere perseuerauit. sanctus, inturbidus, nullius repentini honoris, adeo non principatus appetens, parum effugerat, ne dignus crederetur.* **Italica legione:** the provinces of Tres Galliae did not ordinarily have a legionary garrison (for auxiliary units see n. below, for the urban cohort at Lyon see 64.3n.). The presence of I *Italica*, an elite unit recently created by Nero for his abortive Eastern campaign (6.2n. *claustra Caspiarum*, with Suet. *Ner.* 19.2), gave extra security to a region troubled by Vindex' uprising and its aftermath (for more details see Chilver 11–12; Syme (1982b) 467). Antonius Naso (20.3n.) was an early tribune in the legion. The legion's eagle went to Italy with Valens (64.3, 2.89.1). Against Otho it fought well (2.41.2 *Italicae legionis uirtute*), against the Flavians less so (3.18.1, 3.22.1; cf. also 2.100.1, 3.14.3). After the Vitellian defeat it was deployed in Illyricum (3.35.1; further details in Ritterling (1924) 1407–17). For the legion's legate see 64.4n. *Manlius Valens.* **ala Tauriana:** like I *Italica* this cavalry unit was temporary reinforcement for the regular garrison of Lyon, an urban cohort (64.3n.; for the name see Cheesman (1914) 24 n. 6, for other auxiliary forces in Gaul see 59.1n. *octo ... cohortes*). Its commander, regular base, and size are unknown, but most *alae* comprised 512 riders in 16 *turmae*, were based near their recruiting area, and were commanded, at this period, by Romans pursuing an equestrian military career (Webster (1998) 145–8, Cheesman (1914) 90–7; for further bibliography see Saddington (1975)). The *ala* was added to Valens' forces (64.3). It is not mentioned by name in the battles on the Po, but is probably among the equestrian units mentioned at 3.18.1 and 3.22.2. It survived the civil war and is later found in N. Africa: *ala* I *Flauia Gallorum Tauriana* (*CIL* VIII 2394, 2395). **Raeticis copiis:** auxiliary troops probably raised in Raetia and based there (see n. above); on their contribution to the Flavian cause see further 67.2 and 68.1n. *Raeticae ... iuuentus.* **mora:** sc. *erat.* **dubitatum:** sc. *est.* For Britain see 9.2n.

60 Trebellius Maximus was appointed to several posts by Nero (*PIR* T 239), including Britain, where his tenure, extended by Galba, was distinguished more by cultural than by military success and was tarnished by the indiscipline of the troops (*Agr.* 16.3–4; see further below). Vitellius names his replacement at 2.65.2. He was *frater Arualis* in 72. **per auaritiam . . . inuisusque:** 6.1n. *alter . . . destruebant.* **Roscius Coelius:** a praetorian legate in 69, he too survived the civil wars and became *frater Arualis*, as well as suffect consul in 81 (*PIR* R 67). His adoptive son (*PIR*[2] P 602) was suffect consul in 108, i.e. during the composition of *H.* T.'s source for this chapter may be Agricola, Coelius' successor (*Agr.* 7.3); the parallel tradition ignores Britain. **uicensimae legionis:** an Augustan foundation with a distinguished record, XX *Valeria Victrix* had been in Britain since 43. *nimia ac formidolosa* in 69, it was slow to declare for Vespasian (*Agr.* 7.3). For its history see Ritterling (1924) 1769–81. **discors:** sc. *Trebellio Coelius* (cf. *A.* 1.55.3 *Segestes . . . discors* (sc. *Arminio*) *manebat*); the implied names supply a subject for *proruperant*, which describes the manner ('unbridled') of the recriminations that follow; cf. *A.* 5.3.1 *tunc uelut frenis exsoluti proruperunt* (sc. *Tiberius et Seianus*). The personal conflict is muted (or omitted) at *Agr.* 16.3, where due attention is given to the political situation (*interuentus ciuilium armorum praebuit iustam segnitiae excusationem . . .*) and its disciplinary consequence (*. . . sed discordia laboratum cum assuetus expeditionibus miles otio lasciuiret*); for bibliography see Chilver *ad loc.* A similar dispute between a provincial legate and a *legatus legionis* is reported in connection with Vespasian's bid for power at 2.85.2, with the difference that these later *simultates*, though a *pessimum facinus*, do not draw in the troops. **ordinem disciplinae** 'chain of command'; it is clear from *Agr.* 7.3 that the governor could not control the legate and that neither commander could control the unruly legion. For the loss of control see also *Agr.* 16.4 *precario mox praefuit*; for the expression see 38.3n. *sine . . . distingueretur.* **modestia exercitus:** for this military virtue cf. 2.12.1 *modestiam disciplinae*, 3.11.2 *uirtutis modestiaeque*, *Agr.* 20.2 *laudare modestiam*, *A.* 1.35.1 *modestia militaris* and *TLL* s.v. 1223.3–14. **corrupta:** sc. *est.* **uentum:** sc. *est.* **aggregantibus . . . alisque:** 54.3n. *asciscitur auxiliorum miles.* **quamquam remoto consulari:** 5.2n. *quamuis capite . . . ablato.*

61.1 Adiuncto Britannico exercitu: 9.2n. **ingens uiribus opibusque:** cf. 2.81.1 *Antiochus uetustis opibus ingens*, *A.* 11.10.3 *regreditur ingens gloria* (sc. *Vardanes*), a usage more common in the poets, e.g. Virg. *Aen.* 11.124 *fama ingens ingentior armis* (sc. *Aeneas*). **itinera bello:** 22.2n. *Othoni . . . comes.* **allicere uel . . . uastare Gallias** 'to win over Gaul or to crush it'. Valens' instructions, based on the imperatives of civil war, seem clear (cf. 2.85.1). But his treatment of those through whose territory he passes, the subject of chh. 63–6, involves random violence from the troops and extortion on his own behalf as well as the mustering of support for Vitellius. For *allicere* cf. 24.1 *alliciendo.* **Cottianis Alpibus:** via (abl. of route: *A&G* 429a) the Mt Genèvre pass. For the route see Murison (1993) 86–90, 93–5; he gives a distance from Cologne to Cremona of 1,312 km, an elapsed time of some eighty-seven days (*c.* 12 January–7 April). **propiore transitu:** Caecina's journey, too, involves more than simple transit; see chh. 67–70. T. omits entirely the march from Moguntiacum, where Caecina was joined by vexillations from its two legions (55.3n.), to Vindonissa, the base of his core unit (61.2n. *legio unaetuicensima*), a distance of some 367 km. For his route thereafter (Augusta Raurica, mod. Augst, over the Great St Bernard pass to Cremona), the distance (565 km), and the time elapsed (some sixty-six days: *c.* 28 January–2 April), see Murison (1993) 90–1, 105–6. **iussus:** sc. *est.*

61.2 ad quadraginta milia: given that Vitellius had in total eleven legions plus auxiliaries at his disposal and did not strip either Britain or the Rhine completely, 'the figures seem much too large' (Murison (1993) 85–6). Murison's estimate, which preserves T.'s ratios, is that 20,000 set out with Valens, 15,000–16,000 with Caecina, and 30,000 with Vitellius (see 2.87.1 for his *sexaginta milia*). The size of the auxiliary garrison in the Germanies in A.D. 69 is not known with certainty, but in 89 and 98 there were more than thirty units, or roughly 17,000 men, in Lower Germany alone (Holder (1999)). For the reader of *H.*, however, the more relevant measure is that of the (modest) forces moving towards Rome on behalf of Vespasian: under Mucianus (2.83.1) one legion and 13,000 men in detachments from others, *modicae uires*; under Primus initially only auxiliaries (3.6.1), though he was gradually reinforced by legions and *uexilla* from Illyricum (3.7.1, 3.19.1). **data:** sc. *sunt.* **legio unaetuicensima:** based at Vindonissa, mod. Windisch, much further south than the other Rhine legions and therefore closer to the Alpine passes into Italy. Like V *Alaudae* (55.2n. *primani quintanique*) XXI *Rapax* was active in the sedition of A.D. 14 (*A.* 1.31.3; cf. *A.* 1.37.2, 45.1). In 69 it responded to news of Vitellius' proclamation by plundering a nearby Helvetian fortification (67.1 nn.). Though involved in Vitellian losses to the Flavians (3.25.3), the legion restored its reputation in the conflict with Civilis (4.68.4, 70.2, 78.1, esp. 5.16.3) and remained on the Rhine thereafter, at Bonna. See further Ritterling (1924) 1781–91. **unaetuicensima:** the MS reading is *una prima et uicensima*; *prima*, an ordinal for the '1' in '21' (cf. 57.1 *legionis primae*), might have entered the text as a marginal gloss. **Germanorum auxilia:** probably native levies, distinct from but often used together with the regular *auxilia*: see 68.1 n. *Raeticae alae cohortesque et ipsorum Raetorum iuuentus* and Saddington (1970) 107. Their assistance, predicted by Valens (52.3 *secutura Germanorum auxilia*), is perhaps attested in the activities of the Batavi and Transrhenani of Caecina's advance guard (2.17.2; see 70.2n. *praemissis . . . cohortibus*). See also 57.2n. *auxilia*. **tota mole belli secuturus:** with non-corporeal referents *moles* indicates magnitude and often, as here, impending or actual calamity (*OLD* 7); *tota mole* describes the portentousness of Vitellius' force, not its comprehensiveness (as the context shows); it also fits the slow progress of his army, which had only been *en route* for a few days when news arrived of the defeat and death of Otho (2.57.2: the suicide was on 16 April) and does not arrive in Rome until mid-July (2.89; for Vitellius' pace cf. 2.87.1 *graui . . . agmine* and see Murison (1993) 143–9; for the notion cf. 2.6.1 *tarda mole ciuilis belli*, 2.74.2 *in tanta mole belli plerumque cunctatio*). *moles belli*, a formula found in Livy and Velleius Paterculus (and others) as well as six times in T., echoes Homeric μῶλος Ἄρηος 'fray of battle' (e.g. *Il.* 2.401), here with some irony since the troops with Vitellius contributed not to his victory but rather to its abuse (see, e.g., 2.73, 2.87.1). Beside Vitellius' overwhelming numbers the force that Vespasian sent against Rome seems nicely calculated: 2.82.3 *sufficere uidebantur aduersus Vitellium pars copiarum et dux Mucianus et Vespasiani nomen.*

62.1 diuersitas: sc. *erat*. **instare miles:** *instare*, here of verbal pressure (*OLD* 7), shows the reversal of roles in Vitellius' army. The pressure is conveyed by anaphora (*dum . . . dum, non . . . neque*) and asyndeton (*inuadendam . . . occupandam*); for the style compare Otho's internal monologue at 21.2. **dum Hispaniae cunctentur:** see 76.1. **non obstare** 'is no impediment' *OLD* 3b. **moras:** paired with *hiems* and subject of *obstare*, delay has a more palpable quality here than at 52.3 *nullam in Flacco Hordeonio moram* (cf. 89.3 *moras . . . afferrent*, 4.68.3 *moras nectens*): 'again the poet, and difficult to translate without losing vigour' (Irvine *ad loc.*). The temporizing arguments of some Flavian supporters are set out in 3.1.2 and rebutted at length in 3.2.1–4. **inuadendam Italiam:** sc. *esse*. **nihil . . . festinatione tutius:** for the argument see 32.2n. *scelera . . . ualescere*. As T. presents it, however, Vitellius' delay is not policy (as is that of Vespasian: 2.82.3), or even fear (cf. *ignauae pacis moras* above), but character: *torpebat Vitellius*. **ubi facto magis quam consulto opus esset:** cf. Sal. *Cat.* 43.3 *facto, non consulto in tali periculo opus esse*; for the change of sequence see Draeger (1882) §27d.

62.2 torpebat . . . adderet: the leisurely flow of this sentence, which both reflects its content and stands in contrast to the insistent style of 62.1, derives from its many pairs (both parallel (*luxu~epulis, inerti~prodigis, temulentus~grauis, ardor~uis*) and antithetical (*militum~ducis, strenuis~ignauis, spem~metum*)), a periphrasis (*fortunam principis . . . praesumebat*), and a contrafactual comparison (*ut si adesset*). **torpebat** contrasts Vitellius with his immediate rival: 71.1 *Otho interim . . . non deliciis neque desidia torpescere. torpere* recurs in another picture of Vitellius' dereliction of duty: 3.36.1 *non parare arma, non alloquio exercitioque militem firmare, non in ore uulgi agere, sed umbraculis hortorum abditus, ut ignaua animalia, quibus si cibum suggeras, iacent torpentque.* For more on Vitellius' *torpor* see 52.4n. *segne ingenium*; for Vespasian's energy cf. 2.82.1 *ipse Vespasianus adire hortari, bonos laude, segnes exemplo incitare.* **fortunam principatus . . . praesumebat:** verb and predicate provide criticism without content, which comes in the abl. phrases. For Vitellius' *fortuna* cf. 77.1; see also 10.3n. *post fortunam.* **inerti luxu ac prodigis epulis:** *inerti luxu* is vague as to content (under the heading of luxury, τρυφή, Dio 65.2.1 lists, beside expensive meals, taverns, gambling, dancers, charioteers and, later, housing; self-indulgence during the march to Italy is not specified) but the adj. contributes to the condemnation. The main charge in all sources is gluttony: 2.62.1 *epularum foeda et inexplebilis libido*, 2.71.1 *luxu et sagina mancipatus emptusque*, 2.95.2 *prodigis epulis et sumptu ganeaque satiare inexplebiles Vitellii libidines*, etc. Illustrated with further details at Suet. *Vit.* 13 and Dio 65.2.2–4.3; see Ash (1999) 98–102. For a similar abstract + concrete pair cf. 35.1 *plausus et immodica studia.* **sagina** 'feed'; in T. only in connection with Vitellius: 2.71.1 (quoted above), 2.88.1 *paratos cibos ut gladiatoriam saginam diuidebat* (sc. *Vitellius*). **ardor et uis militum . . . implebat:** cf. *D.* 24.1 *uim et ardorem Apri nostri*, *Agr.* 8.1 *temperauit Agricola uim suam ardoremque compescuit.* **strenuis . . . adderet:** for the definition of a leader's role cf. *Agr.* 21.1 *laudando promptos et castigando segnes*; for the form see 6.1n. *alter . . . destruebant.* **instructi intentique:** although the alliterative formula is historiographical (e.g. Sal. *Jug.* 53.5, Liv. 1.15.2, 6.29.1; cf. 4.69.3 *instruendo bello intentus*), the scene also owes something to Virg. *Aen.* 5.137 *intenti exspectant signum*; see further on *laetum . . . acciperetur* below. **nomen . . . prohibuit:** Plutarch (*G.* 22.7) and Suetonius (*Vit.* 8.2) have similar wording (see App. 1) but place the information differently, Plutarch between the salutation by Valens and the accession of Upper Germany, Suetonius immediately after the latter. T.'s placement avoids the oddity of a reference to Vitellius' victory in the first hours of his movement's existence. It also adds irony to the list of techniques T. uses against Vitellius in this chapter: 'the name "Germanicus" was attached to him in much the same way as, these days, a different label is affixed to a new and supposedly improved product to increase its sales (the passive construction is no accident)' (Morgan (1993c) 327; see further on *laetum augurium* below). *statim*, however, seems more relevant to a placement such as that of Plutarch or Suetonius, since the content of ch. 62 is temporally very vague. Wellesley suggests moving the passage to 57.1 after *consalutauit*. Better to assume that T. has retained some of the language of the common source in a context to which it is not perfectly suited; for this see 27.2n. *innixus liberto*, 31.1 n. *insidiis et simulatione*. For Vitellius' concern with nomenclature (and T.'s scorn for it) see also 2.62.2 *praemisit in urbem edictum, quo uocabulum Augusti differret, Caesaris non reciperet, cum de potestate nihil detraheret*, 3.58.3 *quin et Caesarem se dici uoluit, aspernatus antea, sed tunc superstitione nominis.* **additum:** sc. *est.*

62.3 laetum augurium . . . acciperetur: 'in a civil war only a savage irony will allow a sophisticated writer like Tacitus to talk of a *laetum augurium*', Morgan (1993c) 325. Suetonius has the same expression: *Vit.* 9.1 *praemisso agmine laetum euenit augurium, siquidem a parte dextra repente aquila aduolauit lustratisque signis ingressos uiam sensim antecessit.* For T.'s allusions to Virgil (*Aen.* 5.137, quoted above) and through Virgil to Ennius' description of Romulus' *augurium* (esp. *omnibus cura uiris uter esset induperator* and *sic exspectabat populus atque ore timebat | rebus utri magni uictoria sit data regni*, *Ann.* 78 and 82–3 Skutsch), as well as for the links between this scene and Otho's bird omen at 2.50.2 see Morgan (1993c). For other omens connected with Otho and those of Vespasian see 22.2 and 2.78.1–2. **laetum augurium:** for appositional comments see 44.2n. *munimentum . . . ultionem*; for the initial placement (and subject matter) cf. *A.* 2.17.2 *interea, pulcherrimum augurium, octo aquilae petere siluas et intrare uisae imperatorem aduertere.* **ipso profectionis die:** *c.* 12–13 January (Murison (1993) 89). **meatu** 'movement along a line, progress' *OLD* 1; used of the phoenix' flight from nest to pyre at *A.* 6.28.5 and twice elsewhere in T.

63–70 Vitellians march: *duo duces, duo itinera*

Having described Vitellius, his two principal commanders, and his men in chh. 61–2, T. now sets two of the three armies in motion towards Rome. The focus is on 'the behaviour of men and armies when the restraints of peace are suddenly removed' (Syme (1958) 170). Valens and Caecina pursue their different routes through Gaul simultaneously; T. accords them sequential panels similar in length but very different in incident. Both may be followed on Map 3. Vitellius himself remains immobile.

Valens' itinerary is given in some detail: Trier, Metz, Toul, Langres, Lyon, Vienne, Luc-en-Diois are the modern names of the towns through which T. tracks him in chh. 63–6. His stated task was to win over the inhabitants of these and the many other settlements through which he passed in marching along the now century-old Roman road, or else to lay the places waste (61.1 *allicere uel, si abnuerent, uastare*). Resistence is nowhere encountered, but the march to the Alps was not uneventful, owing to the brutality of the men and the greed of both men and general. The panel's conclusion shows that winning over Gaul lost out to wringing profit and pleasure from it (66.3).

For Caecina T. gives not an itinerary but a small war against the Helvetii, a people sadly diminished since Caesar's day. Though 'a relatively impressionistic and imprecise narrative' (Morgan (1994c) 111), it displays Caecina's military competence: he summons allies (67.2), coordinates troop movements (68.1), uses his forces efficiently (68.2), takes prompt advantage of opportunities that arise (70.1), and weighs strategic alternatives (70.2–3). The campaign might almost be one of Caesar's, as the unadorned report of the capitulation of the capital, Avenches, suggests: 68.2 *missi qui dederent ciuitatem, et deditio accepta*; on the Caesarian underpinning of chh. 63–70 see Morgan (1994c). Ch. 70 looks both forward to N. Italy (70.1 n. *Mediolanum . . . Vercellas*) and back to Valens' march: Valens began with a *laetum augurium* (62.3), Caecina ends with a *laetum . . . nuntium* (70.1), Valens ends *ad Alpes* (66.3), Caecina goes up and over (70.3).

The invasion narratives should be read in conjunction with the Flavian march on Rome, which was also, but differently, in two parts; correspondences are noted below.

The parallel tradition has little information about Valens' march and none at all about Caecina's (62.3n. *laetum augurium*, 66.2n. *Valentem . . . emptum*, 66.3n. *lento . . . agmine*). For discussions of and bibliography on this section see Ash (1999) 38–41 and esp. Morgan (1994c).

63.1 et . . . quidem: 5.2n. **Treueros:** 53.3n.; their capital, Augusta Treuerorum, mod. Trier, was a week's march from Cologne (163 km), a standard day's march being 15 *milia passuum*, or about 22 km (Murison (1993) 89). **Diuoduri . . . temperauere:** the main clause of eight words (plus a four-word parenthesis) is followed by a thirty-one word appendix. **Diuoduri:** mod. Metz, 83 km beyond Trier. **quamquam . . . exceptos:** 43.1n. **raptis:** the tense indicates priority not to the main verb *terruit* but to *mitigati* and *temperauere*. **ob praedam aut spoliandi cupidine:** for concrete and abstract in tandem cf. 35.1 *in plausus et immodica studia*; for the formal *uariatio* see Sörbom (1935) 85. **furore et rabie et causis incertis:** 57.2n. *instinctu et impetu et auaritia. furore et rabie* is a doublet familiar from poetry: Lucr. 4.1117 *redit rabies eadem et furor ille reuisit*, Virg. *Aen.* 5.801–2 *saepe furores | compressi et rabiem tantam*, Ov. *Tr.* 2.1.150 *aequalis rabies continuusque furor*, Lucan 4.420 *redeunt rabies furorque*, 7.551 *hic furor hic rabies*, 10.72 *in media rabie medioque furore* (on the Lucan parallels see Robbert (1917) 65); also Sen. *Thy.* 27–8, Sil. 1.71, and Stat. *Theb.* 7.810. **eoque:** 13.3n. **difficilioribus remediis:** abl. of description (*NLS* §83). **mitigati** 'placated' (cf. *OLD* 4); similarly in the prelude to the sack of Cremona (3.32.1 *nec procul caede aberant, cum precibus ducum mitigatus est miles*), where the soldiers' restraint is short-lived and *excidium urbis* ensues. Both scenes prepare the way for the terrifying 'sack' of Rome by the Flavians: 4.1–2, esp. 4.2.1 *quasi Cremonensem praedam rapere*. The end of this series is reached when Cerealis' troops contemplate but refrain from sacking Trier (4.72.1–2). The next city sacked in *H.* is Jerusalem. On sacking cities see Ziolkowski (1993). **temperauere** 'refrained from' *OLD* 3a. **caesa tamen ad quattuor milia hominum:** sc. *sunt*; cf. Caes. *Gal.* 2.33.5 *occisis ad hominum milibus quattuor.*

63.2 cum magistratibus et precibus 'with magistrates (at their head) and entreaties (on their lips)' (Alford, *ad loc.*). **stratis . . . feminis puerisque:** in supplication, cf. 3.10.2 *supplices manus tenderet* (sc. *Flauianus*), *humi plerumque stratus*, *A.* 16.31.1 *primum strata humi . . . post altaria et aram complexa.* **quaeque alia . . . tendebantur** = *tentisque iis rebus quae placamenta . . . erant*, parallel in function to *stratis . . . feminis puerisque*. The omission of the participle yields an expression more compressed than similar passages at 23.1 *querelas et ambiguos . . . sermones quaeque alia turbamenta uulgi* and elsewhere (2.4.1, *A.* 2.56.2, 11.3.1, *A.* 16.2.2). **placamenta:** a rare word, properly of divinities (e.g. *A.* 15.44.2 *deum placamentis*), but cf. Apul. *Soc.* 13.6 *proinde ut nos pati possunt* (sc. *daemones*) *omnia animorum placamenta*. See also 58.2n. *ut . . . Crispinus*.

64.1 in ciuitate Leucorum: Tullum, mod. Toul, some 53 km beyond Metz. The date is *c.* 24–6 January (Murison (1993) 88–9). **nec**

'but . . . not' *OLD* 5. **permotus:** sc. *est.* **Gallis cunctatio exempta est:** illustrated in chh. 64–6 for the Gallic tribes along Valens' route; for Aquitania and Narbonensis see 76.1. **par:** sc. *erat.*

64.2 Lingonum ciuitas: Andematunnum, mod. Langres, 93 km beyond Toul (53.3n., 59.1 n.). **benigne excepti:** sc. *milites.* **modestia certauere:** cf. Liv. 27.45.11 *modestia certare milites ne quid ultra usum necessarium sumerent.* For occasional *modestia* in the Vitellian ranks see 52.3n. *modesti quietique*; more often they show excess (e.g. 62.1, 3.70.4). **cohortium:** 59.1 n. *octo . . . cohortes.* **intemperie** 'outrageous behaviour' *OLD* 3; a sample is given at 2.27.2 *cohortes Batauorum . . . superbe agebant, ut cuiusque legionis tentoria accessissent, coercitos a se quartadecimanos, ablatam Neroni Italiam atque omnem belli fortunam in ipsorum manu sitam iactantes*; cf. 2.28.1 *turbidas,* 2.66.1 *ueterem aduersus quartadecimanos discordiam,* 4.19.1 *intumuere.* Civilis, on the other hand, claims at 4.17.3 that whatever *militaris disciplina* the Roman forces had came from these Batavians. Elsewhere T. uses *intemperies* of weather (2.94.1, *A.* 16.13.1); here it makes a contrast with *modestia.* **iurgia primum, mox rixa:** mutual irritation is still present at 2.27.2 (*corrupta iurgiis aut rixis disciplina*) and at 2.66.2 it escalates (*a conuiciis ad caedem transiere*). By 2.68.1–2 the problem has spread: *erupere legionarii in perniciem auxiliorum* (sc. *Gallorum*) *ac duae cohortes interfectae* (cf. 2.88.1 *manente legionum auxiliorumque discordia*). After his victory Vitellius tried to curb the Batavians, with disastrous results (2.69.1). Ignoring their later summons to Italy these cohorts eventually defeated the legion stationed at Bonn (4.20) and joined Civilis in the siege of Vetera. **animaduersione** 'punishment' *OLD* 3; thirteen times in Cicero and fairly widely spread in other prose authors, but only here in T. and absent from Sallust. **oblitos . . . imperii:** the tribe's history lends irony to the charge: *G.* 29.1 *populus* (sc. *Batauorum*) . . . *in eas sedes transgressus in quibus pars Romani imperii fierent* (with Rives (1999) *ad loc.*); see also 59.1 n. *ferox gens.* Cerealis uses similar language in rebuking troops at 4.77.3 *Gallici foederis oblitos.* The corresponding virtue is *reuerentia imperii* (55.4n.). **admonuisset** 'had rebuked' *OLD* 5; for the construction cf. *A.* 14.62.3 *accitum eum Caesar operae prioris admonet.*

64.3 Aeduos: the Aeduan capital Augustodunum, mod. Autun, lay west of the Roman road, but the Aeduan town Cabillonum, mod. Chalon-sur-Saône, was on it some 125 km beyond Langres. The Aedui, who had supported Vindex, were identified as a desirable and deserving target of violence by Gauls who had remained loyal to Rome (51.4). Precaution was warranted: the Aedui joined rebellions in 21 as well as 68 (*A.* 3.43.1). But when a rebellion gathered momentum in their vicinity later in 69 they policed themselves (2.61). For an individual Aeduan supporter of Vitellius see 3.35.2. The tribe is not mentioned in connection with Civilis' rebellion. **quaesita:** sc. *est.* **belli causa:** for Caecina's army cf. 67.1. **Lugdunenses:** Lugdunum, mod. Lyon, is 245 km, or nearly two weeks' march (including some days of rest), beyond Langres. **legio Italica et ala Tauriana:** 59.2nn. **cohortem duodeuicensimam:** an urban cohort based in Lyon, attached, it seems, to the mint (Freis (1967) 28–31). Josephus, in reviewing Rome's forces in A.D. 66, says that Gaul was held in check by 1,200 soldiers (*BJ* 2.373), which fits reasonably well with evidence from the Gallic revolt of A.D. 21, where the initial phases reveal an urban cohort at Lyon (*A.* 3.41.1: *c.* 480 men) and an *ala* based at Trier (*A.* 3.42.1; *c.* 512 men). The number of this cohort is disputed (see Chilver *ad loc.*); it was replaced by the new *cohors* I *Flauia urbana* shortly after Vespasian's accession. See further 4.2n. *urbanum militem.*

64.4 Manlius Valens: probably the C. Manlius Valens who as *consul ordinarius* at the age of ninety in A.D. 96 gave his name to the year of Domitian's assassination and Nerva's accession (Dio 67.14.5 with Murison (1999) *ad loc.*; *PIR*² M 163) and the legionary legate of *A.* 12.40.1 (A.D. 52); his recent prominence may help explain the presence of this singular datum in *H. Contra*, Chilver. **bene de partibus meritus:** 59.2n. *Italica legione.* **infamauerat** 'had defamed' *OLD* 2, again with Valens as subject at 3.62.2 *Verginium . . . infamauit.* For the tendency of an emperor's closest advisors to frustrate the services of others cf. 26.2 *consilii quamuis egregii . . . inimicus*; for a similar case, differently resolved, under Vespasian see 3.52.3, with 4.80.2–3.

65.1 ueterem . . . discordiam: cf. 2.66.1 *ob ueterem aduersus quartadecimanos discordiam.* For discussion of the rivalry see Fabia (1902); no incidents are known. **et Viennenses:** the site of Vienna, mod. Vienne, was a crossing point of the Rhone occupied by Celts (Allobroges) from the fifth century B.C. on, but of modest importance. Caesar made Vienne an honourary Latin colony (*Colonia Iulia Viennensium*; honorary because no Roman colonists joined the indigenous population) in about 50 B.C. (Lyon, by contrast, was purely Roman, Cologne a mixed population of Ubii and military colonists). The city's status was upgraded under Augustus and Tiberius, and its importance is evident from Claudius' Lyon speech (*ILS* 212, col. II 10–11): *ornatissima ecce colonia ualentissimaque Viennensium quam longo iam tempore senatores huis curiae confert* (for senators, indeed consuls, from Vienne see 59.2n. *Valerius Asiaticus*, 77.2n. *Pompeius Vopiscus*, Syme (1958) 592 on Bellicus Natalis). But despite its success in Roman terms Vienne supported Vindex' revolt (cf. Vell. 2.121.1 for an earlier uprising) and was a source of concern even after his defeat (2.66.3 *Viennenses timebantur*). It did not, however, play an active role in the *imperium Galliarum* of 70. For references and further discussion see Pelletier (1982), Rivet (1988) 305–10. **proximum bellum:** the revolt of Vindex, which Vienne joined and Lyon opposed. **multae in uicem clades:** sc. *erant*. The only known detail is a siege of Lyon: 65.2 *obsessam ab illis coloniam suam*. For attributive *inuicem* ('reciprocally' *OLD* 3), a compact form of expression found already in Livy (e.g. 3.71.2 and 10.11.7 *multis inuicem cladibus*), cf. 75.1 *omnibus inuicem gnaris*, 4.37.3 *magnisque inuicem cladibus*, *Agr.* 24.1 *magnis inuicem usibus*, *G.* 37.3 *multa inuicem damna*. See also 46.4n. *bonis postea principibus*. **crebrius infestiusque quam ut:** for adverbs introducing a free-standing comment on an already complete sentence cf. 66.3 *adeo minaciter ut*, 74.2 *promptius quam ut*. Heubner supplies parallels from other authors. For a similar stylistic effect see 44.2n. *munimentum ... ultionem*. **reditus Lugdunensium:** what Galba confiscated is not known; for discussion see Fabia (1902) 110–11. **multus ... honor:** sc. *erat*. **uno amne discretis conexum odium:** separated by the Rhone and 31 km, in fact. The mixing of abstract (*odium*) and concrete (*amne*) and the juxtaposition of opposites (*discretis conexum*) makes an epigram of what in Livy (23.31 *utraque* (sc. *aedis*) *in Capitolio est, canali uno discreta*) and Pliny (*Nat.* 5.70 *a ceteris Iudaeis Iordane amne discreta* (sc. *Peraea*)) is perfectly bland.

65.2 euersionem: at Quint. *Inst.* 8.3.67–9 *euersio* is a one word equivalent for the description of an *urbs capta*; cf. *H.* 5.8.3 *urbium euersiones*. Putting *Viennensium* in place of *urbis* emphasizes the violence of a sack; cf. Quint. *Decl.* 293.1 *iuste peterem etiam hostium euersionem*. **obsessam ... relinquerent:** Lyon's *exhortatio* has an appropriately passionate style: asyndeton (*obsessam ... adiutos ... conscriptas, irent ... exscinderent*), isocolon and homoioteleuton (*causas odiorum praetenderant* and *magnitudinem praedae ostendebant*), exaggeration (*in praesidium Galbae, sedem Gallici belli, cuncta illuc externa ac hostilia, partem exercitus*, see nn.), violent language (*euersionem, exscinderent*), poetic periphrasis (*irent ultores*), ponderous sounds (*prosperarum aduersarumque rerum socios*), and euphemism (*si fortuna contra daret*). **obsessam:** sc. *esse*. **coloniam suam:** i.e. *Romanam*: see below and 51.5n. *Lugdunensis colonia*. **conscriptas nuper legiones in praesidium Galbae:** if this refers to a contribution by Vienne to Vindex' force (6.2n. *opprimendis Vindicis coeptis*; for *legio* of non-Roman units see *OLD* 2), *in praesidium Galbae* exaggerates the help given thereby to the hated Galba, who remained safely in Spain until after Vindex' defeat (6.1 n. *tardum Galbae iter*). However, T. nowhere else uses *legio* of a non-Roman unit. Another possibility is that Galba added men from Vienne to his legions, perhaps especially to *legio* VII *Galbiana* (cf. 2.11.1 *septima a Galba conscripta*, and for conscription in Gaul later in the civil war see 2.57.1, 4.19.2); in this scenario *legiones* is an exaggeration. For legionaries from Vienne see Pflaum (1978). **secreta:** sc. *erat.* **irent ultores:** cf. V. Flac. 3.308 *tuos irem nunc ultor in hostes* and, perhaps, the most famous appositional *ultor*: Virg. *Aen.* 4.625 *exoriare aliquis nostris ex ossibus ultor.* Parallels for a substantive in apposition to the subject of *ire* are, outside of T. (here and 2.11.1 *pedes ire*), mostly poetic: *TLL* s.v. *eo* 637.37–44. **sedem Gallici belli:** a puzzling charge. At 3.32.2 (and the other parallels listed by Heubner) *sedes belli* refers to the site (not the source) of fighting, but no fighting is known there from Vindex' rebellion and if another war is meant the charge is far-fetched. **cuncta illic externa ac hostilia:** cf. T. on Vienne at 66.1 *uetustas dignitasque coloniae ualuit*, where *uetustas* and *dignitas* are no doubt ironic, but *colonia* is accurate (65.1 n. *et Viennenses*); according to Chilver *ad loc.*, a 'palpably tendentious plea'. **partem exercitus:** another exaggeration, on any of the explanations advanced: Lyon was home to numerous veterans (Fabia (1902) 114), or a source of army recruits (Syme (1939) 478 n.1), or a troop base (Chilver, Hellegouarc'h). **contra daret** 'turn out adversely'; cf. *A.* 15.13.2 *ualidam quoque et laudatam antiquitatem, quotiens fortuna contra daret, saluti consuluisse*, 3.18.1 *ubi fortuna contra fuit.*

66.1 uelamenta et infulas: symbols of supplication. *uelamenta* are olive branches with a wrapping of wool fillets (cf. Virg. *Aen.* 8.128 *uitta comptos... praetendere ramos*), *infulae* headbands traditionally worn by envoys. The phrasing is standard: 3.31.2 *mox uelamenta et infulas... ostentant*, Liv. 25.25.6 *legati... cum infulis et uelamentis uenerunt, precantes ut a caedibus et ab incendiis parceretur*, 30.36.4 *uelata infulis ramisque oleae... nauis*, 37.28.1 *oratores cum infulis et uelamentis ad Romanum miserunt*, etc. See also 63.2n. *stratis... puerisque.* **uestigia** 'feet' (by metonymy: *OLD* 3), preferable in shape and sound to *pedes.* For the scene cf. 36.2. **addidit Valens... sestertios:** T. often ends lists of causes on a pragmatic (and sometimes morally dubious) note: cf. 46.1 n. *plerisque... respicientibus*, 57.2n. *instinctu... auaritia.* 300 HS was a third of the soldier's annual salary (Alston (1994)); for other bribes see 5.1 n. *neque dari donatiuum*, 24.1 n. *centenos nummos.* **uetustas dignitasque:** the abstract nouns give a hint of the *preces* that were no doubt uttered in Vienne as well as earlier (63.2; cf. *uerba Fabi salutem incolumitatemque . . . commendantis*). Juxtaposed with *sestertii* they seem mere window-dressing. For the singular verb with a compound subject see Draeger (1882) §29a. **accepta:** sc. *sunt.* **publice . . . priuatis:** for the *uariatio* cf. *A.* 6.45.1 *modicus priuatis aedificationibus ne publice quidem nisi duo opera struxit* and Sörbom (1935) 96–7. **armis multati** 'penalized by confiscation of their weapons' *OLD* 1a; cf. *G.* 12.2 *equorum pecorumque numero conuicti multantur.* **priuatis et promiscuis copiis:** the antithesis with *armis* suggests that *promiscuus* here means 'of all sorts' (*OLD* 2b; cf. *A.* 12.7.1 *promisca multitudo*, 14.20.5 *coetu promisco*); it conveys the frantic efforts of the Viennenses to show themselves compliant. See also 47.1 n., 84.4n.

66.2 Valentem . . . emptum: sc. *esse*; the soldiers give voice to their suspicions during a riot in which Valens is stoned and forced to flee in a slave's clothing and his quarters are pillaged (2.29.1). Further profits accrued from the planning of his itinerary (66.3, note *uenditante duce*), from the enrolment of new praetorian and urban cohorts (2.93.2, note *ambitu*), and from his power in the capital (2.92.2 *inuaserant domos hortos opesque imperii*); see also 2.56.2 *ob lucra et quaestus infamis* and 2.95.3 *inter Vinios Fabiosque, Icelos Asiaticos* (where he is paired with Galba's grasping minister, Vinius). Rapaciousness is also the theme of Plutarch's one substantial passage on Valens (*O.* 6.4 'Fabius Valens' pursuit of money was satisfied neither by plunder from the enemy nor by thefts and bribes from the allies') as well as that of Dio (64.10.1 'So eager was Valens for money and so thorough in amassing it from every source, that . . . '). Mucianus, by contrast, contributes from his own funds to Vespasian's war chest, at least initially, and sets an example for others in so doing (2.84.2). **accensis . . . cupidinibus:** illustrated in 66.3; cf. 3.40.1 *Fabius interim Valens multo ac molli concubinatorum spadonumque agmine segnius quam ad bellum procedens* and 3.41.1 *sed Valens ne in tanto quidem discrimine infamia caruit, quo minus rapere illicitas uoluptates adulterisque ac stupris polluere hospitum domus crederetur; aderant uis et pecunia et ruentis fortunae nouissima libido.* **senex:** Valens' age is not known; a legionary legate would ordinarily be in his thirties. Manlius Valens, at sixty-three, was unusually old (64.4n.). Caecina's relative youthfulness worked against Valens in the estimation of the soldiers (2.30.2 *uigore aetatis*). Convalescence from an illness prevents his deployment later in the year: 2.99.1 *infirmitas tardabat.*

66.3 lento . . . agmine: in retrospect his soldiers thought Valens had been deliberately delaying: 2.30.1 *fraude et cunctationibus Valentis proelio* *defuissent.* Plutarch, too, reports criticism that ascribes Valens' slow progress to his rapaciousness and accuses him of dangerously delaying his arrival in Italy: *O.* 6.4 'It was thought that, travelling slowly (βραδέως ὁδεύων) because of this, he arrived too late for the first battle.' Neither author assents to the charge; T., however, later makes a pointed comment about Mucianus' more judicious pace: 2.83.1 *Mucianus . . . non lento itinere, ne cunctari uideretur, neque tamen properans, gliscere famam ipso spatio sinebat.* **ductus:** sc. *est.* **itinerum spatia et statiuorum mutationes** 'marching distances and changes to the (schedule of) rest-days' along the Roman road to the pass. **uenditante duce foedis pactionibus:** the second abl. abs. explains (and comments on: *foedis*) the first. **aduersus possessores agrorum** 'with property owners'; *aduersus* indicates a relationship, not a necessarily hostile one (cf. 10.3 *nec Vespasiano aduersus Galbam uotum aut animus*, 35.2 *aduersus blandientes incorruptus*, *A.* 15.59.5 *foedis aduersus Neronem adulationibus*). The expression here has no exact parallel, but for *aduersus* with other words that themselves imply a relationship (here *pactio*) cf. *A.* 3.29.2 (*necessitudo*) and Apul. *Soc.* 129 (*communio*). **adeo minaciter ut:** 65.1 n. *crebrius infestiusque quam ut.* **Luco:** Lucus Augusti, mod. Luc-en-Diois, 164 km beyond Vienne. According to Plin. *Nat.* 3.37 it was a town with Latin rights (where ex-magistrates had Roman citizenship), not a *municipium* (where all with local citizenship did); T.'s usage may be loose; for the differences in status see Sherwin-White (1973a) 337–50. **pecunia mitigaretur:** placation is usually accomplished via speech (e.g. 63.1, 69, 81.2), sentiment (3.60.3, *A.*1.13.6 *periculo talis uiri mitigatus est*), or time and satiety (*A.* 6.38.1 *tempus preces satias mitigabant*). **sic . . . peruentum:** sc. *est*; the phrase 'gains enormously in bite from its brevity' (Morgan (1994c) 114). From Luc to the Mt Genèvre pass the army marched some 161 km over nearly three weeks (Murison (1993) 86–7, Köster (1927) 22); on T.'s omission of all incidents from this period see Morgan (1994c) 104–8.

67.1 plus . . . Caecina: competition between Vitellius' two legates, initiated in the diptych at 52.3–53.1 (where Valens rouses Vitellius, Caecina his soldiers) and evident here, remains an important theme in Book 2. At 2.30.2–3 T. has Vitellius' soldiers making the comparison; at 2.99.2 Vitellius himself. The rivalry reaches such a pitch that the two men give conflicting orders at 2.101.2 (cf. also 2.30.3 *hinc aemulatio ducibus*; 2.92.1–2, and Plut. *O.* 6.5). The competition was eventually won by Valens, a victory that was thought to have encouraged Caecina's betrayal of Vitellius (2.93.2, 2.99.2). **plus praedae ac sanguinis . . . hausit** 'drew more blood and booty'; cf. 68.2 *multa hominum milia caesa, multa sub corona uenundata. haurio* is used of financial 'withdrawals' as well as of bloodshed (cf. Cic. *Agr.* 2.32 *sumptum haurit ex aerario, Sest.* 93 *haurire cotidie ex ... Syriae gazis innumerabile pondus auri*); *praeda*, unique as its object, capitalizes on both its violent and its financial sense. T. gives few details about Caecina's route (61.1 n. *propiore transitu*), but 'We can deduce from known Roman roads in the area that he went via Salodurum, Aventicum and Octodurus to Augusta Praetoria, which is just inside Italy' (Murison (1993) 90). **armis uirisque ... clara:** cf. Sal. *Jug.* 57.1 *armis uirisque opulentum* (of Zama), Liv. 23.30.6 *opulentam quondam armis uirisque* (of Croton). **memoria nominis:** here the third term, unlike that of the formula used earlier (51.2n. *uiri arma equi*), shows Helvetian resources to be insubstantial; cf. 30.2 *uacua nomina*, 55.4 *oblitterata iam nomina* and, for the series of three abl., 57.2n. *instinctu ... auaritia.* The memory of the Helvetii was preserved in Caes. *Gal.* 1.1–29, esp. 1.1.4 *reliquos Gallos praecedunt quod fere cotidianis proeliis cum Germanis contendunt.* On the paucity of Helvetian notables as Roman officers and senators see Syme (1977) 136–7. **initium bello:** adnominal dat. (22.2n. *Othoni ... comes*). The narrative goes back to January. The confiscation and the letters to Pannonia (see below) presumably occurred shortly after Upper Germany declared for Vitellius (57.1). **auaritia ac festinatio** 'impatient greed' (Davies (1989)) or 'covetous haste' (Alford); a similar hendiadys is used of Antonius Primus' troops at 3.50.3 *festinatio atque auiditas.* **rapuerant:** perhaps a pun on the legion's name (cf. 2.43.1 *unaetuicensima, cui cognomen Rapaci*; see 61.2n.). The tense shows that the legion acted before Caecina's arrival. **castelli:** not securely identified; for bibliography see Chilver *ad loc.* **olim** 'for a long time past' *OLD* 2. **tuebantur** 'looked after' *OLD* 6.

67.2 epistulis quae nomine Germanici exercitus ad Pannonicas legiones ferebantur: cf. 74.3 *epistulas ... nomine Germanici exercitus ad praetorias et urbanas cohortes.* For the legions in Pannonia see 9.2n. *excitae ... legiones.* **proximam quamque culpam** 'every injury immediately'. **mota:** sc. *sunt.* Forms of *esse* are omitted throughout this narrative. **direptus ... locus:** for a similar incident told in more gruesome detail and involving Otho's forces see 2.13.1–2. Civilian settlements were also victimized at the outset of sedition in A.D. 14 (*A.* 1.20.1). **in modum municipii exstructus locus:** cf. 4.22.1 *longae pacis opera, haud procul castris in modum municipii exstructa* (of the civilian district outside the fortress at Vetera) and *A.* 1.20.1 *Nauporto, quod municipii instar* *erat.* **amoeno salubrium aquarum usu frequens:** Aquae Heluetica, mod. Baden on the Limmat, 8 km east of their camp at Vindonissa (and out of their route towards Italy via Augusta Raurica, mod. Augst; 61.1 n. *propiore transitu*). On the omission of place names in chh. 67–70 see Syme (1977) 130–1, Morgan (1994c) 106–7. **Raetica auxilia:** 68.1 n.

68.1 feroces: sc. *erant.* **Claudium Seuerum:** not mentioned elsewhere, and surprisingly bereft of identifying material here, 'as though a known character' (Syme (1977) 133); see also Morgan (1994c) 110. **non arma noscere, non ordines sequi, non in unum consulere:** for anaphora and failures of military discipline cf. 2.12.3 *temere collectis, non castra non ducem noscitantibus* (of emergency levies), 2.93.1 *sed miles ... urbe tota uagus, non principia noscere, non seruare uigilias neque labore firmari* (of Vitellian troops in Rome), 3.18.1 *non laxare ordines, non recipere turbatos, non obuiam ire*, 3.76.2 *non uigilias agere, non intuta moenium firmare* (of a garrison of gladiators and rowers), and esp. *A.* 4.25.2 *hostibus ... omnium nesciis non arma, non ordo, non consilium* (of Numidian forces); cf. also Sal. *Jug.* 99.2 *Mauri atque Gaetuli ... neque fugere neque arma capere neque omnino facere aut prouidere quicquam poterant.* **arma noscere:** for *arma* as *ars armorum* see *TLL* s.v. 594 59–82; cf. Col. 1 *praef.* 4 *armorum et militiae gnaros*, Mela 1.47 *armorum ignari*, Quint. *Inst.* 2.12.2 *armorum inscius*, Flor. *Epit.* 1.34.10 *arma nescirent.* **ordines sequi:** another abbreviated expression, since *ordines* are usually *seruati*, while *sequi* governs *signa* (see Hellegouarc'h for parallels); these standard military procedures are often mentioned together, e.g. Liv. 30.35.6 *signa sequi et seruare ordines*, and (slightly altered) Sal. *Jug.* 80.2 *ordines habere, signa sequi.* Sallust abbreviates, but less drastically, at *Jug* 51.1 *neque signa neque ordines obseruare*; T. has another variation at 4.18.3 *legionarius miles ... arma ordinesque retinebat.* **in unum consulere** 'take common counsel' *OLD* 3b; cf. 4.70.1 *ne duces quidem in unum consulere*, where each *dux* pursues a different strategy, and esp. *Agr.* 12.2 *nec aliud ... pro nobis utilius quam quod in commune non consulunt.* **exitiosum:** sc. *erat* (for the mood see *NLS* §200i); 'this sentence gives the possibilities and the situation as they were for the Helvetii' (Alford). **intuta:** 33.2n. **obsidio** 'a state of siege'; cf. 33.1 *obsidionem ... toleraturus*, *Agr.* 22.2 *aduersus moras obsidionis annuis copiis firmabantur*, *A.* 15.29.3 *exercituum Romanorum caedes aut obsidio.* **dilapsis ... moenibus:** of the capital Aventicum, presumably (68.2n.). **Raeticae alae cohortesque et ipsorum Raetorum iuuentus:** for similar groupings cf. 2.58.1 *decem nouem cohortes, quinque alae, ingens Maurorum numerus* and 3.5.2 *Sextilius Felix cum ala Auriana et octo cohortibus ac Noricorum iuuentute*; for the terminology see Saddington (1970). The size of Raetia's garrison at this period is not known. For native levies in Rome's service see also 2.12.3 *iuuentus*, 2.97.2 *iuuentus*, 4.12.3 *domi delectus eques*, and 57.2n. *auxilia*, 61.2n. *Germanorum auxilia*. **undique populatio et caedes:** troops from the Rhine and Raetia seem to have progressed separately (note *medio* below) through the territory of a disorganized people, killing, capturing (68.2 *sub corona uenundata*), looting and destroying as they went. The delay occasioned when the Roman forces, now joined (68.2 *Germanis Raetisque*), stopped to root out refugees from the *mons Vocetius* was brief. **medio:** 12.2n. *tota ciuitate*. **uagi** 'scattered' *OLD* 4. **palantes** often denotes military disarray, e.g. 4.18.3 *legionarius miles . . . arma ordinesque retinebat, Vbiorum Treuerorumque auxilia foeda fuga dispersa totis campis palantur*, 4.60.2 *pugnacissimus quisque in uestigio, multi palantes*, 4.70.4 *plebes omissis armis per agros palatur*. **montem Vocetium:** for discussion of various identifications see Dürr (1973), who suggests that the Helvetii took refuge near the village of Wöschnau (from *Vocetiana aua*), site of a pre-Roman fortification, the Refugium Eppenberg.

68.2 depulsi: sc. *sunt*. **cohorte Thracum:** one of at least three different units so named and normally stationed in Germany at this time (Cichorius (1900) s.v. *cohors* 335–6, 340–1, Cheesman (1914) 178–9, Holder (1999) 246); all three were *cohortes equitatae*, i.e. infantry cohorts in which some soldiers were mounted and ordinarily used 'for general purpose work, skirmishing, patrolling, reconnaissance, escort duty and messengers' (Webster (1998) 149–50). Clearly the Helvetii do not require Caecina's best troops. **caesa:** sc. *sunt*. **multa sub corona uenundata:** a formula for the sale of captives (Gel. 6.4.3 *mancipia iure belli capta coronis induta ueniebant et idcirco dicebantur 'sub corona' uenire*; see further *TLL* s.v. *corona* 985.1–18), indicating that this sale, unlike Valens' (66.3), was official; cf. *A.* 13.39.4. *imbelle uulgus sub corona uenundatum, reliqua praeda uictoribus cessit* (sc. *Corbulo*). **dirutis omnibus:** the structures dismantled were presumably those of Helvetian settlements through which the troops passed; for *diruo* cf. 4.65.1 *muros . . . augere nobis quam diruere tutius est*, 5.9.1 *muri Hierosolymorum diruti*, 5.19.2 *diruit molem a Druso Germanico factum*, *A.* 15.17.3 *diruta quae . . . communiuerat Corbulo*. **Auenticum gentis caput:** mod. Avenches, 170 km from Augst along the Roman road to the pass. Its status as a *ciuitas*-capital was due to Augustus; whether he built on the foundations of a native settlement is not clear. By 69 its civic façade, at least, was thoroughly Romanized (Frei-Stolba (1976) 384–91). Vespasian upgraded the city to colonial status (*Colonia Pia Flauia Constans Emerita Heluetiorum Foederata*); for discussion and bibliography see van Berchem (1981). **infesto agmine:** *infesto* is Andresen's emendation for M's *in/sto*: (1899) 17. T. uses it of another fear-inducing *agmen* at *A.* 1.69.1: *infesto Germanorum agmine Gallias peti*; *agmine infesto* is a Livian formula (4.22.2, 5.18.11, 7.20.6, cf. 2.26.2, etc.). The point is that the Roman force is now directed, terrifyingly, at a single target. **missi:** sc. *sunt.* **Iulium Alpinum:** mentioned only here, but presumably a connection of the contemporary C. Julius Alpinus Classicianus, an imperial procurator in Britain under Nero (*A.* 14.38.3; *PIR*² C 145). **ueniae uel saeuitiae Vitellii:** the natural antithesis would have been *ueniae uel poenae*; *saeuitiae* makes punishment cruel.

69 haud facile dictu est: the authorial intervention, which T. uses nowhere else (but cf. *A.* 12.24.2 *facile cognitu*), makes a break between scenes. **placabilem:** after this word's second syllable a page of M is missing. The gap, which extends through *incertum* in 75.2, is filled by *recentiores* based on copies made before the loss. (On the *recentiores* see Tarrant (1983) 409.) The consensus of these MSS is taken to represent M, which sometimes needs emendation (see 70.2nn. *ala Petriana*, *Petronium Vrbicum*); where they disagree a satisfactory text may be found in some (see below on *ciuitatis*, 70.1 *reuocati*, 70.3 *hibernis . . . Alpibus*) or none (71.2n. *sed . . . adhibens*). **ciuitatis excidium . . . temperabat:** cf. 63.1 *ab excidio ciuitatis temperauere*; shared vocubulary links the scenes, which end very differently. **ciuitatis:** some descendants of M read *ciuitatis* (which yields sense), others *nouitatis* (which doesn't); see Wellesley's app. crit. for details. **poscunt:** sc. *milites*; cf. 45.2n. *expostulabant.* **uerbis et minis** 'threatening words'; for the hendiadys cf. 3.24.2 *minis ac uerbis prouocatos.* **Claudius Cossus:** only here. **ut est mos:** 7.3n. **uulgus mutabile:** sc. *erat*; cf. 80.2 *uulgus, ut mos est, cuiuscumque motus noui cupidum*, 2.29.2 *ut est uulgus utroque immodicum*, 5.8.3 *mobilitate uulgi.* See also 25.2n. and Newbold (1976), whose statistics show fickleness to be the second most common attribute of the Tacitean *uulgus*, as well as T.'s habit of generalizing about this 'stock character' (89). **subitis:** 7.3n. **impetrauere:** sc. *milites.*

70.1 laetum . . . nuntium: the echo of Valens' *laetum augurium* (62.3) is one of the few verbal links between the parallel journeys (Morgan (1994c) 105). **alam Silianam:** cf. 2.17.1 *aperuerat iam Italiam bellumque* *transmiserat... ala Siliana.* For the unit's history see Cichorius (1894) s.v. *ala* 1260–61. **accessisse** 'had joined' (59.2n.); cf. 2.81.1 *Syria omnis in eodem sacramento fuit. accessere... Sohaemus... Antiochus... mox... Agrippa*, 2.58.1 *accessisse partibus utramque Mauretaniam*, 4.70.2 *accessit ala Singularium.* **pro consule Vitellium... habuerant:** more than a decade earlier, though the years are not certain (9.1 n., with Thomasson (1960) II.39–40). **exciti** 'having been ordered to move'; cf. 2.66.1 *remitti eos in Britanniam unde a Nerone exciti erant*, *A.* 15.6.4 *addita quinta legione quae recens e Moesis excita erat.* Whether the *ala* actually reached Alexandria is not clear from T.'s *ut...praetermitterentur.* Another unit intended for Nero's Parthian expedition, which was being planned in 66 (6.2n. *claustra Caspiarum*; for the date see Chilver 9–11), did reach Alexandria (31.3). It is possible that this *ala* was among the 2,000 troops recently arrived from 'Libya' that enabled the governor of Egypt to quell a riot in Alexandria in 66 (Jos. *BJ* 2.494). If so, the different conditions and locations in January of these units from Africa and Germany that had both reached Italy from Alexandria in the summer of 68 are left unexplained. See Murison (1993) 14–15, Chilver 9–11 and Heubner *ad loc.* for various reconstructions. Heubner replaces *exciti*, which must have been in M (see Wellesley's app. crit.), with *acciti.* **ut... ob:** on the *uariatio* of final clause ~ prep. phrase see Martin (1953) 93–4. **reuocati** 'recalled (from their original mission)' *OLD* 1b; cf. 6.2 *quos idem Nero electos praemissosque ad claustra Caspiarum... opprimendis Vindicis coeptis reuocauerat.* Another unit readied in vain for the Parthian expedition was the *legio Italica* (59.2n.). For other troops summoned to Italy in the spring of 68 cf. 9.3 *excitae a Nerone legiones, dum in Italia cunctantur.* The reading of M is difficult to discern here. Both *remorati* and *prouocati* have strong support but yield inadequate sense; *reuocati*, which is less well attested but gives better sense (cf. 6.2 quoted above), may be an emendation; see Wellesley's app. crit. for the details. **instinctu decurionum:** cf. *A.* 1.32.3 *paucorum instinctu*; with *instinctus* personal agency (rather than passion or experience) is first found in Sallust (*H.* 2. fr. 6 *matris instinctu*); cf. also Suet. *Ves.* 7.3 *instinctu uaticinantium.* **decurionum:** commanders of the *ala*'s thirty-two-man *turmae*; see further Holder (1980) 88–90. **obstricti** 'attached by ties of loyalty' *OLD* 5; cf. *A.* 14.7.4 *praetorianos toti Caesarum domui obstrictos.* **famam Germanici exercitus:** cf. 2.58.2 *magna per prouincias Germanici exercitus fama*, mentioned again at 2.21.4 and 3.9.4. **Mediolanum ac Nouariam et Eporediam et Vercellas:** mod. Milan, Novara, Ivrea, Vercelli, all located north of the Po along one of the roads to Placentia. Reported with a more negative tone at 2.17.1 *aperuerat iam Italiam bellumque transmiserat, ut supra memorauimus, ala Siliana, nullo apud quemquam Othonis fauore, nec quia Vitellium mallent, sed longa pax ad omne seruitium fregerat faciles occupantibus et melioribus incuriosos. florentissimum Italiae latus, quantum inter Padum Alpesque camporum et urbium, armis Vitellii . . . tenebatur.*

70.2 compertum: sc. *est.* **praemissis Gallorum Lusitanorumque et Britannorum cohortibus:** auxiliary units, presumably from the regular garrison of the Germanies; for the specific units see Cichorius (1900) s.v. *cohors.* T. mentions none subsequently. **Germanorum uexillis:** among these are probably the Batavi and Transrhenani mentioned as part of the advance guard at 2.17.2 (see also 61.2n. *Germanorum auxilia*). For other auxiliary detachments cf. 2.11.2 *equitum uexilla,* 2.6.1 *uexillarios e cohortibus.* **ala Petriana:** more fully, the *ala Augusta Gallorum Petriana bis torquata miliaria ciuium Romanorum,* based in Moguntiacum in A.D. 56 (Cichorius (1894) s.v. *ala* 1244). After Vitellius' death the *ala*'s commanding officer, Claudius Sagitta, urged rebellion on the governor of Africa, without success (4.49.2). The name, epigraphically attested (see Cichorius (1894)), was garbled in M (*alpe triaria*; see Wellesley's app. crit. for the various scribal and scholarly emendations). **cunctatus est num** 'hesitated over whether'. Both Morgan (1994c) 121–3 and Chilver *ad loc.* discuss the historical Caecina's aims. That troops approaching N. Italy from Illyricum could be attacked from Raetia is clear from the precautionary measures taken against the forces in Raetia later in the year (see below on *Noricum*). But T.'s focus is on character, not strategy. Caecina's hesitation highlights the factors that proved decisive, his concern for the safety of his advance guard and his desire for glory (70.3), both of which contrast favourably with Valens' preoccupations *en route* (66.2nn.). For Mucianus' hesitation at a similar juncture see 2.83.2. For the indirect question the closest parallel is Plin. *Ep.* 6.16.11 *cunctatus paulum an retro flecteret,* the earliest Sal. *Cat.* 52.31 *uos de crudelissimis parricidis quid statuatis cunctamini?*; see further *TLL* 1395.26–36. **Raeticis iugis:** via the Arlberg pass; for the abl. cf. 61.1 *Cottianis Alpibus . . . Poeninis iugis,* 70.3 *Poenino itinere.* **Noricum:** Raetia's neighbour across the Inn, likewise garrisoned with auxiliary forces, which later in the year were used to prevent Vitellius' supporters from interfering with the march of the Danube legions to Italy (3.5.2). On the province see also 11.2n. and Alföldy (1974). **Petronium Vrbicum:** his cognomen is preserved on an inscription from his provincial capital (*CIL* III 11551;

see *PIR*² P 322) but was truncated in M (to *urbi* or *urbis*; see Wellesley's app. crit.). **interruptis fluminum pontibus:** 'Petronius' breaking down the bridges over the various rivers (the Inn above all) meant that he could neither attack nor be attacked. In the circumstances it was by no means certain that he was *fidus Othoni*, but he could be thought so (*putabatur*) – and ignored' (Morgan (1994c) 111).

70.3 plus gloriae: sc. *fore.* **Noricos . . . cessuros:** sc. *esse*; 11.3n. *in pretium belli cessurae erat.* **Poenino itinere :** 61.1n. *propiore transitu.* **subsignanum militem:** legionaries, as at 4.33.1 *subsignano milite media firmare, auxilia passim circumfusa.* **graue legionum agmen:** a Livian expression (28.14.8, cf. 32.5.9, 35.30.7; T. uses variations at 2.22.1 *densum legionum agmen* and 2.87.1 *graui . . . agmine*) that here acknowledges, quietly, the difficulty of getting an army, with its full train of baggage and attendants, through a high Alpine pass. For the emphasis on weight cf. *A.* 4.73.1 *aestuaria aggeribus et pontibus traducendo grauiori agmini firmat*, Liv. 31.39.2 *montes, quam uiam non ingressurum graui agmine Romanum sciebat* (sc. *Philippus*). **legionum:** one full legion (XXI *Rapax*) and detachments from two (IV and XXII: 55.3n. *quarta . . . tendentes*); similarly at 2.22.1 (quoted above), but cf. also 67.2 *legionem.* **hibernis adhuc Alpibus:** the date is mid-March (Caecina reaches Placentia, mod. Piacenza, some 280 km further on, by the end of the month: see Murison (1993) 105). The reference to the Alps at the end of Caecina's journey parallels that at the end of Valens' (66.3). Some descendants of M read *alpibus*, others *niuibus*, which is more likely to have replaced *alpibus* than to have been replaced by it; see Wellesley's app. crit. for details.

71–79 Otho in Rome: *munia imperii*

With the Vitellians *en route* to Italy, T. returns to Otho in Rome. The narrative of chh. 71–9 follows on from ch. 50 and covers mid-January to early March. As experienced in Rome, the period was a grim one: fear prevailed, even when its causes were well hidden (71.1).

The narrative begins with Otho's first independent acts: his pardon of Marius Celsus (ch. 71), his punishment of Tigellinus (ch. 72), and his delaying tactics vis-à-vis Calvia Crispinilla (ch. 73). Chh. 74–5 treat a series of exploratory exchanges between Otho and Vitellius and reveal the inevitability of war. Ch. 76 assesses the forces on each side: with Otho stands Illyricum (and later Judaea, Syria, and Africa), with Vitellius Spain and

Gaul. Geography decides: *nusquam fides aut amor* (76.1). But Otho's attention is not yet on war, and chh. 77–8 describe his benefactions to various civilian groups: the ruling elite in Rome (77.2–3), provincials (78.1), the urban *plebs* (78.2). Though very different from Galba's disciplinary *acta* (ch. 20), they are equally ineffectual. In ch. 79 fighting begins, but not the fighting we expect: on the Danube front the Rhoxolani invade Moesia. The fight against an external enemy – easily won by Roman forces – forms a striking backdrop to the rioting praetorians of chh. 80–5.

Narrating as they do the bulk of Otho's principate, these chapters share a number of incidents with his biographies, and from these overlapping details differences of organization, selection, emphasis, and style emerge with particular clarity in this section.

71.1 spem 'expectation' *OLD* 2. For Otho's reputation see below on *formidinis*, 13.3nn., 21.1n. *inopia . . . toleranda*, 22.1n. *mollis*, 50.1, 50.3, 2.31.1. **non . . . torpescere:** at 62.2 *torpebat* characterizes Vitellius (see n.). *torpescere* is Sallustian (*Cat.* 16.3, *Jug.* 2.4). On the historic inf. used singly see 46.3n. *fatigari*; on inchoative verbs see 32.2n. *ualescere.* **dilatae:** sc. *sunt.* **eoque:** 13.3n. **formidinis:** cf. the fear ascribed to Otho's contemporaries at Plut. *O.* 1.3 'a shuddering fear that it was not a man, but some genius of retribution or avenging spirit that had suddenly fallen upon the state'. Dio is closer in spirit to T.: 64.8.3 'his life and habits . . . caused alarm'; cf. also 64.8.2[1] 'It did not escape notice that his rule would be more licentious and harsh than Nero's.' **Marium Celsum:** 14.1n., 45.2n. *simulatione . . . iussum.* T.'s version of the pardon, a 'reconciliation comedy' (Heubner *ad loc.*), is less favourable to Otho than Plutarch's. He removes the ceremonial context (see on *Capitolium*), supplies a selfish motivation (*clementiae titulus*), and alters the conversation between the two men, making Celsus speak first, Otho second. His Celsus is contumacious (71.2 *ultro*), his Otho conciliatory rather than magnanimous (*nec quasi ignosceret*). In fact it is Celsus, not Otho, who ends up with a *titulus uirtutis* in T.'s narrative (71.3 *eandem uirtutem*; cf. 71.1 *falsae uirtutes*). **Capitolium:** Plut. *O.* 1.1 connects the pardon with a sacrifice in the temple on 16 March. **clementiae titulus**: cf. 75.2 *Vitellius uictor clementiae gloriam tulit. clementia* implies power and is therefore a *uirtus* vaunted early and often by emperors (e.g. Aug. *RG* 3.1–2, 34.2, Sen. *Cl.* 1.1.2–4). For *titulus* 'claim to fame' (*OLD* 7) cf. Liv. 31.15.10 *liberatae per se Graeciae titulum*, Ov. *Met.* 7.56 *titulum seruatae pubis Achiuae.*

71.2 fidei crimen: 59.1n. **exemplum ultro imputauit:** cf. Plut. *O*.1.2 'Celsus replied... that the charge itself gave proof of his character'; *ultro* 'in addition to everything else' (*OLD* 3) makes T.'s Celsus seem more aggressive. On *imputare* see 38.2n. and cf. 2.60.1 *proditionem ultro imputabant* (of Otho's generals addressing a victorious Vitellius) and 2.85.1 *posse imputari Vespasiano quae apud Vitellium excusanda erant* (why some *Othoniani* joined Vespasian). **nec:** 34.1n. **sed ne hostem metueret conciliationes adhibens** 'but, so that he need not fear (sc. Celsus) as an enemy, bringing to bear conciliatory remarks'. This emendation (Halm's) best aligns the passage with its parallel at Plut. *O.* 1.1, where one of Otho's conciliatory expressions is reported: 'he urged him rather to forget the cause of his imprisonment than to remember that of his release'; see Wellesley's Appendix Critica for the manuscript evidence and other emendations. For the plural of *conciliatio* cf. Suet. *Aug.* 17.1 *societatem semper dubium et incertam reconciliationibusque uariis male focilatam* ('kept warm'). *adhibere* is a technical term for the application of remedies, *OLD* 7; here, as at 4.72.3 *uocem precesque adhibere non ausi lacrimis et silentio ueniam poscebant*, the remedies are words. For *hostis* of a personal enemy cf. 27.1 *domesticum hostem* and 3.38.3 *in urbe et sinu cauendum hostem.* **uelut fataliter:** cf. 50.1 *uelut... fataliter electos.* **integra et infelix:** *infelix* in the short term, since he backed another loser in Otho. He had a distinguished career thereafter (14.1n.). Sound links *integra* and *infelix* but sense divides them; from the tension arises an epigram.

71.3 eandem uirtutem: his *uirtutes* at 45.2 were *industria* and *innocentia*, to which T. adds *fides* at 71.2 and *uigor* at 87.2. For the paradox cf. Liv. 5.26.8 *eandem uirtutem et oderant et mirabantur.*

72.1 par... disparibus: cf. 2.7.2 *boni malique causis diuersis studio pari bellum omnes cupiebant.* The paronomasia highlights the juxtaposition of Celsus' pardon and Tigellinus' punishment; in Plutarch (*O.* 2) the two episodes are separated by material that T. puts later (77.2n. *consul ipse,* 90.1n. *reliquias... conuersas*). T. adds episodes from the reign of Galba, not entirely successfully (72.1n. *impetrato... exitio*), and information about Tigellinus' political rise (72.1 *Ofonius... strepere*), while omitting some details (Tigellinus' disease (Plut. *G.* 17.4) and his suicide ruse (72.3n. *deformes moras*)). The story's exemplary value is declared by the moral commentary (72.1nn. *exsultatio, uirilia scelera,* 72.2*haud dubie... impunitatis,* 72.3nn. *foedam uitam, exitu... inhonesto*) and the high-impact style (72.1n. *quia uelocius erat,* 72.3nn. *inter... oscula, deformes moras, sectis... faucibus*). **exsultatio** connects this scene with others on mob behaviour (4.2n. *primo gaudentium impetu*, 4.3n. *plebs sordido et circo ac theatris sueta*); Plutarch, by contrast, connects the punishment of Tigellinus with Otho's other support-winning measures: *O.* 2.1 'Nothing so won the Romans over to Otho (ᾠκειώσατο πρὸς αὑτόν) as the treatment of Tigellinus.' **consecuta:** sc. *est.* **impetrato Tigellini exitio:** *impetrato* suggests that Tigellinus' punishment was achieved against some resistance. The resistance was Galba's: in every other source the call for punishment is heard first under Galba, who issued an edict denying the request (Plut. *G.* 17.4, Suet. *G.*15.2, Dio 64.3.3). Plutarch even reports Galba's justification ('he declared that Tigellinus was wasting away with consumption and had not much longer to live, and advised them not to exasperate the government or force it to be tyrannical'), but denies him credit for mildness by implying that Vinius, bribed by Tigellinus, had engineered the pardon (cf. 72.2 *apud Galba Titi Vini potentia defensus*). The blending of the two episodes is responsible for the odd picture in 72.3 of crowds in Rome persisting in full cry for Tigellinus' death until (*donec*! see n.) it occurred in Sinuessa, several days' journey from Rome. **Ofonius Tigellinus:** praetorian prefect from 62, implicated in many of the crimes and scandals of Nero's last years (murder: *A.* 14.57, 16.14.3, 16.18.3, 16.20.2; persecution of Octavia: *A.* 14.60.3; fire: *A.* 15.40.2; parties: *A.* 15.37; trip to Greece: Dio 63. 12.3–13.1, etc.; further references in *PIR*² O 91). According to Plutarch (*G.* 17.3) he was 'the man who made Nero worthy of death'. He was instrumental in the suppression of the Pisonian conspiracy (*A.* 15.58.3, 15.72.1, Suet. *Ner.* 15.2), but after Nero's death he was forced from office by Nymphidius Sabinus (5.1 n.). **parentibus . . . pueritia . . . senecta:** abl. of quality. The negative colouring of the associated adj. makes a striking background for the high offices mentioned next. **foeda pueritia:** he was exiled in 39 for adultery with the *princeps*' sister Agrippina (Dio 59.23.9). Various other allegations survive in a scholium to Juvenal 1.155 (see *PIR*²). For his *impudica senecta* see below. **praefecturam . . . uitiis adeptus:** at *A.* 14.51.2 Tigellinus' *uetus impudicitia* and *infamia* moved Nero to appoint him praetorian praefect (similarly Dio 62.13.3); cf. 14.57.1 *malas artes quibus solis pollebat*, 15.50.3 *per saeuitiam impudicitiamque Tigellinus in animo principis anteibat.* **alia praemia uirtutum:** e.g. influence (*A.* 14.48.1), legacies (*A.* 16.17.5, 16.19.3), *horti* (*A.* 15.40.2). **quia uelocius erat:** for the scorn cf. *A.* 16.17.3 *acquirendae potentiae breuius iter credebat per procurationes.* **crudelitatem:** he is the very type of cruelty for Juvenal (1.155–7), a man liable to punish criticism with burning at the stake; cf. *A.* 15.58.3 *Tigellini* *saeuas percunctationes*, 15.61.2; Dio associates him with the torture of Epicharis (62.27.3, for which see *A.* 15.57.1–2), T. with the torture of a freedman (*A.* 16.20.2). **auaritiam:** less prominent in T.'s portrait, but perhaps hinted at *A.* 16.14.3. Dio reports bribes extracted by Tigellinus for protection from Nero: 62.28.4, 63.21.2; cf. 71.2 *haud dubie seruauerat.* **uirilia scelera:** the qualities of the manly control (*uirile seruitium*) exercised by Agrippina include *seueritas, superbia, impudicitia*, and *cupido auri immensa* (*A.* 12.7.3). Cf. also Sal. *Cat.* 24.1 on Sempronia: *multa saepe uirilis audaciae facinora commiserat.* **corrupto ad omne facinus Nerone:** in public opinion, according to Plutarch (*G.* 17.2), Tigellinus was 'the tyrant's tutor and trainer'. T. illustrates the relationship at *A.* 14.57–9 (introduced by *ualidiorque in dies Tigellinus et malas artes, quibus solis pollebat, gratiores ratus si principem societate scelerum obstringeret, metus eius rimatur*), where Tigellinus is indirectly responsible for the deaths of two eminent men; see also above on *Ofonius Tigellinus.* He was directly responsible for the party described at length (*ut exemplum*) at *A.* 15.37.1–4. And at *A.* 15.61.2 he and Poppaea are named *saeuienti principi intimum consiliorum.* **quaedam ignaro ausus:** Tigellinus inflames Nero against rivals for his own influence (*A.* 15.50.3, 16.18.3). Perhaps also meant are the bribes he extracted for protection from Nero (see above on *auaritia*). **desertor ac proditor:** cf. Plut. *G.* 17.3 'betrayed and forsook him'. The details are not known, though betrayal is also mentioned at Jos. *BJ* 4.492. The reproach is a standard one: 2.44.1, *A.* 2.10.1 (with Heubner *ad loc.*). **flagitauere:** sc. *ii*, the antecedent of *quibus . . . et quibus.*

72.2 Titi Vini potentia defensus: sc. *est.* See above on *impetrato Tigellini exitio.* Plutarch gives more circumstantial detail: *G.* 17.5 'Tigellinus celebrated his safety with sacrifices and prepared a splendid feast, and Vinius, rising from beside the emperor after dinner, went to a drinking bout at Tigellinus' house, taking along his marriageable daughter.' Tigellinus gave her gifts of money and jewellery. **seruatam ab eo filiam:** no details are known. For Crispina see 13.2n. **haud dubie seruauerat:** *haud dubie* signals T.'s deviation from the tradition preserved by Plutarch (*G.* 17.2), namely, that Tigellinus 'won over Vinius with large bribes'. T.'s version prompts a general reflection on corruption in high places (*quia . . . impunitatis*). **quippe tot interfectis:** 72.1n. *Ofonius Tigellinus.* For the construction see 32.1n. *quippe . . . postulaturis.* **effugium in futurum:** sc. *erat*; for the *uariatio* with a causal abl. (*clementia*) cf. 12.3n. *odium.* **cura:** sc. *erat.* **uices** 'reciprocal exchange' *OLD* 4a–b.

72.3 recenti Titi Vini inuidia: 7.1n., 12.3. **concurrere . . . strepere:** historic inf. **ubi plurima uulgi licentia:** 32.1n. *in circo aut theatro*; cf. Plin. *Nat.* 34.62 *tanta populi Romani contumacia fuit ut theatri clamoribus reponi apoxyomenon* (a statue) *flagitauerit.* **in circum ac theatra . . . donec:** locations and conjunction match those of Plutarch's Galba episode (see above on *impetrato . . . exilio*): *G.* 17.4 'in all the theatres and circuses they would not cease demanding him until they were quelled by an edict of the emperor'; for the location cf. 4.3 *plebs sordida et circo ac theatris sueta.* **effusi** agrees with the plural sense of *populus.* **Sinuessanas aquas:** Terme di San Ricco, near Mondragone, in Campania. From Plut. *O.* 2.3 we learn that Tigellinus had an estate there (τοὺς περὶ Σινόεσσαν ἀγρούς) and boats waiting to take him into exile. Claudius went there for his health (*A.* 12.66.1); the waters were said to cure barrenness in women and insanity in men (Plin. *Nat.* 31.8). **supremae necessitatis:** the phrase encourages comparison with more honourable deaths (3.1n. *supremae . . . necessitates*). According to Plutarch *O.* 2.3, Otho simply sent a summons, to which Tigellinus responded by taking his own life (see below on *deformes moras*). **inter stupra concubinarum et oscula:** a more shocking scenario than that of Plut. *O.* 2.2, which connects the sex ('unholy and unspeakable grovellings with filthy prostitutes . . . ') with Tigellinus' final illness, not his suicide ('. . . for which his unbridled nature panted as he himself was dying a painful death'). **deformes moras:** solemn and vague where Plutarch is matter-of-fact (*O.* 2.3): Tigellinus tried to bribe the messenger and, failing this, asked him to wait while he shaved. Whereupon he cut his throat. **sectis nouacula faucibus:** without the story of Tigellinus' ruse (see n. above) these details seem incongruous and, after the euphemism *suprema necessitas*, vulgar. Other deaths by razor are less graphic: *A.* 11.3.2 *uenas exsoluit*, *A.* 15.63.2 *bracchia ferro exsoluunt*, *A.* 16.35.1 *porrectis . . . uenis.* **infamem uitam:** in Plut. *O.* 2.2 the assessment of Tigellinus' lifestyle – 'the most extreme punishment and the equivalent of many deaths' – is focalized by 'reasonable men'. **exitu sero et inhonesto:** 3.1n. *laudatis . . . exitus*; cf. 3.84.5 (on Vitellius) *deformitas exitus misericordiam abstulerat.*

73 Caluia Crispinilla: another disreputable adherent of Nero's, not mentioned in the *Annals* or the parallel tradition here, but part of Nero's train on the trip to Greece, with his 'wife' Sporus her particular charge (Dio 63.12; *PIR*² C 363). On the source see Townend (1964) 353. **uariis frustrationibus** replays, in abstract terms (cf. 3.9.2 *per uarias moras*), Otho's rescue of Celsus (45.2). No details are known. **aduersa . . . fama** 'with harm to the reputation'; abl. of attendant circumstances (*NLS* §43.5ii). **Clodium Macrum:** 7.1 n. **famem . . . molita:** cf. Stat. *Theb.* 4.11 *Argiuisque sitim Bacchus molitur.* Vespasian had the same idea in Alexandria: 3.48.3 *ut . . . urbem . . . fame urgeret.* Threats to the grain supply caused instant consternation in Rome (see, e.g., 4.38.2). According to Josephus, Africa fed Rome eight months of the year, Alexandria four (*BJ* 2.383, 386). Crispinilla's subsequent popularity shows the inability of the populace (*totius . . . ciuitatis*!) to attend to its own most crucial interests. **consulari matrimonio:** her husband is not known. No name is necessary for conveying the shocking (to T.) fact that a consular, any consular, married such a woman. **potens pecunia et orbitate:** *captatio* 'inheritance-hunting' figures prominently in social criticism of the imperial period. In T.: *G.* 20.3 *nec ulla orbitatis pretia*, *D.* 6.2 *orbitati . . . dari*, *A.* 3.25.1 *praeualida orbitate*, 13.19.2 *ne opibus et orbitate . . . poteretur*, 13.42.4 *testamenta et orbos . . . capi*, 13.52.2 *ualuit . . . pecuniosa orbitate et senecta*, 14.40.1 *orbitate et pecunia insidiis obnoxius.* See Champlin (1991) 87–102 with his App. 4 and Muecke (1993) on Hor. *Sat.* 2.5.

74.1 crebrae . . . epistulae: in Plut. *O.* 4.2–3 Otho's overtures follow news of Illyricum's support (76.1 in T.), but cf. Murison (1999) 61 'Tacitus . . . in placing this item soon after Otho's accession will have applied a common-sense corrective.' When Civilis and Classicus make overtures to Cerealis on sharing power in the *imperium Galliarum* (4.75.1) he does not reply, in fact he imprisons the messenger. **muliebribus blandimentis:** 22.1 n. *mollis.* **infectae:** for the metaphor see 4.1 n. *quid . . . aegrum.* **pecuniam et gratiam et quemcumque quietis locum prodigae uitae legisset:** cf. Plut. *O.* 4.2 'a large sum of money and a city in which he might spend an easy and enjoyable life in peace'. The other sources report other offers: Suet. *O.* 8.1 *consortem imperii generumque se Vitellio obtulit*, Dio 64.10.1 'joint rule'. **quietis locum:** one branch of M's descendants offers *locum*, the other *locis*, which Heubner adopts with a further slight change (*e quietis locis*). **primo mollius:** cf. Plut. *O.* 4.3 'feigning calm at first', describing Vitellius' response. **stulta utrimque et indecora simulatione:** T. applies Plutarch's 'feigning' (κατειρωνευόμενος) to both and editorializes. **quasi rixantes:** another insertion, making the point that this was not a quarrel, but a conflict on which depended the fates of many. For the implicit antithesis cf. *D.* 26.4 *non pugnat sed rixatur.* **stupra ac flagitia . . . obiectauere:** cf. Plut. *O.* 4.3 'But thereafter in anger they wrote abusing one another with many shameful insults.' Plutarch mentions extravagance, effeminacy, lack of military experience, and debt. Their subordinates were also exchanging letters (2.30.2). **inuicem** 'reciprocally' *OLD* 3. **neuter falso:** wonderfully brief; cf. Plut. *O.* 4.3 'not falsely, but foolishly and ridiculously, seeing that one was insulting the other with reproaches that fit both'. For public opinion on the two see 50.1 and 50.3.

74.2 quos Galba miserat: 19.2n. **rursus...misit:** cf. Suet. *O.* 8.1 *auctor senatui fuit mittendae legationis, quae doceret electum iam principem, quietem concordiamque suaderet.* T. doesn't specify the mission of either deputation (neither accomplished anything) but rather the self-interested behaviour of the senators involved (19.2 *ambitu ... metus ... spes*, 74.2 *promptius*). **legionem Italicam:** 59.2n. **quae Lugduni agebant:** in addition to the *legio Italica*, the *ala Tauriana* (59.2n.) and an urban cohort (64.3n.). **specie senatus:** Otho made the most of the legitimacy conferred by the senate on his principate (see 47.1, 84.3). For the thought cf. 76.2 *erat grande momentum in ... praetexto senatus.* **promptius quam ut:** 65.1 n. *crebrius ... ut.* If the defection of these senators increased Vitellius' authority, or detracted from Otho's, no one mentions it. **simulationem officii:** 'Their real purpose was to watch the behaviour of the senators, but still more to make contact with the Vitellian legionaries' (Chilver *ad loc.*). Otho also deputes praetorians to watch their own commanders (87.1). **antequam legionibus miscerentur:** on the dangers of 'mixing' see 32.1 n. *mixtis*, and cf. 9.2n. *nec uitiis nec uiribus miscebantur.* The ease of spreading disloyalty is illustrated at 25.1, 54.1–3.

74.3 addidit...Fabius Valens: this detail suggests that the deputation, *qua* deputation, got no further than Valens, who sent the praetorians back to Rome (letters in hand), the senators on to Vitellius; see Fabia (1913). **epistulas:** for letters, again *nomine Germanici exercitus*, to the Pannonian legions cf. 67.2. Vespasian wrote in his own name, to great effect (3.3, cf. 2.86.4). **tanto ante traditum:** Vitellius was acclaimed on 2 and 3 January (57.1 nn.), Otho on the 15th; the exaggeration conveys Valens' tone.

75.1 promissis ... ac minis: exemplified (in reverse order) in the *ut*-clause. **neque** 'but ... not' *OLD* 5. **mutata:** sc. *est.* **missi:** sc. *sunt.* **Vitellianis impune:** they were undetected, but not unsuspected (85.2). **per tantam hominum multitudinem mutua ignorantia fallentibus:** cf. *A.* 4.74.4 *quippe Romae ... magnitudine urbis incertum quod quisque negotium pergat,* in a similar geographical antithesis.

75.2 ipsi filioque eius: L. Salvius Otho Titianus was Otho's older brother, cos. 52, *frater Arualis* by 58, procos. Asiae 65 with Agricola as his quaestor (*Agr.* 6.2 *proconsul ad omnen auiditatem pronus*; *PIR* s 111). He was cos. II with his brother from 26 January; Otho entrusted to him first Rome (90.3) then the military campaign (2.23.5, 2.33.3, 2.39.1). He won little credit thereby, and was pardoned by Vitellius: 2.60.2 *pietate et ignauia excusatus.* His son, L. Salvius Otho Cocceianus, whom Otho thought of adopting (Plut. *O.* 16.2), was with Otho at Brixellum (2.48.2) and survived until the reign of Domitian, when he was executed for celebrating his uncle's birthday (Suet. *Dom.* 10.3). **mater ac liberi:** Vitellius' mother, Sextilia, gets a fine cameo at 2.64.2. His children remained safe under Otho (2.47.2, 2.38.2), but the son who was hailed as 'Germanicus' (2.59.3 *infanti filio*, 3.67.2 *paruulus filius*) was killed on Mucianus' orders (4.80.1; cf. Suet. *Vit.* 18.1, Dio 65.22). For his daughter (cf. 59.2n. *Valerius Asiaticus*) Vespasian eventually arranged a marriage (Suet. *Ves.* 14.1). His first son predeceased him (Suet. *Vit.* 6.1). **stetit** 'continued to exist' *OLD* 17. **incertum an metu:** the expected alternative *an clementia* is expressed instead by an independent sentence; cf. 23.1n.

76.1 primus . . . secutae: Otho's supporters are more numerous, but also more distant than Vitellius' (59.2, 70.1), and none contributed materially, such was the speed with which the campaign was concluded. **fiduciam:** similar news produced *superbia* and *socordia* in Vitellius (2.73). **ex Illyrico nuntius:** for the Danube garrison see 9.2n. *excitae . . . legiones.* On their support for Otho see 2.11.1. On the late arrival at Bedriacum of a large portion of the force see Murison (1993) 96–9. **allatum:** sc. *est.* **Cluuius Rufus:** 8.1n. **conuersam:** sc. *esse.* **Aquitania**, lying between the Loire and the Pyrenees, was an ungarrisoned province. It was not involved in any of the incidents of Gallic unrest described in *H.*, which centred on the Rhine and the legions based there (cf. 51.3, 54.1, 57.2, etc.). Its initial declaration for Otho in the face of the German armies' prior proclamation of Vitellius was brave, but futile. **Iulio Cordo:** not mentioned elsewhere. **in uerba Othonis obstricta:** for other oath formulas see 36.2n. *praeire sacramentum*, 36.3 *sacramentum eius accepit*, 55.1n. *adactae*, 76.2. For *obstringere* 'bind' (*OLD* 4), cf. 54.3 *obstringuntur . . . legiones.* **nusquam . . . amor:** sc. *erat*; for the *uariatio* see 12.3n. *odium.* **mutabantur:** sc. *prouinciae.* For the theme see 11.2–3. **facili transitu:** for authorial comment in an abl. abs. appendix see Intro. §14.

76.2 longinquae prouinciae et quicquid . . . mari dirimitur: the relative clause restates the subject; cf. 85.3 *in clamore . . . et ubi.* The military potential of the area is reviewed (in calculating Vespasian's resources) at 2.6.2. For other phrases referring to this general area see *A.* 2.43.1 *prouinciae quae mari diuiduntur* with Goodyear (1981) *ad loc.*; documents use *transmarinae prouinciae* (*Tab. Siar.* fr. I 15, *SCPP* 31). **grande momentum:** 59.1 n. *grande momentum sociae aut aduersae*; for the *uariatio* cf. 12.3n. *odium.* **praetexto senatus:** 74.2n. *specie senatus*; for the phrase see 19.2n. *maiore . . . laturus* and cf. Sen. *Ep.* 71.9 *illud pulcherrimum rei publicae praetextum, optimates.* **prior auditus:** sc. *Otho*; cf. Liv. 6.2.9 *tantum Camillus auditus imperator terroris intulerat.* **Iudaicum exercitum Vespasianus:** 10.3nn. **Syriae legiones:** 10.1 n. **Mucianus:** 10.1–2nn. **sacramento Othonis adegere:** reported with more context at 2.6.1 *sacramentum Othonis acceperat uterque exercitus, pernicibus, ut assolet, nuntiis et tarda mole ciuilis belli, quod longa concordia quietus Oriens tum primum parabat.* **tenebantur:** cf. 3.12.1 *quae prouinciae Vespasiano tenebantur*; *obtinere* (cf. 79.5 *Moesiam obtinens*) is the more usual term.

76.3 idem Africae obsequium: sc. *erat*; three words for the main clause, thirty-five for the appendix. **obsequium** 'allegiance' *OLD* 3; cf. *G.* 29.2 *est in eodem obsequio et Mattiacorum gens*, Plin. *Ep.* 10.17b.1 *prouinciam intraui, quam in eo obsequio, in ea erga te fide quam . . . mereris inueni.* **initio . . . festinauit:** cf. 2.79.1 *initium ferendi ad Vespasianum imperii Alexandriae coeptum, festinante Tiberio Alexandro.* **initio Carthagine orto:** founded by Julius Caesar and reorganized by Augustus, Colonia Julia Karthago was the chief city of Roman Africa, well on its way at this point to becoming the second great city of the West (after Rome; see Rives (1995) 22–7). It was the seat of the governor of Africa Proconsularis (a post held earlier by Galba, Vitellius, and Vespasian, but not Otho) and of the provincial administration; for the province's military complement see 7.1 n. *Clodii Macri.* **neque exspectata . . . auctoritate:** both the failure to follow the governor's lead and the initiative taken by an imperial freedman illustrate the civil war's disrupting effect on established hierarchies. **Vipstani Aproniani:** cos. 59 (*A.* 14.1.1), *frater Arualis* from 57 until his death in 86; *PIR* v 465. **Crescens:** only here, but for a possible reference to his later career see *PIR*[2] c 1576. **nam et hi . . . partem se rei publicae faciunt:** for another freedman playing a public role see on Moschus in 87.2n. †*immutatus*†. As in Book 1, so elsewhere T.'s references to freedmen in public service incorporate gratuitous insults: 3.12.3: *is quoque inter duces habebatur*, 5.9.3 *ius regium seruili ingenio exercuit*, *A.* 12.60.4 *cum Claudius libertos, quos rei familiari praefecerat, sibique et legibus adaequauerit*, 13.2.2 *Pallas . . . modum* *liberti egressus*, 14.39.2 *dux et exercitus . . . seruitiis oboedirent*; cf. T.'s admiration for the absence of publicly active *liberti* in Germany: *G.* 25.2 *liberti non multum supra seruos sunt, raro aliquod momentum in domo, numquam in ciuitate.* Pliny expresses the same outrage at great length in *Ep.* 8.6 and 7.29. Aubrion (1991) 2632 points out that no freedman gets an obituary from T., not even prominent ones such as Pallas (Pliny's *bête noire*) and Narcissus. **epulum plebi:** public dinners are a widely attested form of benefaction both in Rome and throughout the empire (see *TLL* s.v. 706.78–707.56; for a recent discussion see D'Arms (1998)); for a freedman host outside of Rome we have Petronius' fictional Trimalchio, who both gave a dinner to the populace (presumably of 'Puteoli') and advertised his generosity on his tomb (*Sat.* 71.9, cf. *Sat.* 45.10). **populus pleraque . . . festinauit** communicates manner, not content, as at 7.3 *festinantes.* Content can be surmised from other 'declaration of allegiance' scenes (flattering speeches: 2.80.2 *in adulationem effusos*; deposition of statues: 3.7.2 *Galbae imagines discordia temporum subuersas in omnibus municipiis*) but T.'s expression pronounces it unimportant. **ciuitates secutae:** sc. *sunt.* For the cities of Roman Africa see *CAH*[2] XI 539–43.

77.1 principatus fortunam: 10.3n. *post fortunam*, 52.3n. *uenienti Fortunae.* **Otho ut in multa pace munia imperii obibat:** for at least a month and a half. The movement order to troops was not sent out until the first week of March (Murison (1993) 95–100). One possibly fatal omission was Otho's neglect of Antonius Primus, *bello non spernendus* (2.86.2). Vitellius showed similar obliviousness, but worse behaviour: 2.73 *ipse exercitusque, ut nullo aemulo, saeuitia libidine raptu in externos mores proruperant.* For the antithesis between *princeps* and rival cf. 2.87.1 *dum haec per prouincias a Vespasiano . . . geruntur, Vitellius contemptior in dies segniorque . . . graui urbem agmine petebat.* **munia imperii:** the measures T. reports in chh. 77–8 (consulships, priesthoods, civil status, municipal affairs, provincial administration, honorific displays) affected the civilian population of the empire starting with the eminent (consuls) and ending with the *plebs*, with various provincial groups between; none was important in the fight with Vitellius. For generosity to military men see 79.5nn. Plutarch and Suetonius have scattered reports of items mentioned here (see nn.); Dio's report is brief but comprehensive: 64.8.2 'As for the senators, he remitted sentences against some and granted various other favours to others; he went regularly to theatres courting the populace; he gave citizenship to foreigners and announced many other measures.' **quaedam** introduces an appendix to a period shaped by the *Vitellio . . . Otho* antithesis. The appendix has the same antithetical structure (*quaedam . . . pleraque*), and is followed by an appendix of its own, *ex praesenti usu properando. quaedam* and *pleraque* are in apposition to *munia*, but the second appendix, an explanation of *contra decus*, requires reinterpretation of *pleraque* as object of *properando*: 'hurrying on (sc. *pleraque*) out of present need'; for the shift cf. 85.3n. *uulgaribus conuiciis.* Some editors (Chilver, Hellegouarc'h) take both *quaedam* and *pleraque* as objects of *properando.* Pliny employs the same antithesis between the dignified and the expedient: *Pan.* 75.3 *cum ex utilitate tum ex dignitate publica fuit.* **ex dignitate . . . contra decus:** where T. gives his own verdict here and below (78.1 *largitione*; cf. 78.2 *inter quae . . . excusata*), Plutarch reports a contemporary reaction (*O.* 1.3, quoted below on *recoluit*). **properando:** cf. 23.1 *appellando* and *inserendo.*

77.2 consul . . . ipse: for the consulships of 69 see Townend (1962) and Chilver's summary *ad loc.* At Plut. *O.* 1.2–3 the consular designations (and priesthoods of 77.3) come between the pardon of Celsus and the death of Tigellinus and the only name given is that of Verginius. **in kalendas Martias** 'up to the first of March'; see Townend (1962) 122. **Verginio:** 8.2nn. **exercitui . . . delenimentum:** 22.2n. *Othoni . . . comes.* **Pompeius Vopiscus:** only here, and in office for a single month (March). **Viennensium:** 59.2n. *Valerius Asiaticus*, 65.1n., 66.1. **honori datum:** sc. *esse consulatum.* **Caelio ac Flauio Sabinis:** Cn. Arulenus Caelius Sabinus (*PIR*² A 1194) and T. Flavius Sabinus (*PIR*² F 354), the latter being the son of Otho's urban prefect (46.1n.) and nephew of Vespasian. They were consuls for April and May, i.e. during the transition from Otho's principate to Vitellius'. The former, who survived to become a distinguished juriconsult under Vespasian, is not mentioned again in the extant books. The latter takes command of Othonian troops at 2.36.2, surrenders them at 2.51, and survives to hold a second consulship in 72. Two sons fall victim to Domitian (2.3n. *nobilitas*); see further Townend (1961), Gilmartin Wallace (1987), B. W. Jones (1992) 44–8. **Arrio Antonino:** not mentioned again by T., but he, like the other men mentioned here, was prominent during the Flavian period. Antoninus was governor of Asia, consul a second time (perhaps in 97), and friend of Nerva (*PIR*² A 1084). Pliny addresses three very complimentary letters to him (4.3, 4.18, 5.15); they exchanged poems. He is one of the potential eye-witness sources for Tacitus (Intro. §17).

77.3 sed . . . recoluit: more detailed and more Roman in sensibility (esp. *auitis ac paternis sacerdotiis*) than Plut. *O.* 1.3 'He honoured with priesthoods those who were preeminent in age or reputation.' **pontificatus auguratusque:** there were sixteen pontifices and sixteen augurs; no Othonian appointment is known. **cumulum dignitatis:** *cumulus* 'pinnacle' (*OLD* 4), in apposition to *pontificatus auguratusque*. 'When magistracies no longer gave real power, priesthoods began to be regarded as higher distinctions' (Alford *ad loc.*), but perhaps not by T.: *Agr.* 44.3 *et consulari ac triumphalibus ornamentis praedito* (sc. *Agricolae*) *quid aliud astruere fortuna poterat?* **recens:** adv. (*OLD recens*²) with *reuersos*. **recoluit** 'renewed a show of respect for' *OLD* 3; cf. 3.7.2 *Galbae imagines ... in omnibus municipiis recoli iussit*, *A.* 3.72.1 *Lepidus ... auitum decus recoluit*. According to Plutarch, Otho's overtures were successful: *O.* 1.3 'Wherefore the citizens of highest birth and greatest influence ... became more cheerful in their hopes for a government which wore a face so smiling' (ἡγεμονίαν ὥσπερ διαμειδιῶσαν). **redditus ... senatorius locus:** sc. *est*. Similarly for Antonius Primus under Galba (2.86.1). Early in Vespasian's reign, however, Mucianus either denies or, probably (*redegit*), cancels the restoration of two other former senators (4.44.2). (But see on *maiestatem* below.) T.'s dislike of interference with the verdicts of the senatorial court (and of the presence of former convicts on the senatorial benches beside him) is clear. See further Talbert (1984) 27–9. **ceciderant** 'they had been condemned' *OLD* 11b; for Cadius Rufus see *A.* 12.22.3 (A.D. 49), for Pedius Blaesus 14.18.1 (A.D. 59). The third name is garbled in the manuscripts of T. and no other source mentions any of the three. Those convicted of extortion were *infames*, ineligible to participate in public life. **ignoscentibus:** fellow senators. **maiestatem:** shorthand for *crimen laesae maiestatis* (*OLD* 3). Part of T.'s point here is that anybody on trial for *maiestas*, a charge nearly impossible to escape (cf. *A.* 1.74.3 *ineuitabile crimen*) for guilty and innocent alike, was taken to be innocent, regardless of other crimes he (or she) may have been charged with (e.g. *A.* 3.38.1, 4.19.4). The other part, however, is that *maiestas* was not the charge against the two identifiable senators here. According to Dio, Vespasian did cancel *maiestas* verdicts issued under Nero and his successors, restoring citizen status to living and dead victims alike (66.9.1 with Murison (1999) *ad loc.* and Henrichs (1968) 74–5 for precedents).

78.1 prouinciarum animos: cf. 4.1 *habitus prouinciarum* (with 8.1n. *hic ... habitus animorum fuit*), 2.4.2 *suspensis prouinciarum ... mentibus*. Otho's overtures reach civilian communities from Spain to Cappadocia. **Hispalensibus ... dedit:** none of his measures in the west outweighed the Vitellian advantages of proximity and brutality, and none is mentioned by any other source. **Hispalensibus et**

Emeritensibus: Hispalis (mod. Seville) and Emerita Augusta (mod. Merida) were presumably known to Otho from his eight years in Lusitania (based in Emerita): 13.3n. *in prouinciam Lusitaniam.* New settlers meant revenue from land not previously cultivated (*A.* 13.31.2 *coloniae Capua atque Nuceria additis ueteranis firmatae sunt,* cf. 14.27.2 and Liv. 43. 17.1). **Lingonibus:** 53.3n. *Treueri ac Lingones.* For their initiative in spreading their dislike of Galba to the German army see 54.1. By 57.2 they had declared for Vitellius. For other Othonian measures addressed to those in the Vitellian sphere cf. 77.2 *exercitui Germanico delenimentum* and *Viennensium honori.* On the text see Chilver *ad loc.* **ciuitatem Romanam:** 8.1n. *recenti ... ciuitatis.* **prouinciae Baeticae Maurorum ciuitates dono dedit:** presumably another revenue-increasing measure. The gift took these peoples out of the hands of the provincial procurator. It is unclear whether it contributed to contemporary turbulence (11.2n. *duae Mauretaniae*). **noua iura:** none known. Cappadocia experienced further rearrangement under Vespasian: see 2.81.2 and Suet. *Ves.* 8.4 with B. W. Jones (2000) *ad loc.* **ostentata magis quam mansura:** cf. *A.* 6.37.2 *initia ... secunda neque diuturna.* For the emendation (Ernesti's) of M's *ostenta* see 52.2n. *ut Vitellius.*

78.2 statuas Poppaeae: 13.3n. Her statues had already been toppled and restored once (*A.* 14.61.1); they presumably went down again after Nero's death. **per senatus consultum:** for a similarly honorific *s.c.* see 4.40.2. **creditus est ... agitauisse:** the reticence of *creditus est* is striking since both Plutarch and Suetonius offer evidence of Othonian initiative in aligning himself with Nero. From Suetonius we learn that Otho reappointed Neronian procurators and freedmen and financed further construction on Nero's *domus aurea* (*O.* 7.1; the former also in Dio 64.8.3 along with an Othonian liaison with Nero's *deliciae* Sporus). In a later passage Suetonius mentions Otho's intended marriage with Nero's last wife, Statilia Messalina (*O.* 10.2). Cf. Plut. *O.* 3.2 'Cluvius Rufus tells us that documents ... were sent to Spain in which "Nero" was added to the name "Otho,"' a report that agrees, at least in part, with Suet. *O.* 7.1 *ut quidam tradiderunt, etiam diplomatidis et primis epistulis suis ad quosdam prouinciarum praesides Neronis cognomen adiecit.* The two also agree that Otho eventually stopped this practice. (The epitome of Dio has only a simple notice: 64.8.2[1] 'he immediately added Nero's name to his own'.) T. may be reserving the 'honouring Nero' theme for Vitellius (2.95.1). More interesting is the possibility that he is omitting this material for the sake of his characterization of Otho: alignment with Nero is not part of Otho's 'platform' in his initial bid for power (36; for his actual connections with Nero see 13.2n. *M. Othone*, 13.3n. *conscium libidinum*; for their similarities 13.4n. *ut similem*), the re-erection of Poppaea's statues is presented as evidence of Otho's love for her (13.3n. *suspectum*) rather than, say, as part of a general revival of things Neronian, and, more generally, T. takes pains to show in Otho qualities of character absent from his Nero (e.g. 22.1 *non erat Othonis mollis et corpori similis animus* and 71.1 *non ... torpescere*, but especially in the story of Otho's end). The connections T. does report involve no Othonian initiative (*fuere qui ... populus et miles*). Other scholars maintain that T.'s omissions reflect his source here (Chilver *ad loc.*, also Townend (1960) 102–3, 106–7 and (1964) 371 n. 79). **spe uulgum alliciendi:** for the populace's pleasure in remembrances of Nero cf. 2.95.1 and on *quibusdam ... acclamauit* below. **imagines Neronis proponerent:** similarly in the parallel tradition (Plut. *O.* 3.1, Suet. *O.* 7.1; cf. Suet. *Ner.* 57 *non defuerunt qui ... imagines praetextatas in rostris proferrent*). Galba himself restored the statues of members of the imperial family murdered by Nero (Dio 64.3.4c). For more on imperial *imagines* see 40.2n. *scelus ... successit.* **quibusdam diebus populus et miles ... Neroni Othoni acclamauit:** also reported, with small variations, in the parallel tradition (Plut. *O.* 3.1 'to give pleasure to the multitude he did not at first refuse to be hailed in the theatres as Nero', Suet. *O.* 7.1 *ab infima plebe appellatus Nero nullum indicium recusantis dedit*) but only T. has the sarcastic *tamquam ... astruerent.* **nobilitatem ac decus astruerent:** for *astruere* 'heap on' (*OLD* 2) cf. *Agr.* 44.3 *consulari ... quid aliud astruere fortuna poterat?* Plin. *Pan.* 46.8 *omnibus ... hanc astruis laudem.* **in suspenso tenuit** 'he kept [the matter] undecided'; cf. Plin. *Ep.* 10.31.4 *rem totam dum te consulerem in suspenso reliqui*; the slight ambiguity arising from the omission of the object of *tenuit* (*rem* or *se*?) is resolved by *uel*: if Otho were himself *in suspenso* (*OLD* 2) one would expect him to feel *both* fear and shame. **uetandi metu uel agnoscendi pudore:** the suggestion of pusillanimity is absent from Plutarch's account, according to which Otho did not *at first* refuse the appellation 'Nero' (which suggests that he did refuse it eventually), and that Otho ceased producing courier-passes under the name 'Nero Otho' when it became clear that the practice offended important men (*O.* 3.1–2).

79.1 ciuile bellum ... externa: the connection between internal and external affairs is cited again after the Flavian victory to show the empire's gradual return to health: 4.72.2 *paruere* (sc. *milites*) *posito ciuium* *bello ad externa modestiores.* **externa sine cura habebantur** introduces the theme of the threat to empire from civil war, which is further developed at 3.46.1–3 (on another incursion across the Danube) and, at great length, in Books 4 and 5 on Civilis. No other source reports the incidents of this chapter, which, in addition to illustrating Otho's reign, give scope to T. the ethnographer. **caesis . . . cohortibus:** the forts of these auxiliary troops would have been closer to the enemy than the legionary fortresses were (see the maps in Webster (1998), ch. 2 'Frontier Systems', esp. p. 60). **Sarmatica gens:** 2.1 n. **Moesiam irruperant:** the province held, besides its auxiliary troops (cf. *cohortibus* above and *auxiliis* below), whose number is unknown, three legions (III *Gallica*, VII *Claudia*, VIII *Augusta*; roughly 15,000 men), only one of which fought the invaders. **ex ferocia et successu:** 51.1 n. *ferox . . . exercitus*; cf. 3.77.4 *miles secundis . . . ferox*, 4.19.1 *intumuere . . . superbia ferociaque*, 4.28.3 *successu rerum ferocior Ciuilis.* **incuriosos:** 13.3n. **tertia legio:** III *Gallica*, recently arrived in Moesia from Syria (10.1 n. *Syriam . . . legiones*). Its discipline (*omnia proelio apta*, etc.) and success here form the background to its unruly behaviour after Otho's death: 2.85.1, Suet. *Ves.* 6.2 with B. W. Jones (2000) *ad loc.*; see also 79.5n. *M. Aponius.*

79.2 apta: sc. *erant.* **dispersi . . . graues . . . adempta equorum pernicitate:** for the *uariatio* cf. 55.1 n. *raris . . . exspectantes.* **lubrico itinerum:** 26.1 n. *incerta noctis.* **uincti:** for the image cf. *Agr.* 32.2 *clausos quodam modo ac uinctos di uobis tradiderunt*, Liv. 28.2.9 *ad caedem eos uelut uinctos praebebant*, also Sal. *H.* fr. 4.67 (on a battle involving *catafracti*) *ceteri uicem pecorum obtruncabantur.* **mirum:** sc. *est.* **ignauum:** sc. *est.* **per turmas** ≈ *turmatim* 'in squadrons (of cavalry)'. **obstiterit** 'was likely to withstand (them)' *OLD* 4; the primary sequence potential subj. is a form of *repraesentatio* (*NLS* §120; 7.2n. *postquam . . . nequiuerint*).

79.3 conti . . . gladii: lances being wielded by riders, swords by dismounted men, the slipping horses (see below) disable the *conti*, the unwieldy body armour the *gladii.* For the distribution of paired terms see 6.1 n. *alter . . . destruebant.* **usui:** sc. *erant.* **lapsantibus equis et catafractarum pondere:** *lapso* 'slip' first here in prose; cf. Virg. *Aen.* 2.551 *in multo lapsantem* (sc. *Priamum*) *sanguine.* The *catafractes* was a coat of mail worn by both horse and rider; cf. Sal. *H.* fr. 4.66 *equites catafracti, ferrea omni specie* and 4.65 *equis paria operimenta erant, namque linteo ferreas laminas in modum plumae annexuerant.* Mailed cavalry was again encountered in Trajan's war in Dacia (see panels 26 and 31 of his Column; Webster (1998) pl. 19). By Hadrian's time the Romans had their own *alae catafractatae* (Arr. *Tact.*

4; Eadie (1967), Mielczarek (1993)). For the scene cf. *A.* 1.65.5 *illi* (sc. *equi*) *sanguine suo et lubrico paludum lapsantes excussis rectoribus disicere obuios, proterere iacentes*. For the *uariatio* see 14.1 n. *siue . . . Lacone instante.* **id:** the antecedent is *catafractes*, the gender from *tegimen.* **ut . . . ita:** 4.2n. **impenetrabile:** sc. *erat.* **inhabile ad resurgendum:** cf. *Agr.* 36.1 *quod* (sc. hand-to-hand fighting) . . . *et hostibus inhabile, nam Britannorum gladii . . . in arto pugnam non tolerabant, A.* 3.43.2 *inferendis ictis inhabiles* (sc. *crupellarii*), *accipiendis impenetrabiles*, Liv. 24.34.5 *telum ad remittendum inhabile imperitis est*, also *G.* 6.1 (of a spear point) *ferro . . . acri et ad usum habili.*

79.4 facilis 'moving easily' *OLD* 11; for the causal abl. cf. *A.* 3.8.2 *incallidus . . . et facilis iuuenta.* **assultans** 'attacking' *OLD* 2; cf. *A.* 12.35.3 *irrupere ferentarius grauisque miles, illi telis assultantes, hi conferto gradu*, which employs the *eminus / comminus* antithesis used here and (with similar weapons) at 2.36.1 *uulneratum eminus lancea strictis gladiis inuaserant.* **ubi res posceret:** cf. *G.* 6.1 (on Germans wielding spears) *eodem telo prout ratio poscit uel comminus uel eminus pugnent.* In frequentative clauses T. uses both subj. (as here and at 85.2 *attulisset*) and ind. (10.2 *quotiens expedierat*, 36.2 *ut . . . aspexerant*); see *NLS* §194n. and 195–6. **inermem:** i.e. without defensive weapons (*OLD* 1 a). **hiemis aut uulnerum:** for the formal parallel between (singular) abstract and (plural) concrete nouns cf. 32.1 *mixtis seruitiis et dissono clamore.* **absumpti:** sc. *sunt.*

79.5 compertum: sc. *est.* **M. Aponius:** suffect consul under Nero (the year not known), *frater Arvalis* since 57 at the latest (*PIR*² A 938). He declared for Vitellius against the inclination of his troops, who favoured Vespasian (2.60.1, 2.74.1; his fellow governors in Dalmatia and Pannonia, *diuites senes*, did likewise: 2.86.3) and, according to T., used the conflict between Vitellius and Otho as a cover for the attempted murder of one of his own legionary legates, rather tarnishing the military laurels he earned here (2.85.2 *pessimum facinus*). He gave Vitellius incomplete information about the defection in Illyricum (2.96.1) and shortly thereafter went over to Vespasian. He is issued orders by his inferiors (a legionary legate and a procurator) at 3.5.1, arrives in the field at 3.9.3, fails to control rioting men at 3.10.3, and is eventually attacked by them (3.11.1). He escaped by hiding in a bath house (3.11.4). This wealth of (mostly unflattering) detail about Aponius may be due to Vipstanus Messalla, whom T. quotes at 3.25.2 and 3.28.1, and who took command of VII *Claudia* after Aponius' assassination attempt on its legate (see below on *Iulianus Tettius*). Aponius' story is like that of Hordeonius Flaccus (9.1 n.), only less violent. He survived to become *proconsul Asiae* under Vespasian. **Moesiam obtinens:** cf. 2.85.2 *Moesiae rector*, 3.11.1 *Moesici exercitus legatum.* **triumphali statua:** on 1 March the Arval Brethren sacrificed *ob laurum positam* (McC–W 2.63–7); the connection between laurel and triumphal honours suggests that the occasion was the good news from Moesia (Murison (1993) 125n. 17), which would put its arrival very shortly before the beginning of Otho's military initiative against Vitellius (77.1 n. *Otho . . . obibat*). On triumphal honours (which T. mentions again at *Agr.* 40.1, 4.4.2, *A.* 12.28.2) see Maxfield (1981) 105–9; T. is always lukewarm about them. **Fuluus Aurelius** had been legate of III *Gallica* since at least 64; though replaced in that post under Vitellius (3.10.1) he survived to serve as consul (twice; the years are not known) and urban prefect under the Flavians (*PIR*² A 1510; Syme (1987a) 615–16). Originating in Nîmes, he was the first known senator in his family; his career illustrates the first part of Otho's maxim at 84.4 *ex uobis* (sc. *militibus*) *senatores.* **Iulianus Tettius:** legate of VII *Claudia*; he must have been openly pro-Flavian after Otho's death, since the governor of his province tried to assassinate him under cover of party strife (2.85.2; see above on *M. Aponius*). He fled south and skirted the civil war thereafter. In Moesia he was replaced by his tribune Vipstanus Messalla (3.9.3). His whereabouts were still unknown on 1 January 70, when desertion of his legion cost him his praetorship (4.39.1). However, when it was learned that he had made his way to Vespasian the office was restored to him (4.40.2). Julianus became cos. suff. in 83 and fought in Domitian's Dacian war in 88 (Dio 67.10.1, with Murison (1999) *ad loc.*; *PIR* T 102). **Numisius Lupus:** legate of VIII *Augusta*, a position he retained under Vitellius (3.10.1); with his legion he joined the Flavian side (*PIR*² N 210). **consularibus ornamentis:** these privileges of dress and precedence in senatorial debate were 'of strictly limited value for a man's advancement. Only tenure of actual magistracies could further his career' (Talbert (1984) 367); two of the legates here are known to have held further office. The *ornamenta* went to all three legionary legates, though only one legion fought, and to no auxiliary officer (so far as T. reports), though they were present at the battle. **tamquam . . . auxisset:** the claim is standard (Aug. *RG* 26.1 *omnium prouinciarum populi Romani . . . fines auxi*, *A.* 1.31.5 *suis uictoriis augeri rem publicam* (spoken by the seditious German army), etc.) but empty when the emperor had as little to do with the victory as Otho did here (despite *suis . . . suis*). **felix bello:** sc. *esset.*

80–85 *seditio*

From success against an external enemy (ch. 79) T. turns to rioting in Rome. The chain of command in the praetorian guard, already undermined by the soldiers' distrust of their officers and by a general lawlessness (both amply illustrated in the narrative of Otho's coup), collapses after a tribune's miscalculation. When a nighttime opening of the arsenal arouses suspicion, soldiers take up weapons, kill the tribune and two centurions, and rush through Rome demanding sight of the emperor they had made (ch. 80). More blood is shed at the Palace, where a state dinner is in progress. Otho's guests – senators and their wives – take a hasty and ignominious departure (ch. 81) and Otho's pleas appease the soldiers for the moment (82.1). The next day a large bribe, a salutary demonstration of their officers' disgust, and a speech by Otho restore order, if not calm (82.2–85.1). Fear is the final note (85.2–3).

The opening fanfare (80.1 *seditio prope urbi excidio fuit*) is justified more by the symptomatic character of this incident, which shows how civil war saps military discipline, than by its (negligible) effect on subsequent events; see Intro. §5. The riot is mentioned more briefly and with some differences of historical detail in the parallel tradition (Plut. *O.* 3.2–8, Suet. *O.* 8.2, Dio 64.9.2–3); for analysis of the strategy and timing of events see Murison (1993) 120–30. Like T., Dio maintains that the riot illustrated the 'daring and lawlessness' that Otho's coup had stimulated in the soldiers (64.9.2). All sources report the killing and wounding of officers, but T. supplies small corroborating details as well: at the outset he shows a praetorian tribune deliberating on how to accomplish a simple task without interference from his men (80.1), at the end he has tribunes and centurions – career soldiers – demand discharge (82.3). Suetonius (whose account is the briefest and least satisfactory) says that the riot showed Otho the praetorians' *animum fidemque erga se* (*O.* 8.1). Plutarch, too, dramatizes praetorian enthusiasm for their emperor (80.2n. *urbem ... petunt*). T. offers instead a variety of (bad) motives (80.2). Dio's view that 'affection for Otho' was accepted as an 'explanation' of the event in the aftermath (64.9.3 'they received money for this, on the grounds that they had acted out of affection for Otho') is the most balanced. T. does not allow the soldiers even that inadequate justification, but throughout insists on their lack of control. The many connections of language or incident linking this and other episodes are noted below.

80.1 Paruo interim initio . . . orta seditio: cf. 2.68.1 *orta seditio, ludicro initio*, introducing a similar event under Vitellius: his soldiers perceive a threat to their *princeps*, rush into his dinner party demanding the blood of his guest, and are restrained with difficulty (2.68.4). Vitellius' response is as mild as Otho's (2.69.1). **unde nihil timebatur** 'in an unexpected quarter' (Fyfe); lit. 'whence nothing was feared', dependent on *orta*, not *paruo . . . initio* (with which it is otiose); cf. Liv. 6.11.2 *seditio, unde minime timeri potuit, a patriciae gentis uiro.* **urbi excidio:** even limited by *prope* this seems exaggerated next to T.'s account, in which a tribune and two centurions were killed, two other officers wounded, and a party of eighty senatorial men and women threatened but not physically harmed (cf. the more limited expressions of Suet. *O.* 8.1 *paene internecione amplissimi ordinis* and Dio 64.9.2 'they would have killed all the guests . . .'). But according to Plut. *O.* 3.5 'The city was in great commotion, expecting to be plundered at once.' See also 83.2n. *tumultus proximi.* **septimam decimam cohortem e colonia Ostiensi:** Claudius established an urban cohort in Ostia to fight fires (Suet. *Cl.* 25.2); for the four city-based cohorts see 4.2n. *urbanum militem*, and for a cohort based in Lyon see 64.3n. T. omits the reason for the summons. This unit may have been intended as a partial replacement for the city cohorts, which were being sent to delay the Vitellian advance (87.1); if so, the change of duty may explain the need for new equipment (Murison (1993) 125–30). There is still a cohort at Ostia after Otho's death (2.63.1). **Vario Crispino tribuno e praetorianis:** only known from this incident, in which he was first suspected then killed by his own men (80.2, Plut. *O.* 3.4); cf. 36.1n. *caueri . . . praepositos.* **data:** sc. *erat.* **aperto armamentario:** the opening of the arsenal at 38.3 initiated the violence against Galba. **affectatio** 'a striving after' (*OLD* 1) is first attested in V. Max (9.1.3) and most common in Quintilian (fourteen times); T. also uses it at *G.* 28.4. In attempting to avoid the attention of his troops Crispinus repeats a tactical error made by Hordeonius Flaccus, with similar results (54.2 *inde atrox rumor*, etc.). **eualuit** 'developed into' *OLD* 1b, though the connection between the starting points (*tempus*, *causa*, *affectatio*) and results (*suspicionem*, *crimen*, *tumultum*) is loose. **uisa . . . arma cupidinem sui mouere:** the link between sight and desire is a commonplace, here deployed uncommonly (cf. e.g. Ov. *Met.* 13.906 *uisae . . . cupidine uirginis haeret*, *Fast.* 6.119 *uisae . . . cupidine captus*); for *cupidinem sui* 'desire for itself' (i.e. in our passage for *arma*) cf. Sen. *Ep.* 119.9 *pecunia . . . nulli non maiorem sui cupidinem incussit*, Zeno (bishop of Verona, fourth century) *Tract.* 2.4.10

(Löfstedt (1971)) *caro . . . in cupidinem sui utrumque sexum . . . inuitans.* **temulentos:** 26.1n.

80.2 tribunos centurionesque proditionis arguit: 36.1nn. *tribunis aut centurionibus, caueri . . . praepositos*; cf. also the execution of centurions in the German army (56.1, 59.1; 58.2). Later in the year T. reports a similar incident on a larger scale, when Vitellian legions reverse Caecina's declaration for Vespasian and throw him into chains (3.13–14). **familiae senatorum . . . armarentur:** for soldiers' (misplaced) suspicions about the senate cf. 2.52.1 *infensum Othoni senatum arbitrabantur.* Senators are in fact offered arms on that occasion, but hastily decline them (2.52.2). Still later they themselves offer to arm their households to help take Rome for the Flavians, but their offer is declined (3.64–5). **pars . . . cupidum:** though his account emphasizes the show of praetorian loyalty to Otho, Plutarch, too, mentions these (fairly predictable) motives for mayhem: *O.* 3.8 'a few of them were plotting to no good end' and *O.* 3.2 'it is uncertain whether . . . they were using this as a pretext for raising disturbance and war'. For the (unflattering) list cf. 19.1 *multi . . . cura.* **motus noui:** 22.1n. **obsequia meliorum nox abstulerat:** see Intro. §11. The form and/or content of this expression suit a variety of contexts, e.g. 3.84.5 (on Vitellius' death) *deformitas exitus misericordiam abstulerat*, 4.36.2 (of seditious soldiers) *omnem pudorem nox ademerat*, *A.* 13.15.2 (of a drunken dinner party at court) *dissimulationem nox et lasciuia exemerat*; for content cf. Caes. *Ciu.* 1.67.3 *at luce multum per se pudorem omnium oculis*, 2.31.7 *huius modi res aut pudore aut metu tenentur, quibus rebus nox maxime aduersaria est.* For the form cf. also Virg. *Aen.* 6.272 *rebus nox abstulit atra colorem.* **seuerissimos centurionum:** Plut. *O.* 3.4 says two (of seventy-two) were killed. For resentment of disciplinarian officers cf. 3.7.1, and for centurions as a particular target cf. *A.* 1.32.1 (on an attack on centurions by their own men) *ea uetustissima militaribus odiis materies et saeuiendi principium* and *A.* 1.23.3 (on the murder of a harsh centurion). **rapta:** sc. *sunt.* **insidentes equis:** 40.2n. *rapidi equis.* Suetonius says they all ran: *O.* 8.2 *omnes nullo certo duce in Palatium cucurrerunt.* **urbem ac Palatium petunt:** the praetorian barracks were outside the walls of Rome (Richardson (1992) 76). By the shortest route the trip to the Palace would have taken about fifteen minutes (Murison (1993) 123). Plutarch's version includes a dramatic exhortation (*O.* 3.4 'they rode to the Palace saying that now was the moment for destroying all of Caesar's enemies at once') that depicts a unanimity (in loyalty, at least as a pretext, to Otho) that would not have suited T.'s account, which stresses the variety of motivations. *petunt* is echoed by *petiuere* (81.2).

81.1 celebre conuiuium: Plut. *O.* 3.4 says there were eighty guests. **qui . . . timebatur:** cf. Plut. *O.* 3.5, which shares much of this material and some of its language but presents it in a different order and with different effect. **trepidi fortuitusne . . . foret:** for the indirect question dependent on an adj. see 14.1n. *anxius . . . erumperet.* **simulare . . . detegi . . . intueri:** historic inf. The first is absent from Plutarch's version. The others have equivalents: *O.* 3.5 'he saw them (= *detegi*) with eyes fastened on him (= *intueri*), speechless and terrified'. **cum timeret Otho, timebatur:** cf. Plut. *O.* 3.5 'fearing (φοβούμενος) for these men Otho was himself fearful (φοβερός) to them'. T.'s epigram concludes a long period, Plutarch's begins one. The antithesis is a common one (see Heubner).

81.2 discrimine . . . suo territus: T. adds this nuance, suggesting that Otho feared his own best supporters. **et . . . iussit:** shorter than Plutarch's version (see App. 1) because T. focuses on ends (*mitigandas, abire*), not means (talking, rousing, doorways). **tum uero . . . petiuere:** where T. has thirty-one words, Plutarch and Suetonius have none. *petiuere* sets this surreptitious departure in contrast with the noisy onrush of the praetorians (80.2 *urbem . . . petunt*); cf. 82.3n. *insignibus.* **tum uero:** 35.1n. **proiectis insignibus:** including at a minimum the *toga praetexta*; cf. Suet. *Jul.* 16.1 (of Caesar as praetor) *dimissis lictoribus abiectaque praetexta domum clam refugit pro condicione temporum quieturus*, Curt. 3.11.11 (of Darius at the battle of Issus) *insignibus quoque imperii, ne fugam proderent, indecore abiectis.* When praetorian officers shed their insignia at 82.3 the scene is less ignominious but more shocking (see n.). **frequentia** 'throng' *OLD* 3b; cf. *D.* 11.3 *nec . . . frequentiam salutantium concupisco, Agr.* 40.3 *notabilis celebritate et frequentia occurentium introitus.* **ut cuique:** sc. *erat.* **incertas latebras** 'obscure hiding places', because with the (socially) obscure (*humillimus cliens*). For the tactic cf. 3.86.3 *per domos clientium semet occultabant* (sc. *magistratus senatoresque*), for the phrase cf. *A.* 3.42.3 *Florus incertis latebris uictores frustratus.* When young Domitian needed to hide from the Vitellians he chose first a priest's lodgings and an Isiac disguise, then the house of a *cliens paternus* (3.74.1).

82.1 foribus . . . Palatii: the detail connects this scene with 35.1 *refractis Palatii foribus.* **coercitus:** sc. *est.* **Iulio Martiale:** 28n. **Vitellio Saturnino praefecto legionis:** only here. It is odd to find a legionary officer beside a praetorian tribune, but it contributes to T.'s picture of the peculiar and pernicious mixing of military units in this period (38.3nn. *sine... distingueretur* and *miscentur*, 53.3n. *paganos*, 54.3n. *asciscitur auxiliorum miles*). T. does not use a standard name for Saturninus' post, which was probably *praefectus castrorum*, a legion's third in command, 'normally a man of fifty or sixty years of age who had risen through the centurionate to become a *primus pilus*... and who spent his whole life in the army' (Webster (1998) 113). Nothing is said about the soldiers on guard duty (38.2n. *cohors togata*); presumably they joined their fellows. **undique:** sc. *erant*. To the brief main clause is added a string of supplementary details (*modo... poscentibus*) concluded by a temporal clause (*donec... cohibuit*), and an unexpected but effective second main clause (*redieruntque... innocentes*). Suetonius conveys less furor (*O.* 8.2 *caedem senatus flagitantes*...) and more gore (... *sic ut erant cruenti*). **lymphatis:** at its other occurrence in T. it again describes rioting soldiers: *A.* 1.32.1 *repente lymphati destrictis gladiis in centuriones inuadunt.* **destinare:** 12.3n. **donec... cohibuit:** twelve words where Plutarch uses eighteen (see App. 1), and Plutarch does not have the comment *contra decus imperii*. Suetonius leaves out the couch and the tears, too: *O.* 8.2 *nec nisi uiso* (sc. *Othone*) *destiterunt.* **inuiti neque innocentes:** the epigram, a moralizing comment absent from the parallel sources, rounds off the section; cf. 20.2n. *gaudium*. For the alliteration cf. 6.1 *inauditi atque indefensi tamquam innocentes perierant*, 71.2 *integra et infelix*. **neque** 'but not' *OLD* 5.

82.2 uelut capta urbe: T. alludes to, but does not much develop, a standard theme of rhetorical scene-painting (Quint. *Inst.* 8.67–71). His quiet scene contrasts with the previous evening's chaos (and with Quintilian's very noisy one: *fragor*, *clamoribus*, *ploratus*, etc.). **clausae:** sc. *sunt* (forms of *esse* must also be supplied with *deiecti* and *plus*); cf. *A.* 2.82.2 *sumpto iustitio desererentur fora, clauderentur domus*. The front doors of town houses would normally be open during the day for the reception of *clientes*. **plus tristitiae quam paenitentiae** 'more sulky than sorry' (Fyfe), lit. 'there was more ill humour (*OLD* 2) than repentance'; cf. 4.2.3 *nemo supplici uultu, sed tristes et truces*, *A.* 1.24.3 (on mutinous legions) *quamquam maestitiam imitarentur contumaciae propiores*. **manipulatim** suggests a return of order. **allocuti sunt... horridius:** for the careers of the two prefects see 46.1 nn. In the events that follow Proculus is the more aggressive (87.2 *criminando... anteibat*, with 87.2n. *plurima fides*), Firmus, about whom less is said, the more ingratiating (2.46.2 *promptissimo Plotio Firmo*), so it is possible that the names and descriptors are arranged chiastically, as elsewhere (6.1 n. *alter . . . destruebant*). But Firmus, as a career soldier, might be expected to have been the harsher disciplinarian (so Chilver).

82.3 in eo: sc. *erat.* **quina milia nummum:** 5,000 HS, twenty months' pay for an ordinary praetorian (Alston (1994)). Plut. (see below) gives the same figure. For its size relative to that of other payments at this time see 5.1 n. *neque dari donatiuum.* **tum . . . ausus:** sc. *est.* More sarcastic than Plut. *O.* 3.7 'after a gift of 1,250 drachmas to each man Otho entered the camp'; cf. 66.1 *tum . . . ualuit.* **abiectis militiae insignibus:** repeating the magistrates' gesture of the preceding evening (81.2). T.'s avoidance of specifics (here, e.g. the centurion's staff (*uites*), the service decorations) makes aligning the two passages easier. **otium** 'discharge' *OLD* 2a. For the officers' frustration cf. 2.36.2. **sensit inuidiam** 'felt the reproach'; cf. Stat. *Theb.* 6.43–4 *sensere Pelasgi | inuidiam et lacrimis excusant crimen obortis.*

83.1 quamquam: 5.2n. *quamuis . . . ablato.* **ambitioso imperio** 'power based on solicitation (sc. of the troops' goodwill)'; cf. 2.12.1 *Suedius Clemens ambitioso imperio regebat, ut aduersus modestiam disciplinae corruptus ita proeliorum auidus* (where the *proelia* are opportunities for pillage (2.12.2); cf. *per turbas et raptus* below). Galba did not hold power on those terms (17.2n. *ambitu*; cf. 18.2 *nec ullum orationi aut lenocinium addit aut pretium*), nor did Augustus (Suet. *Aug.* 42.1 *salubrem magis quam ambitiosum principem*). V. Max. 2.7.2 (writing *de militari disciplina*) cites the precedent of Metellus, who stripped indulgences from his soldiers and proceeded to win victories against an enemy *cuius tergum sub ambitioso imperatore Romano militi uidere non contigerat.* For Otho's approach see 36.3 *omnia seruiliter pro dominatione*; for Galba, Vitellius, and Vespasian see 5.2n. *legi . . . emi.* **non posse principatum scelere quaesitum subita modestia et prisca grauitate retineri:** echoing Piso (30.1) with a cynical corollary of Sal. *Cat.* 2.4 *imperium facile iis artibus retinetur quibus initio partum est* (cf. Vell. 2.57.1 *semper praedixerant Caesari ut principatum armis quaesitum armis teneret*). **prisca grauitate:** Otho won't make Galba's mistake of attempting to impose an old-fashioned virtue (18.3). **ita disseruit:** the third speech to praetorians in this book, the second speech by Otho; his next and last is at 2.47. Its structure is 'ruffle' then 'soothe' (85.1): he scolds the praetorians for the breach of military discipline (which his own actions – see chh. 23–6 – have undone), then describes the (very mild) punishment he intends, and concludes with exaggerated rhetoric about the value of one of his party's assets, the senate. The speech that Plutarch summarizes from this occasion has quite different emphases: *O.* 3.8 'He praised the crowd for being well-disposed to and supportive of him, but said that some few were intriguing for no good end, bringing reproach to his moderation and his supporters' steadiness; he said they ought to share in his anger and join him in punishing these.' Instead of strengthening their partnership in crime, T.'s Otho urges on the praetorians the importance of discipline (sounding much like Aemilius Paullus: 84.2n. *uobis ... relinquite*) and the glory of the senate (going further even than Cicero on this – 84.4nn. *auspicato* and *immortalem* – and echoing Pompey, who also lost: 84.3nn. *Italiae ... iuuentus* and *senatus ... est*). By the end of the speech its connection with reality is tenuous (84.4nn. *domibus ... stare, aeternitas ... firmatur, ex ... nascuntur*). If Otho's words ring hollow because of their failure to reflect the inevitable collapse of discipline and the irrelevance of the senate to a power struggle based on military might, they exhibit a wealth of stylistic effects. He teases with a paradoxical beginning, requesting that the soldiers restrain their affection for him and rein in their courage (83.2; cf. *nimia pietas*), soothes with euphemisms about the previous day's riot (83.2 *tumultus proximi*, 83.4 *consternatione proxima*), and dazzles with a choice metaphor at the end (84.3 *cuius splendore ... sordes et obscuritatem ... praestringimus*). Along the way we find assonance (84.2 *fortissimus ... quietissimus, paucorum ... duorum*), asyndeton (83.4 *centurionis ... imperatoris*, 84.3 *nationes ... imaginem ... senatus*), polyptoton (83.3 *omnes ... omnia*; 84.1 *quem ... quas ... quid*; 84.1 *ne ... ne ... ut*), and two 'ladders' (84.1 *miles ... tribuno*, 84.4 *ex uobis ... principes*). Contributing to the rich emptiness of the style are abstract nouns (83.3 *ratio, occasionum uelocitas, auctoritas, rigor disciplinae*, 84.1 *discursu, confusione*, 84.4 *congestu, aeternitas*), synonyms (83.2 *temperamentum ... modum, affectus ... amorem ... caritatis, animum ... uirtutuem ... fortitudinis*, 83.3 *palam ... cunctis praesentibus*, 84.1 *seditionem ... discordiam, imprecentur ... optabunt*, 84.3 *imperii ... omnium prouinciarum, splendore ... gloria, sordes ... obscuritatem, alumni ... iuuentus, sanguinem ... caedem*, 84.4 *parente ... conditore, continuum et immortalem*), and bland generalizations (83.2 *quae multos exercitus in discordiam egere* and *saepe honestas rerum causas ... perniciosi exitus consequuntur*, 84.2 *parendo potius ... res militares continentur* and *fortissimus in ipso discrimine exercitus ... quietissimus*). Occasional punctuation is provided by short sentences (83.3 *imus ad bellum*, 84.2 *paucorum culpa fuit, duorum poena erit*), rhetorical questions (83.4 *an et illic ... ?, unus alterue ... ?*), and invective (84.1 *satellitibus*, 84.3 *Germani*). Though empty and even false, the words were *grate accepta* (85.1).

For the themes and language of this speech see Keitel (1987) 75–7 and (1991) 2780–3.

83.2 commilitones: 37.1 n. **tumultus proximi:** Otho's references to the riot convey disorder but ignore casualties; cf. 83.4 *consternatione proxima*, 84.1 *discursu ... tenebris ... rerum omnium confusione*. **non cupiditate uel odio:** sc. *erat*, source abl.; cf. 80.1 *paruo ... initio* (*A&G* §403.2a, Draeger (1882) §56b). **acrius quam considerate:** for the *uariatio* of degree cf. *Agr.* 4.6 *uehementius quam caute*; this Tacitean usage is imitated by Ammianus at 21.16.9 *acrius ... quam ciuiliter*. T. has (the more usual) parallel comparatives at 4.40.3 *ambitiosius quam honestius*.

83.3 ratio rerum: vague, but perhaps equivalent to 3.51.1 *ratio belli* 'the nature of war'. **multa etiam centuriones tribunosque tantum iuberi expediat** equates the officers' access to inside knowledge with that of the *gregarius miles*, addressing the division between men and officers that figured so prominently in the riot.

83.4 illic: i.e. *in bello*. **nocte intempesta** 'in the dead of night'. **neque enim plures ... insanisse crediderim:** Otho turns a blind eye to the (large) numbers involved and to the praetorians' motives, despite his awareness of the role greed and a general taste for mayhem played in the riot (83.1). Galba and Vitellius also display wilful blindness, but less blatantly: 7.2n. *an ... scrutaretur*, 49.3n. *amicorum ... ignarus*.

84.1 pro me: sc. *fecistis*; cf. 36.3n. *omnia ... dominatione*, 89.2n. *quod raro alias*. **satellitibus** signals invective: 4.50.3 *satellitem uocabat*, 4.58.5 (a Roman general to troops who have joined the enemy) *uobis satellitibus*, *A.* 2.45.3 *fugacem Maroboduum appellans* (sc. *Arminius*) ... *proditorem patriae, satellitem Caesaris*, 16.22.2 *et habet* (sc. *Thrasea*) *sectatores uel potius satellites*. **ne ... ne ... ut:** for the addition of object clauses to a verb (*optabunt*) already supplied with direct objects cf. 26.1 n. *sed ne ... destinaretur*. **miles centurioni ... centurio tribuno:** the same rhetorical figure (a 'ladder': *Rhet. Her.* 4.34–5 *climax*) is used by Livy for this thought: 8.34.7 *cum ... non miles centurionis, non centurio tribuni ... pareat imperio*. T. uses it again at the end of Otho's speech: 84.4 *ex uobis senatores ... ex senatoribus principes*. **ut** is a correction in M for a word that M's copies read variously *tot* and *hinc* (see Wellesley's app. crit.). It is rather bland for Otho's crescendo here; Wellesley emends to *at*.

84.2 parendo ... sciscitando: impersonal gerundives (the implied 'subject', *milites*, is not the subject of the sentence, *res militares*). The parallels are poetic: Virg. *Ecl.* 8.71 *cantando*, *Geo.* 2.50 *habendo*, 3.454 *tegendo*, etc. **quietissimus:** sc. *est.* **uobis arma et animus sit; mihi consilium et . . . regimen relinquite:** cf. 3.20.1 *diuisa inter exercitum ducesque munia: militibus cupidinem pugnandi conuenire, duces prouidendo, consultando . . . prodesse*, from another speech attempting to instil discipline in self-willed troops, with even less success than Otho's (see 3.21.1). The principles were tried and true (cf. Liv. 44.34.2–5). **duorum:** identity unknown; cf. 85.1n. **abolete:** 47.1n.

84.3 caput imperii et decora omnium prouinciarum: 'One seems to be reading Cicero on the senate of the Republic' (Alford *ad loc.*). For *caput* cf. *A.* 1.13.4 *quousque patieris, Caesar, non adesse caput rei publicae?* where the *caput* is the *princeps*. If with *decora omnium prouinciarum* T. is referring to the presence of provincial elites in the senate (as he does at 4.74.1), that expression, too, is somewhat anachronistic, since there were as yet senators from only a small number of (mostly western) provinces; see Chilver *ad loc.* **cum maxime:** 29.2n. **Germani:** an insulting label for Roman troops, all citizens, stationed in Germany. **Italiae alumni et Romana uere iuuentus:** *alumnus*, in its three other occurrences in speech in T., signals ties of affection: e.g. *A.* 1.44.1 (soldiers on young Caligula) *rediret legionum alumnus*, 2.37.4 '*diui Augusti alumnos ab inopia defende*', 12.11.3 (Claudius on a Parthian prince) *extollit laudibus alumnum urbis.* For the tone of *Romana iuuentus* cf. Luc. 2.532 (Pompey's exhortation to his men) *o uere Romana manus.* **splendore et gloria:** 'His picture of the Senate's *gloria* and *splendor* is ludicrous when juxtaposed with the senators' craven flattery of him in the next chapter (85.3)' (Keitel (1991) 2782); cf. 55.4 *senatus populique Romani oblitterata iam nomina.* The senate was not among the factors that determined allegiances in ch. 76. **praestringimus** 'we eclipse' *OLD* 3c; cf. Quint. *Inst.* 10.1.92 (on Domitian) *ceterarum fulgore uirtutum laus ista* (sc. *poetae*) *praestringitur.* **senatus nobiscum est:** cf. App. *BC* 2.72 (Pompey's exhortation) 'on our side in this fight are . . . this great number of men, some from the senate, some knights'; cf. 88.3n. *irritamenta libidinorum.*

84.4 domibus et tectis et congestu lapidum stare: for *stare* 'depend on' (*OLD* 21) cf. Enn. *Ann.* fr. 156 Skutsch *moribus antiquis stat res Romana uirisque.* The same original underlies 2.69.2 *et uires luxu corrumpebantur, contra ueterem disciplinam et instituta maiorum, apud quos uirtute quam pecunia res Romana melius stetit.* For the sentiment cf. Liv. 5.54.2 (from Camillus' speech) *in superficie tignisque caritas nobis patriae pendet?* This old theme (at least as old as the Athenians' abandonment of Athens in 480 B.C.), which rests on an antithesis between a city's fabric and its folk, is not ideally suited to a civil war context or to Otho's larger point, the superior value of the senate when set against Vitellius' *nationes aliquae* and *imago exercitus.* **intercidere ac reparari promisca sunt** 'can one and all fall and be rebuilt'; for *promiscus*, which is used with an inf. only here, see also 47.1 n., 66.1 n. **aeternitas rerum . . . mea cum uestra salus incolumitate senatus firmatur:** in contemporary documents these boons depend rather on the safety of the *princeps*: e.g. the vows of the Arval Brethren (McC–W 13.37–42 on Domitian) *ex cuius incolumitate omnium salus constat*, Plin. *Pan.* 67.3 *nuncupare uota . . . pro salute principum, ac propter illos pro aeternitate imperii solebamus*; cf. also McC–W 13.46–7 *custodieris . . . aeternitatem imperii, quod suscipiendo ampliauit* (sc. *princeps*). For T.'s attitude toward such slogans see 15.1 n. *deorum hominumque consensu.* **pax gentium:** cf. McC–W 32, on an Othonian coin, *pax orbis terrarum.* **auspicato** 'with good omens' (*OLD* 2), a much-used impersonal abl. abs. (*NLS* §93n.2); cf. 3.72.1 *sedem Iouis Optimi Maximi auspicato . . . conditam.* In Livy's story of the institution of the senate (1.8.7) no auspices are taken. In Cicero, too, though the city is founded with divine approval (*Rep.* 2.5.1 *urbem auspicato condere . . . dicitur* (sc. *Romulus*)), the senate is not (*Rep.* 2.14). **immortalem:** another term generally applied to Rome or the *res publica* (Cic. *Rab. Perd.* 33 *si hanc ciuitatem immortalem uultis, si aeternum hoc imperium*, etc.; *Marc.* 22 *cum res publica immortalis esse debeat*), not the senate. **ex uobis senatores, ita ex senatoribus principes nascuntur:** the first part of this 'ladder' (84.1 n. *miles . . . tribuno*) speaks most directly to Otho's audience and exaggerates the upward mobility possible. Even equestrian status was beyond the reach of most, though municipal eminence as a decurion (town-councillor) was common (Durry (1938) 289–303). The second half was conspicuously true in 69, and again with Nerva and Trajan.

85.1 oratio ad perstringendos mulcendosque militum animos 'the speech, (calculated) to ruffle and soothe the soldiers' spirits'. Both *perstringere* and *mulcere* have their basis in physical effect (scraping, caressing). *perstringere* (whose prefix means 'along the surface': cf. Cic. *Agr.* 2.67 *solum tam exile et macrum est quod aratro perstringi non possit*) is used of mild scolding, often with an adverb or other expression that further lightens the verb (*leuiter, breuiter, cursim, oblique, carptim*): e.g. *A.* 2.59.2 *cultu habituque eius lenibus uerbis perstricto.* For (*per*)*stringere animos* cf. Curt. 5.9.1 *praesentis periculi species omnium simul corda animosque horrore perstrinxerat* and Virg. *Aen.* 9.294 *animum* (sc. *Iuli*) *patriae strinxit pietatis imago.* On *mulcere* see 39.2n. For *ad* expressing purpose ('calculated') and dependent on a noun cf. 54.3 *consensu ad* *bellum* and 2.35.1 *constantia... ad proelia*, in both of which passages, as here with *oratio*, the governing noun has a verbal or adjectival notion that facilitates the construction. For a similar thought expressed more conventionally cf. *A.* 14.62.1 *uarius sermo et ad metum atque iram accommodatus*. Some editors produce this construction here by adding a modifier for *oratio* (e.g. *apta* Meiser, *parata* C. Heraeus, *peropportuna* Wellesley), a procedure for which a corruption in M (*perodperstringendos*; the first *per* probably a false start on *perstringendos*) provides specious justification. **modus** 'limited extent' *OLD* 6, similarly at 2.29.3 *ille* (sc. *Valens*) *utili moderatione non supplicium cuiusquam poposcit.* **in duos:** Plutarch adds 'whose execution would anger no one', for which thought cf. 58.2 *punienti uilior.* **animaduerti** 'to be dealt with' *OLD* 8; both the euphemism (for execution) and the impersonal passive reflect Otho's mildness. One may contrast the punishment of mutineers at *A.* 1.29.4 *interfici iubet* and *A.* 1.44.1 *puniret noxios.* **accepta:** sc. *sunt*, neuter plur. agreeing with the compound subject *oratio... et... modus* (*A&G* §287.3). **qui coerceri non poterant:** another indication of the reversed roles of *miles* and *dux* (33.1 n. *illatus*). **facies belli:** cf. 4.22.2 *mixta belli ciuilis externique facie.* This striking but rather vague expression is illustrated by the twenty-eight word abl. abs. *militibus... obiecerat.* T. found the metaphor in Sallust: *Jug.* 46.5 *in Numidiam procedit, ubi contra belli faciem tuguria plena hominum, pecora cultoresque in agris erant.* For the scene cf. 4.1.1–3. **ut nihil in commune turbantibus, ita sparsis per domos** 'though there were no further riots, yet here and there among the houses...'; for concessive *ut... ita* see 6.1 n. **occulto habitu:** i.e. disguised by their lack of military dress (cf. 5.22.2, of soldiers awakening to an attack on their camp, *ruunt per uias... pauci ornatu militari*), particularly of the *sagum*, the cloak which distinguished soldier from civilian (cf. Cic. *Phil.* 5.31 *tumultum decerni... sagum sumi dico oportere*, 7.21 *arma, saga, bellum flagitauerunt*); darker than e.g. *tunicati* (*D.* 7.4 *tunicatus hic populus*) and more compact than other references to disguise, e.g. 2.29.1 *Valens seruili ueste... tegebatur*, and *A.* 13.25.1 *Nero... ueste seruili in dissimulationem sui compositus*. At 2.56.1 civilians don military garb: *fuere qui inimicos suos specie militum interficerent.* **maligna cura** 'with unkind attention', a bold oxymoron, hard to parallel; closest are the *malae curae* of Tiberius at *A.* 3.37.2. **nobilitas... obiecerat:** cf. 2.3n. *nobilitas*, 4.1.1 *si quem procerum habitu aut iuuenta conspexerant, obtruncare*, and, for the inverse, 3.31.2 *gregarius miles... ignobilitate tutior.* For abstract subjects of active verbs see Intro. §11. Otho's soldiers behaved badly, but successive waves of victors (Vitellians 2.56, Flavians 4.1) proved worse.

85.2 Vitellianos ... milites uenisse in urbem ... plerique credebant: correctly as to fact but not motive (75.1). **plena:** sc. *erant.* **uix secreta domuum sine formidine:** for the theme see 2.3nn. *corrupti, quibus ... oppressi.* On generalization see Walker (1968) 51–2. **plurimum trepidationis:** sc. *erat.* **in publico** 'in public places' (Irvine), sc. *erat.* In public places reactions could be observed by unfriendly eyes, a topos much used by T. Women are accused *ob lacrimas* (*A.* 6.10.1), senators watched for guilty expressions (2.50.1, *A.* 3.53.1). Even sighs were noted (*Agr.* 45.2 *suspiria nostra subscriberentur*; see also *A.* 1.11.3, 4.69.3, 4.70.2). **ut ... conuersis** 'since people changed in mood and appearance each time rumour reported something new' (cf. 27.2 *animum ex euentu sumpturi*, 2.85.2 *ex nuntiis cunctabundus aut properans*). The piquancy of the expression lies in the fact that in the event of bad news mood and appearance would conflict (despair under a cheerful mien). *conuersis* is abl. abs. referring to the people implicit in *in publico*; *animum* and *uultum* are acc. of respect, a construction regular only in poetry (*NLS* §19) and ordinarily dependent on nominatives (e.g. 4.20.3 *frontem tergaque ac latus tuti*; Draeger (1882) §39). For the subj. see 79.4n. *ubi res posceret.* **diffidere dubiis ac parum gaudere prosperis:** *diffidere* (abs.) 'despair'. *dubiis* = *aduersis*, a circumstantial abl. parallel to *prosperis*; cf. *A.* 12.5.3 *prosperis dubiisque sociam.* In Rome in A.D. 69 it was impolitic to speak of bad news (the growing strength of the Vitellians, 26.1, 50.1 *nouus insuper de Vitellio nuntius exterruit, ante caedem Galbae suppressus*, 76.1–2; Vespasian in the East, 50.4; 3.54.1–3 elaborates on this theme); for good news cf. 76.1–2, 79.5.

85.3 arduus rerum omnium modus: sc. *erat*, 'there was strenuous moderation in all things', an oxymoron. **ne contumax:** sc. *esset.* Silence, criticism (*libertas*), and flattery (*adulatio*) appear to be possible responses, but not sincere support for Otho. On *contumax* see 3.1n. **nota:** sc. *erat.* As senator Otho had a long training in flattery under Nero (*A.* 13.45.4 *flagrantissimus in amicitia Neronis habebatur*, cf. 13.12.1, 46.1–3) and more recently under Galba (Otho must have been prominent among those who flattered *effusius*, 19.1). Implicit is a contrast with Julio-Claudian rulers bred to command. **uersare ... torquere:** historic inf. (likewise *iacere*), *uersare* 'vary' and *torquere* 'twist' are used figuratively in a remarkably impressionistic description of a senate meeting dominated by fear, self-interest, deceit, and noise; no actual business is reported. The senate does little in *H.* but struggle to keep the favour of the men who controlled the soldiers (e.g. 45.1n. *alium ... populum*, 47.1n. *omnes principum honores*). There is a brief flicker of activity in Crispus' trial (2.10; see 90.1 n. *commendata patribus re publica*), and a false start at 2.53, but 'normal' business – speeches, *sententiae*, votes – appears only when Vespasian has come to power (4.6). **hostem ac parricidam:** cf. the name-calling at Sal. *Cat.* 31.8 *obstrepere omnes, hostem* (sc. *Catilinam*) *et parricidam uocare* and *A.* 15.73.3 *increpuit... hostem ac parricidam uocans.* **uulgaribus conuiciis** 'commonplace reproaches' (such as *hostis* and *parricida*), dependent, notionally, on a verb of reproach (*increpare* uel sim., with Vitellius as the object) for which T. substitutes *probra iacere* 'cast insults' in the parallel clause; for a similar shift see 77.1 n. *quaedam.* Caution, learned after an earlier brush with danger (47.1 n. *conuicia ac probra*), is a more scrupulous censor later (90.2n. *nulla Vitellii mentione*). Most of Otho's supporters eventually made their peace with Vitellius (e.g. 2.60, 2.62, 2.71.2). **uera probra:** for the material see 74.1 nn. *stupra ac flagitia... obiectauere, neuter falso*; for the expression cf. *A.* 1.44.1 *uera exprobrari.* **in clamore ... et ubi:** for the epexegetic relative clause cf. 76.2 *longinquae prouinciae et quidquid... mari dirimitur.* **sibi ipsi obstrepentes:** cf. Cic. *de Orat.* 3.50 *ut quodam modo ipsi sibi in dicendo obstrepere uideantur* (where, however, confusion is an unintended consequence).

86 *prodigia et fulminum monitus et futurorum praesagia*

In supernatural phenomena and the causes ascribed to them – a theme announced in the 'table of contents' (3.2) – Tacitus found a narrative device that suited the dark colours in which he painted imperial history. (Lucan achieves a similar colouring with his exhaustive catalogue of prodigies at 1.522–83.) On a narrow definition *prodigia* were events that the senate declared significant of divine feeling towards the Roman state (Linderski (1993) 58). Typical *prodigia* were lightning strikes and other weather signs, earthquakes, eclipses, odd newborns (both animal and human), and peculiar behaviour in the animate and inanimate world (Wülker (1904) 6–26). Prodigies 'suggested that the gods were unfavourable to Rome as a whole, rather than just a single action... they did not foretell anything in particular, but merely put forward a general warning of disaster unless appropriate precautions were taken' (Levene (1993) 4). During the Republic prodigies were reported from all over Italy, and their expiation ('appropriate precautions') via sacrifice was a regular item of business for the consuls before they set out for their provinces (cf. Liv. 33.26.6 *priusquam... ipsi consules ab urbe mouerent, procurare, ut assolet, prodigia quae nuntiabantur iussi*; this is a Livian formula). Expiatory rites were believed to restore the *pax deorum* – divine goodwill toward Rome (e.g. Liv. 36.37.6 *placatis dis nunc uotis rite soluendis nunc prodigiis expiandis*) – whereupon the consuls proceeded to their campaigns without any lingering shadow of divine displeasure; on state cult and the *pax deorum* see Liebeschuetz (1979) 9, Linderski (1993) 56–8. Livy, whose history is the fullest source of information on prodigies, tells us that by his day attention to traditional prodigies had waned (43.13.1 *neglegentia*; cf. T.'s comment at *A.* 14.12.1 *quae* (sc. *prodigia*) *adeo sine cura deum eueniebant, ut multos post annos Nero imperium et scelera continuauerat*). Thus when the Tiber flooded in A.D. 15, rather than expiating the prodigy with guidance from the Sibylline books (as one senator urged), Tiberius asked a senatorial commission to look into flood control (*A.* 1.76.1, and cf. his response to the fire at *A.* 4.64.1; for the connection of the Sibylline books and prodigies see Liv. 22.9.8).

Under the principate omens (which were not controlled by official rituals of acceptance and expiation) came into prominence instead. More content-based than prodigies, they were believed to foretell success or disaster for a particular undertaking or individual (Levene (1993) 5–6) and were thus ideally suited to the principate. Omens foretelling the advent or doom of emperors are collected in great numbers by Suetonius, for example (Wallace-Hadrill (1983) 189–97; in general Liebeschuetz (1979) 56–60).

Both prodigies and omens had a place in the historical tradition. Lists of prodigies and expiations were a regular item of new year's business in Books 21–45 of Livy's history, appearing in at least forty-three of the fifty-one years covered by those books (prodigy-less years are 201 B.C., 195, 189, 185, 184, 171; lists for 175 and 170 might have stood where there are now lacunas in the text). Omens, on the other hand, contributed to the *exaedificatio* of important narratives (e.g. the second Punic war disaster at Lake Trasimene, which has a full crop in both Livy and his source Coelius Antipater: Liv. 22.3.11–14, *HRR* fr. 20). Livy is avowedly old-fashioned in his attention to this material (see 43.13.1); neither Caesar nor Sallust favours it (Caesar only at *Ciu.* 3.105.3–6, part of which is quoted at 86.1 n. *ab occidente ... conuersam*, and Sallust, with a dismissive notice, at *Cat.* 30.2: *simul id quod in tali re solet, alii portenta atque prodigia nuntiabant, alii conuentus fieri* etc.).

T. adapts the annalistic model for prodigies and omens to his own uses (see Ginsburg (1981) 100, Syme (1958) 521–3; on the annalists see Briscoe (1973) 16–17, 88, Luterbacher (1908) 10–13, Drews (1988) 289–99). In the *Annals*, for example, he employs prodigies as a familiar part of the yearly cycle by including them in some of the diminuendo miscellanies at year-end (*A.* 13.58, 15.22.2, 15.47.1, 16.13.1), but he makes more use of them both as a measure of the irrationality of those who read significance into natural or fortuitous events (86.3, cf. *A.* 1.28.1 *miles rationis ignarus*, 4.64.1 *fortuita ad culpam trahentes*), and as a narrative ornament (on Otho's suicide 2.50.2, the *supremus dies* of Jerusalem 5.13.1, the end of Claudius' reign *A.* 12.64.1, Boudicca's revolt 14.32.1, the Pisonian conspiracy 15.47.1). T.'s *prodigia* are considerably more sinister than Livy's both because of their irregular distribution (see the lists above and also *A.* 12.43.1–2, 13.24, 14.12.2, 14.22) and because he so rarely mentions expiation (only here and at *A.*13.24.2; for unexpiated prodigies and omens see Liebeschuetz (1979) 155–66).

In the present passage T. is at his most annalistic. The indirect statement list is a traditional form (86.1 n. *omissas*), some of the reported prodigies are traditional (earlier occurrences are noted below), and so is the expiation (87.1 n. *lustrata urbe*). But T.'s occasional departures from traditional reportage (see below on *diuersis auctoribus* and *plura alia*) betray the artificiality of the treatment.

86.1 prodigia . . . diuersis auctoribus uulgata: for Republican procedure cf. (e.g.) Liv. 22.1.14 on the prodigies that preceded Trasimene: *his* (sc. *prodigiis*) *sicut erant nuntiata, expositis auctoribusque in Curiam introductis consul de religione patres consuluit.* For T.'s *uulgata* the Livian formula is *nuntiata*. A variety of sources (*diuersis*) is implicit in a formula such as *prodigia Romae uisa et peregre nuntiata* (Liv. 28.11.6, 34.45.6, 40.19.1), but the human agency of the report is not as prominent as T. makes it. In fact Livy generally mentions *auctores* only when they were questionable (e.g. 5.15.1 *prodigia . . . quia singuli auctores erant parum credita spretaque*; cf. 5.23.7, 27.11.3, 43.13.6). The increased attention to (and fabrication of) prodigies in times of trouble was a familiar phenomenon (e.g. 4.26.2, Cic. *Div.* 2.58 (quoted 86.1 n. *plura alia*), Sal. *Cat.* 30.2 (quoted above), Luc. 1.469, 473). **terrebant . . . omissas:** T. dissociates himself from superstition both by siting the effect of the prodigies in the past (*terrebant*, cf. *A.* 14.32.1 *ad metum trahebantur*) and by reporting them in indirect statement (see on *omissas*). **in uestibulo Capitolii:** the principal temple on the Capitoline hill, the Capitolium housed three gods, Jupiter Optimus Maximus in the central nave, Juno Regina and Minerva in smaller *cellae* to the left and right respectively (see on *cella Iunonis* below). Begun in the regal period and dedicated at the beginning of the Republic, the original temple survived the sack of Rome by the Gauls but was twice destroyed by civil war (83 B.C., A.D. 69; for T.'s account of its history see 3.72.1–3). Rebuilt each time with greater magnificence (Cic. *Ver.* 2.4.69), though on the same basic plan (Richardson (1992) 221–4), it survived as an emblem of the stability of Rome until the sixth century (*pignus imperii*, 3.72.1, cf. 4.54.2, Virg. *Aen.* 9.448–9, Hor. *Carm.* 3.3.42, 3.30.8–9, etc.). As such, it was frequently associated with omens and prodigies (e.g. *A.* 13.24.2, Cic. *Cat.* 3.19, *Div.* 1.16, 1.19, Liv. 1.55.5–6, Liv. *per.* 14, Dio 41.14.3, 42.26.1–3, 55.1.1, 73.24.1, etc.). The vestibule of the temple was unusually deep; it was one of the regular meeting places of the Republican senate (Taylor and Scott (1969) 557–68; diagram in Richardson (1992), fig. 19). Gifts to the gods from foreign powers and successful generals were on display, as were bronze tablets inscribed with laws (Cic. *Cat.* 3.19). **omissas:** sc. *esse* (also omitted with *conuersam, prolocutum, insolitos*) indirect statement dependent on *uulgata*, a device also used by Livy (Levene (1993) 19–20, 25), gives formal expression to the author's role as (merely) a transmitter of prodigy lists. Plutarch interprets: *O.* 4.4 'as if she were no longer able to control (the chariot)'. For expiated prodigies involving statue activity cf. Liv. 27.11.3 (statuette falls from goddess' crown into her hand), 40.59.7 (statues of gods turn their heads away from a *lectisternium*; Obsequ. 42 (statue stands on head), 43 (statue acquires veil), 70 (statue turns from south to north at fourth hour). Similar is the frequently attested moving of the 'spears of Mars' (Liv. 24.10.1, 40.19.2; Obsequ. 36, 47, 50; Gel. 4.6.1–2). Statues also cry (Liv. 40.19.2, 43.13.4; Obsequ. 6, 28a), bleed (Liv. 27.4.14; Obsequ. 70), and sweat (Liv. 22.1.12, 22.36.7; Dio 48.50.4). Further references in Wülker (1904) 13–14. **bigae cui Victoria institerat:** Heubner and Chilver suggest that this was a replica of the Victory-driven two-horse chariot dedicated by Hiero of Syracuse in 216 B.C. to demonstrate his confidence in Rome's ability to defeat Hannibal (Liv. 22.37.5; the work itself almost certainly perished in the fire of 83 B.C. (D. H. 4.62.5–6)). Parallels for the replication of a work of art (as opposed to a cult statue) are hard to come by: cf. *A.* 15.41.1 *reparari nequibant* and the wistful perfects of Cic. *Ver.* 2.4.129 *unum illud Macedonicum* (sc. *signum Iouis*) *quod in Capitolio uidimus*, *Cat.* 3.19 *quem* (sc. *Romulum*) *inauratum in Capitolio, paruum atque lactentem . . . fuisse meministis*, Plin. *Nat.* 34.38 (quoted in n. below), 35.14 *isque clupeus supra foras Capitolinae aedis usque ad incendium primum fuit*). **cella Iunonis:** four-fifths the size of the central hall, it contained a cult-statue of the goddess and an altar (Serv. ad *Aen.* 3.134), and dedications such as the bronze dog that Pliny admired (*Nat.* 34.38). **speciem:** for the language cf. *A.* 11.21.1

oblata ei species muliebris ultra modum humanum (of a vision that appeared to Curtius Rufus and foretold his future success), and Suet. *Cl.* 1.2 *species barbarae mulieris humana amplior uictorem tendere ultra sermone Latino prohibuisset* (of a vision that stopped the elder Drusus' advance in Germany). In content this *species,* which refrains from speech and from precise signification, is closer to Livy's apparitions: 21.62.5 *uisos* (sc. *homines*) *nec cum ullo congressos,* 24.10.10 *aram in caelo speciesque hominum circum eam ... uisas,* 24.44.8 *nauium longarum species,* 42.2.4 *classis magnae species,* all from lists of expiated prodigies. **ab occidente in orientem conuersam:** although couched in a traditional-seeming list of prodigies expiated by a traditional sacrifice (87.1 n. *lustrata urbe*) this prodigy differs from most of Livy's statue prodigies (see on *omissas* above) in the apparent specificity of its message. In content it is closer to omens reported by Caesar (*Ciu.* 3.105.3 (on the day of a victory) *constabat ... simulacrum Victoriae ... ad ualuas se templi limenque conuertisse*), and by T. himself: *A.* 14.32.1 *nulla palam causa delapsum Camuloduni simulacrum Victoriae ac retro conuersum, quasi cederet hostibus.* In treating the statue's shift as a prodigy (and by keeping it separate from the omens that persuaded Vespasian to challenge Vitellius, 2.78.1–4) T. is resisting Flavian propaganda, which touted the turn to the East as an omen of the advent of Vespasian (Suet. *Ves.* 5.7 *nuntiabantur et ex urbe praesagia: ... comitia secundi consulatus ineunte Galba statuam Diui Iuli ad orientem sponte conuersam*). Since according to Suetonius the event occurred at some time in the last quarter of 68 (Galba's 'election'), the Flavian interpretation relies heavily on hindsight. T. focuses instead on the effect at the time (*terrebant*). Plutarch reports that the prodigy 'is said to have happened during the time when Vespasian was at last openly trying to seize the supreme power' (i.e. in the summer of 69, cf. 2.79; see Chilver). **prolocutum ... bouem:** cf. Plin. *Nat.* 8.183 *est frequens in prodigiis priscorum bouem locutum*; what the animal actually said is rarely recorded (in only one of the twenty-three occurrences listed by Hornstein). T. uses a compound verb where other authors have *locutus,* despite his regular preference for uncompounded forms (Goodyear (1972) ad *A.* 1.57.4). **insolitos animalium partus:** peculiar newborns appear very frequently in prodigy lists (e.g. *A.* 12.64.1, 14.12.2, 15.47.1–2; for other authors see Wülker (1904) 14–15). T. refrains from giving the kind of details that Livy provides (e.g. 27.11.5 boy with elephant head, 31.12.7 lamb with pig's head, Obsequ. 40 (based on Livy) baby born with his abdomen open *ut nudum intestinum conspiceretur*). See further below. **plura alia rudibus saeculis etiam in pace obseruata, quae nunc tantum**

in metu audiuntur: cf. Cic. *Div.* 2.58 *atque haec* (sc. *prodigia*) *in bello plura et maiora uidentur timentibus, eadem non tam animaduertuntur in pace; in metu et periculo cum creduntur facilius, tum finguntur impunius*; the balance and measure of Cicero's version contrast with T.'s inconcinnity. *obseruata* and *audiuntur* are non-technical terms (see on *uulgata* above), and stress private reactions, not official prodigy-management methods. With *plura alia* T. again departs from Livian practice: a comparable 'catch-all' phrase appears only once in forty-three lists (21.62.1 *in quis*); in both passages the expression discredits the phenomena so casually reported. **tantum in metu** 'only in perilous times'; cf. 3.58.3 *in metu consilia prudentium et uulgi rumor iuxta audiuntur.* In antithesis with *in pace* T.'s *in metu* replaces Cicero's obvious *in bello.* T. varies both halves of the common doublet at *A.* 15.45.1 *prospere aut in metu.*

86.2 sed . . . impleuit: the nine-word main clause lacks a verb, and is outweighed by a twenty-seven-word abl. abs. expanded by a relative clause, another abl. abs., a participle, and a *non modo . . . sed etiam* construction (Intro. §14). **praecipuus et cum praesenti exitio etiam futuri pauor:** sc. *erat* 'there was particular fear, with both present damage and future (danger)'; cf. 4.65.1 *metus futuri.* T. follows Livy's lead in buttressing prodigies with a natural disaster: e.g. 30.38.10 *inter quae* (sc. *prodigia*) *etiam aquarum insolita magnitudo in religionem uersa* (also 35.21.2–5). **inundatione Tiberis:** for the causal abl. cf. 2.32.1 *prouinciam Narbonensem incursu classis et aduerso proelio contremuisse.* Plutarch, too, says people considered the flood an unfavourable omen (*O.* 4.5). According to Pliny, Tiber floods were more frightening than destructive (*Nat.* 3.55; see Becher (1985) for examples). T. stresses natural causes and effects by giving physical explanations for the collapse of the bridge and the spread of water (see nn.), and by mentioning real damage (deaths, *fames*, collapsed buildings). **immenso auctu:** sc. *aquarum*; instrumental abl. with *proruto.* **ponte sublicio:** *sublicius* 'on pillars'. Earliest of the Tiber bridges at Rome, this narrow wooden structure possessed a special sanctity, so that *pontifices* (rather than censors or *curatores uiarum*) oversaw its maintenance (Varro *L* 5.83 deriving '*pontifex*' from *pons* and *facere*, Plut. *Num.* 9.3, D. H. 2.73.1, 3.45.2), and its occasional destruction was considered a prodigy (Dio 37.58.3–4; in a joke at Cic. *Qfr.* 3.7.1). It was one of the structures rebuilt by Augustus (*RG* 20.5). **strage:** instrumental abl. with *refusus*; for the *uariatio* see 14.1n. *siue . . . Lacone instante.* **obstantis molis:** i.e. of the fallen bridge. **refusus** 'poured out of its normal course' *OLD* 1b; cf. Sen. *NQ* 3.11.2 *ut amisso canali suo flumina . . . refundantur.* **iacentia et plana**

urbis loca sed secura eius modi casuum: *loca*, which makes the expression unusually full (even Livy is briefer: 38.28.4 *Tiberis duodeciens Campum Martium planaque urbis inundauit*), eases the transition from the adjectives of location (*iacentia, plana*) to the personifying *secura*, for which cf. Sen. *NQ* 6.1.2 *Campaniam numquam securam huius* (sc. *terrae motus*) *mali.* **rapti:** sc. *sunt.* **in tabernis et cubilibus:** the antithesis with *e publico* indicates that this doublet defines 'indoors' (i.e. when the flood carries away entire buildings with shops on the ground floor and apartments above), but *cubilibus* – a surprising partner for *tabernis* (cf. 3.83.1 *abditos in tabernis aut si quam in domum*, Juv. 3.303–4 *clausis domibus... catenatae... tabernae*) – adds the pathos of death taking its victims unaware: cf. Liv. 9.37.3 *semisomnos in cubilibus suis... caedes oppressit* (see further *TLL* s.v. 1271.52–63). **in uulgus** sc. *erat*; for *uulgus* 'general public' see *OLD* 1 b. **inopia quaestus et penuria alimentorum:** the low-lying parts of the city included market areas, whose destruction would interrupt both the income of shop-owners (cf. Cic. *Qfr* 3.7.1 (on losses in a flood of 54 B.C.) *tabernae plurimae*) and the supply of goods, including food, for sale (Plut. *O.* 4.5 reports that the grain market was under water in 69). **corrupta:** sc. *sunt.* **insularum fundamenta:** *insulae*, the multi-storey buildings that crowded ancient Rome, were vulnerable to every variety of urban disaster: Juv. 3.193 *nos urbem colimus tenui tibicine fultam.* With the destruction here cf. the more stylized report at *A.* 1.76.1 *continuis imbribus auctus Tiberis stagnauerat; relabentem secuta est aedificiorum et hominum strages* and Horace's even more ominous list: *Carm.* 1.2.13–16 *uidimus flauum Tiberim retortis | litore Etrusco uiolenter undis | ire deiectum monumenta regis | templaque Vestae.* **remeante** 'going back (to its normal course)'; elsewhere T. uses *remeo* (a poetic synonym for *redeo* and *regredior* that he and Pliny the Elder pressed into service: T. sixteen times, Pliny twenty-two, Caesar never, Cicero once, Sallust never, Livy three times, Virgil twice, Statius twelve times) only of persons (e.g. *A.* 14.25.2 *patrias in sedes remeauere*).

86.3 utque: the focus shifts as we move from event to outlook. **quod** 'the fact that'; the subj. reflects the thinking of contemporaries (*NLS* §240). **uia Flaminia:** the principal road between Rome and the Po valley, via Ariminum (mod. Rimini) and the Adriatic coast. Galba travelled it *en route* from Spain in 68 (6.2n. *trucidatis*). After crossing the Tiber at the *pons Muluius* it follows the river valley for about four miles (Ashby (1970) 247–51). Suetonius locates the obstruction at the twentieth milestone (*O.* 8.3); T. emphasizes the ominous significance of what was blocked. **iter belli:** cf. 4.49.2 *itinera audendi*; for the gen. cf. also Ov. *Ars* 2.37 *iter caeli*, Caes. *Ciu.* 1.4.5 *Asiae Syriaeque itinere*. T. also uses dat. (e.g. 61.1 *itinera bello*); other authors prefer prep. phrases (e.g. Cic. *Att.* 13.42.1 *iter ad bellum*).

87–90 *bello consilia*

Against the foreboding background of chh. 80–6 (soldiers undisciplined, senators useless, portents terrifying, nature hostile) T. begins the account of Otho's military effort. A three-part operation was planned, with praetorian and urban cohorts from Rome and detachments of the seven Danube legions converging to confront the Vitellians in the Po valley, while a fleet-based expedition attempted to delay the Alpine crossings. In chh. 87–8 T. mentions only what Otho could initiate with troops available in Rome; the movement of the Danube legions is reserved for Book 2. Otho's strategy has been much studied; for discussion with further bibliography see Chilver 264–73, Murison (1993) 81–119, Syme (1958) App. 30, Wellesley (1971) 33, 38–41. T. himself gives priority to the problems besetting Otho's forces, which, despite the military might and loyalty of the men (87.1), suffered under a crippling confusion of authority (87.1–2). He adds a long tirade on the folly of Rome's aristocracy, now sadly decayed (88.2–3) and another on her populace (89.1–2). In the final chapter Otho leaves for the front (90). The book ends with all forces poised for conflict.

87.1 lustrata urbe: lustration, a ritual of boundary protection and purification in which the officiant proceeds three times around the pomerium before sacrificing a pig, a sheep, and an ox, was a regular form of prodigy expiation (e.g. Liv. 3.29.9 (458 B.C.), 21.62.7 (218 B.C.), 35.9.5 (193 B.C.), 39.27.5 (186 B.C.), 44.18.6–7 (167 B.C.), Obsequ. 12 (166 B.C.), Plin. *Nat.* 10.36 (107 B.C.), Obsequ. 44 (102–1 B.C.), Obsequ. 46 (99 B.C.); also *A.* 13.24 (A.D. 55)). Restoring the *pax deorum* was a necessary preliminary to successful campaigns, and T. follows Livy's practice in juxtaposing expiation and the beginning of a campaign. Otho's traditionalist response to supernatural signs contrasts with that of Galba (18.1 *contemptor talium ut fortuitorum*; see also 22.1–3 and 89.3n. *conditorum anciliorum*). **expensis** 'having been weighed (in the mind)' *OLD* 5; cf. *A.* 14.35.2 *copias armatorum ... causas belli secum expenderent.* **bello consiliis:** 22.2n. *Othoni ... comes.* **quando Poeninae Cottiaeque Alpes et ceteri**

Galliarum aditus Vitellianis exercitibus claudebantur: the interpretation of this causal clause has important consequences for the understanding of Othonian strategy and for T.'s reputation as a military historian. The principal difficulty lies in *Vitellianis exercitibus*, which has been construed with *claudebantur* as both instrumental abl. ('closed by' Chilver *ad loc.*, with discussion; Heubner) and dat. of disadvantage ('inaccessible to' Wellesley (1971) 47 n. 56). Abl. is easy syntactically (cf. 2.32.1 *clausam Alpibus... transpadanam Italiam*, 3.50.3 *teneri praesidiis Appenninum rebantur*; cf. Plut. *O.* 5.1 'Caecina and Valens were reported already in possession of the Alps'), but goes beyond what T. has told us (the passes of the Pennine and Cottian Alps are blocked by Valens and Caecina (61.1) but nothing is said about *ceteri aditus*) and imputes to Otho the unlikely strategy of invading Gaul, when stopping the invaders at the Po was, most historians agree, his plan (87–90n.). The dat. seems to yield the sensible strategy of attracting Vitellian forces to southern France before they could march on Italy, but requires that *aditus Galliarum* mean 'approaches from Gaul' (for which Caesar, at least, uses *aditus ex Gallia atque Hispania* (*Ciu.* 2.1.2)). Two points of Latinity can guide interpretation: (*a*) the ind. represents T.'s analysis of Otho's strategy (*NLS* §242a), which may be incorrect, and (*b*) there is an antithesis between *Galliarum* and *Narbonensem Galliam* (similarly at 2.32.1, 3.41.3 and implicit at *A.* 11.24.3; see 8.1 n. *Galliae*). The dat., which requires a shift of perspective from Vitellians to Otho, muddies this antithesis, while the abl. reinforces it: since (*quando*) crossing into Gaul (i.e. Tres Galliae) was inadvisable (not to say impossible), Otho sent a force to harass Narbonese Gaul (which had declared for Vitellius and expected protection: 2.14.1, 2.28.1 *cura socios tuendi*). Attacking before the Vitellians crossed the Alps might not have been sound strategy, but it does seem to be T.'s view of what Otho initially hoped to do (2.11.2 *quem* (sc. *Caecinam*) *sisti intra Gallias posse sperauerat*; cf. 2.12.1 *aggrediendae... prouinciae Narbonensis... duces dederat*). At 2.28.2 T.'s Vitellians, too, allude to the possibility of Narbonensis becoming the main theatre of war. **Narbonensem Galliam aggredi statuit:** the Othonian rampage in the maritime Alps (in which Agricola's mother perished, *Agr.* 7.1) is described at 2.12–15, 28. The chronology of the expedition (which only T. mentions) is unclear. Wellesley (1971) 47 and Chilver (*ad loc.*) date it to late February, Murison (1993) 102–3 ties the departure date to Otho's summons to the Danube legions (3/4 March) and argues that it delayed Valens, who detached troops to confront it, for about fifteen days (10/11–24/5 March). **reliquos caesorum:**

6.2n. *trucidatis...militum.* **saeuitia Galbae:** T.'s assessment here echoes Otho's at 37.3, but see 49.2n. *magis...uirtutibus.* **in numeros legionis composuerat** 'arranged into the units of a legion'; cf. 4.66.1 (of Civilis hastily organizing Gallic troops) *iuuentute...per cohortes composita.* In T.'s account these survivors were marines aspiring to legionary status who were attacked and imprisoned by Galba, then satisfied, somehow, by Otho. The standard phrases for enrolling troops in a (pre-existing) legion are *in numeros referre* (cf. Plin. *Ep.* 3.8.4 *neque enim adhuc nomen in numeros relatum est,* with Davies (1989) 17) and *in numeros distribuere* (cf. Plin. *Ep.* 10.29.2 *ut iam dixerant sacramento ita nondum distributi in numeros erant tirones*). T.'s avoidance of these phrases may be interpreted in two ways. Either he denotes the standard procedure with non-standard vocabulary, or his unusual phrase denotes an unusual procedure, perhaps the formation of something that looked like a legion, but wasn't quite one (cf. 4.66.1 quoted above), or the conscription of an entirely new legion (an emergency measure adopted by both Nero and Vitellius: 6.2n. *trucidatis...militum*). If T.'s phrase refers to a new formation of either type these troops vanish from the literary and epigraphic record. It seems more likely that T. imagines these marines to have been enrolled in Nero's ex-marine legion, I *Adiutrix*, which was in Rome at the time (6.2, 36.3). His emphasis on that unit's loyalty to Otho then makes good sense: it served Otho's cause energetically at Bedriacum (2.43.1; cf. 2.23.2 *pugnandi ardore*, 2.24.3), whence Vitellius sent it off to Spain *ut pace et otio mitesceret* (2.67.2), and its loyalty outlived Otho (3.44). But see 6.2n. *trucidatis...militum* for the confused record on these troops. **honoratae...militiae:** in their terms of service (twenty-six years rather than twenty, lower pay, citizenship on discharge rather than enlistment) and opportunities for profit (the Mediterranean fleets saw little military activity during the first two centuries A.D.: Starr (1993) 167–208, Reddé (1986) 323–453) marines ranked below the legionaries. For hopes of betterment raised by the disturbances of 68–9 cf. the opportunistic accession of marines to the Flavian cause at 3.50.3. **urbanas cohortes:** 4.2n. *urbanum militem.* Their contribution to the expedition (2.12–15, 28) is not specified. **plerosque e praetorianis:** their number is unclear. Five praetorian cohorts and their prefect Licinius Proculus (see below) accompanied the advance guard to the Po (2.11.2), and the remaining seven were divided between Otho (2.11.3) and this expedition. See 2.14.2–3 for their importance in the expedition's principal battle. **ipsis ducibus consilium et custodes:** deadpan irony well rendered by Wellesley 'to...give the generals the benefit of their advice and protection'; for the idea cf. 74.2 *simulationem officii*, for the irony cf. *ad obseruandam honestiorum fidem* below.

87.2 Antonio Nouello: he did nothing of note in Narbonensis (2.12.1 *Antonio Nouello nulla auctoritas*) and is unknown elsewhere. **Suedio Clementi:** cf. 2.12.1 *Suedius Clemens ambitioso imperio regebat, ut aduersus modestiam disciplinae corruptus, ita proeliorum auidus*. He survived the civil wars and prospered under Vespasian and Titus, serving as praetorian tribune, imperial administrator in Pompeii (*ILS* 5492, 6438 b–d), and *praefectus castrorum* in Egypt (*CIL* III 33). On his career see Dobson (1978) 207–8; *PIR* s 687). **primipilaribus:** 31.2n. **Aemilio Pacensi:** 20.3n. **permissa:** sc. *est*. **curam nauium:** untechnical language; cf. 2.24.3 *curam peditum Paulinus, equitum Celsus sumpsere* and contrast 2.100.3 *Lucilius Bassus... Rauennati simul Misenensi classibus a Vitellio praepositus*. Freedmen had displaced equestrian fleet prefects during the reigns of Claudius and Nero (the most notorious being Anicetus, prefect from A.D. 59–61, *A.* 14.3–8, 62), but equestrians (including Bassus (above) and the elder Pliny) managed the fleets thereafter (Starr (1993) 30–8). **†immutatus†** is the reading of some copies of M (which is here missing), others offer *inuitatus* and *imitatus*. None is satisfactory. Heubner takes *immutatus* as 'changed' (cf. *D.* 24.2, *A.* 6.2.2, 11.29.2; the text is uncertain at *H.* 2.100.2), but there are no parallels for *immutare ad* as he explains it, namely, that Moschus was still *praefectus classis*, but had the additional assignment (*immutatus*) of keeping an eye on his betters, *ad obseruandam honestiorum fidem*. Wellesley adopts *inuitatus*, explaining '*Moschus praemiis promissis minis inuitatus est*' (in app. crit.), but by itself *inuitatus* is too bare (cf. 2.82.3 *praemio inuitarent*). *imitatus* is nonsense. Wellesley lists seventeen suggested emendations. Whatever word (if any) modifies Moschus, T.'s point is clear: Moschus' mission was comparable to that of another Neronian freedman, Polyclitus: *A.* 14.39.1 *ad spectandum Britanniae statum missus est e libertis Polyclitus*. Polyclitus' invidious authority over his superiors, a legate and a procurator (the legate – Suetonius Paulinus, on whom see below – was recalled) receives extended comment (14.39.1–3); e.g. *mirabantur* (sc. *barbari*) *quod dux et exercitus tanti belli confector seruitiis oboedirent*. See also 76.3n. *nam...faciunt*. **peditum equitumque copiis:** T. now turns to the forces sent to delay the Vitellians at the Po until the Danubian legions should arrive. For its constituents see 2.11.2, for its operations 2.18–26. **Suetonius Paulinus:** cos. suff. *c.* 43, cos. II 66 (*PIR* s 694). Militarily the most distinguished of the three commanders (hence *auctoritatem Paulini*, cf. 90.2, 2.32.1 *nemo illa tempestate militaris* *rei callidior habebatur*, 2.37.1 *uetustissimus consularium et militia clarus*), Paulinus had commanded troops in Mauretania as long ago as A.D. 41 (Dio 60.9), but was renowned primarily for his achievements in Britain (A.D. 58–61; *Agr.* 5.1, 14.2, 16.2, *A.* 14.29–39). He and Celsus inflicted a serious defeat on Caecina in the battle *ad Castores* (2.24–6 *res egregiae*) and his was the (unheeded) voice of prudent delay in Otho's war council (2.32; cf. 2.25.2 *cunctator natura et cui cauta potior consilia cum ratione quam prospera ex casu placerent*). Vitellius pardoned him (2.60.1). He left a written account of a journey he made in Africa (Plin. *Nat.* 5.14–15), and it is possible that T. drew from him details of both the British campaigns and the *ad Castores* battle (Syme (1958) 765; T.'s father-in-law, Agricola, was a close connection). His death is nowhere recorded. **Marius Celsus:** 14.1 n. **Annius Gallus:** suffect consul under Nero sometime between 62 and 68, perhaps at an advanced age (hence *maturitatem Galli*; *PIR*[2] A 653), he was put in charge of these troops and crossed the Po to preserve contact with the legions *en route* from the Danube. His subordinates had better success than he (Spurinna at Placentia, 2.18–22, Martius Macer near Cremona, 2.23.3). Gallus had difficulty controlling the exuberant legion of ex-marines (I *Adiutrix*) and was injured when his horse fell (2.33.1), so he took no part in the Othonian success *ad Castores* (2.24–6). Otho's brother eventually replaced him in command (2.23.4). Gallus supported his consular colleagues in urging delay (2.33.1) and calmed the troops after the defeat at Bedriacum (2.44.2). He survived Vitellius' principate and later appears in command of Flavian forces (4.68.1, 5.19.1). **rectores** 'commanders' *OLD* 4c. **destinati:** sc. *sunt.* **plurima fides** 'his greatest reliance' *OLD* 12b; that the praetorian prefect, an *eques*, could surpass in importance (if not rank) distinguished consular commanders is an aspect of the principate that T. found unpalatable (cf. *A.* 4.74.3–5 on Sejanus' pre-eminence). Otho's reliance was ill placed: Proculus gives bad advice at 2.33.1 (*imperitia properantes* (sc. *Proculus et Titianus*)) and is responsible for *culpa* at 2.37.1. He shows less spirit than his men at 2.44 and succeeds in excusing himself to Vitellius (2.60.1). His career is not elsewhere attested. **urbanae militiae impiger:** backhanded praise, since *urbana militia* is practically an oxymoron (cf. 2.19.1 *is labor urbano militi insolitus*, and 2.21.4 contrasting the *robur* of the German legions with urban troops, *segnem et desidem et circo ac theatris corruptum militem*); contrast the unqualified 2.5.1 *Vespasianus acer militiae* and 3.43.1 *strenuus militiae.* For *impiger* see 53.1 n. **bellorum insolens:** the plural is concrete (*A&G* §100c), emphasizing Proculus' absence from Rome's wars. **ut cuique erat** 'respectively'; lit. 'as each had (these qualities)'. **prauus . . . anteibat:** for the expression cf. Sal. *Hist.* fr. 1.77.13 *antea . . . boni malos facile anteibant, nunc . . .*); for the behaviour see 64.4n. *infamauerat.*

88.1 sepositus: sc. *est.* 10.1 n. *mox . . . sepositus.* **Cornelius Dolabella** was a candidate for adoption by Galba (Plut. *G.* 23.1; 13.2n. *non . . . aliquem*), but the precise relationship between the two is unclear (see *PIR*[2] c 1347). At some point Galba had disbanded a German bodyguard unit on the grounds that it was partial to Dolabella (Suet. *G.* 12.2). Otho tightens the restraints on him here; Vitellius has him killed (2.63–4). T. stresses his innocence (*nullum ob crimen*) and the danger of social eminence and connection with the emperor (cf. 2.3n. *nobilitas*). Plutarch's version is more strongly suggestive of protective custody: *O.* 5.1 'Dolabella, a man of noble family, made the praetorians suspect revolutionary intent, so Otho, fearing either him or someone else, sent him away with heartening words (παραθαρρύνας) to the city of Aquinum.' T. treats Dolabella's eventual death as a revealing sample (*specimen*) of Vitellius' principate: it is instigated by an intimate friend (2.63.1; cf. 2.3n. *quibus . . . oppressi*), exposes a weakness in Flavius Sabinus (46.1 n.), introduces an unpleasant female (2.63.2 *Triaria, L. Vitelli uxor, ultra feminam ferox*), suggests sexual jealousy in Vitellius (2.64.1 *quod Petroniam uxorem eius mox Dolabella in matrimonium accepisset*), and illustrates a soldier's indifference both to his emperor's orders (and reputation) and to killing: 2.64.1 *uocatum* (sc. *Dolabellam*) *. . . deuertere Interamnium atque ibi interfici iussit. longum interfectori uisum: in itinere ac taberna proiectum humi iugulauit, magna cum inuidia noui principatus, cuius hoc primum specimen noscebatur.* Dolabella's son (by Vitellius' ex-wife) became consul in 86. **coloniam Aquinatem:** Aquinum, mod. Aquino, on the via Latina some 105 km from Rome, Juvenal's hometown (*Sat.* 3.319). **neque arta custodia neque obscura:** cf. the antithesis between 'respectful custody' and chains at 3.12.3 *Bassus honorata custodia . . . Atriam peruectus a praefecto alae . . . uincitur.* Dolabella left Aquinum for Rome after Otho's death (2.63.1). **multos e magistratibus:** the difficult straits of the capital's elite receive extended (but not sympathetic) treatment from T. (118 words *multos . . . tutissimi*; cf. 4.3 *patres laeti*, 19.1 *patrum fauor aderat*, 35.1 *equitum plerique ac senatorum . . . ruere*, etc. 45.1 *ruere cuncti*, etc., 81.2 *trepidi*, 2.52.2 *trepidi*). Plutarch is much briefer (*O.* 5.1: 22 words; see App. 1). **ministros bello:** 22.2n. *Othoni . . . comes.* **comitum specie:** more sarcastic than Plut. *O.* 5.1 'men to share his journey' (συνεκδήμους). **Lucium Vitellium:** behind his brother in the *cursus honorum*, and presumably younger, he was suffect consul in 48 and succeeded Aulus as governor of Africa (*PIR* v 501). He plays a prominent role during his brother's principate beginning at 2.54.1 with a meeting of senators after Otho's defeat. The picture that emerges is not flattering: he leads the senate in condemning the traitor Caecina (3.37.1 *atrocis* . . . *sententiae*), manipulates Vitellius into executing a personal enemy (3.38, a long narrative introduced by *mors* . . . *famosa*), and captures Tarracina with signal cruelty (3.76–7, esp. 3.77.2 *Iulianus* . . . *ad L. Vitellium perductus et uerberibus foedatus in ore eius iugulatur*); his wife's contribution is equally noxious (3.77.2 *superbe saeueque egisset*; for Triaria see also above on Dolabella). This episode elicits a character sketch: 3.77.4 *L. Vitellio, quamuis infami inerat industria, ne uirtutibus, ut boni, sed quo modo pessimus quisque, uitiis ualebat* (cf. also 3.38.2 *omni dedecore maculosum*). He surrenders to the Flavians at 4.2.1 and is promptly killed, whereupon he gets an epitaph 4.2.3 *par uitiis fratris, in principatu eius uigilantior, nec perinde prosperis socius quam aduersis abstractus*. Suetonius adds that he entertained the new *princeps* extravagantly: *Vit.* 13.2 *famosissima* . . . *cena data ei aduenticia a fratre, in qua duo milia lectissimorum piscium, septem auium apposita traduntur.* **cultu** 'respect' *OLD* 11; cf. Sal. *Jug.* 5.7 *eodem cultu quo liberos suos habuit* (sc. *Iugurtham*).

88.2 motae: sc. *sunt.* **urbis curae:** reiterated in *nullus ordo metu* . . . *uacuus.* The components of the *urbs* (*primores senatus* . . . *nobilitas* . . . *eques* . . . *uulgus*) are surveyed top to bottom, as in 4.3; at 35.1 the order is reversed. **quanto:** for other passages where T. omits *tanto* from the correlative pair see GG IIB2c; for another variation see 12.3n. *eodem auctu.* **pauidi:** sc. *erant.*

88.3 irritamenta libidinum: cf. 2.62.1 *irritamenta gulae* and see 20.1n. *instrumenta uitiorum.* Like Otho's pride in the (useless) allegiance of the senate (84.3n. *senatus nobiscum est*), this detail aligns his party with Pompey's: Caes. *Ciu.* 3.96.1 *in castris Pompei uidere licuit trichilas structas, magnum argenti pondus expositum, recentibus caespitibus tabernacula constrata* . . . *tabernacula protecta hedera multaque praeterea quae nimiam luxuriam et uictoriae fiduciam designarent.* T. is less detailed but more outraged. **sapientibus . . . tutissimi:** the motives of Vespasian's partisans are similarly mixed: 2.7.2 *optimus quisque amore rei publicae, multos dulcedo praedarum stimulabat, alios ambiguae domi res; ita boni malique causis diuersis, studio pari, bellum omnes cupiebant.* **sapientibus:** sc. *erat.* **spe uana tumens:** Miller (1987b) 98 compares Virg. *Aen.* 11.854 (on Arruns, who has just killed Camilla) *fulgentem armis ac uana tumentem*, and Sil. 17.429 *Clytium* . . . *uana tumentem*: 'Apart from the inevitable Silius example, which has become almost a guarantee of Virgilian influence, the combination of *uana* and *tumeo* appears to be found only in Virgil and Tacitus.' T. has varied the hexameter line-end by borrowing Livy's *uana praedae spes* (23.42.12). **afflicta fide:** the abl. abs. is causal 'since their (financial) credit had been impaired'; *OLD* s.v. *fides* 5. For the metaphor cf. Suet. *Ves.* 4.3 *prope labefacta iam fide*, for the idea 2.7.2 *ambiguae domi res* as a stimulant for bellicosity; for both cf. Luc. 1.180 *concussa fides et multis utile bellum.* Cf. also 30.2 *fides . . . illaesa.* **ac** connects the first two modifiers of *multi* (the descriptive abl. *afflicta fide* and *alacres*); for *ac . . . et* cf. *A.* 12.46.1. (The series *et . . . ac* is more common: e.g. 43.1 *occurrens . . . et . . . exprobrans ac . . . uertendo.*) Heubner prints Nolte's emendation *anxii.* **per incerta tutissimi:** an unexpected and paradoxical phrase concludes the critique of those who desire war.

89.1 uulgus et . . . populus: 35.1 nn. *non populus tantum* and *imperita plebs*, 50.1 n. *non senatus modo . . . sed uulgus quoque.* **magnitudine nimia:** causal abl. with *expers populus* 'because its size was too great', cf. 8.1 *tamquam in tanta multitudine*, 33.2 *tantae multitudinis*, 75.1 *tantam hominum multitudinem*, all on Rome's populace. This fits the context (the ills of war are just now beginning to be felt by the masses). Others take *magnitudine* with *communium curarum*; for discussion see Hellegouarc'h, who takes it with both. **sentire:** historic inf. (46.3n. *fatigari*). **conuersa . . . fuit:** twenty-nine-word abl. abs. appended to a thirteen-word main clause. **intentis** 'made more severe' *OLD* 5; cf. Plin. *Ep.* 4.9.17 *senatui . . . licet et mitigare leges et intendere.* **perinde:** 30.3n. **attriuerant** 'had impoverished' *OLD* 3b; cf. *G.* 29.1 *nec publicanus atterit* (sc. *Germanos*).

89.2 ex quo: sc. *tempore.* **res Caesarum:** 1.1 n. *ut alienae.* **pacis aduersa:** 50.2n. *saeuae pacis.* In the 'table of contents' at 2.2–3 T. offers a list of *aduersa* from the Flavian period, many of which have counterparts under Tiberius and Gaius (see nn.). For the oxymoron cf. Juv. 6.292 *nunc patimur longae pacis mala.* **Scriboniani . . . incepta:** a rebellion in A.D. 42, not long after Claudius' accession, headed by a governor of Dalmatia with two legions at his disposal: Suet. *Cl.* 13.2 *bellum ciuile mouit Furius Camillus Scribonianus*, etc. Its adherents were ruthlessly punished: Dio 60.15–16. T.'s narrative is lost. **simul audita et coercita:** sc. *erant*; cf. Suet. *Cl.* 13.2 *intra quintum diem oppressus est.* Rapid victory is conveyed by similar expressions elsewhere: cf. *A.* 3.47.1 *tum demum Tiberius ortum patratumque bellum senatu scripsit*, Liv. 44.32.5 *hoc . . . bellum prius perpetratum quam coeptum Romae auditum est.* **Nero nuntiis magis et rumoribus quam armis depulsus:** sc. *erat*; for discussion and bibliography see Murison

(1993) 1–26. Plutarch uses a different antithesis (*G.* 29.1 Galba brought down Nero 'by his reputation (δόξηι) rather than by his strength (δυνάμει)') and places it in Galba's epitaph. The epitaph in T. (49.2) has no equivalent phrase. **quod raro alias:** sc. *factum est.* Praetorians accompanied campaigning emperors (e.g. Claudius in Britain: Durry (1938) 367), but there were few such occasions during the long peace. Bérard (1988) cites examples of urban cohorts in external campaigns under Domitian and Trajan, none earlier. **deducti:** sc. *sunt.* **a tergo:** sc. *erat.* **si ducibus aliis bellatum foret** 'had the war been fought under different leaders', with *longo bello materia* (sc. *erat*), a comment by T. based on hindsight. For his assessment of the actual conflict between Otho and Vitellius see 2.38.2 *quod singulis uelut ictibus transacta sunt bella, ignauia principum factum est.*

89.3 moras religionemque: the second term explains the first (GG s.v. *-que* AIIa). Religious observance (see n. below) would have delayed Otho until 23 March at the earliest, eight days. Here religion seems a delaying tactic on the part of Otho's advisors (*fuere qui . . . afferrent*) and Otho's haste reasoned (*cunctationem . . . exitiosam*). In Suet. (*O.* 8.3 *nulla ne religionum quidem cura*) the same episode illustrates Otho's impiety. Suetonius' Otho also ignores *aduersissima auspicia* (*O.* 8.3; not in T. or Plut.). **nondum conditorum ancilium:** cf. Suet. *O.* 8.3 *motis necdum conditis ancilibus, quod antiquitus infaustum habetur.* The story of the twelve *ancilia* (round shields) is told at Ov. *Fast.* 3.365–96: the first was a gift from Jupiter to Numa, eleven copies were made to keep its identity hidden. The Salii carried them about Rome from 1–23 March. These days were also inauspicious for marriage (Ov. *Met.* 3.392–6) and journeys (Liv. 37.33.6 *dies . . . religiosi ad iter*). **Caecina . . . transgressus exstimulabat:** for the expression cf. Liv. 3.35.3 *demissa . . . in discrimen dignitas . . . stimulabat Ap. Claudium.* On the '*ab urbe condita*' expression as subject see 18.1 n. *obseruatum . . . dirimendis.*

90.1 pridie Idus Martius: 14 March, a day on which the Arval Brethren made vows on Otho's behalf (McC–W 2.14 *pro salute et reditu*). **commendata patribus re publica:** the senate's only known action during the remainder of Otho's principate was the trial of Annius Faustus (2.10), a *delator* active under Nero and easy to attack because his rank was only equestrian. **reliquias Neronianarum sectionum nondum in fiscum conuersas:** cf. Plut. *O.* 1.3 'to all senators who had been exiled under Nero and restored under Galba he gave back as much of each man's property as he found unsold'; this was one of Otho's conciliatory measures, the rest of which T. reports in ch. 77. *sectio* is the 'buying up (of confiscated property) at auction' (*OLD* 2; cf. 20.1n. *hasta et sector*), so T.'s expression is slightly illogical (if property was actually bought surely the revenue went straight to the *fiscus*), but *sectio* is the term that best conveys an invidious aspect of confiscations, namely, that others besides the *fiscus* could profit: *A.* 13.23.1 *Paetus quidam, exercendis sectionibus famosus*, Suet. *Vit.* 2.1 (invective on the origins of Vitellius' family) *filius sectionibus... uberius compendium nanctus*; cf. Cic. *Phil.* 2.64 *exspectantibus omnibus quisnam esset tam impius, tam demens, tam dis hominibusque hostis, qui ad illud scelus sectionis auderet accedere*, etc. **reuocatis ab exilio:** Galba recalled Nero's exiles (4.3n. *clientes... erecti*) and Otho began the restoration of their dignity (77.3nn. *recoluit, reditus... senatorius locus*), but they are still waiting for money (from Vitellius) at 2.92.2 *flebilis et egens nobilium turba, quos ipsos liberosque patriae Galbae reddiderat, nulla principis misericordia iuuarentur.* No mention of assistance (if any) from Vespasian survives. At *A.* 15.73.2 T. reports information on the Pisonian conspiracy from exiles *qui post interitus Neronis in urbem regressi sunt.* **iustissimum donum:** for the acc. in apposition to, and commenting on, the sentence see 44.2n. *munimentum... ultionem.* **exactione** 'the execution (of a plan)' *OLD* 3. **usu sterile:** for the agricultural metaphor cf. 3.1n. *uirtutum sterile saeculum.*

90.2 aduersum... disseruit: onto this five-word main clause (preceded by thirteen subordinated words), are appended forty-two words of commentary (*inscitiam... credebatur*); Intro. §14. **nulla Vitellii mentione:** for the caution cf. 2.30.3 *duces partium Othonis quamuis uberrima conuiciorum in Vitellium materia abstinerent*, 3.9.4 *simul uirtus Germanici exercitus laudibus attollebatur, Vitelli modica et uulgari mentione, nulla in Vespasianum contumelia.* **ipsius:** sc. *erat.* **Galeri Trachali:** cos. 68 with Silius Italicus and later Nero, speech-writer for Otho, in-law (perhaps) of Vitellius (cf. 2.60.2 *Trachalum aduersus criminantes Galeria uxor Vitellii protexit*), and governor of Africa under the Flavians (*PIR*[2] G 30). His career inscription survives (*CIL* V 5812 = McC–W 255). Quintilian's tributes to Trachalus' oratorical performances (*Inst.* 10.1.119, 12.5.5–6) show that his talents were wasted as a ghost-writer. **erant qui... noscerent** may be a trace of eyewitness testimony (Intro. §17). **crebro fori usu celebre:** Quintilian describes a memorable performance at *Inst.* 12.5.6: speaking in one of four trials being held simultaneously in the noisy Basilica Julia, Trachalus drew the attention and, finally, praise of all four courts: *hoc uotum est et rara felicitas.* **latum et sonans** 'copious and sonorous'. *latus* is a frequent antithesis to 'compressed' or 'cut short': e.g. Quint. *Inst.* 10.1.106 *ille concludit astrictius, hic* *latius*, Plin. *Ep.* 20.19 *non amputata et abscissa oratio, sed lata et magnifica et excelsa* (*OLD* 6). For *sonans* (*OLD* 3) cf. Sen. *Ep.* 114.14 (on contemporary rhetorical style) *splendidis uti ac sonantibus et poeticis* (sc. *uerbis*); the related stylistic term *sonus* 'sonority' is usually associated with a genre or setting (e.g. *D.* 10.4 *coturnum uestrum aut heroici carminis sonum*; *OLD* s.v. 3), but cf. Quint. *Inst.* 10.1.67–8 (a stylistic comparison of Euripides and Sophocles): *grauitas et coturnus et sonus Sophocli uidetur esse sublimior.* At *Inst.* 12.10.11 Quintilian mentions among rhetorical virtues the *sonus Trachali.*

90.3 clamor uocesque . . . publicum: for the scene cf. 32.1 *uniuersa iam plebs Palatium implebat* (with nn.). **nimiae et falsae:** sc. *erant*, characterizing the cries of support as unreliable (cf. 35.1 *ignauissimus quisque et, ut res docuit, in periculo non ausurus, nimii uerbis, linguae feroces*) and insincere (cf. 45.1 *quanto . . . magis falsa erant quae fiebant, tanto plura facere*) and linking this passage with earlier crowd scenes. **ut in familiis:** for the analogy cf. 22.1, where Otho's slaves are *corruptius quam in priuata domo habiti.* **priuata cuique:** sc. *erat*; for the antithesis with *decus publicum* cf. 19.1 *priuatas spes agitantes sine publica cura* (on senators under Galba; cf. 45.1 n. *alium . . . populum*) and 2.7.2 *optimus quisque amore rei publicae, multos dulcedo praedarum stimulabat, alios ambiguae domi res.* The reading of all but two MSS is *simulatio*, which Wellesley accepts, but *priuata simulatio* can hardly yield the required sense 'self-interested pretence'. *stimulatio*, which often expresses motives (cf. 25.2 *suspensos . . . animos diuersis artibus stimulant*, 2.7.2 quoted above, and *A.* 2.46.3 *propriae . . . causae stimulabant*) makes a better parallel for the causal abl. *metu*, *amore*, and *ex libidine*, and a more effective antithesis with *uile. priuata stimulatio* does convey self-interest, while the scene itself (with *nimiae et falsae*) guarantees the insincerity of the crowd's enthusiasm. **profectus:** Suetonius sets his departure on 15 March (*O.* 8.3). **quietem urbis curasque imperii . . . fratri permisit:** Titianus was soon summoned from Rome to take charge of the war (2.23.5). The former task would in ordinary circumstances be the responsibility of the urban prefect, currently Flavius Sabinus (46.1 nn. *Flauium Sabinum* and *praefecere*).

APPENDICES

1 PARALLEL PASSAGES SHOWING STRONG VERBAL SIMILARITIES

N.B. The translations from Plutarch and Dio replicate the original syntax and word order as closely as possible.

5.2 accessit Galbae uox pro re publica honesta, ipsi anceps, legi a se militem, non emi.
Plut. *G.* 18.2 'He made a statement befitting a great general, saying that he was accustomed to levy soldiers, not to buy them.'
Suet. *G.* 16.1 iactauit legere se militem non emere consuesse.
Dio 64.3.3 'He said, "I am accustomed to levy soldiers, not to buy them."'

6.2 introitus in urbem trucidatis tot milibus inermium militum infaustus omine
Plut. *G.* 15.4 'neither a happy nor an auspicious omen for Galba entering the city through much slaughter and so many bodies'

7.2 seu bene seu male facta parem inuidiam afferebant.
Plut. *G.* 18.1 'Even his moderate measures were criticized.'

7.3 seruorum manus subitis auidae et tamquam apud senem festinantes
Plut. *G.* 16.4 'Vinius, seeing that Galba was weak and old, took his fill of good fortune on the ground that its beginning practically coincided with its ending.'

9.1 legatum Hordeonium Flaccum spernebat, senecta ac debilitate pedum inualidum, sine constantia, sine auctoritate.
Plut. *G.* 18.4 'Flaccus, physically incapacitated by acute gout and without practical experience, was a complete cipher to them.'

9.1b A. Vitellius aderat, censoris Vitellii ac ter consulis filius. id satis uidebatur.
Suet. *Vit.* 7.3 excepit uelut dono deum oblatum (sc. Vitellium), ter consulis filium.
Dio 64.4.2 'all that counted was his good birth' (εὐγένεια).

12.1 rupta sacramenti reuerentia
Suet. *G.* 16.2 obsequium rumpere ausi

13.1 Potentia principatus diuisa in Titum Vinium consulem Cornelium Laconem praetorii praefectum; nec minor gratia Icelo Galbae liberto, quem anulis donatum equestri nomine Marcianum uocitabant.

Suet. *G.* 14.2 regebatur trium arbitrio, quos una et intra Palatium habitantes nec umquam non adhaerentes paedagogos uulgo uocabant. ii erant T. Vinius legatus eius in Hispania, cupiditatis immensae; Cornelius Laco ex assessore praefectus praetorii, arrogantia socordiaque intolerabilis; libertus Icelus, paulo ante anulis aureis et Marciani cognomine ornatus ac iam summae equestris gradus candidatus.

13.3 in prouinciam Lusitaniam specie legationis seposuit.

Suet. *O.* 3.2 sepositus est per causam legationis in Lusitaniam.

13.4 Otho comiter administrata prouincia primus in partes transgressus nec segnis et, donec bellum fuit, inter praesentes splendidissimus, spem adoptionis statim conceptam acrius in dies rapiebat.

Plut. *G.* 20.1 'He made himself neither unpleasant nor hateful to his subjects ... When Galba revolted he was the first of the governors to go over to him.'

Suet. *O.* 3.2–4.1 prouinciam administrauit quaestorius per decem annos, moderatione atque abstinentia singulari. ut tandem occasio ultionis data est, conatibus Galbae primus accessit; eodemque momento et ipse spem imperii cepit magnam.

14.2 Piso M. Crasso et Scribonia genitus

Plut. *G.* 23.1 'Piso, son of Crassus and Scribonia'

17.1 Pisonem ferunt statim intuentibus et mox coniectis in eum omnium oculis nullum turbati aut exsultantis animi motum prodidisse.

Plut. *G.* 23.3 'As for Piso, those present marvelled perceiving from his voice and his expression that he received so great a benefit without astonishment, though not without feeling.'

18.1 Quartum idus Ianuarias, foedum imbribus diem, tonitrua et fulgura et caelestes minae ultra solitum turbauerant.

Plut. *G.* 23.2 'Great signs from heaven accompanied his setting out, and when he began his speech and announcements in the camp there was so much thunder and lightning, so much rain and darkness, that it was clear that heaven neither favoured nor approved an act of adoption that would lead to no good.'

19.1 quadriduo, quod medium inter adoptionem et caedem fuit
Plut. *G.* 24.1 'It was not the work of four days to change the allegiance of a healthy army, and only so many days intervened between the adoption and the murder.'

20.1 bis et uiciens miliens sestertium donationibus Nero effuderat; appellari singulos iussit, decima parte liberalitatis apud quemque eorum relicta. at illis uix decimae super portiones erant, isdem erga aliena sumptibus quibus sua prodegerant.
Plut. *G.* 16.2 'The gifts that Nero had given to the people of stage and palaestra were all recalled, except for the tenth part. When he got small and niggardly sums (for most had squandered what they had received, being improvident and satyr-like individuals) he sought out people who had bought or received anything from these and exacted it from them.'
Suet. *G.* 15.1 liberalitates Neronis non plus decimis concessis . . . reuocandas curauit exigendasque, ut et si quid scaenici ac xystici donatum olim uendidissent, auferretur emptoribus, quando illi pretio absumpto soluere nequirent.

22.1 non erat Othonis mollis et corpori similis animus.
Plut. *G.* 25.1 'In spirit he was not enfeebled, as per the softness and effeminacy of his body.'
Suet. *O.* 12.1 tanto Othonis animo nequaquam corpus aut habitus competit.

22.2 e quibus (sc. mathematicis) Ptolemaeus Othoni in Hispania comes, cum superfuturum eum Neroni promisisset, postquam ex euentu fides, coniectura iam et rumore senium Galbae et iuuentam Othonis computantium persuaserat fore ut in imperium ascisceretur.
Plut. *G.* 23.4 '. . . Ptolemaeus, who frequently expressed confidence in his prediction that Nero would not kill Otho but would predecease him, while Otho would survive and rule the Romans (for having shown the former to be true he thought that Otho should not despair of the latter).'
Suet. *O.* 4.1 qui (sc. Seleucus mathematicus) cum eum olim superstitem Neroni fore spopondisset, tunc ultro inopinatus aduenerat imperaturum quoque breui repromittens.

24.1 quotiens Galba apud Othonem epularetur, cohorti excubias agenti uiritim centenos nummos diuideret.

Plut. *G.* 20.4 'Whenever he entertained Galba he gave a bribe to the cohort on guard duty, an *aureus* to each man, thus appearing to honour Galba but reducing his power and courting the favour of the troops.'

Suet. *O.* 4.2 quotiens cena principem acciperet, aureos excubanti cohorti uiritim diuidebat.

24.2 adeo animosus corruptor ut Cocceio Proculo speculatori de parte finium cum uicino ambigenti uniuersum uicini agrum sua pecunia emptum dono dederit.

Suet. *O.* 4.2 cuidam etiam de parte finium cum uicino litiganti adhibitus arbiter totum agrum redemit emancipauitque.

25.1 Barbium Proculum tesserarium speculatorum et Veturium optionem eorundem

Plut. *G.* 24.1 'Among those were Veturius and Barbius, the one an *optio*, the other a *tesserarius*.'

25.1b pretio et promissis

Plut. *G.* 24.1 'some with money, others with hopes' (τοὺς μὲν ἀργυρίῳ, τοὺς δὲ ἐλπίσι)

27.1 sacrificanti pro aede Apollinis Galbae haruspex Vmbricius tristia exta et instantes insidias ac domesticum hostem praedicit.

Plut. *G.* 24.2 'Early that day Galba offered sacrifice on the Palatine with his friends present. The officiant, Umbricius, as soon as he took the victim's entrails into his hands and studied them, said (not through enigmas but directly) that there were signs of a great disturbance and that danger and treachery threatened the life of the emperor.'

Suet. *G.* 19.1 sacrificanti mane haruspex identidem monuit caueret periculum, non longe percussores abesse.

27.1–2 nec multo post libertus Onomastus nuntiat exspectari eum ab architecto et redemptoribus, quae significatio coeuntium iam militum et paratae coniurationis conuenerat. Otho, causam digressus requirentibus, cum emi sibi praedia uetustate suspecta eoque prius exploranda finxisset, innixus liberto per Tiberianam domum in Velabrum, inde ad miliarium aureum sub aedem Saturni pergit.

Plut. *G.* 24.4 'Onomastus his freedman arrived and said that the builders (ἀρχιτέκτονας) were waiting for him at home. This signalled the moment when Otho had to meet up with the soldiers.

Saying, therefore, that he had bought an old house and wanted to show things he was suspicious about to the sellers, he went off. Proceeding through what is called the *domus Tiberiana* he came to the Forum, where stands the gilded column at which all the roads that cut across Italy terminate.'

Suet. *O.* 6.2 deinde liberto adesse architectos nuntiante, quod signum conuenerat, quasi uenalem domum inspecturus abscessit proripuitque se postica parte Palati ad constitutum (the plan was described earlier: praemonitis consciis, ut se in foro sub aede Saturni ad miliarium aureum opperirentur).

Dio 64.5.3 'He hurried off as if on some other errand.'

27.2 ibi tres et uiginti speculatores consalutatum imperatorem... strictis mucronibus rapiunt.

Plut. *G.* 25.1 'Here, they say, the first to receive him and salute him as emperor numbered no more than three and twenty.'

Suet. *O.* 6.3 imperator consalutatus inter faustas acclamationes strictosque gladios ad principia deuenit.

28 Stationem in castris agebat Iulius Martialis tribunus. is magnitudine subiti sceleris, an corrupta latius castra et, si contra tenderet, exitium metuens, praebuit plerisque suspicionem conscientiae.

Plut. *G.* 25.3 'Of tribunes the one on guard at the camp, Martialis – they say he was not a conspirator and was surprised by the unexpected and frightened – allowed them to enter.'

29.1 sacris intentus fatigabat alieni iam imperii deos, cum affertur rumor

Plut. *G.* 25.4 'At the Palatine the news was immediately announced to Galba, who was still at the sacrifice with the entrails in his hands.'

29.2 Piso pro gradibus domus uocatos in hunc modum allocutus est: (a speech follows).

Plut. *G.* 25.4 'Piso went out and met with the praetorians on guard duty.'

31.2 Missus et Celsus Marius ad electos Illyrici exercitus Vipsania in porticu tendentes.

Plut. *G.* 25.5 'To the Illyrian unit camped in the so-called *porticus Vipsania* was sent Marius Celsus.'

31.3 Germanica uexilla diu nutauere, inualidis adhuc corporibus et placatis animis, quod eos a Nerone Alexandriam praemissos atque inde

rursus longa nauigatione aegros impensiore cura Galba refouebat.
Suet. *G.* 20.1 ii (sc. Germaniciani) ob recens meritum, quod se aegros et inualidos magno opere fouisset, in auxilium aduolauerunt.

33.2 Vinium Laco minaciter inuasit, stimulante Icelo.
Plut. *G.* 26.1 'Icelus and Laco . . . assailed Vinius vehemently.'

34.2 occisum in castris Othonem uagus primum et incertus rumor.
Plut. *G.* 26.1 'Many a report circulated to the effect that Otho had been killed in the camp.'

35.2 Obuius in Palatio Iulius Atticus speculator cruentum gladium ostentans occisum a se Othonem exclamauit. et Galba 'commilito,' inquit 'quis iussit?'
Plut. *G.* 26.1–2 'After a short time was seen Julius Atticus, a praetorian of some distinction. He was approaching with drawn sword and shouting that he had killed the emperor's enemy. Shoving his way through those ahead of him he showed Galba his bloody sword. Galba, looking at him, said "Who gave the order?"'
Suet. *G.* 19.2 iis ut occurreret prodiit tanta fiducia, ut militi cuidam occisum a se Othonem glorianti 'quo auctore?' responderit.
Dio 64.6.2 'A certain soldier, holding out his drawn and bloody sword, approached him and said, "Take heart, emperor, for I have killed Otho and there is no further cause for fear." Believing him, Galba said "And who ordered you to do this?"'

37.5 minore auaritia ac licentia grassatus esset T. Vinius si ipse imperasset.
Suet. *G.* 14.2 his (sc. Vinio, Lacone, Icelo) diuerso uitiorum genere grassantibus

40.1 Agebatur huc illuc Galba uario turbae fluctuantis impulsu.
Plut. *G.* 26.3 'His litter was swept hither and thither (δεῦρο κἀκεῖ) as if in a swell, and often threatened to capsize.'

40.1b completis undique basilicis ac templis, lugubri prospectu
Plut. *G.* 26.4 'seeking the porticoes and galleries of the Forum, as if to spectate'

41.1 uexillarius comitatae Galbam cohortis (Atilium Vercilionem fuisse tradunt) dereptam Galbae imaginem solo afflixit.
Plut. *G.* 26.4 'When Atillius Vergilio dashed down a statue of Galba . . .'

41.2 alii suppliciter interrogasse quid mali meruisset, paucos dies exsoluendo donatiuo deprecatum

Suet. *G.* 20.1 sunt qui tradant, ad primum tumultum proclamasse eum: 'quid agitis, commilitones? ego uester sum et uos mei.' donatiuum etiam pollicitum.

Dio 64.6.4 'saying only this: "But what evil have I done?"'

41.2b plures obtulisse ultro percussoribus iugulum: agerent ac ferirent, si ita e re publica uideretur.

Plut. *G.* 27.1 'Stretching out his neck he said, "Go ahead, if this is better for the people of Rome."'

Suet. *G.* 20.1 plures autem prodiderunt obtulisse ultro iugulum et ut hoc agerent ac ferirent, quando ita uideretur, hortatum.

41.3 de percussore non satis constat: quidam Terentium euocatum, alii Laecanium, crebrior fama tradidit Camurium quintae decimae legionis militem.

Plut. *G.* 27.2 'The man who killed him, according to most writers, was a certain Camurius from Legio XV. Some report that it was Terentius, others Lecanius, still others Fabius Fabullus, who they also say cut off Galba's head and carried it wrapped in a cloak, since its baldness made it difficult to hold.'

42 ... non esse ab Othone mandatum ut occideretur. quod seu finxit formidine seu conscientiam confessus est ...

Plut. *G.* 27.4 '... confessing that he was party to the conspiracy against Galba. For he cried out that he was dying contrary to Otho's intention.'

43.1 Insignem illa die uirum Sempronium Densum aetas nostra uidit.

Plut. *G.* 26.4–5 'No one kept them off or supported him except one man, the only one among the thousands seen by the sun who was worthy of the Roman empire. He was Sempronius Densus, a centurion.'

Suet. *G.* 20.1 illud mirum admodum fuerit, neque praesentium quemquam opem imperatori ferre conatum et omnes qui arcesserentur spreuisse nuntium excepta Germanicianorum uexillatione.

Dio 64.6.4–5 'Sempronius Densus, a centurion, defended him as long as he was able ... I have recorded this man's name as well, because he is most worthy of mention.'

43.2 missu Othonis nominatim in caedem eius (sc. Pisonis) ardentis

Plut. *G.* 27.3 'They say that Otho, when the head (sc. of Galba) was brought to him, cried out, "This is nothing, soldiers. Show me Piso's head!"'

44.2 certatim ostentantibus cruentas manus qui occiderant, qui interfuerant, qui uere qui falso ut pulchrum et memorabile facinus iactabant.

Plut. *G.* 27.5 'Many who had had no part in the murder smeared their hands and swords with blood and showed them off and asked for rewards.'

44.2b plures quam centum uiginti libellos praemium exposcentium ob aliquam notabilem illa die operam Vitellius postea inuenit, omnesque conquiri et interfici iussit.

Plut. *G.* 27.5 'They submitted petitions to Otho. In fact 120 of them were later found out by means of their petitions. All of these Vitellius sought out and killed.'

Suet. *Vit.* 10.1 centum autem atque uiginti quorum libellos Othoni datos inuenerat exposcentium praemium ob editam in caede Galbae operam conquiri et supplicio affici imperauit (sc. Vitellius).

45.1 Alium crederes senatum, alium populum

Plut. *G.* 28.1 'as if they (sc. the senate) were now other men or the gods were different gods'

46.1 urbi Flauium Sabinum praefecere, iudicium Neronis secuti, sub quo eandem curam obtinuerat, plerisque Vespasianum fratrem in eo respicientibus.

Plut. *O.* 5.2 'As prefect of the city he appointed Flavius Sabinus, Vespasian's brother, either as a show of respect for Nero (for Sabinus had the office from Nero, while Galba removed him) or else, as is more likely, he was demonstrating good will and trust to Vespasian by elevating Sabinus.'

47.2 Otho cruento adhuc foro per stragem iacentium in Capitolium atque inde in Palatium uectus

Plut. *G.* 28.1 'They gave him the titles of Caesar and Augustus, while the headless bodies in consular robes lay strewn in the forum.'

48.2–3 legatum Caluisium Sabinum habuerat, cuius uxor mala cupidine uisendi situm castrorum per noctem militari habitu ingressa, cum uigilias et cetera militiae munia eadem lasciuia temptasset, in ipsis principiis stuprum ausa. et criminis huius reus Titus Vinius arguebatur. igitur iussu C. Caesaris oneratus catenis, mox mutatione temporum dimissus

Plut. *G.* 12.1–2 'While still young and a soldier in his first year of service, under Calvisius Sabinus, he brought into camp by night his commander's wife, a loose woman, she wearing military garb, and seduced her in the headquarters, the building that the Romans call the Principia. On account of this Gaius Caesar imprisoned him, but when he (sc. Gaius) died, he (sc. Vinius) with great good fortune was released.'

48.3 seruili deinceps probro respersus est, tamquam scyphum aureum in conuiuio Claudii furatus. et Claudius postera die soli omnium Vinio fictilibus ministrari iussit.

Plut. *G.* 12.2 'Dining with Claudius Caesar he carried off a silver cup. When Claudius heard, he invited him back to dinner the next day, and when he came he ordered the servants to bring out and set before him nothing silver but only earthenware.'

49.1 Galbae corpus diu neglectum et licentia tenebrarum plurimis ludibriis uexatum dispensator Argius e prioribus seruis humili sepultura in priuatis eius hortis contexit.

Plut. *G.* 28.3 'The body of Galba Helvidius Priscus took up with Otho's permission. The freedman Argius buried it.'

Suet. *G.* 20.2 sero tandem dispensator Argiuus et hoc (sc. caput) et ceterum truncum in priuatis eius hortis Aurelia uia sepulturae dedit.

Dio 64.6.3 'They abused his body in various ways.'

49.2 quinque principes prospera fortuna emensus

Plut. *G.* 29.1 'having lived during five emperors' reigns with honour and reputation'

49.2b uetus in familia nobilitas, magnae opes

Plut. *G.* 29.1 'a man inferior to few Romans in birth or wealth, indeed in wealth and birth superior to all his contemporaries'

52.4 collegium Caesaris

Plut. *G.* 22.5 'colleague, in a manner of speaking, of Claudius Caesar'

53.1 corpore ingens

Plut. *O.* 6.3 'with a huge body' (σώματος μεγάλου; Hardy (1890) notes the Latinate construction of Plutarch's phrase).

55.3–4 dirumpunt imagines Galbae, quarta legio promptius, duoetuicensima cunctanter, mox consensu. ac ne reuerentiam imperii exuere uiderentur, senatus populique Romani oblitterata iam nomina sacramento aduocabant.

Plut. *G.* 22.3 'Going up to the statues of Galba they overturned them and dragged them down. After swearing allegiance to the senate and the Roman people they dispersed.'

56.2 Nocte . . . epulanti Vitellio nuntiat

Plut. *G.* 22.6 'he announced it to Vitellius in the evening, while many were feasting with him'

57.1 superior exercitus, speciosis senatus populique Romani nominibus relictis, tertium nonas Ianuarias Vitellio accessit.

Plut. *G.* 22.8 'And straight away Flaccus' force cast aside their fine and democratic oaths of allegiance to the senate and swore to Vitellius that they would do what he commanded.'

Suet. *Vit.* 8.2 consentiente deinde etiam superioris prouinciae exercitu, qui prior a Galba ad senatum defecerat.

62.2 nomen Germanici Vitellio statim additum; Caesarem se appellari etiam uictor prohibuit.

Plut. *G.* 22.7 'He tolerated their application of the name Germanicus to him, though he did not accept that of Caesar.'

Suet. *Vit.* 8.2 cognomen Germanici delatum ab uniuersis cupide recepit, Augusti distulit, Caesaris in perpetuum recusauit.

62.3 Laetum augurium Fabio Valenti exercituique quem in bellum agebat

Suet. *Vit.* 9.1 praemisso agmine laetum euenit augurium.

71.1 Marium Celsum . . . acciri in Capitolium iubet.

Plut. *O.* 1.1 '. . . having ordered Marius Celsus to be brought to him'.

71.2 Celsus constanter seruatae erga Galbam fidei crimen confessus, exemplum ultro imputauit.

Plut. *O.* 1.1 'When Celsus replied neither ignobly nor insensibly, saying that the charge against him gave proof of his character, for he was charged with having been a supporter Galba could rely on . . .'

72.1 Par inde exsultatio disparibus causis consecuta impetrato Tigellini exitio.

Plut. *O.* 2.1 'But nothing so gladdened all Romans alike and won their acceptance for him (sc. Otho) as the treatment of Tigellinus.'

72.1b corrupto ad omne facinus Nerone . . . ac postremo eiusdem desertor ac proditor
Plut. *G.* 17.3 'The man who made Nero deserving of death and abandoned and betrayed him in that state . . .'

72.3 in circum ac theatra effusi seditiosis uocibus strepere, donec
Plut. *G.* 17.4 'in all the theatres and circuses they would not cease demanding him, until'

74.1 ab Othone ad Vitellium epistulae offerebant pecuniam et gratiam et quemcumque quietis locum prodigae uitae legisset.
Plut. *O.* 4.2 'He (sc. Otho) wrote to Vitellius counselling him to think like a soldier and saying that he would give him money and a city in which he could live an easy and pleasant life at peace.'

74.1b paria Vitellius ostentabat, primo mollius, stulta utrimque et indecora simulatione; mox quasi rixantes stupra ac flagitia inuicem obiectauere, neuter falso.
Plut. *O.* 4.3 'He (sc. Vitellius) wrote back, feigning calm at first. But thereafter in anger they wrote abusing one another with many shameful insults, not falsely (οὐ ψευδῶς μέν), but foolishly and ridiculously, seeing that one was insulting the other with reproaches that fit both.'

76.1 iurasse in eum Dalmatiae ac Pannoniae et Moesiae legiones
Plut. *O.* 4.1 '. . . the armies of Pannonia and Dalmatia and Moesia, along with their leaders, chose Otho'.

77.2 ceteri consulatus ex destinatione Neronis aut Galbae mansere.
Plut. *O.* 1.2 'For all those who had been designated by Nero or Galba he preserved their consulships.'

77.3 sed Otho pontificatus auguratusque honoratis iam senibus cumulum dignitatis addidit.
Plut. *O.* 1.2 'With priesthoods he honoured those who were distinguished by age or reputation.'

81.1 cum timeret Otho, timebatur.
Plut. *O.* 3.5 'Fearing for these men he was himself fearful to them' (φοβούμενος γὰρ ὑπὲρ τῶν ἀνδρῶν αὐτὸς ἦν φοβερὸς ἐκείνοις).

81.2 et praefectos praetorii ad mitigandas militum iras statim miserat et abire propere omnes e conuiuio iussit.
Plut. *O.* 3.5 'He both (ἅμα) sent off the prefects, ordering them to talk with the soldiers and calm them, and (ἅμα) roused his guests and sent them out through a different door.'

82.1 donec Otho contra decus imperii toro insistens precibus et lacrimis aegre cohibuit

Plut. *O.* 3.7 'Then upright on the couch he addressed them at length and pleaded with them and spared not even tears. With difficulty he sent them away.'

86.1 in uestibulo Capitolii omissas habenas bigae cui Victoria institerat

Plut. *O.* 4.4 'Everyone saw that in the Capitolium the reins of the Nike standing on a chariot had been loosed from her hands as if she was no longer able to control it.'

86.1 b statuam diui Iulii in insula Tiberini amnis sereno et immoto die ab occidente in orientem conuersam

Plut. *O.* 4.4 'The statue of Gaius Caesar on the island in the river Tiber, without the occurrence of either seismic movement or wind, turned from west to east.'

Suet. *Ves.* 5.7 statuam Diui Iuli ad orientem sponte conuersam

88.1 in quis et Lucium Vitellium, eodem quo ceteros cultu, nec ut imperatoris fratrem nec ut hostis

Plut. *O.* 5.1 'he included among them Lucius, Vitellius' brother, not adding to or detracting from his dignity'.

89.3 fuere qui proficiscenti Othoni moras religionemque nondum conditorum ancilium afferrent; aspernatus est omnem cunctationem ut Neroni quoque exitiosam.

Suet. *O.* 8.3 expeditionem autem impigre atque etiam praepropere incohauit, nulla ne religionum quidem cura, sed et motis necdum conditis ancilibus.

90.1 reliquias Neronianarum sectionum nondum in fiscum conuersas reuocatis ab exilio concessit.

Plut. *O.* 1.3 'To all senators exiled by Nero and recalled by Galba he gave whatever of each man's property he found still unsold.'

2 EPIGRAMS AND *SENTENTIAE*

1.4 ubi sentire quae uelis et quae sentias dicere licet

2.1 ipsa etiam pace saeuum

2.3 et quibus deerat inimicus per amicos oppressi

3.2 non esse curae deis securitatem nostram, esse ultionem

6.1 inauditi atque indefensi tamquam innocentes perierant

7.3 eadem ... nouae aulae mala, aeque grauia, non aeque excusata

10.2 cui expeditius fuerit tradere imperium quam obtinere
10.3 post fortunam credidimus
11.3 annum sibi ultimum, rei publicae prope supremum
13.2 non tam unum aliquem fouebant quam alium
16.4 nec totam seruitutem pati possunt nec totam libertatem
16.4 Galba quidem ... tamquam principem faceret, ceteri tamquam cum facto loquebantur
17.1 imperare posset magis quam uellet
20.2 tam pauperes forent quibus donasset Nero quam quibus abstulisset
22.1 in ciuitate nostra et uetabitur semper et retinebitur
24.2 quem nota pariter et occulta fallebant
25.1 suscepere duo manipulares imperium populi Romani transferendum et transtulerunt
30.1 libido ac uoluptas penes ipsum ..., rubor ac dedecus penes omnes
30.2 Nero ... uos destituit, non uos Neronem
32.1 eodem die diuersa pari certamine postulaturis
36.3 omnia seruiliter pro dominatione
37.1 nec priuatum me uocare sustineo princeps a uobis nominatus, nec principem alio imperante
38.2 non potest laudari nisi peractum
38.3 praecipuum pessimorum incitamentum quod boni maerebant
39.1 optima uiderentur quorum tempus effugerat
45.1 quantoque magis falsa erant quae fiebant tanto plura facere
45.2 Othoni nondum auctoritas inerat ad prohibendum scelus; iubere iam poterat
46.2 per latrocinia et raptus aut seruilibus ministeriis militare otium redimebant
47.1 Exacto per scelera die nouissimum malorum fuit laetitia
48.1 ad hoc tantum maiori fratri praelatus est ut prior occideretur
48.4 prauus aut industrius eadem ui
48.4 testamentum Titi Vinii magnitudine opum irritum, Pisonis supremam uoluntatem paupertas firmauit
49.2 alieno imperio felicior quam suo
49.3 quod segnitia erat, sapientia uocaretur
49.4 omnium consensu capax imperii, nisi imperasset
50.3 deteriorem fore qui uicisset
52.2 ipsa uitia pro uirtutibus interpretabantur

52.4 ut concupisceret magis quam ut speraret
54.3 faciliore inter malos consensu ad bellum quam in pace ad concordiam
55.1 insita mortalibus natura propere sequi quae piget inchoare
56.1 unde plures erant omnes fuere
58.2 apud saeuientes occidere palam, ignoscere non nisi fallendo licebat
59.1 damnatos fidei crimine
63.2 non quidem in bello sed pro pace tendebantur
65.1 uno amne discretis conexum odium
71.2 fidei crimen confessus
71.2 fides integra et infelix
77.3 quod auaritia fuerat, uideri maiestatem
81.1 cum timeret Otho, timebatur
82.1 inuiti neque innocentes
85.3 tumultu uerborum sibi ipsi obstrepentes
87.2 prauus et callidus bonos et modestos anteibat
88.3 per incerta tutissimi

3 NOTES PERTAINING TO PARALLEL INCIDENTS REPORTED UNDER TWO OR MORE *PRINCIPES*

(G = Galba, O = Otho, V = Vitellius, F = Vespasian)

4.2 *finis Neronis* (GOVF), 4.3 *usurpata ... licentius* (GF), 5.1 *neque dari donatiuum* (GF), 6.1 *alter ... destruebant* (GF), 6.1 *cruentum* (GF), 6.2 *trucidatis ... militum* (GVF), 7.2 *an ne ... scrutaretur* (GVF), 8.1 *recenti ... ciuitatis* (GOVF), 8.1 *in ... leuamento* (GF), 13.1 *potentia principatus* (GOV), 13.1 *anulis donatum* (GVF), 13.1 *discordes* (GV), 18.2 *quartam ... fore* (GV), 20.3 *exauctorati* (GF), 21.2 *merito perire* (GO), 27.2 *miraculo* (OF), 41.1 *uexillarius ... imaginem* (GVF), 44.1 *nullam ... dicitur* (OF), 45.1 *nec ... temperans* (OF), 45.2 *Othoni ... poterat* (OVF), 45.2 *simulatione ... iussum* (OVF), 47.2 *in ... uectus* (OV), 52.2 *auiditate imperandi* (GOVF), 53.1 *flagitari* (GV), 54.2 *nec ... aberant* (OV), 55.3 *dirumpunt ... turbantibus* (OVF), 57.2 *auxilia* (VF), 58.1 *astu subtraxit* (VF), 58.2 *occidere ... fallendo* (OV), 59.1 *fidei crimine* (OVF), 60 *discors* (GF), 61.2 *ad ... milia* (VF), 61.2 *tota ... secuturus* (VF), 62.2 *torpebat* (OVF), 63.1 *mitigati* (VF), 64.4 *infamauerat* (VF), 66.2 *Valentem ... emptum* (VF), 66.3 *lento ... agmine* (VF), 67.2 *direptus ... locus* (OV), 70.2 *cunctatus ... num* (VF), 71.2 *exemplum ... imputauit* (OV), 74.1 *crebrae ... epistulae*

(VF), 74.3 *epistulas* (VF), 76.1 *fiduciam* (OV), 77.1 *Otho ... obibat* (OV), 77.3 *reditus ... locus* (GOF), 80.1 *Paruo ... seditio* (OV), 80.2 *tribunos ... arguit* (OV), 83.4 *neque ... crediderim* (GOV), 90.1 *reuocatis ab exilio* (GOV)

4 NOTES ILLUSTRATING DIFFERENCES BETWEEN *HISTORIES* I AND THE PARALLEL TRADITION

1 different context

5.2 *senium ... auaritiam*, 7.2 *seu ... facta*, 7.3 *tamquam ... festinantes*, 8.1 *tamquam ... multitudine*, 12.1 *rupta ... reuerentia*, 13.1 *potentia principatus*, 17.1 *statim ... oculis*, 19.1 *quadriduo*, 21.1 *proximus destinaretur*, 30.2 *Nero ... Neronem*, 36.1 *caueri ... praepositos*, 37.5 *grassatus esset*, 40.2 *inermem et senem*, 48.2 *Titus Vinius*, 49.2 *uetus ... nobilitas*, 53.1 *decorus ... incessu*, 55.4 *non ... locutus*, 62.2 *nomen ... prohibuit*, 72.1 *par ... disparibus*, 72.1 *impetrato ... exitio*, 72.3 *infamem uitam*, 77.2 *consul ... ipse*, 85.1 *in duos*, 89.2 *Nero ... depulsus*, 90.1 *reliquias ... conuersas*

2 different tone or detail

5.1 *praeuentamque gratiam*, 5.2 *ne ... cetera*, 6.1 *inualidum senem*, 7.2 *fuere ... abstinuisse*, 7.3 *imperatores ... comparantibus*, 8.2 *abducto ... amicitiae*, 8.2 *superbia ... uictoriae*, 9.1 *debilitate pedum*, 10.1 *Licinius Mucianus*, 13.1 *Icelo ... liberto*, 13.2 *destinabantur*, 13.2 *rei ... subisse*, 13.3 *aemulatione luxus*, 13.3 *eoque ... seposuit*, 13.3 *conscium libidinum*, 13.4 *primus ... splendidissimus*, 13.4 *spem ... rapiebat*, 14.2 *moris ... seuerus*, 20.1 *isdem ... manerent*, 20.1 *repeti*, 20.3 *exauctorati*, 21.1 *inopia ... toleranda*, 22.1 *non ... animus*, 23.1 *studia ... affectauerat*, 25.1 *Barbium ... eorundem*, 25.1 *pretio ... promissis*, 27.1 *audiente ... interpretante*, 27.2 *sellae*, 28 *suspicionem conscientiae*, 31.3 *nutauere*, 34.2 *multi arbitrabantur*, 35.1 *thorace*, 36.1 *non ... circumdarent*, 41.2 *trepidatione ferentium*, 42 *de ... ambigitur*, 42 *conscius sceleris*, 44.2 *certatim ... ultionem*, 45.2 *Othoni ... poterat*, 45.2 *simulatione ... iussum*, 47.1 *exacto ... laetitia*, 47.1 *omnes ... honores*, 47.2 *in ... uectus*, 47.2 *quaesitis ... capitibus*, 49.1 *dispensator ... contexit*, 49.2 *quinque ... emensus*, 49.2 *magnae opes*, 49.3 *famae ... uenditator*, 49.3 *pecuniae ... parcus*, 49.4 *apud ... Hispaniam*, 49.4 *omnium ... imperasset*, 52.2 *comitatem bonitatemque*, 52.2 *ipsa ... interpretabantur*, 53.2 *praeuentus erat*, 55.3 *dirumpunt ... turbantibus*, 56.2 *nocte ... nuntiat*, 60 *Roscius Coelius*, 62.2 *inerti ... epulis*, 71.1 *formidinis*, 71.1 *Marium Celsum*, 72.1 *exsultatio*, 72.2 *Titi ... defensus*, 72.2 *haud ... seruauerat*, 72.3 *Sinuessanas aquas*, 72.3 *supremae necessitatis*, 72.3 *inter ... oscula*, 72.3 *deformes moras*, 73

Caluia Crispinilla, 74.1 *pecuniam . . . legisset*, 74.1 *stupra . . . obiectauere*, 74.2 *rursus . . . misit*, 77.1 *ex . . . decus*, 77.3 *sed . . . recoluit*, 78.1 *Hispalensibus . . . dedit*, 78.2 *creditus . . . agitauisse*, 78.2 *quibusdam . . . acclamauit*, 78.2 *uetandi . . . pudore*, 79.1 *externa . . . habebantur*, 80.2 *seuerissimos centurionum*, 81.1 *celebre conuiuium*, 81.1 *qui . . . timebatur*, 81.2 *discrimine . . . territus*, 81.2 *tum . . . petiuere*, 82.1 *undique*, 82.1 *donec . . . cohibuit*, 82.3 *tum . . . ausus*, 88.1 *comitum specie*, 88.1 *Lucium Vitellium*, 89.3 *moras religionemque*

3 different chronology
14.1 *nihil . . . certum*, 20.1 *proxima. . . cura*, 20.3 *exauctorati*, 35.2 *Iulius . . . speculator*, 47.2 *in . . . uectus*, 72.1 *impetrato . . . exitio*, 74.1 *crebrae . . . epistulae*, 86.1 *ab . . . conuersam*

4 different facts (i.e. somebody has made a mistake)
6.2 *trucidatis . . . militum*, 7.3 *praepotentes liberti*, 20.2 *triginta . . . praepositi*, 22.2 *e quibus*, 40.2 *rapidi equis*, 43.1 *insignem . . . uidit*, 46.1 *praefecere*, 86.3 *uia Flaminia*

SELECT BIBLIOGRAPHY

EDITIONS OF *HISTORIES* I

The following editions (and commentaries and translations) are cited by name alone. In notes on the text of *Histories* I the names Heubner and Wellesley refer to their respective critical editions; elsewhere they refer to Heubner's commentary and Wellesley's translation.

Alford, M. (1912). *Tacitus: Histories, book I.* London.

Chilver, G. E. F. (1979). *A historical commentary on Tacitus' Histories I and II.* Oxford.

Church, A. J. and W. J. Broddribb. (1894). *The History of Tacitus.* New ed. London.

Fyfe, W. H. (1997). *Tacitus: The Histories,* revised and edited by D. S. Levene. Oxford.

Godley, A. D. (1924). *The Histories of Tacitus, books I and II.* London.

Goelzer, H. (1921). *Tacite: Histoires.* Vol. I. Paris.

Hellegouarc'h, J. (see below under Wuilleumier)

Heraeus, C. (1929). *Cornelii Taciti Historiarum libri qui supersunt. Erster Band, Buch I und II.* 6th ed. by W. Heraeus. Leipzig.

Heubner, H. (1963). *P. Cornelius Tacitus, Die Historien. Band I, erstes Buch.* Heidelberg.

(1978). *P. Cornelii Taciti libri qui supersunt. Tom II. Fasc. I. Historiarum Libri.* Stuttgart.

Irvine, A. L. (1952). *Tacitus, Histories books I & II.* London.

Ritter, F. (1834–6). *Cornelii Taciti opera.* Bonn.

Spooner, W. A. (1891). *Cornelii Taciti Historiarum libri qui supersunt.* London.

Tyler, W. S. (1860). *The Histories of Caius Cornelius Tacitus.* New York.

Valmaggi, L. (1891). *Il libro primo delle Storie.* Turin.

Wellesley, K. (1972). *Tacitus: The Histories.* Harmondsworth.

(1989). *Cornelius Tacitus, II.1, Historiae.* Leipzig.

Wuilleumier, P., H. Le Bonniec, and J. Hellegouarc'h. (1987). *Tacite, Histoires livre I.* Paris.

BOOKS AND ARTICLES CITED

Adams, J. N. (1972). 'The language of the later books of Tacitus' *Annals*', *CQ* 22: 350–73.

(1973). 'The vocabulary of the speeches in Tacitus' historical works', *BICS* 20: 124–44.

Alföldy, G. (1969). *Fasti Hispanienses: senatorische Reichsbeamte und Offiziere in den spanischen Provinzen des römischen Reiches von Augustus bis Diocletian.* Wiesbaden.

(1974). *Noricum*, transl. A. Birley. London.

(1995). 'Bricht der schweigsame sein Schweigen? Eine Grabinschrift aus Rom', *MDAI(R)* 102: 251–68.

Alston, R. (1994). 'Roman military pay from Caesar to Diocletian', *JRS* 84: 113–23.

Andresen, G. (1899). *In Taciti Historias studia critica et palaeographica.* Berlin.

Ash, R. (1999). *Ordering anarchy: armies and leaders in Tacitus' Histories.* Ann Arbor.

Ashby, T. (1970). *The Roman Campagna in classical times.* New ed. by J. B. Ward-Perkins. London.

Aubrion, E. (1991). 'L'*eloquentia* de Tacite et sa *fides* d'historien', *ANRW* II 33.4: 2597–688.

Baillie Reynolds, P. K. (1926). *The vigiles of imperial Rome.* London.

Baldwin, B. (1981). 'Three notes on Tacitus, *Histories* I', *Maia* n.s. 33: 43–4.

Barton, T. (1994). *Ancient astrology.* London.

Becher, I. (1985). 'Tiberüberschwemmungen: die Interpretation von Prodigien in augusteischer Zeit', *Klio* 67: 471–9.

Bérard, F. (1988). 'Le rôle militaire des cohortes urbaines', *MEFRA* 100: 159–82.

Berchem, D. van (1981). 'Avenches colonie latine?', *Chiron* 11: 221–8.

Birley, A. (2000). 'The life and death of Cornelius Tacitus', *Historia* 49: 230–47.

Bishop, M. C. and J. C. N. Coulston (1993). *Roman military equipment from the Punic wars to the fall of Rome.* London.

Bradley, K. R. (1978a). 'The chronology of Nero's visit to Greece', *Latomus* 37: 61–72.

(1978b). *Suetonius' Life of Nero: an historical commentary.* Collection Latomus 157. Brussels.

Brink, K. O. (1944). 'A forgotten figure of style in Tacitus', *CR* 58: 43–5.

Briscoe, J. (1973). *A commentary on Livy Books xxxi–xxxiii.* Oxford.

Brunt, P. A. (1959). 'The revolt of Vindex and the fall of Nero', *Latomus* 18: 531–59.

(1960). 'Tacitus on the Batavian revolt', *Latomus* 19: 494–517 (= *Roman imperial themes*, ch. 3).

(1977). '*Lex de imperio Vespasiani*', *JRS* 67: 95–116.

(1983). '*Princeps* and *equites*', *JRS* 73: 42–75.

Chalon, G. (1964). *L'édit de Tiberius Iulius Alexander: étude historique et exégétique.* Bibliotheca Helvetica Romana 5. Olten.

Champlin, E. (1991). *Final judgments: duty and emotion in Roman wills 200 B.C.–A.D. 250.* Berkeley.

Chausserie-Lapree, J.-P. (1969). *L'expression narrative chez les historiens Latins: histoire d'un style.* Paris.

Cheesman, G. L. (1914). *The auxilia of the Roman imperial army.* Oxford.

Chevallier, R. (1975). 'Gallia Lugdunensis: bilan de 25 ans de recherches historiques et archéologiques', *ANRW* II 3: 860–1060.

Chilver, G. E. F. (1957). 'The army in Roman politics, A.D. 68–70', *JRS* 47: 29–35.

Chilver, G. E. F. and G. B. Townend (1985). *A historical commentary on Tacitus'* Histories *iv and v.* Oxford.

Christes, J. (1995). 'Das persönliche Vorwort des Tacitus zu den *Historien*', *Philologus* 139: 133–46.

Cichorius, C. (1894). '*Ala*', *RE* I: 1223–70.

(1900). '*Cohors*', *RE* IV: 231–356.

Courbaud, E. (1918). *Les procédés d'art de Tacite dans les Histoires.* Paris.

Courtney, E. (1980). *A commentary on the Satires of Juvenal.* London.

Cousin, J. (1951). 'Rhétorique et psychologie chez Tacite: un aspect de la "deinosis"', *REL* 29: 228–47.

Cramer, F. H. (1964). *Astrology in Roman law and politics.* Philadelphia.

Crook, J. A. (1955). *Consilium principis: imperial councils and counsellors from Augustus to Diocletian.* Cambridge.

D' Arms, J. H. (1974). 'Tacitus, *Histories* 4.13 and the municipal origins of Hordeonius Flaccus', *Historia* 23: 497–504.

(1998). 'Between public and private: the *epulum publicum* and Caesar's *horti trans Tiberim*', in (edd.) M. Cima and E. La Rocca, *Horti Romani: atti del convegno internazionale* (Roma, 4–6 maggio 1995). Rome. 33–43.

Davies, R. H. (1989). *Service in the Roman army.* New York.

Deman, A. (1956). 'Tacite, *Histoires* 1.67–8', in *Hommages à Max Niedermann*. Collection Latomus 23. Brussels. 90–101.

Dobson, B. (1978). *Die Primipilares: Entwicklung und Bedeutung, Laufbahnen und Persönlichkeiten eines römischen Offizierranges*. Cologne.

Doppelfeld, O. (1975). 'Das römische Köln I: Ubier-*oppidum* und *colonia Agrippinensium*', *ANRW* II 4: 715–82.

Draeger, A. (1882). *Über Syntax und Stil des Tacitus*. 3rd ed. Leipzig.

Drews, R. (1988) 'Pontiffs, prodigies, and the disappearance of the *Annales Maximi*', *CP* 83: 289–99.

Drinkwater, J. F. (1975). 'Lugdunum: natural capital of Gaul?', *Britannia* 6: 133–40.

(1983). *Roman Gaul: the three provinces, 58 B.C.–A.D. 260*. Ithaca.

Dürr, C. (1973). 'Tacitus, *Mons Vocetius*', *Ort und Wort* 1: 1–19.

Duncan-Jones, R. P. (1981). 'The wealth of Gaul', *Chiron* 11: 217–20.

Durry, M. (1938). *Les cohortes prétoriennes*. Paris.

Eadie, J. W. (1967). 'The development of Roman mailed cavalry', *JRS* 57: 161–73.

Eck, Werner (1982). 'Jahres- und Provinzialfasten der senatorischen Statthalter von 69/70 bis 138/39', *Chiron* 12: 281–362.

Edmondson, J. C. (1990). 'Romanization and urban development in Lusitania', in (edd.) T. Blagg and M. Millett, *The early Roman empire in the west*. Oxford. 151–78.

Engel, R. (1977). 'Das Charakterbild des Kaisers A. Vitellius bei Tacitus und sein historischer Kern', *Athenaeum* n.s. 55: 345–68.

Evelyn White, H. G. and J. H. Oliver (1938). *The temple of Hibis in El Khargeh oasis. Part II: Greek inscriptions*. New York.

Fabia, P. (1893). *Les sources de Tacite dans les Histoires et les Annales*. Paris.

(1902). 'La querelle des Lyonnais et des Viennois', *Revue d'Histoire de Lyon* 1: 106–18.

(1912). 'La journée du 15 janvier 69 à Rome: confrontation des témoignages de Tacite, Plutarque, Suétone et Dion Cassius', *RPh* n.s. 36: 78–129.

(1913). 'L'ambassade d'Othon aux Vitelliens (Tacite, *Hist.* 1.74)', *RPh* n.s. 37: 53–61.

Fantham, E. (1996). *Roman literary culture from Cicero to Apuleius*. Baltimore.

Feldman, L. (1991). 'Proto-Jewish intimations in Tacitus' account of Jewish origins', *REJ* 150: 332–60.

Fishwick, D. (1987). *The imperial cult in the Latin west.* Volume I.1. Leiden.

Fletcher, G. B. A. (1964). *Annotations on Tacitus*. Collection Latomus 71. Brussels.

(1971). 'On some passages in Tacitus, *Histories* I and II', *Latomus* 30: 383–5.

Frei-Stolba, R. (1976). 'Die römische Schweiz: ausgewählte staats- und verwaltungsrechtliche Probleme in Frühprinzipat', *ANRW* II 5.1: 288–403.

Freis, Helmut. (1967). *Die cohortes urbanae*. Epigraphische Studien 2. Beihefte der Bonner Jahrbucher, 21. Cologne.

Fuhrmann, M. (1960). 'Das Vierkaiserjahr bei Tacitus: über den Aufbau der *Historien* Buch II–III', *Philologus* 104: 250–71.

Furneaux, H. (1884–91). *The Annals of Tacitus*. 2 vols. Oxford.

Gibson, B. J. (1998). 'Rumours as causes of events in Tacitus', *MD* 40: 111–29.

Gilmartin, K. (1975). 'A rhetorical figure in Latin historical style: the imaginary second person singular', *TAPA* 105: 99–121.

Gilmartin Wallace, K. (1987). 'The Flavii Sabini in Tacitus', *Historia* 36: 343–58.

Ginsburg, J. (1981). *Tradition and theme in the* Annals *of Tacitus.* New York.

Goodyear, F. R. D. (1972). *The Annals of Tacitus. Vol. 1: Annals 1.1–54*. Cambridge.

(1981). *The Annals of Tacitus. Vol. 2: Annals 1.55–81 and Annals 2*. Cambridge.

Groag, E. (1897). 'Zur Kritik von Tacitus' Quellen in den *Historien*', *Jahrbücher für cl. Phil.*, Supplementband 23: 711–98.

Gruen, E. S. (1974). *The last generation of the Roman Republic*. Berkeley.

Hardy, E. G. (1890). *Plutarch's lives of Galba and Otho*. London.

Harrison, S. J. (1994). '*Ferox scelerum*? A note on Tacitus, *Annals* 4.12.2', *CQ* 44: 557–9.

Hassall, M. W. C. (1970). 'Batavians and the Roman conquest of Britain', *Britannia* 1: 131–6.

Henrichs, A. (1968). 'Vespasian's visit to Alexandria', *ZPE* 3: 51–80.

Herkommer, E. (1968). *Die Topoi in den Proömien der römischen Geschichtswerke*. Dissertation, Eberhard-Karls-Universität, Tübingen.

Heubner, H. (1935). *Studien zur Darstellungskunst des Tacitus* (*Hist.* I, 12–II, 51). Würzburg.

(1963). 'Männer, Pferde, Waffen', *Gymnasium* 70: 226–30.

Holder, P. A. (1980). *Studies in the auxilia of the Roman army from Augustus to Trajan*. Oxford.

(1999). '*Exercitus pius fidelis*: the army of Germania Inferior in A.D. 89', *ZPE* 128: 237–50.

Hopkins, K. (1983). *Death and renewal.* Cambridge.

Hornstein, F. (1961). '*Bos locutus* (zu Varro, *De re rust.* II.5.5)', *RhM* 104: 148–51.

Husband, R. W. (1915). 'Galba's assassination and the indifferent citizen', *CP* 10: 321–5.

Jones, B. W. (1992). *The emperor Domitian.* London.

(2000). *Suetonius, Vespasian.* London.

Jones, C. P. (1971). *Plutarch and Rome.* Oxford.

Kajanto, I. (1965). *The Latin cognomina.* Societas Scientiarum Fennica. Commentationes Humanarum Litterarum 36.2. Helsinki.

Keitel, E. (1987). 'Otho's exhortations in Tacitus' *Histories*', *G&R* 34: 73–82.

(1991). 'The structure and function of speeches in Tacitus' *Histories* I–III', *ANRW* II 33.4: 2772–94.

Kennedy, D. (1996). 'Parthia and Rome: eastern perspectives', in (ed.) D. Kennedy, *The Roman army in the east. JRA* supplementary series no. 18. Ann Arbor. 67–90.

Kenney, E. J. (1990). *Apuleius: Cupid & Psyche.* Cambridge Greek and Latin Classics. Cambridge.

Köster, F. (1927). *Der Marsch der Invasionsarmee des Fabius Valens vom Niederrhein nach Italien (Anfang 69 n. chr.) Untersuchungen über Tacitus, Historien* I 61–66, II 14–15, 27–30. Dissertation. Münster.

Kragelund, P. (1987). 'Vatinius, Nero and Curiatius Maternus', *CQ* 37: 197–202.

Laet, S. de (1949). *Portorium: étude sur l'organisation douanière chez les Romains, surtout à l' époque du Haut-Empire.* Brussels.

Lahusen, G. (1983). *Untersuchungen zur Ehrenstatue in Rom. Literarische und epigraphische Zeugnisse.* Rome.

Leeman, A. D. (1973). 'Structure and meaning in the prologues of Tacitus', *YCS* 23: 169–208.

Levene, D. S. (1993). *Religion in Livy.* Mnemosyne Supplementband 127. Leiden.

Levick, B. (1985). 'L. Verginius Rufus and the four emperors', *RhM* 128: 318–46.

(1999). *Vespasian.* London.

Lewis, N. (1983). *Life in Egypt under Roman rule.* Oxford.

Liebeschuetz, J. H. G. (1979). *Continuity and change in Roman religion.* Oxford.

Linderski, J. (1993). 'Roman religion in Livy', in (ed.) W. Schuller, *Livius: Aspekte seines Werkes. Xenia* 31. Konstanz. 53–70.

(1995). *Roman questions: selected papers.* Heidelberger althistorische Beiträge und epigraphische Studien 20. Stuttgart.

Löfstedt, B. (1971). *Zenonis Veronensis Tractatus.* Corpus Christianorum, series Latina, 22. Turnhout.

Lowe, E. A. (1929). 'The unique manuscript of Tacitus' *Histories*', in *Casinensia.* Monte Cassino. 257–72.

Luce, T. J. (1989). 'Ancient views on the causes of bias in historical writing', *CP* 84: 16–31.

(1991). 'Tacitus on "History's highest function": *praecipuum munus annalium* (*Ann.* 3.65)', *ANRW* II 33.4: 2904–27.

Luterbacher, F. (1908). *Der Prodigienglaube und Prodigienstil der Römer.* 2nd ed. Burgdorf.

Marincola, J. (1999). 'Tacitus' prefaces and the decline of imperial historiography', *Latomus* 58: 391–404.

Martin, R. H. (1953). '*Variatio* and the development of Tacitus' style', *Eranos* 51: 89–96.

(1981). *Tacitus.* London.

Martin, R. H. and A. J. Woodman (1989). *Tacitus, Annals book IV.* Cambridge Greek and Latin Classics. Cambridge.

Maxfield, V. A. (1981). *The military decorations of the Roman army.* Berkeley.

McBain, B. (1982). *Prodigy and expiation: a study in religion and politics in Republican Rome.* Collection Latomus 177. Brussels.

Meer, L. B. van der (1987). *The bronze liver of Piacenza: analysis of a polytheistic structure.* Amsterdam.

Mellor, R. (1993). *Tacitus.* New York.

Mielczarek, M. (1993). *Cataphracti and clibanarii: studies on the heavy armoured cavalry of the ancient world.* Lodz.

Millar, F. (1977). *The emperor in the Roman world (31 BC–AD 337).* Ithaca.

Miller, N. P. (1964). 'Dramatic speech in Tacitus', *AJP* 85: 279–96.

(1977). 'Tacitus' narrative technique', *G&R* 24: 13–22.

(1987a). 'The most unmilitary of historians?', in (edd.) A. Bonanno and H. C. R. Vella, *Laurea corona: studies in honour of Edward Coleiro.* Amsterdam. 170–3.

(1987b). 'Virgil and Tacitus again', *Proceedings of the Virgil Society* 18: 87–106.

Mommsen, T. (1866). 'Zu Sallustius', *Hermes* 1: 427–37.
(1870). 'Cornelius Tacitus und Cluvius Rufus', *Hermes* 4: 295–325.
(1899). *Römisches Strafrecht.* Leipzig.
Morgan, M. G. (1992). 'Dispositions for disaster: Tacitus, *Histories* 1.31', *Eranos* 90: 55–62.
(1993a). '*Commisura* in Tacitus, *Histories* 1', *CQ* 43: 274–91.
(1993b).'Tacitus, *Histories* 1.58.2', *Hermes* 121: 371–44.
(1993c). 'Two omens in Tacitus' *Histories* (2.50.2 and 1.62.2–3)', *RhM* 136: 321–9.
(1993d). 'The unity of Tacitus, *Histories* 1.12–20', *Athenaeum* 81: 567–86.
(1994a). 'The long way round: Tacitus, *Histories* 1.27', *Eranos* 92: 93–101.
(1994b). 'A lugubrious prospect: Tacitus, *Histories* 1.40', *CQ* 44: 236–44.
(1994c). 'Rogues march: Caecina and Valens in Tacitus, *Histories* 1.61–70', *MH* 51: 103–25.
(2000). 'Clodius Macer and Calvia Crispinilla', *Historia* 49: 467–87.
Muecke, F. (1993). *Horace: Satires II.* Warminster.
Murison, C. L. (1979). 'Some Vitellian dates: an exercise in methodology', *TAPA* 109: 187–97.
(1991a). 'The historical value of Tacitus' *Histories*', *ANRW* II 33.3: 1686–1713.
(1991b). *Suetonius: Galba, Otho, Vitellius.* London.
(1993). *Galba, Otho, and Vitellius: careers and controversies.* Spudasmata 52. Hildesheim.
(1999). *Rebellion and reconstruction, Galba to Domitian: an historical commentary on Cassius Dio's Roman History, Books 64–7 (A.D. 68–96).* Atlanta.
Newbold, R. F. (1976). 'The *uulgus* in Tacitus', *RhM* 119: 85–92.
Nipperdey, K. L. (1877). 'Emendationes Historiarum Taciti', in *Opuscula.* Berlin. 199–222.
Norden, E. (1909). *Die antike Kunstprosa vom VI. Jahrhundert v. Chr. bis in die Zeit der Renaissance.* Leipzig.
Nutting, H. C. (1920). 'The ablative as an appositive', *CP* 15: 389–92.
(1928). 'Tacitus, *Histories* 1.13', *CQ* 22: 172–5.
Ogilvie, R. M. (1965). *A commentary on Livy, books 1–5.* Oxford.
Ogilvie, R. M. and I. Richmond (1967). *Cornelii Taciti de vita Agricolae.* Oxford.

Otto, A. (1890). *Die Sprichwörter und sprichwörtlichen Redensarten der Römer.* Leipzig.

Pelletier, A. (1982). *Vienne antique: de la conquête romaine aux invasions alamanniques.* Le Coteau.

Pflaum, H.-G. (1978) *Les fastes de la province de Narbonnaise.* Paris.

Plass, P. (1988). *Wit and the writing of history: the rhetoric of historiography in imperial Rome.* Madison.

Pomeroy, A. J. (1991). *The appropriate comment: death notices in the ancient historians.* Studien zür klassischen Philologie 58. Frankfurt am Main.

Potter, D. S. (1994). *Prophets and emperors: human and divine authority from Augustus to Theodosius.* Cambridge, Mass.

Prosopographia imperii Romani saec. I, II. III. (1933–). 2nd ed., edited by E. Groag et al. Berlin. (= *PIR*²).

Raepsaet-Charlier, M.-Th. (1987). *Prosopographie des femmes de l'ordre sénatorial (Ier–IIe siècles).* Louvain.

Reddé, M. (1986). *Mare nostrum: les infrastructures, le dispositif et l'histoire de la marine militaire sous l'empire romaine.* Rome.

Reinach, S. (1909–12). *Répertoire de reliefs grecs et romains.* 3 vols. Paris.

Rey-Coquais, J.-P. (1978). 'Syrie romaine, de Pompée à Dioclétien', *JRS* 68: 44–73.

Richardson Jr., L. (1992). *A new topographical dictionary of ancient Rome.* Baltimore.

Rickman, G. (1980). *The corn supply of ancient Rome.* Oxford.

Ritterling, E. (1924). '*Legio*', *RE* XII: 1376–1820.

Rives, J. B. (1995). *Religion and authority in Roman Carthage from Augustus to Constantine.* Oxford.

(1999). *Tacitus, Germania.* Oxford.

Rivet, A. L. F. (1988). *Gallia Narbonensis: southern France in Roman times.* London.

Robbert, L. (1917). *De Tacito Lucani imitatore.* Göttingen.

Robinson, H. R. (1975). *The armour of imperial Rome.* New York.

Robinson, O. F. (1992). *Ancient Rome: city planning and administration.* London.

Rüger, C. B. (1979). 'Ein Siegesdenkmal der legio VI victrix', *Bonner Jahrbucher* 179: 187–200.

Rutledge, S. H. (2001). *Imperial inquisitions: prosecutors and informants from Tiberius to Domitian.* London.

Saddington, D. B. (1970). 'The Roman *auxilia* in Tacitus, Josephus and other early imperial writers', *Acta Classica* 13: 89–124.

(1975). 'The development of the Roman auxiliary forces from Augustus to Trajan', *ANRW* II 3: 176–201.

Sage, M. M. (1990). 'Tacitus' historical works: a survey and appraisal', *ANRW* II 33.2: 851–1030.

Schunk, P. (1964). 'Studien zur Darstellung des Endes von Galba, Otho und Vitellius in den *Historien* des Tacitus', *SO* 39: 38–82.

Scott, R. T. (1968). *Religion and philosophy in the Histories of Tacitus*. Papers and monographs of the American Academy in Rome 22. Rome.

Shatzman, I. (1974). 'Tacitean rumours', *Latomus* 33: 549–78.

Sherwin-White, A. N. (1966). *The Letters of Pliny: a historical and social commentary*. Oxford.

(1973a). *The Roman citizenship*. 2nd ed. Oxford.

(1973b). 'The *tabula* of *Banasa* and the *Constitutio Antoniniana*', *JRS* 63: 86–98.

Shotter, D. C. A. (1967). 'Tacitus and Verginius Rufus', *CQ* 17: 370–81.

(1978). 'Tacitus and Marius Celsus', *LCM* 3: 197–200.

Shumate, N. (1997). 'Compulsory pretense and the "theatricalization of experience" in Tacitus', in (ed.) C. Deroux, *Studies in Latin literature and Roman history* 8, Collection Latomus 239. Brussels. 364–403.

Sinclair, P. (1995). *Tacitus the sententious historian: a sociology of rhetoric in Annales 1–6*. University Park, Penn.

Smallwood, E. M. (1967). *Documents illustrating the principates of Gaius, Claudius and Nero*. Cambridge.

Solodow, J. B. (1978). *The Latin particle quidem*. American Classical Studies 4. Boulder.

Sörbom, G. (1935). *Variatio sermonis Tacitei aliaeque apud eundem quaestiones selectae*. Uppsala.

Spence, S. (2001). *Poets and critics read Vergil*. New Haven.

Starr, C. G. (1993). *The Roman imperial navy 31 B.C.–A.D. 324*. 3rd ed. Chicago.

Sumner, G. V. (1976). 'The career of Titus Vinius', *Athenaeum* n.s. 54: 430–6.

Syme, R. (1939). *The Roman revolution*. Oxford.

(1958). *Tacitus*. 2 vols. Oxford.

(1977). 'Helvetian aristocrats', *MH* 34: 129–40.

(1982a). 'The marriage of Rubellius Blandus', *AJP* 103: 62–85.

(1982b). 'Partisans of Galba', *Historia* 31: 460–83.

(1986). *The Augustan aristocracy*. Oxford.

(1987a). 'Prefects of the City, Vespasian to Trajan', in *Estudios de derecho romano en honor de Alvaro d'Ors*. 2 vols. Pamplona. 2.1057–74. (= *Roman papers* 5.608–21)

(1987b). 'The word *opimus*: not Tacitean', *Eranos* 85: 111–14.

Talbert, R. J. A. (1984). *The senate of imperial Rome*. Princeton.

Tarrant, R. J. (1983). 'Tacitus', in (ed.) L. D. Reynolds, *Texts and transmission: a survey of the Latin classics*. Oxford. 406–9.

Taylor, L. R. and R. T. Scott (1969). 'Seating space in the Roman senate and the *senatores pedarii*', *TAPA* 100: 529–82.

Thomasson, B. E. (1960). *Die Statthalter der römischen Provinzen Nordafrikas von Augustus bis Diocletianus*. 2 vols. Lund.

(1984–90). *Laterculi praesidum*. 3 vols. Gothenburg.

Townend, G. B. (1960). 'The sources of the Greek in Suetonius', *Hermes* 88: 98–120.

(1961). 'Some Flavian connections', *JRS* 51: 54–62.

(1962). 'The consuls of A.D. 69/70', *AJP* 83: 113–29.

(1964). 'Cluvius Rufus in the *Histories* of Tacitus', *AJP* 85: 337–77.

Tuplin, C. J. (1989). 'The false Neros of the first century A.D.', in (ed.) C. Deroux, *Studies in Latin literature and Roman history* 5. Brussels. 364–404.

Turner, E. G. (1954). 'Tiberius Julius Alexander', *JRS* 44: 54–64.

Vitucci, G. (1956). *Ricerche sulla praefectura urbis in età imperiale*. Rome.

Walker, B. (1968). *The Annals of Tacitus*. Manchester.

(1976). 'A study in incoherence: the first book of Tacitus' *Histories*', *CP* 71: 113–18.

Wallace-Hadrill, A. (1983). *Suetonius: the scholar and his Caesars*. New Haven.

Watson, G. R. (1974). 'Documentation in the Roman army', *ANRW* II 1: 493–507.

Weaver, P. R. C. (1972). *Familia Caesaris: a social study of the emperor's freedmen and slaves*. Cambridge.

Webster, G. (1998). *The Roman imperial army of the first and second centuries A.D.* 3rd ed. Norman.

Wellesley, K. (1967). 'In defense of the Leiden Tacitus', *RhM* n.s. 110: 210–24.

(1971). 'A major crux in Tacitus: *Histories* II. 40', *JRS* 61: 28–51.

Wiedemann, T. (1999). 'Valerius Asiaticus and the regime of Vitellius', *Philologus* 143: 323–35.

Wölfflin, E. (1888). 'Abolefacio – abolla', *ALL* 5: 107–15 and 118–19.

(1898). 'Galbanus, galbianus', *ALL* 10: 282.

Wolski, J. (1993). *L'empire des Arsacides.* Louvain.

Woodman, A. J. (1983). *Velleius Paterculus: The Caesarian and Augustan narrative (2.41–93).* Cambridge classical texts and commentaries 25. Cambridge.

(1988). *Rhetoric in classical historiography: four studies.* London.

(1995) '*Praecipuum munus annalium*: the construction, convention, and context of Tacitus, *Annals* 3.65.1', *MH* 52: 111–26.

Woodman, A. J. and R. H. Martin (1996). *The Annals of Tacitus, book 3.* Cambridge.

Wülker. L. (1904). *Die geschichtliche Entwicklung des Prodigienwesens bei den Römern: Studien zur Geschichte und Überlieferung der Staatsprodigien.* Leipzig.

Yavetz, Z. (1965). 'Plebs sordida', *Athenaeum* 43: 295–311.

Ziolkowksi, A. (1993). '*Urbs direpta*, or how the Romans sacked cities', in (edd.) J. Rich and G. Shipley, *War and society in the Roman world.* London. 69–91.

INDEXES

1 LATIN WORDS

abolere 47.1
ad 85.1
adeo 9.1
adhibere 71.2
aduersus 66.3
affectatio 80.1
alius 29.1
alumnus 84.3
ambitiosus 83.1
animaduersio 64.2
anxius 14.1
arma 68.1
aula 7.3
auspicato 84.4
auxilia 61.2

casus 2.1
circa 13.2
citus 53.1
clamor 32.1
coercere 11.1
comitia 14.1
commilito 29.2
concieo 4.2
consensus 15.1
consumere 42
contumacia 3.1
cruentus 6.1
cunctus 2.3
cupido sui 80.1

decus 51.2
deorum 15.1
desum + inf. 36.3
domus 37.5
donec + subj. 35.1
dubia 85.2

efferatus 21.1
effugium 43.1
-ere, -erunt 1.1
et quidem 5.2
ex 57.2

fama 5.2
famosus 10.1
feralis 37.3
ferocia 51.1
fessus 12.2
fides 59.1
fingere 21.1
forma 5.2

grassari 37.5

haesitatio 39.2
haud dubie 7.1
haurire 41.3, 67.1
hiare 12.3
horror 37.3
hostis 71.2

iam uero 2.2
illecebrae 10.2
immanitas 16.2
imperare 52.2
impigre 53.1
imputare 38.2
incitamentum 38.3
inclinare 42
incuriose 13.3
indere 51.3
infringere 1.1
ingenium 51.2
ingens 61.1
inhabilis 79.3
inoffensus 48.3
inopia 21.1
instinctus 70.1
instinguere 22.3
insuper 36.1
interest 1.1

intutus 33.2
iter 86.3

latus 90.2
ludibrium 2.1
lymphatus 82.1

magnus 2.2
maiestas 77.3
materies 51.5
matrimonium 22.2
miscere 32.1
moles 61.2
momentum 59.1
mos 7.3
mulcere 39.2

nobilitare 2.1
nutare 31.3

oblitteratus 55.4
occupare 40.1
opimus 2.1

paganus 53.3
palor 68.1
penes 57.1
perinde 30.3
petulanter 13.3
placamenta 63.2
plures 1.1
praegrauis 21.1
praetextus 19.2
prensare 36.2
primores 25.2
principalis 13.3
proinde 21.2
promisce 47.1
prospectus 40.1

quamquam 9.2
quamuis 5.2

recolere 77.3
rector 16.1
refundere 86.2
remeare 86.2
reuerentia 12.1

sagina 62.2
satelles 84.1
scortum 13.3
secreta 22.2
sonans 90.2
strenuus 52.3
subita 7.3

tamquam 7.3, 8.2
-tor 22.3, 38.3, 49.3
trini 2.1
tum uero 35.1
turbamentum 23.1

uocitare 13.1
ut . . . ita 4.2
uulgus 25.2, 69

2 GENERAL INDEX

'ab urbe condita' construction 18.1, 26.1, 89.3
ablative: 2.3, 8.1, 12.2, 22.2; description 31.3; gerundive 52.1; lists 12.2, 57.2, 67.1, 90.3; locative 12.2, 55.4; route 61.1, 70.2
abl. abs. appendixes 20.1, 22.1, 24.2, 27.1, 32.1, 39.2, 40.1, 47.1, 63.1, 76.1, 76.3, 85.1, 86.2, 89.1; *see also* 51.2, 77.1, 90.2
abstract nouns: 1.1, 2.2, 12.1, 15.4, 16.2, 17.2, 22.2, 32.1, 35.1, 44.2, 45.2, 51.4, 55.2, 62.2, 63.1, 65.1, 66.1, 73, 79.4, 83.1, 85.1
accusative in apposition to sentence 44.2
adjectives: substantive + partitive gen. 4.3; with *ex* 57.2
adverbs: attributive 46.4; in apposition to sentence 65.1;
Aedui 64.3
Aemilius Pacensis 20.3

agon 32.2
ala Tauriana 59.2
alliteration: 6.1, 9.2, 25.1, 34.2, 45.1, 45.2, 62.2, 82.1
alternatives 7.2, 14.1, 18.1, 42, 75.2; unexpressed 8.2, 23.1
Ammianus 1.3, 14.1, 22.3, 23.1, 43.2, 53.1, 83.2
anaphora 32.2, 36.3, 44.2, 45.1, 56.1, 62.1, 68.1
Annius Gallus 87.1
antithesis: 8.1, 9.1, 10.2, 33.2, 36.3, 49.3, 68.2, 87.1
Aponius, M. 79.5
Arrius Antoninus 77.2
astrology 22.1
asyndeton 2.3, 6.1, 8.1, 34.2, 35.2, 44.1, 45.1, 62.1, 65.2, 83.1
attraction 5.1, 15.2
Aventicum 68.2

Batavi 59.1
brevity: 4.2, 7.2, 8.2, 11.2, 12.2, 13.2, 13.3, 17.2, 19.1, 26.1, 29.1, 32.1, 46.4, 56.3, 59.1, 63.2, 66.3, 68.1, 85.1

Caecina Alienus: description 52.3, 53.1, 66.2; size of army 61.2; route to Italy 61.1, 67–70 *passim*, 89.3; defection 53.1, 66.2
Calpurnius Piso Licinianus, L. *see under* Piso
Calvia Crispinilla 73
Capitolium 86.1
Catiline 7.2, 10.2
chiasmus 1.4, 8.2
chronology: 7.1, 12.1, 14.1, 20.1, 20.3, 26.1, 35.2, 46.1, 47.2, 74.1; *see also* dates
Cicero 2.2, 6.1, 10.2, 13.3, 16.1, 16.2, 17.2, 23.1, 27.1, 36.1, 37.5, 38.3, 39.2, 51.2, 51.4, 64.2, 84.3, 86.1, 86.2
Cingonius Varro 6.1
Civilis: *see* Julius Civilis
claustra Caspiarum 6.2
Clodius Macer, L. 7.1
Cluvius Rufus 6.1, 8.1, 78.2
cohors Thracum 68.2
cohorts, urban 4.2, 64.3
Cologne 56.2
conditionals 26.1
constructio ad sensum 27.2, 35.1, 46.3
Cornelius Dolabella 2.3, 13.2, 15.2, 21.1, 46.1, 88.1
Cornelius Laco *see under* Laco

dates: 18.1, 19.1, 26.1, 27.1, 55.1, 55.3, 56.2, 57.1, 90.1
dative: adnominal 22.2, agent 34.2, gerundive expressing purpose 6.2
delatores 2.3
donatives 5.1
Ducenius Geminus 14.1

euphemism 16.1, 65.2, 72.3, 85.1
extispicy 27.1

Fabius Valens: description 7.1; age 66.2; competition with Caecina 7.3, 67.1; route to Italy 11.2, 59.2, 61.1, 63–6 *passim*; size of army 61.2; greed 66.2; letters; 74.3; oath 53.2; at Vesontio 55.2; treachery 7.2, 8.2; 7.2, 66.2
Flavius Sabinus 46.1
Flavius Vespasianus 10.3
flood 86.2
Fonteius Capito 7.1, 7.2
freedmen 46.5, 58.1, 76.3; *see also* Icelus

Galba: nobilis 2.3; age 5.2; march to Rome 6.1; reputation 4–7 *passim*, 18.2–3, 35.2, 41.1, 83.1, 87.1; advisors 6.1, 13.1–2, 31.3, 32.2–33, 34.1, 37.5, and *see also* Icelus, Laco, Vinius; executions 6.1; administration 12–20 *passim*; and Civilis 59.1; and Otho 13.4, 21.1, 37–8; and Piso 14.1, 15–16 *passim*, 18.1; and Tigellinus 72.1; and Verginius Rufus 8.2; and Vespasian 10.3; and Vindex 6.2, 8.1; and Gaul 8.1, 65.1–2; quotations 5.2, 35.2,

Galba: (*cont.*)
41.2; last day 27–44 *passim*; assassination 41.1–3; burial 49.1; obituary 49.2–4; avenged 44.2; *see also* Appendix 3
genitive, objective, 46.4
gerundive: abl. 52.1; expressing purpose 6.2, 18.1; impersonal 84.2
gloss 52.2, 55.4, 61.2

hendiadys 36.1, 52.1, 60, 67.1, 69
homoioteleuton 37.5
Hordeonius Flaccus 9.1

Icelus 7.3, 13.1, 37.5, 46.5
impressionistic writing: 55.1, 63–70, 85.3
inchoative verbs 32.2
infinitive, historic 46.3
inheritance-hunting 73
irony and sarcasm 16.1, 22.1, 29.1, 32.1, 34.2, 36.3, 37.1, 41.2, 45.1, 46.1, 47.1, 56.3, 57.2, 61.2, 62.2, 62.3, 64.2, 66.1, 87.1

Julius Alexander, Tib. 11.1
Julius Civilis 59.1
Julius Vindex 6.2, 8.1
Junius Blaesus 59.2

Laco, Cornelius 6.1, 14.1, 24.2, 26.2, 31.2, 33.1, 35.1, 39.2, 46.5, 47.2
lacus Curtius 41.2
'ladder' (rhet. fig.) 84.1
legions 9.2, 10.2, 11.1, 51.3; I 55.2; I *Italica* 59.2; IV *Macedonica* 55.3; V *Alaudae* 55.2; VII *Galbiana* 6.2; XV *Primigenia* 55.2; XVI 55.2; XX *Valeria Victrix* 60; XXI *Rapax* 61.2; XXII *Primigenia* 55.3
lex curiata 15.1
lex sacrata 18.2
Licinius Mucianus 2.1, 6.2, 7.2, 10.1–2, 52.3, 61.2, 66.2–3, 70.2, 75.2, 77.3
Licinius Proculus 46.1, 82.2, 87.1–2
Lingones 53.3
Livy 1, 1.1, 1.3, 4.2, 4.3, 6.1, 9.2, 12.1, 13.3, 16.1, 21.1, 26.1, 27.1, 32.2, 33.2, 34.1, 35.1, 36.1, 37.1, 39.2, 46.2, 46.4, 47.1, 49.2, 50.2, 51.1, 51.2, 52.3, 53.1, 61.2, 62.2, 64.2, 65.1, 68.2, 70.3, 71.3, 79.2, 80.1, 84.1, 84.4, 86, 87.1, 88.3, 89.3
Lucan 2.1, 2.2, 3.2, 6.2, 12.2, 16.2, 32.1, 59.1, 63.1, 84.3, 86.1, 88.3
Lugdunum 51.5
Lusitania 13.3
lustration 87.1

Manlius Valens 64.4
marines 6.2, 87.1
Marius Celsus 14.1, 31.2, 45.2, 71.1–2, 87.2
metaphor 2.1, 3.1, 4.3, 5.1, 10.1, 12.2, 12.3, 13.2, 13.3, 15.4, 16.1, 16.2, 21.1, 26.1, 29.1, 31.3, 35.1, 37.3, 37.4, 40.1, 48.3, 48.4, 49.3, 51.4, 58.2, 74.1, 84.3, 85.1, 88.3, 90.1
miliarium aureum 27.2

Nymphidius Sabinus 5.1, 20.3, 25.1, 30.2, 72.1

oaths 36.2
obituaries 48.2–4, 49.2–4
Ofonius Tigellinus 72
omens 6.2, 70.1, 86
omission: of correlative 14.2, 88.2, of name 5.2, of preposition 4.2, 12.2, of protasis 33.1, of *quam* 30.3, of subject 4.2, 7.2, 13.1, 38.3, 45.2, 51.4, of *utrum* 17.2,
Otho, M. Salvius: description 13.2, 21.1, 50.4; *luxuria* and *mollitia* 21.1, 22.1, 30.1, cf. 71.1; astrology 22.1–2, 27.1; defection 21–6 *passim*; coup 27–8, 36–43 *passim*; administration 71–90 *passim*; preparations for war 87–90; speeches 21.1–2, 37–38.2, 83.2–84; and Cluvius Rufus 76.1; and Galba 13.4; and Marius Celsus 14.1, 45.2, 71.1; and Nero 13.2–4,

30.1, 78.2; and Piso 43.2, 44.1; and Poppaea 13.3, 22.2, 78.2; and Vinius 13.2, 42; and Vitellius 74.1; and praetorians 20.3, 23–5, 80–5 *passim*, and *see also* defection and coup; and senate 45.1, 47.1, 77.3, 84.3, 85.3, 88.1; brother 75.2, 90.3; suicide 3.1; *see also* Appendix 3
oxymoron 21.1, 30.1, 39.2, 54.3, 85.1, 85.3, 87.2

paradox 2.1, 2.3, 15.3, 32.1, 40.1, 56.1, 71.3
paronomasia 72.1
participle, substantive 4.2, 43.2
passive, impersonal 2.3, 17.2, 85.1
periodic sentences 4.1, 5.1, 14.1, 15.1, 32.2, 48.2, 81.1, 87.1
personification 17.2, 34.2, 86.2
Petronius Turpilianus, P. 6.1
Piso Licinianus: description 14.2, 17.1, 19.1; exile 4.3; and Galba 14.1, 15–16; adoption 18.1; and praetorians 29.2–30, 34.1, 39.1; and Otho 21.1, 43.2, 83.1; wife 47.2; death 43.2, cf. 33.2; obituary 48.1; will 48.3
Pliny the Elder 1.1, 2–3, 10.1, 13.2, 16.1, 21.1, 86.2, 87.2
Pliny the Younger 1.4, 2–3, 6.1, 8.2, 14.1, 15.1, 15.3, 16.1, 70.2, 76.3, 77.1
Plotius Firmus 46.1
Poppaea 13.2, 13.3, 22.2, 72.1, 78.2
praetorian guard 4.2, 5.1, 5.2, 6.1, 20.3, 21–6 *passim*, 27.2, 28, 29.2–30 *passim*, 31.1, 31.2, 36–44 *passim*, 46.1, 55.3, 66.2, 74.2, 74.3, 80–5 *passim*, 87.1, 89.2
prepositional phrases, attributive 11.2, 16.2, 21.1, 24.1, 25.1, 26.2, 30.2, 42, 43.2, 44.1, 66.3, 68.1, 74.1, 84.3, 85.1
prodigies 3.2
Ptolemaeus 12.3, 22.2

relative pronoun, connecting 24.2, parenthetical 37.2
repraesentatio 7.2
Roscius Coelius 60

Sallust 1, 1.1, 2.3, 3.2, 4–11, 6.1, 10.1, 10.2, 10.3, 11.3, 13.3, 21.1, 22.3, 23.1, 24.2, 26.1, 33.2, 35.1, 35.2, 36.3, 37.5, 45.1, 46.2, 46.3, 49.3, 51.1, 51.2, 52.2, 52.3, 53.1, 53.2, 56.3, 62.1, 64.2, 67.1, 68.1, 70.1, 70.2, 71.1, 72.1, 79.2, 85.1, 85.3, 86, 87.2, 88.1
Salvius Otho, M. *see under* Otho
Salvius Otho Titianus, L. 75.2, 90.3
second person address 10.2
Sempronius Densus 43.1
Statius 1.2, 2.2, 2.3, 6.1, 16.2, 37.3, 40.1, 41.1, 42, 73, 82.3, 86.2
Suedius Clemens 87.1
Suetonius Paulinus 87.1
Sulpicius Galba, Ser. *see under* Galba
syllepsis 9.2, 67.1

technical language: avoided 52.1, 53.1, 86.1, 87.1; used 6.2, 20.3, 27.1, 66.1
Thucydides 37.1, 52.2
Tigellinus 72.1
tmesis 20.1
Trebellius Maximus 60
Treueri 53.3

uariatio: 10.3, 23.1, 46.1; abl. ~ abl. abs. 14.1, 44.2, abl. ~ *per* + acc. 20.3, abl. ~ prep. phrase 46.2, abl. ~ purpose clause 7.2, abl. of respect ~ adj. 6.2, abl. abs. ~ adj. 55.1, abl. abs. ~ participle 17.1, adj. ~ *in* + acc. 12.3, adverb ~ prep. phrase 32.2, dat. ~ conditional clause 22.1, inf. ~ abstract noun 15.4, noun ~ participle 14.2, of modifier 32.1, of mood 1.2, 15.2, of person 15.3, *palam* ~ *secreta* 10.2, participle ~ temporal clause 7.1
uia Flaminia 86.2
uigiles 46.1
urban cohorts 4.2, 64.3

Valerius Asiaticus 59.2
Verania Gemina 47.2
Verginius Rufus, L. 6.2, 8.2, 12.1, 52.3
Vespasian 10.3, 50.4; *see also* Appendix 3
Vienna 65.1
Vindex *see under* Julius Vindex
Vinia Crispina 13.2
Vinius, T.: consulship 1.1; greed 37.5; and Galba 6.1, 32.2; and Otho 13.2; and Piso 34.1; and Tigellinus 72.2; assassination 42; burial 47.2; obituary 48.2–4
Virgil 2.3, 3.1, 6.1, 6.2, 12.2, 13.2, 18.1, 29.1, 32.2. 36.2, 39.2, 40.2, 42, 44.1, 44.2, 47.2, 48.4, 51.1, 51.4, 59.2, 61.1, 62.2, 62.3, 65.2, 66.1, 79.3, 80.2, 84.2, 85.1, 88.3
Vitellius, A.: description 9.1, 15.4, 52, 53.2, 62.2; gluttony 62.2; acclamation 57.1–2; army 61.2; advisors 7.2, 15.4, 26.2, 67.1; nomenclature 62.2; executions 12.1, 44.2, 58.2, 59.1, 88.1; preparations for march on Rome 55–70 *passim*; family 14.2, 75.2, 88.1; and Cluvius Rufus 8.1; and Cornelius Dolabella 88.1; and Flavius Sabinus 46.1; and Otho 74.1; and Valens 52.3, 57.1; and Valerius Asiaticus 59.2; and Vespasian 55.1; and Batavians 59.1, 64.2; and praetorians 20.3, 25.2; betrayed 55.3, 67.1, 79.5; *see also* Appendix 3
Vitellius, L. 88.1
Vmbricius 27.1

Lightning Source UK Ltd.
Milton Keynes UK
26 September 2009

144207UK00001B/1/A